ABSOLUTE
BEGINNER'S
GUIDE

TO

A+ Certification

Mark Edward Soper

800 East 96th Street,
Indianapolis, Indiana 46240

Absolute Beginer's Guide to A+ Certification

International Standard Book Number: 0-7897-3062-6

Library of Congress Catalog Card Number: 029236730628

Printed in the United States of America

First Printing: February 2004

07   06   05   04   4   3   2   1

Trademarks

All terms mentioned in this book that are known to be trademarks or service marks have been appropriately capitalized. Que Publishing cannot attest to the accuracy of this information. Use of a term in this book should not be regarded as affecting the validity of any trademark or service mark.

Warning and Disclaimer

Every effort has been made to make this book as complete and as accurate as possible, but no warranty or fitness is implied. The information provided is on an "as is" basis. The author and the publisher shall have neither liability nor responsibility to any person or entity with respect to any loss or damages arising from the information contained in this book or from the use of the CD or programs accompanying it.

Bulk Sales

Que Publishing offers excellent discounts on this book when ordered in quantity for bulk purchases or special sales. For more information, please contact

U.S. Corporate and Government Sales
1-800-382-3419
corpsales@pearsontechgroup.com

For sales outside of the U.S., please contact

International Sales
+1-317-428-3341
international@pearsontechgroup.com

Associate Publisher
Greg Wiegand

Executive Editor
Rick Kughen

Development Editors
Rick Kughen
Todd Brakke

Managing Editor
Charlotte Clapp

Production Editor
Jessica McCarty

Indexer
Mandie Frank

Proofreader
Jennifer Timpe

Technical Editor
David Eytchison

Publishing Coordinator
Sharry Gregory

Multimedia Developer
Dan Scherf

Interior Designer
Anne Jones

Cover Designer
Anne Jones

Page Layout
Brad Chinn
Susan Geiselman
Julie Parks

Graphics
Tammy Graham
Laura Robbins

Contents at a Glance

Table of Contents

About the Author

Mark Edward Soper is president of Select Systems and Associates, Inc., a technical writing and training organization located in Evansville, Indiana. Get more information at the Select Systems Web site at www.selectsystems.com. Mark is a 20-year veteran of the computer industry whose first technical articles appeared in the late 1980s. Mark has written more than 140 articles on topics ranging from computer upgrades to laser printer tips and tricks, Internet access, and new features in Windows for publications such as *Maximum PC*, *PCNovice/SmartComputing Guides*, *PCNovice*, *SmartComputing*, the *PCNovice/SmartComputing Learning Series*, *WordPerfect Magazine*, *The WordPerfectionist*, and *PCToday*.

Mark has taught computer troubleshooting and other technical subjects to thousands of students from Maine to Hawaii since the early 1990s. He is an A+ Certified hardware technician and a Microsoft Certified Professional.

This is the second book Mark has written in the *Absolute Beginner's Guide* series: He is also the author of *Absolute Beginner's Guide to Cable Internet Connections*. Mark is also the author of Que's *PC Help Desk in a Book.* Mark has also written for other publishers in the Pearson Education family, including the recent *TechTV's Upgrading Your PC, Second Edition* for Peachpit/TechTV Press (http://www.peachpit.com) and *The Complete Idiot's Guide to High-Speed Internet Connections* for Alpha Books.

Mark is the coauthor of Que's *Upgrading and Repairing PCs: Field Guide* and its predecessors (the *Technician's Portable Reference* series) and he has also contributed to many other Que books in this series, including *Upgrading and Repairing PCs* from the 11th Edition to the current 15th Anniversary Edition; *Upgrading and Repairing Networks, Second Edition*; *Upgrading and Repairing Laptop Computers*; and *Upgrading and Repairing PCs, 12th Edition, Academic Edition*.

Mark has also contributed to several volumes in Que's *Special Edition* series, including: *Special Edition Using Windows Millennium*; *Special Edition Using Windows XP Home Edition*; *Special Edition Using Windows XP Home Edition, Bestseller Edition*; *Special Edition Using Windows XP Professional*; and *Special Edition Using Windows XP Professional, Bestseller Edition*. Mark is also a contributor to *Platinum Edition Using Microsoft Windows XP*.

Watch for details about these and other book projects at the Que Web site at http://www.quepublishing.com.

Mark welcomes comments at mesoper@selectsystems.com.

Dedication

To Jarvis Danger McKinney, my grandson. A true "absolute beginner."

—Mark E. Soper

Acknowledgments

This author would be just another typist without the support of many people who have contributed to this book in particular and my growth as a writer in general.

I want to thank

Almighty God—who encourages each of us to discover the work we should do and is pleased when we perform that work with integrity.

Cheryl—who has taught me how to keep my audience in mind as I write, and who makes it wonderful to come home after long hours of writing and rewriting.

Ian and Jeremy—who explore the artistic and entertainment side of technology.

Kate and Hugh—who are responsible for the latest "absolute beginner" in the family.

Ed and Erin—he keeps the computers running at his university, and she keeps him running.

Greg Wiegand—who gave this project the thumbs-up and built the terrific team that helped put it together.

Rick Kughen—who has overseen this book from start to finish and made sure it's the best in its class.

Todd Brakke—whose critiques made the book even better.

David Eytchison—who helped exterminate technical glitches.

Sharry Gregory—who kept everything organized and kept those checks coming!

Charlotte Clapp—who kept chapters flowing in the right directions.

Jessica McCarty—who made sure that grammar and spelling weren't neglected in the quest for technical excellence.

Mandie Frank—who made sure the index helps you find what you need—fast.

Dan Scherf—who made the CD an essential and easy-to-use part of this book.

And everybody else at Que who works together to make sure you get the best computer books on the market.

Finally, to Jim Peck, who helped give me the opportunity to teach PC troubleshooting around the country back in 1992, and Scott Mueller, whose work has been a constant inspiration to me since 1988.

—Mark Edward Soper

We Want to Hear from You!

As the reader of this book, *you* are our most important critic and commentator. We value your opinion and want to know what we're doing right, what we could do better, what areas you'd like to see us publish in, and any other words of wisdom you're willing to pass our way.

As an associate publisher for Que Publishing, I welcome your comments. You can email or write me directly to let me know what you did or didn't like about this book—as well as what we can do to make our books better.

Please note that I cannot help you with technical problems related to the topic of this book. We do have a User Services group, however, where I will forward specific technical questions related to the book.

When you write, please be sure to include this book's title and author as well as your name, email address, and phone number. I will carefully review your comments and share them with the author and editors who worked on the book.

Email: feedback@quepublishing.com

Mail: Greg Wiegand
Associate Publisher
Que Publishing
800 East 96th Street
Indianapolis, IN 46240 USA

For more information about this book or another Que Publishing title, visit our Web site at www.quepublishing.com. Type the ISBN (excluding hyphens) or the title of a book in the Search field to find the page you're looking for.

Do You Need This Book?

The A+ Certification from CompTIA is the industry standard for entry-level computer technicians. If you want to work in the computer industry, getting the A+ Certification is a great way to start. The skills measured by the A+ Certification Exams are valuable in virtually any computer technology position, from help desk and system repair to Windows support and network installation. In fact, many major companies require A+ Certification for their information technology (IT) employees and supervisors. Thus, getting the A+ Certification can be a faster way to get started in IT and go further, faster.

Even if your long-term goal is network administration or programming, the A+ Certification is useful because it covers the essentials of both hardware and operating systems.

There are two exams you must pass to receive A+ Certification:

- Core (which measures hardware skills)
- Operating Systems (which measures Windows and network skills)

There are many ways to prepare for these exams: Classes, self-study manuals, and books abound. So, why this book?

This book is especially written for the "absolute beginner" in A+ Certification. In other words, I wrote this book for you.

Who are you, my reader? If you're like a lot of the readers of this series, you're probably not working in the IT field full time yet, although you probably like computers (and probably have one or two at home). You might know a lot about some parts of the computer field (such as gaming or multimedia), but you might have big gaps in your knowledge of business-oriented versions of Windows, networking, or other topics essential to A+ Certification. Whatever your level of experience, you're looking for an A+ Certification study guide that doesn't assume you're already an expert, but doesn't talk down to you. If this describes you, welcome.

If you're already in the field, but don't have the A+ Certification yet, you've still discovered the right book for your needs. This book reminds you of the facts and techniques you've already learned, shows you new information you don't know, and helps correct any misconceptions and bits of misinformation you might have picked up on the way.

This book is designed to help you pass the A+ Certification Exams. It doesn't try to give you the entire history of personal computers (22 years and counting if you start with the IBM PC) or try to turn you into an expert who knows everything about everything in the IT field. Instead, it's geared specifically to the knowledge base you *must* know to pass the latest (November 2003) versions of the exams and points you in the right direction to continue to learn.

What You Need to Begin

To get the greatest benefit from this book, you need to have a PC running at least one of the versions of Windows covered on the A+ Certification Exam (Windows NT 4.0/95/98/Me/2000/XP). If you are planning to build or upgrade a computer to use for studying for the exams, I'd recommend installing Windows 98 and Windows 2000 or XP in a dual-boot configuration. (See Chapter 16, "Operating System Installation," for details.)

Although the book has many illustrations of different hardware components and Windows screen shots, if you like to learn by doing, it's also helpful to have the following equipment:

- *A PC for experimentation*—I don't recommend using your only computer for experimentation, but you don't need the latest and greatest PC either. Compare the requirements for Windows versions listed in Chapter 16 to the features of clearance and closeout computers (new or used) sold by various online and local vendors, and you'll see that you can pick up a low-cost desktop computer for experimenting with any recent version of Windows. If you have retained components from computer upgrades you've done, you might be able to build a PC from older parts.

- *A working Internet connection (dial-up or broadband)*—This is vital for performing many of the hands-on labs I provide on the CD packaged with the book.

- *Additional equipment*—Computer components such as hard drives, a CD-ROM drive, network cards and cables, and a printer help you perform experiments and build different configurations. Each hands-on lab exercise on the CD packaged with the book provides a detailed list of what I recommend.

note

Don't break your piggy bank to pick up components. Check with friends, co-workers, or the IT guys at your company to see if you can borrow hardware. Other sources include swap meets, computer fairs, and the junk piles at local computer stores.

■ *Additional books for reference*—I've jammed so much into this book that it also includes a CD that contains the last two chapters of the book along with lots of additional material. However, if you're looking for even more in-depth hardware coverage, I recommend my book *TechTV's Upgrading Your PC, Second Edition* (TechTV Press/PeachPit, 2003) and Scott Mueller's *Upgrading and Repairing PCs, 15th Anniversary Edition* (Que, 2003). I cover even more hardware and software troubleshooting techniques and methods in my book *PC Help Desk in a Book* (Que, 2002), which features dozens of flowcharts and symptom tables.

How This Book Is Organized

This book has 21 chapters, 1 appendix, and study content on the CD packaged with the book. The following sections are included in print form in the book:

■ Chapter 1, "A+ Objectives for the 2003 Exam Revisions," cross-references the official A+ Certification Exam objectives for the latest (November 2003) A+ Certification Exams to the relevant sections of the book. Use this chapter to help you focus on any weak spots in your knowledge of A+ Certification objectives.

■ Chapter 2, "PC Anatomy 101," provides you with a complete outside-in tour of typical desktop and portable computers. If you've never popped the top off your PC before, let this chapter be your guide.

■ Chapter 3, "How Computers Measure and Transfer Data," gets you up to speed on how computers store, count, and transfer information.

■ Chapter 4, "The Motherboard and CPU," brings you the whole story on how motherboards and processors (CPUs) work together and how they are installed and kept cool.

■ Chapter 5, "Power Supplies and Circuit Testing," introduces you to the unsung hero of system stability, the power supply. You also learn how to test the electrical circuits in your computer and protect your PC with surge suppressors and battery backup units.

■ Chapter 6, "BIOS and CMOS Configuration," provides full coverage on how the BIOS chip on the motherboard tells the rest of the computer what to do, how it reports problems, and how you can adjust its default settings.

■ Chapter 7, "RAM," helps you master the bewildering varieties of memory chips and modules. Learn how to install them and discover that with some versions of Windows, you *can* have too much RAM.

- Chapter 8, "Input/Output Devices and Cables," shows you the differences between parallel and serial ports and their more recent siblings, helps you figure out where to plug in your mouse and keyboard, and how modems work.

- Chapter 9, "Video," helps you master video cards and monitors.

- Chapter 10, "Printers," introduces you to new technologies such as thermal and dye sublimation as well as covering the mainstream inkjet and laser printers on everybody's desk.

- Chapter 11, "Installing and Configuring Common Peripherals," shows you how and where to connect popular peripherals such as digital cameras, PDAs, and network devices.

- Chapter 12, "Portables," demonstrates the many ways that portables differ from desktop computers. With more portable computers now being sold than desktops, chances are there's a portable in *your* future.

- Chapter 13, "Safety and Recycling," shows you how to clean, recycle, and dispose of computer equipment the right way. It also covers how to work inside your PC, so read this chapter first!

- Chapter 14, "Storage," covers the selection, installation, and configuration of removable media, hard disk, and floppy and optical storage devices.

- Chapter 15, "Preparing Hard and Floppy Drives with Windows," shifts the focus from hardware to software. Learn how to turn an out-of-the-box hard disk into storage for your ever-increasing collection of data.

- Chapter 16, "Operating System Installation," guides you through the process of installing Windows versions from NT 4.0 through XP from start to finish. This chapter also shows you how to create a dual-boot configuration (two operating systems in one computer).

- Chapter 17, "Operating System Upgrades," shows you how to replace an old Windows version with a newer version and how to finish bringing your system up to date with service pack and Windows Updates installations.

- Chapter 18, "Using and Optimizing Windows," helps you understand the Windows startup process, how to configure Windows after it starts, and how to use Windows's most important GUI and command-line tools.

- Chapter 19, "Installing and Configuring Hardware in Windows," shows you how to install, configure, and use printers and other types of hardware the Windows way.

- Chapter 20, "Troubleshooting Windows and Windows Applications," helps you deal with "broken" Windows installations and stubborn applications.

- Chapter 21, "Networking and Internet Connectivity," covers both the hardware (network card and cable) and software (network protocols and Windows features) that make networks work.

- Appendix A, "CD-ROM Instructions," helps you get the most from the jam-packed CD-ROM packaged with this book. The CD includes Chapters 22, 23, a CD Supplement, a Windows command reference, and the Glossary. It also includes a first-class self-test engine, hands-on labs, study notes, and practice test questions for each chapter you can take with you anywhere (they're in Adobe Acrobat .PDF format) and actual BIOS beep code samples you can play through your PC's speakers. The CD is an integral part of this book, so be sure to use it.

The following chapters and materials are found on the CD:

- Chapter 22, "Troubleshooting Principles," teaches you the methods of troubleshooting and gives you plenty of help with troubleshooting hardware and operating system problems.

- Chapter 23, "Preparing to Take the A+ Certification Exams," shows you how to sign up for the exams and prepare to get a passing score.

- The CD Supplement provides additional technical information on SCSI configuration, touchscreen monitors, and printer options.

- Study Guide sections for Chapters 2–22, including hands-on labs, a glossary for each chapter, and practice test questions and answers.

- The Windows command reference provides detailed syntax and examples.

- The PrepLogic Practice Exam, Preview Edition.

  See Appendix A to learn how to use the contents of the CD.

> **tip**
>
> I've also included a helpful glossary on the CD included with this book, which provides real-world definitions of the key terms and concepts highlighted in each chapter.
>
> This glossary comes in two formats. First, you'll find it in printable PDF format. Print it out and include with your binder of study materials. Second, I've included the glossary in Windows Help file format, which means you can copy the Help file to your hard drive and search the glossary for terms. I believe you will find this to be an asset to your A+ studies.

How to Use This Book

There are many strategies you can use to get the most from this book, depending upon your experience with PCs and your preferred method of test preparation:

- *The "rookie" reader*—If you're new to the PC technical field, start at the beginning and read to the end (including the chapters on CD). Chapters 1–3 lay a solid foundation for later chapters. Don't forget to turn on your PC to read the CD chapters, view the study labs and hands-on exercises for each chapter, and install the glossary.

- *The "do-it-yourself" reader*—Run, don't walk, to your favorite PC and fire it up to get access to the hands-on labs for each chapter on the CD. Turn to the matching chapter in the book for added insight into the labs and for additional ideas for experiments.

- *The "just for review" reader*—Start with Chapter 1 to find out what you need to review, and then jump to the chapters and sections that cover the topics you need. Remember to use the study labs and glossary on the companion CD to complete your review.

- *The "I know Windows, but not hardware" reader*— Concentrate on Chapters 1–14 as well as 21 and 22. Use the hands-on labs on the companion CD to boost your confidence and skill level.

- *The "I know hardware, but not Windows" reader*— After reading Chapters 1 and 3, dig into Chapters 15–22. Use the hands-on labs on the companion CD to try the essential features of Windows.

No matter what type of reader you are, be sure to read Chapter 23 on the CD to master the test-taking process.

Conventions Used in This Book

Commands, directions, and explanations in this book are presented in the clearest format possible. The following items are some of the features that make this book easier for you to use:

- *Glossary terms*—For all the terms that appear in the glossary on the CD, you'll find the first appearance of that term in the text in **bold**. These terms and definitions are also found in the companion CD's Study Lab section for each chapter.

- *Notes*—Information related to the task at hand, or "inside" information is provided in this format to make it easy to find.

■ *Tips*—Pieces of information that are not necessarily essential to the current topic but that offer advice or help you to save time are presented as Tips.

■ *Cautions*—Notes explaining the need to be careful when performing a particular procedure or task are presented as Cautions.

Page references in the index that are preceded by "PDF:" can be found in the elements on the CD.

1

A OBJECTIVES FOR THE 2003 EXAM REVISIONS

This chapter cross-references every objective listed on the A+ Certification Exam to a particular section of this book or the companion CD. I created this cross-reference chapter for one specific reason: to make it as easy as possible for you to use this book to prepare for the exams—and pass them.

The objectives that make up both the Core Hardware and Operating Systems exams are designed to accurately represent the knowledge base you should possess as an entry-level computer technician. If you're like most candidates for A+ Certification, you probably have a lot of knowledge of certain objectives, but little or no knowledge or experience with others. If this describes your situation, this chapter was made for you. Find the objectives you need to study and go straight to the location in the book or companion CD that has the information you need. In some cases, you might find two or more references. Be sure to go to each one to get all the information I've made available to you on that objective. You might prefer to read the book and CD content straight through and come back to this chapter later to review the areas that need more attention. Either way, I think you'll find this cross-reference chapter a worthwhile tool.

note

Don't forget to perform the hands-on labs, install and use the glossary, and study the other CD content to further improve your grasp of every objective.

A+ Objectives for the 2003 Core Hardware Exam

Domain 1.0: Installation, Configuration, and Upgrading

Section	Objective	Subobjective	Page Range
1.1	Identify the names, characteristics of system modules. Recognize these modules by sight or definition.	Motherboard	103–115
		Firmware	41
		Power supply	159–163
		Processor/CPU	125–132
		Memory	219, 222–227
		Storage devices	431–434 443–450 466–480
		Display devices	296–298, 300–302, PDF:999–1001
		Adapter cards	108–112
		Ports	47–55
		Cases	121–124
		Riser cards	113–115

Domain 1.0   (continued)

Section	Objective	Subobjective	Page Range
1.2	Identify basic procedures for adding and removing field-replaceable modules for desktop systems. Given a replacement scenario, choose the appropriate sequences.	Motherboard	115–121
		Storage device	
		FDD	432–436
		HDD	446–448, 470, 481
		CD/CD-RW	473–475
		DVD/DVD-RW	473–475
		Tape drive	480–481
		Removable storage	480–481
		Power supply	
		AC adapter	389–391
		AT/ATX	163–165
		Cooling system	
		Fans	157–158
		Heatsinks	135–136, 138–140
		Liquid cooling	147
		Processor/CPU	135–140
		Memory	237
		Display devices	308–312
		Input devices	
		Keyboard	278–279
		Mouse/pointer devices	280
		Touchscreen	PDF:1000–1001
		Adapters	
		Network Interface Card (NIC)	786–787
		Sound card	286–288
		Video card	308–310
		Modem	273–274
		SCSI	468
		IEEE-1394/FireWire	292–293
		USB	268–269
		Wireless	369–370 789

Domain 1.0 (continued)

Section	Objective	Subobjective	Page Range
1.3	Identify basic procedures for adding and removing field-replaceable modules for portable systems. Given a replacement scenario, choose the appropriate sequences.	**Portable components:**	
		Storage device	
		FDD	406
		HDD	404–406
		CD/CD-RW	406
		DVD/DVD-RW	406
		Removable storage	406
		Power sources	
		AC adapter	389–391
		DC adapter	389–391
		Battery	391–392
		Memory	409–410
		Input devices	
		Keyboard	384–385
		Mouse/pointer devices	387–388
		Touchscreen	PDF:1000–1001
		PCMCIA/mini-PCI adapters	
		Network Interface Card (NIC)	395–401, 787
		Modem	395–401
		SCSI	395–401
		IEEE-1394/FireWire	395–401
		USB	395–401
		Storage (memory and hard drive)	395–401 404–407
		Docking station/port replicators	401–403
		LCD panel	382–383
		Wireless	
		Adapter/controller	369–370, 395–401, 786–787
		Antennae	369–370 395–401

Domain 1.0   (continued)

Section	Objective	Subobjective	Page Range
1.4	Identify typical IRQs, DMAs, I/O addresses, and procedures for altering these settings when installing and configuring devices. Choose the appropriate installation or configuration steps in a given scenario.	Legacy devices (for example, ISA sound card)	75–81
		Specialized devices (for example, CAD/CAM)	75–81
		Internal modems	75–81, 259, 701
		Floppy drive controllers	433–434
		Hard drive controllers	439
		Multimedia devices	75–81
		Network Interface Cards (NICs)	75–81
		I/O ports	
		Serial	259
		Parallel	251–252
		USB ports	75–81
		IEEE-1394/FireWire	75–81
		Infrared	372–373
		Also read	703–712
1.5	Identify the names, purposes, and performance characteristics of standardized/common peripheral ports, associated cabling, and their connectors. Recognize ports, cabling, and connectors by sight.	**Port types**	
		Serial	254–255
		Parallel	246–250
		USB ports	264–267
		IEEE-1394/FireWire	290–291
		Infrared	373–374
		Cable types	
		Serial (straight through versus null modem)	257–258
		Parallel	248–251
		USB	265–268
		Connector types	
		DB-9 (serial)	254–255
		DB-25 (serial)	254–255
		RJ-11	271–272, 277
		RJ-45	277, 783

Domain 1.0 (continued)

Section	Objective	Subobjective	Page Range
		DB-25 (parallel)	246–248
		Centronics (parallel)	246–248
		PS2/MINI-DIN	278–280
		USB	264–265
		IEEE-1394	55, 290–291
		Also read	47–48 57
1.6	Identify proper procedures for installing and configuring common IDE devices. Choose the appropriate installation or configuration sequences in given scenarios. Recognize the associated cables.	**IDE interface types**	
		EIDE	444–447
		ATA/ATAPI	444–447
		Serial ATA	447–449
		PIO	457–458
		RAID (0, 1, and 5)	453
		Master/slave/cable select	442–444
		Devices per channel	443
		Primary/secondary	443–444
		Cable orientation/requirements	442–443
1.7	Identify proper procedures for installing and configuring SCSI devices.	**SCSI interface types**	
		Narrow	463–467
		Fast	463–467
		Wide	463–467
		Ultra-Wide	463–467
		LVD	463–467
		HVD	463–467
		Internal versus external	463–468
		SCSI IDs	
		Jumper block/DIP switch settings (binary equivalents)	468, PDF:1002–100:
		Resolving ID conflicts	PDF:901–927
		RAID (0, 1, and 5)	453

Domain 1.0 (continued)

Section	Objective	Subobjective	Page Range
		Cabling	
		Length	PDF:1004–1005
		Type	480–481
		Termination requirements (active, passive, auto)	468–469 PDF:1005
1.8	Identify proper procedures for installing and configuring common peripheral devices. Choose the appropriate installation or configuration sequences in given scenarios.	Modems and transceivers (dial-up, cable, DSL, ISDN)	269–276 763–771, 786–789
		External storage	481
		Digital cameras	363–367
		PDAs	368–369
		Wireless access points	369–370 789
		Infrared devices	372–274
		Printers	333 680–682
		UPS (Uninterruptible Power Supply) and suppressors	170–175
		Monitors	298–301 310–312
1.9	Identify procedures to optimize PC operations in specific situations. Predict the effects of specific procedures under given scenarios.	**Cooling systems**	
		Liquid	146–147
		Air	146–147
		Heatsink	146–147
		Thermal compound	146–147
		Disk subsystem enhancements	
		Hard drives	456–463
		Controller cards (for example, RAID, ATA-100, and so on)	453
		Cables	
		ATA/IDE	442–443
		Ethernet (RJ-45)	782–784
		Parallel	250–251
		NICs	788–789
		Memory	143–144
		Additional processors	145

Domain 1.0 (continued)

Section	Objective	Subobjective	Page Range
1.10	Determine the issues that must be considered when upgrading a PC. In a given scenario, determine when and how to upgrade system components.	Drivers for legacy devices	696–701
		Portable adapter card bus types and characteristics	395–401
		Desktop adapter card bus types and characteristics	108–112
		Cache in relationship to motherboards	241–243
		Memory capacity and characteristics	222–230
		Processor speed and compatibility	124–132 144–145, 147
		Hard drive capacity and characteristics	405–406 438–443
		System/firmware (BIOS) limitations	208–209 454–456
		Power supply output capacity	
		Desktop	150–152
		Laptop batteries	388–392

Domain 2.0: Diagnosing and Troubleshooting

Section	Objective	Subobjective	Page Range
2.1	Recognize common problems associated with each module and its symptoms, and identify steps to isolate and troubleshoot the problems. Given a problem situation, interpret the symptoms and infer the most likely cause.	**I/O ports and cables**	
		Serial	257–258 PDF:854–856
		Parallel	250–251 PDF:850–853
		USB ports	PDF:856–859
		IEEE-1394/FireWire	PDF:871–872
		Infrared	372–374 PDF:872
		SCSI	PDF:901–902

Domain 2.0   (continued)

Section	Objective	Subobjective	Page Range
		Motherboards	
		CMOS/BIOS settings	207–208 PDF:845
		POST audible/visual error codes	183–187
		Peripherals	PDF:850–877
		Computer case	
		Power supply	165–169
		Slot covers	156
		Front cover alignment	155
		Storage devices and cables	
		FDD	PDF:895–898
		HDD	PDF:898–902
		CD/CD-RW	PDF:903–910
		DVD/DVD-RW	PDF:903–910
		Tape drive	PDF:910–912
		Removable storage	PDF:910–912
		Cooling systems	
		Fans	202–204 PDF:844
		Heatsinks	PDF:844
		Liquid cooling	147
		Temperature sensors	202–204
		Processor/CPU	PDF:844–845
		Memory	PDF:846–849
		Display device	312–320 PDF:873–874
		Input devices	
		Keyboard	PDF:862–863 PDF:867–888
		Mouse/pointer devices	PDF:862–863 PDF:867–888
		Touchscreen	PDF:1001–1002

Domain 2.0 (continued)

Section	Objective	Subobjective	Page Range
		Adapters	
		Network interface card (NIC)	786–788
		Sound card	PDF:869–871
		Video card	312–320 PDF:873–874
		Modem	PDF:859–862
		SCSI	PDF:901–902
		IEEE-1394/FireWire	PDF:871–872
		USB	PDF:856–859
		Portable systems	
		PCMCIA (PC Card)	PDF:892–893
		Batteries	PDF:890–892
		Docking stations/port replicators	PDF:894–895
		Portable unique storage	PDF:912–913
2.2	Identify basic troubleshooting procedures and good practices for eliciting problem symptoms from customers.	Troubleshooting/isolation/ problem determination procedures	PDF:824–829
		Determine whether hardware or software problem	PDF:829–833
		Gather information from user	
		Customer environment	PDF:827–829
		Symptoms/error codes	PDF:828–829
		Situation when the problem occurred	PDF:825–826

Domain 3.0: Preventive Maintenance, Safety, and Environmental Issues

Section	Objective	Subobjective	Page Range
3.1	Identify the purpose of various types of preventive maintenance products and procedures and when to use/perform them.	Liquid cleaning compounds	413–414
		Types of materials to clean contacts and connections	414 PDF:841
		Non-static vacuums (chassis, power supplies, fans)	414–415
		Clean monitors	413–414
		Clean removable-media devices	437–438
		Ventilation, dust, and moisture control on the PC hardware interior	153–157
		Hard disk maintenance (defragging, scan disk, CHKDSK)	649–652
		Verify UPS (Uninterruptible Power Supply) and suppressors	170–174
3.2	Identify various safety measures and procedures, and when/how to use them.	**ESD (electro-static discharge) precautions and procedures**	
		What ESD can do, and how it might be apparent, or hidden	418–419
		Common ESD protection devices	419–422
		Situations that could present a danger or hazard	422–424
		Potential hazards and proper safety procedures relating to	
		High-voltage equipment	422–426
		Power supply	422–423
		CRTs	424–426

Domain 3.0   (continued)

Section	Objective	Subobjective	Page Range
3.3	Identify environmental protection measures and procedures, and when/how to use them.	**Special disposal procedures that comply with environmental guidelines**	
		Batteries	415–416
		CRTs	416–417
		Chemical solvents and cans	416
		MSDS (Material Safety Data Sheet)	417–418

Domain 4.0: Motherboard/Processors/Memory

Section	Objective	Subobjective	Page Range
4.1	Distinguish between the popular CPU chips in terms of their basic characteristics.	Popular CPU chips (Pentium-class compatible)	125–127
		Voltage	125–128
		Speeds (actual versus advertised)	143
		Cache Level 1, 2, 3	132–135
		Sockets/slots	129–132
		VRMs	125–128, 130
4.2	Identify the types of RAM (random access memory), form factors, and operational characteristics. Determine banking and speed requirements under given scenarios.	**Types of memory**	
		EDO RAM (Extended Data Output RAM)	229–230
		DRAM (Dynamic Random Access Memory)	229–230
		SRAM (Static RAM)	229–230
		VRAM (Video RAM)	229–230
		SDRAM (Synchronous Dynamic RAM)	229–230
		DDR (Double Data Rate)	229–230
		RAMBUS	229–230

Domain 4.0   (continued)

Section	Objective	Subobjective	Page Range
		Form factors (including pin count)	
		SIMM (Single Inline Memory Module)	222–228
		DIMM (Dual Inline Memory Module)	222–228
		SoDIMM (Small Outline DIMM)	222–228
		MicroDIMM	
		RIMM (Rambus Inline Memory Module)	222–228
		Operational characteristics	
		Memory chips (8-bit, 16-bit, and 32-bit)	222–230 220–221
		Parity chips versus non-parity chips	221
		ECC versus non-ECC	220–221
		Single sided versus double sided	226
4.3	Identify the most popular types of motherboards, their components, and their architecture (bus structures).	**Types of motherboards**	
		AT	107, 113–115
		ATX	108, 113–115
		Communication ports	
		Serial	113–115
		USB	113–115
		Parallel	113–115
		IEEE-1394/FireWire	103–105 290–291
		Infrared	372–373
		Memory	
		SIMM	222–228
		DIMM	222–228
		RIMM	222–228
		SoDIMM	222–228
		MicroDIMM	222–228

Domain 4.0 (continued)

Section	Objective	Subobjective	Page Range
		Processor sockets	
		Slot 1	129–132
		Slot 2	129–132
		Slot A	129–132
		Socket A	129–132
		Socket 7	129–132
		Socket 8	129–132
		Socket 423	129–132
		Socket 478	129–132
		Socket 370	129–132
		External cache memory (level 2)	241–243
		Bus architecture	
		ISA	108–112
		PCI 32-bit	108–112
		PCI 64-bit	108–112
		AGP 2X, -4X, and 8X (Pro)	108–112
		USB (Universal Serial Bus)	105–108, 115
		AMR (audio modem riser) slots	PDF:1006–1007
		CNR (communication network riser) slots	PDF:1006–1007
		Basic compatibility guidelines	147 PDF:843–844
		IDE (ATA, ATAPI, Ultra-DMA, EIDE)	105–108
		SCSI (Wide, Fast, Ultra, LVD)	463–467
		Chipsets	103–105 107–108
4.4	Identify the purpose of CMOS (Complementary Metal-Oxide Semiconductor), what it contains, and how to change its basic parameters.	**CMOS settings**	
		Default settings	194–195
		CPU settings	141–143
			197–199

Domain 4.0   (continued)

Section	Objective	Subobjective	Page Range
		Printer parallel port—Uni/bidirectional, disable/enable, ECP, EPP	199–201 248–253
		COM/serial port—memory address, interrupt request, disable	199–201 259–261
		Floppy drive—enable/disable drive or boot, speed, density	195–197 206–207
		Hard drive—size and drive type	195–197
		Memory—speed, parity, non-parity	198–200
		Boot sequence	206–207
		Date/time	195–197
		Passwords	197
		Plug and Play BIOS	191–194 204–206
		Disabling onboard devices	199–201
		Disabling virus protection	191–194
		Power management	201–202
		Infrared	199–201

Domain 5.0: Printers

Section	Objective	Subobjective	Page Range
5.1	Identify printer technologies, interfaces, and options/upgrades.	**Technologies**	
		Laser	344–352
		Ink dispersion (inkjet)	338–344
		Dot matrix	333–338
		Solid ink	355–357
		Thermal	352–353
		Dye sublimation	353–355
		Interfaces	
		Parallel	246–248
		Network	PDF:1007

Domain 5.0 (continued)

Section	Objective	Subobjective	Page Range
		SCSI	PDF:1007
		USB	264–269
		Infrared	372–374
		Serial	254–264
		IEEE-1394/FireWire	290–293
		Wireless	PDF:1007
		Options/upgrades	
		Memory	347–349
		Hard drives	PDF:1007
		NICs	PDF:1007
		Trays and feeders	PDF:1007
		Finishers (for example, stapling and so forth)	PDF:1008
		Scanners/fax/copier	PDF:1008
5.2	Recognize common printer problems and techniques used to resolve them.	Printer drivers	357–358
		Firmware updates	357–358
		Paper feed and output	PDF:878
			PDF:880
			PDF:883
		Calibrations	PDF:342 PDF:890
		Printing test pages	687, 689 PDF:878–881 PDF:885
		Errors (printed or displayed)	PDF:882–884
		Memory	688–689 PDF:882–883
		Configuration	687–689 PDF:880–881 PDF:883, PDF:885 PDF:887–888
		Network connections	PDF:913–922
		Paper jam	PDF:878, PDF:883 PDF:890

Domain 5.0 (continued)

Section	Objective	Subobjective	Page Range
		Print quality	PDF:877–881 PDF:882, PDF:884 PDF:886–887 PDF:889–890
		Safety precautions	423
		Preventive maintenance	336, 341, 351–352 355–357, PDF:886–887
		Consumables	416 337 339–340 343–344 345–347 349–356
		Environment	416

Domain 6.0: Basic Networking

Section	Objective	Subobjective	Page Range
6.1	Identify the common types of network cables, their characteristics, and connectors.	**Cable types**	
		RG-6 (coaxial)	782–786
		RG-8 (coaxial)	782–786
		RG-58 (coaxial)	782–786
		RG-59 (coaxial)	782–786
		Plenum/PVC	782–786
		UTP CAT3	782–786
		UTP CAT5/e	782–786
		UTP CAT6	782–786
		Fiber (single and multimode)	782–786
		Connector types	
		BNC	782–786
		RJ-45	782–786
		AUI	782–786
		ST/SC	PDF:918
		IDC/UDC (token ring)	PDF:918

Domain 6.0 (continued)

A+ Objectives for the 2003 Operating Systems Exam

Domain 1.0: Operating System Fundamentals

Section	Objective	Subobjective	Page Range
1.1	Identify the major desktop components and interfaces and their functions. Differentiate the characteristics of Windows 9x/Me, Windows NT 4.0 Workstation, Windows 2000 Professional, and Windows XP.	Contrasts between Windows 9x/Me, Windows NT 4.0 Workstation, Windows 2000 Professional, and Windows XP	618–619
		Major operating system components	
		Registry	614–617, 621–624
		Virtual memory	671–674
		File system	489–500
		Major operating system interfaces	
		Windows Explorer	625–630
		My Computer	625
		Control Panel	631–634
		Computer Management Console	647–649
		Accessories/System Tools	641–646
		Command line	663–670, PDF:1009–1032
		Network Neighborhood/ My Network Places	792, 801–802, 804–805, PDF:918–922,
		Taskbar/systray	634–636
		Start Menu	636–640
		Device Manager	703–712
1.2	Identify the names, locations, purposes, and contents of major system files.	**Windows 9x–specific files**	
		`Io.sys`	603–606
		`Msdos.sys`	607–610
		`WIN.COM`	613–614
		`Autoexec.bat`	611
		`Command.com`	664
		`Config.sys`	610–611
		`HIMEM.SYS`	611–612
		`Emm386.exe`	611–612

Domain 1.0 (continued)

Domain 1.0 (continued)

Section	Objective	Subobjective	Page Range
1.4	Identify basic concepts and procedures for creating, viewing, and managing disks, directories (folders), and files. This includes procedures for changing file attributes and the ramifications of those changes (for example, security issues).	**Disks (partition types)**	
		Active partition	507–509
		Primary partition	501–503
		Extended partition	501–503
		Logical partition	509–510
		Disks (file systems)	
		FAT16	489–496
		FAT32	496–498
		NTFS4	498
		NTFS5.x	498–499
		Directory (folder) structures (root directory, subdirectories, and so on)	
		Create folders	PDF:1019–1020
		Navigate the directory structure	PDF:1019–1020
		Maximum depth	655–656
		Files	
		Creating files	653
		Filenaming conventions (most common extensions, 8.3, maximum length)	654–655
		File attributes—Read Only, Hidden, System, and Archive attributes	657–660
		File compression	658–660
		File encryption	659–660
		File permissions	660
		File types (text versus binary file)	654
1.5	Identify the major operating system utilities, their purpose, location, and available switches.	**Disk management tools**	
		DEFRAG.EXE	651–652
		FDISK.EXE	506–510
		Backup/Restore utility (MSbackup, NTBackup, and so forth)	623, 641–643
		ScanDisk	649–651 PDF:1010

Domain 1.0   (continued)

Section	Objective	Subobjective	Page Range
		CHKDSK	649–651 PDF:1011
		Disk Cleanup	645
		Format	511–513, 517–521
		System management tools	
		Device Manager	703–712
		System Manager	647–649
		Computer Manager	647–649
		MSCONFIG.EXE	747–748
		REGEDIT.EXE (view information/back up Registry)	614–616 622–623
		REGEDT32.EXE	622–623
		SYSEDIT.EXE	618
		SCANREG	617
		COMMAND/CMD	664
		Event Viewer	648–649, PDF:824
		Task Manager	PDF:922–923
		File management tools	
		ATTRIB.EXE	PDF:1021–1022
		EXTRACT.EXE	745–751
		Edit.com	PDF:1028–1029
		Windows Explorer	625–630

Domain 2.0: Installation, Configuration, and Upgrading

Section	Objective	Subobjective	Page Range
2.1	Identify the procedures for installing Windows 9x/Me, Windows NT 4.0 Workstation, Windows 2000 Professional, and Windows XP, and bring the operating system to a basic operational level.	Verify hardware compatibility and minimum requirements	532–540
		Determine OS installation options	541–542
		Installation type (typical, custom, other)	546
		Network configuration	546, 553 558, 560–561

Domain 2.0 (continued)

Section	Objective	Subobjective	Page Range
		File system type	543
		Dual-boot support	530–532 545–548 561–567
		Disk preparation order (conceptual disk preparation)	
		Start the installation	543–550 552–553 555–561
		Partition (9x/Me)	544
		Format drive (9x/Me)	545
		Partition and format drive (NT 4.0)	552–553
		Partition and format Drive (2000/XP)	556–558
		Run appropriate setup utility	
		Setup	545, 563–564
		Winnt	552
		Installation methods	
		Bootable CD	530–532 544, 552, 555
		Boot floppy	484–489 544, 552 555
		Network installation	548–550 553 567
		Drive imaging	568–569
		Device driver configuration	
		Load default drivers	550 554 568
		Find updated drivers	550–551 554 568
		Restore user data files (if applicable)	570

Domain 2.0 (continued)

Section	Objective	Subobjective	Page Range
		Identify common symptoms and problems	570–572, 580–581, 590–592, 598–599
2.2	Identify steps to perform an operating system upgrade from Windows 9x/Me, Windows NT 4.0 Workstation, Windows 2000 Professional, and Windows XP. Given an upgrade scenario, choose the appropriate next steps.	Upgrade paths available	576–579 581 592
		Determine correct upgrade startup utility (for example, WINNT32 versus WINNT)	487–489
		Verify hardware compatibility and minimum requirements	576–577 581–582 592–595
		Verify application compatibility	582 593–595
		Apply OS service packs, patches, and updates	580 587–590 596–598
		Install additional Windows components	641
2.3	Identify the basic system boot sequences and boot methods, including the steps to create an emergency boot disk with utilities installed for Windows 9x/Me, Windows NT 4.0 Workstation, Windows 2000 Professional, and Windows XP.	**Boot sequence**	
		Files required to boot	
		Boot steps (9x)	604
		Boot steps (NT based)	619
		Alternative boot methods	
		Using a Startup disk	725–726 732–733
		Safe/VGA-only mode	727–731 734–736
		Last Known Good Configuration	735
		Command Prompt mode	729–730
		Boot to a system restore point	718–720 747–748
		Recovery Console	750–752
		Boot.ini switches	620–621 732, 748 751

Domain 2.0 (continued)

Section	Objective	Subobjective	Page Range
		Dual boot	530–532, 545–548 561–567
		Create emergency disks with OS utilities	484–488 623 643 733
		Create emergency repair disks (ERDs)	554 623 643
2.4	Identify procedures for loading/ adding and configuring device drivers and the necessary software for certain devices. drivers	**Device driver installation**	
		Plug and Play (PnP) and non-PNP devices	693–696
		Install and configure device	700–701
		Install different device drivers	703–712
		Manually install a device driver	703–712
		Search the Internet for updated device drivers	580 587–590 596–598 700–701
		Use unsigned drivers (driver signing)	700–701
		Install additional Windows components	641
		Determine if permissions are adequate for performing the task	660
2.5	Identify procedures necessary to optimize the operating system and major operating system subsystems.	Virtual memory management	671–674
		Disk defragmentation	651–652
		Files and buffers	606, 610–611
		Caches	461–463 646–647, 677
		Temporary file management	675–676

Domain 3.0: Diagnosing and Troubleshooting

Section	Objective	Subobjective	Page Range
3.1	Recognize and interpret the meaning of common error codes and startup messages from the boot sequence, and identify steps to correct the problems.	**Common error messages and codes (boot failure and errors)**	
		Invalid boot disk	523–525, 741–743
		Inaccessible boot device	451–453, 455–456 741–743
		Missing NTLDR	732
		Bad or missing Command interpreter	725
		Common error messages and codes (Startup messages)	
		Error in `CONFIG.SYS` line XX	724–725
		`Himem.sys` not loaded	725
		Missing or corrupt `Himem.sys`	726 733
		Device/service has failed to start	746–747
		A device referenced in `SYSTEM.INI/WIN.INI/` Registry is not found	726–727
		Event Viewer—Event log is full	733–734
		Failure to start GUI	738–739
		Windows protection error	727
		User-modified settings cause improper operation at startup	613–614 727–731 734–736
		Registry corruption	617, 621–623
		Use the correct utilities	
		Dr. Watson	737–738
		Boot disk	484–487 726
		Event Viewer	647–649
3.2	Recognize when to use common diagnostic utilities and tools. Given a diagnostic scenario involving one of these utilities or tools, select the appropriate steps needed to resolve the problem.	**Utilities and tools (Startup disk)**	
		Required files for a boot disk	485–487, 604, 664
		Boot disk with CD-ROM support	486–487
		Utilities and tools (Startup Modes)	
		Safe Mode	728–731

Domain 3.0 (continued)

Section	Objective	Subobjective	Page Range
		Safe Mode with command prompt	728–731
		Safe Mode with networking	728–731
		Step-by-Step/Single step mode	728–731
		Automatic skip driver (ASD.exe)	707, 716–717
		Diagnostic tools, utilities, and resources	
		User/installation manuals	PDF:833–834
		Internet/Web resources	PDF:833–834
		Training materials	PDF:833–834
		Task Manager	PDF:922–923
		Dr. Watson	737–738
		Boot disk	484–487 726
		Event Viewer	647–649
		Device Manager	703–712
		WinMSD	PDF:924
		MSD	PDF:924
		Recovery CD	569–570
		CONFIGSAFE	PDF:925–926
		Elicit problem symptoms from customers	PDF:825–826
		Have customer reproduce error as part of the diagnostic process	PDF:825–826
		Identify recent changes to the computer environment from the user	PDF:825–826
3.3	Recognize common operational and usability problems and determine how to resolve them.	**Troubleshooting Windows-specific printing problems**	
		Print spool is stalled	746–747
		Incorrect/incompatible driver for print	692–693 PDF:887–889
		Incorrect parameter	687–693

Domain 3.0 (continued)

Section	Objective	Subobjective	Page Range
		Other common problems	
		General protection faults	737
		Bluescreen error (BSOD)	738–739
		Illegal operation	737
		Invalid working directory	744
		System lockup	744–745
		Option (sound card, modem, input device) will not function	703–712
		Application will not start or load	744 PDF:924–925
		Cannot log on to network (option—NIC not functioning)	745
		Applications don't install	746
		Network connection	PDF:913–922
		Viruses and virus types	
		What they are	752–753
		TSR (Terminate-Stay-Resident) programs and viruses	753
		Sources (floppy, emails, and so forth)	753–754
		How to determine presence	754

Domain 4.0: Networks

Section	Objective	Subobjective	Page Range
4.1	Identify the networking capabilities of Windows. Given configuration parameters, configure the operating system to connect to a network.	**Configure protocols (TCP/IP)**	
		Gateway	793 796
		Subnet mask	793 794–795
		DNS (and domain suffix)	776–777 793 796
		WINS	793 795–796

Domain 4.0 (continued)

Section	Objective	Subobjective	Page Range
		Static address assignment	792–794
		Automatic address assignment (APIPA, DHCP)	792–794 PDF:914
		Configure IPX/SPX (NWLink)	796
		Configure AppleTalk	796–797
		Configure NetBEUI/ NetBIOS	797
		Configure client options	
		Microsoft	801–802
		Novell	801–802
		Verify the configuration	809 PDF:1031–1032
		Understand the use of the following tools	
		IPCONFIG.EXE	PDF:1031
		WINIPCFG.EXE	PDF:1032
		PING	PDF:1029–1030
		TRACERT.EXE	PDF:1030
		NSLOOKUP.EXE	PDF:1030
		Share resources (understand the capabilities/limitations with each OS version)	798–804
		Set permissions to shared resources	798–800
		Network type and network card	778–781
4.2	Identify the basic Internet protocols and terminologies. Identify procedures for establishing Internet connectivity. In a given scenario, configure the operating system to connect to and use Internet resources.	**Protocols and terminologies**	
		ISP	774
		TCP/IP	773
		Email (POP, SMTP, IMAP)	777–778
		HTML	775
		HTTP	774
		HTTPS	774
		SSL	774
		Telnet	776
		FTP	776

Domain 4.0 (continued)

Section Objective	Subobjective	Page Range
	DNS	776–777
	Connectivity technologies	
	Dial-up networking	763–766
	DSL networking	767–769
	ISDN networking	766–767
	Cable	769–770
	Satellite	770–771
	Wireless	771
	LAN	759, 772
	Install and configure browsers	
	Enable/disable script support	808
	Configure proxy settings	807–808
	Configure security settings	808–809
	Firewall protection under Windows XP	809

2

PC ANATOMY 101

You can walk into most furniture stores and see a 3D cardboard facsimile of a computer: It's the kind of thing that stores put on display to help you realize that the computer desk on sale this week will, in fact, hold a computer. What is it about a real computer that makes it different than the cardboard phony?

The real computer has a **central processing unit (CPU)** to create and modify information; instructions, to tell the CPU what to do; a place to store the instructions and the output they produce (data); and a workspace where the CPU can work with instructions and data. These essential parts can be broken down into three categories: hardware, software, and firmware. By contrast, the cardboard PC clone at the furniture store doesn't have any of these.

As a computer technician, you will be dealing on a day-to-day basis with the three major parts of any computing environment. Whether you're working on a computer, printer, or component such as a video card, you must determine whether the problem involves hardware, software, firmware, or a combination of these three.

Hardware Overview

Hardware is the physical part of computing. From disk drives to printer cables, from speakers to printers, hardware is the part of computing you can pick up, move around, open, and close. Although hardware might represent the glamorous side of computing (whose computer is faster, has a larger hard disk, more memory, and so on), it can do nothing without software and firmware to provide instructions. Hardware failures can take place because of loose connections, electrical or physical damage, or incompatible devices.

Software Overview

Software provides the instructions that tell hardware what to do. The same computer system can be used for word processing, gaming, accounting, or Web surfing by installing and using new software. Software comes in various types, including operating systems, application programs, and utility programs.

Operating systems provide standard methods for saving, retrieving, changing, printing, and transmitting information. The most common operating systems today are various versions of Microsoft Windows. The 2003 version of the A+ Certification Exam focuses on all recent 32-bit desktop versions of Windows (Windows 9x and Me, Windows NT 4.0 Workstation, Windows 2000 Professional, and Windows XP). Because operating systems provide the "glue" that connects hardware devices and applications, they are written to work on specified combinations of CPUs and hardware.

note

The CD included with this book contains important Study Lab material for this chapter, as well as Chapters 3–22 in this book. The Study Lab for each chapter contains terms to study, exercises, and practice tests—all in printable PDF format (Adobe Acrobat Reader is included on the CD, too). These Study Lab materials will help you gear up for the A+ Exam. Also, the CD includes an industry-leading test engine from PrepLogic, which simulates the actual A+ test so that you can be sure that you're ready when test day arrives. Don't let the A+ test intimidate you. If you've read the chapters, worked through the Study Lab, and passed the practice tests from PrepLogic, you should be well prepared to ace the test!

Also, you'll notice that some words throughout each chapter are in bold format. These are study terms that are defined in the Study Lab. Be sure to consult the Study Lab when you are finished with this chapter to test what you've learned.

Operating system commands come in two major types: internal and external. **Internal commands** are those built into the operating system when it starts the computer. **External commands** require that you run a particular program that is included with the operating system.

Application programs are used to create, store, modify and view information you create, also called **data**. Because an operating system provides standard methods for using storage, printing, and network devices to work with information, applications must be written to comply with the requirements of an operating system and its associated CPUs. A+ Certification does not require any knowledge of application programs, but to provide the best technical support, you should learn the basics of the major applications your company supports, such as Microsoft Office, Corel WordPerfect Office, Adobe Photoshop, and many others.

Certifications are available for major operating systems and applications, and seeking certifications in these areas can further improve your chances of being hired and promoted.

Utility programs are used to keep a computer in good working condition or to set up new devices. In the operating system chapters, you'll learn how to use the major utilities that are included with Windows.

Because these utilities have limited capabilities, you might also want to invest in other utility programs, such as Symantec's Norton System Works or PowerQuest's Drive Image or Partition Magic, for use in your day-to-day work; however, only standard Windows utilities, such as ScanDisk, Fdisk, Disk Management, Defrag, and others, are covered on the A+ Certification Exam.

Firmware Overview

Firmware represents a middle ground between hardware and software. Like hardware, firmware is physical: a chip or chips attached to devices such as motherboards, video cards, network cards, modems, and printers. However, firmware is also software: Firmware chips (such as the motherboard BIOS) contain instructions for hardware testing, hardware configuration, and input/output routines. In essence, firmware is "software on a chip," and the software's job is to control the device to which the chip is connected.

Because firmware works with both hardware and software, changes in either one can cause firmware to become outdated. Outdated firmware can lead to device or system failure or even data loss.

Until the mid-1990s, the only way to change firmware was to remove the chip and replace it with one containing new instructions. Most firmware today is *flashable*, meaning that its contents can be changed through software. You'll learn more about the most common type of firmware, the motherboard BIOS, in Chapter 6, "BIOS and CMOS Configuration."

Memory: RAM and ROM

There are two types of **memory** in a computer: RAM and ROM. In the early days of personal computing, some vendors made their systems sound more impressive by adding these two totals. However, their function in computer systems is very different.

The contents of **RAM (random access memory)** can be accessed in any order and can change instantly. They are in constant flux as you start a computer; load its operating system and drivers for particular devices; load an application; create, store, change, and copy data; and shut down the computer.

Programs are loaded into RAM; until data is stored, it exists only in RAM (that's why you should save your work so often!). The "enemies" of data stored in RAM include

- System crashes and lockups
- User error (forgetting to save before you close a program)
- Power failures

Because most types of RAM must receive a steady dose of electricity to keep its contents around, even momentary power failures can destroy its contents. Because all data must be created or changed in RAM before it's stored, you must make sure that RAM is working correctly. In Chapter 7, "RAM," you'll learn more about adding, configuring, and using RAM.

ROM stands for **read-only memory**, meaning that although its contents, like those of RAM, can be accessed in any order, ROM's contents can't be changed by normal computer operations. So, what is ROM good for?

Because ROM's contents don't change when a system is powered down or restarted, it's the perfect storage place for firmware. As we saw earlier, firmware is the "software on a chip" used to control various devices in the computer. ROM isn't suitable for software storage, however, because its capacity is too limited for today's large programs. And, of course, ROM can't be used to store data files that are constantly changing.

note

Flash memory, also called Flash RAM, is a special type of RAM that uses electricity to change its contents, but doesn't require electricity to maintain its contents. It is used in BIOS chips and in storage for digital music players and digital cameras.

The way that ROM chips have been made has changed several times over the years. Originally, ROMs contained a permanently etched pattern; later, ROMs were made of reprogrammable materials that could be changed through controlled ultraviolet light or electricity. Because the chip had to be removed from the motherboard for replacement or reprogramming, changing the contents of ROMs was difficult and inconvenient. If you think that opening up a single system to change its ROM chip is a pain, imagine performing the same job on dozens of PCs!

Fortunately, current ROMs can be reprogrammed with software. This process is called **flashing** the ROM and is performed with the BIOS firmware found on motherboards and in modems, among other devices. Want to learn more? The reasons for upgrading ROMs and the methods used are covered in Chapter 6.

Dissecting Your Computer

Before you can troubleshoot your computer, you need to understand what a computer is and how it's put together. A computer (or PC, for personal computer) is not a single unit, but is instead a collection of hardware subsystems including

- Video
- Storage
- Input devices
- Printers and other output devices
- Audio
- Networking
- Processor
- Memory
- Power
- Motherboard

Whenever a computer stops working, you can trace it back to the failure of one or more of these subsystems (the device and its cables). What controls the subsystems?

These subsystems are controlled by two types of software:

- A system **BIOS (basic input/output system)** chip on the motherboard (an example of "software on a chip," or firmware)
- The operating system and its device drivers (files that tell Windows how to use your PC's hardware)

Hardware and operating system software are both used by application programs such as Microsoft Office, Adobe Photoshop, Quicken, and many, many others to create, change, store, print, and transmit information.

With even the simplest devices and software depending upon so many other factors, troubleshooting your computer can be a challenge. But, if you don't know the details of what's inside a typical computer and how all this hardware and software relates to each other, it's just about impossible.

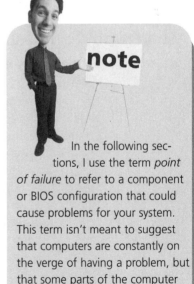

note

In the following sections, I use the term *point of failure* to refer to a component or BIOS configuration that could cause problems for your system. This term isn't meant to suggest that computers are constantly on the verge of having a problem, but that some parts of the computer are more likely to cause problems than others.

This chapter introduces you to the major components you will find in typical computers, including those prone to being a **point of failure**. Think of it as an anatomy lesson, but without the formaldehyde or nasty smells.

The Outside Story of Typical Computers

Although the "inside" story of computers is even more complicated than the outside, don't neglect taking a good look at the outside of your system when it's time to troubleshoot a computer problem. You also need to check out the outside of the computer when it's time to plug in a peripheral to see if there's a suitable connector for it.

The outside of the computer is where you'll find

- Cable connections for external peripherals such as cable modems, printers, monitors, and scanners
- Drive bays for removable-media and optical drives
- The power supply fan and voltage switch
- The power cord between the computer and the wall outlet (and between external peripherals such as monitors and printers and the wall outlet)
- The power switch, reset button, and signal lights

All in all, the outside of the computer is a good place to start when your computer has stopped working, even if you're not sure if that's where the problem lies.

The Front View of a Typical Desktop Computer

A typical "desktop" computer actually sits on the floor in most offices, and resembles Figure 2.1.

The case shown in Figure 2.1 is sometimes referred to as a *mid-tower* case. This computer has room for up to six internal drives (three in 5.25-inch bays and three in 3.5-inch bays; one of the 3.5-inch bays can't be seen in Figure 2.1).

CD-ROMs, CD-RWs, DVD-ROMs, and similar optical drives, as well as large removable-media drives, such as the Castlewood Orb and Iomega Jaz, use 5.25-inch drive bays. Floppy drives, hard drives, and smaller removable-media drives, such as Iomega Zip and SuperDisk LS-120/LS-240, use 3.5-inch drive bays. 3.5-inch drives also can be installed in 5.25-inch drive bays with special mounting brackets.

As Figure 2.1 also shows, you can add other types of devices to the 5.25-inch drive bays, such as the Sound Blaster Audigy Drive (a breakout box for this popular sound card), cooling fans, drive-selection switches, and front-mounted connectors for IEEE-1394 and USB ports.

The front panel of a typical desktop computer with some higher-end internal peripherals. The components seen here vary from PC to PC.

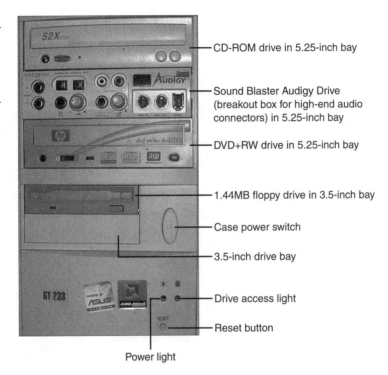

CD-ROM drive in 5.25-inch bay

Sound Blaster Audigy Drive (breakout box for high-end audio connectors) in 5.25-inch bay

DVD+RW drive in 5.25-inch bay

1.44MB floppy drive in 3.5-inch bay

Case power switch

3.5-inch drive bay

Drive access light

Reset button

Power light

Note that the Sound Blaster Audigy Drive has connectors for some types of speakers and other multimedia devices. Some cases also feature built-in USB, serial, and IEEE-1394a ports. Unfortunately, front-mounted ports are still quite rare. Most devices still connect to the rear of the computer, which makes it more difficult to fix problems caused by loose cables and gets your knees dusty.

Points of Failure on the Front of a Computer

The front of the computer might provide valuable clues if you're having problems with a system. In case of problems, check the following common points of failure for help:

- *Can't read CD or DVD media*—The drive door on the CD-ROM or other optical drive might not be completely closed or the media might be inserted upside down; press the eject button to open the drive, remove any obstacles, reseat the media, and close the drive.

tip

You also can eject optical media with Windows Explorer under My Computer. Right-click on the drive and select Eject. If the drive doesn't eject the media, there could be a problem with the drive's data cable, cable connection, or power connection.

■ *Can't shut down the computer with the case power switch*—The case power switch is connected to the motherboard on ATX and Micro-ATX systems, not directly to the power supply as with older designs. The wire might be loose or connected to the wrong pins on the motherboard. Keep in mind that most systems require you to hold in the power button for about four seconds before the system will shut down. If the computer crashes, you might need to shut down the computer by unplugging it or by turning off the surge suppressor used by the computer. Some ATX power supplies have their own on-off switches, but this is not commonplace.

■ *Can't see the drive access or power lights*—As with the case power switch, these lights are also connected to the motherboard. These wires might also be loose or connected to the wrong pins on the motherboard.

■ *Can't use USB, IEEE-1394, or digital camera (serial) ports on the front of the system*—Some systems have these ports on the front of the computer as well as the rear. Front-mounted ports are connected with extension cables to the motherboard. If the cables inside the case are loose, the ports won't work. If the ports are disabled in the system BIOS, the ports won't work.

As you can see from this section, in many situations, you will need to open the case to resolve a problem, even though the symptoms might first manifest themselves outside the computer. To learn more about the typical components found in a PC, see "Inside a Typical PC," later in this chapter.

note

The term *desktop computer* is a bit misleading today because few computers actually sit on the user's desk anymore (when I started working with computers in 1983, real desktop computers were virtually all there were). However, this term survives to describe computers that

• Use standard internal components such as motherboards, processors, memory, drives, sound cards, and video cards

• Can be upgraded and rebuilt by the user without special tools

• Use separate input devices (keyboard, mouse, or other pointing device)

Most (but not all) desktop computers are multipiece units with a separate keyboard and monitor, although the iMac has inspired a few compact "all-in-one" PCs, which incorporate a monitor.

The Rear View of a Typical Desktop Computer

If the video has gone missing in action, you can't connect to the Internet, or your printer refuses to print, it's time to check out the rear of the computer.

Figure 2.2 shows the rear of a typical desktop computer when common peripheral cables are attached, while Figure 2.3 shows the rear of the same computer after the cables are removed.

FIGURE 2.2

The rear panel of a typical desktop computer with common external peripheral cables attached.

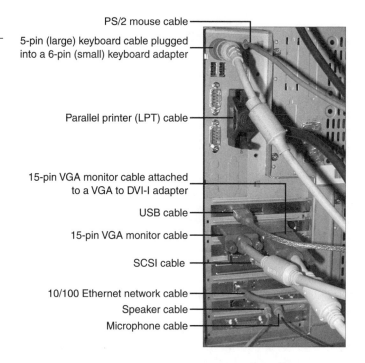

PS/2 mouse cable

5-pin (large) keyboard cable plugged into a 6-pin (small) keyboard adapter

Parallel printer (LPT) cable

15-pin VGA monitor cable attached to a VGA to DVI-I adapter

USB cable

15-pin VGA monitor cable

SCSI cable

10/100 Ethernet network cable

Speaker cable

Microphone cable

Figures 2.2 and 2.3 are typical of computers built in local computer shops (also called "box shops") from standard parts. However, the rear panel of a computer purchased in a retail store or sold as a corporate workstation might more closely resemble the rear panel shown in Figure 2.4. These computers often have built-in sound and VGA video ports (visible in Figure 2.4), and some might also include built-in 10/100 Ethernet ports.

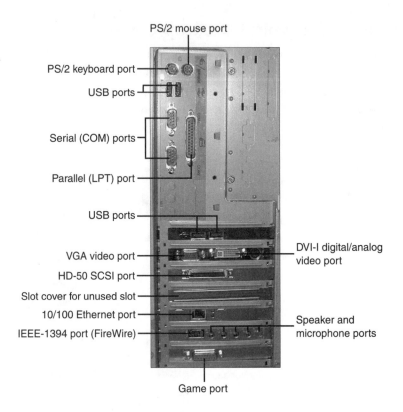

FIGURE 2.3

The rear panel of a typical desktop computer with built-in ports (top) and ports on add-in cards (bottom).

PS/2 mouse port

PS/2 keyboard port

USB ports

Serial (COM) ports

Parallel (LPT) port

USB ports

VGA video port

HD-50 SCSI port

Slot cover for unused slot

10/100 Ethernet port

IEEE-1394 port (FireWire)

DVI-I digital/analog video port

Speaker and microphone ports

Game port

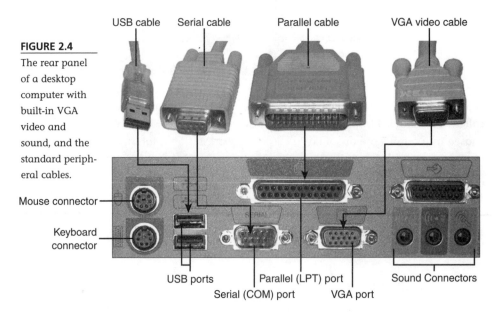

FIGURE 2.4

The rear panel of a desktop computer with built-in VGA video and sound, and the standard peripheral cables.

USB cable   Serial cable   Parallel cable   VGA video cable

Mouse connector

Keyboard connector

USB ports

Serial (COM) port

Parallel (LPT) port

VGA port

Sound Connectors

The computers pictured in Figures 2.2–2.4 use motherboards that are members of the ATX family of motherboard designs. The ATX design, and its more compact siblings, Micro-ATX and Flex-ATX, are found in virtually all computers sold since 1997; the ATX family is far and away the most common industry–standard motherboard form factor used today.

What are the differences between ATX, Micro-ATX, and Flex-ATX? ATX motherboards have six or seven expansion slots inside; Micro-ATX motherboards, which are used most frequently in low-cost retail-store computers sold for home use, normally have three or four expansion slots. Flex-ATX motherboards have no more than two expansion slots, and often have no expansion slots at all; they are used most often in small form-factor and slimline PCs used as corporate workstations.

tip

Although the cables shown in Figure 2.4 are distinctly different from one another, some cables (such as speaker and microphone cables) use the same type of connector. How can you tell what's what? Most recent computers, motherboards, and peripherals use the PC99 color coding standards. See them online at http://www.pcdesguide.org/documents/pc99icons.htm.

Older types of computers use different types of motherboards that have built-in ports mounted under the expansion slots (LPX) or have built-in ports wired to connectors mounted in the expansion slots (Baby-AT). See Chapter 4, "The Motherboard and CPU," for more information about the ATX family, Baby-AT, and LPX motherboard designs.

Above the rear panel details shown in Figures 2.2–2.4 is the power supply (see Figure 2.5). Power supplies actually convert high-voltage AC power into the low-voltage DC power used inside the computer. Because conversions of this type create heat, the power supply has a fan to cool itself and also help overall system cooling.

Although a few power supplies can switch between 115-volt and 230-volt (V) services automatically, most use a sliding switch.

Learn more about the power supply in Chapter 5, "Power Supplies and Circuit Testing."

Sliding AC voltage selector (set for 115V)

Power supply fan

FIGURE 2.5

A typical power supply mounted in a computer.

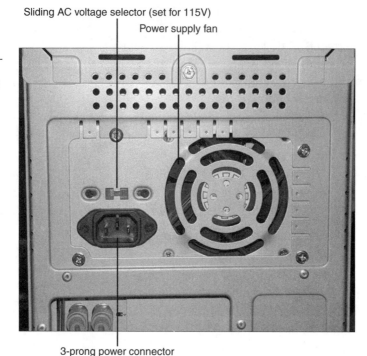

3-prong power connector

The Parallel Port

The parallel port, previously shown in Figure 2.4, is one of the oldest multipurpose interfaces found on a typical PC. The parallel port uses a DB-25F connector, and was originally designed for use with parallel printers. However, it has since been adapted for use with removable-storage drives of varying types (Zip, SuperDisk, CD-ROM, CD-RW), scanners, and for direct parallel (Direct Cable Connection or LapLink) file transfer. The parallel port is included as part of most ATX and Micro-ATX computers' rear panels as shown in Figure 2.4, but it can also be built into an add-on card, which can be installed into the PCI or ISA expansion slots on the motherboard.

Don't be surprised if you work on PCs without parallel ports. The USB port can do every job the parallel port can do, and so-called "legacy-free" computers don't include built-in parallel ports.

If the parallel port is built into the motherboard, as in Figure 2.4, it is considered an ISA device and its IRQ (normally IRQ 7) cannot be shared with other devices. For more details on the hardware resources used by the parallel port, see "Hardware Resources," later in this chapter.

The Serial Port

The serial port, shown in Figure 2.4, was introduced along with the parallel port on the first PCs. The original serial ports used a DB-25M connector, but virtually all serial ports in recent years have used a DB-9M connector as seen in Figure 2.4. The serial port was originally intended for use with analog (dial-up) modems and serial printers, but has been most often used in more recent times for data transfer with programs such as Direct Cable Connection or LapLink, battery backup (UPS/SPS) signaling, PDA docking station connections, or connections for pointing devices such as mice.

Like the parallel port, the serial port is also being replaced by the USB port. Although most recent computers still have one or two serial ports built into the motherboard, legacy-free computers don't have any serial ports. Serial ports can also be added to the ISA or PCI expansion slots on the motherboard.

If the serial port is built into the motherboard, it is an ISA device and it cannot share its IRQ with devices other than serial ports. Although COM 1 and COM 3 "share" IRQ 4, and COM 2 and COM 4 "share" IRQ 3, in practice this means only that COM 1 or COM 2 can be used only when COM 3 or COM 4 is not being used, and vice versa. For more details on the hardware resources used by the serial port, see "Hardware Resources," later in this chapter.

The SCSI Interface

Here's an interface you won't see nearly as often as serial or parallel ports: SCSI. SCSI cards are installed only when a particular device needs to connect via SCSI.

The SCSI interface can have several forms, depending upon the type of SCSI card installed in your computer (it's rare to have a motherboard with built-in SCSI). The most common types of SCSI connectors are shown in Figure 2.6.

The HD-68 pin connector is used for high-performance Wide SCSI devices such as hard drives and tape backups. The other three interfaces are used for various types of Narrow SCSI devices, including CD-ROM, CD-R, and CD-RW drives; scanners; and removable-media drives. Most SCSI cards can support internal and external devices.

The 25-pin connector shown in Figure 2.6 is found primarily on low-cost SCSI cards bundled with scanners or Zip drives. It uses the same DB-25F connector used by the parallel port, but is not interchangeable. To determine if a 25-pin adapter on the rear of your system is a SCSI port, use these methods:

- A 25-pin SCSI connector will usually say SCSI on the card bracket at the rear of the computer or be marked with the SCSI SE SCSI symbol shown in Figure 2.7.

■ Open the Device Manager display of onboard hardware to see if a SCSI device is listed; note that the Promise Ultra IDE controller built into some motherboards is listed under SCSI Devices in Device Manager, but is used for IDE/ATA devices. A true SCSI card will list SCSI in the device description in Device Manager.

FIGURE 2.6

Typical SCSI interfaces: HD-68 (top), HD-50 (second from top), DB25 (third from top), and Centronics 50 (bottom).

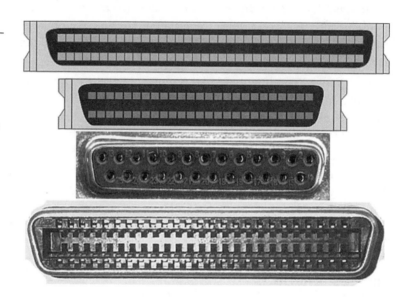

FIGURE 2.7

Logos used to mark SCSI ports and cables. SE signaling is used by narrow SCSI devices. LVD signaling is used by most Wide SCSI devices. LVD/SE ports can work with LVD or SE devices.

SCSI Logos

Single-ended (SE)

Low-Voltage Differential (LVD)

Low-Voltage Differential/ Single-ended (LVD/SE)

Most SCSI cards plug into the PCI slot on the motherboard or the PC Card slot found in notebook computers. In these cases, the IRQ used by the card can be shared with other devices. However, older SCSI cards used ISA, EISA, or VL-Bus slots (EISA and VL-Bus were based on ISA); EISA IRQs can be shared with other EISA cards only, while ISA and VL-Bus cards can't share IRQs at all. Narrow SCSI (25-pin or 50-pin interface) cards support up to seven unique devices plus the host adapter, while Wide SCSI (68-pin) cards support up to fifteen unique devices plus the host adapter. External SCSI devices have two ports, enabling you to create a daisy-chain of devices. Each device plugged into a SCSI card must have a unique device ID, and the end of the daisy-chain of devices must be terminated. For more details about SCSI interfaces, daisy-chaining, and device configuration, see Chapter 14, "Storage."

The USB Interface

The USB interface (refer to Figure 2.4) is replacing serial, parallel, and PS/2 mouse and keyboard ports. Some legacy-free systems feature only USB ports for external expansion, while others still have PS/2 keyboard ports, but leave other types of expansion up to the USB port. The original version of the USB port, USB 1.1, has speeds up to 12 megabits per second (Mbps), while the newer USB 2.0 standard, also called hi-speed USB, has speeds up to 480Mbps and is backward-compatible with USB 1.1. Most recent computers built through mid-2002 include built-in USB 1.1 ports, but computers built from mid-2002 on might include both USB 1.1 and USB 2.0 ports. Both USB 1.1 and USB 2.0 ports can be added to systems through the use of a PCI or PC Card add-on card.

USB ports can be used for keyboards, mice and pointing devices, scanners, printers, removable-media drives, hard drives, optical drives, direct data transfer, modems, and networking. USB ports are thus the most versatile ports built into modern PCs.

USB devices can be daisy-chained, as can SCSI and IEEE-1394a devices, but there are several differences between how these technologies work, as shown in Table 2.1.

Table 2.1   SCSI, IEEE-1394a, and USB Compared

Interface	How Devices Are Daisy-Chained	Maximum Number of Devices	How Devices Are Configured	Maximum Speed
SCSI	Direct connection between devices	7 or 15 (depends upon host adapter type)	Unique device ID; last device in daisy-chain must be terminated	10Mbps up to 640Mbps; speeds beyond 40Mbps are used primarily for hard drives
USB	Multiport hubs	Up to 127	Plug-and-play configuration in Windows	1.1: 12Mbps 2.0: 480Mbps
IEEE-1394a	Multiport hubs or direct connection between devices	Up to 16 with daisy-chaining; up to 63 through the use of hubs	Plug-and-play configuration in Windows	400Mbps

The USB ports built into the computer are known as root hubs; most computers have at least two. External hubs, also called generic hubs, are connected to root hubs to allow multiple USB devices to share a single root hub. Different USB devices use different amounts of power. Bus-powered hubs (hubs that take power from the USB root hub) can provide no more than 100 milliamps (mA) of power to each device, while self-powered hubs can provide the full 500mA of power required by some USB devices. Because USB root hubs, whether built into the motherboard or an add-on card, are PCI devices, they can share IRQs with other PCI devices.

USB 1.1 devices can run at 1.5Mbps (keyboards, mice, and pointing devices) or at speeds of 12Mbps (scanners, printers, and other devices). 1.5Mbps is referred to as low-speed USB 1.1, while 12Mbps is referred to as full-speed USB 1.1. Because low-speed devices can slow down full-speed USB 1.1 devices when they are plugged into the same USB 1.1 root hub, I recommend that you use separate root hubs for low-speed and full-speed USB 1.1 devices. However, if you have USB 2.0 ports (also called hi-speed USB ports), USB 2.0 is capable of managing both USB 1.1 and USB 2.0 devices at their top speeds. For more information about USB ports, see Chapter 8, "Input/Output Devices and Cables."

The IEEE-1394a Interface

The IEEE-1394a interface (see Figure 2.8), commonly referred to as IEEE-1394, FireWire, FireWire 400, or i.Link, is designed to be a high-speed replacement for SCSI, parallel, and other **legacy port** types.

As Table 2.1 indicates, IEEE-1394a is much faster than USB 1.1, but a bit slower than USB 2.0. The major differences between IEEE-1394a and USB, aside from speed, is that IEEE-1394a can be used to connect devices without using a computer and provides enough power to run drives and scanners (when used with a six-wire cable), whereas USB 1.1 and USB 2.0 require that a computer be used to control the connection and can't provide sufficient power for some types of devices. For these reasons, IEEE-1394a is very popular for use with DV camcorders and other multimedia devices. The speed of IEEE-1394a and its increasing popularity has also made it a popular choice for external hard drives. IEEE-1394a ports are occasionally built into a computer's motherboard, but are more often installed into PCI slots or CardBus PC Card slots. For more information about IEEE-1394a ports, see Chapter 8.

Points of Failure on the Rear of Your Computer

The most likely point of failure on the rear of your computer is peripheral cabling. Fortunately, more and more devices use the lightweight USB cable shown in Figure 2.4 instead of the bulky, heavy serial and parallel cables also shown in Figure 2.4. Note that serial, parallel, and VGA cables all use thumbscrews; if you don't fasten the thumbscrews to the connector on the computer, the cables won't connect tightly, which can cause intermittent or complete peripheral failure. Most SCSI cables use locking clips to hold them in place. If the clips aren't engaged, this can cause intermittent or complete SCSI peripheral failure.

FIGURE 2.8

SCSI (left) and IEEE-1394a (right) host adapters installed in a typical PC.

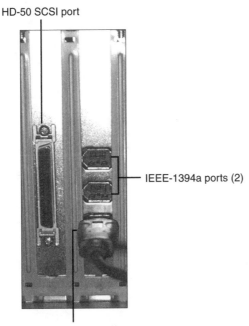

HD-50 SCSI port

IEEE-1394a ports (2)

Cable attached to IEEE-1394a port

Newer types of peripheral cables such as USB and IEEE-1394a are pushed into place and are very lightweight. No thumbscrews or other locking devices are needed. However, these cables can also be pulled out of the socket easily, precisely because they are lightweight and support a feature called hot-swapping. Hot-swap devices can be freely connected and disconnected while the PC's power is on.

The power supply shown in Figure 2.5 is another likely point of failure. If the three-prong power cable is not plugged all the way into the computer, the system might not start up at all, or might shut down unexpectedly. If the voltage selector switch is not set correctly, the computer will not start at all, and if the power supply is set

caution

When you attach cables to the ports at the rear of the computer, avoid tangling them together. Tangled cables can cause electrical interference with each other, leading to erratic performance of external devices such as your printer or monitor. Also, tangled cables put extra stress on ports, which can cause malfunctions or port failure.

for 115V and is plugged into a 230V supply, the power supply and possibly other parts of the computer will be destroyed.

All Around a Laptop Computer

Notebook computers use the same types of peripherals, operating system, and application software as desktop computers use. However, notebook computers vary in several ways from desktop computers:

- Most notebook computers feature integrated ports similar to those found in recent desktop computers (such as USB 1.1 or 2.0 ports and 10/100 Ethernet network ports) as well as one or more PC Card (PCMCIA) slots and a 56 kilobits per second (Kbps) modem.

- Some notebook computers support swappable drives, but less-expensive models require a trip to the service bench for a drive upgrade.

- More and more notebook computers use combo DVD-ROM/CD-RW drives to enable one optical drive to perform the work of two.

- Many notebook computers don't have an internal floppy drive, but rely on CD-RW or removable-media drives on USB connections to transfer or back up data.

- Notebook computers have integrated pointing devices built into their keyboards; most use a touchpad, but a few (primarily IBM and some Toshiba models) have a pointing stick (which is better is a matter of personal preference).

Figure 2.9 shows you a composite view of a typical notebook computer, a Compaq Presario 700-series.

Points of Failure on a Notebook Computer

As with desktop computers, cabling can be a major point of failure on notebook computers. However, notebook computers also have a few unique points of failure. The PC Card (PCMCIA card) represents a significant potential point of failure for the following reasons:

- If a PC Card is not completely pushed into its slot, it will not function.

- If a PC Card is ejected without being stopped by using the PC Card system tray control, it could be damaged.

- Many PC Cards designed as 10/100 Ethernet network adapters or 56Kbps modems use dongles similar to the one pictured in Figure 2.9. If the dongle is damaged, the card is useless until a replacement dongle is obtained.

FIGURE 2.9

Rear, left, and right views of the author's Compaq Presario 700-series notebook computer.

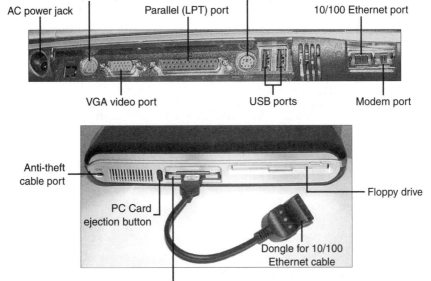

PS/2 keyboard port
AC power jack
PS/2 mouse port
Parallel (LPT) port
10/100 Ethernet port
VGA video port
USB ports
Modem port

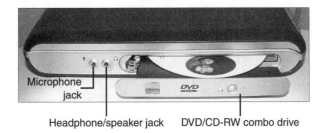

Anti-theft cable port
Floppy drive
PC Card ejection button
Dongle for 10/100 Ethernet cable
10/100 Ethernet PC Card inserted in PC Card slot

Microphone jack
Headphone/speaker jack
DVD/CD-RW combo drive

■ Some notebook computers that have the 32-bit CardBus version of the PC Card slot require the user to enable CardBus compatibility in the system BIOS, or else CardBus cards (used by USB 2.0, IEEE-1394a, and other high-bandwidth PC Card devices) will not work.

For more information on PC Card and CardBus devices, see Chapter 12, "Portables."

Although a notebook computer's drives are much more rugged than those found in desktop computers, they are much more expensive to replace if damaged. Although some mid-range and high-end notebook computers offer swappable drives, most lower-priced models do not. You can perform an upgrade to a hard disk without special tools on many models, but replacement of other types of drives on systems that don't support swappable drive bays can be expensive.

Although drives are expensive to replace on notebook computers, the biggest potential expense is the LCD screen. Most recent computers use active-matrix LCD panels in place of the dimmer (but less expensive to fix) passive-matrix panels once common.

Inside a Typical PC

As you have already learned, some problems that manifest themselves on the outside of the computer come from problems inside the computer. If you ever add memory, add an internal drive, upgrade your processor or motherboard, or add a card to your computer, you will need to work with the interior of the computer to complete these tasks.

The interior of a typical desktop computer is a crowded place, as Figure 2.10 shows.

FIGURE 2.10

The interior of a typical PC using an ATX motherboard.

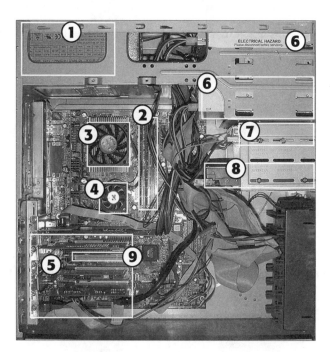

1. Power supply
2. Memory modules
3. Processor with fan/heatsink
4. North Bridge chip with fan/heatsink
5. Add-on cards
6. Optical drives
7. Floppy drive
8. Hard drive
9. Empty PCI slot

Each of the devices highlighted in Figure 2.10, as well as the data, signal, and power cables that connect them to the motherboard and power supply, can cause significant system problems if they fail.

Expansion Slots

Although today's systems have more built-in ports than ever, sooner or later you might want (or need) to add a new port or card type. That's a job for an expansion slot.

Typical mini-tower and full-tower desktop computers have three or more expansion slots, some of which might already be used for factory-installed devices such as video cards, network cards, or modems. Most computers have several PCI slots, and many also have a single AGP slot for high-speed video. Although AGP slots are faster than PCI slots, they are configured the same way in the system BIOS.

See "PCI Configuration" in Chapter 6 for details.

Most recent systems have no more than one ISA slot, and many no longer have ISA slots at all. ISA cards are much slower than PCI cards, and some can't be installed with Windows's normal plug-and-play automatic detection. You should avoid using ISA slots for upgrading your system if possible. Figure 2.11 compares AGP, PCI, and ISA slots.

caution

If you're not familiar with working inside your PC, read "Working Inside Your PC," later in this chapter, for help in opening the case and preventing damage to components inside your PC.

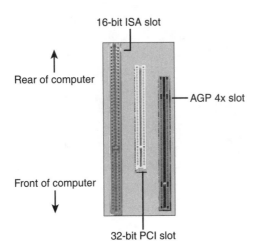

FIGURE 2.11

ISA, PCI, and AGP slots compared.

16-bit ISA slot

Rear of computer

AGP 4x slot

Front of computer

32-bit PCI slot

Regardless of the type of expansion slot an add-on card uses, you need to push the card connector all the way into the expansion slot when you install a card, as shown in Figure 2.12.

Card bracket not flush with rear edge of case

Bracket not flush with rear case wall

Connector not pushed down into slot

FIGURE 2.12

A video card partly inserted into the slot (top) and fully inserted into the slot (bottom).

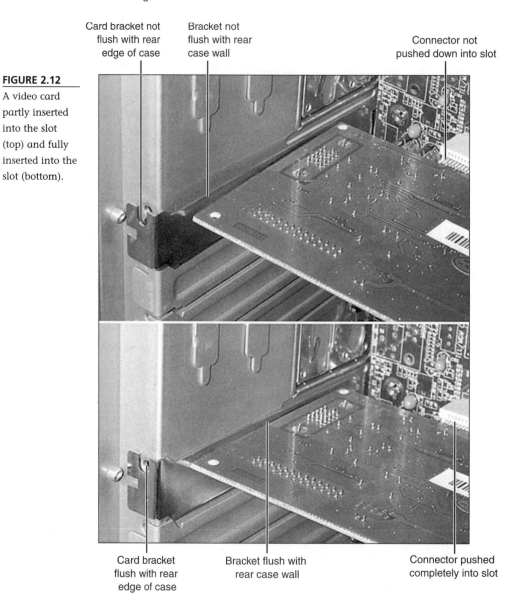

Card bracket flush with rear edge of case

Bracket flush with rear case wall

Connector pushed completely into slot

After the card is properly inserted into the expansion slot, you need to fasten the card to the case with a screw.

Points of Failure Inside the Computer

Some of the problems you could encounter because of devices inside your computer include

- *Overheating*—Failure of the fans in the power supply or those attached to the processor, North Bridge chip, or video card can cause overheating and can lead to component damage. Each fan shown in Figure 2.10 is connected to the motherboard to obtain power. Some case-mounted or older processor fans use a standard four-wire drive power connector instead (shown later in Figure 2.15).

- *Loose add-on cards* (see Figure 2.12)—A loose add-on card might not be detected by plug-and-play or the Windows Add New Hardware Wizard, or might have intermittent failures after installation.

- *Inability to start the computer*—A loose processor or memory module can prevent the computer from starting (see Figures 2.13 and 2.14).

- *Drive failures*—If drives are not properly connected to power or data cables, or are not properly configured with jumper blocks, they will not work properly (see Figures 2.15 and 2.16).

- Multimedia failures—If the analog or digital audio cable running from the CD-ROM or other optical drive to the sound card is disconnected, you might not be able to hear CD music through the speakers. Some high-end sound cards also have connections to an external breakout box for additional speaker or I/O options. Be careful when you work inside a computer to avoid disconnecting these cables (see Figure 2.17).

- *Front panel failures*—The tiny cables that connect the case power switch, reset switch, and status lights are easy to disconnect accidentally if you are working near the edges of the motherboard (see Figure 2.23).

- *Battery failure*—The battery (see Figure 2.23) maintains the system settings that are configured by the system BIOS. The settings are stored in a part of the computer called the CMOS, more formally known as the non-volatile RAM/real-time clock (NVRAM/RTC). If the battery dies (the average life is about two to three years), these settings will be lost. After you replace the battery, you must re-enter the CMOS settings and save the changes to the CMOS before you can use the system.

- *BIOS chip failure*—The system BIOS chip (see Figure 2.23) can be destroyed by electro-static discharge (ESD) or lightning strikes. However, BIOS chips can also become outdated. Although some systems use a rectangular socketed BIOS chip like the one shown in Figure 2.23, others use a square BIOS chip that might be socketed or surface-mounted. In both cases, software BIOS upgrades are usually available to provide additional BIOS features, such as support for newer processors and hardware.

The following sections introduce you to these components and how they work.

FIGURE 2.13

A socket-based processor before (left) and after (right) serious problems were corrected.

Heatsink not locked into place   Fan connected to motherboard

Fan not connected

Processor socket lever not locked into place

Processor socket lever locked into place

Heatsink locked into place

FIGURE 2.14

A memory module before (top) and after (bottom) being locked into its socket.

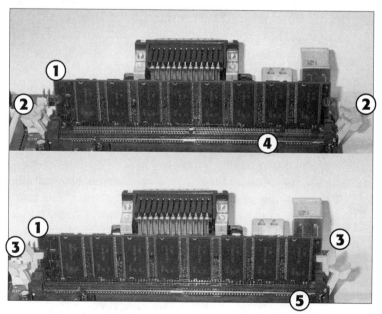

1. DIMM memory module
2. Module locks in open position
3. Module locks in closed position
4. Memory module edge connector before module fully inserted
5. Memory module edge connector after module fully inserted

The ATA/IDE Interface

Virtually every desktop computer built since the mid-1990s has featured two ATA/IDE interfaces on the motherboard. Each ATA/IDE interface can handle one or two drives, including hard drives, optical drives, and removable-media drives. Thus, you can install up to four ATA/IDE drives into a typical desktop computer.

The ATA/IDE interface uses a 40-pin connector (see Figure 2.15), which connects to a 40-wire or 80-wire ATA/IDE cable (both cable types use the same connector). This cable has three connectors, which go to the following locations:

- ATA/IDE interface on the motherboard
- Master drive
- Slave drive

40-wire cables, which are now becoming outdated, support device speeds up to UltraDMA/33 (33 megahertz [MHz]). 80-wire cables support all older devices plus the latest drive speeds up to 133MHz (UltraDMA/133). Because most ATA/IDE drives on the market today run at UltraDMA/100 or UltraDMA/133 speeds, you should not use 40-wire cables with hard disk drives anymore.

Each ATA/IDE interface uses an IRQ: IRQ 14 is used for the primary interface, and IRQ 15 is used for the secondary interface. These IRQs cannot be shared with other devices. For details, see "Hardware Resources," later in this chapter.

tip

Want to install more ATA/IDE drives? Add a PCI-based ATA/IDE host adapter. Some of these cards also support ATA RAID or Serial ATA, which can provide greater speed, data security, or easier installation. See Chapter 14 for more information about ATA RAID and Serial ATA.

caution

Most ATA/IDE drives and motherboard host adapters are designed to accept cables only when they are properly connected. The usual method is to match a *key* on one side of the cable plug (refer to Figure 2.15) with a matching cutout on the cable connector. However, some low-cost cables don't feature keying, making it easy to install them incorrectly. If you use such a cable, note that the colored stripe indicating pin 1 on the cable is usually on the same side of the cable as the power supply connector. Check the motherboard (shown later in Figure 2.16) for markings.

Even if you aren't installing a new drive, if you move existing ATA/IDE cables around inside your computer to gain access to memory, processor, or other components, you need to recheck the cable connections, both to the drive and to the motherboard. It's very easy to accidentally pull these cables loose. Whether a cable is completely removed or only partially detached, drives do not function properly.

Figure 2.16 shows a typical ATA/IDE motherboard connector.

Audio Hardware

Although more and more motherboards feature built-in sound, serious gamers and hardcore audio fans still insist on a separate sound card. Many high-end sound cards, such as the Creative Labs Sound Blaster Audigy shown in Figure 2.17, can be connected to breakout boxes that provide additional audio connectors and controls, and some also feature onboard IEEE-1394a ports.

Both motherboard-integrated audio and separate sound cards can also be connected to CD-ROM and other optical drives with four-wire analog or two-wire digital audio cables, also shown in Figure 2.17.

caution

The original ATA/IDE drive cable, which contained 40 wires, enabled users to select primary (master) and secondary (slave) drives with *jumper blocks* on the rear or bottom of the drives. Some vendors, such as Western Digital, supported a no-jumper-block configuration for single hard drives. Most drives are labeled with the correct jumper settings as well as with the correct orientation for the power and data cables. If your drive lacks this information, look up the drive model on the vendor's Web site.

However, in most new systems today, ATA/IDE hard drives are connected with an 80-wire ATA/IDE cable. This enables ATA/IDE drives such as hard drives, CD-RW drives, or DVD drives to be jumpered as *Cable Select*, giving control of master/slave settings to the cable. Most of these cables are color coded. With color-coded cables, the black connector at one end of the cable is used for master, the middle (gray) connector is used for slave, and the blue end of the cable connects to the system board or other ATA/IDE host adapter.

FIGURE 2.15

A typical ATA/IDE CD-ROM drive before (top) and after (bottom) typical cabling and configuration problems have been corrected.

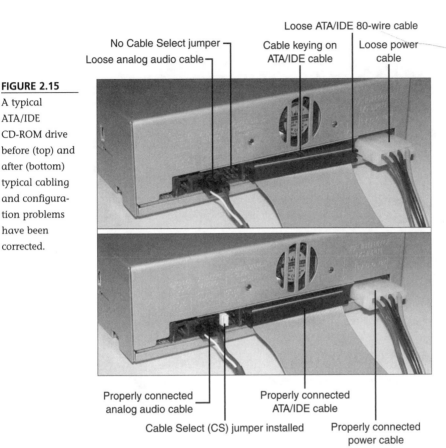

No Cable Select jumper —
Loose analog audio cable —
Loose ATA/IDE 80-wire cable
Cable keying on ATA/IDE cable
Loose power cable

Properly connected analog audio cable
Properly connected ATA/IDE cable
Cable Select (CS) jumper installed
Properly connected power cable

FIGURE 2.16

A typical ATA/IDE motherboard drive connector (top) and the DIP switches used on some motherboards for system configuration (left).

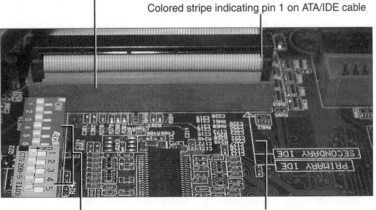

Blue motherboard ATA/IDE drive connector
Colored stripe indicating pin 1 on ATA/IDE cable

Motherboard marking for pin 1 on ATA/IDE connectors
DIP switches for motherboard configuration

FIGURE 2.17

The top edge of a typical high-end sound card (a Sound Blaster Audigy Platinum) with multiple cable connections.

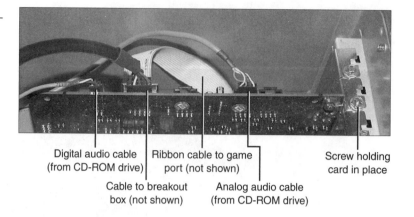

Digital audio cable (from CD-ROM drive)

Ribbon cable to game port (not shown)

Screw holding card in place

Cable to breakout box (not shown)

Analog audio cable (from CD-ROM drive)

Working Inside Your PC

If you've never opened up a computer before, it can be pretty overwhelming. In this section, I'm going to help you get started with practical advice on how to

- Open the case.
- Protect your system against electrostatic discharge (ESD).
- Connect internal and external data cables.
- Install a PCI card.

Opening the Case of a Desktop PC

I recommend that you look at your system manual for case-opening instructions, particularly if you have a retail-store system made by HP or Compaq. Depending upon the type of case you have, you might need to remove just one or two screws, or maybe a handful. If you're opening the case to gain access to the motherboard, you might need to do more than just take the cover off the system.

note

Some systems can transfer CD music through the standard ATA/IDE cable and don't require a separate patch cable. If you can play music CDs through your speakers and your system doesn't use analog or digital audio cables, don't worry about it. Most CD-ROM and other types of optical drives include analog or digital audio cables, but if you need replacements, most computer stores also stock them.

So-called "white box" systems are usually pretty straightforward to open, because they use case designs made for user access instead of low cost. Figure 2.18 shows the rear of two typical cases used by white-box computer dealers or as replacement cases. The computer on the left has a single screw holding the covers in place. After this screw is removed, the top panel must be removed before the side panels can be removed. The computer on the right uses four screws per side to hold the side panels in place, but the side panels can be removed without removing the top cover. The right-side panel can even be swung out and latched back into place for faster card and drive installation.

Screws holding side panel in place

Screw hole (releases top panel)   Screw holes (release side panel)

FIGURE 2.18
Two generic cases compared to each other.

Retail-store systems often use a single-piece molding that slips off the rear of the chassis. It can be held in place by several screws.

Taking ESD Precautions

After you open your PC, what should you do next?

Ideally, you should wear a commercial wrist strap made for ESD protection and clip it to an unpainted metal part on the computer you are servicing, as in Figure 2.19, before you touch any other part of the interior of your computer.

caution

Be sure to unplug the system before you open the case.

Don't mix up the screws used for the case with screws used for holding expansion cards or drives in place. Keep them separate. Label empty film or medicine containers and use one for each type of screw you remove.

Attaching cable with alligator
(grounding) clip to wrist strap

FIGURE 2.19

A wrist strap
and some suit-
able places to
clip it inside the
system.

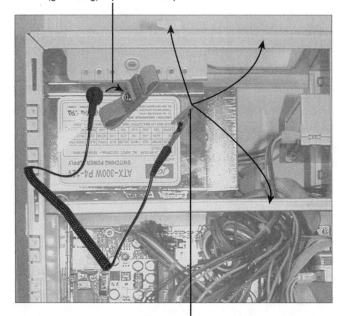

Bare metal parts of chassis that are suitable
locations to attach the grounding clip

When you put the wrist strap on, make sure the metal plate on the inside of the
strap touches bare skin; don't wear it over a shirt or sweater, and make sure it's comfortably snug. When the wrist strap is connected to a metal part of the chassis with
the alligator clip on the end of the cable that snaps onto the wrist strap, it equalizes
the electrical potential of your body and the computer to prevent ESD discharge.

However, if you don't have a wrist strap, touch unpainted metal on the chassis or
the power supply before you touch or remove any cables or other parts. If possible,
keep touching the chassis or power supply while you work.

For more details on ESD protection, see Chapter 13, "Safety and Recycling."

Connecting Internal and External Data Cables

Connecting internal and external drives and devices is critical if you want to have
reliably working PCs. Here are a couple of examples of how to do it right:

Attaching Cables to the Floppy Drive and Controller

The floppy drive uses a 34-pin cable that has a twist at one end. This end of the cable connects to the floppy drive (A: drive). The middle connector is used for the B: drive (if present; not supported on some machines). The connector with the untwisted end plugs into the floppy controller on the motherboard. The colored marking on the cable and the twist indicate the pin 1 side of the cable. This is important to note because floppy drives and controllers are not always keyed to prevent incorrect installation.

The floppy drive is powered by a small 4-pin power cable. There is a small cut-out in the center of the connector on the drive that corresponds to a projection on the cable.

Figure 2.20 shows how the floppy drive cable and power cable connect to the rear of a typical floppy drive and to the floppy controller.

To install the cables

1. Take the ESD precautions discussed in "Taking ESD Precautions," earlier in this chapter, after you open the case and before you touch the cables or other components.

2. Be sure to line up the keying on the cable (if any) with the cut-out on the floppy drive and controller connectors.

3. Push the cable firmly but gently into place.

4. Make sure the ridge on the power cable connector faces away from the drive; the power cable can be forced into place upside down, but this will destroy the drive when the power is turned on.

5. Push the power cable connector firmly but gently into place. If you don't have a spare 4-wire connector for the floppy drive, you can purchase an adapter, which converts the large Molex connector used for hard disks into a floppy drive power connector. You can also purchase a Y-splitter, which can power a floppy drive and a hard drive.

The installation of an ATA/IDE hard disk or other drive type is similar in many ways, but the cables used are different and the drives must be correctly jumpered.

For more information on floppy drives and hard drives, cables, and floppy media, see Chapter 14.

caution

If any pins are bent on the floppy drive, controller data, or power connectors, carefully straighten them with a pair of needlenose pliers before installing the cables.

FIGURE 2.20

Connecting data and power cables to a typical 3.5-inch floppy drive (top) and floppy controller on motherboard (bottom).

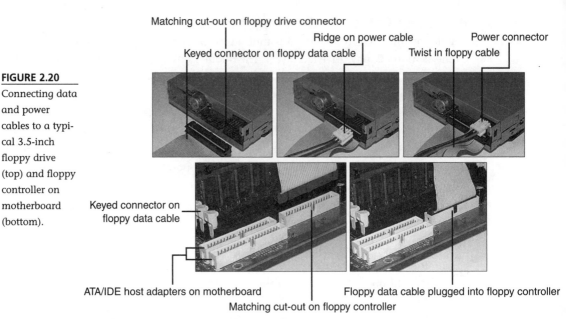

Matching cut-out on floppy drive connector

Ridge on power cable

Power connector

Keyed connector on floppy data cable

Twist in floppy cable

Keyed connector on floppy data cable

ATA/IDE host adapters on motherboard

Matching cut-out on floppy controller

Floppy data cable plugged into floppy controller

Attaching the VGA Cable to a Video Card or Port

The VGA cable has as many as 15 wires that are routed into a connector the same size as a serial (COM) port. Consequently, it is one of the heaviest cables you need to connect to a PC. If you don't attach it correctly, you could have poor-quality images on your monitor, and if the cable falls off, you won't have any picture at all.

Depending upon the computer, the VGA port might be located on a card built into an expansion slot, or might be clustered with other ports at the rear of the computer. In either case, the port and the cable are the same.

Figure 2.21 shows how the VGA cable should be connected to the VGA port.

To connect the VGA cable to the VGA port

1. Turn the thumbscrews so they are completely retracted. If they are not completely retracted, they could prevent proper connection.

2. Check the VGA cable for bent pins, but don't panic if you see a few pins that appear to be missing. Most VGA monitors don't use all 15 pins. Carefully straighten any bent pins you find.

3. Line up the cable with the port and carefully push the cable into the port.

4. Fasten the thumbscrews tightly but evenly to hold the cable in place.

For more information about graphics cards and cables, including installing and configuring cards that support multiple displays, see Chapter 9, "Video."

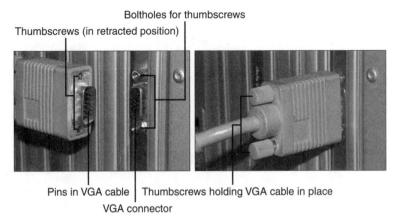

FIGURE 2.21

Connecting a
VGA cable to a
VGA port.

Installing a PCI Card

Most systems have at least one open PCI card slot; it's the standard card type used
for most devices. If you need to add an internal modem, a network adapter, a USB
2.0, an IEEE-1394a, a hard disk, or a SCSI host adapter to a desktop PC, you will add
a PCI card that includes the necessary port.

Figure 2.22 shows the process of adding a PCI card (specifically, a Serial ATA hard
disk host adapter) to a typical system. The procedure for installing an AGP-based
video card is similar, except that the AGP slot is used.

To add a PCI card

1. Shut down the system and unplug it.

2. Open the system.

3. Follow the ESD precautions discussed in "Taking ESD Precautions," earlier in
   this chapter.

4. Remove the slot cover behind the PCI slot you want to use.

5. Line up the connector on the bottom of the card with the slot.

6. Carefully push the card into place until it locks into place. Make sure the
   bracket on the card fits between the rear edge of the motherboard and the
   outer wall of the case.

7. Fasten the card into place using the screw you removed from the slot cover in
   step 4.

8. Attach any cables required between the card and other devices.

9. Double-check your work; then close up your system and follow the instructions provided with the card for driver installation and card configuration.

Removing the slot cover   Inserting the PCI card

FIGURE 2.22

Installing a
Serial ATA card
into a PCI slot.

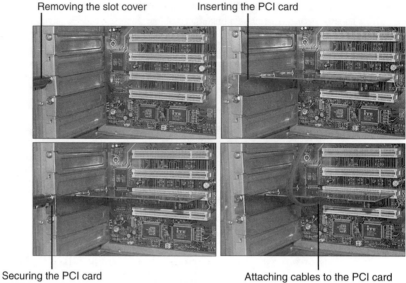

Securing the PCI card   Attaching cables to the PCI card

For more information about installing cards and configuring them, see Chapter 8, "Input/Output Devices and Cables"; Chapter 9, "Video"; Chapter 14, "Storage"; Chapter 19, "Installing and Configuring Hardware in Windows"; and Chapter 21, "Networking and Internet Connectivity."

The System BIOS

The system BIOS chip shown in Figure 2.23 is responsible for configuring many parts of your computer, including

- Floppy, optical, and hard drive configuration
- Memory size and speed
- Drive boot sequence
- Built-in port configuration
- System security
- Power management
- Plug-and-play hardware configuration
- Processor compatibility and speed setting

Essentially, the BIOS acts as a restaurant menu of possible choices, and the CMOS RAM (which might be a separate chip or built into the South Bridge on some chipsets) stores the selections made from the menu of choices. When you received your computer from the factory, default selections were already stored in the BIOS, but as you add devices or customize your computer to perform certain operations, you might need to make additional choices. The battery shown in Figure 2.23 maintains the contents of CMOS memory; a typical battery lasts for two years or longer.

System BIOS chip

Front-panel cables for system power
button, status lights, and PC speaker

Battery

FIGURE 2.23

The front-panel
cables, BIOS
chip, and bat-
tery on a typical
motherboard.

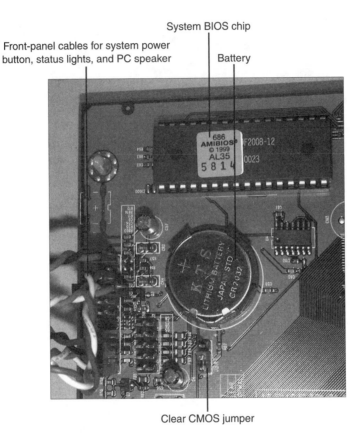

Clear CMOS jumper

How the BIOS Displays Your PC's Components

Although some computers display only a system manufacturer's logo at startup, forcing you to read the system manual to determine which key to press to start the BIOS setup program, others, particularly "white box" computers that use a collection of components from various vendors, or systems that use a replacement motherboard, can provide you with a lot of useful information at startup.

Figure 2.24 shows a typical example of the BIOS chip's POST (power-on self-test) program detecting onboard storage (the memory size is displayed briefly on many systems first). The display also shows which key to press to start the setup program.

FIGURE 2.24

A typical startup screen displaying detected drives, chipset, and BIOS information.

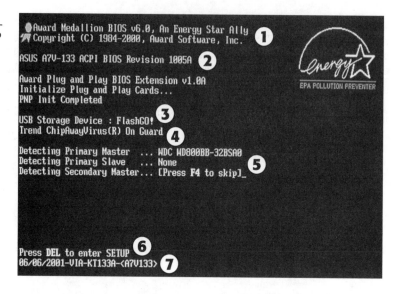

1. BIOS vendor and release information
2. Motherboard vendor and model number
3. USB storage device(s)
4. Anti-virus feature enabled

5. Detected ATA/IDE drives
6. How to start the BIOS setup program
7. BIOS date and chipset information

Many systems that display information similar to that shown in Figure 2.24 also display a condensed listing of onboard hardware before starting Windows (see Figure 2.25). Because this information should not change on a day-to-day basis unless you change your system configuration (BIOS changes or hardware upgrades), displaying this information at startup is a valuable aid to troubleshooting a sick system.

One of the reasons it's so important to display this information when you start your computer (if your system permits it) is because you will know immediately if there are any changes in your hardware configuration. If the configuration information displayed some day at startup differs from the normal information you see, it might mean that

- Someone has changed the system's normal BIOS configuration.
- The computer has reverted to default settings for troubleshooting or other reasons.
- The computer's battery is failing, causing stored setup information to be lost or corrupted.
- The hardware inside your computer has failed, or has been removed/replaced.

FIGURE 2.25

A typical system
configuration
screen displayed
at system
startup.

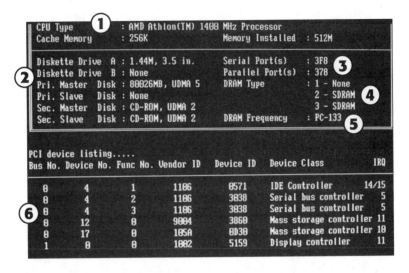

1. Processor type, speed, and
   memory size information
2. Drive information
3. I/O port addresses for serial
   and parallel ports
4. Memory slot usage
5. Memory speed
6. Onboard PCI devices

For more information on using the BIOS and CMOS setup to configure the system,
correct configuration problems, or to determine the system's configuration, see
Chapter 6.

Hardware Resources

There are four types of hardware resources used by both onboard and add-on card
devices:

- IRQ
- I/O port address
- DMA channel
- Memory address

Each device needs its own set of hardware resources, or needs to be a device that can
share IRQs (the only one of the four resources that can be shared). Resource conflicts
between devices can prevent your system from starting, lock up your system, or even
cause data loss.

IRQs

IRQs, or **interrupt requests**, are a series of 8 or 16 lines that run between the CPU and both built-in and expansion card devices. Most devices use at least one IRQ. As the name implies, IRQs enable devices to interrupt the CPU to signal for attention when they need to send or receive data. Without IRQs, the CPU would run in isolation, never pausing to take care of any devices. The IRQ can be compared to a telephone's ringer. When the telephone rings, you pick it up. If the ringer is broken, you would never know if you were getting a telephone call. The different IRQs can be compared to a multiline phone in which each line is set aside for a different department. At least one IRQ is used by most major add-on cards (network, SCSI, sound, video, modem, and IEEE-1394) and major built-in system components such as ATA/IDE host adapters, serial, parallel, and USB ports.

Because IRQs are used to handle different hardware devices, there's a simple rule of thumb: Generally, no two ISA devices should have the same IRQ assignment. While COM 1 and COM 3 serial ports are both assigned to IRQ 4, and COM 2 and COM 4 are both assigned to IRQ 3, this is not a true exception; if COM 1 and COM 3 are used at the same time, they stop working, and ditto for COM 2 and COM 4. PCI devices typically support IRQ sharing with Windows 95 OSR 2.x (Windows 95B), Windows 98, Windows Me, Windows 2000, and Windows XP, as well as Windows Server 2003 if the motherboard's design and configuration permit it.

The number of total IRQs available to you depends on the types of cards and expansion slots you use. Eight-bit ISA expansion slots, such as those used in the original IBM PC and PC/XT, could use IRQs up to 7 only. The ISA 16-bit and wider expansion slots can use up to IRQ 15. The typical and default IRQ usage appears in Table 2.2.

tip

Many computers sold at retail stores do not display the POST and configuration information screens shown in Figures 2.24 and 2.25 as configured from the factory. To display this information, start the computer's BIOS setup program and look for a BIOS option called Quiet Boot. Disable this option and save your changes. Some systems have an option called Boot-Time Diagnostic Screen instead; enable this option and save your changes. When your computer restarts, it should display hardware information.

Note that if your BIOS doesn't have an option such as Quiet Boot or Boot-Time Diagnostic Screen, you might not be able to view your hardware configuration at bootup.

Table 2.2 Typical IRQ Usage

IRQ	Standard Function	Bus Slot	Resource Type	Recommended Use
0	System timer	No	System	—
1	Keyboard controller	No	System	—
2	Second IRQ controller cascade to IRQ 9	No	System	—
8	Real-time clock	No	System	—
9	Available (might appear as IRQ 2)	Yes	PCI	Network Interface Card or VGA*
10	Available	Yes	PCI	USB*
11	Available	Yes	PCI	SCSI host adapter*
12	Motherboard mouse port/ available	Yes	ISA/PCI	Motherboard mouse port
13	Math coprocessor	No	System	—
14	Primary IDE	Yes	PCI	Primary IDE (hard disks)
15	Secondary IDE/ available	Yes	PCI	Secondary IDE (CD-ROM/tape)
3	Serial Port 2 (COM 2:)	Yes	ISA	COM 2:/internal modem
4	Serial Port 1 (COM 1:)	Yes	ISA	COM 1:
5	Sound/Parallel Port 2 (LPT2:)	Yes	ISA	Sound card*
6	Floppy disk controller	Yes	System	Floppy controller
7	Parallel Port 1 (LPT1:)	Yes	ISA	LPT1:

On systems that use ACPI power management or support IRQ sharing, PCI versions of some or all of these devices might share IRQs.

IRQs are used by the system in the following way: You issue a command DIR C:>LPT1 on the keyboard (IRQ 1). The IRQ is routed to the CPU, which "looks" at the keyboard and interprets the command. It uses IRQ 14 (IDE hard disk interface) to pass the command to the hard disk. Because the user has asked to print the command

(>LPT1), the CPU uses IRQ 7 to "wake up" the parallel port and print the directory listing. Meantime, the system timer (IRQ 0) has kept everything working. As you look at the printout, you see the date- and timestamps next to the file listings, letting you know that the real-time clock (IRQ 8) is also on the job. Thus, even a simple operation uses several interrupt requests on several different lines.

Although Table 2.2 shows you traditional IRQ usage, you should realize that your computer might list much different IRQ usage and still work correctly. Here's why:

- If your computer is a so-called "legacy-free" system without serial, parallel, or PS/2 mouse and keyboard ports, or if you have manually disabled them, IRQs 3, 4, 7, and 12 will also be treated as PCI IRQs on most recent systems. This means they can be used for PCI cards not listed on the chart, such as IEEE-1394a host adapters, SCSI host adapters, video capture cards, add-on multi-I/O (serial/parallel) adapters, and so forth.

- Beginning with late versions of Windows 95 and continuing on to today's Windows XP versions, PCI devices can share IRQs on most systems. Although ISA devices such as built-in serial, parallel, and PS/2 mouse ports each need an exclusive IRQ, two or more PCI devices (as well as AGP video cards) can share IRQs as shown later in Figure 2.27.

I/O Port Addresses

The system resource used even more often than IRQs, but one that causes fewer problems, is the **I/O port address**. The I/O port address is used to pass information between a given device and a system. Even simple devices that don't require an IRQ to function need one or more I/O port addresses. If you compare the IRQ to a telephone ringer, the I/O port address can be compared to the telephone transmitter and receiver, which do the actual work of sending and receiving your voice after you pick up the ringing telephone.

Your computer has 65,535 I/O port addresses (numbered hexadecimally), but uses only a relative few of them. Addresses might be followed by an "h", indicating hexadecimal.

Each device uses an exclusive range of I/O port addresses for the actual transmission of data to and from the device. For situations in which two devices (such as COM 1 and COM 2) share a single IRQ, the I/O port addresses are still unique to each device. Often, information about an add-on card will list only the starting address, but you should know both the first and last I/O port address used by the device to keep from overlapping addresses, which will cause the devices to fail. There are thousands of I/O port addresses available in today's computers, so resource conflicts are rare unless a user tries to assign two serial ports to the same address (refer ahead to Figure 2.28).

As you can see from Figure 2.26, different types of devices use different amounts of I/O address space. Some devices use a continuous "block" of addresses, such as the LPT1 (parallel) port, which uses eight addresses (0378-037Fhex). Others use only one or two addresses, or sometimes just a (literal) bit of a single address. For example, most systems don't have a secondary floppy controller, so the addresses reserved for it (0370–0375, bit 7 of 0377) will be available for another device.

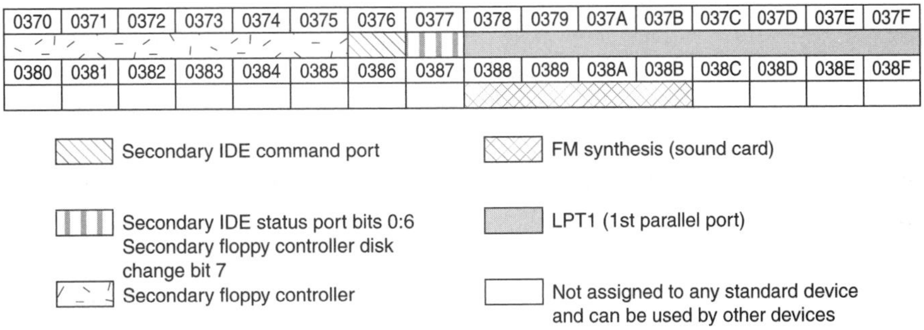

FIGURE 2.26

A section of the I/O port address map appears here. Devices listed use the port addresses listed if they are present.

0370	0371	0372	0373	0374	0375	0376	0377	0378	0379	037A	037B	037C	037D	037E	037F

0380	0381	0382	0383	0384	0385	0386	0387	0388	0389	038A	038B	038C	038D	038E	038F

Secondary IDE command port

Secondary IDE status port bits 0:6
Secondary floppy controller disk change bit 7
Secondary floppy controller

FM synthesis (sound card)

LPT1 (1st parallel port)

Not assigned to any standard device and can be used by other devices

I/O port addresses are used by the system in the following way: You issue a command DIR C:>LPT1 on the keyboard. The keystrokes pass through the keyboard interface's I/O addresses 0060h, 0064h. When the hard disk receives the command to read the directory listing, the command is given through I/O port 03F6, and the status is monitored through bits 0:6 of I/O port 03F7. When the directory listing is redirected to the printer, the output is routed through LPT1's I/O port addresses 0378–037F.

As you look at I/O port address usage in your computer, you might see two different components, which are working but are displaying the same I/O port address per the Windows Device Manager. In these cases, the devices listed use the same I/O port address as a way to communicate with each other. For example, the AMD-751 chipset processor to AGP controller and the TNT2 AGP video card in my computer use the same I/O port addresses to facilitate communication with each other as shown in Figure 2.27.

DMA (Direct Memory Access) Channels

As you saw earlier in this chapter, the CPU is responsible for many tasks, including that of being a sort of "traffic cop," overseeing the transfer of information between itself, memory, and various devices. Although a police officer on the corner of a busy intersection helps keep bumper-to-bumper rush-hour drivers on their best behavior, this manual stop-go-stop process isn't the fastest way to get around town—or around the motherboard.

The expressway, beltway, or freeway that bypasses surface streets, traffic lights, and hand-signaling police officers is a faster way to travel when conditions are favorable. Similarly, bypassing the CPU for memory to add-on board transfers (either direction) is also a faster way to travel.

This process of bypassing the CPU is called **Direct Memory Access (DMA)**. DMA transfers can be done in two ways; some DMA transfers (such as those done by tape backup drives or by PCI cards using bus-mastering) do not require a particular DMA channel; however, some devices, such as popular ISA sound cards and the ECP mode of the parallel port, require that we select an unused DMA channel. Table 2.3 lists the standard DMA channel uses. In Table 2.3, standard uses appear in **bold** type, and typical uses (which can change) are shown in *italic* type.

Table 2.3 Standard and Typical DMA Channel Uses

DMA Channel #	Use	Notes
0	*Some sound cards*	Requires 16-bit ISA or PCI card*
1	*Sound card*	Sound Blaster standard; also used by "clones"
2	**Floppy drive**	
3	*LPT port in ECP mode*	Some systems offer DMA 1 as an alternative setting
4	**System reserved**	
5	*Sound card*	Requires 16-bit ISA or PCI card*; some sound cards use only DMA 1 or use DMA 0 instead of 5
6		Requires 16-bit ISA card
7		Requires 16-bit ISA card

PCI sound cards use DMA only if used in a Sound Blaster emulation mode.

Because DMA is used for high-speed data transfer, and because there are relatively few DMA channels, some users are tempted to "share" them between ISA devices. Never do this. If two devices using DMA are used at the same time, a catastrophic loss of data could result. Because the CPU is not involved in DMA transfers, there's no "traffic cop" in case of disaster!

One of my favorite "disaster" stories was related by longtime *Byte* magazine columnist Jerry Pournelle in July 1994. He installed a sound card on a system that already had an unusual hard disk interface that used DMA; both devices were set to DMA 5.

When he tried to record sound samples with the sound card, the flow of hard disk data and the flow of sampled sound "collided" on DMA 5, wiping out the entire contents of his hard disk! DMA conflicts are rare, especially now that ISA cards are not used by most systems, but they're never funny.

Memory Addresses

The physical memory (RAM) installed into the computer is divided into **memory addresses**; each address equals a byte of RAM. For normal operations, the system automatically determines which memory address to use for retrieving existing information or for temporary location of new memory addresses. These addresses are also given in hexadecimal notation.

Like DMA channels, memory addresses are also abundant in computers. Add-on cards that have their own BIOS chips (some SCSI, some ATA/IDE, and some network cards, as well as all VGA and 3D video cards) or add-on cards that have RAM (video cards and a few network cards), however, must use unique memory addresses that are found in the range between 640 kilobytes (KB) and 1 megabyte (MB). Because there's abundant memory address space and relatively low demand for memory addresses, conflicts are rare unless you manually configured a card to use an address already in use by another device. Memory managers such as EMM386.EXE that can be used to support MS-DOS software running under Windows 9x can also use memory addresses that are not in use by cards.

Viewing Hardware Resources in Use

You can view the current resource usage in your computer with the Windows Device Manager. To see the resource usage for a particular device, open the Device Manager, open the device's properties sheet, and click Resources. You can also use the Windows System Information program to view resource usage. For details, see Chapter 18, "Using and Optimizing Windows."

If you need to install non-PnP devices, or if you are concerned about installing devices that have limited configuration options, you can also view all the resources currently in use. With Windows XP and Windows 2000, start the Device Manager, select View, Resources by Type, and click the plus sign (+) next to each category. Figure 2.27 shows the DMA channel, IRQ, and a portion of the memory resource usage in one of my computers, which runs Windows XP. Figure 2.28 shows a portion of the I/O port address usage in the same computer. With Windows 9x/Me, double-click the computer icon at the top of the Device Manager listing to see resource usage.

FIGURE 2.27

The Windows XP
Device Manager
configured to
display IRQ,
DMA, and
memory address
usage.

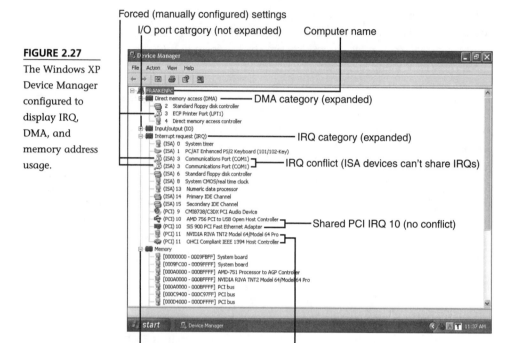

Forced (manually configured) settings
I/O port catrgory (not expanded)
Computer name
DMA category (expanded)
IRQ category (expanded)
IRQ conflict (ISA devices can't share IRQs)
Shared PCI IRQ 10 (no conflict)
Memory category
(expanded)
Shared PCI IRQ 11 (no conflict)

FIGURE 2.28

The Windows XP
Device Manager
configured to
display a por-
tion of the I/O
port address
usage.

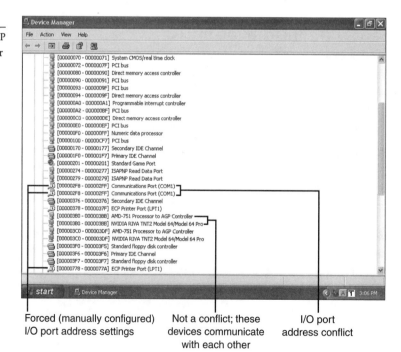

Forced (manually configured)
I/O port address settings
Not a conflict; these
devices communicate
with each other
I/O port
address conflict

Note that in these two figures, forced (manually configured) settings are indicated with a white circle containing a blue *i*. Forced settings are seldom a good idea (plug-and-play configuration usually works much better, especially with Windows XP). Additionally, if two ISA devices have been forced to use the same hardware resource (such as the COM ports in Figures 2.27 and 2.28, which are both set to use the same IRQ and I/O port address), you have a hardware conflict that will prevent the devices from working.

Study Lab

Don't miss the Study Lab materials found on the CD accompanying this book. Each Study Lab is tailored to the individual chapters in this book, meaning that you'll quickly be able to determine which topics you understand well enough to pass the exam and which topics need more study. The Study Labs are presented in printable PDF format so that you can take them with you to study at work, on the road, or even in your car just before test time!

THE ABSOLUTE MINIMUM

Here are the high points of this chapter. Read these just before you take your exam, or any time to find out what topics you need to review in more detail.

- All computers contain hardware, software, and firmware.

- There are two types of memory: RAM (contents change as programs and data are loaded, created, and saved) and ROM (contents can't be changed under normal circumstances).

- Hardware subsystems such as video, drives, memory, and others are controlled by the system BIOS on the motherboard and by the operating system and its device drivers.

- The outside of the computer typically has cable connections for peripherals, drive bays for removable-media drives, the power supply, and the power switch.

- The inside of the computer contains the motherboard, add-on cards, memory modules, the processor, and internal drives (hard disk, floppy disk, and optical drives).

- The BIOS controls built-in components and displays the installed components on some systems.

- IRQs range from 0–15 and are used to request attention from the CPU.

- I/O port addresses are used to transmit information between the system and a particular device. There are 65,535 I/O port addresses.

- DMA channels are used by ISA devices to bypass the processor for faster device-memory transfers. DMA channels range from 0 to 7.

- Memory addresses are used by devices with built-in ROM or RAM chips.

- The Windows Device Manager and Windows System Information display current hardware (IRQ, DMA, I/O port address, and memory address) usage.

3

HOW COMPUTERS MEASURE AND TRANSFER DATA

How do computers measure information? By the byte. It's the basic unit of measurement for all parts of the computer that involve the storage or management of information (RAM, storage, ROM). Here are a few examples:

- Software stored on a floppy or hard disk occupies a finite number of bytes.

- RAM is measured in megabytes (1MB = 1,000,000 bytes).

- Drive capacity is measured in gigabytes (1GB = 1,000,000,000 bytes).

Understanding bytes and the other measurements derived from bytes is essential to choosing the correct sizes for RAM configurations, storage media, and much more. Some of the A+ Certification test questions typically deal with RAM and hard disk size measurements, as will your day-to-day work.

So, what's a byte? If you are storing text-only information in the computer, each character of that text (including spaces and punctuation marks) equals a byte. Thus, to calculate the number of bytes in the following sentence, count the letters, numbers, spaces, and punctuation marks:

```
"This book is written by Mark Edward Soper."
123456789012345678901234567890123456789012341234
        |          |          |          |
        10         20         30         40
```

From this scale, you can see that the sentence uses 44 bytes. You can prove this to yourself by starting up Windows Notepad (or using MS-DOS's EDIT) and entering the text just as you see it printed here. Save the text as EXAMPLE.TXT and view the directory information (MS-DOS) or the File properties. You'll see that the text is exactly 44 bytes.

Do most computer programs store just the text when you write something? To find out, start up a word-processing program, such as Windows WordPad or Microsoft Word. Enter the same sentence again, and save it as EXAMPLE.If you use WordPad, save the file as a Rich Text Format (.RTF) file and as a Microsoft Word (.DOC) file. Depending upon the exact version of WordPad or Microsoft Word you use, the file takes up much more space. For example, WordPad for Windows XP saves text as an RTF file, using 243 bytes to store the file. The same sentence takes 19,968 bytes when saved as a .DOC file by Microsoft Word XP!

What happened? The next section explains this apparent oddity.

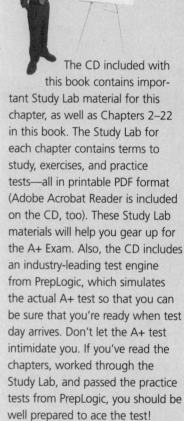

note

The CD included with this book contains important Study Lab material for this chapter, as well as Chapters 2–22 in this book. The Study Lab for each chapter contains terms to study, exercises, and practice tests—all in printable PDF format (Adobe Acrobat Reader is included on the CD, too). These Study Lab materials will help you gear up for the A+ Exam. Also, the CD includes an industry-leading test engine from PrepLogic, which simulates the actual A+ test so that you can be sure that you're ready when test day arrives. Don't let the A+ test intimidate you. If you've read the chapters, worked through the Study Lab, and passed the practice tests from PrepLogic, you should be well prepared to ace the test!

Also, you'll notice that some words throughout each chapter are in bold format. These are study terms that are defined in the Study Lab. Be sure to consult the Study Lab when you are finished with this chapter to test what you've learned.

File Overhead and Other Features

When data you create is stored in a computer, it must be stored in a particular arrangement suitable for the program that created the information. This arrangement of information is called the **file format**.

A few programs, such as MS-DOS Edit and Windows Notepad, store only the text you create. What if you want to boldface a certain word in the text? A text-only editor can't do it. All that Edit and Notepad can store is text. As you have seen, in text-only storage, a character equals a byte.

In computer storage, however, pure text is seldom stored alone. WordPad and other word-processing programs such as Microsoft Word and Corel WordPerfect enable you to **boldface**, underline, *italicize*, and make text larger or smaller. You can also use different fonts in the same document (see Chapter 10, "Printers," for more about that).

Most modern programs also enable you to insert tables, create columns of text, and insert pictures into the text. Some, such as Microsoft Word, have provisions for tracking changes made by different users. In other words, there's a whole lot more than text in a document.

To keep all this non-text information arranged correctly with the text, WordPad and other programs must store references to these additional features along with the text, making even a sentence or two into a relatively large file, even if none of the extra features is actually used in that particular file. Thus, for most programs, the bytes used by the data they create is the total of the bytes used by the text or other information created by the program and the additional bytes needed to store the file in a particular file format.

Because different programs store data in different ways, it's possible to have an apparent software failure take place because a user tries to open a file made with program A with program B. Unless program B contains a converter that can understand and translate how program A stores data, program B can't read the file, and might even crash. To help avoid problems, Windows associates particular types of data files with matching programs, enabling you to open the file with the correct program by double-clicking the file in Explorer or File Manager. You'll learn more about file associations in Chapter 18, "Using and Optimizing Windows."

Numbering Systems Used in Computers

Three numbering systems are used in computers: **decimal**, **binary**, and **hexadecimal**. Decimal is also known as base 10. Binary is also known as base 2, and hexadecimal is also known as base 16. Here's an illustration to help you remember the basic differences between them.

You already are familiar with the decimal system: Look at your hands. Now, imagine your fingers are numbered from 0–9, for a total of 10 places. Decimal numbering is sometimes referred to as base 10.

The binary system doesn't use your fingers; instead, you count your hands: One hand represents 0, and the other 1, for a total of two places. Thus, binary numbering is sometimes referred to as base 2.

The hexadecimal system could be used by a pair of spiders who want to count: One spider's legs would be numbered 0–7, and the other spider's legs would be labeled 8, 9, A–F to reach a total of 16 places. Hexadecimal numbering is sometimes referred to as base 16.

Decimal Numbering System

We use the decimal or base 10 system for everyday math. A variation on straight decimal numbering is to use "powers of 2" as a shortcut for large values. For example, drive storage sizes often are defined in terms of decimal bytes, but the number of colors that a video card can display can be referred to as "24-bit" (or 2^{24}), which is the same as 16,777,216 colors.

Binary Numbering System

All data is stored in computers in a stream of 1s (on) and 0s (off). Because only two characters (0 and 1) are used to represent data, this is called a "binary" numbering system. Text is converted into its numerical equivalents before it is stored, so binary coding can be used to store all computer data and programs.

tip

Although all data in the computer is stored as a stream of binary values (0s and 1s), most of the time you will use decimal ("512MB of RAM") or hexadecimal ("memory conflict at C800 in upper memory") measurements. The typical rule of thumb is to use the system that produces the smallest *meaningful* number. If you need to convert between these systems, you can use any scientific calculator, including the Windows Calculator program (select View, Scientific from the menu).

Table 3.1 shows how you would count from 1 to 10 (decimal) in binary.

Table 3.1 Decimal Numbers 1–10 and Binary Equivalents

Decimal	1	2	3	4	5	6	7	8	9	10
Binary	1	10	11	100	101	110	111	1000	1001	1010

Because even a small decimal number occupies many places if expressed in binary, binary numbers are usually converted into hexadecimal or decimal numbers for calculations or measurements.

There are several ways to convert a decimal number into binary:

- Use a scientific calculator with conversion.
- Use the division method.
- Use the subtraction method.

To use the division method

1. Divide the number you want to convert by 2.
2. Record the remainder: If there's no remainder, enter 0. If there's any remainder, enter 1.
3. Divide the resulting answer by 2 again.
4. Repeat the process, recording the remainder each time.
5. Repeat the process until you divide 0 by 2. This is the last answer.
6. When the last answer is divided, the binary is recorded from Least Significant Bit (LSB) to Most Significant Bit (MSB). Reverse the order of bit numbers so that MSB is recorded first and the conversion is complete. For example, to convert the decimal number 115 to binary using the division method, follow the procedure listed in Figure 3.1.

tip

Table 3.2 provides a listing of powers of 2, but you can use the Windows Calculator in scientific view mode to calculate any power of two you want. Just enter 2, click the x^y button, and enter the value for the power of 2 you want to calculate (such as 24). The results are displayed instantly (you add the commas). Use the Edit menu to copy the answer to the Windows Clipboard, and use your program's Paste command to bring it into your document. Sure beats counting on your fingers!

FIGURE 3.1

Converting decimal 115 to binary with the division method.

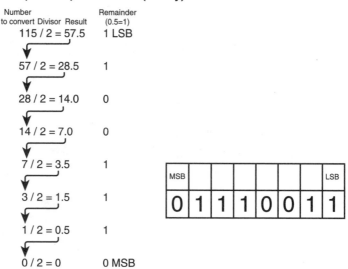

115 (decimal) = 01110011 (binary)

Number to convert	Divisor	Result	Remainder (0.5=1)
115	/ 2 =	57.5	1 LSB
57	/ 2 =	28.5	1
28	/ 2 =	14.0	0
14	/ 2 =	7.0	0
7	/ 2 =	3.5	1
3	/ 2 =	1.5	1
1	/ 2 =	0.5	1
0	/ 2 =	0	0 MSB

MSB							LSB
0	1	1	1	0	0	1	1

If you use a scientific calculator (such as the scientific mode of the Windows Calculator) to perform the conversion, keep in mind that any leading zeros will be suppressed. For example, the calculation in Figure 3.1 indicates the binary equivalent of 115 decimal is 01110011. However, a scientific calculator will drop the leading zero and display the value as 1110011.

To use the subtraction method

1. Look at the number you want to convert and determine the smallest power of 2 that is greater than or equal to the number you want to subtract. Table 3.2 lists powers of 2 from 2^0 through 2^{17}. For example, 115 decimal is less than 2^7 (128) but greater than 2^6 (64).

2. Subtract the highest power of 2 from the value you want to convert. Record the value and write down binary 1.

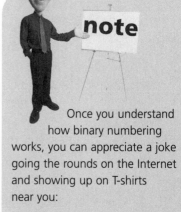

note

Once you understand how binary numbering works, you can appreciate a joke going the rounds on the Internet and showing up on T-shirts near you:

"There are 10 kinds of people in the world—those who understand binary and those who don't." T-shirts are available from Think Geek (www.thinkgeek.com).

3. Move to the next lower power of 2. If you can subtract it, record the result and also write down binary 1. If you cannot subtract it, write down binary 0.

4. Repeat step 3 until you attempt to subtract 2^0 (1). Again, write down binary 1 if you can subtract it, or binary 0 if you cannot. The binary values (0 and 1) you have recorded are the binary conversion for the decimal number. Unlike the division method, this method puts them in the correct order; there's no need to write them down in reverse order.

For example, to convert 115 decimal to binary using the subtraction method, see Figure 3.2.

FIGURE 3.2

Converting 115 decimal to binary with the subtraction method.

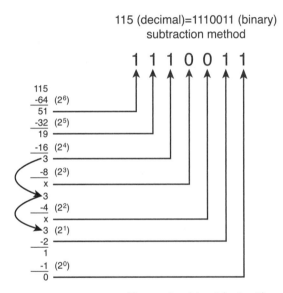

Table 3.2 Powers of 2

Power of 2	Decimal Value	Power of 2	Decimal Value
2^0	1	2^9	512
2^1	2	2^{10}	1024
2^2	4	2^{11}	2048
2^3	8	2^{12}	4096
2^4	16	2^{13}	8192
2^5	32	2^{14}	16384
2^6	64	2^{15}	32768

Table 3.2 (continued)

Power of 2	Decimal Value	Power of 2	Decimal Value
2^7	128	2^{16}	65536
2^8	256	2^{17}	131072

Hexadecimal Numbering System

A third numbering system used in computers is hexadecimal. Hexadecimal numbering is also referred to as base 16, a convenient way to work with data because 16 is also the number of bits in 2 bytes or 4 nibbles. Hexadecimal numbers use the digits 0–9 and letters A–F to represent the 16 places (0–15 decimal). Hexadecimal numbers are used to represent locations in data storage, data access, and RAM. Table 3.3 shows how decimal numbers are represented in hex.

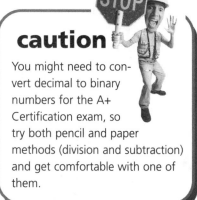

caution

You might need to convert decimal to binary numbers for the A+ Certification exam, so try both pencil and paper methods (division and subtraction) and get comfortable with one of them.

Table 3.3 Decimal and Hexadecimal Equivalents

Decimal	0	1	2	3	4	5	6	7	8	9	10	11	12	13	14	15
Hexadecimal	0	1	2	3	4	5	6	7	8	9	A	B	C	D	E	F

To convert decimal to hexadecimal, use the same division method listed previously, but use 16 rather than 2 as the divisor.

Figure 3.3 demonstrates how to use this conversion process to convert the decimal number of 65,536 (the start of upper memory) to its hexadecimal equivalent (A0000).

Note that if you use the Windows Calculator in scientific mode to perform this conversion that you will get an answer of 100000. The initial value 10 is the numeric equivalent of hex A (refer to Table 3.3).

The most typical uses for hexadecimal numbering are

- Upper memory addresses for add-on cards and for memory-management use
- I/O port addresses for use with an add-on card

FIGURE 3.3

Converting 65,536 decimal to hexadecimal.

65,536 (decimal) = A0000 (hex)

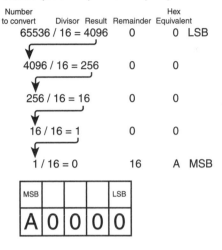

Binary Versus Decimal MB/GB

Although a byte represents the basic "building block" of storage and RAM calculation, most measurements are better performed with multiples of a byte. All calculations of the capacity of RAM and storage are done in **bits** and **bytes**. Eight bits is equal to one byte.

Table 3.4 provides the most typical values and their relationship to the byte.

Table 3.4 Decimal and Binary Measurements

Measurement	Type*	Number of Bytes/Bits	Calculations	Notes
Bit		1/8 of a byte	Byte/8	
Nibble		1/2 of a byte	Byte/4 (4 bits)	
Byte		8 bits	bit*8	
Kilobit (Kb)	D	1,000 bits		
Kibibit (Kib)	B	1,024 bits		1
		(128 bytes)		
Kilobyte (KB)	D	1,000 bytes		
Kibibyte (KiB)	B	1,024 bytes		2
Megabit (Mb)	D	1,000,000 bits	1 kilobit^2	
Mebibit (Mib)	B	1,048,576 bits	1 kibibit^2	

Table 3.4   (continued)

Measurement	Type*	Number of Bytes/Bits	Calculations	Notes
		(131,072 bytes)		[3]
Megabyte (MB)	D	1,000,000 bytes	1,000KB	
Mebibyte (MiB)	B	1,048,576 bytes (1,024KiB)	1 kilobyte[2]	[4]
Gigabit (Gb)	D	1,000,000,000 bits	1 kilobit[3]	
Gibibit (Gib)	B	1,073,741,824 bits	1 kibibit[3]	[5]
Gigabyte (GB)	D	1,000,000,000 bytes	1 kilobyte[3]	
Gibibyte (GiB)	B	1,073,741,824 bytes	1 kibibyte[3]	[6]

D=Decimal   B=Binary

[1]*Also known as binary kilobit*

[2]*Also known as binary kilobyte*

[3]*Also known as binary megabit*

[4]*Also known as binary megabyte*

[5]*Also known as binary gigabit*

[6]*Also known as binary gigabyte*

Until December 1998, the terms kilobit, kilobyte, megabit, megabyte, gigabit, and gigabyte were officially used to refer both to decimal and binary values. A great deal of confusion in the industry has been caused by the indiscriminate use of both types of measurements for hard disk storage. Although the binary multiples shown in Table 3.4 are an IEC standard, many vendors in the computer business don't yet use the term kibibits or other binary multiples yet.

Floppy and hard disk manufacturers almost always rate their drives in decimal megabytes (multiples of 1 million bytes) or decimal gigabytes (multiples of 1 billion bytes), which is also the standard used by disk utilities, such as CHKDSK, ScanDisk, and FORMAT. However, most BIOSs and the MS-DOS/Windows FDISK and Windows NT/2000/XP Disk Management utilities list drive sizes in mebibytes (binary megabytes) or gibibytes (binary gigabytes). Mebibytes are also used to specify the size of rewritable and recordable CD and DVD media. Although the actual number of bytes is identical, the differences in numbering are confusing.

tip

Because the industry has not yet widely adopted the terms kibi, mebi, and gibi, the A+ Certification Exam might use KB, MB, and GB to refer to either type of numbering system.

Take a hard disk rated by its maker as 8.4GB. This is 8,400,000,000 bytes (decimal). However, when the drive is detected and configured by the BIOS and partitioned with FDISK, its size is listed as only 7.82GB (binary GB—more accurately referred to as GiB). At first glance, you might believe you've lost some capacity (see Figure 3.4).

However, as you've already seen, there is a substantial difference between the number of bytes in a binary gigabyte and one billion bytes. This different numbering system, not any loss of bytes, accounts for the seeming discrepancy. Use this information to help explain to a customer that the "missing" capacity of the hard disk isn't really missing (see Figure 3.5).

FIGURE 3.4

The capacity of an 8.4GB hard disk size is 8.4 billion bytes (top bar), but most BIOSs and Windows FDISK/Disk Management measure drives in binary gigabytes (bottom bar).

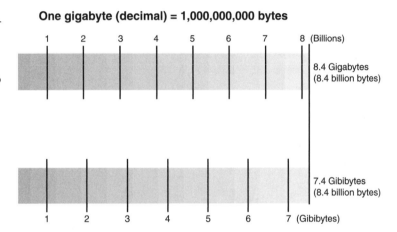

One gigabyte (decimal) = 1,000,000,000 bytes

8.4 Gigabytes
(8.4 billion bytes)

7.4 Gibibytes
(8.4 billion bytes)

One gibibyte = 1,073,741,824 bytes

FIGURE 3.5

A gibibyte (or binary gigabyte) has over 73 million more bytes than a decimal gigabyte (1 billion bytes).

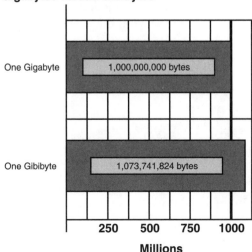

Gigabytes versus Gibibytes

One Gigabyte — 1,000,000,000 bytes

One Gibibyte — 1,073,741,824 bytes

250   500   750   1000

Millions

Use the values in Table 3.4 to convert between decimal and binary values for drive sizes or other measurements. For the exam, keep in mind that values that can be divided by 1,000 are decimal, while values that can be divided by 1,024 are binary.

Serial Versus Parallel Information Transfer

Information flows through the computer in many ways. The CPU is the central point for most information. When you start a program, the CPU instructs the storage device to load the program into RAM. When you create data and print it, the CPU instructs the printer to output the data.

Because of the different types of devices that send and receive information, two major types of data transfers take place within a computer: parallel and serial. These terms are used frequently, but if you're not familiar with the differences between them, check out Figure 3.6.

FIGURE 3.6

Parallel data transfers move data 8 bits at a time, whereas serial data transfers move 1 bit at a time.

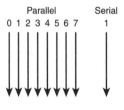

Parallel Information Transfers

Parallel transfers use multiple "lanes" for data and programs, and in keeping with the 8 bits = 1 byte nature of computer information, most parallel transfers use multiples of 8. Parallel transfers take place between the following devices:

- CPU and RAM
- CPU and interface cards (see Chapter 8)
- **LPT** (printer) port and parallel printer
- **SCSI** port and SCSI devices
- **ATA/IDE** host adapter and ATA/IDE drives
- RAM and interface cards (either via the CPU or directly with DMA)

Why are parallel transfers so popular?

- Multiple bits of information are sent at the same time.
- At identical clock speeds, parallel transfers are faster than serial transfers because more data is being transferred.

However, parallel transfers also have problems:

■ Many wires or traces (wire-like connections on the motherboard or expansion cards) are needed, leading to interference concerns and thick, expensive cables.

■ Excessively long parallel cables or traces can cause data to arrive at different times. This is referred to as *signal skew* (see Figure 3.7).

■ Differences in voltage between wires or traces can cause *jitter*.

FIGURE 3.7

Parallel cables that are too long can cause signal skew, allowing the parallel signals to become "out of step" with each other.

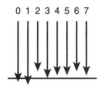

As a result of these problems some compromises have had to be included in computer and system design:

■ Short maximum lengths for parallel, ATA/IDE, and SCSI cables

■ Dual-speed motherboards (running the CPU internally at much faster speeds than the motherboard or memory)

Fortunately, there is a second way to transmit information: serial transfers.

Serial Transfers

A **serial** transfer uses a single "lane" in the computer for information transfers. This sounds like a recipe for slowdowns, but it all depends on how fast the speed limit is on the "data highway."

The following ports and devices in the computer use serial transfers:

■ Serial (also called **RS-232** or COM) ports and devices

■ **USB** (Universal Serial Bus) 1.1 and 2.0 ports and devices

■ Modems (which can be internal devices or can connect to serial or USB ports)

■ **IEEE-1394** (**FireWire**, i.Link) ports and devices

■ **Serial ATA** (SATA) host adapters and drives

Serial transfers have the following characteristics:

- One bit at a time is transferred to the device.
- Transmission speeds can vary greatly, depending on the sender and receiver.
- Very few connections are needed in the cable and ports (one transmit, one receive, and a few control and ground wires).
- Cable lengths can be longer with serial devices. For example, an UltraDMA/66 ATA/IDE cable can be only 18 inches long for reliable data transmission, whereas a Serial ATA cable can be almost twice as long.

Although RS-232 serial ports are slow, newer types of serial devices are as fast or faster than parallel devices. The extra speed is possible because serial transfers don't have to worry about interference or other problems caused by running so many data lines together.

For more information about serial, parallel, USB, and IEEE-1394 ports, see Chapter 8, "Input/Output Devices and Cables." For more information about RAM, see Chapter 7, "RAM." For more information about ATA/IDE, Serial ATA, and SCSI, see Chapter 14, "Storage."

Study Lab

Don't miss the Study Lab materials found on the CD accompanying this book. Each Study Lab is tailored to the individual chapters in this book, meaning that you'll quickly be able to determine which topics you understand well enough to pass the exam and which topics need more study. The Study Labs are presented in printable PDF format so that you can take them with you to study at work, on the road, or even in your car just before test time!

THE ABSOLUTE MINIMUM

Here are the high points of this chapter. Review these just before you take the exam to brush up on the major topics and help you identify what you need to review.

- The basic unit of measurement for storage or information management is the byte.

- When stored as plain text, one character uses one byte of disk space.

- Other file formats require more space than .TXT (plain text) files because they reserve space for formatting and document management information stored as part of the file.

- Binary numbering uses two digits, 0 and 1. Binary is also called base 2.

- Decimal (base 10) uses digits 0–9.

- Binary (base 2) uses digits 0–1.

- Hexadecimal (base 16) uses digits 0–9 and A–F.

- Decimal numbers can be converted to binary or hexadecimal numbers through a process of division.

- Decimal values such as kilo, mega, and giga are based on multiples of 1,000.

- Binary values such as kibi, mebi, and gibi are based on multiples of 1,024.

- Parallel transfers use eight wires or multiples of eight wires for data.

- Serial transfers use a single wire (or pair or wires) for data.

- Parallel transfers are faster than serial transfers performed at the same speed.

- Fast serial interfaces such as USB, IEEE-1394, and Serial ATA are as fast or faster than parallel interfaces and will eventually replace most parallel-based interfaces.

4

THE MOTHERBOARD AND CPU

For several years, I taught computer-troubleshooting classes around the country using computers that were never enclosed in a case. To allow students to see the essentials of the computer (and save space), we assembled all the essential parts of each computer on antistatic mats on each group's table. They worked! This proves that the computer is the sum of the components inside the case and, as you will see in this chapter, the motherboard is the central connector among all the components that make up the computer.

The Motherboard

The **motherboard** represents the logical foundation of the computer. In other words, everything that makes a computer a computer must be attached to the motherboard. From the **CPU** to storage devices, from RAM to printer ports, the motherboard provides the connections that help them work together.

Take a close look at a motherboard, and you'll see fine copper-colored wire traces on the top and bottom that run between different parts of the motherboard. These wire traces are portions of the motherboard's bus structure. In a city, a bus takes passengers from one point to another; in a computer, a bus carries signals from one component to another.

The motherboard is essential to computer operation in large part because of the two major buses it contains: the **system bus** and the **I/O bus**. Together, these buses carry all the information between the different parts of the computer.

The System Bus

The system bus carries four different types of signals throughout the computer:

- Data
- Power
- Control
- Address

To help you understand this concept, let's take an imaginary trip to Chicago and compare the city to a typical motherboard. If you were on the Sears Tower observation deck overlooking downtown Chicago one evening, you would first notice the endless stream of cars, trucks, and trains carrying people and goods from everywhere to everywhere

note

The CD included with this book contains important Study Lab material for this chapter, as well as Chapters 2–22 in this book. The Study Lab for each chapter contains terms to study, exercises, and practice tests—all in printable PDF format (Adobe Acrobat Reader is included on the CD, too). These Study Lab materials will help you gear up for the A+ Exam. Also, the CD includes an industry-leading test engine from PrepLogic, which simulates the actual A+ test so that you can be sure that you're ready when test day arrives. Don't let the A+ test intimidate you. If you've read the chapters, worked through the Study Lab, and passed the practice tests from PrepLogic, you should be well prepared to ace the test!

Also, you'll notice that some words throughout each chapter are in bold format. These are study terms that are defined in the Study Lab. Be sure to consult the Study Lab when you are finished with this chapter to test what you've learned.

else along well-defined surface routes (the expressways and tollways, commuter railroads, Amtrak, and airports). You can compare these routes to the data bus portion of the system bus, which carries information between RAM and the CPU. If you've ever listened to a station such as Chicago's WBBM (760AM), you've heard how traffic slows down when expressway lanes are blocked by construction or stalled traffic. In your computer, wider data buses that enable more "lanes" of data to flow at the same time promote faster system performance.

Now, imagine that you've descended to street level, and you've met with a local utility worker for a tour of "underground Chicago." On your tour, you will find an elaborate network of electric and gas lines beneath the street carrying the energy needed to power the city. You can compare these to the power lines in the system bus, which transfer power from the motherboard's connection to the power supply to the **integrated circuits** (**ICs** or **chips**) and expansion boards connected to the motherboard.

Go back to street level, and notice the traffic lights used both on city streets and on the entrance ramps to busy expressways, such as the Eisenhower and the Dan Ryan. Traffic stops and starts in response to the signals. Look at the elevated trains or at the Metra commuter trains and Amtrak intercity trains; they also move as directed by signal lights. These signals, which control the movement of road and rail traffic, can be compared to the control lines in the system bus, which control the transmission and movement of information between devices connected to the motherboard.

Finally, as you look around downtown, take a close look at the men and women toting blue bags around their shoulders or driving electric vans and Jeeps around the city. As these mail carriers deliver parcels and letters, they must verify the correct street and suite addresses for the mail they deliver. They correspond to the address bus, which is used to "pick up" information from the correct memory location among the megabytes of RAM in computer systems and "deliver" new programs and changes back to the correct memory locations.

The I/O bus connects storage devices to the system bus and can be compared to the daily flow of commuters and travelers into the city in the morning, and out again in the evening.

Between them, the system and I/O buses carry every signal throughout the motherboard and to every component connected to the motherboard.

Essential System Components Found on the Motherboard

Because the motherboard contains the system and I/O buses, it isn't surprising that the most central components to computing are found attached to the motherboard, as listed in Table 4.1.

Table 4.1 Components Located on All Motherboards

Component	Use	How Attached to Motherboard	Notes
CPU	Computational "brains" of computer	Dedicated socket or slot[1]	A few CPUs are soldered in place
RAM (random access memory)	Programs are loaded into this for operation; data resides here until saved to storage device	Dedicated sockets and/or soldered	RAM can be upgraded to limits determined by CPU type and motherboard design
ROM (read-only memory)	Firmware containing drivers for standard devices; power-on self-test	Dedicated socket	Most common ROM is the ROM BIOS
Keyboard connector	Attach keyboard	Soldered	Can be damaged by careless insertion/ removal of keyboard cable
CMOS/RTC chip[2]	Records BIOS settings; keeps date and time	Soldered	Some contain their own battery
Battery[2]	Maintains contents of CMOS/RTC chip	Soldered, socketed, or cabled	Many different types on older systems
Cache RAM	Holds a copy of last memory locations read for faster performance	Dedicated socket or surface mounted	Introduced with 386-based systems; common with 486 and Pentium; Pentium II and newer processors include all cache RAM inside the CPU
Expansion slots	Enables expansion of computer's capabilities with new ports and so forth	Soldered in place	ISA, VL-Bus, EISA, MCA, PCI, and AGP types
Chipset	A set of chips (usually two) on the motherboard that replace many individual chips	Soldered in place	Most motherboards use a chipset that includes a North Bridge chip with a high-speed interface to memory and a South Bridge chip with interfacing to ATA and USB ports, PCI and ISA buses, and Super I/O chip and BIOS chip

Table 4.1 (continued)

Component	Use	How Attached to Motherboard	Notes
Super I/O chip	Chip that replaces serial, parallel, and keyboard controller chips; connects with BIOS chip on some systems	Soldered in place	Might be integrated into the South Bridge chip on some recent chipsets
BIOS chip	Chip that contains setup options and POST (power-on self-test) for system	Soldered in place or socketed	Connect to the Super I/O chip or South Bridge chip

[1]*"Dedicated" means that the socket or slot can only be used for the device listed.*

[2]*This component is found in all PCs using an Intel 286–class CPU or above but is rarely found in PCs using an 8088 or 8086 CPU. Most of these computers used switches to set configuration options and didn't have built-in RTC (real-time clocks).*

Until the mid-1990s, components such as hard drive and floppy drive controllers, sound cards, network cards, and serial and parallel ports were added to typical systems through the use of add-on cards.

Integrated Motherboard Ports

During the first decade or so of the PC era, if you wanted to add a port, you added a card. To avoid using up all the expansion slots, some companies developed multi-I/O cards, which combined serial, parallel, and other ports on a single card. However, from the mid-1990s to the present, motherboards have included more and more ports and expansion connections that formerly required add-on cards. Ports added to the motherboard are often referred to as **integrated ports**.

Table 4.2 lists components that are included in recent motherboard designs.

Table 4.2 Components Found on Recent and Current Motherboards

Component	Use	Form Factor	Notes
ATA/IDE interface	Runs ATA/IDE and ATAPI storage devices (hard drives, optical drives, and removable-media drives)	40-pin connector (two rows of 20)	Most recent systems feature two; each interface supports two drives.

Table 4.2 (continued)

Component	Use	Form Factor	Notes
Floppy	Runs floppy-interface storage devices	34-pin connector (two rows of 17)	Older systems can support two drives with the single interface; some newer systems support only one drive.
PS/2 mouse port	Connector for PS/2 mouse	Mini-DIN 6-pin connector	Most systems with this port also have a PS/2 keyboard port.
COM (serial) port	Connector for serial devices	DB-9 male (DB-25 male is obsolete, but can be converted to DB-9)	Systems might feature one or two.
LPT (parallel) port	Connector for parallel devices	DB-25 female	Most systems feature one.
USB (Universal Serial Bus) port	Connector for USB devices and hubs	USB Type A connector	Four or more are typical on desktop systems. Some systems have a mix of USB 1.1 and USB 2.0 (Hi-Speed USB) ports.
XGA video	Connector for VGA-class monitors	DB-15 female	Some systems with integrated graphics also feature an AGP port.
Audio	Speaker and microphone connection for WAV and MIDI playback and WAV recording	Mini-jacks for microphone and speakers	Some systems offer 4-channel or 6-channel sound.
IEEE-1394 (FireWire) port	Connector for DV camcorders and high-speed drives and scanners	6-pin or 4-pin IEEE-1394 connector	One to three might be found, primarily in legacy-free systems.

Why integrated ports? They provide clear benefits to both users and technicians setting up a system. For users, integrated ports provide lower system purchase prices, faster component performance, centralized control of components through the ROM BIOS and CMOS, and an interior less crowded with add-on cards. In other words, you might have a slot or two available in a brand-new system for future upgrades.

For technicians, the major benefits of integrated components are during initial setup: Fewer components need to be installed to bring a system to meet standard requirements and components can be enabled or disabled through the BIOS setup program. Very handy!

However, when systems must be repaired or upgraded, integrated components can be troublesome. If an integrated component fails, you must either replace the motherboard or disable the component in question (if possible) and replace it with an add-on card. Check out Figures 4.1 and 4.2 to see the locations of these components on typical Baby-AT and ATX motherboards. Note that although Baby-AT motherboards and ATX motherboards both feature a large number of built-in ports, ATX motherboards have a cluster of ports built into the rear of the motherboard and Baby-AT motherboards must use clumsy header cables to route external ports to the rear of the case.

FIGURE 4.1

Major components on a typical Baby-AT motherboard with integrated ports. Header cables are used to route serial, parallel, PS/2 mouse, and USB ports (if present) to the rear of the system.

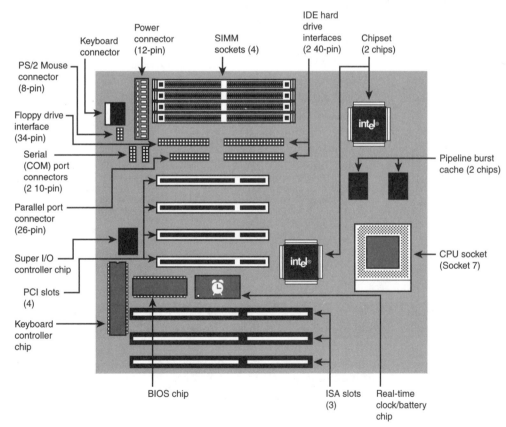

FIGURE 4.2

Major components on a typical ATX motherboard. All ATX motherboards have a cluster of I/O ports (serial, parallel, PS/2 mouse and keyboard, USB, and others) at the rear of the motherboard.

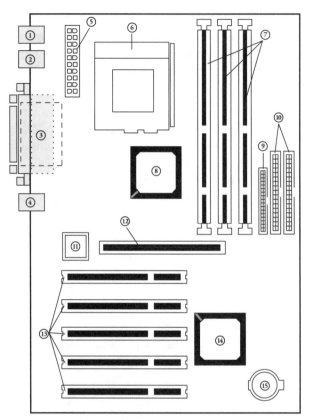

1. PS/2 mouse and
   keyboard ports
2. USB and (optional)
   10/100 Ethernet ports
3. Parallel port (serial and/or
   XGA graphics ports not shown)
4. Audio ports
5. ATX power connector
6. CPU (processor) socket

7. Memory sockets
8. North Bridge chip
9. Floppy interface
10. ATA/IDE interfaces
11. BIOS chip
12. AGP slot
13. PCI slots
14. South Bridge chip
15. Battery

Recognizing Expansion Slot Types

What components are fastest inside your PC? In order of speed, the CPU accesses **cache** memory at the fastest speed, followed by main memory, and then cards mounted in expansion slots.

Most systems have mixtures of two or more of the slot types discussed in the following sections.

tip

The A+ Certification Exam, as well as your day-to-day work, tests your ability to recognize the different expansion slot types and be able to choose the most appropriate slot for a given type of card.

Table 4.3 compares expansion slot designs by speed, data bus width, and suggested uses; you must know the speed and bus width of these slots for the exam. Most systems today primarily have PCI expansion slots, but one or two ISA slots are found on some older systems still in use. Most modern systems include either an AGP slot and/or video built into the motherboard chipset.

Table 4.3 Technical Information About Expansion Slot Types

Slot Type	Bus Width	Slot Speed	Status	Suggested Uses
ISA	8-bit, 16-bit	Approximately 8MHz	Obsolete	Modems, serial and parallel ports
EISA	32-bit	Approximately 8MHz	Obsolete	Server-optimized network interface cards (NICs), all ISA cards
VL-Bus	32-bit	25–33MHz[1]	Obsolete	Video, IDE hard disk, all ISA cards
PCI	32-bit, 64-bit[2]	25–33MHz, 66MHz	Current	Video, network, SCSI, sound card
AGP	32-bit	66MHz[3]	Current	Video

[1]*Runs at full speed of 486SX/DX processors (25–33MHz); runs at bus speed of 486DX2/SX2/DX4 processors (25–33MHz).*

[2]*64-bit and 66MHz versions found mostly on network servers and high-performance workstations.*

[3]*All versions of AGP have the same clock speed, but AGP 1x performs one transfer per clock cycle. AGP 2x, 4x, and 8x perform 2, 4, or 8 transfers per clock cycle, increasing throughput accordingly.*

If ISA, PCI, and AGP are just abbreviations to you, read on to learn more.

ISA

The oldest slot type is **ISA (Industry Standard Architecture)**. ISA slots come in two forms: a slot with a single long connector, which can send or receive 8 bits of data, and a 16-bit or AT-style slot, which adds a shorter connection in line with the original connector. This 8-bit slot was developed for the IBM PC in 1981; the 16-bit or AT-style slot adds a shorter connector to the first one. It sends or receives 16 bits of data per operation and was developed for the IBM AT in 1984(!).

Although a few older systems still contain one or two ISA slots, the ISA slot is now considered obsolete for all except industrial computing uses. Many systems that contain ISA slots have at least one that's called a *shared* slot—a pair of tightly spaced slots that share—or a single slot cover at the back in the case. One slot or the other, but not both, can be used. Refer to Figure 4.3 to see a typical ISA slot compared to a PCI slot.

Obsolete variations on ISA include EISA and VL-Bus. Both were 32-bit versions of the ISA but have been obsolete for many years.

PCI

Starting in 1993–1994, the **PCI (Peripheral Component Interconnect)** slot rapidly replaced VL-Bus slots (a 32-bit version of the ISA slot) in both late-model 486-based machines and in most Pentium-class computers. Most computers today have PCI slots and an AGP slot, or PCI slots only. Figure 4.3 compares the most common type of PCI slot, the 33MHz, 32-bit version to a 16-bit ISA slot.

The *combo* or *shared* slot design shown in Figure 4.3 uses one slot cover at the rear of the system. You can choose whether you want to use the slower ISA slot or the faster PCI slot. Combo slot designs are common among the last generation of computers to feature ISA slots, meaning you won't see these on most newer PCs.

FIGURE 4.3

An ISA slot (top) and a PCI slot (bottom) in a shared or combo configuration. Only one of the slots can be used at a time.

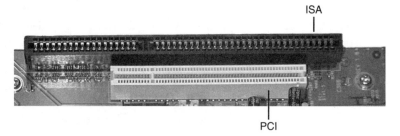

ISA

PCI

AGP

The PCI slot is a whole lot faster than the ISA slot, but with more and more devices using this slot, video performance began to suffer. Intel developed the **Accelerated Graphics Port**, or **AGP** slot, in 1996 strictly for high-speed video: You can't use AGP slots for anything but video. Although low-cost desktop systems and servers might use integrated video along with or instead of an AGP slot, most midrange and high-end desktop systems now feature some type of AGP slot. As Table 4.3 indicates, even the first-generation AGP slot, AGP 1x, was twice as fast as a typical PCI slot. All types of AGP slots can temporarily "borrow" system memory when creating 3D textures.

There are several variations on the AGP slot in use, depending upon the age of the system and the intended use of the system, as shown in Figure 4.4.

FIGURE 4.4

PCI slots compared to an AGP 1x/2x slot (top), an AGP 4x/8x slot (middle) and an AGP Pro/Universal slot (bottom).

1. PCI slots	5. AGP Pro slot cover
2. AGP 1x/2x (3.3v) slot	6. AGP 4x/8x retaining latch
3. AGP 4x/8x (1.5v) slot	7. AGP 1x/2x key
4. AGP Pro/Universal slot	8. AGP 4x/8x key

Note that the AGP 1x/2x and AGP 4x/8x slots have their keys in different positions. This prevents installing the wrong type of AGP card into the slot. AGP 1x/2x cards use 3.3V, whereas most AGP 4x cards use 1.5V. AGP 8x cards use 0.8 or 1.5V. The AGP Pro/Universal slot is longer than a normal AGP slot to support the greater electrical requirements of AGP Pro cards (which are used in technical workstations). The protective cover over a part of the slot is intended to prevent normal AGP cards from being inserted into the wrong part of the slot. The slot is referred to as a *universal* slot because it supports both 3.3V and 1.5V AGP cards.

caution

Note that an AGP Pro slot cover might be removed after a system has been in service for awhile, even if an AGP Pro card wasn't inserted in a computer. If you see an AGP Pro slot without a cover and you're preparing to install an AGP card, cover the extension with a sticker to prevent damaging a standard AGP card by inserting it improperly.

Figure 4.5 shows how typical AGP, PCI, and ISA cards compare to each other. Note that the components of AGP and PCI cards are on the opposite side from the components on ISA cards.

FIGURE 4.5

A typical PCI graphics card (top left) compared to a typical ISA network card (top right) and a typical AGP graphics card with a Universal connector (bottom).

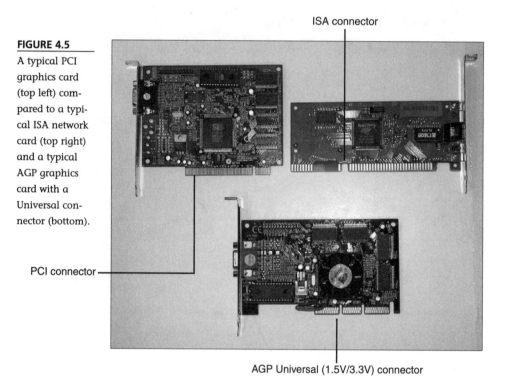

ISA connector

PCI connector

AGP Universal (1.5V/3.3V) connector

Motherboard Types

There are several basic motherboard designs:

- Baby-AT
- LPX
- ATX family (ATX, Micro-ATX, Flex-ATX, Mini-ITX)
- NLX

The most common of these in recent systems include the **ATX** family and the **NLX**. The others (**Baby-AT** and **LPX**) are found primarily in older systems that are obsolete but might still be in service on a desktop near you.

The following tables and accompanying illustrations indicate the major differences between the different motherboard types.

ATX Motherboards Compared to Other Models

The ATX family of motherboards was introduced in 1996, and has since become the dominant choice for all types of desktop computers. Odds are good that most computers you've used since the late 1990s have motherboards that belong to the ATX family. The full-size ATX and **Micro-ATX** motherboard designs have replaced the Baby-AT motherboard designs in full-size and mid-size tower systems, whereas the NLX and **Flex-ATX** motherboard designs have replaced the LPX in slimline and small form-factor corporate desktop computers.

Figure 4.6 compares the layouts of these motherboards to each other.

The major distinguishing factors of each motherboard design can be summarized thus:

■ Baby-AT models have expansion slots, which run parallel to the long edge of the motherboard. Built-in mouse, serial, parallel, and USB ports (if present) require header cables to be run between the ports on the motherboard and the rear of the case. Most Baby-AT motherboards use a 12-pin power connector.

■ ATX-family motherboards have expansion slots that run parallel to the short edge of the motherboard. They have a two-row cluster of ports on the rear of the motherboard (see Figure 4.7). ATX motherboards use a 20-pin power connector.

■ LPX motherboards have a proprietary riser card running from the middle of the motherboard. Some use a vertical riser card as shown in Figure 4.6, in which add-on cards are parallel to the motherboard, whereas others use a T-shaped riser card in which add-on cards are at the normal 90-degree angle to the motherboard. LPX motherboards have a single row of

tip

As you maintain, troubleshoot, and upgrade systems, you must be able to recognize each of these motherboard types.

Recognizing different motherboard types will enable you to determine whether

- The computer uses a standard motherboard and can be upgraded by changing its motherboard

- The computer uses a proprietary motherboard that cannot be interchanged

note

The Mini-ITX design created by VIA Technologies is similar to a Flex-ATX motherboard, but VIA's own C3 or Eden processors are built into the motherboard instead of being removable.

built-in ports along the rear edge of the motherboard. LPX motherboards use the same power connector as Baby-AT motherboards.

■ NLX motherboards also use a riser card, but the motherboard connects to the riser card along the right edge (as viewed from the front). NLX motherboards have a two-row cluster of ports along the rear edge of the motherboard. NLX motherboards are powered by the riser card connector.

FIGURE 4.6

Baby-AT and ATX-family motherboards (top) compared to LPX and NLX motherboards (bottom).

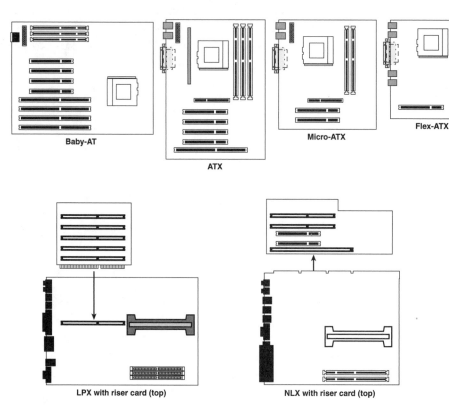

Baby-AT

ATX

Micro-ATX

Flex-ATX

LPX with riser card (top)

NLX with riser card (top)

See Chapter 5, "Power Supplies and Circuit Testing," for details about the differences in power supplies and connectors.

Figure 4.7 compares typical built-in port configurations found on the rear of ATX-family, LPX, and NLX motherboards.

Note that ATX and NLX port arrangements are similar (both have two rows), whereas the LPX ports are arranged in a single row. Keep in mind that there are lots of variations in the ports built into different systems.

FIGURE 4.7

Typical ATX (top), NLX (middle), and LPX (bottom) port configurations. Some motherboards might vary from these examples.

1. PS/2 mouse and keyboard ports
2. USB ports
3. Parallel (LPT) port
4. Game port
5. Serial (COM) port
6. VGA port
7. Onboard audio ports
8. 10/100 Ethernet port

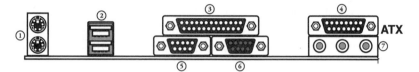

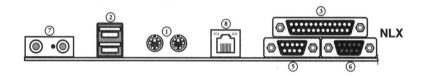

Upgrade Options for Different Types of Motherboards

ATX-family motherboard upgrades, particularly for systems using ATX or Micro-ATX motherboards, are plentiful. Baby-AT motherboards and systems are obsolete, and the only motherboards available are old designs that don't support current processor and memory module types. Because of differences in riser card location and design, LPX-based systems generally cannot be upgraded with new motherboards. NLX systems are designed for fast motherboard exchanges (they use a standardized riser card), but very few third-party NLX motherboards are available. They've been used primarily by vendors manufacturing corporate-class workstations instead of upgradeable PCs.

Motherboard Installation and Removal

What keeps a motherboard from sliding around inside the case? Most ATX-family motherboards are held in place by screws that are fastened to brass spacers. Baby-AT motherboards use a combination of brass spacers and screws along with plastic **stand-off** spacers.

If you look at an unmounted motherboard from the top, you can see that motherboards have several holes around the edges and one or two holes toward the middle of the motherboard. When a Baby-AT motherboard is installed in a computer, you'll see that one or two of the holes have a screw in them that attaches to a brass spacer, which itself is attached to the bottom or side of the case. The remainder of the holes have the top of a plastic spacer inserted in them; the bottom of the spaces fits into a teardrop-shaped mounting hole on the bottom or side of the computer case. ATX-family motherboards, on the other hand, usually are attached to brass spacers either built into the case or a removable motherboard tray.

⇨   Before you start working with motherboards or other static-sensitive parts, **see** "Electro-Static Discharge (ESD)," **p. 418**, for ESD and other precautions you should follow.

Step-by-Step Motherboard Removal (ATX and Baby-AT)

Removing the motherboard is an important task for the computer technician. For safety's sake, you should remove the motherboard before you install a processor upgrade as well as if you need to perform a motherboard upgrade.

To remove ATX or Baby-AT motherboards from standard cases, follow these steps:

1. Disconnect all external and internal cables attached to add-on cards after labeling them for easy reconnection.

2. Disconnect all ribbon cables attached to built-in ports on the motherboard (I/O, storage, and so on) after labeling them for easy reconnection.

3. Disconnect all cables leading to internal speakers, key locks, speed switches, and other front-panel cables after labeling them for easy reconnection. All these cables must be removed before the motherboard can be removed. Marking them enables you to properly attach them to the new motherboard (see Figure 4.8).

4. Remove all add-on cards and place them on an antistatic mat or in (not on top of) antistatic bags.

⇨   **See** "Electro-Static Discharge (ESD)," **p. 418**, for details about ESD precautions.

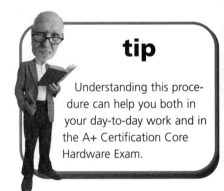

tip

Understanding this procedure can help you both in your day-to-day work and in the A+ Certification Core Hardware Exam.

tip

You can purchase premade labels for common types of cables, but if these are not available, you can use blank address labels.

FIGURE 4.8

Front-panel cables attached to a typical motherboard, which control the case speaker, drive and power lights, and so on.

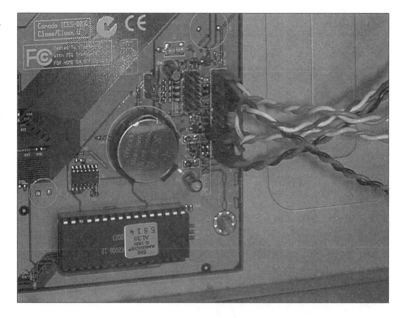

5. Disconnect the power-supply leads from the motherboard. The new motherboard must use the same power-supply connections as the current motherboard.

↪ **See** "Power Supplies and Circuit Testing," **p. 149**, for details about power supply connections.

   Unscrew the motherboard mounting screws and store for reuse; verify that all screws have been removed.

6. Remove the heatsink and the processor before you remove the motherboard and place them on an antistatic mat. Removing these items before you remove the motherboard helps prevent excessive flexing of the motherboard and makes it easier to slip the motherboard out of the case. However, skip this step if the heatsink requires a lot of downward pressure to remove and if the motherboard is not well supported around the heatsink/processor area.

caution

Easy does it with the screwdriver! Whether you're removing screws or putting them back in, skip the electric model and do it the old-fashioned way to avoid damaging the motherboard. If your motherboard is held in place with hex screws, use a hex driver instead of a screwdriver to be even more careful.

If your motherboard uses plastic spacers, follow this additional step:

7. Gently push the motherboard toward the front of the case (for desktop units) or toward the bottom of the case (for tower units) to release the plastic stand-off spacers from the mounting grooves, as shown in Figure 4.9. To release the motherboard from the case, remove the screws, and then push the motherboard to release the plastic stand-off spacers from the teardrop-shaped mounting holes.

FIGURE 4.9

Most Baby-AT motherboards are held in place by plastic stand-off spacers.

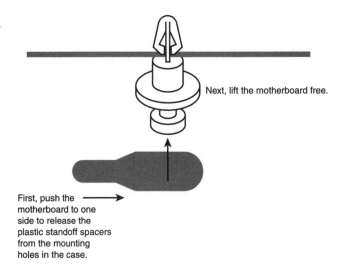

Next, lift the motherboard free.

First, push the → motherboard to one side to release the plastic standoff spacers from the mounting holes in the case.

For all types of motherboards, continue with this step:

8. Lift the motherboard and plastic stand-off spacers out of the case and place on an antistatic mat. If the motherboard is an ATX or Mini-ITX type, remove the **I/O shield** (the metal plate on the rear of the system that has cut-outs for the built-in ports) and store it with the old motherboard. If the motherboard is a Baby-AT type, remove the external connectors for serial, parallel, and other ports from the case and store with the old motherboard. Sometimes they will be attached to punch-outs in the case; more often, they are attached to slot covers. Use the appropriate-sized hex driver or screwdriver to remove them.

9. If you are planning to install a replacement motherboard, use a pair of pliers to squeeze together the tops of the plastic spacers in the old motherboard. Then, push them from the top until they fall out of the motherboard. They can be inserted into the new motherboard. These spacers come in different heights for use with different types of cases.

Motherboard Removal (NLX)

NLX motherboards are designed for fast, easy removal. Follow this procedure:

1. Disconnect cables from any installed add-on cards as described earlier.

2. Remove any add-on cards, remembering to handle the cards by their edges.

3. Pull the motherboard release lever to disconnect the motherboard from the NLX riser.

4. Slide the motherboard out of the case.

Preparing the Motherboard for Installation (All Types)

Before you install the new motherboard into the computer, perform the following steps:

1. Install the desired amount of memory. See Chapter 7, "RAM," for details.

2. Install the processor (CPU) and heatsink as described later in this chapter.

3. Configure CPU speed, multiplier, type, and voltage settings on the motherboard if the motherboard uses jumpers or DIP (Dual Inline Pin) switches. Note that many recent motherboards use BIOS configuration options instead.

To learn more about configuring the motherboard for a particular CPU, see "The CPU" later in this chapter.

Making these changes after the motherboard is installed in the computer is normally very difficult.

Step-by-Step Motherboard Installation (ATX/Baby-AT)

After you have prepared the motherboard for installation, follow these steps to install the motherboard:

1. Place the new motherboard over the old motherboard to determine which mounting holes should be used for standoffs (if needed) and which should be used for brass spacers. Matching the motherboards helps you determine that the new motherboard will fit correctly in the system.

2. Move brass spacers as needed to accommodate the mounting holes in the motherboard. If your case uses plastic stand-off spacers, remove them from the old motherboard and push them through the bottom of the appropriate holes on the new motherboard (as described earlier in this chapter). The spacers prevent the motherboard from shorting out on the bottom of the case.

3. If the motherboard is ATX, place the I/O shield and connector at the back of the case. Line up the mounting holes on these motherboards with the brass spacers.

   If the motherboard is a Baby-AT, place the new motherboard into the case, and make sure the plastic stand-off spacers (if used) are lined up in the correct teardrop-shaped mounting grooves at the bottom or sides of the case.

4. Gently push a Baby-AT motherboard into place until the plastic stand-off spacers snap into the mounting grooves (if present). Make sure the board is level and parallel with the side or bottom of the case. Avoid flexing the motherboard; excessive flex can damage the system or I/O bus wires and destroy the motherboard.

5. If the motherboard uses an I/O shield, make sure it is correctly positioned at the rear of the case. The I/O shield is marked to help you determine the port types on the rear of the motherboard. If the port cut-outs on some I/O shields are not completely removed, remove them before you install the shield.

6. Determine which holes in the motherboard have brass stand-off spacers beneath them and secure the motherboard using the screws removed from the old motherboard (see Figure 4.10).

Brass standoff   I/O shield   Rear of computer

FIGURE 4.10

An ATX I/O shield and motherboard during installation.

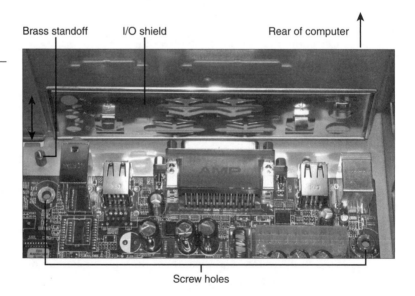

Screw holes

7. Reattach the wires to the speaker, reset switch, IDE host adapter, and power lights.

8. With a Baby-AT motherboard, attach the new ribbon cables supplied with the motherboard's I/O ports if present (these might be called header cables in the documentation that came with your Baby-AT motherboard). These are normally attached to slot covers, but if your case has punch-outs for these ports, knock out the holes, remove the ports from the slot covers, and attach them to the case. This will prevent the loss of usable slots.

9. Reattach the ribbon cables from the drives to the motherboard's IDE and floppy disk drive interfaces. Match the ribbon cable's colored side to pin 1 on the interfaces.

10. Reattach the power supply connectors to the motherboard.

11. Insert the add-on cards you removed from the old motherboard; make sure your existing cards don't duplicate any features found on the new motherboard (such as sound, ATA/IDE host adapters, and so on). If they do, and you want to continue to use the card, you must disable the corresponding feature on the motherboard.

12. Attach any cables used by front-mounted ports such as USB, serial, or IEEE-1394 ports to the motherboard and case.

Step-by-Step Motherboard Installation (NLX)

After you have prepared the motherboard for installation, follow these steps to install the motherboard:

1. Line up the replacement motherboard with the motherboard rails located at the bottom of the case.

2. Slowly push the motherboard into place. After the motherboard is connected to the riser card, it stops moving.

3. Lift and push the motherboard release lever to lock the motherboard into place.

4. Replace the side panel. If the side panel cannot be replaced properly, the motherboard is not installed properly.

Case Selection and Replacement

Planning a major system upgrade? Building a computer from scratch? Helping to select a system to buy? Better think about choosing the right computer case (also called an *enclosure* or *chassis*) for the job.

Selecting the right case for a desktop computer is important if you

■ Need to build a new PC from the ground up

■ Provide input for the purchase of prebuilt systems

■ Upgrade a system by moving components into a new case

There are three major types of cases used in typical systems:

■ Tower cases

■ Desktop cases

■ Slimline cases

Figure 4.11 compares the layouts of typical mid-tower, micro-tower, convertible desktop/tower, and Slimline/small form-factor cases.

FIGURE 4.11

Typical tower (top) and desktop (bottom) case form factors compared to each other.

1. Case
2. 5.25-inch drive bays (external)
3. Slimline 5.25-inch drive bays (internal)
4. 3.5-inch drive bays (internal)
5. Motherboard
6. Power supply
7. Slimline 5.25-inch drive bay (external)
8. 3.5-inch drive bays (external)
9. Additional 3.5-inch internal drive bays (mid/full only)

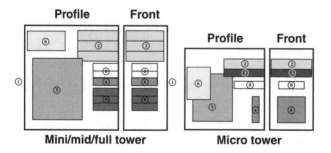

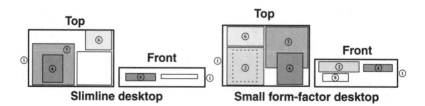

There are more differences between these case types than Figure 4.11 shows: For the gory details, read on!

Tower Cases

Tower cases get their name from their layout: The case stands upright on the short side.

Current mini-, mid-, and full-tower cases are designed to work with all types of ATX and Mini-ITX motherboards and ATX power supplies; older models are designed for Baby-AT motherboards and LPX power supplies. They differ in the number of 3.5-inch and 5.25-inch drive bays available. Generally, cases in these categories have five or more total drive bays and provide the greatest flexibility in system design and component choice.

How can you tell which cases work with ATX motherboards and which are designed for Baby-AT or LPX motherboards? Tower cases designed for ATX and Mini-ITX motherboards have a cut-out on the back side for the I/O shield and have an on-off switch that connects to the motherboard, whereas cases designed for the Baby-AT motherboard are designed to use the hardwired power switch, which is part of the LPX power supply. LPX motherboards have a single row of ports along one edge of the rear of the case.

Tower-based, low-cost retail systems sold for home and small-office use typically use a micro-tower configuration. Some micro-tower systems support as many as five drives, whereas others support no more than three. Some use ATX power supplies, whereas others use the lower-power SFX power supplies. The major distinguishing factor separating micro-tower from larger tower cases is the motherboard types supported: Micro-tower designs support only Micro-ATX, Flex-ATX, and Mini-ITX motherboards.

Desktop Cases

A traditional desktop case stands upright on the long side. Although desktop cases with internal layouts comparable to tower cases were once quite popular, they are scarce today. Some vendors produce so-called convertible cases, which can be used in both tower and desktop configurations. These systems typically offer removable drive bays, which enable optical drives to run in the flat position whether the case is upright (tower) or lying down (desktop). Some vendors also provide removable feet, which can be attached to stabilize the system when it is used as a tower.

Slimline and Small Form-Factor Cases

Corporate desktop computers that formerly used the LPX form factor now often use a **Slimline** or **small form-factor** design that supports the NLX, Micro-ATX, or Flex-ATX motherboard designs. These systems can be used in an upright or desktop position, but unlike with tower or convertible tower/desktop cases, the optical drive in a

Slimline or small form-factor case must be one that can be run in a vertical position. These case designs might not use industry-standard power supplies, making them more expensive and difficult to maintain.

Factors for Selecting the Best Case for the Job

Consider the following factors when selecting a case form factor:

■ *Expandability*—Mid-tower and full-tower cases support the widest range of motherboards and largest number of internal ATA, Serial ATA, and SCSI drives. However, if USB 2.0 or IEEE-1394 external drives are used, any case form factor offers satisfactory expansion opportunities.

■ *Ease of servicing and upgrading*—Mid-tower and full-tower cases are the easiest to work with for internal memory, drive, add-on card and processor upgrades, and for routine maintenance.

■ *Space required*—If space is at a premium, a Slimline desktop computer that can be used in an upright position takes the least amount of space, whereas a tower system placed on the floor uses the most amount of space.

Selecting a Motherboard Upgrade

If you need to upgrade the motherboard in a system, consider the following factors:

■ *Case and power supply form factors*—The replacement motherboard must fit into the current case to be a workable upgrade. Note that if you move to a **Pentium 4** motherboard that you might need to upgrade the power supply.

■ *Processor and memory compatibility*—While you might be able to reuse the existing memory or processor with a new motherboard, reusing these components might limit the performance or future upgrade path of your system.

■ *Support for advanced hardware*—A motherboard that supports the latest technologies (**Athlon XP** or Pentium 4 processors, AGP 8x, USB 2.0, IEEE-1394, Serial ATA, six-channel audio, 10/100 or Gigabit Ethernet, and so on) provides greater upgrade options than a motherboard lacking support for these technologies.

■ *Adequate number of PCI expansion slots*—Although motherboards with a large number of onboard peripherals reduce the need for expansion slots, you should select a motherboard that offers at least one open PCI expansion slot if the case form factor permits it. An open slot allows for future expansion.

■ *Vendor support*—A motherboard is only as good as the vendor that supplies and supports it. Check the quality of the documentation, the warranty, and the availability of support files (BIOS, chipset, audio, and so forth) before selecting a particular motherboard.

The CPU

One of the most important components found on any motherboard is the **CPU**, or **central processing unit**. The CPU is the brains of the computer, requesting information from devices, modifying and creating information, and then sending information to devices. It's also the first component your friends will ask you about when you buy a new PC! Recognizing different CPU types is very important in determining

- Which computers are capable of performing certain tasks
- Which computers are obsolete
- Which computers can be updated through a CPU change

The following tables provide an overview of CPU types, including their speed, voltage, and socket type. Use Table 4.4 along with the illustrations to help you recognize the major CPUs.

tip

The 2003 version of the A+ Certification Exam covers Pentium, Pentium-equivalent, and newer processors.

What makes a particular CPU fit (or not fit) into a particular motherboard? The motherboard and processor must both support the same processor type, same voltage, same socket type, and same clock speed. Although adapters can be used to adjust voltage and clock speeds and to convert some slot-based motherboards to use socketed processors of the same processor family, adapters cannot change a CPU's pinout to enable a Pentium 4 to fit in place of an AMD Athlon XP CPU, for example.

There are actually two clock speeds that must be considered when you match a processor to a motherboard. Starting with 486DX2 CPUs, CPUs began to have two clock speeds: a **core clock speed** (the speed at which operations took place inside the CPU) and a slower system bus speed (the speed at which RAM memory was accessed). When comparing systems with similar core clock speeds, the one with the faster system bus speed is preferred because it can access RAM faster.

Table 4.4 lists the physical characteristics of major CPU types, starting with the Intel Pentium. Use this table to verify compatibility with motherboards and to make sure that the system is correctly configured. Table 4.4 lists chips in order by socket or slot type used. Most chips on these charts were produced by Intel. Use the footnotes to determine additional manufacturing sources and other notes. The chip types are defined later, in Table 4.5.

Table 4.4 Physical Characteristics of Intel Pentium and Newer Processors (Desktop Versions)

Processor	Clock Speed Range	System Bus	Core Voltage	Socket Type	L2 Cache
Pentium	60–66MHz	Same	5V	**Socket 4**	No
Pentium	75–200MHz	50, 60, and 66MHz	3.3V	**Socket 5**, 7	No
Pentium MMX	200–233MHz	66MHz	2.8V	**Socket 7**	No
AMD K5	100–166MHz	66MHz	3.3V	Socket 5, 7	No
AMD K6	166–300MHz	66MHz	2.9–3.2V	Socket 7, Super 7	No
AMD K6-2	266–550MHz	66–100MHz	2.2V	Socket 7, Super 7	No
AMD K6-III	400–450MHz	100MHz	2.4V	Socket 7, Super 7	Yes
Cyrix 6x86	80–150MHz	40–66MHZ	2.8–3.52V	Socket 7, Super 7	No
Cyrix 6x86MX, MII	100–300MHz	50–100MHz	2.2–2.9V	Socket 7, Super 7	No
Pentium Pro	150–200MHz	60–66MHz	3.1–3.3V	**Socket 8**	Yes
Pentium II	233–333MHz	66MHz	Auto VRM[1]	Slot 1	Yes
Pentium II	350–450MHz	100MHz	Auto VRM[1]	Slot 1	Yes
Celeron	266–400MHz	66MHz	Auto VRM[1]	Slot 1	Yes
Pentium III	450–600MHz	100MHz	Auto VRM[1]	Slot 1	Yes
Pentium III	600MHz–1.1GHz	100MHz	Auto VRM[1]	**Socket 370**	Yes
Celeron	300–766MHz	66MHz	Auto VRM[1]	Socket 370	Yes
Celeron	800MHz–1.4GHz	100MHz	Auto VRM[1]	Socket 370	Yes
Pentium III	533MHz–1.4GHz	133MHz	Auto VRM[1]	Socket 370	Yes
AMD Athlon	500MHz–1GHz	200MHz	Auto VRM[1]	Slot A	Yes
AMD Athlon	650MHz–1GHz	200MHz	Auto VRM[1]	**Socket A**	Yes
AMD Athlon	1–1.4GHz	266MHz	Auto VRM[1]	Socket A	Yes
AMD Duron	550MHz–1.3GHz	200MHz	Auto VRM[1]	Socket A	Yes
AMD Athlon XP	1.333GHz (1500+)–2.2GHz (3200+)[2]	266MHz, 333MHz, 400MHz	Auto VRM[1]	Socket A	Yes
Pentium 4	1.3–1.8GHz[2]	400MHz	Auto VRM[1]	**Socket 423**	Yes

Table 4.4   (continued)

Processor	Clock Speed Range	System Bus	Core Voltage	Socket Type	L2 Cache
Pentium 4	1.4–3.2GHz²	400MHz, 533MHz, 800MHz	Auto VRM¹	**Socket 478**	Yes
Celeron	1.7–2.4GHz²	400MHz	Auto VRM¹	Socket 478	Yes

¹*Voltage level set by processor*

²*Processor in current production; maximum speeds listed might increase*

As you prepare for the A+ Certification Exam, note in particular the processor sockets and speed ranges used by each processor. Note also that the Celeron name actually refers to a series of low-cost (slower, less L2 cache) versions of the Intel Pentium II, Pentium III, and Pentium 4 processors.

Core Voltage

The *core voltage* is the voltage that the motherboard feeds to the processor. Most Socket 5–, Socket 7–, and Super Socket 7–compatible CPUs use a variety of different voltage settings, depending on clock speed and design revisions. Motherboards that use these CPUs must be used with voltage regulators set to the correct voltage to avoid CPU damage. Voltage regulators are built into many motherboards, or they can be "sandwiched" between the CPU socket and the CPU. Voltage regulators must be set to the correct voltage for the particular CPU model installed or the CPU can be damaged.

Fortunately, CPUs that use Socket 370, Slot 1, Slot A, or Socket A feature automatic voltage regulation, enabling the CPU to set the correct operating voltage without any "help" from the user. Some motherboards using these CPUs might enable the user to vary the voltage from the default settings for special purposes. Note that

tip

So-called "Super 7" or "Super Socket 7" motherboards use the standard Socket 7 processor socket, but also add support for different voltages and processor/ system bus speeds required by Pentium-class processors from AMD and Cyrix.

caution

Some processors are marked with two voltage levels: the core and the I/O. Make sure you set the voltage regulator to the core (lower) voltage level. Set a processor that is supposed to run at 2.2V to run at 3.3V, and you'll have a fried processor!

early motherboards might not be able to adjust to the voltage requirements of some later processors in a particular processor family.

Physical CPU Packaging Types

CPUs have been packaged in many different forms since the first IBM PC was produced in 1981. During the lifespan of any given CPU, more than one physical packaging type can be used. Thus, you always should physically examine a system that you want to upgrade with a new CPU. Make sure you determine which slot or socket type it has so you know which packaging type to ask for. Some desktop computers have soldered CPUs that cannot be removed for replacement or upgrading.

Table 4.5 defines the packaging types used for both older and current processors, as seen previously in Table 4.4.

caution

Most processors listed in Table 4.4 represent different families of models that use different voltage levels and processor sockets/slots. You should physically examine any system and check its documentation to verify the exact CPU type and socket in use and to determine compatible processors before replacing or upgrading the CPU.

Table 4.5 Major Physical Chip Packaging Types

Package Type	Major Uses	Package Name and Note
DIP	8088, 8086	Dual Inline Pin.
	Early 80287 math co-processors	A rectangular, ceramic chip with easily bent thin metal legs down the long sides of the chip. A recessed "dimple" at one end corresponds with a similar cutout at one end of the socket for keying.
		This packaging type is no longer used for CPUs but is still used for BIOS (firmware) chips used on motherboards, video cards, SCSI host adapters, and network cards. BIOS DIPs have fewer pins than CPU DIPs, and often have a sticker indicating the manufacturer over the top of the chip.
PLCC	80286, 80387SX math co-processor	Plastic Leaded Chip Carrier.
	BIOS chip (recent systems)	A square, ceramic chip with protruding contacts on all four sides. These slightly springy metal contacts hold the chip in place but don't provide a reliable keying method; a special PLCC chip puller is recommended if you work on systems using these types of chips.

Table 4.5   (continued)

Package Type	Major Uses	Package Name and Note
PQFP	80386SX	Plastic Quad Flat Pack.
	BIOS chip (recent systems)	A square, ceramic chip that resembles the PLCC but is surface-mounted to the motherboard.
PGA	80486DX, 80386DX	Pin Grid Array.
	Pentium 60 and 66, Pentium Pro, most later models	A square, ceramic chip with several rows of pins on the underside, leaving the middle open. Introduced with some 80286 models, PGA is also the basis for all subsequent socketed processors from the Pentium 75MHz all the way through the latest Pentium 4 and AMD Athlon XP processors. **See** "PGA Variations," later in this chapter.
SECC	Early Pentium II	Single Edge Contact Cartridge.
		The first slot-mounted CPU in the Intel family, the cartridge is a shell that encloses an SEC (Single Edge Contact) module with the Pentium II CPU and Level 2 cache.
		Other slot-mounted packages used for later Pentium II, Pentium III, and Celeron include SECC2 (simplified design) and SEPP (no cartridge shell). Adapters using SEPP are available to enable PPGA-based Celeron and Pentium III processors to attach to Slot 1 motherboards.

PGA Variations

The PGA chip/socket design is the basis for all recent socketed chips. Some socketed chips move the processor core to the top of the processor for better cooling. These include FC-PGA (Flip-Chip Pin Grid Array) and FC-PGA2 used by some Socket 370 (Pentium III and Celeron) processors; AMD Athlon and Duron (Socket A) and all Socket 478 processors (Pentium 4 and Celeron); OLGA (Organic Land GA) used by Socket 423 Pentium 4 processors; and OPGA (Organic Pin Grid Array) used by AMD Athlon XP.

Socket and Slot Types

Most Pentium-class and newer CPUs fit into square sockets of various types (the Pentium Pro's socket is rectangular); see Figure 4.12 for a comparison of these sockets. These sockets have different pinouts and electrical characteristics, making it important that you match the CPU you want to use to the sockets designed to handle it. You should note the most popular CPUs that use each socket type for the test (see Table 4.6).

Table 4.6 CPU Socket Types for Pentium and Newer CPUs

Socket Type	For CPU Types	Number of Pins	Voltage
Socket 4	Pentium 60/66	273	5V
Socket 5	Pentium 75–133, OverDrive	320	3.3/3.5V
Socket 7[1]	Pentium 75–233, MMX; AMD K5, K6; Cyrix 6x86, MII	321	Uses voltage regulator on motherboard
Socket 8	Pentium Pro	387	Automatic voltage regulation
Socket 370 (PGA 370)	Celeron; Pentium III[2] VIA C3	370	Automatic voltage regulation
Socket A (Socket 462)	Athlon, Duron, Athlon XP	462	Automatic voltage regulation
Socket 423	Pentium 4 (early version)	423	Automatic voltage regulation
Socket 478	Pentium 4 (current), Celeron	478	Automatic voltage regulation
Socket 603	Xeon	603	Automatic voltage regulation

[1]*Super Socket 7 is an unofficial term for Socket 7 motherboards, which support processors faster than 233MHz (AMD K6 and Cyrix 6x86, 6x86MX, and MII).*

[2]*There are three versions of Socket 370 that vary by pin assignment and voltage. Verify processor compatibility for a particular Socket 370 motherboard before you upgrade processors.*

Starting with Socket 3 (used for 486 CPUs), CPU sockets typically feature a so-called Zero Insertion Force (ZIF) socket design, with a handle that you raise to release the CPU and lower to clamp the CPU in place.

tip

Most CPU sockets have the socket name molded into the top of the socket for easy identification.

FIGURE 4.12

Processors and sockets from Pentium to Pentium 4.

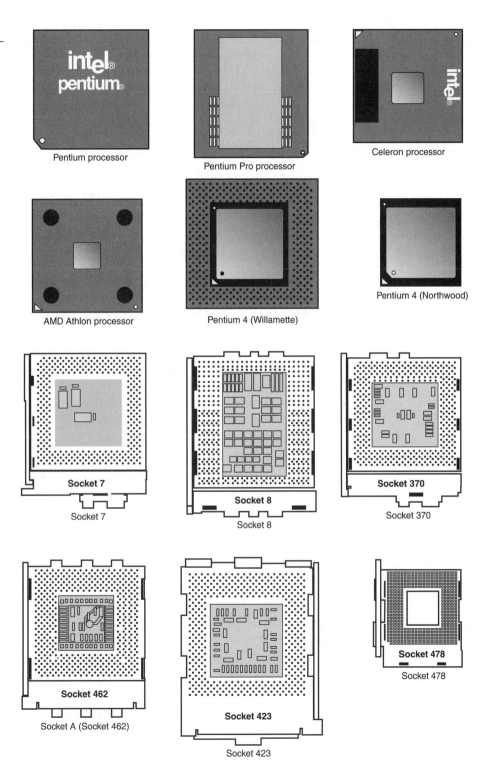

Pentium processor

Pentium Pro processor

Celeron processor

AMD Athlon processor

Pentium 4 (Willamette)

Pentium 4 (Northwood)

Socket 7

Socket 8

Socket 370

Socket A (Socket 462)

Socket 423

Socket 478

Table 4.7 lists the major CPU slot types. Slot-mounted processors are no longer produced, although many systems using slot-mounted processors are still in use.

Table 4.7 CPU Slot Types

Slot Type	Also Known As	For CPU Types
Slot 1[1]	SEC-242	Intel Pentium II, Celeron
Slot A	N/A	AMD Athlon
Slot 2	SEC-330	Intel Pentium II Xeon, Pentium III Xeon

[1]*Adapters known as slot-kets can be used to adapt Socket 370 processors for use on Slot 1 motherboards.*

Internal CPU Characteristics Affecting Performance

Besides core and bus clock speeds, there are other factors that influence the true speed of a CPU:

- *The register size and data bus*—These refer to the width of data that can be accessed in each CPU operation; the register size refers to data management inside the CPU, whereas the data bus refers to data transfer between the CPU and RAM. Some CPUs have a bottleneck created by having a data bus narrower than the register size; having a data bus wider than the register size increases speed by enabling the CPU to perform two data-transfer operations at the same time.

- *The presence or absence of a math co-processor circuit to perform faster floating-point math (used by CAD and spreadsheet programs)*—Although most CPUs prior to the Pentium used a separate math co-processor, the Pentium and all newer CPUs covered on the A+ Certification Exam have a built-in math co-processor.

- *The amount of RAM the CPU can access*—Larger amounts are better, although the actual motherboard design limits most systems to far less RAM than the CPU can use.

- *The presence or absence of cache RAM (RAM that holds a copy of main memory for faster access by the CPU)*—**L1 cache** is part of the CPU itself; Level 2 cache is found in various locations as listed in Table 4.8. Small L2 cache sizes or no L2 cache at all slows down the system.

- *The amount and speed of cache RAM*—Larger and faster cache RAM improves system speed, especially for operations that take place entirely or primarily in RAM.

Table 4.8 Locations for Level 2 Cache

Processor Model	Level 2 (L2) Cache Location	Notes
Pentium, Pentium MMX, AMD K5, AMD K6, K6-2	Motherboard	Size and type varies; some motherboards have removable cache chips or no cache, whereas others have permanently installed cache.
K6-III	Processor	This model is rare.
Pentium Pro	Processor	L2 cache runs at full processor speed.
Pentium II, Celeron 300A and faster, Pentium III (Slot 1 versions)	Processor assembly	L2 cache runs at half processor speed.
Celeron 266–300 (non-A)	None	Lack of L2 cache causes very slow performance.
AMD Athlon (Slot A)	Processor assembly	L2 cache runs at half or less of processor speed.
Pentium III, Celeron (Socket 370); AMD Athlon (Socket A), Duron, Athlon XP (all); Pentium 4, Celeron (all)	Processor die	On-die L2 cache runs at full processor speed.

Table 4.9 reviews these internal characteristics of the same CPUs listed in Table 4.8. Check out Table 4.9 when you need to determine the best optimization methods for a given CPU and when looking for CPUs for servers and other tasks requiring large amounts of memory. Note that CPUs used in notebook computers might have different specifications.

For the A+ Certification Exam, you should know which processors include both L1 and L2 cache.

⇨ For more information on how cache memory works, **see** "Cache RAM and Main Memory," **p. 240**.

All processors listed in Table 4.9 have built-in math co-processors, 32-bit internal registers (they handle 32 bits of data internally), and a 64-bit external data bus. However, they vary in the maximum amounts of memory supported, the size of L1 cache, and the presence (and speed) of L2 cache.

Table 4.9 Internal Characteristics of Major CPUs—Pentium and Newer

CPU	Max Memory	L1 and L2 Cache	L2 Cache Speed
Pentium	4GB	16KB - L1	N/A
Pentium MMX	4GB	32KB - L1	N/A
AMD K5	4GB	16KB - L1	N/A
AMD K6	4GB	64KB - L1	N/A
AMD K6-2	4GB	64KB - L1	N/A
Pentium Pro	64GB	16KB - L1; 256KB, 512KB, 1GB - L2	CPU speed
Pentium II	64GB	32KB - L1 512KB - L2	Half CPU speed
Pentium III	64GB	32KB - L1 512KB - L2	Half CPU speed
Pentium III	64GB	32KB - L1 256KB - L2	Full CPU speed
"Coppermine" Pentium III	64GB	32KB - L1 512KB - L2	Full CPU speed
"Tualatin" Celeron (266–300MHz)	64GB	32KB - L1	N/A
Celeron[1] (300A and up)	64GB	32KB - L1 128KB - L2	Full CPU speed
Celeron[2]	64GB	32KB - L1 256KB - L2	Full CPU speed
AMD Athlon Slot A	8TB	128KB - L1 512KB - L2	Half to one third CPU speed
AMD Athlon Socket A	8TB	128KB - L1 512KB - L2	Full CPU speed
AMD Duron	8TB	128KB - L1 64KB - L2	Full CPU speed
AMD Athlon XP	8TB	128KB - L1 256KB - L2	Full CPU speed
AMD Athlon XP "Barton"	8TB	128KB - L1 512KB - L2	Full CPU speed
Intel Pentium 4	64GB	20KB - L1 256KB - L2	Full CPU speed

Table 4.9   (continued)

CPU	Max Memory	L1 and L2 Cache	L2 Cache Speed
Intel Celeron[3]	64GB	20KB - L1 128KB - L2	Full CPU speed
Intel Pentium 4 HT Tech[4]	64GB	20KB - L1 512KB - L2	Full CPU speed

[1]*Slot 1 and Socket 370 versions are based on the Pentium II/III.*

[2]*Socket 370 version is based on the Pentium III "Tualatin" (has large heat spreader across most of the processor top).*

[3]*Socket 478 version of the Celeron is based on the Pentium 4.*

[4]*HT Technology versions of the Pentium 4 can simulate a dual-processor computer with just one processor.*

As you can see from Table 4.9, different versions of a processor might have significant differences in the size and speed of L2 cache. The size and speed of L2 cache should be considered when selecting a new processor for a system. Note also that the Celeron and AMD **Duron** processors are economy versions of the Pentium II/III/4 and AMD Athlon/Athlon XP. Moving from a Socket 478 Celeron to a Pentium 4 and from a Duron to an Athlon XP processor boosts L2 cache size and usually increases processor speed as well.

CPU Installation and Removal

CPUs are one of the most expensive components found in any computer. Because a CPU can fail, or more likely, need to be replaced with a faster model, knowing how to install and remove CPUs is important. On the A+ Certification Exam, you should be prepared to answer questions related to the safe removal and replacement of Pentium-class or higher CPUs.

The methods used for CPU removal vary according to two factors: the CPU type and the socket/slot type.

As you saw in Tables 4.4 and 4.5, almost all CPUs are socketed. Before the development of the **ZIF socket**, the processor was held in place by tension on the chip's legs, pins, or leads. Thus, to remove these chips, you must pull the chip out of the socket. Because the chip's legs, pins, or leads are fragile, special tools are strongly recommended for removing chips that are not mounted in ZIF sockets.

Refer to Table 4.4 for a definition of each of the following physical chip packaging types; Table 4.5 cross references chip types to the recent CPU types that use them.

Before removing and installing any CPU or other internal component, be sure to review and follow the ESD precautions discussed in Chapter 13, "Safety and Recycling."

PGA-Type CPUs (Pentium, Pentium Pro, and Later Models)— No ZIF Socket

Pentium-class and newer socketed processors (refer to Table 4.4) use some version of the **PGA (Pin Grid Array)** design (refer to Table 4.5) and are usually installed in ZIF sockets; these sockets have a handle that can be lifted to release the processor. However, you might encounter a few Pentium-class processors that are not installed in ZIF sockets. You should use a chip extractor to remove these processors from their sockets.

If the CPU has a removable heatsink or fan that is attached to the motherboard, remove the heatsink before removing the CPU. These heatsinks have a horizontal bar that attaches to the motherboard on two sides of the CPU. Squeeze or push the clip down at one end to release the bar and work it loose from the other side of the CPU. Then, disconnect the CPU fan (if included) from its power source and lift the assembly away. Then use one or two PGA chip extractors to remove the PGA chip; this tool resembles a small rake. These extractors are often supplied with 486 or Pentium-class chip upgrades.

1. Slide the chip extractor's "fingers" under any side of the CPU (see Figure 4.13). If you have two chip extractors, place the second one on the opposite side of the CPU.

FIGURE 4.13
Insert the PGA chip extractor under the side of the CPU and gently push down on the handle to loosen the CPU; move the extractor to the opposite side and repeat until the chip can be removed.

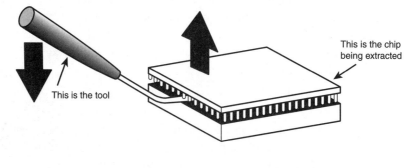

This is the chip being extracted

This is the tool

2. Push gently down on the handle of the chip extractor to pry up the CPU. If you have only one extractor, move the extractor to the opposite side and repeat; do *not* try to remove the chip with a single application of the extractor because the uneven force will bend the CPU's pins and might damage the socket.

3. Repeat until the chip is free; place it in antistatic packaging.

With the old chip removed, it's time to install a new chip. To insert a PGA-type CPU into a motherboard without a ZIF socket, find the corner of the chip that is cut off (beveled) and might also be marked with a dot; this indicates pin 1. The underside of some chips might be marked with a line pointing toward pin 1. Then follow these steps:

1. Line up the pin 1 corner with the corner of the socket also indicated as pin 1 (look for an arrow or other marking on the motherboard). If you put the chip in with pin 1 aligned with the wrong corner and apply the power, you will destroy the chip.

2. Gently press the chip into the socket. Make sure you are pressing evenly on all sides of the chip because uneven force will cause pins to bend. Stop when the chip is firmly in the socket (see Figure 4.14).

3. Attach the heatsink or fan if required at this time.

Beveled corner of 486SX CPU indicating pin 1

FIGURE 4.14

Line up the beveled corner (also marked with a dot) of a socketed CPU with pin 1 on the socket.

Pin 1 marking on motherboard

PGA-Type CPU in a ZIF Socket

ZIF sockets are used on almost all desktop systems using Pentium-class or newer socketed processors including the Athlon XP and Pentium 4. They allow easy installation and removal of the CPU.

What makes ZIF sockets easy to work with? They have a lever which, when released, loosens a clamp that holds the CPU in place.

If the CPU has a removable heatsink or fan that is attached to the motherboard, remove the heatsink before removing the CPU. Some of these heatsinks have a horizontal bar that attaches to the motherboard on two sides of the CPU. Others, such as the one shown in Figure 4.13, have a spring-loaded clip on one side and a fixed lug on the opposite side. Pentium 4 and Celeron processors that use Socket 478 use heatsinks that attach to a frame around the processor. Here's how to remove the heatsink and the processor:

1. Push the clip or bar down at one end to release it and work it loose from the other side of the CPU. With Socket 478, release the screws that hold the CPU fan to the motherboard.

2. Disconnect the active heatsink (if included) from its power source and lift the assembly away (Figure 4.15).

3. Push the lever on the ZIF socket slightly to the outside of the socket to release it.

4. Lift the end of the lever until it is vertical (see Figure 4.15). This releases the clamping mechanism on the CPU.

FIGURE 4.15

After the heatsink fan is disconnected from power (left) to reveal the processor (center), the lever on the ZIF socket (right) can be lifted to release the processor.

5. Grasp the CPU on opposite sides, making sure not to touch the pins, and remove it from the socket. Put it into antistatic packaging.

To insert a PGA-type CPU into a ZIF socket, find the corner of the chip that is marked as pin 1 (usually with a dot or triangle). The underside of some chips might be marked with a line pointing toward pin 1. Then follow these steps:

1. Line up the pin 1 corner with the corner of the socket also indicated as pin 1 (look for an arrow or other marking on the motherboard). If you put the chip in with pin 1 aligned with the wrong corner and apply the power, you will destroy the chip.

2. Make sure the lever on the ZIF socket is vertical; insert the CPU into the socket and verify that the pins are fitting into the correct socket holes.

3. Lower the lever to the horizontal position and snap it into place to secure the CPU.

4. Before attaching the heatsink or fan, determine if the heatsink has a thermal pad (also called a phase-change pad) or if you need to apply thermal compound to the processor core (refer to Figure 4.15). Remove the protective tape from the thermal pad or apply thermal compound as needed. Attach the heatsink or fan.

5. To secure the heatsink or fan on motherboards other than those using Socket 478, make sure that the retaining clip is securely in place around the lug on one side of the processor socket. Then, push down the locking clip until it fastens to the locking lug on the other side. For Socket 478, remove the old heatsink mounting mechanism if necessary, install the new one, and attach the heatsink to the mounts on the support mechanism.

Slot-Type CPU (SECC, SECC2, SEPP, or AMD Athlon Slot A)

You won't see many slot-type CPUs anymore, but if you need to install one on a motherboard, make sure the motherboard has a retention mechanism attached. If the motherboard doesn't have one, you will need to remove the motherboard from the case to attach a retention mechanism.

To remove a slot-type CPU

1. Push down on the retainers at each end of the CPU to release the CPU from the retention mechanism.

2. Disconnect the power lead to the CPU fan (if present).

3. Remove the CPU and fan/heatsink from the retention mechanism. The CPU slides straight up from the slot.

To attach a slot-type CPU

1. Attach the CPU retention mechanism to the motherboard. Leave the foam backing on the bottom of the motherboard while pushing the supports into place. Lift up the motherboard and secure the retention mechanism with the screws supplied.

   Some motherboards are shipped with the retention mechanism already installed, so this step might not apply to you. If the retention mechanism is folded against the motherboard, unfold it so the supports stand straight up.

2. Attach the fan and heatsink to the CPU if not already attached; some CPUs have a factory-attached heatsink/fan, whereas others require you to add it in the field.

3. Match the pinouts on the bottom of the CPU to the motherboard's slot; note that the slot has two sides of unequal length, making it easy to match the slot with the CPU.

4. Insert the CPU into the retention mechanism; push down until the retaining clips lock the CPU into place. Figure 4.16 shows the CPU in place.

5. Connect the power lead from the fan (if present) to the motherboard or drive power connector as directed.

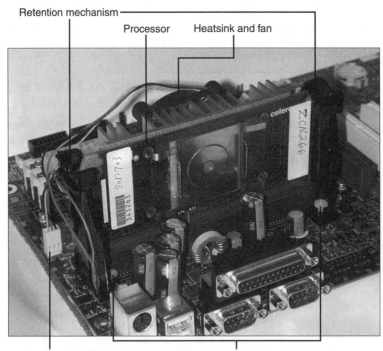

Retention mechanism ———

Processor   Heatsink and fan

FIGURE 4.16

A Slot 1–based Celeron CPU after installation. The heatsink and fan are attached to the rear of the CPU.

Processor power connection   Support pins (two on each side of processor)

Processor (CPU) Optimization

Because the CPU is the "brains" of the computer, and because faster data flow to and from the CPU is a critical factor in overall performance, you need to know how to optimize the CPU's performance. This can be done by making changes in the motherboard's CPU configuration and in the configuration of devices that communicate directly with the CPU.

Adjusting Speed and Multiplier Settings

As you saw earlier in this chapter, most recent CPUs have two clock speeds: an internal or *core* clock speed, and an external or *bus* clock speed (also called the **CPU frequency**). The CPU's core clock speed is a multiple of the system bus speed. The **Front-Side Bus (FSB) speed** on recent systems (the speed at which the CPU connects with memory) is a multiple of the CPU frequency (system bus speed). As Table 4.4 demonstrates, different types of processors have wide variations in FSB speeds. For example, the first AMD Athlon XP processors have an FSB running at 266MHz (133MHz×2), whereas the latest models have an FSB running at 400MHz (200MHz×2). Early Pentium 4 processors have an FSB running at 400MHz (100MHz×4), whereas the latest models have an FSB running at 800MHz (200MHz×4).

A motherboard's capability to use a given CPU depends in part on its support for the CPU's bus (frequency) speed and **clock multiplier**. Some motherboards provide you with a single speed/multiplier setting that makes the correct adjustments for you or detects the correct settings automatically by querying the processor.

Other motherboards require you to set the CPU bus speed and multiplier to the correct options. These settings can be made on the motherboard with jumper blocks, through the CMOS setup program, or automatically by the CPU. Your motherboard or system manual will have a listing of the correct jumper or CMOS setup options to select for all CPUs supported by your motherboard.

Some motherboards have a chart of correct jumper or DIP switch settings silk-screened to the top surface. Jumpers are small pins that are used on many motherboards to configure these settings; you must place a jumper block (a small plastic device with a metal insert) over two pins to choose a setting. DIP switches are small switches that can be flipped to one position or the other with a small screwdriver.

Most recent motherboards use BIOS settings instead of DIP switches or jumpers to configure FSB and clock multiplier settings. Figure 4.17 shows the configuration options for a system using a 1.4GHz Athlon processor.

FIGURE 4.17

The CPU clock multiplier. (M) times the CPU frequency (F) equals the CPU clock speed (S). This system has a 1.4GHz Athlon processor installed (10.5×133MHz= 1,400MHz or 1.4GHz).

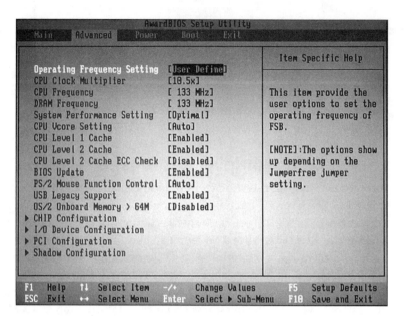

If you don't set the speed jumpers or BIOS settings correctly, your system will not run at the correct specifications. Whenever you replace an old CPU with a new, faster CPU, you must set these options correctly. Otherwise, you are running the chip at the wrong speed, which is called **overclocking** (faster than normal) or **underclocking** (slower than normal). Note that some motherboards do *not* allow bus speed or multiplier changes, meaning that specially designed, upgraded CPUs with the capability to override the motherboards' limitations must be used. If you run the processor at faster-than-normal speeds, you could damage the processor or other components due to overheating.

You also will need to change the voltage setting on many motherboards if you change to a faster CPU on a Socket 7 or Super Socket 7 motherboard. These motherboards, unlike Slot 1, Socket 370, Slot A, Socket 478, or Socket A–based motherboards, require you to select the correct voltage for the CPU you install. If you don't select the correct voltage setting, you might damage the CPU.

Some processor manufacturers sell several different processors that have the same model designation and clock speed but have different CPU frequencies and FSB speeds as well as L2 cache sizes. For this reason, knowing the model number and clock speed of a given processor is not enough to properly install it if you need to configure the motherboard or BIOS speed settings manually. Table 4.10 provides examples of processors that have the same clock speed but use different settings. Note that the processor clock speed is derived from the CPU frequency and clock multiplier.

Table 4.10 Recent Processors Compared by CPU Frequency/FSB Speeds

Processor	Clock Speed	CPU Frequency (F)	Clock Multiplier (M)	FSB Speed	(F×M)
AMD Athlon XP 2600+	2.133GHz	133MHz	16	266MHz	(F×2)
AMD Athlon XP 2600+	2.083GHz	166MHz	12.5	333MHz	(F×2)
AMD Athlon XP 3000+	2.167GHz	166MHz	13	333MHz	(F×2)
AMD Athlon XP 3000+	2.1GHz	200MHz	10.5	400MHz	(F×2)
Intel Pentium 4 2.6GHz	2.6GHz	100MHz	26	400MHz	(F×4)
Intel Pentium 4 2.6GHz	2.6GHz	200MHz	13	800MHz	(F×4)
Intel Pentium 4 2.8GHz	2.8GHz	133MHz	21	533MHz	(F×4)
Intel Pentium 4 2.8GHz	2.8GHz	200MHz	14	800MHz	(F×4)

Thus, to configure a processor correctly, you need to know the following:

- Clock speed
- CPU frequency (bus)
- Clock multiplier

Increasing Memory Size and Speed

The CPU must access data in memory (RAM) before it can perform functions on that data. Thus, CPU performance can be optimized through the following system upgrades:

- Increasing the size of installed memory
- Using faster memory (if supported by the processor and motherboard)
- Upgrading to a processor with faster clock speed and larger L2 cache

Installing more memory is the easiest way to improve the performance of any system. Increasing RAM memory in the system optimizes CPU performance by providing a larger pool from which to draw program code and data. Inadequate RAM forces the CPU to request the correct information from storage devices, which are much slower than RAM.

Systems running Windows 9x/Me can be upgraded to 512MB of RAM. Upgrades beyond 512MB are not recommended with these versions of Windows because of memory-address conflicts between RAM and AGP video (graphics) cards. Systems running Windows NT/2000/XP can be upgraded beyond this level. Systems running RAM-intensive functions and handling large amounts of data benefit most from a RAM upgrade.

Although any given processor model is designed to work at a particular clock multiplier and CPU frequency setting, most can work with a variety of memory speeds. The exact details vary with the motherboard. If the motherboard can use faster memory than the current memory installed, such as 333MHz (PC2700) DDR memory instead of 266MHz (PC2100) DDR memory, performance can be boosted by changing to faster memory. See Chapter 7 for details.

Increasing cache memory in the system provides an even faster shortcut for the CPU's access to information. You can compare cache memory to an ATM; it's usually faster to go to the ATM for money than it is to go inside the bank and stand in line. However, you can't use the ATM for all transactions; sooner or later you'll need to go inside the bank. Similarly, cache memory is like an ATM for information; it's faster to retrieve the information from cache memory than from main memory *if* the information is available there. Cache memory retains a copy of the last information read from main memory, so for repeated reads of the same memory locations, cache memory is used rather than main memory. However, if cache memory doesn't have the correct information, your system will retrieve the information you need from main memory (the "bank" in this comparison). Although Pentium-, K5-, and K6-based systems used L2 cache on the motherboard, more recent processors include the L2 cache in the CPU. Thus, upgrading the processor is the only way to increase cache size with most systems.

As already noted, different processor models in the same processor family have differences in clock speed, FSB speed/CPU frequency, and L2 cache size. Selecting a faster processor that also offers an increase in FSB speed and L2 cache size boosts system performance. Note that you might need to replace existing memory with faster memory to take full advantage of a faster processor.

Selecting the Best CPU Upgrade

There are two philosophies you can follow for processor upgrades:

- Choose the fastest processor upgrade that works with the existing motherboard, power supply, memory, and other onboard hardware.
- Choose the fastest available processor, even if it requires other components to be replaced, such as motherboard, memory, power supply, and so forth.

Which philosophy rules? It depends upon your upgrade budget! To determine which processors work with your existing hardware, check the documentation for the system or motherboard you want to upgrade. The vendor's Web site is recommended rather than consulting the original manual because the vendor might have updated the list of supported processors and have BIOS updates listed that might need to be installed before a faster processor can be installed.

If you want to change only the processor, the best upgrade is one that

- Increases overall performance by a substantial amount (15% or more at least)
- Supports your existing motherboard and memory

Installing Additional CPUs

Some motherboards in servers and technical workstations are designed to work with two or more processors. Before installing a second processor in these motherboards, verify the following:

- *Multiple-processor support in the operating system*—Windows NT 4.0/2000/XP Professional support multiple-processor systems, whereas Windows 9x/Me/XP Home Edition do not.

- *Availability of a processor that matches the characteristics of the installed processor*—At a minimum, the second processor should have the same clock speed, L2 cache size, FSB speed, and CPU frequency as the original processor. See the vendor's Web site for additional considerations.

- *Processors designed for multiple-processor use are recommended*—The AMD Athlon MP and the Intel Xeon series are built for multiple-processor mother-boards, whereas other processors, such as the AMD Athlon and Athlon XP, and the Intel Pentium III and Pentium 4, can work in a multiple-processor configuration but aren't optimized for it. Frequently, processors made for multiple-CPU motherboards have more L1 or L2 cache memory than conventional processors.

- *Consider upgrading memory*—For maximum performance, each processor should have access to the same amount of memory originally available for the first processor. Thus, you should double the memory size in a given system when you add a second processor.

- *Verify the system type identified by Windows*—If Windows NT/2000/XP have identified your system as a multiprocessor system in the Device Manager, Windows is ready to recognize the additional processor. However, if Windows recognizes your system as a standard motherboard, open the Windows Device Manager, select the motherboard, and update the driver. If this doesn't work, you need to reinstall Windows after installing the second processor. Back up all data first!

- *Verify BIOS configuration settings*—Some systems have more than one setting in the BIOS for MPS version. Consult with the system/motherboard vendor for the recommended MPS version to use for your multiple-processor operating system.

- *Determine the method used to configure Windows for multiple-processor support.*

Processor Cooling

All processors covered by the A+ Certification Exam require a heatsink. A heatsink is a finned metal device (occasionally plastic on very old processors) that radiates heat away from the processor. In almost all cases, an *active heatsink* (a heatsink with a fan) is required for adequate cooling, unless the system case is specially designed to aim air directly over the processor.

Although aluminum has been the most common material used for heatsinks, copper has better thermal transfer properties, and is frequently specified for processors faster than 1.5GHz. Some active heatsinks use a copper contact plate along with a larger-than-normal aluminum cooling area instead of an all-copper design (see Figure 4.18) to support faster processors (which normally produce more heat than slower models) at a cost lower than that of an all-copper design.

FIGURE 4.18

A large active heatsink with a copper contact plate (left) compared with a smaller, all-aluminum version (right). The larger model is designed for faster, hotter processors.

To allow for proper heat transfer between the processor and the heatsink, a thermal transfer material must be used. Heatsinks supplied with boxed processors might use a preapplied phase-change material on the heatsink, whereas OEM processors with third-party heatsinks usually require the installer to use a paste or thick liquid thermal grease or silver-based compound.

If the thermal material is preapplied to the heatsink, make sure you remove the protective tape before you install the heatsink. If a third-party heatsink is used, or if the original heatsink is removed and reinstalled, carefully remove any existing thermal transfer material from the heatsink and processor die surface. Then, apply new thermal transfer material to the processor die before you reinstall the heatsink on the processor.

Most active heatsinks for recent processors plug into a processor fan connection on the motherboard. The 3-pin connection enables the system BIOS to monitor fan revolutions. Many recent systems also monitor processor temperature. The cooler the processor runs, the more efficient it is and the lower the risk of instability and system crashes due to overheating.

Liquid Cooling Systems

Liquid cooling systems for processors are now available as add-on solutions. Some are integrated into a custom case, whereas others can be retrofitted into an existing system that has openings for cooling fans. Liquid cooling systems attach a liquid cooling unit instead of an active heatsink to the processor; some also offer liquid cooling for the North Bridge chip and graphics card chip. A pump moves the liquid (which might be water or a special solution, depending upon the cooling system) through the computer to a heat exchanger, which uses a fan to cool the warm liquid and back to the processor. Liquid cooling systems are designed primarily for very high-performance systems, especially overclocked systems. It's essential that only approved cooling liquids and hoses be used in these systems; unauthorized types of liquids or hoses could leak and corrode system components.

Compatibility Guidelines for Processors

Before installing a processor upgrade, verify that the processor you want to install is supported by the motherboard. It's annoying to discover that your computer won't recognize a new processor because you didn't check for BIOS upgrades before you installed the new processor.

Active heatsinks are designed for particular processor/socket types and processor speed ranges. Don't reuse the heatsink from an old processor with a newer, faster processor unless you verify compatibility with the new processor.

Some heatsinks are so large that they can damage voltage regulator components located next to the processor socket on some motherboards. Check the dimensions of any heatsink wider than the processor socket against clearances around the processor socket before you install it.

Study Lab

Don't miss the Study Lab materials found on the CD accompanying this book. Each Study Lab is tailored to the individual chapters in this book, meaning that you'll quickly be able to determine which topics you understand well enough to pass the exam and which topics need more study. The Study Labs are presented in printable PDF format so that you can take them with you to study at work, on the road, or even in your car just before test time!

THE ABSOLUTE MINIMUM

Here are the high points of this chapter. Review these just before you take the exam to brush up on the major topics and help you identify what you need to review.

- The motherboard is the heart of the computer because it contains connectors for the CPU, main and cache RAM, I/O ports, and expansion slots.

- Motherboards can be categorized by their shape, the presence of I/O ports, their processor, and the type(s) of expansion slots they use.

- The most common motherboard family today is the ATX family.

- Choosing the correct expansion cards for a particular task will improve system performance and allow for the best use of the system interior.

- Most systems in use today use PCI and AGP cards. ISA cards are obsolete but can still be found in some systems.

- The most important part of the motherboard is the CPU or processor.

- CPUs can be classified by their internal and external clock speed, internal and external data bus, memory address size, and amounts and speeds of L1 and L2 cache.

- Recent processors have full-speed L2 cache and fit into sockets. Older processors might lack L2 cache or have slow L2 cache.

- Upgrading the processor improves performance if the core clock speed is faster, the FSB is faster, and the L2 cache is larger and/or faster than with the old processor.

5

Power Supplies and Circuit Testing

Power issues are largely ignored by most computer users, but a properly working power supply is the foundation to correct operation of the system. When the power supply stops working, the computer stops working, and when a power supply stops functioning properly—even slightly—all sorts of computer problems can take place. From unexpected system reboots to data corruption, from unrecognized bus-powered USB devices to system overheating, a bad power supply is bad news. The power supply is vital to the health of the computer. So, if your computer is acting "sick," you should test the power supply to see if it's the cause. To keep the power supply working properly, use surge suppression and battery backup (UPS) units.

The power *supply* is really misnamed: It is actually a power *converter* that changes high-voltage **alternating current (AC)** to low-voltage **direct current (DC)**. There are lots of wire coils and other components inside the power supply that do the work, and during the conversion process, a great deal of heat is produced. A fan in the power supply dissipates the heat created by the operation of the power supply. That same fan also helps to cool the rest of the computer. Figure 5.1 shows a typical desktop computer's power supply. You can use the label attached to the power supply to determine its **wattage** rating and see important safety reminders.

How can you tell if a power supply meets minimum safety standards? Look for the backward UR logo, which indicates the power supply has the UL and UL Canada safety certifications as a component (the familiar circled UL logo is used for finished products only). The CE mark indicates the power supply has met the requirements of the European Union for power supplies.

Power Supply Ratings

In previous chapters, you've learned about bits, nibbles, bytes, base 2, base 10, and base 16. Here's another measurement for you: watts. There are all types of complex calculations for watts, but they aren't important in this case. What is important to realize is that power supplies are rated in watts, and the more watts a power supply provides, the more devices it can safely power.

note

The CD included with this book contains important Study Lab material for this chapter, as well as Chapters 2–22 in this book. The Study Lab for each chapter contains terms to study, exercises, and practice tests—all in printable PDF format (Adobe Acrobat Reader is included on the CD, too). These Study Lab materials will help you gear up for the A+ Exam. Also, the CD includes an industry-leading test engine from PrepLogic, which simulates the actual A+ test so that you can be sure that you're ready when test day arrives. Don't let the A+ test intimidate you. If you've read the chapters, worked through the Study Lab, and passed the practice tests from PrepLogic, you should be well prepared to ace the test!

Also, you'll notice that some words throughout each chapter are in bold format. These are study terms that are defined in the Study Lab. Be sure to consult the Study Lab when you are finished with this chapter to test what you've learned.

Output levels by type   Power supply type, rating, and special features

FIGURE 5.1

A typical power supply label. This power supply supports the ATX-12V connection required by motherboards for the Pentium 4 processor.

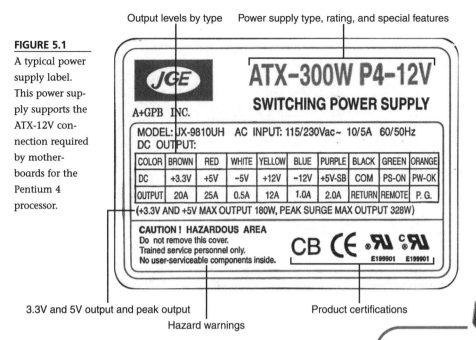

3.3V and 5V output and peak output

Hazard warnings

Product certifications

Typically, power supplies in tower-case (upright case) machines use 300-watt or larger power supplies, reflecting the greater number of drives and cards that can be installed in these computers. Power supplies used in smaller desktop computers have typical ratings of 145 watts or less. The power supply rating is found on the top of the power supply, along with safety rating information and amperage levels produced by the power supply's different DC outputs.

If you have a processor that runs faster than 1GHz, a mid-range or high-end gaming 3D card, or multiple hard or optical drives *and* your power supply is under 300 watts, you're just asking for trouble. Fast processors and 3D graphics cards along with multiple drives are notorious power munchers.

What happens if you connect devices that require more wattage than a power supply can provide? A big problem we call an *overload*.

caution

In the replacement market, unlabeled power supplies are often bad news. If you're shopping for a replacement power supply, and you're not buying from one of the major vendors such as Antec or PC Power and Cooling, avoid unlabeled models because you literally don't know what you're getting.

However, don't assume that all unlabeled power supplies are questionable. Some computer vendors prefer to use unlabeled power supplies in new equipment. If you find an unlabeled power supply in a system you bought new, contact the system vendor for information about it.

An overloaded power supply has two major symptoms:

- Overheating.

- Spontaneous rebooting (cold boot with memory test) due to incorrect voltage on the **Power Good** line running from the power supply to the motherboard. See Figure 5.7, later in this chapter, for details.

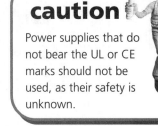

caution

Power supplies that do not bear the UL or CE marks should not be used, as their safety is unknown.

Here's a good rule of thumb: If your system starts spontaneously rebooting, replace the power supply as soon as possible. However, power supply overheating can have multiple causes; follow the steps listed in the section "Causes and Cures of Power Supply Overheating," later in this chapter, before replacing an overheated power supply.

To determine whether Power Good or other motherboard voltage levels are within limits, perform the measurements listed in the section "Determining Power Supply DC Voltage Levels" later in this chapter.

Multivoltage Power Supplies

Most power supplies are designed to handle two different voltage ranges:

- 110–120V/60 cycle
- 220–240V/50 cycle

Standard North American power is now 115–120V/60-cycle AC (the previous standard was 110V). The power used in European and Asian countries is typically 230–240V/50-cycle AC (previously 220V). Power supplies typically have a slider switch with two markings: 115 (for North American 110–120V/60-cycle AC) and 230 (for European and Asian 220–240V/50-cycle AC). Figure 5.2 shows a slider switch set for correct North American voltage. If a power supply is set to the wrong input voltage, the system will not work. Setting a power supply for 230V with 110–120V current is harmless; however, feeding 220–240V into a power supply set for 115V will destroy the power supply.

Voltage selector switch

FIGURE 5.2

A typical power supply's sliding voltage switch set for correct North American voltage (115V). Slide it to 230V for use in Europe and Asia.

AC power cord connection

Causes and Cures of Power Supply Overheating

Got an overheated power supply? Not sure? If you touch the power supply case and it's too hot to touch, it's overheated. Power supplies can overheat, causing system failure and possible component damage, due to any of the following causes:

- **Overloading**
- Fan failure
- Inadequate air flow outside the system
- Inadequate air flow inside the system
- Dirt and dust

Use the following sections to figure out why in any given situation:

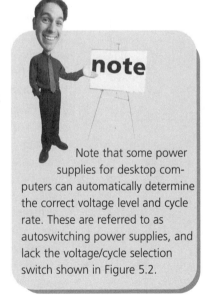

note

Note that some power supplies for desktop computers can automatically determine the correct voltage level and cycle rate. These are referred to as autoswitching power supplies, and lack the voltage/cycle selection switch shown in Figure 5.2.

Overloading

An overloaded power supply is caused by connecting devices that draw more power (in watts) than the power supply is designed to handle. As you add more card-based devices to expansion slots and install more internal drives in a system, the odds of having an overloaded power supply increase, especially if your current power supply is 300 watts or less.

If a power supply fails or overheats, check the causes listed in the following sections before determining whether you should replace the power supply. If you determine that you should replace the power supply, purchase a unit that has a higher wattage rating.

Use the following methods to determine the wattage rating needed for a replacement power supply:

- Whip out your calculator and add up the wattage ratings for everything connected to your computer that uses the power supply, including the motherboard, processor, memory, cards, drives, and bus-powered USB devices. If the total wattage used exceeds 70% of the wattage rating of your power supply, you should upgrade to a larger power supply. Check the vendor spec sheets for wattage ratings, or

- If you have amperage ratings instead of wattage ratings, multiply the amperage by the volts to determine wattage and then start adding. If a device uses two or three different voltage levels, be sure to carry out this calculation for each voltage level, and add up the figures to determine the wattage requirement for the device.

  For example, a system with a typical mid-range Athlon XP processor (2200+), AGP graphics card, two optical drives (DVD-ROM and CD-RW), 512MB of RAM, and four add-on cards uses over 220 watts (W) of power. A system with this configuration needs at least a 350W power supply ($350 \times .7 = 245$). The additional power over the minimum requirement provides a margin of safety, room for further expansion, and helps to handle the peak power requirements used at startup.

note

Some power supplies now feature power factor correction (PFC), which uses special circuitry to achieve an efficiency of 95% or more, as opposed to the 70%–75% efficiency of standard power supplies. Thus, when comparing two power supplies with the same wattage rating, the power supply with PFC makes more wattage available to the system.

■ Use an interactive power supply
sizing tool such as the one provided
by PC Power and Cooling
(`www.pcpowerandcooling.com`).

Fan Failure

The fan inside the power supply cools it and is
partly responsible for cooling the rest of the computer. If the fan fails, the power supply and the
entire computer are at risk of damage. The fan
also might stop turning as a symptom of other
power problems.

If the fan stops immediately after the power
comes on, this usually indicates incorrect input
voltage or a short circuit. If you turn off the system
and turn it back on again under these conditions, the
fan will stop each time.

To determine whether the fan has failed, listen to
the unit; it should make less noise if the fan has
failed. You can also see the fan blades spinning
rapidly on a power supply fan that is working correctly. If the blades aren't turning, the fan has
failed.

If the system starts normally but the fan stops turning later, this indicates a true fan failure instead of
a power problem.

Inadequate Air Flow Outside the System

The power supply's capability to cool the system
depends in part on free airflow space outside the
system. If the computer is kept in a confined area (such as a closet or security
cabinet) without adequate ventilation, power supply failures due to overheating
are likely.

Even systems in ordinary office environments can have airflow problems; make sure
that several inches of free air space exist behind the fan output for any computer.

tip

The PC Power and Cooling
Web site is a great way to
learn about power supplies.
Poke around inside it to see
different shapes and sizes,
and try the sizing tool with
different answers to see
how the equipment inside the PC
affects the recommended power
supply size.

note

Note that if the fan has
failed because of a short
circuit or incorrect input voltage,
you will not see any picture
onscreen because the system cannot operate.

Inadequate Air Flow Inside the System

As you have seen in previous chapters, the interior of the typical computer is a messy place. Wide ribbon cables used for hard and floppy drives, drive power cables, and expansion cards create small **air dams** that block air flow between the heat sources, such as the motherboard, CPU, drives, and memory modules, and the fan in the power supply.

You can do the following to improve air flow inside the computer:

- Use cable ties to secure excess ribbon cable and power connectors out of the way of the fans and the power supply.

- Replace any missing slot covers.

- Make sure that auxiliary case fans and CPU fans are working correctly.

- Use Serial ATA drives in place of conventional ATA hard drives (assuming the system supports Serial ATA); Serial ATA drives use very narrow data cables.

caution

Should you try to replace a standard power supply fan? No. Because the power supply is a sealed unit, you would need to remove the cover from most power supplies to gain access to the fan. The wire coils inside a power supply retain potentially *lethal* electrical charges. Instead, scrap the power supply and replace it with a higher-rated unit. See "Removal and Replacement of the Power Supply" later in this chapter.

Dirt and Dust

Most power supplies, except for a few of the early **ATX power supplies**, use a cooling technique called **negative pressure**; in other words, the power supply fan works like a weak vacuum cleaner, pulling air through vents in the case, past the components, and out through the fan.

Vacuum cleaners are used to remove dust, dirt, cat hairs, and so on from living rooms and offices, and even the power supply's weak impression of a vacuum cleaner works the same way.

When you open a system for any kind of maintenance, look for the following:

- Dirt, dust, hair, and gunk clogging the case vents

- A thin layer of dust on the motherboard and expansion slots

- Dirt and dust on the power supply vent and fans

Yuck! You never know what you'll find inside of a PC that hasn't been cleaned out for a year or two. So how can you get rid of the dust and gunk? You can use either a vacuum cleaner especially designed for computer use or compressed air to remove dirt and dust from inside the system. If you use compressed air, be sure to spread newspapers around the system to catch the dirt and dust. See Chapter 13, "Safety and Recycling," for more information.

Auxiliary Fans

Most systems today rely on more than the power supply fan to cool the system's interior. Auxiliary fans can be attached to the following:

- The CPU's heatsink
- The case
- A card mounted in an expansion slot
- An empty drive bay
- Motherboard North Bridge chip
- Chipset on graphics (video) card

Although most systems include an active heatsink (heatsink with fan) for the CPU (processor) and a front-mounted case fan, you can add other fans to help cool the system and reduce the possibility of power supply failure. Existing fans and additional fans you add should be checked for proper working order and cleaned regularly.

Figure 5.3 shows a typical rear case fan. You can plug fans like this into the three-prong chassis fan connection found on many recent motherboards or into the 4-pin Molex drive power connector used by hard drives. If the motherboard power connector is used, the PC Health or hardware monitor function found in many recent system BIOS setup programs can monitor fan speed. See Chapter 6, "BIOS and CMOS Configuration," for a typical example.

caution

Unfortunately, the more fans you install in a system, the noisier the system can be. While a few gaming PCs have variable-speed fans that spin more slowly when the system requires less cooling, most fans run at a constant speed. With typical systems, if the noise level coming from the system is much lower one day, don't enjoy the quiet. Instead, make sure the fans inside the case are still working.

Rear case fans are available in various sizes up to 120mm. The fan shown in Figure 5.3 is an 80mm model; measure the opening at the rear of the case (see Figure 5.4) to determine which fan size to purchase.

Figure 5.4 shows the rear case fan, North Bridge fan, and CPU fan after installation in a typical system. This system has two 80mm openings for case fans; a fan is already installed in one opening, and there's room for another.

FIGURE 5.3

A rear case fan that can be plugged into the motherboard or into a Molex power connector.

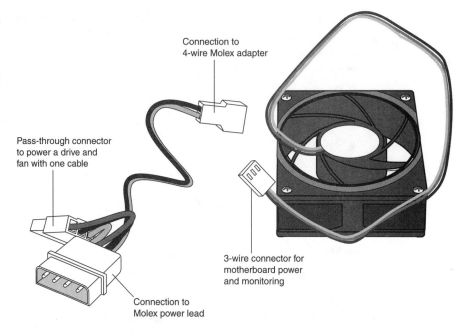

Connection to
4-wire Molex adapter

Pass-through connector
to power a drive and
fan with one cable

3-wire connector for
motherboard power
and monitoring

Connection to
Molex power lead

FIGURE 5.4

A system with a rear case fan, North Bridge chip fan, and CPU fan. An additional rear case fan could be installed later.

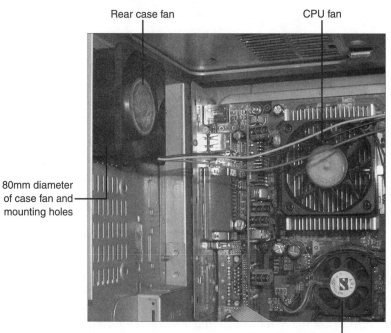

Rear case fan

CPU fan

80mm diameter
of case fan and
mounting holes

North Bridge chip fan

Replacement Power Supply Form Factors and Connectors

When you shop for a power supply, you also need to make sure it can connect to your motherboard. There are two major types of power connectors on motherboards:

- 12-pin, modeled after the original IBM PC power connector and used on Baby-AT and LPX motherboards (see Figure 5.5)

- 20-pin, used by all motherboards in the ATX family (see Figure 5.6) and by the NLX riser card (which provides power to the NLX motherboard)

Figure 5.7 lists the pinouts for these connectors. Note that only 5V and 12V DC power levels are supported by 12-pin (LPX) power supplies, whereas ATX power supplies also support 3.3V DC power levels.

caution

Another difference between ATX and LPX connectors is that the ATX connector uses specially shaped holes and a locking clip for positive keying, whereas the LPX 12-pin connector requires the user to properly align the black wires of connectors P8 and P9 to make a correct connection. If the LPX power supply wires are not oriented correctly, the motherboard could be damaged when the power is turned on.

FIGURE 5.5

Twin 6-pin power connectors are used on LPX and other power supply types that attach to motherboards with a 12-pin connector.

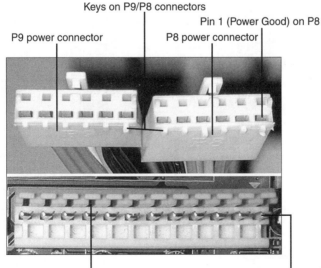

Keys on P9/P8 connectors

Pin 1 (Power Good) on P8

P9 power connector

P8 power connector

Cut-outs for P9/P8 connector keys on motherboard power connector

Pin 1 (Power Good) on motherboard power connector

FIGURE 5.6

The ATX power supply has a single 20-pin power connector. The extra connectors (compared to the LPX design in Figure 5.5) provide support for 3.3V and for software- or keyboard-controlled power down. Many of these power supplies don't have an external power switch for that reason.

Release lever on ATX/SFX power supply connector

Pin 1 on power supply connector

Locking tab on motherboard power connector

Pin 1 on motherboard power connector

FIGURE 5.7

Pinouts for an ATX power connector (left) and Baby-AT (LPX) power connector (right). The color coding in the figure represents the standard wire colors used.

ATX Power Connector Pinout

+3.3v	Orange	11		1	Orange	+3.3v
−12v	Blue	12		2	Orange	+3.3v
Ground	Black	13		3	Black	Ground
PS-On	Green	14		4	Red	+5v
Ground	Black	15		5	Black	Ground
Ground	Black	16		6	Red	+5v
Ground	Black	17		7	Black	Ground
−5v	White	18		8	Gray	Power Good
+5v	Red	19		9	Purple	+5v Standby
+5v	Red	20		10	Yellow	+12v

XT/AT/LPX Power Connector

	1	Orange	+5v (Power Good)	
	2	Red	+5v	
	3	Yellow	+12v	P8
	4	Blue	−12v	
	5	Black	Ground	
	6	Black	Ground	
	1	Black	Ground	
	2	Black	Ground	
	3	White	−5v	P9
	4	Red	+5v	
	5	Red	+5v	
	6	Red	+5v	

Most systems that still use the 12-pin power supply connector use a type of power supply referred to as **Slimline**, LPX, or PS/2. Slimline power supplies have a power switch that connects directly to the power switch on the front of the case. Systems that use the 20-pin power supply with a full-size ATX motherboard (refer to Chapter 4, "The Motherboard and CPU") use ATX power supplies. However, systems that use the smaller Micro-ATX and Flex-ATX motherboards typically use an **SFX** (small form factor) power supply. SFX power supplies might have internal or external cooling fans, and can have the AC power connector on the short side (most versions) or the long side (used by some eMachine and HP computers that use micro-tower cases). ATX and SFX power supplies do not use a cable-mounted power switch, although some ATX power supplies have a built-in on-off switch.

Figure 5.8 shows how these power supplies compare physically to each other.

FIGURE 5.8

Rear view of typical LPX (top), ATX (middle), and SFX-L (bottom) power supplies.

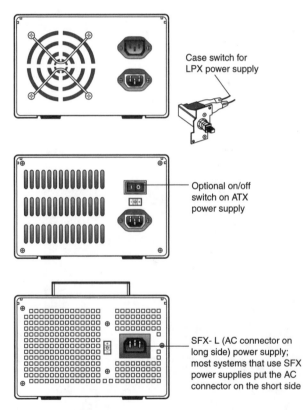

Case switch for LPX power supply

Optional on/off switch on ATX power supply

SFX- L (AC connector on long side) power supply; most systems that use SFX power supplies put the AC connector on the short side

If your wattage calculations or your tests (covered later in this chapter) agree that it's time to replace the power supply, make sure the replacement will

- Have the same power supply connectors as the original.
- Have the same form factor (shape, size, and switch location).
- Have the same or higher wattage rating; a higher wattage rating is highly desirable.
- Support any special features required by your CPU and motherboard. For example, motherboards that support the Pentium 4 processor use a 4-pin connection known as the **ATX-12V** connector as well as the standard 20-pin ATX connector. Some motherboards use a 6-pin connector known as the **auxiliary** connector as well as the normal 12-pin or 20-pin connector. See Figure 5.9.

caution

Most Dell computers built from September 1998 through 2000 use a proprietary version of the 20-pin ATX power supply connector. Dell's version doesn't have any 3.3V wires, so if you plug a standard power supply into a Dell PC that uses the proprietary version, or use a regular motherboard as an upgrade for a model that has the proprietary power supply, stand by for smoke and fire! See "Avoiding Power Supply Hazards," later in this chapter, for all the gory details.

FIGURE 5.9

ATX-12V (left) and auxiliary (right) power connectors.

To ensure reliability, a power supply should have a UL (Underwriters Laboratory) or CE (European) rating; these are the leading international standards associations for powered devices. Many very low-cost power supplies lack either rating and can produce erratic voltage levels and might represent a significant high-voltage hazard.

It's also desirable to select a power supply that has enough Molex (large four-wire) and floppy drive (small four-wire) connectors to support the drives and case fans you plan to use in the system (see Figure 5.10). If your power supply doesn't have enough connectors, you can add Y-splitters to divide one power lead into two, but these can short out and can also reduce your power supply's efficiency.

FIGURE 5.10
Molex (left) and small (right) drive power connectors.

 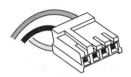

Removal and Replacement of the Power Supply

If you've done your homework (checked compatibility and size and dug up the case-opening instructions for your PC), installing a new power supply is one of the easier repairs around. You don't need to fiddle with driver CDs or Windows Update to get the new one working. But, you do need to be fairly handy with a screwdriver or nut driver.

Typical power supplies are held in place by several screws that attach the power supply to the rear panel of the computer. The power supply also is supported by a shelf inside the case, and screws can secure the power supply to that shelf. To remove a power supply, follow these steps:

1. Shut down the computer. If the power supply has an on-off switch, turn it off as well.

2. Disconnect the AC power cord from the computer.

3. Open the case to expose the power supply, which might be as simple as removing the cover on a desktop unit, or as involved as removing both side panels, front bezel, and case lid on a tower PC. Consult the documentation that came with your computer to determine how to expose the power supply for removal.

4. Disconnect the power supply from the motherboard.

5. Disconnect the power supply from all drives.

6. Disconnect the power supply from the case and CPU fans.

7. Remove the power supply screws from the rear of the computer case (see Figure 5.11).

8. Remove any screws holding the power supply in place inside the case. (Your PC might not use these additional screws.)

9. Disconnect the power supply switch from the case front (if present).

10. Lift or slide the power supply from the case.

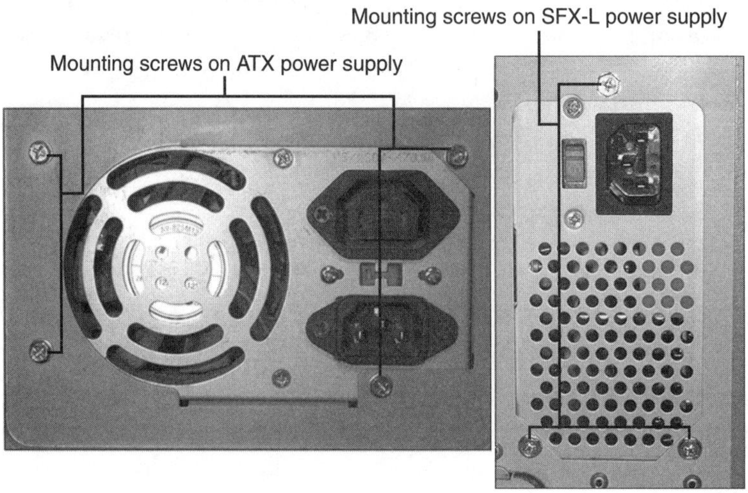

FIGURE 5.11

Mounting screws on typical ATX (left) and SFX-L (right) power supplies.

Mounting screws on SFX-L power supply

Mounting screws on ATX power supply

Before installing the replacement power supply, compare it to the original, making sure the form factor, motherboard power connectors, and switch position match the original.

To install the replacement power supply, follow these steps:

1. Lower the power supply into the case.

2. Connect the power supply switch to the case front (if present; this applies to Slimline/LPX power supplies).

3. Attach the power supply to the shelf with screws if required.

4. Attach the power supply to the rear of the computer case; line up the holes in the unit carefully with the holes in the outside of the case.

5. Connect the power supply to the case, CPU fans, drives, and motherboard.

6. Attach the AC power cord to the new power supply.

7. Turn on the computer. On systems with both a front and rear power switch, turn on the rear one first.

8. Boot the system normally to verify correct operation, and then run the normal shutdown procedure for the operating systems. If necessary, turn off the system with the front power switch only.

9. Close the case and secure it.

Testing Power Supplies with a Multimeter

How can you find out that a defective power supply is really defective? How can you make sure that a cable has the right pinouts? Use a **multimeter**. A multimeter is one of the most flexible diagnostic tools around. It is covered in this chapter because of its usefulness in testing power supplies, but it also can be used to test coaxial, serial, and parallel cables, as well as fuses, resistors, and batteries (see Table 5.1).

Multimeters are designed to perform many different types of electrical tests, including

- DC voltage and polarity
- AC voltage and polarity
- **Resistance** (Ohms)
- Diodes
- **Continuity**
- Amperage

All multimeters are equipped with red and black test leads. When used for voltage tests, the red is attached to the power source to be measured, and the black is attached to ground.

Multimeters use two different readout styles: digital and analog. **Digital multimeters** are usually **autoranging**, which means they automatically adjust to the correct range for the test selected and the voltage present. **Analog multimeters**, or non–autoranging digital meters, must be set manually to the correct range and can be damaged more easily by overvoltage. Figure 5.12 compares typical analog and digital multimeters.

Multimeters are designed to perform tests in two ways: in series and in parallel. Most tests are performed in **parallel** mode, in which the multimeter is not part of the circuit but runs parallel to it. On the other hand, amperage tests require that the multimeter be part of the circuit, so these tests are performed in **series** mode. Many low-cost multimeters do not include the ammeter feature for testing amperage (current), but you might be able to add it as an option.

Figure 5.13 shows a typical parallel mode test (DC voltage for a motherboard CMOS battery) and the current (amperage) test, which is a serial-mode test.

FIGURE 5.12

Typical analog (left) and digital (right) multimeters. Photos courtesy of Colacino Electric Supply, www.colacino. com.

FIGURE 5.13

A parallel-mode (DC current) test setup (left) and an amperage (current) serial-mode test setup (right).

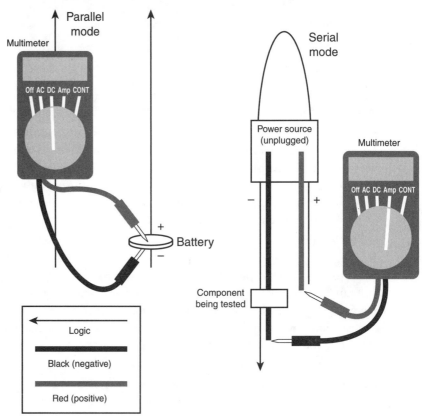

Table 5.1 Using a Multimeter

Test to Perform	Multimeter Setting	Probe Positions	Procedure
AC voltage (wall outlet)	AC	Red to hot, black to ground.	Read voltage from meter; should be near 115V in North America.
DC voltage (power supply outputs to motherboard, drives, batteries)	DC	Red to hot, black to ground (see next section for details).	Read voltage from meter; compare to default values.
Continuity (cables, fuses)	CONT	Red to lead at one end of cable; black to corresponding lead at other end.	No CONT signal indicates bad cable or bad fuse.
		For a straight-through cable, check the same pin at each end. For other types of cables, consult a cable pinout to select the correct leads.	Double-check leads and retest to be sure.
Resistance (Ohms)	Ohms	Connect one lead to each end of resistor.	Check reading; compare to rating for resistor.
			A fuse should have no resistance.
Amperage (Ammeter)	Ammeter	Red probe to positive lead of circuit (power disconnected!); black lead to negative lead running through component to be tested.	Check reading; compare to rating for component tested.

The following section covers the procedure for using a multimeter to diagnose a defective power supply.

Determining Power Supply DC Voltage Levels

You can use a multimeter to find out if a power supply is properly converting AC power to DC power. Here's how: Measure the DC power going from the power supply to the motherboard. A power supply that does not meet the measurement standards listed in Table 5.2 should be replaced.

You can take the voltage measurements directly from the power supply connection to the motherboard. Both 12-pin and 20-pin power connectors are designed to be back-probed as shown in Figure 5.14; you can run the red probe through the top of the power connector to take a reading (the black probe uses the power supply enclosure or metal case frame for ground).

The multimeter also can be used to check the Power Good or Power OK line by pushing the red lead through the open top of the power connector. See Table 5.2 for the acceptable voltage levels for each item.

Red probe from multimeter back-probing +12V line
DC voltage readout

FIGURE 5.14

Testing the +12V line on an ATX power supply. The voltage level indicated (+11.92V) is well within limits.

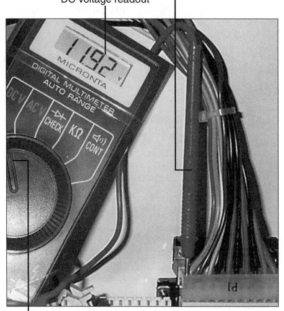

Multimeter's mode selector switch set to DV voltage

Table 5.2   Acceptable Voltage Levels

Rated DC Volts	Minimum Acceptable	Maximum Acceptable
+5.0	+4.8	+5.2
−5.0	−4.8	−5.2
−12.0	−11.4	−12.6
+12.0	+11.4	+12.6
+3.3	+3.14	+3.5
Power Good (pin 1 on P8) (pin 8 Power OK on ATX)	+3.0	+6.0

If a power supply fails any of these measurements, replace it and retest the new unit.

Avoiding Power Supply Hazards

To avoid shock and fire hazards when working with power supplies, follow these guidelines:

- *Never disassemble a power supply or push metal tools through the openings in the case.* Long after you shut off the system, the wire coils inside the power supply retain potentially fatal voltage levels. If you want to see the interior of a power supply safely, check the Web sites of leading power supply vendors such as PC Power and Cooling.

caution

- *If you are replacing the power supply in a Dell desktop computer, determine whether the computer uses a standard ATX or Dell proprietary ATX power supply.* Many Dell computers built from September 1998 through 2000 use a nonstandard version of the ATX power supply with a different pinout for the power connector. Install a standard power supply on a system built to use a Dell proprietary model, or upgrade from a Dell motherboard that uses the Dell proprietary ATX design to a standard motherboard, and you can literally cause a power supply and system fire!

  The proprietary Dell version of the 20-pin ATX connector has no 3.3V (orange) lines, and its Power Good (gray wire) line is pin 5, not pin 8 as with a standard ATX power supply. The 3.3V (orange) wires are routed to the 6-pin Dell proprietary auxiliary connector. With any Dell computer, check the pinout before ordering and installing a replacement.

- Always *use a properly wired and grounded outlet for your computer and its peripherals.* You can use a plug-in wiring tester to quickly determine if a three-prong outlet is properly wired; signal lights on the tester indicate the outlet's status (see Figure 5.15).

tip

PC Power and Cooling (www.pcpowerandcooling.com) makes a line of Dell-compatible power supplies; adapters to convert off-the-shelf power supplies to work with Dell proprietary motherboards are available from several vendors.

FIGURE 5.15

An **outlet tester** like this one can find wiring problems quickly. This outlet is wired correctly.

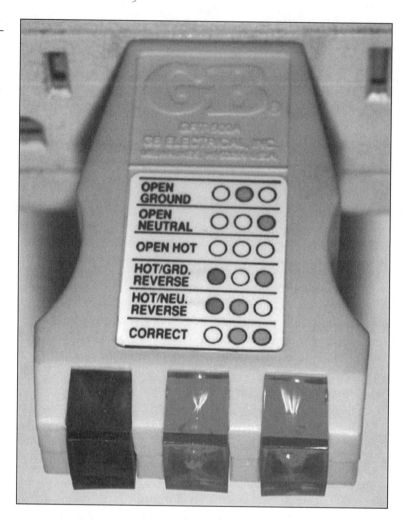

Power Protection Types

Question: How well can a power supply work if it has poor-quality AC power to work with?

Answer: Not very well.

Because computers and many popular computer peripherals run on DC power that has been converted from AC power, it's essential to make sure that proper levels of AC power flow to the computer and its peripherals. There are four problems you might run into:

- Overvoltages (spikes and surges)
- Undervoltages (brownouts)
- Power failure (blackouts)
- Noisy power (interference)

Extremely high levels of transient or sustained overvoltages can damage the power supply of the computer and peripherals, and voltage that is significantly lower than required will cause the computer and peripherals to shut down. Shutdowns happen immediately when all power fails. A fourth problem with power is interference; "noisy" electrical power can cause subtle damage, and all four types of problems put the most valuable property of any computer, the data stored on the computer, at risk. Protect your computer's power supply and other components with appropriate devices:

- **Surge suppressors**, which are also referred to as surge protectors
- Battery backup systems, which are also referred to as UPS or SPS systems
- Power conditioning devices

Surge Suppressors

Stop that surge! While properly designed surge suppressors can prevent power surges (chronic overvoltage) and spikes (brief extremely high voltage) from damaging your computer, low-cost ones are often useless because they lack sufficient components to absorb dangerous surges. Surge suppressors range in price from under $10 to close to $100 per unit.

Both spikes and surges are overvoltages: voltage levels higher than the normal voltage levels that come out of the wall socket. **Spikes** are momentary overvoltages, whereas **surges** last longer. Both can damage or destroy equipment and can come through data lines (such as RJ-11 phone or RJ-45 network cables) as well as through power lines. In other words, if you think of your PC as a house, spikes and surges can come in through the back door or the garage as well as through the front door. Better "lock" (protect) all the doors. Many vendors sell data-line surge suppressors.

How can you tell the real surge suppressors from the phonies? A surge suppressor must have a **UL-1449** rating to be considered a "true" surge protector. Many low-cost units labeled "surge suppressors" actually have a different UL rating (UL-1363) for a multioutlet strip ("transient voltage tap"). Although UL-1363 units can provide a minimal level of protection against modest overvoltages, UL-1449–rated units are recommended for significant protection. An alternative rating to look for is the IEEE-587 Category A rating; high-quality surge suppressors will normally have both

UL-1449 and IEEE-587 Category A ratings (IEEE-587 Category B applies to major feeders and local branch circuits, and Category A applies to outlets and long branch circuits).

Beyond the UL-1449 rating, look for the following features to be useful in preventing power problems:

- A low UL-1449 let-through voltage level (400V AC or less). This might seem high compared to the 115V standard, but power supplies have been tested to handle up to 800V AC themselves without damage.
- **IEEE-587A** let-through voltage rating of under 100V.
- A covered-equipment warranty that includes lightning strikes (one of the biggest causes of surges and spikes).
- A high joule rating. Joules measure electrical energy, and surge suppressors with higher joule ratings can dissipate greater levels of surges or spikes.
- Fusing that will prevent fatal surges from getting through.
- Telephone, fax, and modem protection if your system has a modem or is connected to a telephone or fax.
- **EMI/RFI** noise filtration (a form of line conditioning).
- Site fault wiring indicator (no ground, reversed polarity warnings).
- Fast response time to surges. If the surge suppressor doesn't clamp fast enough, the surge can get through.
- Protection against surges on hot, neutral, and ground lines.

If you use surge protectors with these features, you will minimize power problems. The site-fault wiring indicator will alert you to wiring problems that can negate ground and can cause serious damage in ordinary use.

In preparing for the A+ Certification Exam, you should pay particular attention to the UL and IEEE standards for surge suppressors and the major protection features just listed.

caution

If you're looking for a way to negate the protection provided by high-quality surge protectors, plug them into an ungrounded electrical outlet. You'll still find them in older homes and buildings.

The two- to three-prong adapter you use to make grounded equipment plug into an ungrounded outlet is designed to be attached to a ground such as a metal water pipe (that's what the metal loop is for). If you can't ground the adapter, don't use a computer or other electronic device with it. If you do, sooner or later you'll be sorry.

UPSs and SPSs

A **UPS (uninterruptible power supply)** is another name for a battery backup unit. A UPS provides emergency power when a power failure strikes (a **blackout**) or when power falls below minimum levels (a **brownout**).

There are two different types of UPS systems: true UPS and SPS systems. A **true UPS** runs your computer from its battery at all times, isolating the computer and monitor from AC power. There is no switchover time with a true UPS when AC power fails because the battery is already running the computer. A true UPS inherently provides power conditioning (preventing spikes, surges, and brownouts from reaching the computer) because the computer receives only battery power, not the AC power coming from the wall outlet. True UPS units are sometimes referred to as **line-interactive** battery backup units because the battery backup unit interacts with the AC line, rather than the AC line going directly to the computer and other components.

An **SPS (standby power supply)** is also referred to as a UPS, but its design is quite different. Its battery is used only when AC power fails. A momentary gap in power (about 1ms or less) occurs between the loss of AC power and the start of standby battery power; however, this switchover time is far faster than is required to avoid system shutdown because computers can **coast** for several milliseconds before shutting down. SPS-type battery backup units are far less expensive than true UPSs, but work just as well as true UPSs when properly equipped with power-conditioning features.

Battery backup units can be distinguished from each other by differences in

note

In the rest of this section, the term *UPS* refers to both true UPS or SPS units except as noted, because most backup units on the market technically are SPS but are called UPS units by their vendors.

Make sure you understand the differences between these units for the exam.

- ▪ *Runtimes*—The amount of time a computer will keep running on power from the UPS. A longer runtime unit uses a bigger battery and usually will cost more than a unit with a shorter runtime. Fifteen minutes is a minimum recommendation for a UPS for an individual workstation; much larger systems are recommended for servers that might need to complete a lengthy shutdown procedure.

tip

■ *Network support*—Battery backup units made for use on networks are shipped with software that broadcasts a message to users about a server shutdown and shuts down the server automatically before the battery runs down.

■ *Automatic shutdown*—Some low-cost UPS units lack this feature, but it is essential for servers or other unattended units. The automatic shutdown feature requires an open RS-232 serial port or USB port and appropriate software from the UPS maker. If you change operating systems, you will need to update the software for your UPS to be supported by the new operating system.

■ *Surge suppression features*—Virtually all UPS units today have integrated surge suppression, but the efficiency of integrated surge suppression can vary as much as separate units. Look for UL-1449 and IEEE-587 Category A ratings to find reliable surge suppression in UPS units.

Always plug a UPS directly into a wall outlet, not into a power strip or surge suppressor.

Buying the Correct-Sized Battery Backup System

Battery backups can't run forever. But then, they're not supposed to. How can you make sure you get enough time to save your files and shut down your computer?

UPS units are rated in **VA (volt-amps)**, and their manufacturers have interactive buying guides you can use online or download to help you select a model with adequate capacity. If you use a UPS with an inadequate VA rating for your equipment, your runtime will be substantially shorter than it should be.

Here's how to do the math: You can calculate the correct VA rating for your equipment by adding up the wattage ratings of your computer and monitor and multiplying the result by 1.4. If your equipment is rated in amperage (amps), multiply the amp rating by 120 (volts) to get the VA rating.

For example, my computer has a 300W power supply, which would require a 420VA-rated UPS (300×1.4) and a 17-inch monitor that is rated in amps, not watts. The monitor draws 0.9A, which would require a 108VA-rated UPS (0.9×120). Add the VA ratings together, and my computer needs a 528VA-rated battery backup unit or larger. Specifying a UPS with a VA rating at least twice what is required by the equipment attached to the UPS will greatly improve the runtime of the battery.

In the previous example, a typical 600VA battery backup unit would provide about seven minutes of runtime when used with my equipment. However, if I used a 1050VA battery backup, I could increase my runtime to more than 20 minutes because my equipment would use only about half the rated capacity of the UPS unit.

Power Conditioning Devices

Although power supplies are designed to work with voltages that do not exactly meet the 120V or 240V standards, power that is substantially higher or lower than what the computer is designed for can damage the system. Electrical noise on the power line, even with power at the correct voltage, also causes problems because it disrupts the correct sinewave alternating-current pattern the computer, monitor, and other devices are designed to use.

caution

You should *not* attach laser printers to a UPS because their high current draw will cause the runtime of the battery to be very short. In most cases, only the computer and monitor need to be attached to the UPS. However, inkjet printers and external modems have low current draw and can be attached to the UPS with little reduction in runtime.

Better-quality surge protectors often provide power filtration to handle EMI/RFI noise problems from laser printers and other devices that generate a lot of electrical interference. However, to deal with voltage that is too high or too low, you need a true power conditioner.

These units take substandard or overstandard power levels and adjust them to the correct range needed by your equipment. Some units also include high-quality surge protection features.

To determine whether you need a power-conditioning unit, you can contact your local electric utility to see if it loans or rents power-monitoring devices. Alternatively, you can rent them from power consultants. These units track power level and quality over a set period of time (such as overnight or longer) and provide reports to help you see the overall quality of power on a given line.

Moving surge- and interference-causing devices such as microwaves, vacuum cleaners, refrigerators, freezers, and furnaces to circuits away from the computer circuits will help minimize power problems. However, in older buildings, or during times of peak demand, power conditioning might still be necessary. A true (line-interactive) UPS provides built-in power conditioning by its very nature (see the previous discussion).

Troubleshooting Power Problems

A dead system that gives no signs of life when turned on can be caused by the following:

- Defects in AC power to the system
- Power supply failure or misconfiguration
- Temporary short circuits in internal or external components
- Power supply or other component failure

With four suspects, it's time to play detective. Use the procedure outlined next to find the actual cause of a dead system. If one of the test procedures in the following list corrects the problem, the item that was changed is the cause of the problem. Power supplies have a built-in safety feature that shuts down the unit immediately in case of short circuit. The following steps are designed to determine whether the power problem is caused by a short circuit or another problem:

1. Check the AC power to the system; a loose or disconnected power cord, a disconnected surge protector, or a surge protector that has been turned off will prevent a system from receiving power.

2. Check the AC voltage switch on the power supply; it should be set to 115V for North America. Turn off the power, reset the switch, and restart the system if the switch was set to 230V.

3. Check the keyboard connector; a loose keyboard connector could cause a short circuit.

4. Open the system and check for loose screws or other components such as loose slot covers, modem speakers, or other metal items that can cause a short circuit. Correct them and retest.

5. With ATX/SFX power supplies, verify that the cable from the front-mounted power switch is properly connected to the motherboard.

6. Check for fuses on the motherboard (mainly found in very old systems). Turn off the power, replace any blown fuse on the motherboard with a fuse of the correct rating, and retest.

7. Remove all expansion cards and disconnect power to all drives; restart the system and use a multimeter to test power to the motherboard and expansion slots per Table 5.2, earlier in this chapter.

8. If the power tests within accepted limits with all peripherals disconnected, reinstall one card at a time and check the power. If the power tests within accepted limits, reattach one drive at a time and check the power.

9. If a defective card or drive has a dead short, reattaching the defective card or drive should stop the system immediately upon power-up. Replace the card or drive and retest.

10. Test the Power Good line at the power supply motherboard connector with a multimeter.

It's a long list, but chances are you'll track down the offending component before you reach the end of it.

Study Lab

Don't miss the Study Lab materials found on the CD accompanying this book. Each Study Lab is tailored to the individual chapters in this book, meaning that you'll quickly be able to determine which topics you understand well enough to pass the exam and which topics need more study. The Study Labs are presented in printable PDF format so that you can take them with you to study at work, on the road, or even in your car just before test time!

The Absolute Minimum

Use this list of chapter highlights as a quick review just before the exam, and to help you find areas you need to study in greater detail.

- Power supplies are rated in watts.
- An overloaded power supply might reboot itself or overheat.
- A power supply set to the wrong voltage cannot start the system.
- Multiply amperage by volts for each power level used by a device to determine its total wattage use.
- Fan failure at startup is usually caused by incorrect input voltage or system shorts.
- The interior of a power supply has *no* user-serviceable components and contains potentially fatal voltage levels.
- Poor cable placement, missing slot covers, dirty case vents, and a lack of case fans are typical reasons for system overheating.
- You can add fans to the case, North Bridge chip, and to hard drive bays to improve airflow.
- Slimline, PS/2, and LPX are all names for the power supply used by most Baby-AT systems.

- Slimline power supplies have two six-pin connectors, which can be installed incorrectly, leading to system failure.

- ATX and SFX power supplies have a keyed 20-pin motherboard connector.

- SFX power supplies are available in two varieties: SFX-L and SFX-S, referring to the location of the AC power cord connection.

- Systems that use the Pentium 4 processor require an ATX-12V connector on the power supply.

- All types of power supplies have two four-wire power connectors: Molex (large connector for hard and optical drives and case fans, and floppy (small connector) for floppy drives and other low-power devices.

- A power supply is held in place by several mounting screws, which must be removed before the power supply can be removed.

- A multimeter can be used to test AC and DC voltage, cables (CONT), and ohms. Some also test amps (current).

- Parallel-mode tests use the multimeter running in parallel to the circuit (DC voltage), whereas series-mode tests (amperage) place the multimeter in the test circuit.

- To determine if a power supply is working correctly, you should test all voltage levels and Power Good.

- Improperly wired outlets, no ground to system, touching the interior of the power supply, and installing a standard power supply on a system designed for a Dell proprietary ATX power supply are all hazardous activities that should be avoided.

- True surge suppressors have a UL-1449 or IEEE-587A rating.

- A true UPS battery backup unit provides battery power to the system at all times.

- Most so-called UPS units are really SPS (standby power supply) units that start up only when AC power fails.

- For adequate runtimes, you should choose a UPS/SPS with a VA rating at least twice the VA of the devices you connect to it.

- Multiply watts by 1.4 or amps by 120 to get the VA rating.

- When troubleshooting power supplies, keep in mind that problems such as loose AC or power switch cables, short circuits, and loose add-on cards can cause system failure. Check these before testing the power supply.

6

BIOS AND CMOS CONFIGURATION

You know what the CPU does—it does the "thinking" for the computer. But, how does the CPU "know" what kinds of drives are connected to the computer? What tells the CPU when the memory is ready to be read or written to? What turns on the USB ports or turns them off? The answer to all these questions is the BIOS. Next to the CPU, the **BIOS (basic input/output system)** chip is the most important chip found on the motherboard.

The BIOS is firmware ("software on a chip"), and it performs a lot of different jobs during system operation. So, is it hardware, software, or firmware?

On systems that use 32-bit versions of Microsoft Windows (Windows 95 or newer), the BIOS doesn't do much after the boot (system startup) process has been completed. However, during the boot process, the BIOS is an extremely critical component. What jobs does the BIOS do? The major tasks performed by the BIOS include

- Configuration and control of devices built into the motherboard; these are sometimes referred to as **standard devices**
- The **power-on self-test (POST)**
- The location of an operating system, to which it turns over control of the system by using the Bootstrap loader

The BIOS doesn't do its job alone. It works with two other important components:

- CMOS memory
- Motherboard battery (also called the CMOS battery)

In the following sections, you'll learn more about how these components work together to control system startup and onboard hardware.

What Does the BIOS Control?

Now that you understand what the BIOS does, it's time to dive into the details.

The BIOS is a complex piece of firmware ("software on a chip") that provides support for the following devices and features of your system:

- Selection and configuration of storage devices connected to the motherboard's host adapters, such as hard drives, floppy drives, and CD-ROM drives
- Configuration of main and cache memory

note

The CD included with this book contains important Study Lab material for this chapter, as well as Chapters 2–22 in this book. The Study Lab for each chapter contains terms to study, exercises, and practice tests—all in printable PDF format (Adobe Acrobat Reader is included on the CD, too). These Study Lab materials will help you gear up for the A+ Exam. Also, the CD includes an industry-leading test engine from PrepLogic, which simulates the actual A+ test so that you can be sure that you're ready when test day arrives. Don't let the A+ test intimidate you. If you've read the chapters, worked through the Study Lab, and passed the practice tests from PrepLogic, you should be well prepared to ace the test!

Also, you'll notice that some words throughout each chapter are in bold format. These are study terms that are defined in the Study Lab. Be sure to consult the Study Lab when you are finished with this chapter to test what you've learned.

- Configuration of built-in ports, such as ATA/IDE and Serial ATA hard disk, floppy disk, serial, parallel, PS/2 mouse, USB, and IEEE-1394 ports

- Configuration of integrated (built into the motherboard chipset) audio, network, and graphics features when present

- Selection and configuration of special motherboard features, such as memory error correction, antivirus protection, and fast memory access

- Support for different CPU types, speeds, and special features

- Support for advanced operating systems, including networks and plug-and-play versions of Windows

- Power management

- Hardware monitoring (processor temperature, voltage levels, and fan performance)

Without the BIOS, your computer would simply be a collection of metal and plastic parts that couldn't interact with one another or do much of anything but gather dust.

Storing System Settings

To enable the BIOS to perform these tasks, two other components on the motherboard work with the BIOS: the CMOS chip, also known as the **NVRAM/RTC (non-volatile RAM/real-time clock)**, and the battery. The **CMOS** stores the settings that you make with the BIOS configuration program and contains the system's real-time-clock circuit. Power from a battery attached to the motherboard is used by the CMOS to keep its settings; thus, the CMOS RAM is "non-volatile" as long as the battery is working (figure about two years or so for the typical battery). Because the battery on the motherboard maintains the CMOS settings, it is often referred to as the CMOS battery. Figure 6.1 shows typical socketed BIOS chips and batteries. Note that the BIOS chip shown on the second motherboard in Figure 6.1 is square, whereas the other one is rectangular. The A+ Certification Exam might ask you to identify these devices on a motherboard and to explain their operation.

Most recent systems use various models of lithium batteries to power the CMOS chip, which can last from two to five years. Figure 6.2 shows three of the many battery types used on motherboards over the years.

The most common batteries you will see in Pentium class and newer systems are the DS12887A-type clock/battery chip seen in Figure 6.2 (left) and the CR2032 lithium battery seen in both Figure 6.1 and Figure 6.2 (center). The AA-size Eternacell in Figure 6.2 on the right was used in many early 286- and 386-based systems made by Zenith Data Systems and others. Some motherboards now feature a non-replaceable lithium battery with an estimated life of 10 years. Knowing that battery types can vary is not as important for the A+ Certification Exam as it will be for your day-to-day work.

FIGURE 6.1

BIOS and batteries on two typical motherboards. The CR2032 battery has become the most common removable battery on Pentium class and newer systems. The AMI BIOS chips' labels list support for "686" (sixth-generation) CPUs such as the Pentium II, Pentium III, and Athlon/Duron/Athlon XP series.

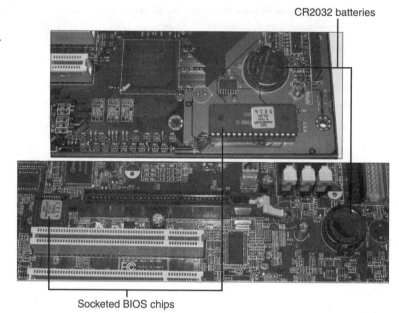

CR2032 batteries

Socketed BIOS chips

FIGURE 6.2

The Dallas Semiconductor DS12887A (left) clock/battery chip, CR2032 lithium battery (center), and the AA-size 3.6 volt (V) Eternacell (right) have all been used in computers for maintaining CMOS settings.

When the battery starts to fail, the clock will start to lose time. Complete battery failure causes the loss of all CMOS configuration information (such as drive types, settings for onboard ports, CPU and memory speeds, and much more). When this takes place, the system cannot be used until you install a new battery and re-enter all CMOS configuration information by using the CMOS configuration program.

Because the battery maintaining settings can fail at any time, and viruses and power surges can also affect the CMOS configuration, you should record important information before it is lost.

How the BIOS, CMOS, and Battery Work Together

The relationship between the BIOS, CMOS, and battery might be difficult to understand, so here's a comparison that can help:

As will become clear later in the chapter, the BIOS, in part, is like a huge digital restaurant menu, offering a dizzying array of system configuration choices. You can accept the normal settings if they work for your hardware or you can make changes.

Don't like the usual menu? At a restaurant you can often substitute salad for the potato and add a bowl of soup to your meal. Similarly, if you don't like the normal BIOS settings, you can use the BIOS setup program to adjust the values stored in the **CMOS (Complementary Metal-Oxide Semiconductor)** chip (often incorporated into the South Bridge or Super I/O chip on recent systems). The BIOS offers you many different options for most system components controlled by the BIOS, but until the settings are stored in the CMOS, the system is unable to run.

A restaurant would go out of business very quickly if it forgot or mixed up your order, so the members of the wait staff use order pads or develop very good memories. The motherboard battery performs the same task for the CMOS memory, providing a trickle of power that enables the CMOS to retain the BIOS settings you choose months and years later (see Figure 6.3).

POST

Every time you turn on your PC, the BIOS performs one of its most important jobs: the POST (power-on self-test). The POST portion of the BIOS enables the BIOS to find and report errors in the computer's hardware. For the POST to work correctly, the system must be configured correctly, as you will see in "System Configuration with the BIOS," later in this chapter.

The POST checks the following parts of the computer:

- The CPU and the POST ROM portion of the BIOS
- The system timer
- Video display (graphics) card

- Memory
- The keyboard
- The disk drives

You hope the POST always checks out OK. But what happens if the POST encounters a problem? The system will stop the boot process if it encounters a serious or fatal error (see the following "Beep Codes" section). During the POST process, the BIOS uses any one of several methods to report problems:

- Beep codes
- POST error messages (displayed on the monitor)
- POST (hex) error codes

FIGURE 6.3

The BIOS chip (top right) offers a wide variety of configuration options, which you select with the BIOS/CMOS setup program (lower left). The CMOS chip stores the choices you make with the assistance of the battery (lower right).

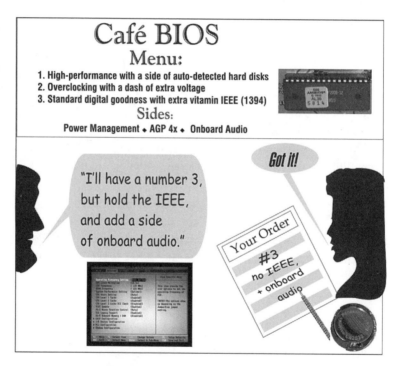

Beep Codes

Beep codes are used by most BIOS versions to indicate either a fatal error or a very serious error. A *fatal error* is an error that is so serious that the computer cannot continue the boot process. A fatal error would include a problem with the CPU, the POST ROM, the system timer, or memory. The *serious error* that beep codes report is a problem with your video display card or circuit. Although systems can boot without video, seldom would you want to because you can't see what the system is doing.

Beep codes vary by the BIOS maker. Some companies, such as IBM, Acer, and Compaq, create their own BIOS chips and firmware. However, most other major brands of computers and virtually all "clones" use a BIOS made by one of the "Big Three" BIOS vendors: **American Megatrends (AMI)**, **Phoenix Technologies**, and Award Software (now owned by Phoenix Technologies).

As you might expect, the beep codes and philosophies used by these three companies vary a great deal. AMI, for example, uses beep codes for over 10 fatal errors. It also uses eight beeps to indicate a defective or missing video card. Phoenix uses beep codes for both defects and normal procedures (but has no beep code for a video problem), and the Award BIOS has only a single beep code (one long, two short), indicating a problem with video.

> **tip**
>
> You can hear actual audio samples of several beep codes on the CD packaged with this book. Check them out!

Because beep codes do not report all possible problems during the startup process, you can't rely exclusively on beep codes to help you detect and solve system problems.

The most common beep codes you're likely to encounter are listed in Table 6.1.

Table 6.1 Common System Errors and Their Beep Codes

	Beep Codes by BIOS Version			
Problem	Phoenix BIOS	Award BIOS	AMI BIOS	IBM BIOS
Memory	Beep sequences: 1-3-4-1 1,3,4,3 1,4,1,1	Beeping (other than 2 long, 1 short)	1 or 3 or 11 beeps 1 long, 3 short beeps	(None)
Video	(none)	2 long, 1 short beep	8 beeps 1 long, 8 short beeps	1 long, 3 short beeps or 1 beep
Processor or motherboard	Beep sequence: 1-2-2-3	(none)	5 beeps or 9 beeps	1 long, 1 short beep

POST Error Messages

Most BIOS versions do an excellent job of displaying **POST error messages** indicating what the problem is with the system. These messages can indicate problems with memory, keyboards, hard disk drives, and other components. Some systems document these messages in their manuals, or you can go to the BIOS vendors' Web site for more information.

POST (Hex) Codes and POST Cards

There are beep codes and text messages to tell you that there's a problem with your computer, but there's also a third way your PC can let you know it needs help.

In Chapter 2, "PC Anatomy 101," you learned about the different ways data passes through the system. One method, used by virtually all devices, is to send data through one of 65,535 I/O port addresses. The POST is no exception; it also uses an I/O port address (usually 80h), sending a series of codes indicating the progress of testing and booting. The hexadecimal codes output by the BIOS change rapidly during a normal startup process as different milestones in the boot process are reached. These codes provide vital clues about what has gone wrong when your system won't boot and you don't have a beep code or onscreen messages to help you. It would be handy if the system came with a little TV screen to display these codes, but it doesn't.

To monitor these codes, you need a **POST card** such as the one shown in Figure 6.4, available from a variety of vendors, including JDR Microdevices (www.jdr.com) and Ultra-X (www.ultra-x.com). These cards are available in versions that plug into either ISA or PCI expansion slots. The simplest ones have a two-digit LED area that displays the hex codes, whereas more complicated (and expensive) models also have additional built-in tests.

The same hex code has different meanings to different BIOSs. For example, **POST code** 31h means "display (video) memory read/write test" on an AMI BIOS, but it means "test base and extended memory" on the Award BIOS, and it is

note

For additional beep codes, see the following resources:

- *AMI BIOS*—http://www.ami.com/support/doc/AMIBIOS-codes.pdf

- *Phoenix BIOS*—http://www.phoenix.com/resources/bios-postcode1.pdf

  (These files require the free Adobe Acrobat Reader, available from Adobe at http://www.adobe.com.)

- *IBM BIOS*—http://www.computerhope.com/beep.htm

caution

Don't mix up your boops and beeps! Many systems play a single short boop (usually a bit different in tone than a beep) when the system boots successfully. This is normal!

not used on the Phoenix BIOS. As with other types of error messages, check your manual or the BIOS maker's Web site for the meaning of any given code.

The worst time to learn how to interpret a POST card is when your system's sick. On the other hand, the best way to learn to use a POST card is to plug it into a healthy system and watch the codes change during a normal system startup. Typically, the codes change very quickly until the final code (often "FF") is reached and the system starts. On a defective system, the codes will pause or stop when a defective item on the system is tested. The cards remove easily and need not be left in systems routinely.

Keep in mind that the system almost always stops after the first error, so a serious problem early in the boot process will stop the system before the video card has been initialized to display error messages.

FIGURE 6.4

This POST card plugs into a PCI slot.

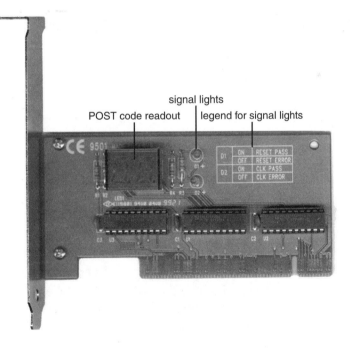

Transferring Control to the Operating System with the Bootstrap Loader

When the POST has done its job, if it finds no errors, it's time for the BIOS to do the next job on its to-do list.

During the POST, it detects drives and other **standard devices**. Many systems display the CPU type, hard disk configuration, floppy disk drive, memory size and type, and ports at the end of the POST (refer to Chapter 2 for details).

Next, the BIOS searches for an operating system on the drives listed in the BIOS configuration as bootable drives. On most systems, bootable drives can be hard disks, floppy disks, or optical disks. A few recent systems can also boot from drives connected to the USB port.

caution

In case you are wondering, ISA is dead, and ISA POST cards aren't far behind. The only reason to get an ISA POST card is if you still support systems with ISA slots. Most systems built in the last two or three years don't have any ISA slots. If there's no slot to use for a POST card, it's useless to you.

The first drive containing an operating system will be used to start the computer, and at that point the BIOS says to the operating system, "Here, you take over," and transfers control of most of the computer to the operating system. The portion of the BIOS responsible for starting the system is called the **bootstrap loader** (from the old expression "pulling yourself up by your bootstraps").

If a drive is listed as a bootable drive but has no media in it, the BIOS skips it and moves to the next drive in the list of bootable drives. If a bootable floppy drive has a non-bootable disk inserted and the system attempts to boot from that drive, the system displays a "non-system disk" error and the boot process stops until you remove the disk from the drive.

Warm and Cold Booting

There are two ways to boot (start) your computer:

- A **cold boot** (or *hard boot*) refers to starting the computer with the power or reset switch, which runs the entire POST and bootstrap process.
- A **warm boot** (or *soft boot*) skips the POST and refers to restarting the computer with the MS-DOS Ctrl+Alt+Del key sequence or the Windows Start, Shutdown, Restart menu.

Figure 6.5 shows a typical screen displayed during a cold boot.

The exact order and contents of the cold boot screen shown in Figure 6.5 vary with the system and with the installed equipment. For example, if you have an ATA RAID or Serial ATA card installed instead of a SCSI card, you would see the information for the BIOS chip on that card in place of the SCSI BIOS information shown in Figure 6.5. If antivirus or plug-and-play is not enabled, those options won't be shown.

What if your system doesn't display this information? Many systems are configured to save a few seconds at startup by not displaying this information. However, if you like to see what's under the hood, you can usually change the default settings.

➪ To learn more about how the BIOS collects and displays critical system information, **see** "How the BIOS Displays Your PC's Components," **p. 73**, for details.

tip

To prepare yourself for the A+ Certification Exam, make sure you can identify the three different methods computers use for identifying errors (beep codes, onscreen codes, and POST codes) and when each method is most appropriate for discovering why a computer cannot boot.

FIGURE 6.5

The screen displayed on a typical Athlon-based system during a cold boot.

BIOS vendor and major version

Motherboard brand and model

Processor type and speed

Onboard memory

Plug-and-Play information enabled

Antivirus BIOS setting enabled

Detected ATA/IDE drives

SCSI BIOS

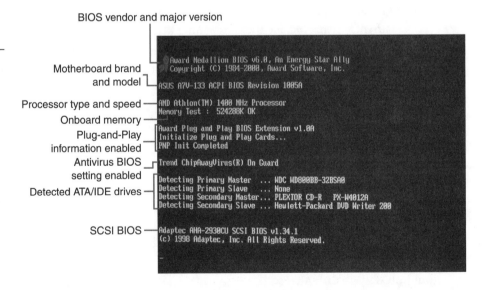

On an MS-DOS–based system whose hard disk and floppy disk drives are connected to the motherboard, the BIOS controls the drives. However, for systems using 32-bit versions of Windows (Windows 95 and NT 4.0 and newer), device drivers are loaded by the operating system to replace the BIOS. Still, without the BIOS, the system would not know what hardware was onboard or whether it was working.

System Configuration with the BIOS

The BIOS starts your computer by locating the operating system on a disk drive. So, you might be wondering, "How does the BIOS know what disk drives are installed?"

Disk drives are some of the most important items that must be configured in the BIOS. If the drive types are not correctly identified in the BIOS, the BIOS will not be able to start the system.

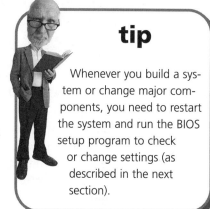

tip

Whenever you build a system or change major components, you need to restart the system and run the BIOS setup program to check or change settings (as described in the next section).

Starting the BIOS Setup Program

On most systems built since the late 1980s, the BIOS configuration program is stored in the BIOS chip itself. Just press the key or key combination displayed onscreen (or described in the manual) to get started.

Although these keystrokes vary from system to system, the most popular keys on current systems include the escape (Esc) key, the Delete (Del) key, the F1 key, the F2 key, the F10 key, and various combinations of Ctrl+Alt+ another specified key.

If you don't know which key to press to start your computer's BIOS setup program, try the keystrokes listed in Table 6.2.

Table 6.2 Common Keystrokes Used to Start the BIOS Setup Program

BIOS	Keystrokes	Notes
Phoenix BIOS	Ctrl+Alt+Esc	—
—	Ctrl+Alt+F1	—
—	Ctrl+Alt+S	—
—	Ctrl+Alt+Enter	—
—	Ctrl+Alt+F11	—
—	Ctrl+Alt+Ins	—
Award BIOS	Ctrl+Alt+Esc	—
—	Esc	—
—	Del	—
AMI BIOS	Del	—
IBM BIOS	Ctrl+Alt+Ins* F1	*Early notebook models; press when cursor is in upper-right corner of screen.
Compaq BIOS	F10	Keystroke actually loads Compaq setup program from hard disk partition on most models; press when cursor is in upper-right corner of screen.

Because the settings you make in the BIOS setup program are stored in the non-volatile RAM of the CMOS, the settings are often called **CMOS settings**.

In the following section, we will review the typical setup process, looking at each screen of a typical sixth-generation (Pentium III/Athlon) system. Setup screens used by other recent processors such as the Pentium 4, Athlon XP, and Athlon 64 are similar.

Step-by-Step CMOS/BIOS Configuration

To do well on the A+ Certification Exam, you need to understand basic CMOS/BIOS configuration. To help you prepare for the exam, this section covers the most important portions of the CMOS/BIOS setup process.

To start the CMOS setup process, press the correct key(s) during the bootstrap process or run the setup program from hard disk or floppy disk after the computer has started. Depending upon the brand and version of BIOS your computer uses, you might see a menu screen only, or you might see the standard CMOS setup screen with a top-level menu as in Figure 6.6 (shown later in this chapter). If you see a menu only, select Standard CMOS Setup to begin.

Table 6.3 provides a detailed discussion of the most important BIOS settings. Use this table as a quick reference to the settings you need to make or verify in any system. Examples of these and other settings are provided in the following sections.

> **tip**
>
> Notebook computers sometimes use a setup program executed within Windows as an alternative to configuring the system with the **BIOS setup** program at system startup.

> **caution**
>
> BIOSs vary widely, but the screens used in the following sections are representative of the options available on typical recent systems; your system might have similar options, but place the settings on different screens than those shown here. Be sure to consult the manual that came with your computer or motherboard before toying with the settings you find here. Monkeying with the settings here can improve performance, but can also wreak havoc on an otherwise healthy PC if you don't know what you're doing. Be warned!

Table 6.3   Major CMOS/BIOS Settings

Option	Setting	Notes	See Figure #
Floppy Drive	Usually 3.5-inch 1.44MB	Set to actual drive type/ capacity; some systems default to other sizes.	6.6
ATA/IDE Drives	Auto	Auto-detects drive type and settings at startup time.	6.6

Table 6.3 (continued)

Option	Setting	Notes	See Figure #
User/Power-On Password	Blocks system from starting if password not known	Enable for security but be sure to record password in a secure place.	6.6
Setup Password	Blocks access to setup if password not known	Both passwords can be cleared on both systems if CMOS RAM is cleared.	6.6
Keyboard	Numlock, auto-repeat rate/delay	Leave at defaults (NumLock On) unless keyboard has problems.	N/A
CPU Clock and Frequency	Set to correct settings for your processor (see Chapter 4, "The Motherboard and CPU")	Faster or higher settings overclock the system but could cause instability; some systems default to low values if system doesn't start properly.	6.7
CPU/Memory Cache	Enabled	Disable only if you are running memory testing software.	6.7
BIOS Update	Disabled	Enable to clear configuration data if you have problems with add-on cards.	6.7
PS/2 Mouse	Varies with mouse type	Disable if you use USB mouse; some systems use a motherboard jumper.	6.7
USB Legacy	Enable if USB keyboard is used	Enables USB keyboard to work outside of Windows.	6.7
CHIP (**Chipset Configuration**)	Set AGP card speed and memory speed to match device speed	Nonstandard AGP or memory settings could cause instability.	6.8
Serial Ports	Disable unused ports; use default settings for port you use	Avoid setting two serial ports to use the same IRQ.	6.9
Parallel Port	EPP/ECP with default IRQ/DMA	Compatible with almost any recent parallel printer or device; be sure to use an IEEE-1284-compatible printer cable.	6.9
Power Management (Menu)	Enable unless you have problems with devices	Enable CPU fan settings to receive warnings of CPU fan failure.	6.10
AC Pwr Loss Restart	Enable restart	Prevents system from staying down if power failure takes place.	6.11

Table 6.3   (continued)

Option	Setting	Notes	See Figure #
Wake on LAN (WOL)	Enable if you use WOL-compatible network card or modem	WOL-compatible cards use a small cable between the card and motherboard.	6.11
Hardware Monitor	Enable display for all fans plugged into the motherboard	Some systems, like this one, primarily report settings with very few options.	6.12
PCI IRQs	Use Auto unless Windows Device Manager indicates conflict or Windows can't configure the device	Sound cards should be installed in a PCI slot that doesn't share IRQs with another slot.	6.13
USB Function	Enable	If motherboard supports USB 2.0 (Hi-Speed USB) ports, be sure to enable USB 2.0 function and load USB 2.0 drivers in Windows.	6.13
PCI/PnP IRQ, DMA, I/O Port Address Configuration (Exclusion)	Leave at defaults unless you have non-PnP ISA cards installed	No changes required on systems without ISA cards (motherboard serial, parallel, and PS/2 mouse ports are ISA but support PnP).	6.14
Boot Sequence	Adjust as desired	With bootable Windows CDs (2000, XP), move CD-ROM (optical) drive before hard drive.	6.15
Plug-and-Play OS	Enable for all except some Linus, Windows NT, MS-DOS	When enabled, Windows configures devices.	6.15
Boot Virus Detection (Antivirus Boot Sector)	Enable	Stops true infections but allows multiboot configuration.	6.15
Primary VGA BIOS	Varies	Use AGP unless you have AGP and PCI graphics (video) cards that won't work unless PCI is primary.	6.15
Assign IRQ to VGA	Enable	Disable frees up an IRQ, but can cause problems in determining primary VGA BIOS.	N/A

Table 6.3 (continued)

Option	Setting	Notes	See Figure #
Write-Protect Boot Sector	Varies	Enable for normal use, but disable when installing drives or using a multiboot system; helps prevent accidental formatting, but might not stop third-party disk prep software from working.	N/A
Shadowing	Varies	Enable shadowing for video BIOS; leave other shadowing disabled.	N/A
LBA Mode	Enable	Disable would prevent MS-DOS or Windows from using more than 504MiB (528.5MB) of an ATA/IDE drive's capacity. Some older systems put this setting in various locations away from the standard setup screen.	N/A
Onboard Audio, Modem, or Network	Varies	Enable if you don't use add-on cards for these functions; disable each setting before installing a replacement card.	N/A
Quiet Boot	Varies	Disable to display system configuration information at startup.	N/A
Boot-Time Diagnostic Screen	Varies	Enable to display system configuration information at startup.	N/A

Automatic Configuration of BIOS/CMOS Settings

Let's be frank—after reading Table 6.3, you might be wondering, "Isn't there an easier way to configure the BIOS?" Well, actually there is, in a way.

Many versions of the AMI and Award (Phoenix) BIOS enable you to automatically configure your system with a choice of these options from the main menu:

- BIOS defaults (also referred to as Original/Fail-Safe on some systems)
- Setup defaults (also referred to as Optimal on some systems)
- Turbo

What exactly do these options configure, and what do they leave out?

These options primarily deal with performance configuration settings in the BIOS such as memory timings, memory cache, and the like. The settings used by each BIOS setup option are customized by the motherboard or system maker.

Use **BIOS defaults** to troubleshoot the system because these settings are very conservative in memory timings and other options. Normally, the **Setup defaults** provide better performance. **Turbo**, if present, speeds up the memory refresh rate used by the system. As you view the setup screens in this chapter, you'll note these options are listed.

With many recent systems, you can select Optimal or Setup defaults, save your changes, and exit, and the system will work acceptably. However, you might want more control over your system. In that case, look at the following screens and make the changes necessary.

Standard CMOS Configuration

The first stop on any trip to BIOSLand is the **Standard CMOS Configuration** screen shown in Figure 6.6. It includes settings for items such as

- Date; the Windows clock is based on this setting.
- Time; the Windows clock is based on this setting.
- Floppy disk drive types for drives A: (first floppy disk drive) and B: (second floppy disk drive); some recent systems support only one floppy disk drive.
- Drives connected to the ATA/IDE interface, such as hard disks, optical drives, and removable media drives.
- User (power-on) and supervisor (access to setup) passwords.

Why are these settings critical?

If the date and time are not set correctly, the Windows clock will show incorrect date and time information. If the drives are not configured correctly, the system can't boot. If you enable password options and forget the passwords, the system can't boot.

To make selections here, you normally press keys to cycle through the different options, including date and time. In the system used as an example in this chapter, values with square brackets around them can be edited by the user, whereas values without brackets (such as memory size) are displayed for your reference, but can't be changed. The triangle symbol shown in Figure 6.6 and other screens means the menu item links to a submenu.

The time must be entered in the 24-hour format (1:00 p.m. = 13:00, and so on). Some systems have an option to enable automatic changes to and from daylight savings time. However, Windows can also be configured to make this adjustment, so make sure you enable this feature in the BIOS or in Windows, but not in both places.

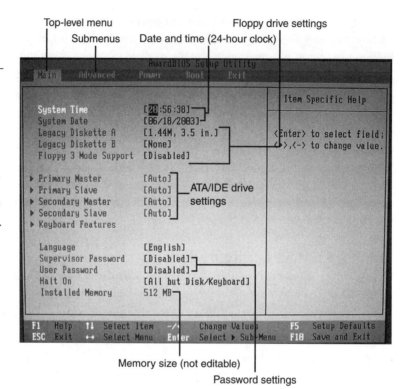

FIGURE 6.6
The standard (main) BIOS setup screen on a typical recent system. This screen also provides a top-level menu for access to other parts of the system BIOS.

Change the default floppy drive types to match your current configuration if necessary.

To select the correct ATA/IDE hard drive type, you can use one of three methods:

- Manually enter the correct settings. These are usually listed on the drive's faceplate. See Chapter 14, "Storage," for details.

- Use **auto-detect** to query the drives for their setup (might be located on the main menu or another submenu) main menu.

- Allow the system to detect the hard drives during every system boot (auto). This is the setting I recommend.

The **Auto** setting shown in Figure 6.6 for primary and secondary master and slave drives refers to drives connected to the ATA/IDE host adapters on the motherboard. Auto configuration enables the computer to detect the drives and use the correct settings at startup.

caution

If you use automatic setup after you make manual changes, all your manual changes will be overridden! Use one of these settings first (I recommend trying Turbo or Setup Defaults); then make any other changes you want.

Many systems also display the amount of memory onboard on this screen, but only extremely old systems based on 386 or older processors require that you manually enter the amount of RAM in the system. The standard setup screen is the single-most important screen in the entire BIOS/CMOS setup process. If the drives are not defined correctly, the system cannot boot.

Security/Passwords

Are you the paranoid type? Perhaps you'd rather not let complete strangers start up your computer or play with the BIOS? If this sounds like you, the Security or Passwords BIOS option is made for you.

You can enable two types of passwords on many systems: a user or power-on password that must be entered to allow any use of the system, and a setup password that must be entered to allow access to the BIOS/CMOS setup.

Because passwords are useful to prevent tampering with system settings, record the system information first, before you enable this feature. Some systems use a separate setup screen for configuring passwords, whereas others use the main setup screen as in Figure 6.6.

Advanced CMOS Configuration

Just as the Standard CMOS Configuration screen helps your system start correctly, the Advanced CMOS Configuration screen helps your system run at the correct speed. As you can see from Figure 6.7, the **Advanced CMOS Configuration** screen (sometimes called **CMOS Features**) is typically used to enable memory caching features in the processor and, on most recent systems, the speeds of the processor and its connection to memory. To learn more about using the processor and memory speed settings, see Chapter 4, "The Motherboard and CPU."

note

Most motherboards have a clear CMOS jumper near the battery that can be used to clear out the CMOS settings if you forget passwords or make other errors in BIOS configuration. Typically, you unplug the system, put the jumper block over the clear CMOS jumper pins for a few moments, and then remove the jumper block. Keep in mind that clearing the CMOS removes all the settings, including the correct ones.

caution

Although some users recommend that you configure the settings for hard drives to user-defined, which will list the exact settings for each hard drive, this can cause a major problem in case your BIOS settings are lost due to a virus, battery failure, or other causes. If you are not an experienced user, I highly recommend you let your computer do the work here.

This system's advanced menu also offers settings for cache memory, USB and PS/2 mouse configuration, BIOS update settings, and has submenus for chipset (CHIP), built-in I/O device, PCI device, and RAM/ROM shadowing. For more information on these options and additional options not shown in Figure 6.7, see Table 6.3 and the following sections.

CHIP (Chipset) Menu

The CHIP menu, also known as the Advanced Chipset/Chipset Features Configuration screen, like the one shown in Figure 6.8, offers many advanced options that vary by the system.

The following are some typical features of this menu:

- *Memory types, speed, and timing*—Adjust the values here to match the memory installed in the system (such as parity, non-parity, SDRAM, EDO, and so on).

- *Configuration of the AGP slot*—On systems with an AGP slot, you might need to select the AGP mode (1x, 2x, 4x, or 8x) and the graphics aperture (the amount of memory space used by the AGP graphics card).

Some computers also place the ATA/IDE host adapter settings on this screen (top of Figure 6.8). Both primary and secondary host adapters should be enabled unless the computer is using a faster ATA/IDE or Serial ATA host adapter card in an expansion slot as a replacement for the onboard host adapters.

For more information on these options and additional options not shown in Figure 6.8, see Table 6.3.

caution

If you don't have all the settings recorded (with screen printouts or by writing them down), enabling power-on or setup passwords can be mighty inconvenient.

Why? If the passwords are lost, users are locked out of the system. Keep in mind that there are two ways that passwords can be stored:

- If the password is stored in the CMOS, you would need to remove the battery or use the clear CMOS jumper on the motherboard to erase the CMOS record of the passwords—and all other settings. This would require reconfiguring the system BIOS from scratch!

- If the password is stored in a special security chip (as on some IBM and Compaq models), you might need to replace the chip if the password is lost.

Before you use the password feature on a particular system, find out how it stores passwords.

Processor (CPU) settings

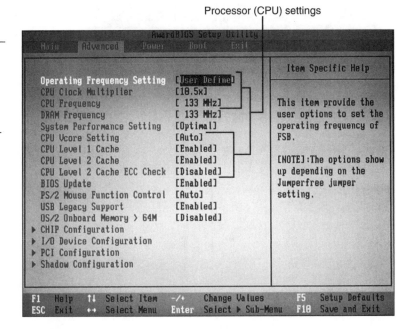

FIGURE 6.7

The Advanced screen on this system enables the user to configure the processor, memory speed, PS/2 mouse, USB legacy (USB keyboard), and has submenus for additional options.

I/O Device Configuration

When I started working with PCs about 20 years ago, the only built-in port on the motherboard was the keyboard port! Every other port you wanted to use required an add-on card. Things have changed a lot today: Although you can still install cards, most systems today have a bunch of built-in ports. Naturally, the system BIOS setup program is responsible for configuring them.

Depending upon the system, you might need to check several BIOS setup screens to verify that your computer's onboard devices are all configured as you desire. The example shown in Figure 6.9 configures serial and parallel port settings only, whereas other ports (USB, PS/2 mouse, ATA/IDE, onboard sound and modem) are configured on different screens on this and some other systems. This menu is sometimes referred to as the Onboard Peripherals menu.

caution

Advanced users can tinker with these settings to improve system speed, but be warned: Wrong settings for memory or AGP video can cause your system to be unstable. Unless you have the leisure to experiment, I recommend you use the Setup Defaults configuration option described earlier to set up this screen.

FIGURE 6.8

The CHIP (chipset) menu on this system is used to configure the AGP slot and memory timings.

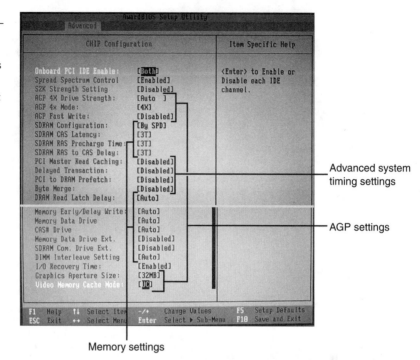

Advanced system timing settings

AGP settings

Memory settings

FIGURE 6.9

A typical I/O device configuration screen.

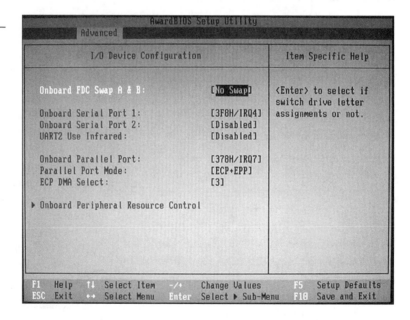

The parallel port setting in Figure 6.9 (ECP/EPP) is recommended for use with virtually any parallel port printer or device, because some devices prefer EPP mode and others prefer ECP mode. Note that you can disable parallel and serial ports if you no longer use parallel or serial devices.

For more information on these options and additional options not shown in Figure 6.9, see Table 6.3.

Power Management Configuration

Have you ever walked into a small office or bedroom where a PC's been running all day long? Boy, it's hot in there! PCs produce a lot of heat, but that's just a byproduct of the kilowatts they gobble up. Nobody minds using power to run a PC that's doing something useful, but a PC running a screen saver uses just as much power as a PC creating payrolls or downloading files.

Power management features in the BIOS (see Figure 6.10) can be used to save power when a system is idle and, on some systems, to protect your processor. Although the savings available from power management might be minimal when only one PC is considered, they really add up when hundreds or thousands of PCs in a company are considered.

Although you might prefer to manage power through the Windows Power Management dialog box, you can enable features such as CPU Fan Check at Power On or Fan Check Beeping through this dialog box on some recent computers. Enabling these settings can help protect your processor from overheating.

Power management works like this: After a user-defined period of inactivity, devices such as the monitor, the hard drive, or even the CPU will go into different low-power modes, such as

- *Standby mode*—Shuts off the hard drive and blanks monitor screens that use Display Power Management Signaling. Move the mouse or press a key to "wake up" the system.

- *Suspend mode*—Turns off the CPU clock to save even more power. Systems that fully support suspend mode enable you to choose a special shutdown option that "remembers" what programs and files were open, and can bring the system back to that state when the power is restored. Suspend to RAM is a variation that stores the system state in RAM for faster recovery after the system is turned on.

In the system shown in Figure 6.10, select the PowerUp Control submenu (see Figure 6.11) to determine the events that can wake up the system from a power-saving mode or use the Power dialog box in Windows. Systems that support ACPI power management perform most configuration tasks in Windows.

Helps protect processor if enabled

FIGURE 6.10

A typical power management setup screen.

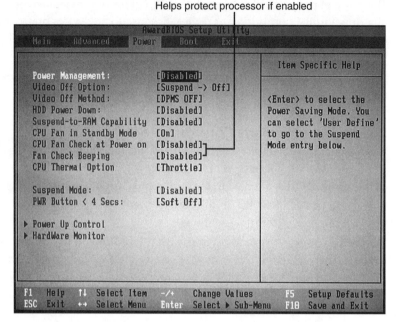

Most recent hardware handles power management properly, but it can be disabled on systems that have problems. If you enable power management, I recommend you enable power-up options to bring the system back to normal operation after a power failure or when activity is detected on modem or network lines (see Figure 6.11).

For more information on these options and additional options not shown in Figures 6.10 and 6.11, see Table 6.3.

Hardware Monitor

As hot as a small room containing a PC can get, it's a whole lot hotter inside the PC itself. Excessive heat is the enemy of system stability and shortens the life of your hardware. Adding fans (see Chapter 5) can help, but if they fail, you have problems.

caution

Power management doesn't always work well, especially with older hardware or if the correct drivers aren't installed to support power management. For example, Epson inkjet printers that connect to the USB port require a special USB driver to work properly on a power-managed system running Windows 98.

The Hardware Monitor screen (sometimes referred to as PC Health) has been added to newer systems to help you make sure that your computer's temperature and voltage conditions are at safe levels for your computer (see Figure 6.12).

FIGURE 6.11

Typical power-up options. This system can be configured to restart automatically if AC power is lost, or when activity is detected on an external modem, internal PCI modem, or network adapter.

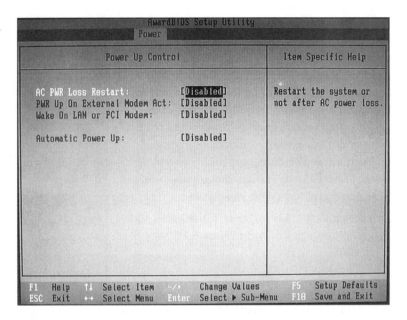

Displays fan speeds for CPU and other fans that are connected to the motherboard

Displays current motherboard and CPU temperatures

FIGURE 6.12

A typical Hardware Monitor screen.

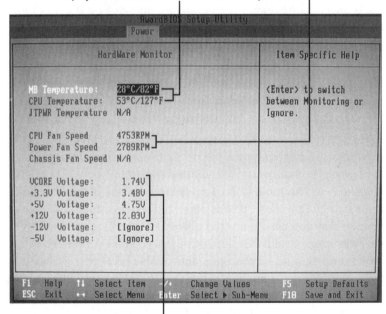

Displays current voltage levels (-12V and –5V are sometimes ignored because very few devices use these levels)

Although it is useful to view temperature and voltage settings in the BIOS setup program, temperature values are usually higher after the computer has been working for awhile (after you've booted to Windows and no longer have access to this screen). Generally, the major value of this screen is that its information can be detected by motherboard or system monitoring programs that run under Windows and enable you to be warned immediately if there are any heat- or fan-related problems with your system.

For more information on these options and additional options not shown in Figure 6.12, see Table 6.3.

PCI Configuration

When ISA and other legacy card types were common, installing add-on cards into a system was a nightmare of IRQ and other conflicts. However, PCI cards (and their faster siblings, AGP cards) are designed to share IRQs (see Chapter 2 for more information about IRQs). IRQ conflicts have always been number one on the list of installation headaches.

Even though IRQ sharing usually works very nicely, you might need to manually configure the hardware resource settings used by PCI (and AGP) cards in a few cases, such as if Windows can't detect a PCI or AGP card you've installed. That's the time to use the BIOS's PCI Configuration screen, such as the example shown in Figure 6.13. On this system, the **PCI Configuration** dialog box is also used to enable or disable USB ports.

If Windows can't configure a PCI device inserted into a particular PCI slot, you might need to change the Auto settings shown in Figure 6.13 to manually selected settings. Note that slots 4 and 5 must use the same IRQ in this example; if cards in these slots can't work with each other, move one of the cards to another slot. There's another way you can deal with balky PCI cards: Give them more IRQs to work with. On older systems with PCI slots, PCI cards could be configured to use only IRQs 9, 10, 11, and 12 (and 12 was often unavailable because it was used by the PS/2 mouse port). Newer systems might also enable PCI cards to use IRQs traditionally used by ISA devices such as serial (IRQs 3 and 4) and parallel ports (IRQ 7). If IRQs below 9 can be used by the PnP BIOS (as in Figure 6.14), disabling serial and parallel ports you don't use makes it easier for Windows and your BIOS to find resource

tip

Figure 6.12 doesn't list values for the power and chassis fans. That's because the fans inside this system aren't connected to the motherboard, and thus can't be monitored by the BIOS. If you install chassis fans, make sure you buy the type that can connect to your motherboard so that you can get the full benefit of your computer's Hardware Monitor feature.

combinations that work correctly for all cards and for motherboard-based devices such as USB and integrated sound.

FIGURE 6.13
A typical PCI
Configuration
screen.

Configures IRQ usage per each PCI slot

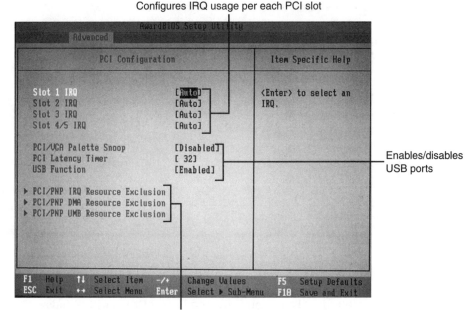

Enables/disables
USB ports

Use to prevent conflicts with ISA devices that aren't PnP compatible

Things get trickier if you have a system that uses non-PnP ISA cards alongside PCI cards. These systems are getting scarcer, but they're still around.

If you don't tell the system which IRQs are used by non-PnP cards, the BIOS might try to assign them to PnP cards, which causes the cards to stop working. What's the solution? Use a Resource Exclusion menu in your system BIOS such as the one shown in Figure 6.14. This menu, known as a **PnP Configuration** menu on some systems, enables you to reserve IRQ settings for use by non-PnP ISA devices (ISA devices, unlike PCI devices, can't share IRQs). Some systems put IRQ, DMA, and I/O port address settings on a single menu, whereas others, like this one, use separate menus for each resource.

For more information on these options and additional options not shown in Figure 6.14, see Table 6.3.

note

A non-PnP ISA card is a card that makes you flip DIP switches or run a special configuration program to set its IRQ and other hardware resources (see Chapter 19, "Installing and Configuring Hardware in Windows," for more information).

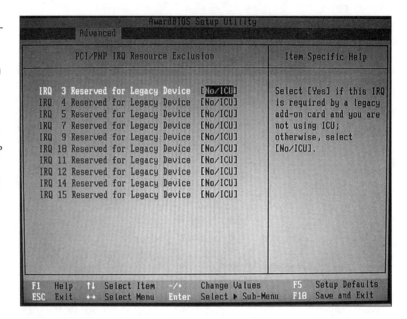

Boot Setup

You can follow all the rules for creating a bootable floppy disk or hard disk covered in Chapter 15, "Preparing Hard and Floppy Drives with Windows," but if the BIOS doesn't list the drives you want to boot from in the correct order, your system won't boot.

The **Boot Configuration** screen (part of the Advanced setup screen on some systems) is used to configure the order in which the computer looks for a bootable device (see Chapter 14, "Storage," for more information), support for PnP operating systems (Windows 95 and newer, but not Windows NT), antivirus BIOS configuration, the primary video card, and related settings (see Figure 6.15). On systems that have ATA or Serial ATA RAID host adapters such as this one, this menu might also enable the RAID array's ATA or Serial ATA BIOS (see Chapter 14 for more information).

I recommend the following boot order with Windows:

1. Floppy drive

2. CD-ROM

3. Primary Master hard disk

If you compare this list to the drive order shown in Figure 6.15, you can see that the CD-ROM drive should be moved up in the boot order. If the CD-ROM is listed after the hard disk, you won't be able to boot from the CD-ROM if the hard disk is bootable.

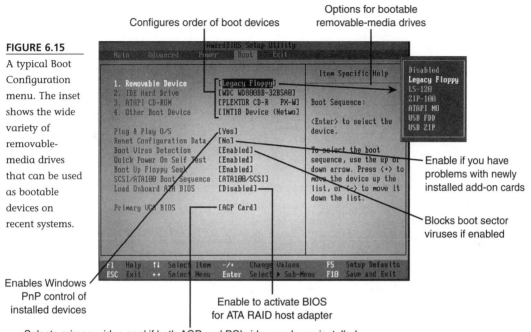

FIGURE 6.15

A typical Boot Configuration menu. The inset shows the wide variety of removable-media drives that can be used as bootable devices on recent systems.

Configures order of boot devices

Options for bootable removable-media drives

Enable if you have problems with newly installed add-on cards

Blocks boot sector viruses if enabled

Enables Windows PnP control of installed devices

Enable to activate BIOS for ATA RAID host adapter

Selects primary video card if both AGP and PCI video cards are installed

For more information on these options and additional options not shown in Figure 6.15, see Table 6.3.

Getting Support for Your BIOS

Chances are, if you've gone through your system's BIOS configuration screens and compared them to the ones listed previously, you've seen some differences. That's inevitable. Some differences come from the specific motherboard chipset and other components installed on the system, whereas other differences come from the different designs used by the different BIOS makers. So, if you're puzzled or confused by a particular BIOS setting, where do you go for help?

Although BIOSs are developed by just a handful of companies (IBM, Compaq, and Acer develop for their own systems, and Phoenix, AMI, and Award for others and for "clone" motherboards), each BIOS is unique to the motherboard it's matched with. Therefore, for specific help with your BIOS (errors, configuring, troubleshooting), your best bet is to go back to the system or motherboard maker.

The relationship of BIOS makers and motherboard makers is similar to the difference between standard and custom vans:

■ A standard van is sold by a dealer who is associated with the van maker. This is similar to the situation with Compaq, IBM, or Acer PCs: The same company makes both the PC and its BIOS.

■ A custom van has been modified from a "bare-bones" cargo van and sold by a third-party company. If you're having problems with the van, it's no longer the van that Ford or Daimler/Chrysler produced. You must go back to the custom van maker for help. This is the situation with Phoenix, AMI, and Award BIOSs; they have been modified by the system and motherboard makers. The BIOS makers' Web sites can provide general help, but not the specifics of your system, because the BIOS is no longer their product after it goes on a motherboard.

tip

BIOS configuration tips are available from the motherboard vendor's Web site, as well as from Wim's BIOS (`www.wimsbios.com`), BIOS Central (`www.bioscentral.com`), and *Phil Croucher's BIOS Companion* (a great reference guide available in printed or electronic form from `www.electrocution.com`).

BIOS Upgrades

The BIOS chip can be regarded as the "glue" that binds the hardware to the operating system. If the BIOS doesn't recognize the operating system or the hardware it communicates with, you're sure to have problems.

Because the BIOS chip bridges hardware to the operating system, you will need to upgrade the BIOS whenever your current BIOS version is unable to properly support

■ New hardware, such as large ATA/IDE hard drives and different types of removable-storage drives

■ Faster CPUs

■ New operating systems and features

■ New BIOS options

Although software drivers can be used as workarounds for hard drive BIOS limitations, a true BIOS upgrade is the best solution for hard disk control, and the only solution if your BIOS can't handle new processors or operating systems.

If you keep your computer for more than a year or so, or if you decide to install a new processor, you might need to upgrade the BIOS. Back in the 1980s into the early 1990s, a BIOS upgrade required a physical chip swap and, sometimes, reprogramming the chip with a device called an EEP-ROM burner. If the replacement or reprogrammed BIOS chip was installed incorrectly into the socket, it could be destroyed.

Fortunately, since the mid-1990s, a **BIOS upgrade** can now be performed with software. The Flash BIOS chips in use on practically every recent system contain a special type of memory that can be changed through a software download from the system or motherboard maker.

Although Flash BIOS updates are easier to perform than the older replace-the-chip style, you still need to be careful. An incomplete or incorrect BIOS upgrade will prevent your system from being accessed. No BIOS, no boot! Regardless of the method, for maximum safety, I recommend the following initial steps:

note

Your car dealer uses a similar process to reprogram the onboard computer in most recent automobiles and trucks.

- Back up important data.
- Record the current BIOS configuration, especially hard disk settings as discussed earlier in this chapter.

Flash BIOS Upgrade

So, you've decided you need a Flash BIOS upgrade. Where do you get it? Don't ask the BIOS manufacturers (Phoenix, AMI, and Award/Phoenix). They don't sell BIOS upgrades because their basic products are modified by motherboard and system vendors (see "Getting Support for Your BIOS" earlier in this chapter).

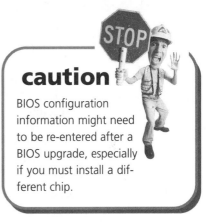

caution

BIOS configuration information might need to be re-entered after a BIOS upgrade, especially if you must install a different chip.

Here are the general steps for performing a Flash BIOS upgrade:

1. For major brands of computers, go to the vendor's Web site and look for "downloads" or "tech support" links. The BIOS upgrades are listed by system model and by version; avoid beta (pre-release) versions.

2. Download the correct BIOS upgrade for your system or motherboard. For generic motherboards, Wim's BIOS page also has links to the motherboard vendors' Web sites.

3. You might also need to download a separate loader program, or the download might contain both the loader and the BIOS image. If the Web site has instructions posted, print or save them to a floppy disk for reference.

4. Next, install the BIOS upgrade loader and BIOS image to a floppy disk. Follow the vendor's instructions.

5. After installation is complete, restart your system with the floppy disk containing the upgrade. Press a key if necessary to start the upgrade process.

   Some upgrades run automatically; others require that you choose the image from a menu, and prompt you to save your current BIOS image to a floppy disk. Choose this option if possible so you have a copy of your current BIOS in case there's a problem.

6. After the update process starts, it takes about three minutes to rewrite the contents of the BIOS chip with the updated information.

7. Remove the floppy disk and restart the system to use your new BIOS features. Reconfigure the BIOS settings if necessary.

On motherboards whose BIOSs can't be upgraded with software, you might be able to purchase a replacement BIOS from vendors such as Micro Firmware (for Phoenix BIOS upgrades at www.firmware.com), eSupport (for Award, AMI, and Phoenix BIOS upgrades at www.esupport.com), or BIOSWorld (www.biosworld.com).

Before you order a BIOS chip replacement, consider the following:

■ BIOS chip upgrades cost about $40–$60 each.

■ Although the BIOS will be updated, the rest of the system might still be out of date.

■ For not much more than the cost of the BIOS chip itself, you might be able to purchase a new motherboard (without RAM

tip

If your system is a generic system (that is, it came with a "mainboard" or "motherboard" manual and other component manuals rather than a full system manual), you need to contact the motherboard maker. Some systems indicate the maker during bootup. Others display only a mysterious series of numbers. You can decode these numbers to get the motherboard's maker. See the following Web sites for details:

- Wim's BIOS page (www.wimsbios.com)

- eSupport (www.esupport.com)

- American Megatrend's BIOS Support page (www.ami.com/support/bios.cfm)

tip

Some motherboards have a jumper on the motherboard that can be set to write-protect the Flash BIOS. Take a quick look at your documentation before you start the process and disable this jumper first. Then, re-enable the write-protect jumper after you're done with the upgrade.

or CPU) that will give you similar BIOS features as well as advanced features that might be missing from your existing motherboard.

If you still need to update the BIOS chip itself, first verify that the vendor has the correct BIOS chip replacement. The replacement needs to

- Plug into your current motherboard; as you saw in Figure 6.1, some BIOS chips are square, while others are rectangular.
- Support your motherboard/chipset.
- Provide the features you need (such as support for larger hard disks, particular processor speeds, and so on).

It might be a different brand of BIOS than your current BIOS. If so, make sure that you have recorded your hard drive information. You will need to re-enter this and other manually configured options into the new BIOS chip's setup program.

caution

While performing a Flash upgrade, make sure that you don't turn off the power to your PC and that you keep children or pets away from the computer to prevent an accidental shutdown (read: your 4-year-old decides to unplug the computer). 'Wait for a message indicating the BIOS upgrade has been completed before you even *think* about touching the computer. If the power goes out during the Flash update, the BIOS chip could be rendered useless.

How does the BIOS vendor know what your system uses? The vendor will identify the BIOS chip you need by the motherboard ID information displayed at bootup. eSupport offers a free download utility to display this information for you. To replace the chip, follow these steps:

1. Locate the BIOS chip on your motherboard after you open the case to perform the upgrade. It sometimes has a sticker listing the BIOS maker and model number. If not, go to step 2.

2. Socketed BIOS chips might be in a DIP-type package (rectangular with legs on two sides) or in a **PLCC** (**Plastic Leaded Chip Carrier**; square with connectors on four sides). The vendor typically supplies a chip extraction tool to perform the removal.

To remove a DIP (the most common type of socketed chip), use the appropriately sized DIP puller tool if you have one. This tool resembles an inverted "U" with small flat hooks on each point. If a DIP puller is not available (ask the BIOS vendor to supply one), you can use a pair of flat-bladed screwdrivers. Follow these steps:

1. Place one end of the tool between the end of the chip and the end of the socket; repeat for the other side.

2. If you are using the DIP puller, gently tighten the tool around the ends of the chip and pull upward to loosen; if you are using the screwdrivers, gently *lift*

upward on both handles to loosen. Pushing down on the screwdriver handles could damage the motherboard.

3. Gently rock the ends of the chip to free it, and straighten any bent pins when you finish removing it.

4. Remove the existing BIOS chip carefully and put it on antistatic material in case you need to reuse it in that system.

5. Align the new BIOS chip's dimple with the matching cutout on one end of the socket.

6. Adjust the legs on the new BIOS chip so it fits into the sockets, and press it down until the legs on both sides are inserted fully.

7. Double-check the alignment and leg positions on the BIOS chip before you start the system; if the chip is aligned with the wrong end of the socket, you'll destroy it when the power comes on.

8. Turn on the system, and use the new BIOS's keystroke(s) to start the setup program to re-enter any information. You might get a "CMOS" error at startup, which is normal with a new BIOS chip. After you re-enter the BIOS data from your printout and save the changes, the system will run without error messages.

A "CMOS Checksum" error is normal after you replace the BIOS chip. However, after you run the BIOS setup program and save the settings, this error should go away. If you continue to see this error, test the motherboard battery. If the battery checks out okay, contact the vendor for help.

Study Lab

Don't miss the Study Lab materials found on the CD accompanying this book. Each Study Lab is tailored to the individual chapters in this book, meaning that you'll quickly be able to determine which topics you understand well enough to pass the exam and which topics need more study. The Study Labs are presented in printable PDF format so that you can take them with you to study at work, on the road, or even in your car just before test time!

THE ABSOLUTE MINIMUM

Here are the highlights of this chapter. Reread these just before the exam to help you find any topics you need to review in more detail.

- The BIOS contains a POST (power-on self-test) routine that tests memory, video, hard drives, floppy disk drives, and other important system components.

- The BIOS also contains a bootstrap program that locates the operating system after the POST and transfers control to it.

- The BIOS uses three methods to report errors: beep codes, onscreen error messages, and BIOS POST codes.

- The BIOS contains tables of supported devices and options; the CMOS is used to store the options chosen with the BIOS setup program.

- The CMOS is battery-backed.

- You must verify correct floppy disk drive and hard drive configurations before a system can be started. These settings are found in the standard CMOS setup screen.

- By making adjustments to other BIOS screens, you can adjust the performance of the system, configure the system for compatibility with Windows PnP–compatible boards, adjust or disable built-in ports, and control power management.

- A BIOS needs to be upgraded when you want to use new hardware, new software, or new features not included in the current BIOS.

- BIOS upgrades can be performed with software (Flash BIOS) or by replacing the chip.

- Recovering from a failed BIOS upgrade might mean replacing the BIOS chip, enabling the recovery function, or disabling write-protection.

7

RAM

When it's time for the CPU to process something, **RAM (random access memory)** is the workspace it uses. RAM is one of two types of memory found in your computer; the other type of memory is ROM (read-only memory). What's the difference? RAM's contents can be changed at any time, whereas ROM's contents require special procedures to change. Think of RAM as a blank sheet of paper and a pencil: You can write on it, erase what you've done, and keep making changes. On the other hand, ROM is like a newspaper. If you want to change what's printed on the newspaper, you must recycle it so it can be reprocessed back into newsprint and sent through the newspaper's printing presses again.

RAM is used for programs and data, and by the operating system for disk caching (to hold recently accessed disk sectors). Thus, installing more RAM improves transfers between the CPU and both RAM and disk drives. If your computer runs short of RAM, Windows can also use the hard disk as a very slow substitute for RAM. The swapfile (Windows 9x/Me) or paging file (Windows NT/2000/XP) is a file on the hard disk used to hold part of the contents of memory if the installed RAM on the system isn't large enough for the tasks currently being performed.

Although the hard disk can substitute for RAM in a pinch, don't confuse RAM with magnetic storage devices such as hard disks. Although the contents of RAM and magnetic storage can be changed freely, RAM loses its contents as soon as you shut down the computer, whereas magnetic storage can hold data for years. Although RAM's contents are temporary, RAM is much faster than magnetic storage: RAM speed is measured in nanoseconds (millionths of a second), while magnetic storage is measured in milliseconds (thousandths of a second).

Even though every computer ever made is shipped with RAM, you will probably need to add more RAM to a computer as time passes. Ever-increasing amounts of RAM are needed as operating systems and applications get more powerful and add more features. Because RAM is one of the most popular upgrades to add to any system during its lifespan, you need to understand how RAM works, what types of RAM exist, and how to add it to provide the biggest performance boost to the systems you maintain.

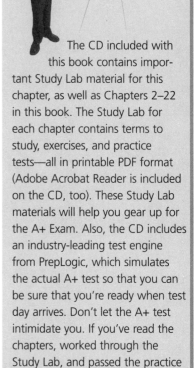

note

The CD included with this book contains important Study Lab material for this chapter, as well as Chapters 2–22 in this book. The Study Lab for each chapter contains terms to study, exercises, and practice tests—all in printable PDF format (Adobe Acrobat Reader is included on the CD, too). These Study Lab materials will help you gear up for the A+ Exam. Also, the CD includes an industry-leading test engine from PrepLogic, which simulates the actual A+ test so that you can be sure that you're ready when test day arrives. Don't let the A+ test intimidate you. If you've read the chapters, worked through the Study Lab, and passed the practice tests from PrepLogic, you should be well prepared to ace the test!

Also, you'll notice that some words throughout each chapter are in bold format. These are study terms that are defined in the Study Lab. Be sure to consult the Study Lab when you are finished with this chapter to test what you've learned.

When you must specify memory for a given system, there are several variables you need to know:

■ *Memory module type (184-pin DIMM, 168-pin DIMM, and so on)*—The module type your system can use has a great deal to do with the memory upgrade options you have with any given system. Although a few systems can use more than one memory module type, in most cases if you want to change to a faster type of memory module, such as from 168-pin DIMM (used by SDRAM) to 184-pin DIMM (used by **DDR SDRAM**), you need to upgrade the motherboard first.

■ *Memory chip type used on the module (SDRAM, DDR SDRAM, RDRAM, and so on)*—Today, a particular memory module type uses only one type of memory. However, older memory module types such as 72-pin SIMM and early 168-pin DIMMs were available with different types of memory chips. You need to specify the right memory chip type in such cases to avoid conflicts with onboard memory and provide stable performance.

■ *Memory module speed (60ns, PC-133, PC800, PC2700, and so on)*—There are three ways to specify the speed of a memory module: the actual speed in **ns (nanoseconds)** of the chips on the module (60ns), the clock speed of the data bus (PC-133 is 133MHz; PC800 is 800MHz), or the throughput (in MBps) of the memory (PC2700 is 2,700MBps or 2.7GBps).

■ *Error checking (parity, non-parity, ECC)*—Most systems don't perform parity checking (to verify the contents of memory) or correct errors, but some motherboards and systems support these functions. Although parity-checked memory mainly slows down the system, ECC memory can correct memory errors as well as detect them. If a system is performing very critical work (high-level mathematics or financial functions, departmental or enterprise-level server tasks), ECC support in the motherboard and ECC memory are worthwhile options to specify.

■ *Allowable module sizes and combinations*—Some motherboards insist you use the same speeds and sometimes the same sizes of memory in each memory socket, whereas others are more flexible. To find out which is true about a particular system, check the motherboard or system documentation before you install memory or add more memory.

■ *The number of modules needed per bank of memory*—Systems address memory in banks, and the number of modules per bank varies with the processor and the memory module type installed. If you need more than one module per bank, as with SIMM memory on a Pentium-class system, and only one module is installed, the system will ignore it. Systems that require multiple modules per bank require that modules be the same size and speed.

■ *Whether the system requires or supports **dual-channel** memory (two identical memory modules instead of one at a time)*—Dual-channel memory treats two matched modules as a single unit, similar to the way that older systems use two or more modules per bank. However, dual-channel memory is faster than single-channel memory, and is becoming common on more and more systems.

■ *The total number of modules that can be installed*—The number of sockets on the motherboard determines the number of modules that can be installed. Very small-footprint systems (such as those that use Micro-ATX, Flex-ATX, or Mini-ITX motherboards) often support only one or two modules, but systems that use full-size ATX motherboards often support three or four modules. Although very old systems dating back to the late 1980s and earlier used standard or proprietary memory boards in expansion slots for additional memory, all memory expansion in more recent systems is done on the motherboard.

If some of these factors aren't familiar to you yet, relax! My job is to make sure you understand them, and by the time you finish this chapter, you'll be well on the road to being a memory expert.

Memory Types and Forms

Physical forms of RAM have changed greatly over the years since the first IBM PC was introduced. Throughout the 1980s, most systems used individual **memory chips** in capacities ranging from 64KB to 1MB. In the late 1980s, **memory modules** (multiple memory chips on a miniature board that we know today as SIMMs, DIMMs, and RIMMs) became popular, and this type of memory is still the standard today, although specific forms and capacities are changing rapidly.

The same physical form (chip or module) can be used for RAM with different speeds, types, and sizes. Memory also can be purchased in forms that enable the system to detect or even correct memory errors.

To specify the correct memory for any given system, you must choose the correct options for that system, including the following (all of which are explained in more detail later in the chapter):

■ *Form factor*—Whether DIMM, SIMM, or another standard or proprietary type, the memory must be designed to fit into the memory upgrade sockets in the system.

■ *Memory type*—You must install memory modules that contain memory chips of the types specified by the system. Normally, all memory in the system should use the same types of chips (EDO, SDRAM, DDR, RAMBUS, and so forth).

- *Memory speed*—Memory chips (and the modules created with those chips) have different speed ratings; you must choose modules that meet the speed requirements of the system you are upgrading. For best results, all memory should be the same speed.

- *Memory capacity (MB)*—You must choose modules that meet the capacity requirements of the system you are upgrading.

- *Socket and module metals*—Whereas the latest RAMBUS modules and DIMM modules and sockets are all gold plated, earlier SIMM modules and sockets could be either tin plated or gold plated. Mixing metals can cause long-term corrosion, leading to memory failures.

All of these factors must be specified correctly to get the correct memory for any given system.

Memory Form Factors

The first fact you need to know when you order memory for a system is what type of memory module it uses. The original form of memory used in the IBM PC, XT, and AT models and other computers of the time (early to mid-1980s) was individual RAM chips, ranging in size from 16Kb to 1Mb. These chips were installed on the motherboard or add-on cards that plugged into expansion slots on the motherboard. Because memory chips are sized in bits, not bytes, it took multiple chips to reach a given capacity. Some add-on cards for memory upgrades were so large that they ran the full length of the case and sometimes contained two layers of chips. Starting in the late 1980s, memory modules (small printed circuit boards [PCBs] with multiple memory chips soldered to them) became popular and continue to be the most common type of memory used today.

Single and Multibit Chips

As you learned in Chapter 3, "How Computers Measure and Transfer Data," eight bits make a byte. A byte is the basic building block used to determine storage and RAM capacity. You might assume that every memory module made uses at least eight chips, one for each bit in a byte. At one time, many 30-pin memory modules did use a chip for each bit. This was relatively simple because a 30-pin SIMM (single inline memory module) is an eight-bit device. However, as processors required memory in larger and larger gulps (Pentium-class and newer processors use a 64-bit data bus), it stopped being practical to use a single chip for each bit on a memory module.

Fortunately, there's a solution. **Multibit chips**, in which each memory chip contains four bits or a multiple of four bits, have been in use even before memory modules were introduced. Consequently, it was relatively simple to start producing memory modules that use multibit chips. Figure 7.1 compares a 30-pin memory module that uses one chip for each bit to two modules that use multibit (four bits per chip) memory chips.

FIGURE 7.1

A 30-pin SIMM that uses a single chip for each bit (top) compared to two 30-pin modules that use four-bit-wide memory chips (middle and bottom). The top and middle memory modules support parity checking (which uses a single chip for the ninth [parity] bit), but the bottom module, which has only eight data bits, does not.

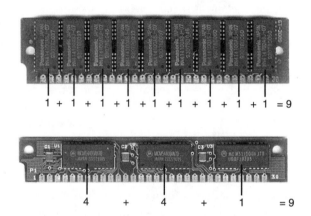
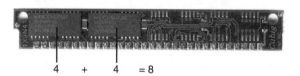

Current memory module designs continue to use multibit chips to reduce chip count, reduce heat, and improve reliability. However, before discussing newer memory modules, it's time to find out why some modules have "extra" bits, such as the top and middle modules shown in Figure 7.1. What does the ninth bit do?

Parity Versus Non-Parity Memory

The "extra" memory bits found on some memory modules, such as those shown in Figure 7.1, are actually used by one of two methods designed to protect the reliability of memory:

- Parity checking
- ECC (error-code correction)

Parity checking, which goes back to the original IBM PC, works like this: Whenever memory is accessed, each data bit has a value of 0 or 1. When these values are added to the value in the parity bit, the resulting checksum should be an odd number. This is called **odd parity**. A memory problem will typically cause the data bit values plus the parity bit value to total an even number. This triggers a parity error, and your system halts with a parity error message. Note that parity checking requires parity-enabled memory and support in the motherboard. On modules that support parity checking, there's a parity bit for each group of eight bits.

The method used to fix this type of error varies with the system. On museum-piece systems that use individual memory chips, you must open the system, push all memory chips back into place, and test the memory thoroughly if you have no spares (using memory-testing software), or replace the memory if you have spare memory chips. If the computer uses memory modules, replace one module at a time, test the memory (or at least run the computer for awhile) to determine if the problem has gone away. If the problem recurs, replace the original module, swap out the second module, and repeat.

Because parity checking "protects" you from bad memory by shutting down the computer (which can cause you to lose data), vendors have created a better way to use the parity bits to solve memory errors using a method called ECC.

Beyond Parity—ECC

For critical applications, network servers have long used a special type of memory called **ECC**, which stands for **Error Correcting Code** memory. This memory enables the system to correct single-bit errors and notify you of larger errors.

More expensive systems today have optional ECC support that can require special ECC-compatible memory or use parity-checked memory along with special motherboard features to enable ECC. The parity bit is used by the ECC feature to determine when the contents of memory are corrupt and to fix single-bit errors. ECC memory actually corrects errors, unlike parity checking, which only warns you of memory errors.

This is recommended for maximum data safety, although parity and ECC do provide a small slowdown in performance in return for the extra safety. ECC memory modules use the same types of memory chips used by standard modules, but they use more chips and might have a different internal design to allow ECC operation. ECC modules, like parity-checked modules, have an extra bit for each group of eight data bits.

To determine if a system supports parity-checked or ECC memory, check the system BIOS memory configuration (typically on the Advanced or Chipset screens). Systems that support parity or ECC memory can use **non-parity** checked memory if parity checking and ECC are disabled. Another name for ECC is *EDAC (Error Detection and Correction)*.

Memory Module Types and Form Factors

All systems built since the early 1990s have used some form of memory module, and most of these systems have used standard versions of these modules.

These modules come in these major types:

- **Single Inline Memory Module (SIMM)**—Has a single row of 30 or 72 edge connectors on the bottom of the module. *Single* refers to both sides of the module having the same pinout.

- **Single Inline Pin Package (SIPP)**—A short-lived variation on the 30-pin SIMM, which substituted pins for the edge connector used by SIMM modules.

- **Dual Inline Memory Module (DIMM)**—The most common form has 168 edge connectors on the bottom of the module. *Dual* refers to each side of the module having a different pinout.

- **Small Outline DIMM (SODIMM)**—A compact version of the standard DIMM module, available in both a 72-pin version (SDRAM) and a 144-pin version (DDR SDRAM) for use in recent-model notebook computers. Some laser and LED printers use a 100-pin SODIMM for memory upgrades.

- **Rambus RDRAM Module**—A memory module using Direct Rambus memory (RDRAM) chips.

Figure 7.2 illustrates SIMM, SIPP, and DIMM modules used in desktop computers. See Figure 7.4 for examples of SODIMMs.

All modules except for certain versions of the 30-pin SIMM and its sibling, the SIPP, use multibit chips to achieve their high capacities. (Refer to Figure 7.1 to compare 30-pin SIMM modules with single-bit and multibit chips.)

note

Kingston Technology has copyrighted the name *RIMM* for its Rambus RDRAM modules, but Rambus RDRAM modules are often referred to as *RIMMs*, regardless of their actual manufacturer.

FIGURE 7.2

Desktop memory modules (SIMM, SIPP, and DIPP) compared.

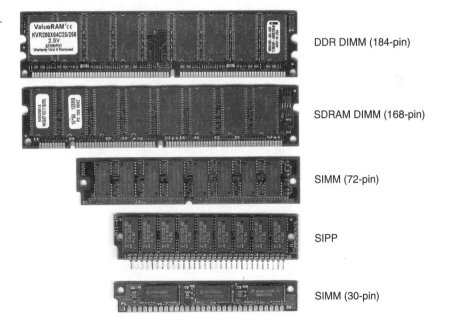

DDR DIMM (184-pin)

SDRAM DIMM (168-pin)

SIMM (72-pin)

SIPP

SIMM (30-pin)

72-pin SIMMs are divided into two major types:

- 32 bits (non-parity)
- 36 bits (parity checked and supports ECC)

The most typical chip arrangements for 72-pin SIMMs include

- Eight chips (4 bits per chip × 8 = 32 bits)
- Two chips (16 bits per chip × 2 = 32 bits)
- Three chips (two chips at 16 bits per chip and one chip at 4 bits for parity/ECC support: 16 × 2 = 32; 32 + 4 = 36)

DIMM modules with 72 bits support ECC error correction, whereas DIMM modules with 64 bits are non-parity.

The first major use of 30-pin SIMMs was in the IBM XT/286, a lower-cost version of the IBM AT introduced in 1986.

30-pin SIMM memory became obsolete in the early 1990s because four of these SIMMs were required to make a single bank of memory with a 386- or 486-class CPU (which have 32-bit data buses). The first major use of 72-pin SIMMs (which provide 32 bits per module) was in the IBM PS/2 Model 50 and above, introduced in 1987. 72-pin SIMMs became the standard in later-model 486s and most Pentiums. However, Pentium and newer systems (which have 64-bit data buses) require two SIMMs to make a bank, and this type of memory has become obsolete.

note

You might run across the term, *Small Outline Rambus Module*. These are compact versions of the standard Rambus module for use in laptop computers.

note

SIPPs resemble 30-pin SIMMs but have projecting pins on the bottom of the module in place of edge contacts; they are seldom used.

The 168-pin DIMM (which provides 64 bits per module) was introduced with the first Pentium II–based systems, and it is also standard on the Pentium III, early Pentium 4, Celeron, AMD Athlon, AMD Duron, and most Super Socket 7 systems. SIMMs and DIMMs can have memory chips (often very thin) on one or both sides of their circuit boards. The difference is in the connectors: SIMMs have either 30-pin or 72-pin connectors and require two or more SIMMs to make the full data width of the Pentium class processor; DIMMs have 168-pin or 184-pin connectors, and each DIMM supplies the full data bus width for Pentium-class and newer processors. Figure 7.3 demonstrates how the data bus width of different processors compares to the memory bus width of various memory modules.

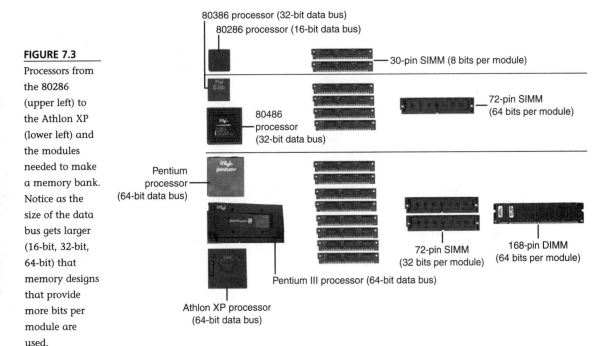

FIGURE 7.3

Processors from the 80286 (upper left) to the Athlon XP (lower left) and the modules needed to make a memory bank. Notice as the size of the data bus gets larger (16-bit, 32-bit, 64-bit) that memory designs that provide more bits per module are used.

As Figure 7.3 illustrates, newer memory module technologies that provide more data bits per module are a virtual necessity with newer processors because they have wider data buses. In fact, hardly any motherboards for Pentium-class processors were ever designed to use 30-pin SIMMs because eight SIMMs were needed per bank. Instead, the wider 72-pin SIMM (32 bits per module) was the typical memory module for Pentium and similar processors such as the AMD K6 series. Similarly, after the Pentium was replaced by newer designs such as the Pentium II, almost all systems used 168-pin or the latest 184-pin DIMM (64 bits per module) instead of a pair of 72-pin SIMMs (32 bits per module). All processors covered on the A+ Certification Exam (Pentium class and newer) have 64-bit data buses.

note

The 30-pin SIMMs used by IBM had different signals on five pins than the so-called "generic" SIMMs used by systems such as the Compaq 386s and many others.

The most common type of memory in use on recent systems is the 184-pin DDR SDRAM DIMM module, a faster version of the 168-pin SDRAM DIMM shown in Figures 7.1 and 7.2. It is used by most recent Pentium 4, Celeron, and Athlon XP systems. Two identical DIMMs must be added at a time for systems that support dual-channel memory.

SODIMMs are small versions of DIMMs used mainly in notebook computers. 72-pin SODIMM modules are 32-bit devices, and 144-pin SODIMM modules are 64-bit devices (see Figure 7.4).

Some high-performance systems use 184-pin or 232-pin RDRAM modules. Figure 7.5 shows a 168-pin RDRAM module; 232-pin modules have a small third connection between two large connectors.

> **caution**
>
> A double-sided SIMM acts like two conventional SIMMs in one, and can be recognized by having data chips on both sides of the module. Some systems work with both double-sided and single-sided SIMM memory modules; others restrict the number of double-sided modules you can use, or you can't use them at all. Read the manual for the system or motherboard to determine whether you can use double-sided SIMMs.

FIGURE 7.4

An SDRAM SODIMM (top) compared to a DDR SODIMM (bottom). Photos courtesy Micron Technology.

Table 7.1 compares the bit widths, sizes, types, and speeds of popular memory modules (though SIPPs are almost never seen today), whereas Table 7.2 compares the
speeds of memory chips used in these modules.

Table 7.1 Memory Modules Compared

Memory Module Type	Bit Widths	Common Sizes (KB/MB)	Common Type	Common Speeds
SIPP (Single Inline Pin Package)	8-bit, 9-bit	256KB, 1MB	FPM	100ns, 80ns
SIMM (Single Inline Memory Module), 30-pin	8-bit, 9-bit	256KB, 1MB, 4MB	FPM	100ns, 80ns, 70ns
SIMM, 72-pin	32-bit, 36-bit	512KB, 2MB, 4MB, 8MB, 16MB, 32MB	FPM, EDO	100ns, 70ns, 60ns
DIMM (Dual Inline Memory Module), 168-pin	64-bit, 72-bit	32MB, 64MB, 128MB, 256MB, 512MB, 1,024MB	SDRAM (EDO)	60ns (EDO) 15ns and faster (SDRAM)[1]

Table 7.1 (continued)

Memory Module Type	Bit Widths	Common Sizes (KB/MB)	Common Type	Common Speeds
DIMM, 184-pin	64-bit, 72-bit	128MB, 256MB, 512MB, 1,024MB, 2,048MB	DDR SDRAM	7.5ns and faster[1]
RAMBUS Memory Module	16-bit, 18-bit (single channel) 32-bit, 36-bit (dual channel)	128MB, 256MB, 512MB	RDRAM	600MHz, 700MHz, 800MHz, 1,066MHz[1]

[1]*Speeds usually specified in throughput (MBps). See Table 7.2 for details.*

Memory Speeds

Memory chips, and the modules built from them, have become faster over the years as Table 7.1 shows. Memory speeds for SIMM and SIPP modules are rated in **nanoseconds (ns)**. However, DIMM, SODIMM, Rambus RDRAM, and SO-Rambus RDRAM memory modules are identified by their throughput or clock speed rather than their ns rating. When you add memory to a system, you should follow these guidelines to ensure that the system will work properly after the memory upgrade is complete:

tip

For the A+ Certification Exam, you should be able to distinguish these modules from each other by appearance, data bus width, and speed.

- New memory added to a system must be at least as fast as the existing memory. If you are adding a second memory module to a system to enable dual-channel memory, the new module must be identical in size and speed to the original module.

- A smaller nanosecond (ns) rating equals faster memory. For example, memory rated at 8ns access time is faster than memory rated at 10ns access time.

- A larger MHz or throughput rating equals faster memory. For example, PC-133 (133MHz) memory is faster than PC-100 (100MHz) memory. PC2700 (DDR 333MHz) memory is faster than PC2100 (DDR 266MHz) memory.

Memory speeds are affected by the type of memory chips used in the module. For typical speed ratings for different types of memory chips (and the modules created with them), see Table 7.2 in the following section.

Memory Chip Types

Several different types of memory chips have been used in memory modules and as chips. Table 7.2 compares the features, uses, and speeds of the most popular chip types.

Most current systems use DDR or standard SDRAM DIMMs, whereas most Pentium-class systems still in service use EDO SIMMs.

caution

Don't mix different types of memory in a system! Differences in timing will usually cause system crashes.

Table 7.2 Memory Chip Types Compared

Memory Chip Type	Features	How Used	Typical Speeds
DRAM (Dynamic RAM)	*Dynamic* refers to the contents; this type of RAM requires frequent recharges of electricity to keep its contents valid	Memory chips in 8088–286 systems; variations include FPM and EDO	100ns or slower
Fast Page Mode (FPM) DRAM (Standard SIMM Memory)	Faster access than regular DRAM by using paging and burst-mode techniques	30-pin and 72-pin SIMM	70ns, 80ns, 100ns
Extended Data Out (EDO) DRAM	Faster access than FPM by overlapping accesses to different memory addresses	72-pin SIMM, a few 168-pin DIMMs	60ns
SRAM (Static RAM)	Many times bulkier and more expensive than same quantity of DRAM; requires electricity much less often than any type of DRAM because it's made from transistors	Used for main memory in some early 386-based systems from PCs Limited (now Dell), Wyse, and others; used for memory cache in newer systems	10ns, 15ns, 20ns and slower
SDRAM (Synchronous DRAM)	Much faster than older DRAM types by running in sync with the processor bus speed	Most 168-pin DIMMs	SDRAM is usually rated by motherboard speed, not by module speed

Table 7.2 (continued)

Memory Chip Type	Features	How Used	Typical Speeds
		speeds of 66MHz	Motherboard (**PC-66**), 100MHz (**PC-100**), and 133MHz (**PC-133**) use different DIMMs
Double-Data-Rate (DDR) SDRAM	Performs two transfers per clock cycle	184-pin DIMMs	Rated in MHz or in throughput (MBps): PC1600 (200MHz/ 1.6GBps), PC2100 (266MHz), PC2700 (333MHz), PC3200 (400MHz)
Rambus Direct RAM (RDRAM)	16-bit (18-bit with parity /ECC) memory chips make two transfers over the Direct Rambus channel per cycle	184-pin RAMBUS module (16-bit) connector) 232-pin RAMBUS module (32-bit dual channel)	Rated in MHz or in throughput: **PC800**: 800MHz, 3.2GBps **PC1066**: 1,066MHz, 4.2GBps Empty RIMM sockets must be occupied by a **continuity module** (resembles a RIMM but without memory)

Memory Banks

All memory must be added in "banks." In systems that use single-channel memory access, a **bank** of memory is the amount of memory (in bits) equal to the data bus of the CPU. Therefore, a bank isn't a fixed amount of memory but varies with the data bus of the CPU. In other words, for a CPU with a 64-bit data bus (Pentium, PII, PIII, Celeron, K6, Athlon, and so on), a bank of memory is the total of one or more identical modules (same type, size, speed,

tip

For the A+ Certification Exam, you need to know the meaning of the major chip type names and their features.

and so on) that add up to 64 bits in width. Refer back to Figure 7.3 to see how different processors and module combinations work together to provide a bank of memory.

A growing number of systems use **dual-channel** memory access. In these systems, two matched 64-bit memory modules (identical in size, speed, and timing) must be used per bank instead of the single 64-bit module that would be used in single-channel mode.

If your system needs multiple modules and you don't add the full number, the system ignores partial banks. See the "Using a RAM Calculator" section later in this chapter to see how to use this information to determine how many modules to add to a system.

Using a RAM Calculator

If you know three variables about a system, you can determine how many memory modules that system needs. You need to know the following:

- The system's data bus width (in bits)
- The data bits in each memory module your system uses (ignore parity or ECC bits, if any)
- Whether the system requires or supports dual-channel memory

To calculate the amount or number of memory modules that your system needs, divide the data bus width (D) by the number of bits per memory module (M) that your system uses. The result will be the number of modules needed (N). Multiply N by 2 for dual-channel systems.

Table 7.3 shows sample calculations for systems you might encounter.

Table 7.3 Calculating Memory Modules Needed

CPU Data Bus Width (D)	Bits per Module (M)	Calculation (D/M)	Number of Modules Needed (N=D/M)	Number of Identical Modules Needed for Dual-Channel System (N×2)
64-bit[1]	64-bit[3]	64/64	1	2
64-bit	32-bit[4]	64/32	2	N/A
32-bit[2]	32-bit	32/32	1	N/A
32-bit	8-bit[5]	32/8	4	N/A

[1] Processors such as Pentium class and newer (including Pentium 4 and Athlon XP)

[2] Processors such as 386 and 486 class (for comparison)

[3] DIMMs and Rambus RDRAM modules

[4] 72-pin SIMM

[5] 30-pin SIMM or SIPP

On systems that use RDRAM modules, you will need to consult the system manual for the details of adding memory. Although each module can function as a bank, some systems use a memory access technique called interleaved memory, which requires that a pair of identical modules be installed in the system.

Specifying Memory Modules

Wouldn't it be nice if you could go to your friendly neighborhood computer store and ask for a "16MB 72-pin SIMM" or a "256MB 184-pin DIMM?" Well, you could, but if the clerk is on the ball, you'll be asked questions in return such as "How fast?", "Do you want parity checking?", "Gold or tin?", "What CL setting?", and more. Provide the wrong information, and you'll get memory you can't use or memory that will slow down the system when you install it instead of speeding it up.

Sometimes you can skip the technicalities, particularly if your system uses proprietary memory, by looking up your computer or motherboard at the interactive Web sites provided by major memory vendors such as Kingston (www.kingston.com) or Crucial (www.crucial.com) to determine the proper memory to use. However, sooner or later, you'll need to understand how to decode the standard designation for any given memory module. As you'll learn in the following sections, the standard designation for any memory module is shorthand for its size, speed, whether it supports parity/ECC, and other information you need. The following sections break down each part of the standard designation for typical memory modules so you know what you're getting.

tip

Buy the largest-capacity modules you can that will work with the system. For example, it's better to use a single 256MB DIMM module than to use two 128MB modules if you need to add 256MB of RAM to a system. This allows you to use fewer modules, which reduces heat and can leave room for additional memory upgrades in the future. However, many older systems can't use the full capacity of newer, larger modules of the same connector type; check the system manual to verify which sizes will work in a given system.

tip

Check your system or motherboard manual to determine what memory types are used by your system. In most cases, vendors will use standard designations such as those shown in the following sections to specify the memory you should use. Systems that use proprietary modules instead might mention particular memory modules made by major vendors instead. In such cases, look up the data sheet for the module to learn more about it.

The methods used for specifying memory modules vary with the type of memory module used by the system. 72-pin SIMMS, 168-pin DIMMs, 184-pin DIMMs and SODIMMs, and Rambus RDRAM modules are covered in the following sections.

Specifying 72-Pin SIMMs

To specify a 72-pin SIMM, you need to specify the following:

- Size (MB)
- Memory type (FPM or EDO)
- Speed (ns)
- Parity/ECC or non-parity
- Socket metal (gold or tin)

> **tip**
>
> If you're wondering what the actual size of a 72-pin SIMM memory module is and all you know is the standard designation (see Table 7.4 for examples), multiply the first number listed in the standard designation by 4 to get the actual size of the module. For example, the 16MB module shown in Table 7.4 is listed as a 4Mx36 module. Multiply 4M by 4 and you get 16(MB).

Table 7.4 shows some examples of 72-pin SIMM specifications.

In the standard designation, 32 is the number of data bits; 36 is the number of data plus parity bits. Note that if EDO is not mentioned, the memory module uses slower FPM memory.

Before you order memory, you should determine which metal is used for the SIMM sockets on your motherboard, gold or tin. Match the metal in the socket to the metal on the memory module contacts to avoid corrosion caused by mixing metals.

Table 7.4   Specifying 72-Pin SIMMs (Examples)

Size	Parity/ Non-Parity	Memory Type	Speed	Connector Standard Type	Designation
4MB	Non-parity	FPM	70ns	Tin	1Mx32-70 tin
16MB	Parity	EDO	60ns	Gold	4Mx36EDO-60 gold

➪   To learn more about the problems that can result from mixing tin and gold connectors, **see** "Avoid Mixing Metals in RAM and Sockets," **p. PDF:846**.

Specifying 168-Pin DIMMs

Some of the factors used to specify a 168-pin DIMM are similar to those used to specify a 72-pin SIMM:

- Size (MB); multiply the first number in the designation by 8 to determine the actual size

- Non-parity (64-bit); ECC (72-bit)

- Memory type (EDO or SDRAM); most memory sold in 168-pin form today is SDRAM, but some older systems use EDO DIMMs

However, there are several new factors you also need to specify:

- The speed of a 168-pin SDRAM DIMM is not listed in ns (nanoseconds), but instead by the clock speed of the memory bus: 66MHz is known as PC-66, 100MHz is known as PC-100, and 133MHz is known as PC-133. EDO memory is 50ns or slower.

- There are three types of memory: *buffered* (which re-drives memory signals to make higher memory amounts possible), *unbuffered* (which doesn't re-drive memory signals), and *registered* (a newer form of buffering). Buffered DIMMs are usually EDO modules and are designed for older PCs or for Macs. Almost all desktop PCs use unbuffered DIMMs, and newer servers might use registered DIMMs.

- DIMMs with SDRAM memory use 3.3v; DIMMs with EDO memory use 5v.

- **CAS Latency**, or CL (the number of clock cycles required between the issuance of a command to memory and the start of data flow). Lower latency (smaller CL number) is faster. SDRAM DIMMs use CAS Latency values of CL2.5 and CL3.

note

Use 36-bit or 72-bit memory modules when your motherboard or system supports parity checking or ECC error correction. If you add 36-bit or 72-bit memory modules to a system that doesn't perform parity checking or ECC error correction, the additional bits are ignored.

note

The examples in Table 7.4 are just a few of the possible configurations available for 72-pin SIMM memory. Smaller and larger sizes are available, and slower speeds (larger ns—or nanoseconds— rating) have also been produced.

■ Standard (168-pin) or small outline modules (used by notebook and portable computers).

Check the manual to determine what speed(s), sizes, types, and CL values to specify for memory.

Table 7.5 provides examples of how typical SDRAM DIMMS are specified.

Table 7.5 Specifying SDRAM DIMMs

Size	ECC	Speed	CAS Latency	Registered	Standard Designation
64MB	No	66MHz	CL3	No	8M×64 66MHz
128MB	Yes	133MHz	CL2.5	No	16M×64 133MHz ECC CL2.5
512MB	Yes	100MHz	CL2	Yes	64M×72 100MHz Registered ECC CL2

Specifying 184-Pin DDR SDRAM DIMMs

The process of specifying DDR SDRAM memory is similar to that of specifying SDRAM memory, except that memory speeds can be specified by MHz (DDR333 is 333MHz) or by a PC factor referring to the memory's throughput in MBps. For example, PC2700 = 2,700MBps = DDR333. CL factors range from CL3 to CL2.

Table 7.6 provides some examples of how to specify DDR SDRAMs.

note

You can normally make the following substitutions:

• PC-133 memory can be used in place of PC-66 or PC-100 memory on most recent systems. However, some systems that use Intel chipsets cannot use PC-133 memory.

• If CL3 memory is not available, CL2.5 memory can be used in its place.

Table 7.6   Specifying DDR SDRAM DIMMs—Typical Examples

Size	ECC	Speed	PC Type	CAS Latency	SODIMM	Standard Designation
128MB	No	266MHz	PC2100	CL2.5	No	DDR266 PC2100 128MB non-ECC CL2.5
256MB	Yes	400MHz	PC3200	CL3	No	DDR400 PC3200 256MB ECC CL3
512MB	No	333MHz	PC2700	N/A	Yes	DDR333 PC2700 512MB SODIMM[1]

[1]*You don't need to specify CAS Latency values for SODIMM memory.*

Specifying Rambus RDRAM Modules

To order a Rambus module, you need to specify the following:

- Memory speed (800MHz or 1,066MHz)
- Memory size
- ECC or non-ECC
- Pin configuration
- Number of devices (chips)

Each device in the standard designation represents an RDRAM chip. Some systems require a specific number of devices in each module.

Table 7.7 provides some examples of how to specify Rambus RIMMs.

note

As you review Tables 7.5 and 7.6, keep in mind that these are just a few examples of the many SDRAM and DDR SDRAM memory module sizes and types on the market. All types of memory in these tables are available in 128MB, 256MB, and 512MB sizes as well as smaller sizes, and DDR memory is also available in a 1GB size. ECC memory is also available in a variety of sizes and types.

Table 7.7   Specifying Rambus RIMMs

Size	ECC	Speed	Pins	# of Devices	Standard Designation
128MB	No	800MHz	232	4	128MB PC800 non-ECC four-device RIMM
256MB	No	1,066MHz	168	2	256MB PC1066 non-ECC two-device RIMM
512MB	Yes	800MHz	168	18	512MB PC80040 ECC 18-device RIMM

Specifying Memory by System or Motherboard Type

As you can see from the preceding sections, there are many variables involved in specifying memory for a particular system. The complexity of the specifications for modern memory modules can make getting the right module difficult. As an alternative, you also can use the following methods to specify memory:

- Check the system or motherboard manual for recommended brands and part numbers.
- Use interactive memory order databases provided by major vendors such as Crucial.com or Kingston.

Installing SIMMs

As with any device, correct orientation of memory modules with their sockets is critical both for your real-world work and for the A+ Certification Exam.

SIMM modules have one end with a cut-off lower corner, corresponding to a projection, or *bump*, at the matching end of the SIMM socket; refer to Figure 7.2, where the cut-off side of the SIMM modules shown is the left side. This provides a keying mechanism designed to keep you from installing the SIMM backward.

To install the SIMM

1. Line up the cut-out end of the SIMM with the correct end of the socket.
2. Insert the SIMM at a 35-degree angle, ensuring that the connector is solidly in the socket, as shown in Figure 7.6. Do not touch the tin- or gold-plated connectors on the bottom of the module; this can cause corrosion or ESD.
3. Push and lift the top of the SIMM until the SIMM is aligned at 90 degrees with the socket and is locked in place. If the SIMM slips out of the socket, double-check the orientation. The bump on the keyed end of the SIMM will force an incorrectly aligned SIMM out of the socket.

FIGURE 7.6

With either a 30-pin or 72-pin SIMM (shown here), insert the SIMM at an angle into the SIMM socket.

Some SIMM sockets are at a 90-degree angle to the motherboard, but many 30-pin SIMM sockets on motherboards or on expansion cards are at a 30-degree angle to the motherboard or expansion card. Determine the approximate insertion angle from the socket, not the board.

Installing DIMMs and Rambus RDRAM Modules

DIMM and Rambus RDRAM module sockets have an improved keying mechanism and a better locking mechanism compared to SIMMs.

To install the DIMM or Rambus RDRAM module

1. Line up the modules' connectors with the socket. Both DIMMs and Rambus modules have connections with different widths, preventing the module from being inserted backwards.

2. Verify that the locking tabs on the socket are swiveled to the outside (open) position.

3. After verifying that the module is lined up correctly with the socket, push the module straight down into the socket until the swivel locks on each end of the socket snap into place at the top corners of the module (see Figure 7.7). A fair amount of force is required to engage the locks. Do not touch the gold-plated connectors on the bottom of the module; this can cause corrosion or ESD.

For clarity, the memory module installation pictured in Figure 7.7 was photographed with the motherboard out of the case. However, the tangle of cables around and over the DIMM sockets in Figure 7.8 provides a much more realistic view of the challenges you face when you install memory in a working system.

When you install memory on a motherboard inside a working system, use the following tips to help your upgrade go smoothly and the module to work properly:

■ If the system is a tower system, consider placing it on its side to make the upgrade easier. Doing this also helps to prevent tipping the system over by accident when you push on the memory to lock it into the socket.

tip

If you need to install two or more SIMMs, make sure you install the SIMMs that will be blocked by other SIMMs first so you don't need to remove any modules to complete the installation.

- Move the locking mechanisms on the DIMM sockets to the open position before you try to insert the module. In Figure 7.8, the locks on the empty socket are in the closed position. Figure 7.7 shows open and closed locks for comparison.

- Move power and drive cables away from the memory sockets so you can access the sockets. Disconnect drive cables if necessary.

- Use a flashlight to shine light into the interior of the system so you can see the memory sockets and locking mechanisms clearly; this enables you to determine the proper orientation of the module and to make sure the sockets' locking mechanisms are open.

- Use a flashlight to double check your memory installation to make sure the module is completely inserted into the slot and locked into place.

- Replace any cables you moved or disconnected during the process before you close up the case and restart the system.

> ## tip
>
> Note the positions of any cables you need to remove before you remove them to perform an internal upgrade. I like to use self-stick colored dots on a drive and its matching data and power cables. You can purchase sheets of colored dots at most office supply and discount stores.

FIGURE 7.7
A DIMM module partly inserted (top) and fully inserted (bottom). The memory module must be pressed firmly into place before the locking tabs will engage.

Locking clips not engaged

Locking clips engaged; module locked in place

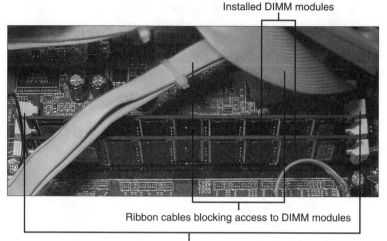

FIGURE 7.8

DDR DIMM memory sockets in a typical system are often surrounded and covered up by drive and power cables, making it difficult to properly install additional memory.

Installed DIMM modules

Ribbon cables blocking access to DIMM modules

Locking mechanism on empty DIMM socket in closed position; must be opened before another module can be installed

Memory and Operating System Limits

Windows 9x/Me cannot use more than 512MB of RAM because the virtual memory cache (Vcache) feature in these versions runs out of available memory addresses if more than 512MB of RAM
is installed. This can lead to erroneous out-of-memory errors when you try to open a DOS prompt. This limitation can also lead
to conflicts with AGP video cards, which also require memory address space, which can conflict with Vcache.

If you want to use more than 512MB of RAM, upgrade to Windows 2000 or Windows XP, because there is no update available for Windows 9x/Me.

Cache RAM and Main Memory

As you learned in Chapter 4, "The Motherboard and CPU," CPUs with **Level 1 (L1)** and/or **Level 2 (L2) cache** RAM perform RAM-bound operations much more quickly than CPUs that lack cache.

There are two reasons why cache RAM helps the CPU perform RAM-bound operations faster:

- Cache RAM is faster than main memory.
- Cache RAM holds a copy of the last-accessed section of main memory.

Because programs and other processes performed by the CPU often use the same section of memory several times before they need to access a new section of memory, checking cache RAM first for information enables a CPU to perform tasks more quickly than if it checked main memory every time. In most situations, the memory section needed by the CPU is stored in cache memory, so the CPU can reuse it.

The order in which the CPU accesses memory is **L1 cache**, then **L2 cache** (if necessary), **L3 cache** (if present, used mostly on server processors such as the Intel Itanium family) and finally, main memory (if necessary). This process is detailed here:

1. L1 cache is checked. If the desired memory location is here, this is a cache *hit* and the CPU uses it.

2. If the desired memory location is not found here, this is a cache *miss* and the CPU then checks L2 cache.

   If the desired memory location is here, this is a cache *hit* and the CPU uses it.

3. If the desired memory location is not found here, this is a cache *miss* and the CPU then checks L3 cache (if present).

   If the desired memory location is here, this is a cache *hit* and the CPU uses it.

4. If the desired memory location is not found here, this is a cache *miss* and the CPU then retrieves the location from main memory.

5. All caches are refreshed with the latest information when the CPU fetches information from main memory, enabling the CPU to use cache memory successfully on future memory accesses.

Locations for Level 2 Cache

L2 cache is built into Pentium II and newer processors (see Chapter 4 for details), but is located on the motherboard of most Pentium and Pentium-class (Socket 4, 5, or 7) processors. Table 7.8 lists the types of L2 cache chips used on Pentium-class motherboards and their typical locations, which are pictured in Figure 7.9.

Table 7.8 Level 2 Cache Types and Uses

Cache Type	Details	Sizes	Typical Systems
SRAM chips	4 or 8 data chips, 1 **TAGRAM** chip (usually socketed)	64KB, 256KB	486 and early Pentium
COAST module	Dedicated slot	256KB	Late-model 486 and some Pentium
Pipeline-burst chips	Rectangular surface-mount chips on motherboard	256KB, 512KB, 1MB	Late-model Pentium, K6

FIGURE 7.9

L2 cache memory on Pentium-class motherboards might be provided by socketed SRAM chips (top), a COAST (Cache On A STick) module (middle), or surface-mounted pipeline-burst cache chips (bottom).

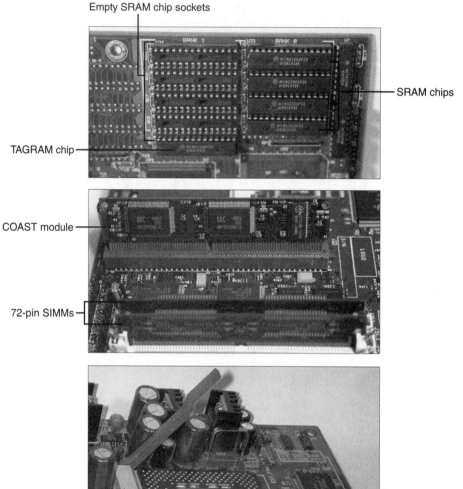

Empty SRAM chip sockets

SRAM chips

TAGRAM chip

COAST module

72-pin SIMMs

Pentium MMX processor

Pipeline-burst cache chips

Locations for L3 Cache

The only current PC processors with built-in L3 cache at this writing are the Intel Itanium family of processors, which are used in very high-performance servers. Some versions of the Intel Xeon used in servers and workstations, and the Intel Pentium 4 Extreme Edition used in high-performance PCs. The rare K6-III processor, which used the same Socket 7 as the Intel Pentium MMX, was the first PC processor to have both L1 and L2 cache onboard. When it was plugged into a motherboard that had onboard cache (as described in the previous section), the onboard cache was treated as L3 cache.

Upgrading Cache RAM

You can upgrade the L2 cache on a Pentium-class system by installing additional SRAM cache chips or a **COAST** module or by installing a motherboard with integrated **pipeline-burst cache** chips. To upgrade the cache on newer systems, replace the processor with a model with more L2 cache.

⇨ **See** "Internal CPU Characteristics Affecting Performance," **p. 132**, for more information on CPUs that contain L2 cache.

Study Lab

Don't miss the Study Lab materials found on the CD accompanying this book. Each Study Lab is tailored to the individual chapters in this book, meaning that you'll quickly be able to determine which topics you understand well enough to pass the exam and which topics need more study. The Study Labs are presented in printable PDF format so that you can take them with you to study at work, on the road, or even in your car just before test time!

THE ABSOLUTE MINIMUM

Here are the high points of this chapter. Review these just before you take the exam to brush up on the major topics and help you identify what you need to review.

- Adding RAM to systems improves performance by minimizing disk accesses and by providing a larger workspace.

- Adding cache RAM to systems improves performance for memory-bound operations. However, recent systems incorporate L2 cache in the processor.

- To add RAM to a system, you must know both the CPU type and the type(s) of modules the system needs to determine the number of memory modules needed.

- SDRAM and DDR SDRAM DIMMs are the most common modules used on recent systems and can be added one at a time to normal (single-channel) systems.

- Dual-channel systems require two identical DIMMs.

- Some advanced systems use RAMBUS modules.

- SIMM speeds are rated in nanoseconds (ns).

- SDRAM and Rambus speeds are rated in MHz (PC-133 or 133MHz SDRAM; PC800 or 800MHz Rambus).

- DDR SDRAM speeds are rated in MHz or in throughput (DDR333 [333MHz] or PC2700).

- CAS Latency (CL) values are used when specifying SDRAM and DDR SDRAM. Smaller CL values are faster.

- Exchanging one module at a time is a good way to determine which module has failed in a system.

- Cache memory should be disabled when main memory is tested.

INPUT/OUTPUT DEVICES AND CABLES

No matter how well a computer is equipped, there will come a time when you want to plug something else into it. From printers to mice to broadband Internet devices, external peripherals of all kinds connect to ports on your computer. If your computer doesn't have the correct port needed for a **peripheral**, you can't use that peripheral until you add the port required. This chapter covers the configuration, setup, and uses of the fundamental input/output ports and devices most computers have in common:

- Parallel port
- Serial port
- Modem
- Keyboard
- Mouse
- Sound card
- USB
- IEEE-1394 (FireWire)

This chapter discusses installation, configuration, cabling, and physical installation issues for these ports and devices. Windows driver installation and configuration issues are discussed in Chapter 19, "Installing and Configuring Hardware in Windows."

Parallel Ports

The **parallel port**, also known as the **LPT (line printer)** port, was originally designed for use with parallel printers. However, don't let the name "LPT port" fool you: the parallel port is among the most versatile of I/O ports in the system because it is also used by a variety of devices, including tape backups, external CD-ROM and optical drives, scanners, and removable-media drives such as Zip drives. Although newer devices in these categories are now designed to use USB or **IEEE-1394** ports, the parallel port continues to be an important external I/O device for systems running Windows 95 and Windows NT 4.0.

The parallel (LPT) port is unusual because it uses two completely different connector types:

- All IBM and compatible computers since the first IBM PC of 1981 have used the **DB-25F** port shown in Figure 8.1, with pins 1–13 on the top and pins 14–25 on the bottom. This is also referred to as the type IEEE-1284-A

note

The CD included with this book contains important Study Lab material for this chapter, as well as Chapters 2–22 in this book. The Study Lab for each chapter contains terms to study, exercises, and practice tests—all in printable PDF format (Adobe Acrobat Reader is included on the CD, too). These Study Lab materials will help you gear up for the A+ Exam. Also, the CD includes an industry-leading test engine from PrepLogic, which simulates the actual A+ test so that you can be sure that you're ready when test day arrives. Don't let the A+ test intimidate you. If you've read the chapters, worked through the Study Lab, and passed the practice tests from PrepLogic, you should be well prepared to ace the test!

Also, you'll notice that some words throughout each chapter are in bold format. These are study terms that are defined in the Study Lab. Be sure to consult the Study Lab when you are finished with this chapter to test what you've learned.

connector. (**IEEE-1284** is an international standard for parallel port connectors, cabling, and signaling.)

■ The port used by parallel printers of all types, however, is the same **Centronics** 36-pin port used since the days of the Apple II and other early microcomputers of the late 1970s, as seen in Figure 8.1. This port is also referred to as the IEEE-1284-B port. It is an edge connector with 36 connectors, 18 per side.

Some recent Hewlett-Packard LaserJet printers also use a miniature version of the Centronics connector known as the **IEEE-1284-C**, which is also a 36-pin edge connector. The 1284-C connector doesn't use wire clips.

Accordingly, a parallel printer cable also has different connectors at each end, as seen in Figure 8.2.

caution

Devices other than printers that plug into the parallel (LPT) port have two connectors: one for the cable that runs from the device to the parallel port, and another for the cable that runs from the device to the printer. Although it's theoretically possible to create a long daisy-chain of devices ending with a printer, in practice you should have no more than one device plus a printer plugged into a parallel port. If you use more than one device, you could have problems getting the devices (not to mention the printer) to work reliably.

FIGURE 8.1

Parallel devices use the Centronics port (top) for printers and some other types of parallel devices, whereas the DB-25F port (bottom) is used for the computer's parallel port. Some external devices also use a DB-25F port.

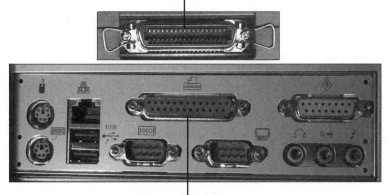

Printer port

Parallel port on computer

FIGURE 8.2

The ends of a typical IBM-style parallel cable. The Centronics 36-pin connector (upper left) connects to the printer; the DB-25M connector (lower right) connects to the computer's DB-25F parallel port.

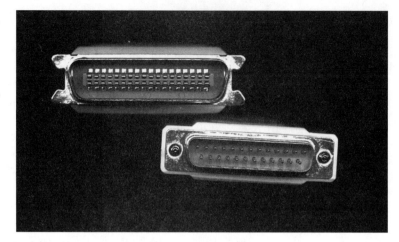

Parallel cables have the pinout described in Table 8.1.

Table 8.1 Parallel Port Pinout (DB-25F Connector)

Pin #	Description	I/O	Pin #	Description	I/O
1	-Strobe	Out	14	-Auto Feed	Out
2	+Data bit 0	Out	15	-Error	In
3	+Data bit 1	Out	16	-Initialize Printer	Out
4	+Data bit 2	Out	17	-Select Input	Out
5	+Data bit 3	Out	18	-Ground (Data bit 0 Return)	In
6	+Data bit 4	Out	19	-Ground (Data bit 1 Return)	In
7	+Data bit 5	Out	20	-Ground (Data bit 2 Return)	In
8	+Data bit 6	Out	21	-Ground (Data bit 3 Return)	In
9	+Data bit 7	Out	22	-Ground (Data bit 4 Return)	In
10	-Acknowledge	In	23	-Ground (Data bit 5 Return)	In
11	+Busy	In	24	-Ground (Data bit 6 Return)	In
12	+Paper End	In	25	-Ground (Data bit 7 Return)	In
13	+Select	In			

Parallel Port Configuration

The configuration of the LPT port consists of

- Selecting the port's operating mode
- Selecting the IRQ, I/O port address, and DMA channel (for certain modes)

⇨ For an overview of how IRQ, I/O port addresses, and DMA channels are used, **see** "Hardware Resources," **p. 75**.

tip

As you prepare for the A+ Certification Exam, you should note that the parallel designation for the LPT port comes from its use of eight data lines (pins 2–9) and that the port has provisions for printer status messages (pins 10–12).

LPT Port Operating Modes

The LPT port can be configured for a variety of operating modes. The options available for a particular port depend on the capabilities of the system. Most systems you're likely to work with should offer all of these modes, although a few digital dinosaurs still kicking around in some offices might not have the IEEE-1284 modes.

Standard Mode

The **standard mode** of the LPT port is the configuration first used on PCs, and it is the only mode available on many 386-based and earlier systems. On some systems, this is also known as *compatible mode*. Although configuration for this mode typically includes both the IRQ and I/O port address, only the I/O port address is actually used for printing. If the parallel port is used in standard/compatible mode, IRQ 7 can be used for another device. The standard mode is the slowest mode (150 kilobytes per second [KBps] output/50KBps input), but it is the most suitable mode for older printers. In this mode, eight lines are used for output, but only four lines are used for input. The port can send or receive, but only in one direction at a time.

This mode will work with any parallel cable.

PS/2—Bidirectional

The next mode available on most systems is the **PS/2** or **bidirectional mode**. This mode was pioneered by the old IBM PS/2 computers and is the simplest mode available on some computer models.

Bidirectional mode is more suitable for use with devices other than printers because eight lines are used for both input and output, and it uses only I/O port addresses. This mode is no faster than compatible mode for printing but accepts incoming data at a faster rate than compatible mode; the port sends and transmits data at 150KBps.

This mode requires a bidirectional printer cable or IEEE-1284 printer cable.

IEEE-1284 High-Speed Bidirectional Modes

Three modes that are fully *bidirectional* (able to send and receive data 8 bits at a time) and are also much faster than the original PS/2-style bidirectional port include

- **EPP (Enhanced Parallel Port)**—Uses both an IRQ and an I/O port address. This is the mode supported by most high-speed printers and drives attached to the parallel port.

- **ECP (Enhanced Capabilities Port)**—Designed for daisy-chaining different devices (such as printers and scanners) to a single port. It uses an IRQ, an I/O port address, and a DMA channel, making it the most resource hungry of all the different parallel port modes.

- **EPP/ECP**—Many recent systems support a combined EPP/ECP mode, making it possible to run devices preferring either mode on a single port.

These modes, which transmit data at up to 2 megabytes per second (MBps) and receive data at 500KBps, have all been incorporated into the IEEE-1284 parallel port standard. Most Pentium-based and newer systems have ports that comply with at least one of these standards. All of these require an IEEE-1284–compliant parallel cable.

These modes are suitable for use with

- High-speed laser and inkjet printers
- External tape-backup drives, optical drives, and Zip drives
- Scanners
- Data-transfer programs such as Direct Cable Connection, Direct Parallel Connection, LapLink, Interlink, and others

Basically, the list includes all of the most recent printers and peripherals that plug into the parallel port.

Types of Parallel Cables

There are three major types of parallel cables:

- *Printer*—Uses the DB-25M connector on one end, and the Centronics connector on the other.

- *Switchbox/Device*—Most use the DB-25M connector on both ends.

- *Data transfer*—Uses the DB-25M connector at both ends and crosses the transmit and receive wires at one end (meaning that two computers can send and receive data, much like a computer network, though much slower).

caution

If you use a switchbox or device cable in place of a data transfer cable, or vice versa, your device or your data transfer process won't work. Fortunately, data transfer cables are usually thinner than switchbox or device cables because only a few of the wire pairs are required for data transfer. However, you might want to label the different types of cables to avoid mixing them up.

Printer and switchbox/device cables can support the IEEE-1284 or earlier bidirectional standards. Here's how they differ internally:

IEEE-1284 cables feature several types of shielding in both the cable and at the printer end of the cable. This shielding is designed to minimize interference from outside sources. Normal cables have minimal shielding.

IEEE-1284 cables use a twisted wire-pair construction internally, running 18 wire pairs to the printer. The wire pairs help minimize *crosstalk* (interference between different wires in the cable). Standard (compatible) cables don't use as many wire pairs, and bidirectional cables use less shielding. As a result, IEEE-1284 cables are both a good deal thicker and more expensive than ordinary or bidirectional printer cables.

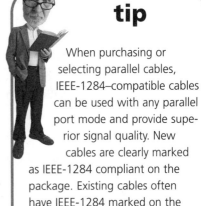

tip

When purchasing or selecting parallel cables, IEEE-1284–compatible cables can be used with any parallel port mode and provide superior signal quality. New cables are clearly marked as IEEE-1284 compliant on the package. Existing cables often have IEEE-1284 marked on the rubberized outer shield of the cable.

Standard and Optional Parallel Port Settings

Parallel ports can be configured as **LPT1**, **LPT2**, and LPT3. When a single parallel port is found in the system, regardless of its configuration, it is always designated as LPT1. The configurations for LPT2 and LPT3, shown in Table 8.2, apply when you have a computer with more than one parallel port.

Table 8.2 Typical Parallel Port Hardware Configuration Settings

LPT Port #	IRQ	I/O Port Address Range
LPT1	7	3BC-38Fh or 378-37Fh
LPT2	5	378-37Fh or 278-27Fh
LPT3	5	278-27Fh

If one of the ports is an ECP or EPP/ECP port, DMA 3 is normally used on most systems along with the IRQ and I/O port address ranges listed here. Some computers default to DMA 1 for an ECP or EPP/ECP parallel port, but DMA 1 will conflict with most sound cards running in Sound Blaster emulation mode.

➪ To learn more about DMA conflicts with sounds cards, **see** "Default Sound Card Hardware Configuration," **p. 288**.

Some 16-bit ISA or PCI-based **multi-I/O cards** can place the parallel port at any available IRQ up to 15. PCI parallel port or multi-I/O (parallel and serial ports and possibly others on the same card) cards can share IRQs with other PCI cards. However, ISA parallel ports, including those built into the motherboard, cannot share IRQs when used in EPP, ECP, or EPP/ECP mode. (These modes use an IRQ.)

How to Configure or Disable Parallel Ports

Depending on the location of the parallel port, there are several ways to configure the port settings. These include

■ BIOS setup program for built-in ports

■ Jumper blocks or DIP switch configuration for I/O cards in expansion slots

■ Plug and Play (**PnP**) mode for use with Windows 9x/Me and Windows 2000/XP

Follow these steps to adjust the configuration of a parallel port built into the system's motherboard:

1. Start the BIOS setup program.

2. Change to the I/O device or peripheral configuration screen (see Figure 8.3).

3. Select the mode, IRQ, I/O port address, and DMA channel if required.

4. Save changes and exit; the system reboots.

FIGURE 8.3

A typical BIOS I/O device configuration screen with the parallel port configured for EPP/ECP mode with default settings.

Parallel port I/O port address/IRQ

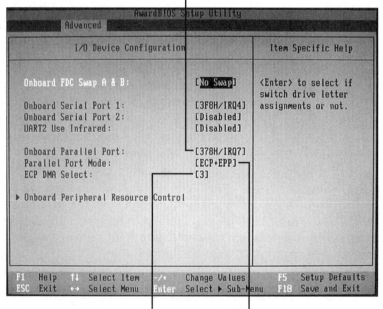

ECP mode select   Parallel port mode

Follow these steps to adjust the configuration of an ISA parallel port card using jumper blocks or DIP switches:

1. Turn off the system's power.

2. Remove the parallel port or multi-I/O card.

3. Adjust the jumper blocks or DIP switches to select the mode, IRQ, I/O port address, and DMA channel if required. Check the card's documentation for details.

    ⇨ To learn more about jumper blocks and DIP switches, **see** "Adjusting Speed and Multiplier Settings," **p. 141**.

4. Reinsert the card into the expansion slot.

5. Restart the system.

PCI-based parallel ports are configured by the PnP (Plug and Play) BIOS; some ISA cards can also be configured by the PnP BIOS. In some cases, you can adjust the settings used by a PnP parallel port or a motherboard-based parallel port with the Windows Control Panel. See Chapter 19 for details.

Adding Additional Parallel Ports

Although you can daisy-chain a printer and another parallel-port device to a single parallel port, you can't connect two printers to the same port unless you use a switchbox. If you want to have two parallel printers that can be used at the same time, or if you want to provide different parallel port devices with their own ports, you need to add a parallel port. What are your options?

You can add additional parallel ports to a system with any of the following:

- ISA-based parallel or multi-I/O card
- PCI-based parallel or multi-I/O card
- USB-to-parallel-port adapter

Install a PCI card in a PCI slot and an ISA card in an ISA slot. ISA cards that are not PnP should be manually configured to use available IRQ, I/O port address, and DMA channel resources. Use the Windows Device Manager to determine available resource settings (see Chapter 19 for details).

tip

A USB-to-parallel-port adapter has a USB Type A connection at one end and a Centronics connection at the other end. This adapter enables you to connect a parallel printer to your USB port so you can use the parallel port for other devices. However, this type of adapter isn't designed to support other types of parallel port devices: If you want to connect a parallel port drive or scanner, you must use a real parallel port.

Serial Ports

The **serial port**, also known as **RS-232** or **COM** (communication) ports (see Figure 8.4), historically has rivaled the parallel port in versatility. Serial ports have been used to connect

- External modems
- Serial mouse or pointing devices such as trackballs or touchpads
- Plotters
- Label printers
- Serial printers
- File transfer programs such as Direct Cable Connection, LapLink, and Interlink

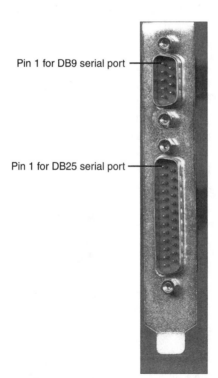

FIGURE 8.4

A 9-pin serial port (DB-9M connector, top) and a 25-pin serial port (DB-25M connector, bottom) on a typical extension bracket from an ISA multi-I/O card. The ribbon cables used to connect the ports to the card can be seen in the background.

Pin 1 for DB9 serial port

Pin 1 for DB25 serial port

How do serial ports compare in speed with parallel ports? Serial ports transmit data one bit at a time (parallel ports send and receive data eight bits at a time), and their maximum speeds are far lower than parallel ports. However, serial cables can carry data reliably at far greater distances than parallel cables. Serial ports, unlike parallel ports, have no provision for daisy-chaining; only one device can be connected to a serial port. It's no wonder that a lot of devices that formerly plugged into the serial port are now calling the USB port "home port."

Serial ports come in two forms:

- ■ **DB-9M** (male)
- ■ **DB-25M** (male)

Either type can be adapted to the other connector type with a low-cost adapter (see Figure 8.5). The difference is possible because serial communications need only a few wires. Unlike parallel printers, which use a standard cable, each type of serial device uses a specially wired cable. DB-9M connectors are used on all but the oldest systems.

Serial Port Pinouts

At a minimum, a serial cable must use at least three wires, plus ground:

- ■ A transmit data wire
- ■ A receive data wire
- ■ A signal wire

Tables 8.3 and 8.4 can be used to determine the correct pinout for any specified serial cable configuration. Unlike parallel devices, which all use the same standard cable wiring, serial devices use differently wired cables. A modem cable, for example, will be wired much differently than a serial printer cable. And different serial printers might each use a unique pinout.

note

The DB-9 (9-pin male) connector is the more common of the two serial port connector types. The 25-pin serial port has many additional pins but is seldom used today. The major difference between it and the 9-pin serial interface is the 25-pin port's support for current loop data, a type of serial communication primarily used for data collection in industrial uses.

Table 8.3   9-Pin Serial Port Pinout

Use	Pin	Direction
Carrier Detect	1	In
Receive Data	2	In
Transmit Data	3	Out
Data Terminal Ready	4	Out
Signal Ground	5	—

Table 8.3   (continued)

Use	Pin	Direction
Data Set Ready	6	In
Request to Send	7	Out
Clear to Send	8	In
Ring Indicator	9	In

Table 8.4 lists the pinouts for the 25-pin connector; unused pins are omitted.

Table 8.4   25-Pin Serial Port Pinout

Use	Pin	Direction
Transmit Data	2	Out
Receive Data	3	In
Request to Send	4	Out
Clear to Send	5	In
Data Set Ready	6	In
Signal Ground	7	—
Received Line Signal Indicator	8	In
+ Transmit Current Loop Data	9	Out
- Transmit Current Loop Data	11	Out
+ Receive Current Loop Data	18	In
Data Terminal Ready	20	Out
Ring Indicator	22	In
- Receive Current Loop Return	25	In

When a 9-pin to 25-pin serial port adapter is used (see Figure 8.5), the pins are converted to the more common 25-pin connector (see Table 8.5).

Table 8.5   9-Pin to 25-Pin Serial Port Converter/Serial Modem Pinout

Use	Pin # (9-Pin)	Pin # (25-Pin)
Carrier Detect (CD)	1	8
Receive Data (RD)	2	3
Transmit Data (TD)	3	2
Data Terminal Ready (DTR)	4	20

Table 8.5   (continued)

Use	Pin # (9-Pin)	Pin # (25-Pin)
Signal Ground (SG)	5	7
Data Set Ready (DSR)	6	6
Request to Send (RTS)	7	4
Clear to Send (CTS)	8	5
Ring Indicator (RI)	9	22

Serial ports assume that one end of the connection transmits and the other end receives.

FIGURE 8.5

A typical DB-25F to DB-9M serial port converter. The DB-25F connector (lower left) connects to the 25-pin serial port and converts its signals for use by devices attaching to the DB-9M port at the other end (upper right).

Types of Serial Cables

Serial cables, unlike parallel cables, can be constructed in many different ways. In fact, cables for serial devices are usually specified by device type rather than port type. This is because different devices use different pinouts.

Some of the most common examples of serial cables include

■ Null-modem (data transfer) cable

■ Modem cable

A null-modem cable enables two computers to communicate directly with each other by crossing the receive and transmit wires (meaning that two computers can send and receive data, much like a computer network, though much slower). The best known of these programs is LapLink, but the Microsoft MS-DOS Interlink and Windows Direct Cable Connection/Direct Serial Connection utilities can also use this type of cable. Although these programs support serial cable transfers, parallel port transfers are much faster and are recommended with MS-DOS and most versions of Windows. However, Windows NT 4.0 and earlier do *not* support using the parallel port for file transfers, so you must use a null-modem cable such as the one shown in Figure 8.6.

3-wire LapLink cable   9-wire serial port extension cable

FIGURE 8.6

A LapLink serial cable with connectors for either 25-pin or 9-pin serial ports. Only three wires are needed, enabling the cable to be much thinner than the 9-pin serial extension cable also shown.

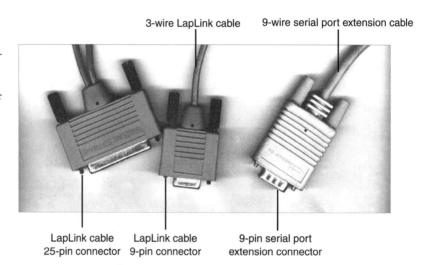

LapLink cable   LapLink cable   9-pin serial port
25-pin connector   9-pin connector   extension connector

A modem cable is used to connect an external modem to a serial port. Some modems include a built-in cable, but others require you to use a DB-9F to DB-25M cable from the 9-pin connector on the serial port to the 25-pin port on the modem. This cable typically uses the same pinout shown in Table 8.5.

What about serial printers? These printers are used primarily with older terminals rather than with PCs, and because different printers use different pinouts, their cables must be custom made. In fact, I've built a few myself. Fortunately, most recent terminals use parallel printers.

Standard IRQ and I/O Port Addresses

Serial ports require two hardware resources: IRQ and I/O port address. Table 8.6 lists the standard IRQ and I/O port addresses used for COM ports 1–4. Some systems and add-on cards enable alternative IRQs to be used.

Table 8.6 Standard Settings for COM (Serial) Ports 1–4

COM Port #	IRQ	I/O Port Address
1	4	3F8-3FFh
2	3	2F8-2FFh
3	4	3E8-3EFh
4	3	2E8-2EFh

Note that serial ports never require a DMA channel (and thus can't have DMA conflicts with other devices). However, there's another way to stumble when working with serial ports: IRQ conflicts. IRQ 4 is shared by default between **COM 1** and **COM 3**; IRQ 3 is shared by default between **COM 2** and **COM 4**. However, with ISA serial ports (including those on the motherboard), sharing does *not* mean that both serial ports can be used at the same time. If a device on COM 1 and a device on COM 3 that share the same IRQ are used at the same time, both devices will stop working and they might shut down the system.

The most common situation that causes such a conflict is the use of a mouse connected to COM 1 and a modem connected to COM 3. Use the modem, and the mouse quits working (and so does Windows).

As you saw in Chapter 2, "PC Anatomy 101," this happens because computers are *interrupt driven*; they use IRQs to determine which device needs to be listened to. When one device (the mouse) is already using the IRQ, the other device (the modem) gets a busy signal.

Just as the only solution to busy signals is a second phone line, the preferred solution to IRQ conflicts is to move the second device using an ISA IRQ to a different IRQ. Your ability to do this depends on the serial port.

tip

You can avoid IRQ conflicts between COM ports by

- Using only two COM ports in your system

- Not using devices connected to COM 1 and COM 3 or COM 2 and COM 4 at the same time

How to Configure or Disable Serial Ports

Depending on the location of the serial port, there are several ways to configure the port settings to select different IRQ and I/O port addresses for a serial port, or to disable the serial port. These include

- BIOS setup program for built-in ports
- Mechanical (jumper blocks or DIP switch) or software configuration for I/O cards in expansion slots
- Plug and Play (PnP) mode for use with Windows 9x/Me/2000/XP

To adjust the configuration of a serial port built into the system's motherboard

1. Start the BIOS setup program.
2. Go to the peripherals configuration screen.
3. Select the serial port you want to adjust.
4. To change the port's configuration, choose the IRQ and I/O port address you want to use, or select Disabled to prevent the system from detecting and using the serial port (see Figure 8.7).
5. Save changes and exit; the system reboots.

Serial port I/O port address/IRQ

FIGURE 8.7

A typical BIOS I/O device configuration screen with the first serial port enabled, the second port disabled, and IR (infrared) support disabled.

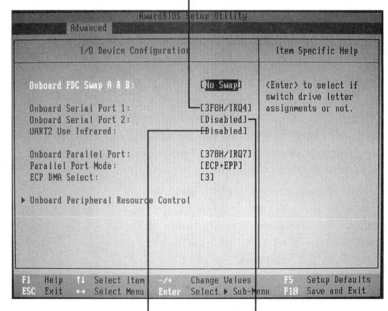

Disabled IR support for serial port

Disabled serial port

To adjust the configuration of an old-school serial port on an I/O card that uses jumper blocks or DIP switches

1. Turn off the system's power.

2. Remove the serial port or multi-I/O card.

3. Locate the jumper blocks or DIP switches for the serial port you want to adjust.

4. Move the jumper blocks or DIP switches to select the IRQ and I/O port address you want to use, or adjust the jumper blocks or DIP switches to disable the port. See the card's manual for details, or look for settings silk-screened on the card.

5. Reinsert the card into the expansion slot.

6. Restart the system.

Many recent systems will display the new port or new configuration during the initial bootup process.

⇨   To learn more, **see** "How the BIOS Displays Your PC's Components," **p. 73**.

To adjust the configuration of a serial port using a configuration program, start the configuration program, select the serial port, select the IRQ and I/O port address desired or select the Disable Port option, save the changes, and exit.

Serial ports on PCI cards are configured by the PnP BIOS. In some cases, you can use the Windows Device Manager to change the port configuration (see Chapter 19 for details).

Serial Port Software Configuration

Unlike parallel ports, serial ports have many different configuration options, making successful setup more challenging. Through software settings at the computer end, and by hardware or software settings at the device end, serial devices can use

■ A wide variety of transmission speeds, from as low as 300bps to as high as 115,200bps or faster

■ Different word lengths (7 bit or 8 bit)

■ Different methods of flow control (XON/XOFF or DTR/DSR)

■ Different methods of ensuring reliable data transmission (even parity, odd parity, no parity, 1-bit or 2-bit parity length)

Although simple devices such as a mouse or a label printer don't require that these settings be made manually (the software drivers do it), serial printers used with PCs running terminal-emulation software, PCs communicating with mainframe computers, serial pen plotters, serial printers, and PCs using modems often do require that these options be set correctly. Both ends of a serial connection must have these configurations set to identical values, or the communications between your computer and the other device will fail.

Figure 8.8 illustrates how Windows XP configures the port speed, flow control, and hardware settings for a serial port connected to an external modem.

FIGURE 8.8

General (left) and Advanced (right) dialog boxes used in Windows XP to configure a serial port connected to an external modem.

Serial Port UARTs

All serial ports are connected to a **UART (Universal Asynchronous Receive Transmit)** chip or a multifunction chip that emulates a UART. The UART chip is the "heart" of the serial port because it does the actual transmitting and receiving of data. If you've ever wondered why some serial ports are faster than others, the UART chips used by the serial ports may be the most likely reason. Problems with serial ports that cannot run fast enough to reliably receive and transmit to a particular device, or are unable to run in a multitasking environment such as Windows, can often be traced back to an obsolete UART chip. There are several major types of UART chips:

- *8250 series*—The 8250 series of UARTs are not fast enough to support modems running faster than 9,600bps. They have no means to buffer received data, and will drop characters if used with Windows. This chip was used primarily in IBM PC and PC/XT-type computers. The 8250B is the best chip of this series, but it's long out of date.

- *16450*—The 16450 UART will run reliably at speeds up to 19,200bps. It was introduced with the IBM AT, but it's also passé.

- *16550A*—This series of UARTs has a 16-byte **FIFO (first in, first out)** buffer for reliable multitasking without data loss and can run at speeds of up to 115,200bps. This is the standard UART used in the serial ports included on virtually all Pentium-class or better motherboards.

- *16650, 16750, 16850, 16950*—These UARTs have 32-byte or larger FIFO buffers (16750 has 64-byte FIFO, 16850/16950 have 128-byte FIFO buffers) and support speeds of 230,400bps up to 921,400bps; special serial port and multi-I/O cards often include one or more of these UARTs.

You can use the Windows 9x/Me (but not Windows 2000/XP) Modem Diagnostics to determine the UARTs installed in a system. Follow this procedure:

1. Open the Control Panel icon.

2. Open the Modems icon.

3. Click the Diagnostics tab (see Figure 8.9).

4. Select a serial port or modem.

5. Click the More Info button.

6. The port or modem's IRQ, starting I/O port address, and UART type will be displayed. Additional information will be displayed if you selected a modem.

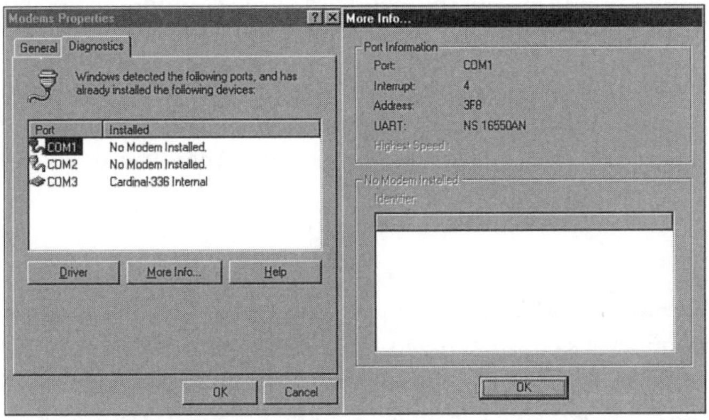

FIGURE 8.9

You can determine the IRQ, I/O port address, and UART type for any COM port or modem in your Windows 9x/Me system with the Diagnostics tab for modems.

In such cases, you can replace obsolete UARTs by disabling the existing serial ports (see "How to Configure or Disable Serial Ports," earlier in this chapter), and then add a faster serial port card containing a fast UART. Systems built since the late 1990s (such as those running Windows 2000 or Windows XP) already have 16550A or faster UARTs (or equivalents) installed so you don't need to worry about having outdated UARTs installed.

Don't like the UART in your system? If a system or I/O card uses a socketed 16450 chip, you can replace it with a 16550A or better chip to upgrade the UART. However, most recent computers and I/O cards use a Super I/O chip that contains a UART equivalent and LPT port inside a custom chip, rather than using a standard UART chip. Some recent motherboards don't even have a separate Super I/O chip; the South Bridge chip on the motherboard contains the Super I/O features plus ATA/IDE ports, USB ports, and other functions. To upgrade these systems, disable the serial port function in the system BIOS and install a serial or multi-I/O card that uses a faster UART. Virtually all serial or multi-I/O cards on the market today use 16550A or faster UARTs or UART equivalents.

Adding Additional Serial Ports

You can add additional serial ports to a system with any of the following:

- ISA-based serial or multi-I/O card
- PCI-based serial or multi-I/O card
- USB-to-parallel-port adapter

Install a PCI card in a PCI slot and an ISA card in an ISA slot. ISA cards that are not PnP should be manually configured to use available IRQ, I/O port address, and DMA channel resources. Use the Windows Device Manager to determine available resource settings (see Chapter 19 for details).

A USB-to-serial-port adapter has a USB Type A connection at one end and a 9-pin serial port at the other end. This adapter enables you to connect a serial device to your USB port so you can use the serial port for other devices.

USB Ports

The **Universal Serial Bus (USB)** port is the most flexible port found on recent PCs—no wonder it's called "universal." It can replace the serial (COM) and parallel (LPT) ports as well as the PS/2 mouse and keyboard ports; these ports are often called **legacy ports**. Some so-called **legacy-free** systems use only USB ports (or sometimes USB and IEEE-1394a ports) for external devices. Most scanners, printers, mouse devices, keyboards, and external drives are now designed to connect to USB ports, and USB ports can also be used for external modems and network connections.

Most recent systems have at least two USB ports, as shown in Figure 8.10.

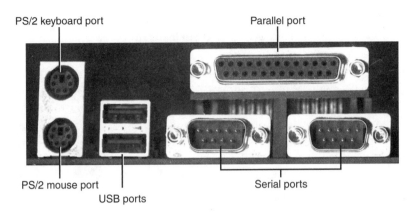

FIGURE 8.10

A typical ATX
motherboard's
I/O port panel
before installa-
tion into a case.
The PS/2 mouse
and keyboard
ports, twin USB
ports, parallel
port, and twin
RS-232 serial
ports are all visi-
ble. Each USB
port can host as
many as 127
USB devices.

PS/2 keyboard port — Parallel port

PS/2 mouse port — USB ports — Serial ports

USB Port Types, Speeds, and Technical Details

There are two standards for USB ports:

- **USB 1.1**
- **USB 2.0** (also called **Hi-Speed USB**)

Both use the same Series A and Series B connectors shown in Figure 8.11 and Series
A and Series B cables shown in Figure 8.12.

FIGURE 8.11

Series A (left)
and Series B
(right) USB
ports. Systems,
add-on cards,
and hubs have
two or more
Series A ports.
Each device that
is connected to a
USB port with a
removable cable
has a single
Series B port.

USB cables use two different types of connectors: **Series A** (also called Type A) and **Series B** (also called Type B). Series A connectors are used on USB root hubs (the USB ports in the computer) and USB external hubs to support USB devices. Series B connectors are used for devices that employ a removable USB cable, such as a USB printer or a generic (external) hub. Generally, you need a Series A–to–Series B cable to attach most devices to a USB root or external hub. Cables that are Series A to Series A or Series B to Series B are used to extend standard cables, and can cause problems if the combined length of the cables exceeds recommended distances.

USB 1.1 ports run at a top speed (**full-speed USB**) of 12 megabits per second (Mbps), **low-speed USB** devices such as a mouse or a keyboard run at 1.5Mbps, and USB 2.0 (Hi-Speed USB) ports run at a top speed of 480Mbps. USB 2.0 ports are backward-compatible with USB 1.1 devices and speeds, and manage multiple USB 1.1 devices better than a USB 1.1 port does.

USB packaging and device markings frequently use the official logos shown in Figure 8.13 to distinguish the two versions of USB in common use. Note that the industry is shifting from using the term *USB 2.0* to *Hi-Speed USB*.

> **tip**
>
> I don't recommend using extension cables or cables that are longer than six feet (especially with USB 1.1 ports); I've seen some devices stop working when longer-than-normal cables were tried. If you need a longer cable run, use a self-powered hub between the PC and the device. The self-powered hub provides the power needed for any USB device and keeps the signal at full strength.

FIGURE 8.12

Series A (left) and Series B (right) USB cables. Connect the Series A connector to a system's USB port and the Series B cable to the USB device.

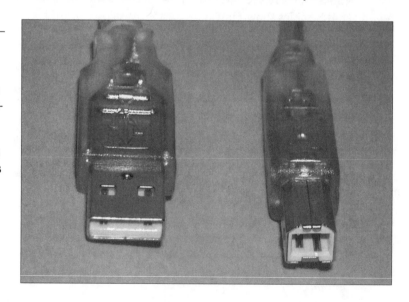

With either version of USB, a single USB port on an add-on card or motherboard is designed to handle up to 127 devices through the use of multiport hubs and daisy-chaining of hubs. Although there was limited support for USB devices in Windows 95 OSR 2.1 and above (Windows 95B and Windows 95C), most USB devices are designed to work with Windows 98 and later versions (Windows NT 4.0 does not support USB). USB devices can be *hot-swapped* (connected and disconnected without turning off the system) with Windows 98 Second Edition and later versions of Windows. The USB ports (each group of two ports is connected to a **root hub**) in the computer use a single IRQ and a single I/O port address, regardless of the number of physical USB ports or devices attached to those ports.

The maximum length for a cable attached to 12Mbps or 480Mbps USB devices is 5 meters, whereas the maximum length for low-speed (1.5Mbps) devices is 3 meters. When a USB root hub is enabled in a computer running Windows, two devices will be visible in the Windows Device Manager: a USB root hub and a PCI-to-USB univer-sal host controller (USB 1.1) or advanced host controller (USB 2.0), which uses the single IRQ and I/O port address required by USB hardware. If an external USB hub is attached to the computer, a **generic hub** also will be listed in the Windows Device Manager (see Figure 8.14). A root hub supports two USB ports. In Figure 8.14, there are two root hubs listed, indicating the system has four USB ports.

FIGURE 8.14

The USB section of the Windows XP Device Manager on a typical system. Note the fork-shaped USB logo next to the category and each device.

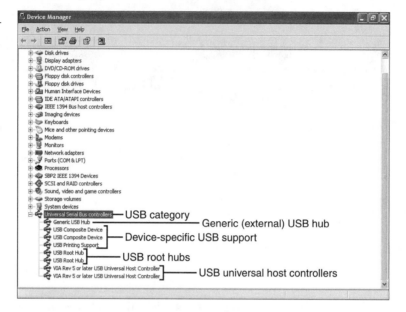

Requirements for USB Operation

Because USB ports were not part of the original IBM PC architecture, they are not supported by the traditional IBM-compatible BIOS as are COM and LPT ports. Instead, you need a recent-model computer with USB ports built in, USB support provided in the system BIOS, and the USB ports enabled in the system BIOS or an add-on card with USB ports plus drivers for your operating system.

Windows 95B OSR 2.1 and above feature a USB driver, but this will not work with all USB devices. For best results, use Windows 98, Windows Me, Windows 2000, or Windows XP, all of which feature integrated USB support. **Hot-swap** capabilities for USB were introduced with Windows 98 Second Edition (Win98SE).

USB 2.0 ports built into recent motherboards are handled as USB 1.1 ports unless USB 2.0 support is enabled in the system BIOS and USB 2.0 drivers are installed.

Adding Additional USB Ports

Need more USB ports? You can add additional USB ports with any of the following methods:

- Motherboard connectors for USB header cables
- Hubs
- Add-on cards

Some motherboards have **header cable** connectors, which enable you to add additional USB ports to the rear or front of the computer. Some motherboard vendors include these header cables with the motherboard, whereas others require you to purchase them separately. Some recent case designs also include front-mounted USB ports, which can also be connected to the motherboard. Because of vendor-specific differences in how motherboards implement header cables, the header cable might use separate connectors for each signal instead of the more common single connector for all signals.

USB generic hubs enable you to connect multiple devices to the same USB port and to increase the distance between the device and the USB port. There are two types of generic hubs:

- Bus-powered
- Self-powered

Bus-powered hubs are typically built into other devices. For example, monitors and USB keyboards often have bus-powered hubs. A bus-powered hub distributes both USB signals and power via the USB bus to other devices. Different USB devices use different amounts of power, and some devices require more power than others do. A bus-powered hub provides no more than 100 milliamps (mA) of power to each device connected to it. Thus, some devices fail when connected to a bus-powered hub.

A **self-powered hub**, on the other hand, has its own power source; it plugs into an AC wall outlet. It can provide up to 500mA of power to each device connected to it. A self-powered hub supports a wider range of USB devices, and I recommend using it instead of a bus-powered hub whenever possible.

Modems

Dial-up or analog modems, which enable computers to communicate with each other over telephone lines, derive their name from the process they perform. A **modem** sending data modulates digital computer data into analog data suitable for transmission over telephone lines to the receiving modem, which demodulates the analog data back into computer form. Modems share two characteristics with serial ports:

- Both use serial communication to send and receive information.
- Both often require adjustment of transmission speed and other options.

In fact, most external modems require a serial port to connect them to the computer; some external modems use the USB port instead.

Modems come in five types: add-on card, external, **PC Card**, motherboard-integrated, and **mini-PCI** card. Add-on card modems for desktop computers, such as the one shown in Figure 8.15, fit into an ISA or PCI expansion slot. External modems plug into a serial or USB port. PCMCIA (PC Card) modems are sometimes built in a combo design that also incorporates a 10/100 Ethernet network adapter. Many recent desktop computers have integrated modems, as do many notebook computers. However, some notebook computers that appear to have built-in modems actually use modems that use the mini-PCI form factor and can be removed and replaced with another unit.

⇨ To learn more about expansion slots, **see** "Recognizing Expansion Slot Types," **p. 108**. To learn more about mini-PCI cards, **see** "Mini-PCI Card Types and Usage," **p. 399**.

Although some high-end add-on card and PC Card modems have a hardware UART or UART-equivalent chip, most recent models use a programmable *digital signal processor (DSP)* instead. Modems with a DSP perform similarly to UART-based modems, but can easily be reprogrammed with firmware and driver updates as needed. Low-cost add-on card and PC Card modems often use *HSP (host signal processing)* instead of a UART or DSP. HSP modems are sometimes referred to as **Winmodems** or **soft modems** because Windows and the computer's processor perform the modulation, slowing down performance. HSP modems might not work with some older versions of Windows or non-Windows operating systems.

External modems, such as the one shown in Figure 8.16, must be connected to a serial or USB port. Serial port versions require an external power source (USB modems are usually powered by the USB port or hub), but the portability and front-panel status lights of either type of external modem make them better for business use in the minds of many users.

> **note**
>
> Properly used, the term *modem* refers only to a device that connects to the telephone line and performs digital-to-analog or analog-to-digital conversions. However, other types of Internet connections such as satellite, wireless, DSL, and cable Internet also use the term *modem*, although they work with purely digital data. When used by itself in this book, however, *modem* refers only to dial-up (telephone) modems.

FIGURE 8.15

A typical PCI **internal modem**. Note the two **RJ-11** connectors on the rear of the modem: They enable you to plug a phone into the modem so you can use the modem or your telephone.

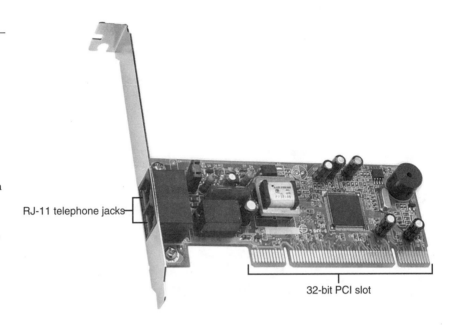

RJ-11 telephone jacks

32-bit PCI slot

Status/activity lights

FIGURE 8.16

A typical external modem that connects to a serial port. Note the reset switch, which enables the user to reset the modem without turning off the computer.

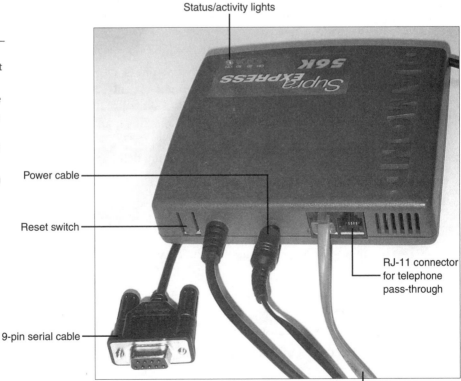

Power cable

Reset switch

9-pin serial cable

RJ-11 connector for telephone pass-through

RJ-11 telephone cable

A typical PC Card modem is shown in Figure 8.17. The modem pictured here uses a **dongle**, a proprietary cable that attaches to one end of the PC Card to enable the modem to plug into a standard telephone jack or telephone line. If the dongle is lost or damaged, the modem can't be used until the dongle is replaced. Some PC Card modems use an integrated or pop-out RJ-11 jack instead of a dongle. (It's one less thing to lose or break as you travel.)

➪ To learn more about PC Card modems, **see** "PC Card (PCMCIA Card) Types and Usage," **p. 395**.

FIGURE 8.17

A typical PC Card modem that uses a dongle (right). Many recent modems feature integrated or pop-out RJ-11 jacks instead of a dongle.

Most modems in use today are designed to run at speeds up to 56Kbps for downloading. However, these so-called **56K modems** are subject to two limitations: FCC regulations limit their top download speed to 53Kbps because of concerns about how much power must be run over the telephone line to reach 56Kbps, and speeds above 33.6Kbps apply only to downloads from *ISPs (Internet service providers)* and their special modems. If you make a direct connection between two PCs, the fastest speed you can have in either direction is just 33.6Kbps (if both modems can run at least that fast).

Modem Configuration and Setup

So, you want to use a dial-up modem. Here's what you need to do before you can use it:

1. The modem must be physically installed in your system or connected to your system.

2. The modem must be turned on (if external) and detected by the system.

3. The correct software drivers must be installed for the modem and operating system in use.

When you use a modem, you're actually creating a connection between your computer and a remote computer. Because serial ports and modems can be configured in many different ways, parameters such as connection speed, word length, and others must be set to match the remote computer's requirements (see "Serial Port Software Configuration" earlier in this chapter for details). If the two ends of the connection don't match, you get gibberish instead of useful information. The default settings for the modem or the serial port attached to an external modem can be overridden by communications software.

Modem Installation

The method used for physical installation of the modem varies with the modem type. To install a PCI or ISA modem

1. Take ESD precautions. (See Chapter 13, "Safety and Recycling," for details.)

2. Open the system and locate an empty slot of the appropriate type.

3. Remove the screw holding the slot cover in place.

4. Remove the slot cover.

5. Install the modem into the slot and fasten it into place with the screw previously used to secure the slot cover.

6. Connect an RJ-11 telephone cable running from the telephone jack in the wall to the line or telco jack on the modem. (Some modems can use either RJ-11 connection for the line connection.)

7. If desired, plug a telephone into the other jack.

8. Close the system and restart it.

9. Install drivers as required. See Chapter 19 for details on Windows modem driver installation and modem configuration.

caution

You can drive yourself crazy trying to make a connection with your modem if you plug the RJ-11 telephone cord into the wrong jack. There are actually three ways to make this mistake:

- Plugging the RJ-11 cord into the phone jack instead of the line or telco jack on the modem.

- Plugging the RJ-11 cord into the slightly larger RJ-45 jack used for 10/100 Ethernet networking.

- Plugging the RJ-11 cord into a HomePNA network card (which also has two RJ-11 jacks) instead of the modem. If you use the HomePNA network, check the network documentation for the correct way to connect your network card and your modem to the telephone line.

To install a PC Card modem

1. Slide the PC Card modem into an empty PC Card slot of the appropriate type (Type II or Type III; see Chapter 12, "Portables," for details).

2. After the operating system indicates the modem has been detected, attach the **dongle** (if appropriate).

3. If the dongle has an RJ-11 plug, connect it to the telephone wall jack.

4. For modems with a pop-out RJ-11 jack, release the jack.

5. Connect an RJ-11 telephone cable between the RJ-11 connector on the PC Card or dongle and the wall jack.

6. Install drivers as required.

To install an external modem

1. Connect the modem to a USB or serial port as appropriate.

2. Connect the modem to AC power and turn it on (if necessary).

3. If the modem is not detected automatically, use the operating system's Modem dialog to detect the modem and install its drivers.

See Chapter 12 for more information about mini-PCI modems.

Standard AT Commands

After you have completed the modem installation and Windows configuration process, you can use either communications software programs included with Windows, such as HyperTerminal, or third-party programs to operate the modem. Communications software uses AT **commands** to operate modems and change their default configuration.

AT stands for *attention*, and the options that follow AT instruct the modem to perform particular operations. These commands were originally created for use with Hayes modems; because most modems use the standard Hayes command set, most of these commands will work with most modems (thus the term, *Hayes Compatible*). Check your modem's documentation for additions and exceptions to this list.

Table 8.7 lists the most important AT commands.

By using a communication program (such as Windows Terminal or HyperTerminal) that enables you to send these commands to the modem, you can learn more about the modem's condition, and be able to troubleshoot problems. The same commands are used by communication software to control the operation of modems.

Table 8.7   Standard AT Commands Used for Modem Control

AT Command	Meaning	Example
ATDT	Tone-dial the telephone number that follows	ATDT5551212
ATDP	Pulse-dial the telephone number that follows	ATDP5551212
+++	Escape sequence: enables you to send the modem a command after you're connected to another modem	+++
ATH	Hangs up the modem	ATH
ATZ	Resets the modem to the configuration referred to by the following number	ATZ0

AT commands can also be used to set the modem's volume, adjust additional dialing options, and perform various diagnostic tests.

S-Registers

AT commands can also be used to view or set **S-registers**, which are used to store or adjust timing and other technical details.

To see the current settings for S-registers and other settings stored in your modem, use this command within your terminal program:

AT

Followed by

AT&V

The information displayed by the AT&V command (see Figure 8.18) will vary from modem to modem. You can alter the values that your modem displays for S-registers and other settings by sending your modem the appropriate AT commands if needed.

Initialization Strings

An **initialization string** is a series of AT& modem commands sent to the modem by the communications program before dialing the number and connecting with the remote computer. AT& commands are used to set special modem options. Normally, you will not need to edit this directly; instead, by selecting the modem and the desired options in the communications program, the program will build the initialization string for you. A typical initialization string for a U.S. Robotics modem is

AT&F&C1&D2X7&H1&R2&K3&B1&A3^M

You can manually edit the initialization string within most communications programs if the settings are incorrect for your modem. See the modem's documentation for the specific AT& commands that apply to that model.

FIGURE 8.18

Using
HyperTerminal
to view the cur-
rent settings for
the author's
Diamond
SupraExpress
external modem
with the AT&V
command.

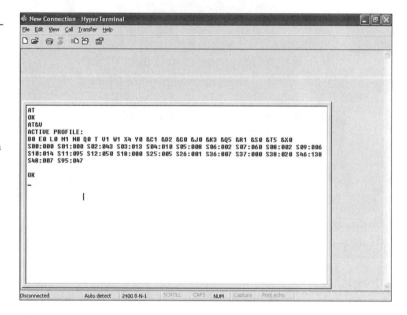

Disabling Call Waiting

Call waiting, which lets you know that you have another incoming call while you're on the telephone, is a great boon when you're expecting a call, but the momentary interruption of your existing call will cause many modems to drop the connection. Consequently, it's an excellent idea to disable call waiting when you use your dial-up modem.

To disable call waiting in most areas, add *70,, to the beginning of the telephone number you use to make your connection. *70 is the code to disable call waiting, and each comma pauses for one second. The momentary pause helps make certain the phone company has implemented the change before you continue with the phone number.

As soon as you hang up the connection, call waiting is activated again automatically.

Cabling

The RJ-11 cable included with most modems could be any of a variety of colors, but it is identical internally to the "silver satin" cable that connects telephones to wall jacks. Run the cable from the "line" jack on the back of the modem to the telephone wall jack.

The "phone" jack on the back of both internal and external modems enables you to plug in your normal telephone and still use it, whether the computer is on or off. The modem will take over the telephone line when it actually is in use.

The RJ-11 plug is keyed to connect only one way. Push down on the locking tab lever on the plug to release it when you need to remove the cable from either the modem or the wall jack. The RJ-11 plug is similar to the **RJ-45** Ethernet network plug, but smaller; it has four connectors, as opposed to the RJ-45 cable's eight (see Figure 8.19).

External modems might use built-in or removable cables to connect to the serial or USB port on the computer.

caution

When you travel, make sure you don't connect your modem to an RJ-11 jack designed for digital phones. The difference in voltage will fry most modems. Look for a data jack in the side of the phone in your hotel or conference room, or contact the front desk for help.

FIGURE 8.19

An RJ-45 network cable (top) compared to an RJ-11 telephone cable (bottom).

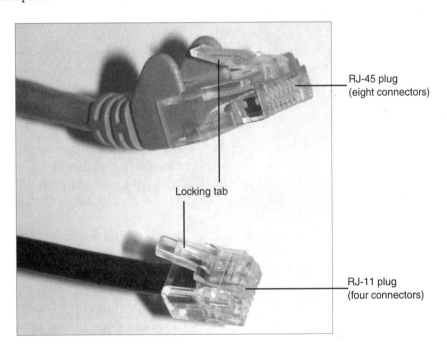

RJ-45 plug
(eight connectors)

Locking tab

RJ-11 plug
(four connectors)

Keyboards

The keyboard remains the primary method used to send commands to the computer and enter data. You can even use it to maneuver around the Windows Desktop if your mouse or other pointing device stops working.

Keyboards can be connected through dedicated keyboard connectors or through the USB port. Extremely old systems use the **5-pin DIN** connector, whereas newer systems use the **6-pin mini-DIN** connector (also called the PS/2 keyboard connector). Both are shown in Figure 8.20.

FIGURE 8.20

Typical 6-pin mini-DIN (left) and 5-pin DIN (right) keyboard connectors.

Both types of keyboards can be interchanged if they are built for IBM AT-type computers or newer by using adapters to change the pinouts and connector.

Some recent systems use the USB port for the keyboard, and any system with USB ports can be equipped with a USB keyboard if the system BIOS supports **USB Legacy mode** and if the system runs an operating system that supports USB ports (Windows 98 or greater).

Installation and Replacement

To install the keyboard using a DIN or mini-DIN jack, turn off the power and insert the connector end of the keyboard cable into the keyboard connector (usually on the back of the computer). No special drivers are required unless the keyboard has special keys, a programmable feature, or is a wireless model that uses a receiver. Note that systems with a PS/2 keyboard port usually also have a PS/2 mouse port. Be sure to use the PS/2 keyboard port. To remove the keyboard, turn off the power before removing the connector end of the keyboard cable from the keyboard connector.

To install a USB keyboard, enable USB Legacy mode in the system BIOS (see Chapter 6, "BIOS and CMOS Configuration," for details); then plug the keyboard into a USB port built into the computer, or into a USB hub plugged into a USB port built into the computer. With Windows 98 Second Edition and newer versions of Windows, the keyboard can be plugged and unplugged as desired without shutting down the system. Note that some USB keyboards include an adapter that enables them to connect to PS/2 keyboard ports (refer to Figure 8.22). USB keyboards are part of the *HID (human interface device)* device category, and Windows installs HID drivers after the keyboard is connected. Have your Windows CD handy to provide the needed drivers.

Figure 8.21 shows the typical location and appearance of these ports on a recent ATX desktop system.

PS/2 mouse port

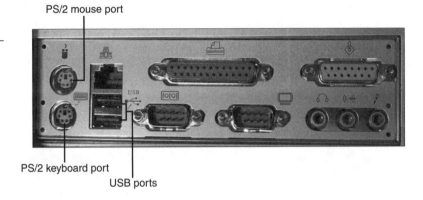

FIGURE 8.21

PS/2 keyboard and USB ports on the rear of a typical system with an ATX-type mother-board.

PS/2 keyboard port

USB ports

Mouse and Pointing Devices

Next to the keyboard, the mouse is the most important device used to send commands to the computer. For Windows users who don't perform data entry, the mouse is even more important than the keyboard. Mouse alternatives, such as trackballs or touchpads, are considered mouse devices because they install and are configured the same way.

Three major interface types are used for mouse devices on systems built since the mid-1990s:

- Serial
- 6-pin mini-DIN (PS/2)
- USB

Most mouse devices supplied with older systems use the PS/2 mouse connector, whereas most recent mouse devices supplied with systems or sold at retail use the USB connector. Older PS/2 mouse devices purchased at retail stores often included a serial connector so the mouse could be used with a serial or PS/2 mouse port. Recent mouse devices purchased at retail are usually designed for the USB port but usually include a PS/2 mouse port adapter.

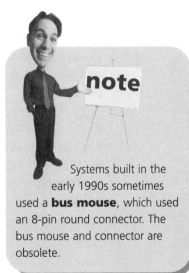

note

Systems built in the early 1990s sometimes used a **bus mouse**, which used an 8-pin round connector. The bus mouse and connector are obsolete.

Figure 8.22 shows typical keyboard and mouse adapters that can be used to convert serial port and USB mouse devices and keyboards to the PS/2 mouse or keyboard ports.

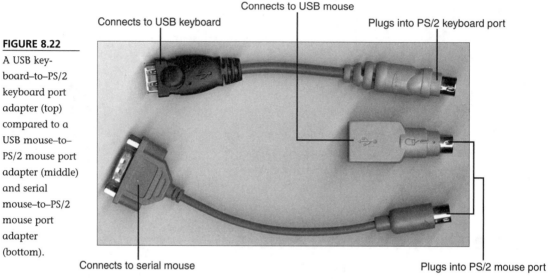

FIGURE 8.22

A USB keyboard–to–PS/2 keyboard port adapter (top) compared to a USB mouse–to–PS/2 mouse port adapter (middle) and serial mouse–to–PS/2 mouse port adapter (bottom).

Connects to USB mouse

Connects to USB keyboard

Plugs into PS/2 keyboard port

Connects to serial mouse

Plugs into PS/2 mouse port

Note that adapters cannot be used successfully unless the mouse (or keyboard) is designed to use an adapter. A mouse designed to use an adapter is sometimes called a **hybrid mouse**.

Installing and Replacing Mouse Devices

The physical installation of a serial or PS/2 mouse is extremely simple. Turn off the computer and plug the mouse into the appropriate connector. Then, restart the computer. That's it!

Unlike keyboards, mouse devices require software drivers. Although many mouse devices today emulate or act like the Microsoft mouse, some require different software drivers. Mouse devices with wheels or toggles for screen scrolling should be installed with the drivers included with the mouse devices, because standard drivers might not support the scrolling feature or additional buttons.

To install a USB mouse, plug it into any USB port on a system running Windows 98 or newer versions. Install any software drivers required.

Mouse Configuration

A serial mouse uses the IRQ and I/O port address of the serial port to which it is connected.

A PS/2 mouse uses IRQ 12; if IRQ 12 is not available, the device using that IRQ must be moved to another IRQ to enable IRQ 12 to be used by the mouse.

A USB mouse uses the IRQ and I/O port address of the USB port to which it is connected. Because a single USB port can support up to 127 devices through the use of hubs, a USB mouse doesn't tie up hardware resources the way other mouse types do.

Mouse Software Installation

The MS-DOS mouse drivers need to be used only if mouse-compatible utility or recreational software that cannot run under Windows will be used on a Windows 9x system (Windows 2000/XP versions can emulate the DOS mouse driver within a DOS session). To install MS-DOS drivers

1. Copy the Mouse.com or Mouse.sys driver from the mouse setup software disk to a folder called \Mouse on the hard drive (C:).

2. Edit the autoexec.bat file and add an entry c:\Mouse\Mouse.com to start the mouse driver during the boot process.

   or

   If the mouse does not have a Mouse.com driver, you can add an entry to the Config.sys file instead to start the mouse during the boot process:
   DEVICE=C:\Mouse\Mouse.sys

For Windows 9x and later versions

1. Open the Control Panel icon.

2. Open the Mouse icon.

3. Select the General tab.

4. Click the Change button.

5. Select the new mouse from the list, or click Have Disk if your mouse isn't listed.

6. Insert the Windows CD-ROM or vendor-supplied driver disk or CD-ROM, or use Browse to indicate its location.

7. Click Finish when the process is completed.

Most mouse devices are configured by software. The most common hardware option is a sliding switch on the bottom of some three-button mouse devices that can be used to select either native mode or Microsoft Mouse Emulation mode, which disables the middle button.

Software configuration allows more options, including

- Switching of left and right mouse buttons
- Speed of mouse pointer movement
- Acceleration factors
- Double-click speed

Third-party mouse driver software for mouse devices with additional buttons or scroll wheels usually has additional configuration options. USB mouse devices or pointing devices are part of the HID category, so Windows installs HID drivers after the USB mouse or pointing device is connected to the system and detected.

With Windows 9x and above, these options are configured through the Mouse icon in the Control Panel.

Mouse Maintenance

There are two types of motion sensors used by typical mouse devices (see Figure 8.23):

- Mechanical/opto-mechanical (ball and rollers)
- Optical

FIGURE 8.23
A mechanical mouse (left) with the retaining ring and ball removed for cleaning compared to an **optical mouse** (right).

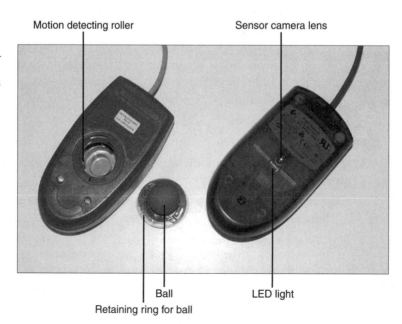

Motion detecting roller   Sensor camera lens

Ball

Retaining ring for ball

LED light

The motion of the mouse ball against a mouse pad, desk, or tabletop can pick up dust and dirt that can cause erratic mouse-pointer movement. The ball and the rollers should be cleaned periodically. Clean the mouse with a specially designed mouse cleaning kit or use a nonabrasive damp cloth to remove gunk from the rollers and the ball.

To remove the mouse ball (as shown in Figure 8.23) for access to the rollers

1. Turn over the mouse; an access cover on the bottom of the mouse holds the ball in place.

2. Follow the arrows on the access cover to turn or slide the cover to one side; lift the plate out of the way to release the ball (refer to Figure 8.23).

3. Turn the rollers until you see dirt or grit; wipe them clean and clean the ball.

4. Shake loose dust and gunk out of the mouse.

5. When the cleaning process is finished, replace the ball and access panel.

Mouse devices that lack a ball normally have optical sensors that pick up movement. Keep the sensors clear of dust and debris and the mouse will work properly; no disassembly is required.

Trackballs can also become dirty. Remove the trackball and clean the rollers to keep the trackball working properly.

Touchpads should be periodically wiped with a dampened cloth to remove skin oils that can prevent proper sensing of finger movements.

Audio Hardware and Sound Cards

With the increase of multimedia applications for PCs, many systems now feature integrated audio hardware. Sound cards with greater 3D audio performance and more options remain popular upgrades. Sound cards can be used for the following tasks:

- Digital conversion of prerecorded audio
- Playback of CD-ROM or Web-based audio content
- Recording of sounds or speech
- Voice control and dictation
- Text-to-speech (computer "reads" text)

Sound cards and systems with **integrated audio** have distinctive internal and external features, as you will see in the following sections.

External Features

Systems with integrated audio have two or three jacks for speakers, microphone, and headset or auxiliary output. Some also feature a 15-pin **game port** (see Figure 8.24). The game port can also be converted to a MIDI port (used for connecting to a MIDI synthesizer) with an optional adapter.

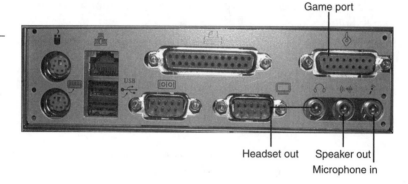

FIGURE 8.24

Game port and audio jacks on the rear of a typical ATX system with integrated audio. Similar connectors can be found on most sound cards.

Low-end sound cards typically have similar connectors. More advanced sound cards as well as better-integrated audio solutions also feature digital output through the **S/PDIF** connector, and some also integrate IEEE-1394a ports for direct connection to digital media sources such as DV camcorders (see Figure 8.25).

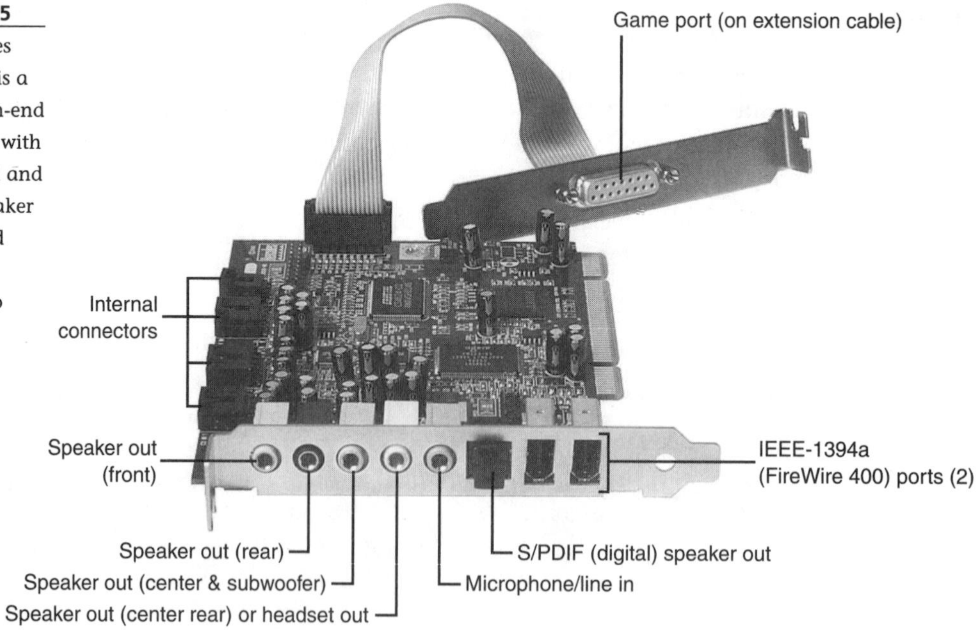

FIGURE 8.25

The Hercules Digifire 71 is a typical high-end sound card with both digital and analog speaker outputs and IEEE-1394a ports. Photo courtesy Hercules.

Game port (on extension cable)

Internal connectors

Speaker out (front)

IEEE-1394a (FireWire 400) ports (2)

Speaker out (rear)

Speaker out (center & subwoofer)

Speaker out (center rear) or headset out

S/PDIF (digital) speaker out

Microphone/line in

Internal Sound Card Features

All sound cards have at least one four-wire internal jack to enable music CDs to be played through the sound card's speakers. Most recent models also feature a two-wire digital audio jack for pure digital CD playback and for fast conversion of digital CD audio into compressed audio files such as MP3 or WMA (a process called **ripping**). Most motherboards with integrated audio have the analog jack, and some also have a digital jack. Figure 8.26 provides a typical example.

Sound cards that feature FM synthesis for MIDI files might also have a connector for a wavetable daughtercard. Some very old ISA sound cards might also feature proprietary or IDE CD-ROM data cable connectors.

Types of Sound Hardware

Sound cards can be installed into the expansion slots of a computer (ISA or PCI), or the equivalent sound circuits can be integrated into the motherboard. Both slot-mounted and integrated sound circuits will be referred to as *sound cards* in this section, except as noted.

Sound cards differ in their capability to handle different forms of audio content. All sound cards can play back digitized sound, but they differ in the quality of sound they can record and play back and in how they play MIDI musical scores:

> **tip**
>
> Most recent sound cards and motherboards use the PC99 color-coding standards for built-in and add-on ports. Although most port types have distinctive shapes and sizes, analog audio jacks are all the same size! Use this guide to keep from plugging stuff into the wrong jacks:
>
> | Port | Color Coding |
> |------|------|
> | Audio line in | Lt. blue |
> | Audio line out | Lime |
> | Microphone | Pink |
> | MIDI/Game port | Gold |
> | Speaker out/Subwoofer | Orange |
> | Right-to-left speaker | Brown |
>
> Get the full story for all port types along with color samples at `http://www.pcdesguide.org/documents/pc99icons.htm`.

- 8-bit sound cards cannot record or play back high-quality sound, but are long obsolete and rare. These old sound cards use only a single-edge connector for the 8-bit portion of the ISA slot.

- 16-bit or better sound cards can record and play back high-quality sound (44 kilohertz [KHz] or higher sampling rate). These cards are 16-bit ISA on older systems or PCI (32-bit) on newer systems.

- **FM synthesis** cards must create artificial versions of musical instruments to play **MIDI** scores. MIDI scores played on this type of sound card have poor musical quality.

FIGURE 8.26

Analog (left) and digital (right) connections between optical drives and a typical sound card. The TAD jack on the sound card can be used to connect a modem with a telephone answering device (TAD) feature, and the AUX_IN jack enables a second optical drive to be connected to the sound card with a four-wire analog audio cable.

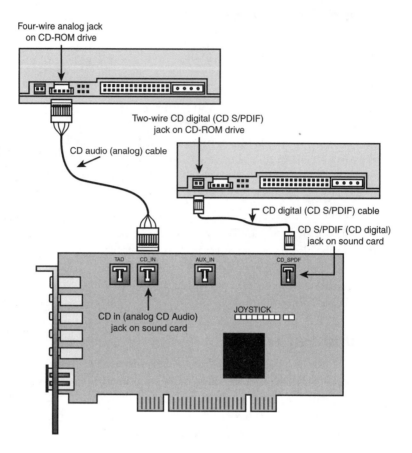

- **Wavetable** cards use actual samples from real musical instruments to play MIDI scores. Some older cards used onboard modules to store audio samples, but most recent cards use system memory for this purpose.

Most recent sound cards use wavetable synthesis.

Physical Installation and Replacement

Sound cards that use jumper blocks for configuration should be set before installation into the system. However, most recent sound cards are configured with software or by Windows 95/98/2000/XP's Plug and Play technology.

Because the sound quality of sound cards can be affected by interference, the best results are obtained if you can install the sound card into a slot that is one slot away from other cards and as far away from the power supply as possible.

Follow this basic procedure to install a sound card:

1. If the system already has onboard sound, disable it to prevent conflicts. Typically, you'll need to restart the system and take a quick trip through the system BIOS setup screens. On some systems, there's only one setting along the lines of Integrated Sound or Integrated Audio to disable. Others might require you to disable several settings, such as in the example in Figure 8.27. Save the changes in the system BIOS and restart the computer.

FIGURE 8.27

A BIOS setup screen from a typical system with onboard audio. You can leave the game port enabled on this system if you need it and the new sound card doesn't have one.

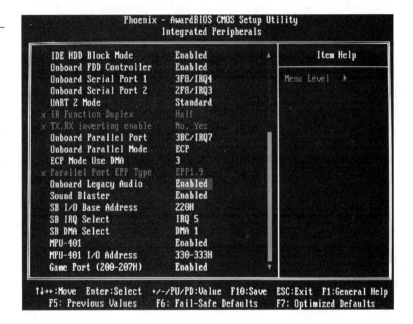

2. If the system has a built-in sound card, open the System Properties sheet's Device Manager and remove references to the sound card (see Figure 8.28). Then, shut down the system and remove the card after you disconnect the cables.

3. Install the new card in an empty slot. If you are upgrading to a better PCI sound card, you can use the same slot. If you are replacing an ISA with a PCI card, you need to use a PCI slot.

tip

As you disconnect cables from the old card, mark them if they are not color coded or if the colors of the new card's jacks don't match the colors used on the original cables.

4. Connect optical drives to the jacks on the inside of the card. Most optical drives include the four-wire audio cable illustrated in Figure 8.26, but you might need to buy a two-wire audio cable from an electronics or computer store if you prefer all-digital sound.

5.   Connect speakers and microphone to the jacks on the rear of the card.

6.   Restart the system and install drivers as needed. You might need the Windows CD (or determine where the .CAB archive files for Windows drivers are located) to install support for some sound card features.

Default Sound Card Hardware Configuration

The default configuration of sound cards differs depending on whether the sound card will be used for MS-DOS programs or for Windows programs. A Plug and Play sound card running under Windows will use any available resources. However, if the card will be used for MS-DOS programs, the card needs to emulate the Creative Labs **Sound Blaster** Plus or Sound Blaster 16 and use the same settings these cards used.

To perform Sound Blaster (SB) emulation, some older sound cards used a special four-wire PC/PCI cable that attached to the motherboard. However, most recent sound cards include a special program that must be run before an MS-DOS program requiring sound can be used in Windows 9x. Windows XP provides built-in SB support for MS-DOS and older Windows programs.

If you need to manually configure a sound card to use the same settings as a Sound Blaster card, use the settings shown in Table 8.8. Note that PCI sound cards emulate DMA settings and can share IRQs, but any ISA sound cards you might still encounter use actual DMA channels and non-shareable IRQs that can conflict with other ISA or PCI devices.

The configuration listed in Table 8.8 is based on the defaults used by the Creative Labs Sound Blaster AWE64 Gold card. Most other brands of sound cards use similar settings.

note

Note also that third-party sound cards might use two sets of settings: a native set and an SB-compatible set. These sound cards thus consume even more hardware resources than those shown in Table 8.8.

Table 8.8   Standard and Optional Hardware Settings for Creative Labs Sound Blaster AWE64 Gold (Options for Some Settings in Parentheses)

Feature	IRQ	DMA 8-Bit	DMA 16-Bit	Starting I/O Port Address
Audio	5 (2,7,10)	1 (0,3)	5 (6,7)	220h (240h, 260h, 280h)
FM synthesis	N/A	N/A	N/A	388h
Joystick port	N/A	N/A	N/A	200h

Table 8.8 (continued)

Feature	IRQ	DMA 8-Bit	DMA 16-Bit	Starting I/O Port Address
MPU-401 (MIDI) standard	N/A	N/A	N/A	330h (300h)
Wave synthesis (select one)	N/A	N/A	N/A	6x0, Ax0, Ex0 (x=0-9,a-f)

This card uses one IRQ, two DMA, and up to *five* different I/O port addresses.

With some cards, you can use the Windows Device Manager to select some "stripped-down" configurations that omit certain features.

Because sound cards are resource hungry, the sound card should be the first add-on card installed in any system.

As Table 8.8 indicates, sound cards have multiple hardware devices onboard. Figure 8.28 shows that the Windows Device Manager displays each hardware component in a sound card as a separate device.

FIGURE 8.28

A sound card's resources might be listed under multiple headings, as seen here: The ENSONIQ AudioPCI, ENSONIQ AudioPCI Legacy Device (for Sound Blaster emulation), and Gameport Joystick are all part of a single sound card.

Sound cards used with MS-DOS (or with the MS-DOS mode of Windows 9x) need

- The appropriate sound card driver to be installed in **Config.sys**.

- A SET statement in Autoexec.bat indicating card type and settings. In Figure 8.29, an actual SET statement used with a wavetable Sound Blaster card is listed, along with a key.

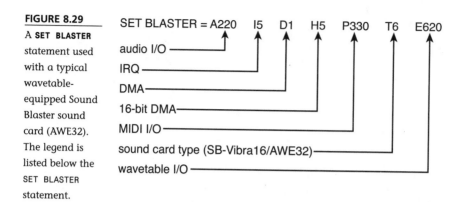

Some third-party ISA sound cards use two different SET statements (one for native mode, and one for SB-compatible mode). These cards might use even more resources than those shown in Figure 8.29.

IEEE-1394 (FireWire)

IEEE-1394 is a family of high-speed bidirectional serial transmission ports that can connect PCs to each other, digital devices to PCs, or digital devices to each other.

The most common version of IEEE-1394 is known as IEEE-1394a, and is also known as **FireWire** 400. Sony's version is known as **i.LINK**. At 400Mbps, IEEE-1394a is one of the fastest and most flexible ports used on personal computers. IEEE-1394a can be implemented either as a built-in port on the motherboard or as part of an add-on card (see Figure 8.30).

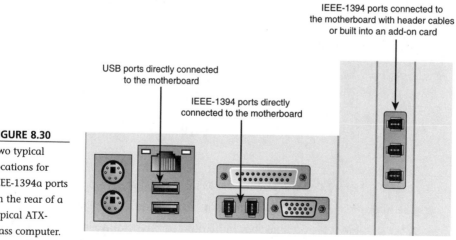

Some IEEE-1394a add-on cards also provide an internal port for the growing number of internal IEEE-1394 devices.

A faster version of the IEEE-1394 standard, IEEE-1394b, was introduced in early 2003. Also known as FireWire 800, 1394b ports and devices transfer data at 800Mbps. Future versions will reach higher speeds.

IEEE-1394 Ports and Cables

Standard IEEE-1394a ports and cables use a 6-pin interface (four pins for data, two for power), but some digital camcorders and all i.LINK ports use the alternative 4-pin interface, which supplies data and signals but no power to the device. Six-wire to four-wire cables enable these devices to communicate with each other.

> **note**
>
> A growing number of high-end sound cards (such as the one shown in Figure 8.25) also feature IEEE-1394a ports. If you're in the market for a high-end sound card, choosing a sound card with a built-in IEEE-1394a port could let one card do the work of two.

IEEE-1394b ports use a 9-pin interface. There are two versions of the IEEE-1394b port: The Beta port and cable are used only for 1394b-to-1394b connections, whereas the Bilingual cable and port are used for 1394b-to-1394a or 1394b-to-1394b connections. Beta cables and ports have a wide notch at the top of the cable and port, whereas Bilingual cables and ports have a narrow notch at the 1394b end, and use either the 4-pin or 6-pin 1394a connection at the other end of the cable. All four cable types are shown in Figure 8.31.

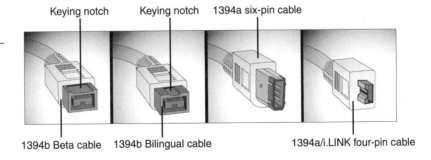

Keying notch   Keying notch   1394a six-pin cable

1394b Beta cable   1394b Bilingual cable   1394a/i.LINK four-pin cable

FIGURE 8.31
1394b and 1394a cable connectors compared.

IEEE-1394–Compatible Devices and Technical Requirements

IEEE-1394–compatible devices include internal and external hard drives, digital camcorders (also referred to as DV camcorders), Web cameras, MP3 players (such as Apple's iPod) and high-performance scanners and printers, as well as hubs, repeaters, and SCSI to IEEE-1394 converters. IEEE-1394 ports support hot-swapping, enabling you to add or remove a device from an IEEE-1394 port without shutting down the system. 1394 ports can also be used for networking.

Up to 16 IEEE-1394 devices can be connected to a single IEEE-1394 port through daisy-chaining. Most external IEEE-1394 devices have two ports to enable daisy-chaining.

Windows 98/Me/2000/XP all include IEEE-1394 support; Windows 95 and Windows NT 4.0 and earlier NT versions do not. IEEE-1394 cards are PCI-based and require the following hardware resources:

■ One IRQ (it can be shared on systems that support IRQ sharing by PCI devices)

■ One memory address range (must be unique)

The exact IRQ and memory address range used by a particular IEEE-1394 card can be determined by using the Windows Device Manager. When an IEEE-1394 card is installed, a device category called 1394 Bus Controller is added to the Device Manager, and the particular card installed is listed beneath that category.

Installing an IEEE-1394 Card

To install and configure the card

1. Turn off the computer and remove the case cover.

2. Locate an available PCI expansion slot.

3. Remove the slot cover and insert the card into the slot. Secure the card in the slot.

4. Some IEEE-1394 cards are powered by the PCI expansion slot, whereas others require a 4-pin connector used by hard drives or floppy drives for power. Connect a power lead if the card requires it; you can use a Y-splitter to free up a power lead if necessary (see Figure 8.32).

5. Close up the system, restart it, and provide the driver disk or CD-ROM when requested by the system.

6. The IRQ and memory address required by the card will be assigned automatically.

1394a six-pin connector

FIGURE 8.32
A typical IEEE-1394a card after installation. This card requires a four-wire power cable and also includes an internal port.

4-wire Molex power cable

Study Lab

Don't miss the Study Lab materials found on the CD accompanying this book. Each Study Lab is tailored to the individual chapters in this book, meaning that you'll quickly be able to determine which topics you understand well enough to pass the exam and which topics need more study. The Study Labs are presented in printable PDF format so that you can take them with you to study at work, on the road, or even in your car just before test time!

THE ABSOLUTE MINIMUM

Use this section for a quick review of the high points of the chapter right before you take your exams.

- The major I/O ports and devices used in computers include the serial and parallel ports, USB and IEEE-1394 ports, mouse devices, modems, keyboards, and sound cards.

- Legacy I/O devices such as serial and parallel ports offer many configuration options, including choices of IRQ, I/O port address, DMA channel, and other options.

- Newer I/O ports such as USB and IEE-1394 are PnP, so they can use any open resources, and can share IRQs with other PCI devices.

- Parallel ports generally are used for printers, but they also can be used for high-capacity removable storage and scanners.

- Serial ports generally are used for mouse devices on older systems and external modems.

- Both parallel and serial ports can be used for direct-connect data transfer.

- USB ports can be used for a wide variety of devices.

- Serial, parallel, and USB ports are generally built into the motherboards of recent systems and can be retrofitted to older systems.

- Keyboard ports can be either 5-pin DIN or the same 6-pin mini-DIN connector used for PS/2 mouse devices, although keyboard and mouse ports cannot be interchanged.

- USB mouse devices and keyboards can be adapted to PS/2 ports with adapters, if so equipped from the factory.

- USB 1.1 and USB 2.0 use the same connectors, but USB 2.0 is much faster (480Mbps versus 12Mbps).

- USB Legacy mode enables USB keyboards to work outside of the Windows GUI.

- Sound chipsets are included on some motherboards.

- PCI sound cards can emulate Sound Blaster cards when necessary.

- Some sound cards and motherboards support digital audio.

- IEEE-1394 ports are almost always added to systems through PCI cards.

- FireWire 400 is another name for IEEE-1394a; it runs at 400Mbps.

- FireWire 800 is another name for IEEE-1394b; it runs at 800Mbps.

- i.LINK is the Sony version of FireWire 400/IEEE-1394a.

- You can enable, disable, or adjust the configuration of both legacy and newer ports built into the motherboard through the system BIOS setup program.

- PnP ports and I/O devices generally request device driver and configuration software when the system is turned on for the first time after the device is installed.

9

VIDEO

The monitor and video card work together to provide real-time notification of the computer's activities to the user. Because you might spend all day (and sometimes all night) gazing into the display, keeping it working to full efficiency is important. This chapter helps you prepare for the A+ Certification Exam by enhancing your understanding of the major types of video cards and displays and showing you how to configure and troubleshoot them.

The Video Card and Monitor

The video card (also known as the **graphics card** or graphics accelerator card) is an add-on card (or circuit on the motherboard of portable computers and some desktop computers) that creates the image you see on the monitor. No video card, no picture!

Video cards have been built using all the major expansion card types covered in Chapter 4, "The Motherboard and CPU," including

- **ISA** (16-bit and 8-bit)
- **EISA**
- **VL-Bus**
- **PCI**
- **AGP**

Don't worry about ISA, EISA, or VL-Bus except to know what these terms mean: Pentium-class and newer systems almost always use either the PCI bus or the AGP bus for add-on cards. However, if your computer is a low-end desktop or a portable, it probably includes chipset-integrated PCI-equivalent or AGP-equivalent video instead of a video card.

➪ For more information about these expansion slot standards, **see** "Recognizing Expansion Slot Types," **p. 108**.

From 1994 to 1997, the most common type of expansion slot used for video cards was PCI. Although PCI is still the leading general-purpose expansion slot type, the advent of the Pentium II CPU led to the development of the AGP expansion slot, which, unlike PCI or the obsolete VL-Bus, is dedicated solely to high-speed video.

Virtually all recent systems that don't have integrated video use AGP cards and some recent systems with integrated video also have AGP slots for future expansion. AGP is the way to go if you're

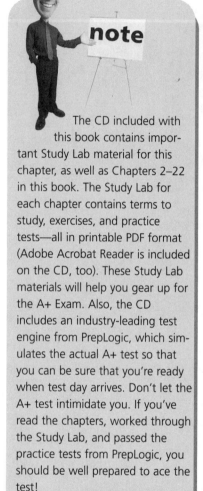

note

The CD included with this book contains important Study Lab material for this chapter, as well as Chapters 2–22 in this book. The Study Lab for each chapter contains terms to study, exercises, and practice tests—all in printable PDF format (Adobe Acrobat Reader is included on the CD, too). These Study Lab materials will help you gear up for the A+ Exam. Also, the CD includes an industry-leading test engine from PrepLogic, which simulates the actual A+ test so that you can be sure that you're ready when test day arrives. Don't let the A+ test intimidate you. If you've read the chapters, worked through the Study Lab, and passed the practice tests from PrepLogic, you should be well prepared to ace the test!

Also, you'll notice that some words throughout each chapter are in bold format. These are study terms that are defined in the Study Lab. Be sure to consult the Study Lab when you are finished with this chapter to test what you've learned.

not satisfied with the performance or features of your integrated video. Figure 9.1 compares AGP and PCI video cards, and Figure 9.2 compares AGP and PCI expansion slots.

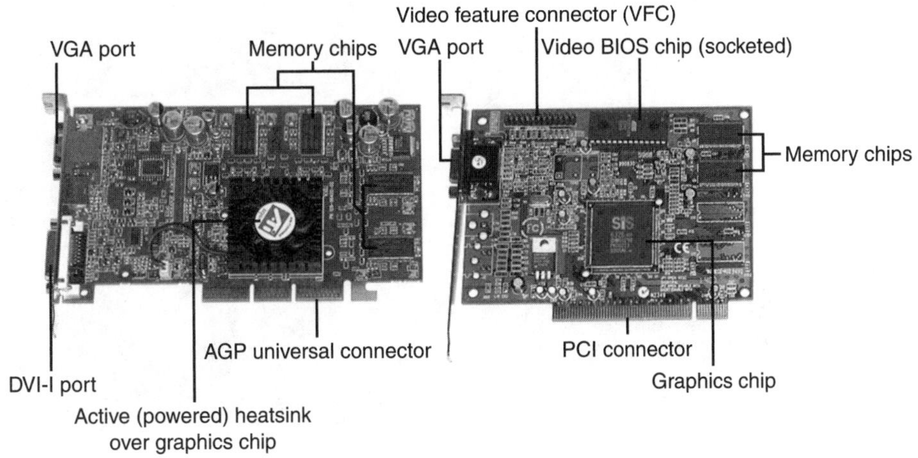

FIGURE 9.1

A typical AGP 4x video card (left) compared to a typical PCI video card (right).

Did you know that there are four major versions of the AGP slot? Three of them are shown in Figure 9.2:

- AGP 3.3 Volt (V) (supports AGP 1x and 2x cards)

- AGP 1.5V (supports AGP 4x and 8x cards); AGP 8x cards actually require only 0.8V, but work in 1.5V slots

- **AGP Universal** (supports AGP 1x through 8x cards); looks like the AGP Pro slot without the extra AGP Pro section (not shown in Figure 9.2)

- **AGP Pro** (supports AGP 3.3V and 1.5V as well as AGP Pro; AGP Pro cards use the additional connector for added voltage)

Note in Figure 9.2 the reversed keying in the 3.3V and 1.5V slots to prevent the wrong type of AGP card from being inserted into the slot. AGP Pro and AGP Universal slots can use both types of cards. Also, most recent 1.5V AGP cards, such as the ATI Radeon 9000 Pro card shown in Figure 9.1, are designed with two cutouts in the slot connector so they can be used in either a 1.5V or 3.3V slot. These cards also have onboard voltage regulators to adjust slot voltage to the card's requirements.

caution

Note that some 3.3V AGP cards also have connectors with two cutouts but aren't designed to fit safely into a 1.5V slot. They can damage newer motherboards. Check compatibility before you install a 3.3V AGP card into a recent motherboard, or you might be sorry!

Keyed AGP 1.5 volt slot (prevents
3.3V cards from being inserted)

Keyed AGP 3.3 volt slot (prevents 1.5V cards from being inserted)

FIGURE 9.2

AGP 3.3V, AGP
Pro, and AGP
1.5V slots com-
pared to a PCI
slot.

Cover over AGP Pro-only section
of AGP Pro slot (prevents non-Pro cards
from being damaged by incorrect insertion)

PCI slot

Understanding the Video Card Accelerator Chip and Video BIOS Chip

All video cards except for the original 1981-vintage IBM *MDA* (*monochrome display adapter*; no pictures, just text) have used a video BIOS chip, which occupies a portion of the upper memory addresses between 640KB (kilobytes) and 1MB (megabyte). The video BIOS chip on **VGA** systems provides the basic VGA features used when your system starts up in text mode and in Windows 9x/Me **Safe Mode** and Windows 2000/XP **VGA Mode**.

The video accelerator chip provides support for higher **resolutions** and color depths along with special acceleration and 3D features. This part of the video card must be enabled by software drivers written for that particular video chipset. Ninety-nine percent of the time, this is how you use your display, which is why installing the right drivers is very important.

Monitor and Connector Types

Regardless of bus type, video cards are primarily distinguished from each other by the type of signal they produce and the type of monitor that must be used with each type of signal.

Almost all **CRT** monitors (monitors with glass picture tubes similar to televisions) have used VGA or developments of VGA since 1989, whereas **LCD** displays can use VGA or one of two high-resolution digital standards (DFP or DVI), which emulate VGA. See the following sections for details.

VGA and Analog Displays

Virtually all systems built from 1989 on have used analog displays based on the VGA (Video Graphics Array) standard developed by IBM in 1987 for its then-new PS/2 line of computers. (They replaced early digital displays that supported monochrome or no more than 16 colors.)

Unlike the monochrome or color digital displays replaced by VGA, an analog display is capable of displaying an unlimited number of colors by varying the levels of red, green, or blue per dot (pixel) onscreen. Practical color limits (if you call over 16 million colors limiting) are based on the video card's memory and the desired screen resolution.

Most analog displays are CRT (cathode-ray tube)-based, using a picture tube that is similar to a TV's picture tube. Some LCD flat-panel displays also accept analog signals but must convert the analog signal to a digital signal internally before displaying the image onscreen. All VGA cards made for use with standard analog monitors use a **DB-15F** 15-pin female connector, which plugs into the **DB-15M** connector used by the VGA port. This connector is the same size as the DB-9 connector used for the older digital video standards and serial ports, but it has three rows of pins.

The picture tubes used in CRT displays typically use one of three technologies to form the image:

- A phosphor triad (a group of three phosphors—red, green and blue). The distance between each triad is called the *dot pitch*.

- An aperture grill, which uses vertical red, green, and blue phosphor strips. The distance between each group is called the *stripe pitch*.

- A slotted mask, which uses small blocks of red, green, and blue phosphor strips. The distance between each horizontal group is also called the *stripe pitch*.

caution

The pins on the DB-15 (and most other connectors) are very small and are made of fairly soft metal, so be careful that you don't bend them when you install or remove the cable, and use the thumbscrews! Always insert and remove the cable with steady forward or back pressure. No wiggling the cables or connectors!

Generally, the smaller the dot or stripe pitch, the clearer and sharper the onscreen image will be. Typical standards for CRT monitors call for a dot pitch of .28 millimeters (mm) or smaller. Generally, low-cost monitors have poorer picture quality than higher-cost monitors of the same size because of wider dot pitch, low refresh rates at their highest resolutions, and poor focus at their highest resolutions.

LCD Digital Display Standards

With the increasing popularity of LCD displays for desktop computers, new digital display technologies have become popular on most mid-range and high-end VGA cards. Two major digital display standards support LCD displays with digital interfaces:

- **Digital Flat Panel (DFP)**—This was adopted as a standard in February 1999 but has been largely superseded by DVI. Fortunately, DFP-compatible panels can be adapted to DVI.

- **Digital Visual Interface (DVI)**—DVI-D versions of this standard support digital-only displays, whereas DVI-I supports both digital and analog displays.

See Figure 9.3 for a comparison of analog VGA, DFP, and DVI connectors. Details about DFP and DVI are listed in Table 9.1.

Both DFP and DVI standards skip the wasteful digital-analog-digital conversion required when you use an analog LCD display with a VGA card. How about software support, though? Luckily, both support VGA resolutions and color depth and are treated as VGA displays by software.

Most recent mid-range and high-end graphics cards have both VGA and DVI-I ports (refer back to Figure 9.1); many of these cards also support dual displays. The DVI-I port can be converted to a VGA port with a plug-in adapter so you can use two VGA-type displays with a single card. As you prepare for the A+ Certification Exam, you should note the differences in appearance among these connections and the major features of the different display standards. Remember, there will be a test!

Table 9.1 LCD Digital Display Standards

Standard	Maximum Resolution	Analog Display Support	Pinout
Digital Flat Panel (DFP)	1,280×1,024	No	2 rows of 10 pins
Digital Visual Interface (DVI-D)	Single link: 1,280×1,024 Dual link: Supports resolutions above 1,280×1,024	No	3 rows of 8 pins (dual link); single link omits pins 4, 5, 12, 13, 20, and 21

Table 9.1 (continued)

Standard	Maximum Resolution	Analog Display Support	Pinout
Digital Visual Interface (DVI-I)	1,280×1,024 for digital displays	Yes	3 rows of 8 pins and 5-pin Micro/Cross analog output

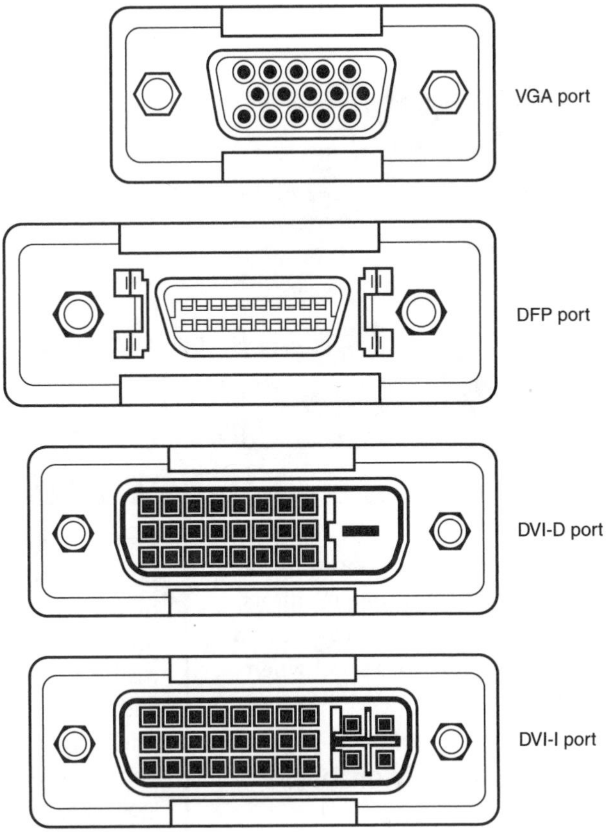

FIGURE 9.3

A comparison of VGA, DFP, DVI-D, and DVI-I ports.

VGA port

DFP port

DVI-D port

DVI-I port

TV-Out Ports

Want to put your PC picture on TV? Many recent graphics cards and the integrated graphics in some desktop and portable computers also include a **TV-out** port, which can be used to connect the computer to TVs, VCRs, and similar devices. Some use a single **RCA jack**, which blends all the TV signals together, but most use an **S-video** jack similar to the one shown in Figure 9.4. S-video splits the signal into two parts (luma and chroma) for a better picture.

Because TVs have a relatively low resolution compared to monitors, expect some loss of sharpness when using a TV for the display. You might need to experiment with resolution settings, font size, and graphics sizes to determine the best settings for use in programs you plan to send through a TV. Note that scan converters are available as retrofits for systems that lack TV-out connectors.

Figure 9.4 shows the VGA, S-video (TV-out) and DVI-I connectors on the rear of a typical recent graphics card and the cables or adapters that can connect to them.

FIGURE 9.4
VGA (left),
S-video/TV-out
(center), and
DVI-I (right)
ports and cable
connectors.

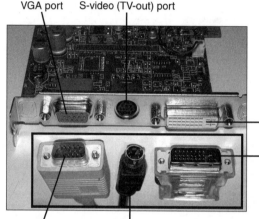

VGA port   S-video (TV-out) port

DVI-I port

DVI-I to VGA adapter

VGA cable   S-video (TV-out) cable

Note that video cards with a VGA port and TV-out port technically support multiple monitors. That means you need to enable the TV-out port in the Windows Display Properties sheet when you want to use it.

VGA Color Depths and Memory Requirements

How high a resolution and how many colors do you want? Memory is the deciding factor (along with the resolutions supported by your monitor).

Table 9.2 lists the most common levels of VGA, the higher-than VGA resolutions, and the video card memory requirements needed to achieve resolutions and color depths in 2D and 3D operations (3D graphics used for gaming require much

caution

Except for the very bottom-of-the-barrel models, virtually all 3D accelerator cards on the market today offer VGA and TV-out. However, vendors often refer to these cards as supporting "dual displays." If you are looking for a replacement video card for a client who wants to support two CRTs or a CRT and an LCD, a system that has only a VGA port and a TV-out port is not sufficient. Make sure you get one that has two VGA ports or a VGA and a DVI-I port (which can be converted to VGA with a low-cost or bundled adapter) as well as TV-out.

larger amounts of memory). Standard VGA is equal to 16 colors at 640×480 resolution. Boring!

Video card colors can be referred to both by the number of colors and by the number of the factor of 2 needed to calculate that number of colors. For example, 24-bit color = 2^{24} = 16,777,216 colors.

16-bit color is sometimes referred to as *high color*. 24-bit and 32-bit color are sometimes referred to as *true color*. When a photograph is viewed on a monitor set for 16-bit color and then on a monitor set for 24-bit or 32-bit color, the 16-bit version of the photograph looks more mottled and grainy than with 24-bit or 32-bit color. This is because the 16-bit color display must use dithering (a process that uses small dots of color to simulate a color not available) to display the photo.

tip

In preparing for the A+ Certification Exam, note in particular the meaning of **8-bit** (256 colors), **16-bit**, and **24-bit color** and that the amount of video memory on the card needed to achieve 24-bit color at a given resolution is twice what is required to achieve 16-bit color. Note that most 3D graphics cards use a **32-bit color** setting instead of 24-bit; however, 32-bit color supports the same number of colors as 24-bit color (the extra bits are used for 3D operations).

Table 9.2 VGA Resolutions and Color Depth (2D/3D Graphics)

Resolution	Number of Colors	Color Depth Bit Rating	Video Card Memory Requirements	
			2D	3D
640×480	16	4-bit	256KB	N/A
640×480	65,536	16-bit	1MB	2MB
640×480	16,777,216	24-bit	1MB	4MB
640×480	16,777,216	32-bit	N/A	8MB
800×600	65,536	16-bit	1MB	4MB
800×600	16,777,216	24-bit	2MB	8MB
800×600	16,777,216	32-bit	N/A	8MB
1,024×768	65,536	16-bit	2MB	8MB
1,024×768	16,777,216	24-bit	4MB	16MB
1,024×768	16,777,216	32-bit	N/A	16MB

Table 9.2 (continued)

| Resolution | Number of Colors | Color Depth Bit Rating | Video Card MemoryRequirements | |
			2D	3D
1,280×1,024	65,536	16-bit	4MB	16MB
1,280×1,024	16,777,216	24-bit	4MB	16MB
1,280×1,024	16,777,216	32-bit	N/A	32MB
1,600×1,200	65,536	16-bit	4MB	16MB
1,600×1,200	16,777,216	24-bit	8MB	32MB
1,600×1,200	16,777,216	32-bit	N/A	32MB

By now you're probably thinking, how do *I* find out how much memory *my* video card (or built-in video) has to work with? To determine the amount of graphics memory, you can use the following methods (try them all or use just one):

■ Click Start, Run. Type **DXDIAG** to run the **DirectX** diagnostics program. Click the Display tab to determine the graphics chipset and memory.

■ Windows XP displays the chipset and amount of memory on the Adapter tab in the **Display Properties** sheet's Advanced dialogs.

■ Some drivers have an information tab to display this information.

■ Systems that use **integrated graphics** subtract the memory used for graphics from the total amount of memory shown on the System Properties sheet's General tab. For example, a system with 256MB of RAM that uses 32MB for graphics displays only 224MB of RAM on the General tab.

■ Third-party diagnostic and reporting software such as SiSoftware Sandra can also be used to determine the amount of memory used by the video card or circuit.

■ Read the manual, especially if you're working with an Intel chipset with integrated graphics. Most of these chipsets vary the amount of memory used for

> **note**
>
> 800×600 resolution is often referred to as *Super VGA*, and 1,024×768 resolution is sometimes referred to as *XGA*. 1,280×1,024 is sometimes called *Super XGA (SXGA)*. Super VGA is sometimes considered to be any color depth and resolution beyond standard VGA.

video according to the operating system you're using and the amount of RAM installed on the system, and the methods listed previously might not provide a valid answer on these systems.

Achieving Higher Resolutions and Color Depths

So, what do you need to achieve the resolution, color depth, and refresh rate you want for pixel-perfect image and video editing and great gaming? You need

- Video card memory as required for the color depth, 2D or 3D mode, and resolution desired

- Video driver customized to the video card and able to set desired color depth and resolution

- Monitor able to use the display resolution desired at a vertical refresh rate high enough to avoid flicker

Vertical refresh rate refers to how quickly the monitor redraws the screen, and is measured in hertz (Hz), or times per second. Typical vertical refresh rates for 14-inch diagonal to 17-inch diagonal monitors vary from 56Hz to 85Hz, with refresh rates over 72Hz causing less flicker onscreen.

The vertical refresh in Windows 9x/Me/2000/XP can be adjusted through the Advanced portion of the Display Properties sheet.

I/O Port, Memory, and IRQ Usage

Now it's time for some numbers (hardware resource numbers, that is). Video cards use at least two, and typically three of the standard hardware resources you first learned about in Chapter 2, "PC Anatomy 101." All video cards must use one or more I/O port address ranges, and all video cards use a section of the system memory map called *upper memory*. Most recent video cards also use an IRQ.

tip

Flicker-free (72Hz or higher) refresh rates are better for the user, producing less eyestrain and more comfort during long computing sessions. Note that LCD monitors never flicker, so the Windows default refresh rate of 60Hz works well with any LCD display.

VGA cards normally use the I/O port address ranges of 3C0–3CFh, whereas some ATI cards also use 2E8–2EFh, which can conflict with COM 4. VGA cards use memory addresses below 1MB of A0000–BFFFF (RAM buffer) and C0000–CFFFF (video BIOS). Various memory ranges above 1MB are also used by PCI and AGP video cards. Recent PCI and all AGP graphics cards use an IRQ assigned automatically by the Plug and Play (PnP) BIOS or Windows. Older video cards often used IRQ 9.

Video Memory

Just as the CPU uses memory on the motherboard as a workspace to create information, the video card uses its own video memory (or main memory borrowed by systems with integrated graphics) as a place to create visual information that is displayed by the monitor. Just as different types of RAM affect the speed of the computer, different types of video RAM affect the speed of the video card.

Video memory comes in almost as many different types as motherboard memory. The following types of memory were reviewed in Chapter 7, "RAM," and their performance on video cards is comparable to their performance on the motherboard:

- *DRAM*—Dynamic RAM
- *EDO RAM*—Extended Data Out RAM
- *SDRAM*—Synchronous DRAM
- *DDR SDRAM*—Double Data Rate SDRAM

Of these four memory types, DDR SDRAM is the fastest and is extremely common on new high-performance video cards; because it is a variation on standard SDRAM (popular for lower-priced video cards), video card makers can easily adapt their designs to use it. DRAM and EDO RAM were often found on older video cards.

Special types of video memory have also been created for the needs of video display:

- **Video RAM (VRAM)** enables data to be read from it and written to it at the same time; this type of operation is referred to as *dual ported*. Video RAM is very fast when compared to DRAM but has not proven to be very popular.
- **Window RAM (WRAM)** is a modified version of VRAM. WRAM is also very fast when compared to DRAM but is not very popular.
- **Synchronous Graphics RAM (SGRAM)** is a faster version of SDRAM with additional circuitry designed especially for video cards. It is very popular on many recent high-performance video cards.

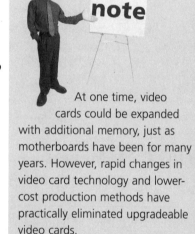

note

At one time, video cards could be expanded with additional memory, just as motherboards have been for many years. However, rapid changes in video card technology and lower-cost production methods have practically eliminated upgradeable video cards.

If a video card needs more memory, you need to yank it out and replace the card because there's no place to add memory to most recent models. Use a model that has more memory plus other advanced features (such as a faster graphics chip and dual-display support) as a replacement.

Common Video Card Bus Types

The video card normally plugs into the same type of expansion slots that other cards do. Systems built before the mid-1990s used one of the following obsolete bus standards:

- ISA
- VL-Bus (VESA Local-Bus)
- EISA (Enhanced ISA)

Current systems feature one of these video interfaces:

- PCI slot
- AGP slot
- Integrated graphics

Built-in video uses two different types of memory:

- Dedicated memory chips on the motherboard; used primarily with portable systems that use a discrete graphics chip instead of chipset-integrated graphics
- Shared main memory (also known as **Unified Memory Architecture [UMA]**); used primarily with systems that use chipset-integrated graphics

There's a double whammy on system performance if your video comes from your motherboard's chipset:

- Built-in video that uses shared main memory normally is slower than video that uses separate memory because main memory and video memory have different characteristics and speeds.
- Sharing main memory means there's less memory for programs. For example, if a system with 256MB of RAM uses 32MB for video, programs only have 224MB of RAM to work with.

What can you do about this?

- If your system shares main memory for video, you normally can adjust how much memory is set aside for video by making adjustments in the system BIOS setup program. As little as 9MB or as much as 64MB of RAM is shared built-in video; the exact amount varies by chipset, operating system, and the amount of main memory installed.
- Install more memory. Many recent systems also increase the amount of memory available for graphics as the total amount of memory increases. Check the system's or chipset's technical documentation for details.

Installing a Video Card

The BIOS settings involving the video card typically include the following:

- *Display type*—VGA is the basis for all system graphics today, so no change from the default of VGA is necessary.

- *AGP speed settings*—Most systems automatically detect the type of AGP card installed and set these accordingly. However, you can override the settings if necessary. For example, enable AGP Fast Write to improve graphics performance, but disable it if the system crashes.

- **Primary VGA BIOS**—If you move from PCI to AGP, be sure to set this to AGP.

- **Graphics aperture** *size*—Use the default size (generally 32MB).

Adjust these settings as needed.

note

You can normally replace built-in video with a video card, but if the built-in video is AGP based and the system has no AGP slots, you'll need to use the slower PCI slots for upgrades (see the next section for details). Keep in mind that video card vendors aren't putting much effort into PCI cards these days; they use the slowest graphics chips and lack other features.

Although all video cards since the beginning of the 1990s are based on VGA, virtually every one uses a unique chipset that requires special software drivers to control acceleration features (faster onscreen video), color depth, and resolution. So, whenever you change video cards, you must change video driver software as well. Otherwise, Windows will drop into a low-resolution, ugly 16-color mode and give you an error message because the driver doesn't match the video card.

Windows 9x/Me/2000/XP also require that you change the monitor driver when you change monitors. Some monitors use a standard plug-and-play driver (which reads the monitor settings from the monitor itself), but others use a model-specific driver that sets up the monitor's resolutions, refresh rates, power management, and other options. When you get a new monitor, look for a driver CD or floppy disk.

Upgrading to a New Video Card in Windows

As you prepare for the A+ Certification Exam, you might want to practice these steps on a working PC to help you prepare for installation questions on the exam. Changing to standard VGA before changing video cards is recommended to avoid system crashes and error messages because all VGA-class video cards will use a standard VGA driver.

To change to Standard VGA before changing video cards with Windows 9x/Me, follow these steps:

1. Open the Display Properties sheet in the Control Panel and click Settings.

2. Select the Advanced Properties button to display the Advanced Properties sheet.

3. Select the Adapter tab.

4. Select the Change button.

5. Select Show All Hardware.

6. Select (Standard Display Types) and choose Standard Display Adapter (VGA), as shown in Figure 9.5.

FIGURE 9.5

Select Standard Display Adapter (VGA), because all video cards are now VGA compatible, and shut down the system before you change your video card.

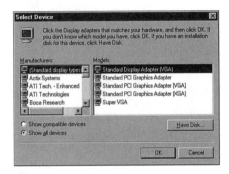

7. When prompted to reboot after accepting the change, shut down the system instead and unplug it.

8. Turn off the monitor.

9. Disconnect the data cable attached to the video card.

10. Remove the old video card.

11. Insert the new video card; use an AGP-based card for best performance if possible; otherwise, use a PCI-based card.

12. To continue with the changeover to the new video card, reattach the data cable to the new video card.

13. Turn on the monitor.

14. Turn on the computer.

15. If the computer supports plug-and-play, the new video card will be detected during the startup process.

16. Provide video drivers as requested; you might need to run an installer program for the drivers.

After the card is installed, choose the color depth, resolution, and refresh rate desired and restart the system.

With Windows 2000/XP, use this procedure:

1. Go into Device Manager and delete the listing for the current graphics card.
2. Shut down the system and unplug it.
3. Turn off the monitor.
4. Disconnect the data cable attached to the video card.
5. Remove the old video card.
6. Insert the new video card; use an AGP-based card for best performance if possible; otherwise, use a PCI-based card.
7. To continue with the changeover to the new video card, reattach the data cable to the new video card.
8. Turn on the monitor.
9. Turn on the computer and press F8 to display the startup menu.
10. Select Enable VGA Mode from the startup menu.
11. Provide video drivers as requested; you might need to run an installer program for the drivers.

Installing a Monitor

The process of installing a new monitor is similar to that used for installing a new video (graphics) card, except that you should change the graphics card refresh rate to 60Hz and use 800×600 resolution with the Windows Display Properties sheet before you change monitors. This prevents damage to the monitor, which can be caused by using too high a refresh rate.

⇨   To learn more about safely adjusting Display Properties, **see** "Adjusting Display Properties in Windows," **p. 314**.

If you need to connect a monitor that uses the VGA DB-15 connector to a graphics card that has a DVI-I connector, you need to attach a DVI-I–to-VGA adapter first (see Figure 9.6). Compare Figure 9.6 to Figure 9.4 to see both connectors on this adapter. Some vendors put this adapter in the package, but you might need to order it.

DVI-to-VGA adapter

VGA cables

FIGURE 9.6

Install a DVI-I-to-VGA adapter (upper left) if you want to attach a VGA display (lower left) to a graphics card whose VGA port is already in use (upper right).

Installing Multiple Displays in Windows 98 and Later Versions

Have you ever had so many program windows open you couldn't find what you were looking for? Windows has the solution! A larger desk(top).

Windows 98 introduced **multiple-display support** to the world of Windows (a quick tip of the hat to Macintosh for pioneering this idea), and all subsequent versions of Windows also support this feature. Multiple-display support originally required the installation of two or more supported video (graphics) cards with monitors into a single system.

After the second or subsequent graphics card and monitor is recognized by the system (sometimes easier said than done) and the drivers are installed, you can drag the windows for email or Web browsers to one display, work with documents in a second display, or place floating menus in one display while you edit a document, graphic, or multimedia project in another display. Take it from a longtime dual-display fan—it's great!

The major problem with multiple-display support using two video cards is in convincing the system to detect the secondary video card. Sometimes the video cards fight over which one's in charge. When cards compete, you lose.

The most common solution is to use the BIOS option for primary VGA BIOS and select the card type you want to use as primary. Because the options are AGP and PCI, this works best when one card is PCI and one is AGP. Generally, it's best to select the AGP card's video BIOS as primary, but you can use the PCI setting if it's the only way a particular combination of graphics cards can work together. It's possible to have a multiple-display system that uses PCI cards only, but it can be more difficult.

Fortunately, the best solution for most users who need two-monitor, multiple-display support—particularly with a system that supports 1.5V or Universal AGP cards—is to replace the existing single-display card with one that supports two or more displays. Video cards based on various mid-range and high-end ATI and nVidia chipsets support two monitors, and cards from Matrox support up to four monitors. Windows 2000 does better with two separate graphics cards than with a so-called **dual head** card, but Windows 98, Windows Me, and Windows XP all work very well with dual-head cards.

After multiple displays are installed (either through adding a card to a single-display system or upgrading to a multiple-display compatible card), use the Windows Display Properties sheet to configure the card(s) and displays. See "Adjusting Display Properties in Windows," later in this chapter, for more information.

tip

If you want to go the dual-card route to support multiple displays, make sure you

- Completely install Windows using the original video card before you install the second video card.
- Assume that onboard video will be disabled when you install a video card into a PCI or AGP slot; it's extremely rare that onboard video will still work, and if it does, it will be treated as the secondary display.

Adjusting Video Displays

Don't like the picture on your monitor? Fix it!

Video adjustments are made by adjusting monitor or display properties, either on the monitor or with the Windows Display Properties sheet. Depending on the monitor, it might be necessary to make changes whenever the picture type changes or the monitor itself can memorize the settings and recall them on demand.

Adjusting Picture Size and Quality Settings with Monitor Controls

Although very old monitors often required the user to manually change horizontal and vertical picture sizes when changing resolutions or switching from VGA graphics (640×480) to VGA text (720×400) resolutions, or from one graphics resolution to another, more recent monitors have built-in,

note

Some portable computers running Windows XP, particularly those with discrete graphics chips instead of integrated graphics, might support DualView, which uses any monitor plugged into the VGA port as a secondary display. To learn more about DualView, see "Video/Graphics Circuitry," in Chapter 12, "Portables."

digitally controlled settings for each supported resolution. You can adjust the horizontal and vertical settings as well as **screen geometry** and other settings with onscreen controls (see Figure 9.7) on most recent monitors. These are activated with push buttons on the front of both CRT and LCD displays, and provide a greater number of adjustments than older types of digital display controls.

Typical picture adjustments available on virtually all monitors include

- Horizontal picture size
- Horizontal picture centering
- Vertical picture size
- Vertical picture centering
- Contrast
- Brightness

Recent CRT and LCD monitors also offer settings for color balance, **color temperature**, **degaussing** (removes color fringing in a CRT display caused by the magnetic fields in the monitor), and options for the language and position of the **onscreen display** (OSD).

FIGURE 9.7

Typical OSD adjustments for CRT and LCD monitors. A portion of an LCD monitor's OSD is shown in the inset at lower right; the other images are from a typical CRT's OSD.

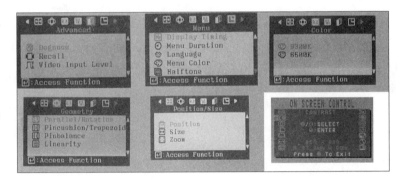

When the vertical and horizontal pictures size and centering controls (sometimes combined into a single zoom control) are used to fill the available screen area on a CRT display, **barrel** (outward curving image sides) and **pincushion** (inward curving image sides) **distortion** can take place (see Figure 9.8) as well as other problems. Use the OSD controls on recent monitors or the interactive push-button geometry controls on older monitors to fix these types of picture distortion. Note that you might need to make these adjustments for each resolution you use. The good news is that monitors "remember" the changes you make for each resolution.

FIGURE 9.8

Typical geometry errors in monitors that can be corrected with digital or OSD controls available on most monitors.

Adjusting Display Properties in Windows

Installing a better video card or bigger monitor is only half the battle when it comes to providing the display quality you need. If you need to adjust

- Screensavers
- Desktop backgrounds
- Color scheme and font sizes
- Resolution and color depth settings
- Multiple monitors
- Vertical refresh rate
- 3D graphics properties
- Color quality
- Desktop theme

...it's time to open the Display Properties sheet in Windows.

To open the Display Properties sheet, open the Display icon in the Windows Control Panel or right-click on an empty part of the Windows desktop and select Properties.

Adjusting Backgrounds, Screensavers, Color Schemes, and Font Sizes

Want to put your favorite photo on the desktop? Click the Desktop tab and select a graphic; use Browse to look in other folders as desired. You can use .BMP and other graphics file formats. You should also choose a color to use for the background. You can also use a color without a photo if you prefer.

To adjust the type of **screensaver**, its settings, and how long it waits before starting, click the Screen Saver tab, select a screensaver, and click the Settings button. The Screen Saver tab also has a button for monitor power saving; it opens the general Power dialog on some versions of Windows.

Click the Appearance tab to select the style and color scheme to use for Windows. If you are working with a user with limited vision, you can enable larger-than-normal font sizes and high-contrast black or white color schemes through this dialog. Use the Effects button to enable various special effects such as onscreen font smoothing and large icons.

Adjusting Resolution, Color Quality, and Multiple Monitor Support

Click the Settings tab to adjust the resolution and color quality (**color depth**) of any display, or to enable multiple displays on a system with two or more monitors (see Figure 9.9).

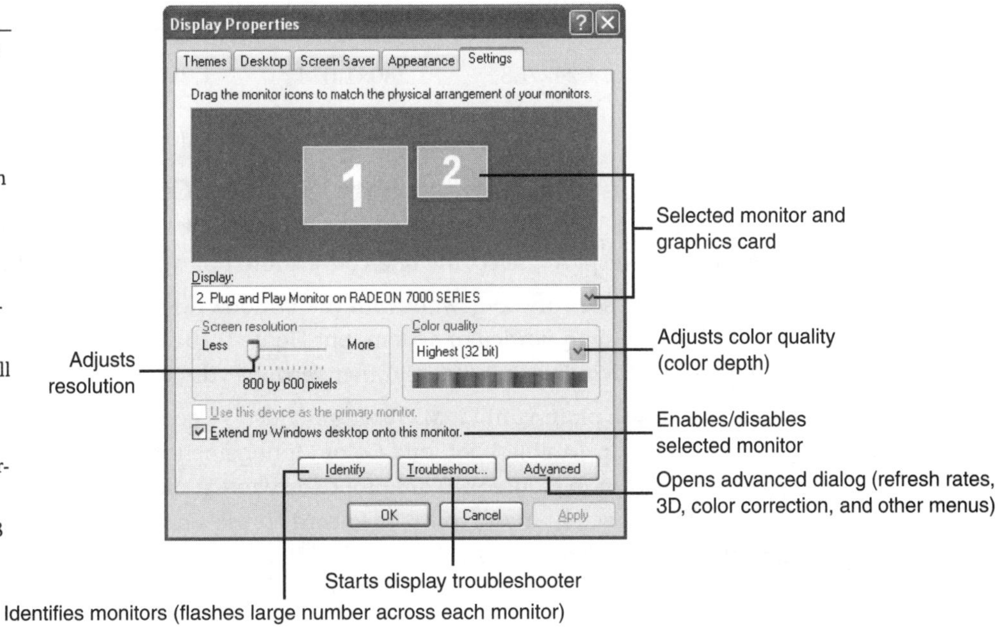

FIGURE 9.9

The Settings tab is "Control Central," the single-most important tab in the Display Properties sheet when you upgrade to multiple monitor support or install a bigger monitor. The Windows XP version is shown, but Windows 98 and others are similar.

Selected monitor and graphics card

Adjusts resolution

Adjusts color quality (color depth)

Enables/disables selected monitor

Opens advanced dialog (refresh rates, 3D, color correction, and other menus)

Starts display troubleshooter

Identifies monitors (flashes large number across each monitor)

Note that until you enable the additional monitor(s) shown in the Settings tab, Windows can't use them. Windows 2000, by the way, has poorer multiple monitor support than Windows 98, Me, or XP: It doesn't support different resolutions or refresh rates with most multiple-display video cards. If you use Windows 2000, you're better off with separate cards.

If you're switching to a larger monitor, check out Table 9.3 for the recommended resolutions to use with various sizes of CRT and LCD displays.

Many CRT monitors in the 15-inch to 19-inch size ranges support higher resolutions than those shown in Table 9.3, but in most cases these resolutions produce poor screen quality. Stick with these recommendations to get easy-on-the-eyes results with both cheap monitors and high-quality displays.

> **tip**
>
> If you've just replaced a tiny monitor with a big one, don't make the all-too-common mistake of forgetting to adjust the screen resolution to make the most of your new display. If you keep the same settings your old display used, your graphics and menus will be enormous (Windows might even complain it can't show you all your menus if you like to install lots of software!), and you'll still be scrolling around and through long Web pages and documents. See Table 9.3 for my picks.

Table 9.3   Recommended Resolutions by Display Size and Type

Display Type/Size	15-inch	17-inch	19-inch	20-inch
CRT	800×600	1,024×768	1,280×1,024	1,600×1,200
LCD	1,024×768	1,280×1,024	1,280×1,024	1,600×1,200

Adjusting Vertical Refresh Rate, 3D, and Color Quality

To make more advanced changes for your display, click the Advanced button. If you have multiple displays, select the one you want to adjust before you click Advanced.

The menus you see vary somewhat with the Windows version, driver version, and video card used on a particular system, but Figure 9.10 is representative of what you'll see on a Windows XP system (other versions vary a bit).

Systems that use plain-vanilla, Microsoft-provided video drivers have the General, Adapter, Monitor, Troubleshoot, and Color Management tabs shown in Figure 9.10. The others shown in Figure 9.10 are proprietary to the driver provided by the video card vendor. However, most recent video card chipsets offer similar features if you download the drivers from the vendor Web site.

Proprietary advanced display dialogs

FIGURE 9.10
The
Troubleshoot tab
on the Windows
XP Advanced
Display
Properties sheet
configured to
disable DirectX
acceleration.

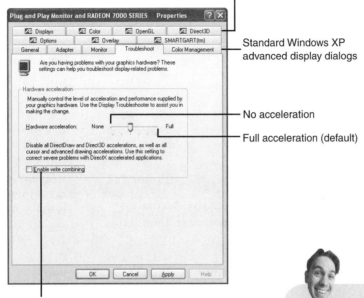

Standard Windows XP
advanced display dialogs

No acceleration

Full acceleration (default)

Disables write combining when cleared
(recommended when using less than full acceleration)

Need to fix your display or your system won't start
or crashes a lot? Use Tables 9.4, 9.5, and 9.6 along
with Figure 9.10 to help you choose the right dialog
to make the adjustments you need to make for best
display quality or to fix startup problems and
crashes.

note

Note that at sizes
below 19-inch that LCD
displays support higher recommended resolutions than CRT
monitors do; this is because the
usable screen size of a CRT monitor is an inch or so smaller than its
total measurement, and because
LCD displays don't have problems
with misalignment, flicker, or poor
focus the way CRT monitors can.
Note also that many CRT monitors
don't support **flicker-free
refresh rates** (72Hz or higher) at
their maximum resolutions.

Table 9.4 Advanced Adjustments for Display Quality and Features

Adjustment Needed	Tab	Menu Item or Button	Notes
Icons and text too small	General	DPI setting	Custom lets you select the setting you want.
Need to update video card driver	Adapter	Properties	Click Driver tab to update driver.
Need to adjust vertical refresh rate to eliminate flicker	Adapter or Monitor (varies by Windows version)	(Screen) refresh rate	Use 72Hz or higher refresh rate (up to limits of monitor) to reduce or eliminate flicker.
Graphics or mouse pointer problems	Troubleshoot (Windows XP) or Performance (other Windows versions)	Hardware Acceleration	Drag to left to reduce acceleration; download and install new mouse and display drivers as soon as possible (refer to Table 9.5).
Colors don't match between screen and printer	Color Management	Add (color profile)	Get color profiles from printer or graphics software vendors.
3D game performance too low	**OpenGL or Direct3D**	Adjust settings for performance	If not available on your system, download the latest driver from your 3D graphics card vendor.
3D game image quality too low	OpenGL or Direct3D	Adjust settings for quality	If not available on your system, download the latest driver from your 3D graphics card vendor.
Color balance, brightness, and contrast need adjusting	Color	Adjust options as needed	Many 3D games are very dark; use Full Screen 3D option (if available) to adjust display for 3D gaming only.

Troubleshooting Frequent Lockups or Startup Problems

A computer that won't start except in VGA or Safe Mode or has frequent lockups or screen corruption when you move your mouse needs upgraded display, mouse, or DirectX drivers. Time to start downloading!

However, as a workaround, you can reduce the video acceleration as shown in Figure 9.10. Use Table 9.5 to determine the best setting to use for the display problem you're having with Windows XP and 2000. With other Windows versions, use Table 9.6 to determine how to adjust the Performance tab's acceleration settings.

Table 9.5 Using Graphics Acceleration Settings to Troubleshoot Windows XP and 2000

Acceleration Setting	Left	One Click from Left	Two Clicks from Left	Two Clicks from Right	One Click from Right	Right
Effects of Setting	No acceleration; use when system won't start except in Safe or VGA Mode	Disables all but basic acceleration	Disables DirectX, DirectDraw, and Direct 3D acceleration (mainly used by 3D games)	Disables cursor and drawing accelerations	Disables mouse and pointer acceleration	Enables full acceleration
Long-Term Solution	Updates display, DirectX, and mouse drivers	Updates display, DirectX, and mouse drivers	Updates DirectX drivers	Updates display drivers	Updates mouse drivers	N/A

Disable write combining, a method for speeding up screen display, whenever you select any setting other than full acceleration to improve stability (see Figure 9.10). Re-enable write combining after you install updated drivers and retry.

Table 9.6 Using Graphics Acceleration Settings to Troubleshoot Other Windows Versions

Mouse Pointer Location	Left	One Click from Left	One Click from Right	Right
Effects of Setting	Disables all acceleration	Basic acceleration only	Disables mouse pointer acceleration	Full acceleration
Solution	Updates display and mouse drivers	Updates display and mouse drivers	Updates mouse drivers	N/A

Lots of settings, but which one to use? If you're not sure which setting is the best for your problem, try this procedure:

1. Start the computer.

2. Open the Troubleshooting or Performance dialog box as described in the previous section.

3. Slide the acceleration pointer one notch to the left from its current position.

4. Click Apply, OK, and then OK again to close the Display Properties dialog box.

5. Use your normal software and perform typical tasks.

6. If the computer now performs acceptably (no more crashes), continue to use this setting until you can obtain and install updated drivers. If the computer continues to have problems, repeat steps 2–5 and move the pointer one step to the left each time until the problems go away or until you can install updated drivers.

Study Lab

Don't miss the Study Lab materials found on the CD accompanying this book. Each Study Lab is tailored to the individual chapters in this book, meaning that you'll quickly be able to determine which topics you understand well enough to pass the exam and which topics need more study. The Study Labs are presented in printable PDF format so that you can take them with you to study at work, on the road, or even in your car just before test time!

THE ABSOLUTE MINIMUM

Here's a quick review of the high points of this chapter. Take a quick stroll through this section before you head out for your exam.

- The AGP slot is used for most card-based video today, although PCI cards are still available.

- There are several standards for AGP slots that vary by voltage and connector. The AGP Universal and AGP Pro slots can use any normal AGP card, and the AGP Pro slot also supports AGP Pro cards.

- CRT monitors use a vacuum tube and are similar to TVs in their basic construction, whereas LCD monitors are similar to active-matrix LCD panels built into portable computers.

- Almost all CRT monitors and most LCD monitors support the analog VGA standard and its higher-resolution descendants.

- The DVI standard is the current standard for digital LCD displays. The DVI-D connector supports digital displays only, whereas the DVI-I connector also supports analog LCD displays through the use of an adapter.

- Many recent video cards and some portable computers' built-in video also feature TV-out. S-video provides a sharper picture than a single RCA jack.

- 24-bit color is the highest color standard supported for business graphics; it is equal to over 16 million colors and is sometimes called *true color*.

- 32-bit color supports the same colors as 24-bit color, but is optimized for 3D graphics.

- 16-bit color supports over 65,000 colors and is sometimes called *high color.*

- You can use DXDIAG, the Display Properties sheet, or third-party software to determine the amount of display memory.

- The amount of display memory and the resolution selected determine what color quality can be used at a particular resolution.

- 3D graphics require much more video memory than 2D graphics or business applications.

- Most recent video cards use SGRAM or some form of SDRAM or DDR SDRAM for display memory.

- Recent video cards no longer provide memory upgrade sockets; replace the video card with a model with more memory and a faster graphics chip if you need more video memory.

- Systems with integrated graphics normally use Unified Memory Architecture to share memory between graphics and system requirements.

- Increasing system memory on systems with integrated graphics can increase the amount of memory available for graphics.

- You should reset the existing video card type to VGA or delete the current card listing in the Windows Device Manager before installing a new video card.

- You should set the refresh rate to 60Hz and the resolution to 800×600 before installing a new monitor to prevent damage to the monitor.

- You can install an additional PCI video card into a system that already has a PCI or an AGP video card to create a multiple-display system, but it's usually better to install a dual-head AGP card.

- Settings such as horizontal and vertical picture size and position, contrast, brightness, and screen geometry can be controlled on the monitor itself.

- TV-out, secondary monitor support, screensavers, refresh rates, and 3D graphics settings are controlled through the Display Properties sheet in Windows.

- The Troubleshoot (Windows XP) or Performance (other versions) tab in the Advanced dialog can be used to reduce or eliminate graphics acceleration for startup or program troubleshooting.

10

PRINTERS

If you want to get what you see on the screen onto a piece of paper, you need a printer.

All printers have the following characteristics in common:

- A method of transferring characters (and often graphics) to paper. Except for a tiny number of specialized printers that use heat-sensitive paper stock, this involves some sort of ink or toner as well as a mechanism to transfer the ink or toner to the paper.
- One or more methods of feeding paper stock.
- An interface that connects the printer with the computer.
- A "language" used by software to send commands to the computer.

The details of these features are what separate the various types of printers from each other.

Let's get started!

The Printing Process

The specifics of the printing process vary with the printer type, but all printers have the same goal: to turn pages created with software into hard copy. Here's an overview of the printing process:

1. An application program in the computer sends a print request to the printer. Unlike MS-DOS applications, which send commands directly to the printer, Windows-based applications send the command to the Windows operating system, which relays the command to the printer.

2. Windows uses a **print queue** to manage print jobs, storing one or more print jobs in the default temporary directory until the printer is ready.

3. After the printer is ready, it receives a stream of data from the computer through its interface. The **data stream** contains commands that begin the printing process, select a page orientation and margins, and select built-in fonts and **typefaces**, or it contains instructions to create fonts and typefaces especially for this print job, depending on the printer and the typefaces and fonts in the document.

   If the data stream is appropriate for the printer, printing works correctly; if the data stream contains commands the printer doesn't recognize, garbage will be printed, with much paper wasting. That's why it's important to use the correct printer driver for your printer.

4. The printer feeds a page and prepares to print the document from the top of the page.

5. When the page is complete, the paper is ejected and the process starts again with the next page of a multipage document or a new document.

Line Versus Page Printers

Some printers print a line at a time, whereas others print a page at a time. What's the difference?

■ **Character/line printers** (dot-matrix, inkjet, thermal, and some types of dye-sublimation printers) immediately move the printhead to the top-left page margin and use ink to begin to print characters and dot patterns line by line to print the page; the **printhead** moves back and forth while the paper advance mechanism moves the paper through the printer.

■ Character/line printers might pause periodically to receive data from the computer or for mechanical reasons.

■ **Page printers** (laser and LED printers, solid-ink printers, and most dye-sublimation printers) wait until the entire page is received before transferring the page to the print mechanism, which pulls the paper through the printer as the page is transferred from the printer to the paper; most page printers use toner, but some color models might use solid ink or special ribbons.

> **tip**
>
> You can expect 9% of the entire exam to cover printers. To do well on the printers portion of the A+ Certification Exam, be sure to pay careful attention to
>
> - How printers create a page (note in particular the steps used by a **laser printer** to create a page)
> - Major components of each printer type covered (the test now includes dye-sublimation, thermal, and solid-ink printers as well as dot-matrix, inkjet, and laser/LED)
> - Typical printer operation and output problems and their solutions
> - How printers are interfaced to the computer

Printer Controls for Text and Graphics

Besides the imaging technology (dot-matrix, inkjet, laser/LED, thermal, or dye-sublimation) used by a printer, the two biggest influences on what page output looks like from a given printer are its typeface and font options and its printer language. The typeface and font options affect how text appears, and the printer language affects how the printer changes fonts and how it creates graphics on the printed page.

Fonts and Typefaces

All printers designed to print text (this leaves out dye-sublimation printers, but includes the rest) have a limited number of **fonts** built in. Depending on the printer, the fonts can have the following characteristics:

- **Scalable fonts** can be printed at any size.
- **Fixed-size fonts** can be printed only at certain sizes.
- **Proportional fonts** use different amounts of space for each letter. Their sizes are given in *points*; 72 points = 1 vertical inch. Most built-in and add-on fonts used today are proportional.
- **Fixed-pitch fonts** use the same amount of space for each letter. **Pitch** describes the horizontal space occupied by each letter; a 10-pitch font, for example, can put 10 characters into a horizontal inch.

Printer fonts are stored in the printer's firmware (software on a chip, you might remember from other chapters). Some older laser and inkjet printers have a provision for font cartridges, enabling them to print more fonts with additional firmware. The rise of scalable-font technologies such as TrueType has caused many recent printer models to omit font cartridge support.

The sample in Figure 10.1 lists the word *hamburgerfons* in Arial, Times New Roman, and Courier New 24-point fonts. The first two are proportional, and the last is fixed pitch. There are 72 points per vertical inch.

FIGURE 10.1

Hamburgerfons in Arial (top), Times New Roman (middle), and Courier New (bottom) fonts. Although each sample is the same size in points, the differences in font design cause each font to appear to be a different size.

hamburgerfons
hamburgerfons
hamburgerfons

Windows (starting with version 3.1) uses scalable **TrueType** fonts that are sent to the inkjet, laser/LED, or **thermal printer** as an outline that can be scaled as necessary for the document. If the printer has the same fonts built into its firmware, they are usually substituted to speed printing.

Dot-matrix printers can also use TrueType fonts but because they must be printed in a slow graphics mode (which also sounds like a dentist's drill), most dot-matrix printers use built-in fonts. The default font for a typical dot-matrix printer can be set with the printer's control panel, as in Figure 10.2, but software settings for fonts in a document override it.

Some printers can print more fonts in portrait mode than landscape mode. **Portrait mode** uses the paper in its normal vertical orientation, whereas **landscape mode** prints as if the paper were inserted horizontally by rotating the fonts and graphics. A dot-matrix printer can print in portrait mode only when using built-in fonts; it must use scalable fonts and print very slowly (rendering the fonts as bitmapped graphics) to produce landscape printouts. Laser/LED and solid-ink printers often feature both types of fonts, and inkjet, laser/LED, and solid-ink printers can print scalable fonts quickly and are better suited to producing landscape documents than dot-matrix.

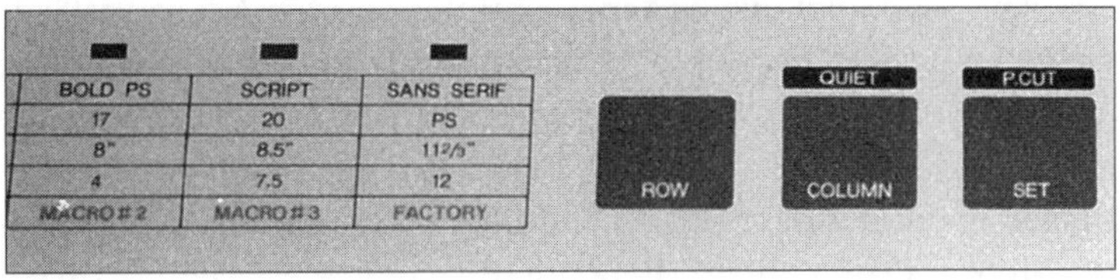

FIGURE 10.2

A portion of a typical dot-matrix printer's font-control panel. A wide range of printer fonts and other settings can be selected from the grid at left by using the control buttons at right.

Printer Languages

Virtually any printer (except for dye-sublimation models) used on a computer is designed to print more than plain text. A printer's capability to work with scalable fonts, select fonts, and create graphics all depend on the features of the **printer language** used by the printer.

The following are common methods of controlling the printer:

- Escape sequences
- Printer Control Language
- PostScript
- Host based

Dot-matrix, inkjet, and simpler dye-sublimation and thermal printers generally use a simple language based on **escape sequences**—commands sent to the printer preceded by the ESC character (ASCII code 27). Epson printers pioneered this method of controlling the printer, and most dot-matrix printers either emulate the Epson ESC-P or ESC-P2 sequences or have their own sequence of commands.

Laser, LED, and solid-ink printers generally use either the **Printer Control Language (PCL)** developed by Hewlett-Packard or Adobe's **PostScript**. PCL is an enhanced version of the escape sequence–based printer control used on dot-matrix printers. Various versions of PCL have been introduced over the years, with more and more features enabling PCL printers to print better graphics and to handle scalable fonts.

PostScript laser, solid-ink, and inkjet printers use the Adobe PostScript language to send commands to the printer. PostScript provides printers with graphics power that is still unrivaled, even by the latest version of PCL (PCL6), and is preferred for graphic arts and advertising uses. Originally, PostScript was used strictly by laser printers, but many high-end inkjet printers—especially large-format models—are also PostScript compatible. There are three different levels of PostScript, with PostScript Level 3 being the most recent and most powerful.

A PostScript printer without a PCL language option cannot be used from an MS-DOS prompt for Print-Screen or other utility tasks, but can be controlled only by an application sending PostScript printer commands. Many PostScript printers also include or emulate PCL to be more flexible. PostScript can be retrofitted to a non-PostScript printer in two ways:

- By adding firmware (in the form of a cartridge or a special memory module); this method is possible with many HP laser printers
- By using a software PostScript driver (also called a raster image processor, or **RIP**) that enables non-PostScript printers to print PostScript

The first method produces faster printing, but the second method works with many additional printers.

The latest type of printer control is host based. A **host-based** printer lacks a built-in interpreter for any of the previously mentioned printer control methods. Instead, it is controlled by the operating system (usually Microsoft Windows). These printers are inexpensive but cannot be used outside Windows, and normally cannot be used as a self-contained printer on a network.

When you are asked on the exam to troubleshoot printer problems, keep these differences in mind.

Paper-Feed Types

Three major types of paper are used with printers:

- Single sheets
- Continuous tractor fed
- Roll paper

Depending on the paper-feed type in the printer, a printer can use one or more of these paper types.

Single-Sheet Feed

The most common type of paper used today is **single sheets**. These are used by laser/LED, inkjet, **thermal transfer**, and dye-sublimation printers and by some impact dot-matrix printers. Most printers that use single sheets have paper trays that hold many sheets for easy printing of multipage documents. A few portable printers, however, require you to feed one sheet at a time.

Impact dot-matrix printers that can handle single sheets use a rubber roller called a **platen**, which is similar to the platen found in typewriters. It rolls the paper through and absorbs the impact of the printhead wires used to form the printed text and graphics.

Because inkjet and laser printers are non-impact, they use small rollers instead of a platen to pull the paper through the printer.

Common problems with single-sheet paper feeds include

- Wrinkled or damaged sheets that will not feed properly
- Damp paper that sticks together

Single-sheet paper feed is the major form of paper feed used today because it makes the production of high-quality printouts easier with most types of printers.

Tractor-Fed Paper

Tractor-fed paper can be easily recognized by its perforated edges. It is most often sold in folded, continuous sheets, with folding on the perforations that enables the pages to be separated after printing. Tractor-fed paper is used by most impact dot-matrix printers, but hardly any other types of printers use it.

Two major types of tractor feeds exist on impact dot-matrix printers:

- Push tractor
- Pull tractor

Both types of tractor feeds use sprockets that fit through the perforations on the edge of tractor-fed paper. The feeders hold the paper in place with retainers that snap over the edges of the paper. Figure 10.3 compares push and pull tractor feeds to each other.

The **push tractor** is located before the printhead in the paper path. Because of this, the push tractor has the advantage of enabling a printed sheet to be removed immediately after printing; this so-called **zero tear-off** feature avoids waste of forms. However, adjustment of the tractor mechanism is critical to avoid jams and the zero tear-off feature must be properly configured through adjusting the paper advance. This type of tractor feed is best used for printing just a few pages at a time on demand, as in point-of-sale billing and receipts.

The **pull tractor** is an older, simpler mechanism. It is located after the printhead in the paper path, and therefore a sheet must be wasted whenever a print job is removed from the printer. The pull tractor tends to be more reliable for long print jobs and is best used for printing reports of many pages in length, such as those used for accounting or payroll.

Most tractor feeds can be adjusted horizontally to handle various widths of paper or to adjust the left margin. A few older, low-end, dot-matrix printers used a simplified variation on the pull tractor called **pinfeed**, which uses nonadjustable sprockets at either end of a platen.

Although tractor feeds have been around since the early days of the PC, they can still cause plenty of trouble: misaligned tractors cause the paper to tear at the page perforations before the page is printed. In addition, with the widespread use of attractive but relatively weak microperforated paper that has nearly invisible perforations, the tractor perforations are likely to pull off as well.

note

Fortunately, tractor-feed mechanisms aren't used in home or office printers anymore. However, wide-carriage dot-matrix printers with tractor-feed mechanisms are still popular in business and industrial use because they can handle multipart forms, print wide reports, and work well in relatively dirty environments.

FIGURE 10.3

A typical dot-matrix printer with a pull tractor feed (top) and a push tractor feed (bottom).

Roll Paper

Continuous roll paper can be sold either in a tractor feed–compatible form (for use with dot-matrix printers) or as a plain roll (for use with inkjet printers). Small and narrow rolls of paper or labels are also used by receipt and point-of-sale printers and bar code printers.

Paper Paths and Paper Problems

Most printers use one or both of the following paper paths for printing:

- Curved paper path
- Straight-through

The more turns the paper must pass through during the printing process, the greater the chances of paper jams.

Curved paper paths are typical of some inkjet and many laser printers as well as dot-matrix printers using push tractors: The paper is pulled from the front of the printer, pulled through and around a series of rollers inside the printer during the print process, and then ejected through the front or top of the printer onto a paper tray (see Figure 10.4). Because the cross-section of this paper path resembles a C, this is sometimes referred to as a *C-shaped paper path*.

Some printers, especially those with bottom-mounted paper trays, have more complex paper paths that resemble an *S*.

A **straight-through paper path** is a typical option on laser printers with a curved paper path. Printers with this feature have a rear paper output tray that can be lowered for use, which overrides the normal top paper output tray. Some also have a front paper tray. Use both front and rear trays for a true straight-through path. Inkjet printers with input paper trays at the rear of the printer and an output tray at the front also use this method or a variation in which the paper path resembles a flattened V.

If you want to avoid jams when you print envelopes and labels, straight-through paper paths rule! However, there's a glitch with laser printers: The pages come out in reverse order because a straight-through tray stacks printed pages face up rather than face down. Beat this problem by using the reverse-order printing command, which stacks the pages in their normal order in a straight-through paper tray.

FIGURE 10.4

A C-shaped paper path on a typical inkjet printer. The paper is pulled face down from the input paper tray and ejected face up into the output tray. The C-curve makes feeding envelopes and thick stock difficult.

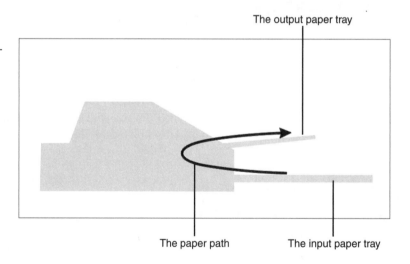

The output paper tray

The paper path

The input paper tray

Interface Types

How do you connect your printer? Most printers in use today are connected through the USB 1.1 or USB 2.0 interface, whereas some printers also have the older parallel (LPT/IEEE-1284) interface. However, some very old dot-matrix and laser printers use the RS-232 serial (COM) interface.

A few high-end inkjet and laser printers can be attached directly to an Ethernet network, but most are networked through a print server or a client PC with file- and printer-sharing software installed.

Dot-Matrix Printers

The dot-matrix printer is so named because it creates the appearance of fully formed characters from dots placed on the page.

The print mechanism of the dot-matrix printer is almost always an impact mechanism: A printhead containing 9–24 fine wires (called **pins**) arranged in one, two, or three columns is used along with a fabric ribbon, similar to typewriter technology. The wires are moved by an electromagnet at high speed against the ribbon to form dot patterns that form words, special characters, or graphics.

Dot-Matrix Printhead Types

The two major types of dot-matrix printheads are

- **9-pin**
- **24-pin**

A third type of dot-matrix printhead uses 18 pins and basically acts like a faster version of a 9-pin printhead.

To create a character, a dot-matrix printer uses a predefined series of columns called a **matrix**, in which each character is formed. As the printhead moves across the paper, commands from the computer rapidly move the 9, 18, or 24 pins in special sequences to form characters or graphics.

Figure 10.5 shows actual print samples from a typical 9-pin printer's draft mode, a typical 24-pin printer's draft mode, and the **Near Letter Quality (NLQ) mode** of the same 24-pin printer.

Figure 10.6 shows how small the printhead is in relation to the rest of the printer. Size is misleading, though, because a damaged printhead will render the rest of the printer useless.

Although 24-pin printheads produce much better-looking text in NLQ mode, their capability to print on multipart forms is limited because of their narrow wires. The smaller diameter causes a lighter impact on the top page, and subsequently even lighter impact on all the remaining pages. Typical form limits for a 24-pin printer are the original plus three non-carbon copies. 9-pin and 18-pin printheads use wider wires, and high-end printers with these printheads can handle up to four or more non-carbon copies as well as the original.

Durability in the field is also better with 9-pin/18-pin printheads; a broken pin in the printhead is more likely to result with the narrower wires used in the 24-pin printhead.

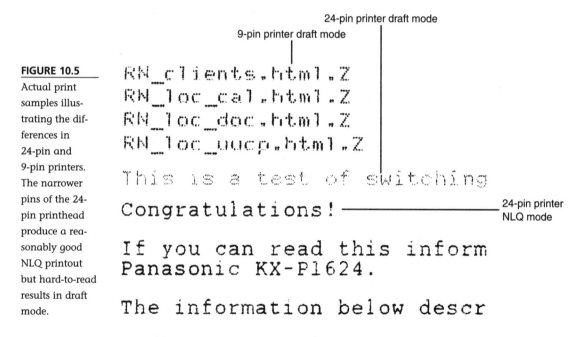

FIGURE 10.5
Actual print samples illustrating the differences in 24-pin and 9-pin printers. The narrower pins of the 24-pin printhead produce a reasonably good NLQ printout but hard-to-read results in draft mode.

Parts of a Dot-Matrix Printer

The components of a typical dot-matrix printer are identified in Figure 10.6.

Impact dot-matrix printers have the following parts moving in coordination with each other during the printing process:

- The paper is moved past the printhead vertically by pull or push tractors or by a platen.

- The printhead moves across the paper horizontally, propelled along the printhead carriage by a drive belt, printing as it moves from left to right.

Bidirectional printing prints in both directions but is often disabled for high-quality printing because it can be difficult to align the printing precisely.

■ The pins in the printhead are moving in and out against an inked ribbon as the printhead travels across the paper to form the text or create graphics.

■ The ribbon is also moving to reduce wear during the printing process.

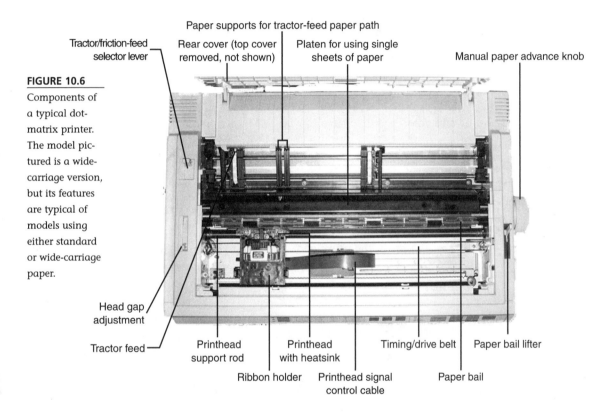

FIGURE 10.6
Components of a typical dot-matrix printer. The model pictured is a wide-carriage version, but its features are typical of models using either standard or wide-carriage paper.

Paper supports for tractor-feed paper path

Tractor/friction-feed selector lever

Rear cover (top cover removed, not shown)

Platen for using single sheets of paper

Manual paper advance knob

Head gap adjustment

Tractor feed

Printhead support rod

Printhead with heatsink

Ribbon holder

Printhead signal control cable

Timing/drive belt

Paper bail

Paper bail lifter

Standard-Carriage Versus Wide-Carriage Models

Many printer manufacturers produce both standard-carriage (8.5×11-inch paper) and wide-carriage models (15.5 inches wide) of some of their dot-matrix printers. The wide-carriage models are preferred for accounting or other occupations requiring very wide printouts. Wide-carriage printers can fit about 80% more text on a line with the same-sized typeface.

Wide-carriage models can be adjusted to use standard paper, but often feature options such as a bottom paper feed for running high volumes of printing.

Periodic Maintenance and Care for Impact Dot-Matrix Printers

To keep an impact dot-matrix printer in top condition

- Change ribbons when the ribbon begins to dry out; the ink in the ribbon also helps lubricate the printhead. Discard frayed ribbons because the fraying can snag a printhead's pins and break them.

- Use platen conditioner to keep the rubber platen supple; a platen that becomes hard can break printheads.

- Adjust the head gap whenever you change from ordinary paper to multipart forms, envelopes, labels, or other thicker-than-normal items, and when you return to normal paper; failure to set the head gap properly can result in smudged printing and broken pins in the printhead.

- Periodically clean out hair, dust, and paper shreds from the printer.

Dot-Matrix Printer Troubleshooting

The following problems are typical of dot-matrix printers; use this information to prepare for troubleshooting questions on the A+ Certification Exam and day-to-day printer troubleshooting.

Typical dot-matrix printer problems include gaps in printed letters, paper jams and torn perforations, and faded printing.

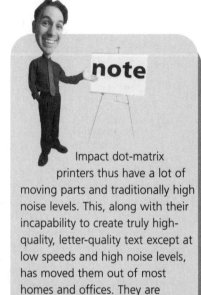

note

Impact dot-matrix printers thus have a lot of moving parts and traditionally high noise levels. This, along with their incapability to create truly high-quality, letter-quality text except at low speeds and high noise levels, has moved them out of most homes and offices. They are largely used for utility tasks (bank receipts, point-of-sale receipts, and warehouse reports) where their capability to print multipart forms is more important than print quality or noise level. Because impact dot-matrix printers use inexpensive ribbons designed to print millions of characters and can use fan-fold or single-sheet papers of all types, they have the lowest cost per page of all printers.

Gaps in Printed Letters

Because of how dot-matrix printers work, a slight amount of space between the dots that make up a dot-matrix letter is normal, especially in draft mode (refer to Figure 10.5). However, if horizontal white space through a letter is noticeable in NLQ mode, this usually indicates that the printer has a bent or broken pin.

When a pin in the printhead has become bent or broken, the printhead must be repaired or replaced. Incorrect head gap settings are a typical cause of bent or broken pins; the head gap must be adjusted to match the thickness of the paper, forms, or label stock inserted in the printer. Another typical cause is the use of a dried-out or damaged printer ribbon; replace the ribbon when print quality fades to protect the printhead and produce sharper, easier-to-read printing.

Paper Jams and Tears at Perforations

Incorrect tractor-feed width and position settings are the typical causes of paper jams and torn sheets. Make sure the tractor feed is adjusted to the correct width, which will make the paper lay flat without putting undue stress on the tear-off perforations. Printers with push and pull tractors must have the tractor-feed and paper-feed options selected correctly to avoid jams and torn sheets.

Faded Printing

If the print is evenly faded, the ribbon is dried out. Replace the ribbon to achieve better print quality and protect the printhead. If the print appears more faded on the top of each line than on the bottom, the head gap is set too wide for the paper type in use. Adjust the head gap to the correct width to improve printing and protect the printhead from damage.

Printhead Won't Move

The printhead should move back and forth during printing; if it won't move, check the drive belt and the gear mechanism. Jammed gears in the printer or a broken drive belt will prevent the drive belt from moving the printhead. Check the drive belt first to see if it is broken, and then check the gears that move the printhead. You might need to disassemble the printer to check the gears.

Paper Won't Advance

The paper advance, whether single-sheet or tractor feed, is also gear driven. Jammed gears will prevent the paper advance from working. You might need to disassemble the printer to check the gears.

Some printers require special tools to remove the plastic shell; contact the printer's manufacturer for detailed disassembly instructions and recommended tools.

Most impact dot-matrix printers have a self-test feature onboard. Use this to determine

- Which firmware the printer is using
- Which fonts and typefaces the printer includes

Normally, the self test is activated by holding down a button, usually the LF (line feed) button, while the printer is turned on. If the printer is wide-carriage, make sure the paper in place is also wide-carriage; if you don't use wide-carriage paper, the printer will try to print on the platen, which could damage the printhead. Note that the printer shown in Figure 10.3 is a wide-carriage model loaded with standard 8.5×11-inch paper.

Inkjet Printers

Inkjet printers (also known as **ink dispersion printers**) represent the most popular type of printer in *small-office/home-office (SOHO)* use today and are also popular in large offices. Their print quality can rival laser printers, and virtually all inkjet printers in use today are able to print both color and black text and photographs.

From a tightly spaced group of nozzles, inkjet printers spray controlled dots of ink onto the paper to form characters and graphics. On a typical 5,760×1,440 dots per inch (dpi) printer, the number of nozzles can be as high as 180 for black ink and over 50 per each color (cyan, magenta, yellow). The tiny ink droplet size and high nozzle density enables inkjet printers to perform the seemingly impossible at resolutions as high as 1,200dpi or above: fully formed characters from what is actually a high-resolution, non-impact, dot-matrix technology.

The printer's maximum resolution is determined from the number, spacing, and size of these nozzles. The printer's print quality, on the other hand, is determined by a combination of resolution, ink droplet size, and paper quality. Two major methods are used to create the ink dots. Most inkjet printers heat the ink to boiling, creating a tiny bubble of ink that is allowed to escape through the printhead onto the paper. This is the origin of the name **BubbleJet** for the Canon line of inkjet printers.

Another popular method uses a **piezo-electric** crystal to distribute the ink through the printhead. This method makes achieving high resolutions easier; the Epson printers using this method were the first to achieve 5,760×1,440dpi resolutions. This method also provides a longer printhead life because the ink is not heated and cooled. Both types of inkjet printers are sometimes referred to as **drop-on-demand** printers.

Inkjet printers are character/line printers. They print one line at a time of single characters or graphics up to the limit of the printhead matrix. Inkjet printers are functionally fully formed character printers because their inkjet matrix of small droplets forming the image is so carefully controlled that individual dots are not visible.

Larger characters are created by printing a portion of the characters across the page, advancing the page to allow the printhead to print another portion of the characters, and so on until the entire line of characters is printed. Thus, an inkjet printer is both a character and a line printer because it must connect lines of printing to build large characters. Some inkjet printers require realignment after each ink cartridge/printhead change to make sure that vertical lines formed by multiple printhead passes stay straight.

Figure 10.7 shows some of the typical components of an inkjet printer.

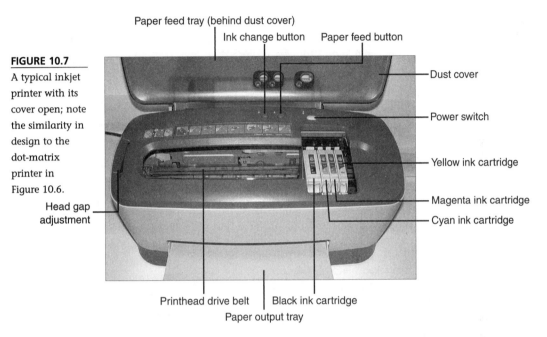

FIGURE 10.7

A typical inkjet printer with its cover open; note the similarity in design to the dot-matrix printer in Figure 10.6.

Inkjet Printers and Ink Cartridges

Many inkjet printers, especially low-cost models, continue to use a large tank of liquid ink for **black** and a separate color tank with individual compartments for each color (typically **cyan**, **magenta**, and **yellow**; some models feature light versions of some of these colors for better photo-printing quality). However, the trend in recent mid-range and high-end models has been for each color to use a separate cartridge. This improves print economy for the user because only one color at a time needs to be replaced. With a tricolor cartridge, the entire cartridge needs to be replaced, even though only one of the colors runs out.

note

Inkjet printers are sometimes referred to as **CMYK** devices because of the four ink colors used on most models: cyan, magenta, yellow, and black.

Inkjet printers produce very attractive pages, but the high cost of inkjet cartridges and the small numbers of pages per cartridge—as well as the higher cost of paper made for inkjet printing—makes inkjets the most expensive general-purpose printer technology on a per-page basis.

How Inkjet Printheads and Ink Cartridges Relate

Depending on the printer, the printhead might be incorporated into the ink tank; be a separate, user-replaceable item; or be built into the printer.

Some inkjet printers feature an extra-wide (more nozzles) printhead or a dual printhead for very speedy black printing. Some models enable the user to replace either the ink cartridge only or an assembly comprising the printhead and a replaceable ink cartridge.

An inkjet printer is only as good as its printhead and ink cartridges. Clogged or damaged printheads or ink cartridges render the printer useless. If an inkjet printer fails after its warranty expires, you should check service costs carefully before repairing the unit. Failed inkjet printers are often "throwaway" models and can be replaced, rather than repaired, even during the warranty period.

Always use the printer's own power switch, which enables the printer to protect the ink cartridges and perform other periodic tasks (such as self-cleaning) properly.

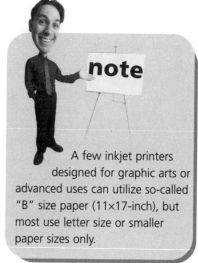

caution

Inkjet printers should *never* be turned off with a surge protector; doing so prevents the printer from self-capping its ink cartridges, which is a major cause of service calls and printer failures. Cleaning the printhead, either with the printer's own cleaning feature, a cleaning utility built into the printer driver, or with a moistened cleaning sheet, will restore most printers to service.

Inkjet Printer Paper-Feed Mechanisms

Most inkjet printers use single sheets of paper, but a few can use continuous paper rolls to create banners. In either case, the inkjet printer uses a series of rollers to pull the paper through the printer. Inkjet printers typically use either a C-shaped paper path (pulling the paper through the front and curving the paper past the printhead and out to the front-mounted tray), as in Figure 10.4, or a straight-through paper path.

note

A few inkjet printers designed for graphic arts or advanced uses can utilize so-called "B" size paper (11×17-inch), but most use letter size or smaller paper sizes only.

Because the rollers usually touch all four edges of the paper, almost all inkjet printers have an unprintable border area of one-quarter to one-half inch; the largest area is often on the bottom of the sheet.

Periodic Maintenance for Inkjet Printers

Most inkjet printers have built-in or software-controlled routines for cleaning the ink cartridges and checking the alignment of two-pass characters. An example appears in Figure 10.8. Use these options when you notice poor-quality printouts.

Some models with dual printheads require you to adjust alignment whenever you use dual black-ink cartridges.

Inkjet printer cleaning kits come in two forms:

- A special sheet and cleaning spray
- A cleaning pad and liquid cleaner

The sheet and spray is used to clean the paper paths in the printer and to remove ink buildup on the printheads. Spray the cleaner onto the sheet, insert it into the printer as directed, and print a few lines of text to clean the printer.

The cleaning pad is designed for models with removable printheads (which are part of the ink cartridge on thermal-inkjet printer models). Soak the pad with the supplied fluid and rub the printhead over it to remove built-up ink.

caution

Because both cleaning liquids and plain water can be used to clean up excess ink (unplug the printer first!), inkjet printers should *not* be used when water resistance is of paramount concern. Inkjet inks are more water resistant today than previously, but a careless spill can still destroy a digital masterpiece printed on an inkjet printer.

FIGURE 10.8

A typical inkjet printer's Utility menu. Printers can also use printer Control Panel options to clean printheads, test printing, or align text.

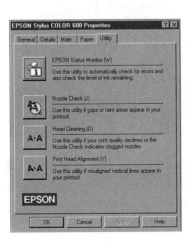

Troubleshooting Inkjet Printers

The following are typical problems and solutions for inkjet printers. Use this list to help you prepare for printer troubleshooting questions you might encounter on the A+ Certification Exam and in your day-to-day work.

Smudged Printing

Smudged print output from an inkjet printer can be caused by dirty printheads or paper rollers and by incorrect resolution and media settings. Clean the printhead by using the printer's built-in cleaning routine. Typically, the cleaning routine can print a test sheet before and after cleaning. Repeat the cleaning process until all colors and black print properly. If the cleaning process doesn't result in acceptable results, remove the printhead and clean it. If the printhead is built into the printer or if the paper-feed rollers or platen have ink smudges, use a cleaning sheet to clean the paper-feed rollers, platen, and printhead.

Check the Printer Properties setting in the operating system to ensure that the correct resolution and paper options are set for the paper in use. Incorrect settings can lead to excessive ink being used for a particular print job, leading to smudged output.

Unlike laser output—which can be handled as soon as the page is ejected—inkjet output, particularly from older printers or output on transparencies or glossy photo paper, often requires time to dry. For best results, use paper specially designed for inkjet printers. Paper should be stored in a cool, dry environment; damp paper also will result in smudged printing.

caution

Make sure that the correct side of the paper is being used! Many specialty inkjet papers (including photo papers) are designed for single-sided printing only. Check the package for an indication of which side of the paper should be used for printing if the difference in surface isn't obvious.

Gaps in Printed Output or Uneven Characters

If uneven characters occur after the ink cartridge has been replaced, you might need to realign the printhead with the printer's utility program or Printer Properties sheet. This process prints out a series of long bars, after which the user selects which bar is properly aligned.

Gaps in printed output usually indicate a partially clogged printhead. See "Smudged Printing" (in the preceding section) for instructions. Replacing the ink cartridge replaces the printhead on some printers, but on other printers the printhead is a separate, removable device or is fixed in position.

No Output at All

Use the printer's self test (activated by pressing a button or button combination on most printers when turned on; it varies by printer) to see if the printer can print any output. If the head moves and the paper advances but there is no output on the page, clean the printheads and retry. Replace ink cartridges if there is still no output.

If the self test fails, check the drive belt; if it is broken or if the drive gears are jammed, the printer must be repaired or replaced. (Low-cost printers usually are not worth repairing.) Try using the paper advance button; if the paper won't advance, check for obstructions, such as stuck labels or torn sheets, in the paper path.

If the self test works right, make sure the printer cable is attached correctly to the printer and computer, and retry the print job. If you get no results, make sure the proper port and driver are selected in Windows. If Windows sends print jobs to the wrong port, the printer won't receive the data and can't print. USB printers require a printer-specific driver as well as working USB ports and USB support in the operating system.

Gibberish Printing

Gibberish printing can be caused by partially attached cables or by using the incorrect printer driver. Turn off the printer and computer if you use parallel or serial port cables before tightening the cable. Restart the printer and system, and retry.

If the printer is attached to the serial port, check the baud rate, word length, parity bits, and flow-control settings for the printer's serial port and the computer's serial port. Both printer and computer must use the same settings to produce correct printing. Adjust the printer's configuration or the computer's serial port settings (using the operating system's serial port Control Panel settings) as needed.

Check the operating system's printer driver. If the driver appears correct, replace the cable and retry. If the results are still garbage, reinstall the printer driver and retry.

If these steps don't solve the problem, the printer might have a damaged logic board or a damaged printhead data/signal cable. Repair or replace the printer.

Using the Self Test on Inkjet Printers

The self test on inkjet printers can be used to

- Check the condition of the nozzles in the printhead.
- Check the firmware (ROM) onboard the printer.

Depending on the model, the test might be brief, or more than one page might be printed.

As with dot-matrix printers, you hold down a specified key (often the paper-feed key) while starting the printer to activate the self-test feature. Some recent printers don't have a self test. In those cases, use the test-print feature in Windows to check the printer.

Laser and LED Printers

Laser and LED printers combine the low noise of an inkjet printer with the waterproof printing of a dot-matrix printer and have a very low cost per page.

Laser/LED printers are similar in many ways to photocopiers:

■ Both use an electrostatically charged drum to receive the image to be transferred to paper.

■ Both use a fine-grained powdered toner that is heated to adhere to the paper.

■ Both must feed the paper through elaborate paper paths for printing.

However, significant differences exist between the photocopier and its computer-savvy sibling:

■ Laser/LED printers produce images digitally, turning individual dots on and off; most copiers, however, are still analog devices.

■ Laser/LED printers work under the control of a computer; copiers have a dedicated scanner as an image source.

■ Laser/LED printers are optimized for both text and graphics, including continuous-tone photos; copiers must choose text or photo modes, with mediocre results at best on anything other than scanned text.

■ Laser/LED printers use much higher temperatures than copiers to bond printing to the paper; using copier label or transparency media in a laser printer can result in damage to the printer due to melted label adhesive, labels coming off in the copier, or melted transparency media.

The essential difference between a laser and an **LED printer** is in the imaging device. The laser

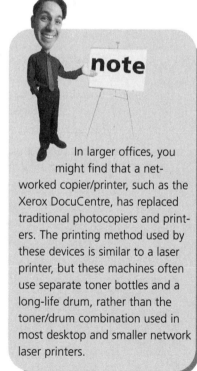

note

In larger offices, you might find that a networked copier/printer, such as the Xerox DocuCentre, has replaced traditional photocopiers and printers. The printing method used by these devices is similar to a laser printer, but these machines often use separate toner bottles and a long-life drum, rather than the toner/drum combination used in most desktop and smaller network laser printers.

printer uses a laser to transfer the image to the drum, whereas an LED printer uses an LED array to perform the same task. Otherwise, these technologies are practically identical. The laser printing process described in the following section also applies to LED printers.

The Laser Printing Process

To master this section, make sure you

- Memorize the six steps involved in laser printer imaging.
- Master the details of each step and their sequence.
- Be prepared to answer troubleshooting questions based on these steps.

The laser printing process often is referred to as the **electrophotographic (EP) process**.

Before the six-step laser printing process can take place, the following events must first take place:

tip

Understanding the sequence of events in the laser printing process is essential to successfully passing the A+ Core Hardware Exam. About 70% of A+ printer questions concern laser printers, and 9% of the entire exam is printer related.

- Laser printers are page based; they must receive the entire page before they can start printing.
- After the page has been received, the printer pulls a sheet of paper into the printer with its feed rollers.

After the paper has been fed into the print mechanism, a series of six steps takes place, which results in a printed page:

1. The excess toner is cleaned from the drum and the electrical charge discharged to prepare for the next page.
2. The image drum is conditioned.
3. The page is written to the drum.
4. The image is developed on the drum with the toner.
5. The toner image of the page is transferred to the paper.
6. The toner image of the page is fused permanently to the paper.

See Figure 10.9 to learn where each of these steps takes place in the printer.

Step 1: Cleaning

To prepare the drum for a new page, the image of the preceding page placed on the drum by the laser (see step 3) is removed by a discharge lamp.

Toner that is not adhering to the surface of the drum is scraped from the drum's surface for reuse.

Step 1 prepares the drum for the conditioning step (step 2).

Step 2: Conditioning

The cylinder-shaped imaging drum receives an electrostatic charge of -600Vdc (DC voltage) from a primary corona wire or conditioning roller. The smooth surface of the drum retains this charge uniformly over its entire surface. The drum is photosensitive and will retain this charge only while kept in darkness.

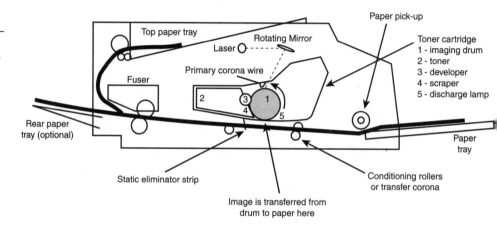

FIGURE 10.9

A typical laser printer's components. The heavy line indicates the paper path; paper enters the printer at the right and is pulled through the printer to either the left output tray or the top output tray.

Step 3: Writing

A moving mirror moves the laser beam across the surface of the drum. As it moves, the laser beam temporarily records the image of the page to be printed on the surface of the drum by reducing the voltage of the charge applied by the charger corona to -100Vdc. Instead of using a laser beam, an LED printer activates its LED array to record the image on the page.

Step 4: Developing

The drum has toner applied to it from the developer; because the toner is electrostatic and is also at -600Vdc, the toner stays on only the portions of the drum that have been reduced in voltage to create the image. It is not attracted to the rest of the drum because both the toner and the drum are at the same voltage, and like charges repel each other. This "like charges repel" phenomenon is the same reason two magnets repel each other.

Step 5: Transferring

While the sheet is being fed into the printer, it receives an electrostatic charge of +600Vdc from a corona wire or roller; this enables it to attract toner from the drum, which is negatively charged (see step 3). As the drum's surface moves close to the charged paper, the toner adhering to the drum is attracted to the electrostatically charged paper to create the printed page.

As the paper continues to move through the printer, its charge is canceled by a static eliminator strip, so the paper itself isn't attracted to the drum.

Step 6: Fusing

The printed sheet of paper is pulled through fuser rollers, using high temperatures (about 350F degrees) to heat the toner and press it into the paper. The printed image is slightly raised above the surface of the paper.

The paper is ejected into the paper tray, and the drum must be prepared for another page.

Color and Monochrome Laser Printers

Most laser printers for home and small office use print with black toner only. However, an increasing number of laser and LED printers also support color printing using the CMYK model.

Conventional color laser printers require four passes to print a color page (one pass per color), but color LED printers can print all four colors in one pass so they print color as fast as black and white.

Memory and Laser Printers

Because a laser printer is a page printer and the graphics, text, and fonts on the page all use memory, the amount of memory in the laser printer determines the types of pages it can print successfully—and on some models, how quickly the pages are printed.

All laser printers are shipped with enough memory to print with built-in typefaces, and most printers sold since the mid-1990s have enough memory for documents containing several scalable TrueType typefaces used by Windows. However, graphics, especially photographs, require a great deal more printer memory.

If a page is sent to a laser printer that requires more memory than the laser printer contains, the laser printer tries to print the page but stops after the printer's memory is full. The printer then displays an error message or blinks error status lights, at which point you must manually eject the page. Only a portion of the page is printed.

If the page requires an amount of memory close to the maximum in the laser printer, most recent laser printers have techniques for compressing the data going to the printer. Although this technique means that more pages can be printed successfully, compressing the data can slow down the print process.

Three options can be used if the pages you need to print require too much memory:

■ Reduce the resolution of the print job. Most laser printers today have a standard resolution of 600dpi or 1,200dpi. Reducing the **graphics resolution** to the next lower figure (from 1,200 to 600dpi or from 600 to 300dpi) will reduce the memory requirement for printing the page by a factor of four. The laser printer's Graphics or Advanced – Printing Defaults – Paper/Quality Properties sheet (see Figure 10.10) enables this factor to be adjusted as needed.

note

If you reduce the graphics resolution, text resolution stays the same, so a document that is not designed for reproduction or mass distribution will still have acceptable quality.

However, graphics resolutions of 300dpi or less produce poor-quality photo output.

FIGURE 10.10

The Graphics Properties sheet in Windows 98 (left) or the Advanced – Printing Defaults – Paper/Quality Properties sheet in Windows XP (right) for a typical laser printer enable you to adjust the graphics resolution from the default of 600dpi to 300dpi or less; text quality is not affected by this option.

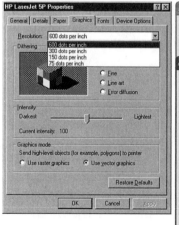
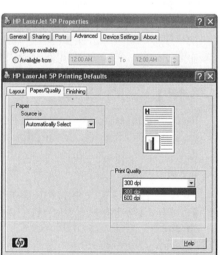

- Eliminate or reduce the size of graphics on the page.
- Convert color photos to black-and-white photos before placing in a desktop publishing document or printing them directly from the file. This can actually enhance the output quality from a monochrome laser printer as well as reduce the memory requirement for pages with photos.

These options are temporary workarounds that are unsatisfactory for permanent use. The best solution to "out-of-memory" problems with a printer, as with the computer, is to add more RAM.

Printers generally use memory modules that are somewhat different from computer memory modules, although they might look similar. Recent laser printers often use a 100-pin SDRAM SODIMM (SDRAM SODIMMs used in portable computers have 144 pins), whereas older models often use 72-pin fast-page or EDO SIMMs. Other types of printer memory expansion include credit card–sized proprietary modules or, on very old printers, slide-in boards that are populated with individual memory chips.

If the printer uses SIMM memory, see Chapter 7, "RAM," for installation tips. If the printer uses SODIMM memory, see Chapter 12, "Portables," for installation tips. However, if the printer uses proprietary modules or slide-in boards, see the printer's own documentation for details.

After the memory is installed in the printer, the printer is ready to use it immediately. However, some Windows printer drivers might not automatically detect the additional RAM. Because many Windows printer drivers try to compress data to fit into the amount of printer RAM known, an inaccurate RAM value will cause slower printing; Windows will ignore printer RAM it doesn't know about. After installing the RAM in the laser printer, open the printer Properties sheet in Windows and reset the total value for printer RAM to the correct value; a typical location for this option is Device Options (Windows 98) or Device Settings (Windows XP).

> **tip**
>
> To avoid memory problems, make sure at least 4 megabytes (MB) or more RAM is installed in 600dpi laser printers using PCL and at least 16MB or more RAM is installed in 600dpi PostScript laser printers; add more RAM for higher resolutions.

Toner Cartridges

Most laser printers use **toner cartridges**, which combine the imaging drum and the developer with toner. This provides you with an efficient and easy way to replace the laser printer items with the greatest potential to wear out.

Depending on the model, a new toner cartridge might also require that you change a wiper used to remove excess toner during the fusing cycle. This is normally packaged with the toner cartridge.

When you install the toner cartridge, be sure to follow the directions for cleaning near the toner cartridge. Depending on the model of laser printer, this can involve cleaning the mirror that reflects the laser beam, cleaning up stray toner, or cleaning the **charging corona wire** on the toner cartridge itself (replaced by **conditioning rollers** on most recent models). If you need to clean the charging corona wire (also called the *primary corona wire* on some models, the laser printer will contain a special tool for this purpose. The printer instruction manual will show you how to clean the item.

Keep the cartridge closed; it is sensitive to light, and leaving it out of the printer in room light can damage the enclosed imaging drum's surface. Figure 10.11 shows a typical laser printer toner cartridge and mirror cleaning tool. The tool above the toner cartridge is used to clean the printer's mirror.

note

Recycled toner cartridges are controversial in some circles, but I've used a mixture of new and rebuilt toner cartridges for several years without a problem. Major manufacturers, such as Apple, HP, and Canon, encourage you to recycle your toner cartridges by enclosing a postage-paid return label in the box.

Reputable toner cartridge rebuilders can save you as much as 30% off the price of a new toner cartridge.

FIGURE 10.11

A typical laser printer toner cartridge. The inset shows the mirror cleaning tool in use after the old toner cartridge has been removed and before the new cartridge is put into position.

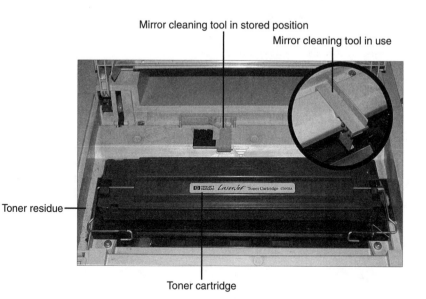

Mirror cleaning tool in stored position

Mirror cleaning tool in use

Toner residue

Toner cartridge

Paper, Labels, and Transparency Stock

Because the laser printer bonds the print to the paper during the fusing process, it can handle a wider range of paper stocks than inkjet printers. However, the same heat that produces an embossed feel to printing can also cause problems if the wrong types of labels or transparencies are used. For best results, follow these guidelines:

caution

When you change a toner cartridge, take care to avoid getting toner on your face, hands, or clothing. It can leave a messy residue that's hard to clean.

- Use paper made for laser or photocopier use. Extremely rough-surfaced specialty papers might not enable the toner to fuse correctly to the paper.

- Use envelopes made for laser printing, especially if the printer doesn't offer a straight-through paper path option. Standard envelopes can lose some of their flap adhesive or have the flap stick to the back of the envelope when used in a laser printer.

- Use only labels made for laser printers; these labels have no exposed backing, requiring you to separate the labels from the backing after printing.

caution

Labels made for copiers have exposed backing, and the labels can come off inside the printer, leading to expensive repairs.

- Use only laser-compatible transparency stock; it can resist the high heat of the fuser rollers better than other types, which can melt and damage the printer.

- Avoid using paper with damaged edges or damp paper; this can cause paper jams and lead to poor-quality printing.

- Load paper carefully into the paper tray; fan the paper and make sure the edges are aligned before inserting it.

Periodic Maintenance for Laser Printers

Because laser printers use fine-grain powdered toner, keeping the inside of a laser printer clean is important in periodic maintenance. Turn off the laser printer before using a damp cloth to clean up any toner spills.

To keep the paper path and rollers clean, use cleaning sheets made for laser printers. To use the sheets

1. Insert the sheet into the manual feed tray on the laser printer.
2. Create a short document with Notepad, WordPad, or some other text editor and print it on the sheet.

As the sheet passes through the printer, it cleans the rollers. If a specialized cleaning sheet is not available, you can also use transparency film designed for laser printers.

Change the toner cartridge as needed, and the ozone filter on models that use one as required.

caution

Never use transparency media not designed for laser printers in a laser printer. Copier or inkjet media isn't designed to handle the high heat present in a laser printer and can melt or warp and possibly damage the printer.

Thermal Printers

Thermal printers use heat transfer to create text and graphics on the paper. Thermal printers are used in point-of-sale and retail environments as well as for some types of portable printing.

Types of Thermal Printing

Thermal printers are available using two different technologies:

- Thermal transfer
- **Direct thermal**

Thermal transfer printers use wax or resin-based ribbons, whereas direct thermal printers use heat-sensitized paper. Some printers can be used in both modes.

The Thermal Printing Process

Although both thermal transfer and direct thermal printing involve heating the elements in a printhead to a particular temperature to transfer the image, there are some differences in operation. The basic process of thermal printing works like this:

1. The printhead has a matrix of dots that can be heated in various combinations to create text and graphics.
2. The printhead transfers text and graphics directly to heat-sensitive thermal paper in direct thermal printing, or to a ribbon that melts onto the paper in thermal transfer printing.

3. If a multicolor thermal transfer printer is in use, each ribbon is moved past the printhead to print the appropriate color.

Figure 10.12 compares direct thermal and thermal transfer printing technologies.

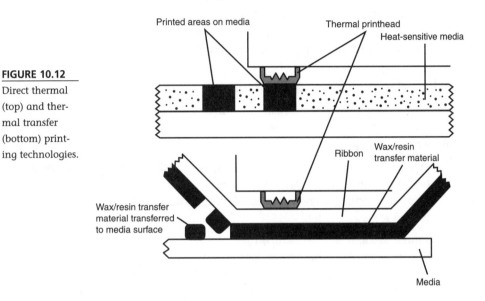

FIGURE 10.12
Direct thermal (top) and thermal transfer (bottom) printing technologies.

Suitable Paper and Label Stock for Thermal Printers

The best paper and label stock to use for thermal printing depends upon the type of thermal printing to be performed.

If the printer uses direct thermal printing, heat-sensitive paper with characteristics matching the printer's design specifications must be used. For portable printers using direct thermal printing such as the Pentax PocketJet series, the usual source for such paper is the printer vendor or its authorized resellers. If the direct thermal printer is used for bar codes or point-of-sale transactions, you can get suitable paper or label stock from bar code or POS equipment suppliers and resellers.

If the printer uses thermal transfer, most smooth paper and label stocks are satisfactory, including both natural and synthetic materials.

Dye-Sublimation Printers

Dye-sublimation (often abbreviated as **dye-sub**) printers are designed to do just one thing: print terrific continuous-tone photographs. Thus, you can't use a dye-sub printer in place of your trusty inkjet or laser/LED printer. However, dye-sub printers produce photo prints as good, if not better, than the best inkjets and are widely used in the "scan, crop, and print-it-yourself" workstations found in many photo departments and camera shops.

Although most dye-sub printers use a printhead rather than a laser mechanism to print, dye-sub printers still qualify as page printers. The photo can't be printed until all the data is received, because the print mechanism must make multiple passes to print all the colors and to apply an optional overcoat used to protect the print.

The Dye-Sublimation Printing Process

Dye-sublimation, like thermal transfer and direct thermal printing, also relies on heat to transfer the image to the media, but the process is very different than with traditional thermal printers:

1. During printing, the printhead heats up to transfer cyan, magenta, yellow, and (sometimes) black dye from special dye-sub ribbons to the paper under computer control (some can print directly from flash or CD media). One pass is used for each color.

2. Unlike thermal transfer, which melts the wax or resin material to the surface of the paper, dye-sublimation dyes turn into a gas when heated and penetrate the surface of the paper. This creates a **continuous-tone** image. Thus, the relatively modest-sounding typical dye-sub resolutions of around 300–400dpi provides better real-world quality than high-resolution inkjet printers.

3. Many recent dye-sub printers apply a protective coating (**overcoat**) to the surface of the print before ejecting it.

Suitable Paper Stock for Dye-Sublimation Printers

Most dye-sub printers sold for home or small-business use fall into the 4×6-inch snapshot size category, although a few are designed to produce enlargements up to about 8×10-inch. Regardless of the size, you should use only media that is made for a particular printer (either by the printer vendor or a reliable third party).

You can get sticker or compact print paper for some printers, and some vendors sell kits that include the paper and the ribbon cartridge needed to print the quantity of paper packaged in the kit.

Periodic Maintenance for Dye-Sublimation Printers

The only periodic maintenance needed for typical dye-sub printers is to change the ribbons and paper when they run out. If the printer uses a separate overcoat cartridge, make sure to change it when it runs out. Overcoating dye-sub prints helps extend their useful life.

Solid-Ink Printers

Solid-ink printers combine features of inkjet and laser printers to produce very fast and high-quality output for office printing requirements. Solid-ink printing was originally developed by Tektronix, but after the purchase of Tektronix by Xerox, all solid-ink printers are manufactured and sold by Xerox.

The Solid-Ink Printing Process

The solid-ink printing process has these major elements:

1. Solid-ink printers use specially shaped bars of ink in the four standard colors used for printing (CMYK):

   - Cyan
   - Magenta
   - Yellow
   - Black

   Each color uses a different shape to prevent misfeeds.

2. The ink is heated and sprayed onto a rotating drum under computer control.

3. Paper is heated and pressed against the drum to transfer the ink from the drum to the paper.

4. The paper is ejected from the printer into the output tray.

Figure 10.13 shows how a typical **solid-ink printer** works. The numbers in Figure 10.13 are explained in the caption.

Suitable Paper Stock for Solid-Ink Printers

Solid-ink printers are designed to use various weights of paper, cover stock, labels, business cards, and envelopes of the same types used in laser printers. These printers can also use photo paper and glossy and coated papers; these are recommended for the best reproduction of high-quality illustrations and photos.

FIGURE 10.13

How a typical solid-ink printer works: The ink loader (1) melts ink into the reservoir (2). The printhead (3) creates the image by depositing ink droplets (4) onto the drum (9). Meanwhile, the paper (5) is pulled past the paper heater (6). The image is transferred to the paper (8) by the pressure of the transfer roller (7) against the drum (9).

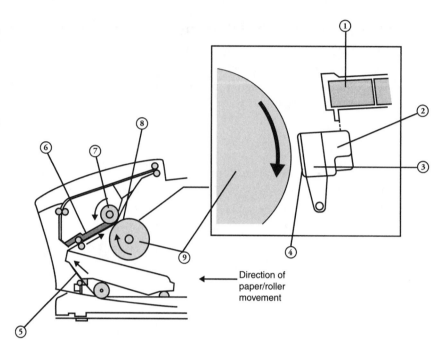

Direction of paper/roller movement

Some printer models use different types of trays or tray settings for different types of media. Be sure to use the correct tray or tray setting when changing media types.

Periodic Maintenance for Solid-Ink Printers

In addition to replacing ink colors and paper as needed, the following maintenance items must be performed periodically on typical solid-ink printers:

- The maintenance roller and counter have a rated lifespan measured by months of use or a certain number of copies (some models offer a standard and extended-life version). Replace these components when they reach their rated lifespan (copies or time in service, whichever comes first).

tip

When you insert paper into any type of printer, be sure to fan the pages before you insert the paper into the tray to prevent sticking.

- The waste tray catches excess ink. Remove it and empty it (discarding the ink) when the tray is full. Most solid-ink printers have an indicator to tell you when to perform this step.

- Components such as the rapid-release guide, maintenance drawer wiper blade, exit rollers, and paper-feed rollers should be cleaned as needed to help solve print-quality problems. See the printer documentation for specific recommendations.

Installing Firmware and Software Drivers

Like any other device, a printer requires software to drive it. MS-DOS and command-prompt programs in Windows can print plain-text output to all printers except PostScript printers. Windows can also output plain text but must use the Generic/Text-only printer driver for this. To use the printer's special fonts, graphics, or other features, printer drivers made for the printer model or for its recommended emulation must be used.

Printer drivers are selected in either applications or the operating system. MS-DOS software uses its own printer drivers; Windows applications use the printer drivers installed in Windows.

Windows printer drivers can be installed from

- The Windows installation CD-ROM
- Installation floppy disks or CD-ROMs supplied with the printer
- Driver files downloaded from the manufacturer's Web site

The most recent and full-featured printer drivers are found on the manufacturer's Web site, followed by the driver disks or CD-ROM included with the printer. These often have enhanced features not found in the standard printer drivers supplied with Windows (such as ink- or toner-level monitoring and head-cleaning routines) and are usually much more recent. However, Microsoft recommends that you use its own printer drivers whenever possible if you are installing a service pack for Windows; service packs might not work correctly if you have a vendor-supplied printer driver installed.

A new printer can be installed at any time; with Windows, any programs that use printers should be closed to enable common files used by all printers to be updated, particularly with Windows 9x/Me.

If you are installing a printer that wasn't packaged with a printer driver made especially for it, use the following options to configure the printer:

■ Download a new driver from the manufacturer's Web site.

■ Check the manual for recommended emulations.

■ For inkjet printers used with an MS-DOS program, choose the most similar inkjet printer made by the same maker, or a dot-matrix printer that the inkjet printer emulates.

■ If you want to use any printer with an MS-DOS program, you need to set up Windows to properly handle print jobs. With Windows 9x/Me, open the Details tab of a local printer's Properties sheet, click Port Settings, and make sure the Spool MS-DOS Print Jobs box is checked. Windows NT 4.0/2000/XP automatically spool print jobs to the printer attached to LPT1.

■ To print to a network printer from Windows, you need to use one of these methods. With Windows 9x/Me, open the Details tab of the printer's Properties sheet, click Capture Printer Port, select LPT1, and specify the path to the network printer. (Replace the text in italics with the actual server and shared printer name on your network.)

`\\`*servername*`\`*printername*

Click the Reconnect at Login box to make the connection persistent.

With Windows NT/2000/XP, open a command-prompt session and enter the following command:

net use lpt1 *servername******printername* **/persistent:yes**

Always use the Windows Test Print feature or create and print an MS-DOS document to see how well the substitute printer driver performs. Acquire and install the correct printer driver as soon as possible.

Study Lab

Don't miss the Study Lab materials found on the CD accompanying this book. Each Study Lab is tailored to the individual chapters in this book, meaning that you'll quickly be able to determine which topics you understand well enough to pass the exam and which topics need more study. The Study Labs are presented in printable PDF format so that you can take them with you to study at work, on the road, or even in your car just before test time!

THE ABSOLUTE MINIMUM

- When printing in Windows, the printer is controlled by Windows and print jobs are held in a print queue before being sent to the printer.

- Character/line printers can start printing as soon as they receive the start of the document.

- Page printers must receive the entire page (including fonts and graphics) before they can start printing.

- TrueType is a popular scalable font technology; Windows has native support for TrueType since version 3.1.

- HP LaserJet printers use PCL (Printer Control Language) as their native language; it is widely emulated by other brands.

- Adobe PostScript has more powerful graphics features, but requires PostScript language commands be sent to activate printing.

- Dot-matrix printers usually have 9-pin or 24-pin printheads. They are best suited for multipart forms.

- Inkjet printers typically support CMYK printing with two or more ink tanks (black/all colors or one for each color).

- Laser and LED printers both use the EP process to print, but LED printers use an LED array to write data to the imaging cartridge instead of a laser.

- The EP (electrophotographic) process has six steps: cleaning, conditioning, writing, developing, transferring, and fusing.

- Replacing the toner cartridge solves many problems with most laser printers because most of the imaging process happens inside the toner cartridge.

- Direct thermal printing uses heat-sensitive paper, whereas thermal transfer printing uses ribbons and can support multicolor printing.

- Dye-sublimation printers use a thermal process that turns dyes into gas to print continuous-tone photographs.

- Solid-ink printers are page printers that use separate CMYK ink blocks to print the page.

- Printer drivers control printers under Windows.

11

INSTALLING AND CONFIGURING COMMON PERIPHERALS

The 2003 revision of the A+ Certification Exams includes coverage of how to install common peripherals used for multimedia, portable, and network functions. If that's why you're reading this chapter, you've turned to the right page.

Interfaces Used for Common Peripherals

You need to connect a peripheral to your PC. Which ports will you use? Although a wide variety of I/O ports were formerly used to connect devices to a PC, most current PCs use just two port types for most peripheral connections:

- USB ports
- IEEE-1394a (FireWire 400/i.Link) ports

Some peripherals also connect to the PC Card or CardBus slots on a portable computer or to the serial port on a desktop or portable computer, but in general, both desktop and portable computers use USB and IEEE-1394a ports for most peripherals other than network devices.

USB and IEEE-1394a ports are supported by Windows 98 and newer versions. Devices using these ports can be hot-swapped in Windows 98 Second Edition and newer versions.

To learn more about these ports, see Chapter 8, "Input/Output Devices and Cables."

How do you connect your PC to a network device? Depending upon the device, you can use either the USB port or the RJ-45 10/100 Ethernet port. If you have a choice, which port is the better bet?

- USB 1.1 ports have a maximum speed of 12Mbps, which is fast enough for broadband Internet devices, but falls far below the 100Mbps speed of Fast Ethernet.
- USB 2.0 (Hi-Speed USB) ports have a maximum speed of 480Mbps, but support USB 1.1 devices at USB 1.1 speeds. If you want the blinding speed of USB 2.0, use USB 2.0 devices with USB 2.0 ports.

note

The CD included with this book contains important Study Lab material for this chapter, as well as Chapters 2–22 in this book. The Study Lab for each chapter contains terms to study, exercises, and practice tests—all in printable PDF format (Adobe Acrobat Reader is included on the CD, too). These Study Lab materials will help you gear up for the A+ Exam. Also, the CD includes an industry-leading test engine from PrepLogic, which simulates the actual A+ test so that you can be sure that you're ready when test day arrives. Don't let the A+ test intimidate you. If you've read the chapters, worked through the Study Lab, and passed the practice tests from PrepLogic, you should be well prepared to ace the test!

Also, you'll notice that some words throughout each chapter are in bold format. These are study terms that are defined in the Study Lab. Be sure to consult the Study Lab when you are finished with this chapter to test what you've learned.

■ 10/100 Ethernet ports run at 100Mbps when connecting with Fast Ethernet devices, and at just 10Mbps when connecting with 10BaseT Ethernet devices.

Given the speeds of these ports, I recommend Hi-Speed USB and 10/100 Ethernet as your best choices, and USB 1.1 if Hi-Speed USB ports or devices are not available.

Connecting Digital Cameras to Your PC

Digital cameras can be connected to your PC through either the USB port or serial port. Most recent digital cameras include a USB patch cable, whereas some older digital cameras might include both a USB and a serial cable, or only a serial cable.

note

Windows NT 4.0 and most versions of Windows 95 don't support USB or IEEE-1394a ports. The last edition of Windows 95 (Windows 95C) included a USB supplement you had to install manually, but the USB supplement doesn't work well with most devices.

Follow this procedure to connect a typical **digital camera** to your computer through the USB or serial ports. These instructions apply to all versions of Windows covered on the A+ Certification Exam.

1. Install the software provided with the camera. The software package included with your camera might include a photo-editing application as well, which might prove useful even if you decide not to install the camera-control software.

2. Connect the cable provided with the camera to the camera; the cable might attach to a mini-USB port or a proprietary connection.

3. Plug the Type A (flat) end of the USB cable from the camera into a USB port on the computer or a USB hub attached to the computer (see Figure 11.1). If a serial cable is used instead, shut down the computer, attach the cable to a serial port on the computer, and restart the computer. For more information about USB and serial ports, see Chapter 8.

4. Turn on the camera; set the camera to Connect mode if necessary. (Consult your camera's documentation for exact details.) After Windows detects the camera, the software provided with the camera should start automatically after a few moments. If not, start the program manually.

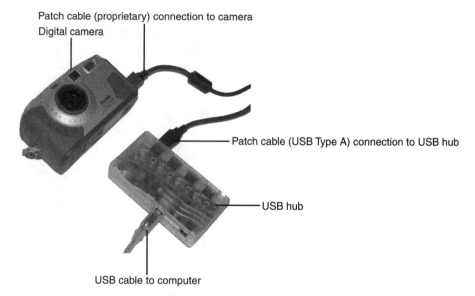

Patch cable (proprietary) connection to camera
Digital camera

Patch cable (USB Type A) connection to USB hub

USB hub

USB cable to computer

FIGURE 11.1

Attaching a dig-
ital camera to a
USB hub.

5. If you didn't install the software provided with the camera, Windows detects
   and installs drivers for the camera (you might need to provide a driver disk
   or CD).

6. Windows Me and XP feature the **Scanner and Camera Wizard** to transfer
   pictures from a digital camera to a folder of your choice. If the Scanner and
   Camera Wizard doesn't start automatically, start the program manually
   (click Start, [all] Programs, Accessories, Scanner and Camera Wizard). Select
   the pictures you want to transfer to your system (see Figure 11.2) and turn off
   the camera when you are finished.

FIGURE 11.2

Using the
Windows XP
Scanner and
Camera Wizard
to transfer pho-
tos from a digi-
tal camera.

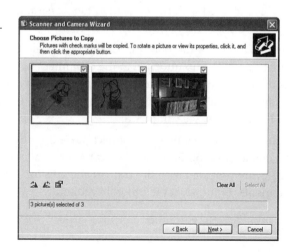

7. If the Scanner and Camera Wizard can't find your digital camera, check My Computer or Windows Explorer to see if the camera is being detected as a removable-media drive. You can drag and drop files from the camera to other drives as needed (see Figure 11.3).

FIGURE 11.3

Using Windows Explorer (My Computer) to transfer files from a digital camera.

Some digital cameras use a **camera dock**, a special type of docking station, instead of a direct USB or serial port connection. Follow the instructions listed next if a camera dock is used.

1. Install the software provided with the camera or camera dock.

2. Connect the camera dock to the computer. Plug the Type A (flat) end of the USB cable from the docking station into a USB port on the computer. This cable might be the same one provided with the camera or a separate cable provided with the camera dock.

3. Plug the camera dock into an AC power source with the cable provided.

4. Turn off the camera and attach the camera to the camera dock (see Figure 11.4).

note

If you use Windows XP or Me, you might be able to use the Camera and Scanner Wizard to transfer pictures from the camera to the computer as an alternative to the software provided with the camera.

5. Press the Connect button on the camera dock to begin transferring pictures to the computer. See the instruction manual provided with the camera or camera dock software for details.

6. Leave the camera in the camera dock to recharge its batteries.

FIGURE 11.4

Attaching a digital camera (top) to a camera dock (bottom).

note

Some digital cameras can be used with either a conventional camera dock or with a printer dock. A printer dock has all the features of a camera dock and also includes a dye-sublimation printer which makes 4×6-inch prints.

Connecting DV Camcorders to Your PC

Digital video (DV) camcorders connect to a PC through the IEEE-1394a (FireWire, i.Link) port for video transfer. Some DV camcorders also include Flash memory capability for use in still image capture, and these models use the USB port, just as normal digital cameras do.

If you don't have Windows Me or Windows XP, you need both an IEEE-1394a port and a third-party digital video capture/editing software to work with digital video. Many IEEE-1394a cards include software for capturing digital video. However, if you use Windows Me or Windows XP, you can use the built-in Scanner and Camera Wizard and Microsoft Movie Maker to capture and edit digital video.

Follow this procedure to connect a typical DV camcorder to your computer through the IEEE-1394a port.

1. Install an IEEE-1394a card if your system doesn't have an IEEE-1394a port. (See Chapter 8 for details.)

2. Turn on the system. Install the drivers for the card and restart the system if necessary.

3. Install the software provided with the camera; with Windows XP or Me, you might be able to use the Camera and Scanner Wizard to transfer pictures from the camera to the computer as an alternative to the software provided with the camera.

4. Connect the appropriate type of IEEE-1394a cable to the camera. Cameras use the four-wire connector shown in Chapter 8. Most computers with built-in IEEE-1394a ports and all IEEE-1394a cards use the six-wire connector shown in Chapter 8, except for Sony's computers with i.Link: The i.Link port uses the same four-wire connector as a DV camcorder.

5. Connect the other end of the IEEE-1394a cable to the IEEE-1394a/FireWire/i.Link port on the computer.

6. If the DV camcorder also captures still images to Flash memory and you prefer to connect the camcorder directly to the PC instead of using a card reader, connect the USB cable provided with the camcorder to the camcorder's USB port.

> **note**
>
> It's imperative that you verify that a particular IEEE-1394a card is compatible with Windows XP. For some reason, Windows XP seems to be fussier than other versions (98, 2000, and Me) about IEEE-1394a support. I recommend you make sure that the card you want to buy has a Windows XP driver included in the package or is listed on the Microsoft Windows Catalog (www.microsoft.com/windows/catalog) Web site.
>
> Keep in mind that if you can't locate a Windows XP driver for your card, you might be able to use a Windows XP driver from a vendor whose card uses the same IEEE-1394a chipset.

7. Plug the Type A (flat) end of the USB cable from the camera into a USB port on the computer or a USB hub attached to the computer.

8. Turn on the camcorder and follow the prompts from the camera's own software or Windows Scanner and Camera Wizard to capture your footage.

9. Follow the camcorder's instructions for transferring still images from the camcorder's Flash memory card.

Connecting PDAs and Pocket PCs to Your PC

PDAs (personal digital assistants) such as Pocket PCs and PalmOS-based devices can be connected to PCs in three ways:

- With a cradle that attaches to the PC with a serial or USB cable
- Direct connect with serial or USB cables
- IrDA (infrared) port

As with digital cameras, you should install the software provided with the PDA first before you connect the PDA to your computer.

After the software is installed, follow this procedure to connect the PDA:

1. Read the instructions included with your PDA. You might need to install the software included with your PDA before you connect it to your PC.

2. Install driver software and perform other preliminary steps as required.

note

If you're working with a system that's so cutting edge it has an **IEEE-1394b (FireWire 800)** port or card instead of an IEEE-1394a card, you can plug the DV camcorder into the card or computer's legacy (bilingual) port, which can accept either 1394b or 1394a connections. See the Apple FireWire 800 briefing (PDF format, requires Adobe Acrobat Reader) at http://www.apple.com/firewire/pdf/FireWire_Tech_Brief-a.pdf for details.

3. Connect the serial or USB cable or **cradle** to the appropriate port on your computer. If the cradle uses AC power, plug the cradle into an AC power source such as a wall outlet or surge suppressor.

4. If a cable is used, connect the other end of the cable to the PDA and turn on the PDA to start the synchronization process. Some cables also provide power to recharge the PDA.

5. If a cradle is used, slide the PDA into the cradle (see Figure 11.5) and turn it on to start the synchronization process. The cradle also recharges the PDA.

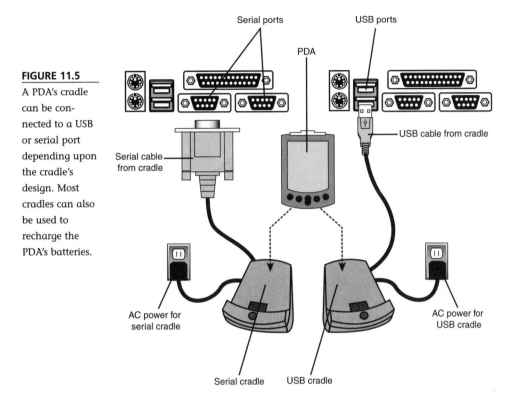

FIGURE 11.5
A PDA's cradle can be connected to a USB or serial port depending upon the cradle's design. Most cradles can also be used to recharge the PDA's batteries.

Connecting Network Devices to Your PC

Network devices such as wireless access points, infrared adapters, and broadband Internet access devices can be connected to your PC with the following methods:

- Direct connection to the RJ-45 (10/100 Ethernet) port
- Direct connection to the USB port
- Wireless Ethernet (Wi-Fi) connection
- Installation of a proprietary module on the motherboard

Read the following sections to learn more.

Connecting Wireless Access Points

Although some **wireless access points (WAPs)** can be configured through a wireless connection established with a compatible wireless Ethernet card, you might prefer to connect a CAT 5 (10/100 Ethernet) cable using the RJ-45 connector between the WAP and your PC to make configuration easier.

The cable should be plugged into the appropriate port on the WAP. If the WAP also contains a **router**, make sure you don't attach the cable to the **WAN** port—this port is used to connect the router to a broadband Internet access device. Use one of the **LAN** ports—they are designed to connect to PCs (see Figure 11.6).

FIGURE 11.6

The rear of a typical WAP, which incorporates a router and a switch. Use the LAN ports (numbered 1–4 in this example) for wired networking or to configure the router.

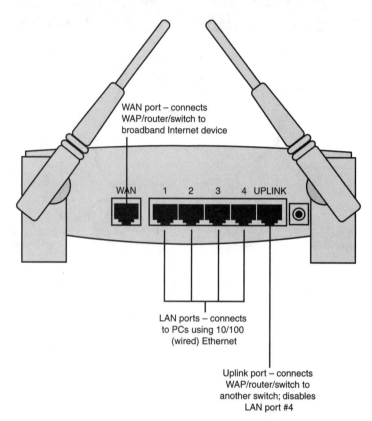

WAN port – connects WAP/router/switch to broadband Internet device

WAN 1 2 3 4 UPLINK

LAN ports – connects to PCs using 10/100 (wired) Ethernet

Uplink port – connects WAP/router/switch to another switch; disables LAN port #4

After the connection is made, follow the instructions provided with the WAP for configuration.

Connecting Broadband Internet Access Devices

You can connect broadband Internet access devices such as cable modems or DSL modems to the USB or 10/100 Ethernet port on your computer. Follow this procedure:

1. If the **broadband Internet access device** supports both USB and 10/100 Ethernet, select the connection type you want to use. I recommend 10/100 Ethernet if your computer and broadband device support it. Otherwise, use USB.

2. Connect the broadband Internet access device to the data cable used by the provider: A **cable modem** uses coaxial cable provided by the **CATV** provider (see Figure 11.7), whereas a **DSL modem** uses a specially provisioned telephone line. See Chapter 21, "Networking and Internet Connectivity," for more details.

3. Connect the USB or 10/100 Ethernet (RJ-45) cable to the port on the broadband device (see Figure 11.7)

4. Connect the other end of the cable to the USB or 10/100 Ethernet port on your computer.

5. Connect the broadband Internet device to AC power with the transformer provided with the unit (see Figure 11.7).

6. Turn on the broadband Internet device if it has a separate on/off switch.

7. Turn on the PC if it was turned off.

8. Install any software provided by the broadband Internet access vendor. You might also need to install Windows network drivers, so have your Windows CD handy.

9. Configure the software as required (user name, password, and so on).

FIGURE 11.7

Power, 10/100 Ethernet, and coaxial cables connected to the rear of a typical cable modem.

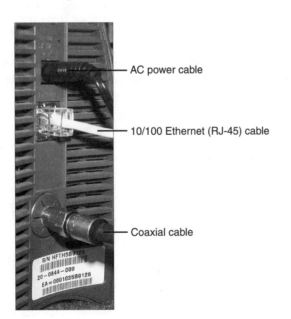

AC power cable

10/100 Ethernet (RJ-45) cable

Coaxial cable

Connecting Infrared Adapters

Infrared adapters for connecting computers to IrDA-compliant printers and other devices aren't all that popular. Nevertheless, the 2003 edition of the A+ Certification Exam expects you to be ready to handle the process of installing and configuring an **infrared adapter**—just in case.

Infrared adapters can be installed in the following locations:

- Inside a desktop PC
- Connected to existing serial or USB ports
- Connected to a printer

Some laser printers, portable inkjet printers, and notebook computers already include IrDA-compliant infrared ports.

Installing an Infrared Port on a PC

Most motherboards that support Pentium or newer processors have a multi-pin infrared port that is compatible with the **IrDA** standard. IrDA is the infrared data transport method supported by the Infrared Data Association. Most motherboards treat the IrDA port as a COM port; the IrDA port is enabled in the system BIOS as a separate component on some motherboards, but other motherboards enable infrared as a setting for one of the COM ports (normally COM 2).

Although the infrared port can be enabled or disabled through the system BIOS, it is useless until a transceiver is attached to the header pins on the motherboard. So, if you want infrared transmissions, where do you get the transceiver? You can get transceivers from the following sources:

- The motherboard maker
- Third-party sources (search Google for "IrDA motherboard" to find them)

In most cases, the transceiver is connected to the motherboard by means of a bracket with a header cable (see Figure 11.8). To install this type of a transceiver, follow this procedure:

1. Shut down the computer and unplug it. Take ESD precautions as described in Chapter 13, "Safety and Recycling."

2. Remove the cover to gain access to the motherboard.

The leading third-party source of IrDA transceivers is ACTiSYS Corporation (www.actisys.com).

3. Remove a slot cover for use by the bracket with the IrDA header cable.

4. Attach the bracket to the rear of the computer in place of the slot cover you removed in step 3.

5. Use the documentation for the motherboard to locate the pins for the IrDA infrared module or infrared port.

6. Connect the cable from the bracket to the header pins on the motherboard. Make sure you match the pinouts of the header cable to the header pins.

7. Connect the transceiver to the bracket you installed in step 4.

8. Plug in the computer and turn it on.

9. Start the BIOS setup program and enable the infrared port. Adjust the settings according to the recommendations for the transceiver or module you are using.

10. Save the changes to the BIOS and restart the computer.

11. If necessary, provide the Windows CD or driver disk to complete the setup process.

tip

As an alternative to installing an internal infrared port, ACTiSYS and other vendors offer IrDA-compatible adapters that can be attached to existing USB and serial ports.

FIGURE 11.8

A typical IrDA transceiver kit designed to connect to the IrDA header pins found on most recent motherboards.

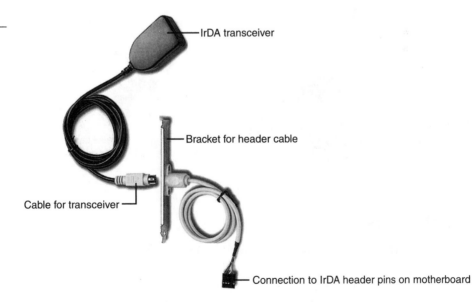

IrDA transceiver

Bracket for header cable

Cable for transceiver

Connection to IrDA header pins on motherboard

Adapting a Parallel Printer to Work with IrDA

Having IrDA support on a desktop or portable computer is useful if you want to print or perform file transfers without wires. However, if you want to print wirelessly, the printer also needs to support IrDA. You can attach an IrDA receiver (see Figure 11.9) to many parallel printers that don't include IrDA support. Follow this basic procedure:

1. Shut down the PC and the printer.
2. Disconnect the parallel cable from the printer's Centronics parallel port.
3. Connect the IrDA receiver to the Centronics port on the printer.
4. Plug the parallel cable back into the IrDA receiver's Centronics port (see Figure 11.9).
5. Make sure the parallel cable is still connected to the PC's parallel port.
6. If the IrDA receiver requires power, plug its AC adapter into a power source.
7. Position the IrDA receiver where it can be seen by the computer(s) from which you want to print.
8. Turn on the computer and the printer.
9. Install any software drivers required by the adapter.
10. Test the adapter by printing from the host PC and by printing from a computer with an IrDA port.

FIGURE 11.9

A typical IrDA parallel printer adapter kit. The printer can still be used by the host PC as well as by other PCs that have IrDA support.

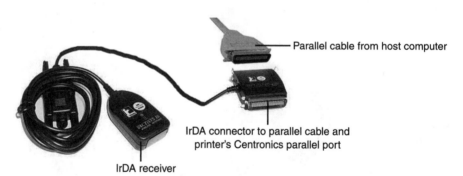

Parallel cable from host computer

IrDA connector to parallel cable and printer's Centronics parallel port

IrDA receiver

Study Lab

Don't miss the Study Lab materials found on the CD accompanying this book. Each Study Lab is tailored to the individual chapters in this book, meaning that you'll quickly be able to determine which topics you understand well enough to pass the exam and which topics need more study. The Study Labs are presented in printable PDF format so that you can take them with you to study at work, on the road, or even in your car just before test time!

THE ABSOLUTE MINIMUM

Use this section for a final review before your test.

- Most recent peripherals connect to the USB or IEEE-1394a ports, although some also use the serial or PC Card connections.

- Network devices can connect to the 10/100 Ethernet or USB ports.

- Digital cameras can connect directly to the PC with a USB or serial cable, via a camera dock connected to the USB port, or via a printer dock connected to the USB port.

- The Windows Me/XP Scanner and Camera Wizard can be used with many digital cameras to preview and transfer pictures.

- Some digital cameras show up as removable drive letters in My Computer/Windows Explorer if the standard Windows drivers are used to install the camera instead of the camera's own customized software.

- PDAs can connect directly to a PC's serial or USB port, or via serial or USB cradles.

- Some cables can also recharge the PDA's batteries, whereas almost all cradles can.

- Broadband Internet access devices such as cable modems or DSL modems can be connected to the PC's 10/100 Ethernet or USB ports.

- Most recent motherboards have IrDA header pins on the motherboard, but the actual transceiver is usually not included.

- IrDA ports can be used for file transfer or printing to IrDA-equipped printers.

- You can add IrDA adapters to serial or USB ports, and adapt parallel printers to work with IrDA-equipped computers.

12

PORTABLES

Portable computers, once regarded as a niche product used primarily by travelers, have become mainstream. They're showing up on desks and bistro tables across the world as well as under an airline seat near you. In May 2003, portable computers outsold desktop computers for the first time! To successfully maintain portable computers, you must understand their unique features and the special challenges they present for repair and upgrades.

Major Components of Typical Portable Computers

What makes portable computers different than desktop computers? They perform the same types of tasks, but Table 12.1 shows you how their hardware differs.

Table 12.1 Portable and Desktop Computers Comparison by Features

Feature	Desktop Computer	Portable Computer
Display	Separate CRT or LCD display connected to VGA port	Integrated LCD plus external VGA port
Keyboard	Standard 101 or 104 key with separate numerical keypad; full-size keys	Compact integrated keyboard with embedded numerical keypad; nonstandard layout of directional keys
Mouse or pointing device	Separate unit; wide choice of types	Integrated into keyboard; can be replaced with external units
Battery use	Battery used for CMOS maintenance only	Battery used to power computer and many peripherals attached to computer; separate battery used for CMOS maintenance
Expansion bus	PCI and ISA slots enable interchange of many different components	Connector for docking station and/or port replicator is proprietary
Hard disk form factor	3.5 inch or 5.25 inch	2.5 inch, with integrated power and data connector
PC Card	Optional card reader	Standard on most systems
Floppy drive location	Internal; a few now use external USB interface	May be internal or external, using hot-swappable proprietary or USB interface
Optical drive location	Internal or external	May be internal or external
Memory expansion	Uses standard DIMM, SIMM, or Rambus modules	Uses proprietary modules or Small Outline (SO) SDRAM, DDR SDRAM, or Rambus modules
CPU upgrades	Common on virtually any model	Not available due to special CPU types used in portable computers
Video	AGP or PCI slot, or integrated into chipset	Integrated into motherboard chipset or separate chip soldered to motherboard

A typical portable computer has the following components:

- Integrated LCD display
- Integrated keyboard with pointing device
- Standard I/O ports
- Integrated drives
- Battery
- Proprietary motherboard with integrated video or 3D graphics and mobile-optimized processor; some memory might be built into the motherboard
- Integrated speakers

Recent systems might also include

- Integrated wired (10/100 Ethernet) or wireless (Wi-Fi) network adapters
- Integrated analog (dial-up) modem
- Advanced I/O ports such as IEEE-1394a and USB 2.0

Tablet PCs are similar to traditional portable computers, but feature a modified version of Windows XP (called Windows XP Tablet Edition), support handwriting recognition, and sometimes have detachable keyboards.

Although portable and desktop computers have many differences, systems that use the same version of Microsoft Windows and have similar CPU types, CPU speeds, and memory sizes are capable of performing work in similar ways. This is definitely not the case with the smallest and newest portable unit, the *Portable Digital Assistant (PDA)*. PDAs differ not only in their size (hand-held), but in their user interface (stylus-based with handwriting recognition or an optional keyboard on some models), their processors, their operating systems, and their storage (fixed or removable flash memory).

note

The CD included with this book contains important Study Lab material for this chapter, as well as Chapters 2–22 in this book. The Study Lab for each chapter contains terms to study, exercises, and practice tests—all in printable PDF format (Adobe Acrobat Reader is included on the CD, too). These Study Lab materials will help you gear up for the A+ Exam. Also, the CD includes an industry-leading test engine from PrepLogic, which simulates the actual A+ test so that you can be sure that you're ready when test day arrives. Don't let the A+ test intimidate you. If you've read the chapters, worked through the Study Lab, and passed the practice tests from PrepLogic, you should be well prepared to ace the test!

Also, you'll notice that some words throughout each chapter are in bold format. These are study terms that are defined in the Study Lab. Be sure to consult the Study Lab when you are finished with this chapter to test what you've learned.

PalmOS PDAs are generally smaller, lighter, and less expensive than Pocket PCs. Pocket PCs use Windows CE, a version of Windows designed for PDA processors, which runs different applications than desktop Windows.

With add-on software such as Documents to Go, both PalmOS- and Windows CE–based PDAs can create documents and exchange data files as well as synchronize contact information and email with desktop computers. However, PDAs should be looked at as a supplement, rather than as a partial replacement, for larger computers.

In the following sections, you'll learn about the distinctive challenges of portable hardware.

Standard I/O Interfaces Used on Portable Computers

Most portable computers feature a wide range of standard I/O connectors that can be used in the same way as those on desktop computers:

- Serial (RS-232) ports (see Chapter 8, "Input/Output Devices and Cables")
- Parallel port (see Chapter 8)
- External VGA (see Chapter 9, "Video")
- PS/2 jack for keyboard/mouse (see Chapter 8)
- USB ports (see Chapter 8)

For details on using these options, see the chapters referenced for each port type.

LCD Display

One of the biggest differences between portable and desktop computers is the display. Desktop computers enable both the screen and graphics cards to be changed; in portable computers, both the screen and graphics cards are built into the system. Although most portables feature an external VGA port, which enables a separate monitor to be plugged into the computer, that is the extent of the video expandability of most portable systems. Some recent systems support DualView, a Windows XP feature that enables supported graphics chipsets to use an external monitor as a true secondary monitor instead of as a mirror of or replacement of the built-in display.

Two major types of **LCD display** screens are used on portables: dual-scan and active-matrix.

Dual-Scan

Dual-scan displays are no longer used on portable computers. However, you might encounter them on older systems. Dual-scan displays are an improved version of **passive-matrix** displays. Both are controlled by an array of transistors along the horizontal and vertical edges of the display. For example, a 1,024×768 resolution display features 1,024 transistors along the horizontal edge of the display and 768 transistors along the vertical. The transistors send out a pulse of energy, and the individual LCDs polarize at varying angles to produce the picture. Dual-scan screens split the screen into a top half and a bottom half for faster response.

Dual-scan LCD displays are dimmer, have slower response times, and feature a narrower viewing angle than active-matrix screens. The main advantage of dual-scan LCD displays is that, until recently, they have been far less expensive to replace when broken. For that reason, many companies have selected portables with dual-scan displays instead of active-matrix displays. Keep in mind that a portable with a dual-scan display cannot be upgraded to an active-matrix display because the interface to the system is completely different.

Active-Matrix

Active-matrix refers to screens that use a transistor for every dot seen onscreen: for example, a 1,024×768 active-matrix LCD screen has 786,432 transistors. The additional transistors put the "active" in active-matrix, making them nearly as bright as CRT displays. They also offer wide viewing angles for easier use by groups of people and tend to display rapid movement and full-motion video with less blur then dual-scan displays.

Until recently, active-matrix LCD displays were more expensive to replace when broken, and computers with these screens were more expensive to buy initially. However, the widespread popularity of active-matrix desktop displays and improvements in production capacity have enabled active-matrix panels to replace dual-scan in all price ranges of portable computers.

Active-matrix LCD displays also are used an increasing number of desktop computers. Unlike portable active-matrix displays, these displays are attached to the video card or built-in video port the same way that standard CRT-based monitors are. Most plug into the VGA port, but some high-end displays use the DVI port found on mid-range and high-end graphics cards.

Video/Graphics Circuitry

The other built-in portion of the display system is the graphics circuitry; portable computers have built-in graphics that can't be interchanged. There are two methods used for graphics support:

- Motherboard chipsets with integrated graphics
- Discrete graphic chip on the motherboard

What are the differences between these?

Motherboard chipsets with **integrated graphics** provide adequate performance for business (2D) graphics and cost less than those with discrete graphics, but must use system memory to display graphics. As a result, portables with this design do poorly at displaying full-motion graphics or 3D animations. If you want to increase the amount of memory available for graphics, you might be able to do so by adding additional system memory. Some systems automatically adjust the amount of memory set aside for graphics depending upon the amount of system memory installed. You can sometimes adjust the amount of memory set aside for graphics with a BIOS setting.

Systems that use a **discrete graphics** chip have faster 3D performance due to these chips' more advanced design and their use of dedicated memory. Recent versions of these chips typically support Windows XP's DualView, which enables an external monitor to be used as a secondary monitor. Typically, you can't increase the amount of graphics memory, but systems with discrete graphics usually have more than enough for both business and light to moderate 3D gaming.

> **tip**
>
> To determine if a portable running Windows XP supports DualView, open the Display properties sheet and click the Settings tab. If two monitor icons are displayed, the system supports DualView. Activate it by attaching a monitor to the external video port. If only one monitor icon is shown, DualView is not supported.

Installation and Removal of LCD Display Panels

LCD display panels built into portable computers are customized for each model of portable computer and require the disassembly of the computer for removal and replacement. You can get replacements from either the vendor or an authorized repair parts depot. Many vendors require that you be an authorized technician before you remove or replace LCD display panels in portable computers. However, the process of replacing the entire LCD display assembly is simpler and *might* be possible for you to perform in the field.

The details of the process for removing an LCD display assembly from a portable computer vary by model, but you can follow these basic steps:

1. Remove the screws holding the display assembly in place.

2. Remove the cover over the monitor connector.

3. Unlatch the LCD panel from the base unit.

4. Rotate the display assembly to a 90-degree angle to the base unit.

5. Lift the display assembly free from the base unit.

6. Remove the cover over the **FPC** cable attachment on the system board; the FPC cable transmits power and data to the LCD display assembly.

7. Disconnect the assembly's FPC cable from the system board.

8. Be sure to save all screws, ground springs, and other hardware that you removed during the disassembly process.

Depending on the vendor, you might be able to purchase a replacement LCD display assembly that can be installed by following the previous steps in reverse order, or you might need to disassemble the display assembly to remove and install the LCD display panel itself. Replacing the LCD display panel (which requires the disassembly of the display assembly) should be performed at a repair depot.

Because of differences in chipsets, BIOSs, and display circuitry between systems with dual-scan and active-matrix LCD panels, dual-scan and active-matrix LCD panels are generally not interchangeable.

> ## caution
>
> Should you do your own LCD display panel replacement? Vendors are of two minds about this. Some vendors provide online documentation, which guides you through the entire process of reducing an intact portable into a pile of parts and rebuilding it. However, this information is primarily intended for professional computer service staff. Portables require specialized tools to deal with their tiny screws and snap-together cases and they contain proprietary parts: If you break an internal drive or an integrated keyboard, you can't run to your favorite electronics superstore for a replacement. You have been warned.

Input Devices

Although portable computers can use the same keyboards, mice and other input devices used by desktop computers, portable users generally use the portable's integrated input devices.

Integrated Keyboards

Portable systems feature keyboards that are designed to be compact in size and light in weight. Internally, the keyboard module attaches to the notebook's main portable computer circuitry with a relatively fragile ribbon cable. In most cases, the keyboard also integrates the primary pointing device (see Figure 12.1).

Portable keyboards also differ from desktop keyboards in their layout:

- An integrated numeric keypad typically occupies the right side of the keyboard; instead of a Num Lock key, the normal letter and number functions are switched to the number pad functions with a special key, often marked Fn (see Figure 12.2).

- The classic "inverted T" layout for directional arrows is sometimes not used because of space limitations.

Because of the portable keyboard's design, it is vulnerable to a heavy touch while typing (easy does it!), abuse of the **pointing device**, and spills, dirt, and dust.

FIGURE 12.1

A typical notebook computer with an integrated pointing device (Toshiba **AccuPoint**, a licensed version of the IBM TrackPoint II), reduced-size function keys, and the special Fn key that switches the normal function keys to special uses, such as power management.

The CD-ROM drive in its removable bay

The ribbon cable that attaches keyboard to motherboard

The function keys, reduced in size to save space

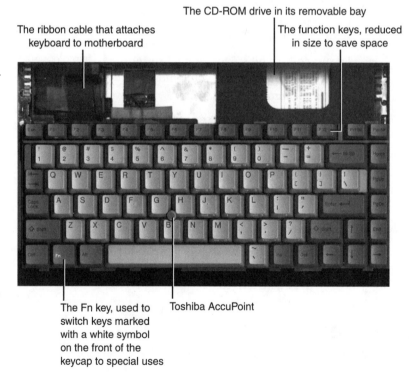

The Fn key, used to switch keys marked with a white symbol on the front of the keycap to special uses

Toshiba AccuPoint

Portable Keyboard Replacement

Replacing a portable keyboard requires the unit to be partially disassembled. Details vary from unit to unit (check with your vendor for the details of the particular model you are repairing), but the following is the basic procedure:

1. Remove the display assembly if the vendor recommends this; some portable systems don't require this step.

2. Remove screws or bezels that hold the keyboard in place.

3. Lift up the keyboard to expose the keyboard cable.

4. Remove any hold-down devices used to hold the keyboard cable in place.

5. Disconnect the keyboard cable from the system board.

6. Remove the keyboard.

tip

If you have purchased a replacement integrated keyboard, it might include detailed disassembly/reassembly instructions.

Contact the parts or system vendor to get this information if your replacement keyboard doesn't include this information.

If the keyboard has an integrated pointing device, such as the IBM TrackPoint II or similar device, this procedure will remove the pointing device but might not replace the buttons.

➪ If the buttons or the pointing device are built into the **palm rest, see** "Replacing Portable Pointing Devices," **p. 387**, later in this chapter.

To install a replacement keyboard, reverse the steps.

note

Note that because of differences in design, form factor, and system board interface, integrated portable keyboards are not usually interchangeable between brands and models.

Mouse and Mouse Alternatives on Portable Computers

Some very old portable computers you might still encounter use clip-on **trackballs** that plug into standard PS/2 or serial mouse ports. Most recent portable computers use one of the following technologies as an alternative to a separate mouse, which can still be used.

IBM TrackPoint II "Eraserhead" Pointing Stick

This mouse alternative (originally called the **TrackPoint II** by IBM) enables the user to keep his or her hands on the keyboard at all times, pushing a small button shaped like a pencil eraser located in the middle of the keyboard to move the mouse pointer. Although this technology was developed by IBM for its portable computers, it has been licensed by several other vendors, including Toshiba and HP (refer to Figure 12.1).

The mouse buttons for the TrackPoint are located beneath the spacebar; some systems use the conventional left and right buttons, but others use buttons arranged vertically, in which the top button corresponds to the left mouse button and the bottom button corresponds to the right mouse button. Newer systems might feature an additional button used to scroll the screen.

The IBM UltraNav found on some recent-model IBM ThinkPad portables combines the features of a **pointing stick** and a **touchpad**; use the System Setup dialog box in Windows to selectively disable either pointing device if desired. Some Dell computers also offer both pointing devices.

Touchpad

This mouse alternative uses a square or rectangular touch-sensitive surface located beneath the spacebar. To move the mouse pointer, the user slides his or her finger on the surface. Clicking and double-clicking can be done by tapping on the trackpad surface with the finger or with the mouse buttons. The Mouse Properties sheet can be used to enable or disable clicking or other touchpad options.

The mouse buttons for the touchpad are also located beneath the spacebar; if the buttons are arranged vertically, the top button corresponds to the left mouse button and the bottom button corresponds to the right mouse button. Newer systems might feature an additional button for scrolling the screen (see Figure 12.2).

Trackball

This mouse alternative, found primarily on older portables, uses a ball similar in size to a mouse ball and is situated below the spacebar. The user rolls the trackball to guide the cursor. The mouse buttons for the trackball are also located beneath the spacebar—as with other pointing devices, the buttons can be arranged horizontally or vertically.

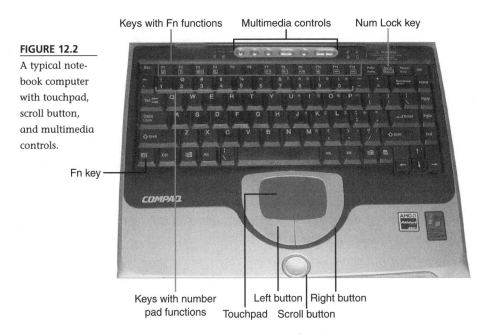

FIGURE 12.2

A typical notebook computer with touchpad, scroll button, and multimedia controls.

Replacing Portable Pointing Devices

Pointing devices in portable computers are normally located in two places:

- *The palm rest*—Used for touchpads and integrated trackballs and for the buttons on some pointing sticks.

- *The keyboard*—Used for integrated pointing sticks, such as the IBM TrackPoint II and later versions.

To replace defective pointing sticks, follow the steps listed in "Portable Keyboard Replacement," earlier in this chapter.

If you need to replace the pointing device built into the palm rest (including buttons used by pointing sticks), you need to partially disassemble the portable computer. Details vary from unit to unit (check with your vendor for details), but the following is the basic procedure.

To remove the palm rest

1. Remove the display panel assembly (if necessary) and keyboard.

2. Turn over the system.

3. Release the clips or screws holding the palm rest in place.

4. Turn the system right side up.

5. Remove the palm rest from the system.

To remove a pointing device, such as a touchpad or others, from the palm rest

1. Disconnect or unscrew the pointing device from the touchpad.

2. Remove the pointing device from the touchpad.

3. You might need to remove the pointing device cable from the pointing device or from the system board; check the specific instructions for the device.

To replace the pointing device, follow these steps in reverse order to install a new pointing device into the palm rest and to reinstall the palm rest into the portable computer.

Power Sources

Portable computers typically have two power sources:

- AC power
- Battery power

Battery power is a vital feature for portable computers, which are frequently used away from an AC power source. Battery life depends on several factors, including

- Battery type
- Recharging practices
- Power-management options
- Memory size
- CPU speed and type
- PC Card type and use

Battery Types

How long should a portable computer's battery last? The rechargeable battery type used by a portable computer has a great deal to do with the amount of time you can use a computer between recharges (the *run time*).

The most common battery types include

- Nickel Metal Hydrite (NiMH)
- Lithium Ion (Li-Ion)
- Nickel-Cadmium (NiCad or NiCd)

note

Portable computers actually have at least two batteries:

- Main battery (used to power the computer)
- CMOS battery (used to maintain CMOS/BIOS settings)

Some also have a third battery called a *RAM* or *bridge* battery. This is used for reserve power or to support suspend/restore functions. In this chapter, *battery* refers to the main battery.

The original rechargeable standard, **NiCad**, has fallen out of favor for use as a notebook computer's main power source because of a problem called the **memory effect**. If NiCad batteries are not fully discharged before being recharged, the memory effect enables the battery to be recharged only to the level it was used. In other words, if you use a NiCad battery and recharge it when it's only 50% exhausted, the memory effect will enable you to use only 50% of the battery's actual capacity. You might be able to correct the memory effect if you'll allow your battery to fully discharge before recharging it; however, the memory effect can permanently affect your battery's condition.

Low-cost notebook computers use **NiMH** batteries instead of NiCad. NiMH batteries have fewer problems with the memory effect and can be used in place of NiCad in most cases.

The most efficient battery technology in widespread use is **Li-Ion**, which has little problem with memory effect, puts out the same power as NiMH, but is about 35% lighter.

NiCad batteries are still used today but as CMOS batteries or as "RAM" or "bridge" batteries, which store a system's configuration when the suspend mode is used.

Batteries for PDAs

PDAs, such as the Palm series or **Pocket PC** models, often use off-the-shelf alkaline or NiMH rechargeable batteries in AA or AAA sizes. These batteries usually can be purchased at local retail stores. Use nonalkaline rechargeable batteries only in systems that are designed for them. Rechargeable alkaline batteries can be used in systems that were designed for standard alkaline batteries. Some units are designed to use rechargeable battery packs.

Battery and Charger Interchangeability

Both battery types and battery form factors prevent free interchange of batteries between different brands—and even different models—of portable computer systems. The Duracell standardized battery packs found in a few models of portable computers have never become widely adopted.

Rechargers, too, are matched to particular brands and models of portable computers.

Power Adapters and Battery Chargers

Most systems use an external AC adapter and battery-charging unit, sometimes referred to as a *brick*. To make portable use easier, some systems build the AC adapter/battery charger into the portable computer and use a special polarized power cord for recharging.

Just as with desktop power supplies, notebook battery recharging systems must be compatible with the local electrical power source. Most portable computers use an automatically switching recharger, capable of handling either European and Asian 50-cycle, 230V power or North American 60-cycle, 115V power (see Figure 12.3). However, a few systems are shipped with a single voltage recharger, requiring that you use a power converter or different recharger if you travel internationally.

FIGURE 12.3

A portion of the label from a typ- ical portable battery charger, which features auto-switching.

Voltage/frequency input and amperage output

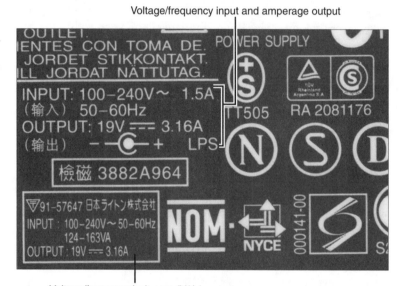

Voltage/frequency/volt-amp (VA) input

If the portable computer doesn't appear to be receiving power from either an exter- nal or internal AC adapter/battery charger, check the following:

- Loose or defective line cord
- Battery failure

Check the line cord for damage or loose connections; reconnect or replace the line cord between the wall outlet and the computer or external AC adapter, and retest the system. If the system still will not start and run correctly, remove the batteries from the portable computer and try to run it from wall current only if the unit will work in this fashion. If the batteries are the problem, the unit should work properly on wall current only—simply replace the batteries.

If both of these tests fail, repair or replace the external AC adapter or computer with the internal AC adapter. Use only manufacturer-approved parts for replacement. Because of differences in battery technology and system boards, internal units from different models of portable computers usually are not interchangeable. Make sure that you replace single-voltage AC adapters with the correct voltage for your country or region.

Battery Replacement

Most batteries in portable computers can be replaced by the user in the field. Generally, replacement batteries fall into two categories:

- *Proprietary batteries that are customized for a particular portable computer model*—You can purchase these batteries from specialized battery stores as well as from the manufacturer of the computer.

- *Industry-standard models that fit into a wide variety of computer and other devices*—These batteries can be purchased at most retail stores. Most computers that use industry-standard AA- and AAA-sized batteries are PDAs.

tip

Battery power is measured in milliampere hours (mAh). The larger the mAh value, the longer the battery will last. If you need to replace the battery in a portable computer, find out if you can get a high-capacity battery (a battery with a larger mAh value) instead of the standard-capacity battery originally supplied with the portable.

Follow this procedure to replace computer batteries:

1. Turn off the computer.

2. Unplug the AC adapter or line cord from the computer.

3. Locate the battery compartment in the unit; it might be secured by a sliding lock or by screws.

4. Remove the cover.

5. Slide or lift out the battery or batteries. If the battery is a flat assembly, it might be held in place by a clip; push the clip to one side to release the battery.

6. Check the battery contacts inside the computer for dirt or corrosion, and clean dirty contacts with a soft cloth.

7. Insert the replacement battery or batteries. Make sure you insert batteries so the positive and negative terminals are in the right directions.

8. Close the cover and secure it.

9. If the battery must be charged before use, plug in the line cord or AC adapter into both the computer and wall outlet. Check the computer's manual for the proper charge time for a new battery.

10. Unplug the system or AC adapter when the battery has been charged for the recommended time period.

> **caution**
>
> Take precautions against ESD when you change the battery: Discharge any static electricity in your body by touching a metal object before you open the battery compartment, and don't touch the contacts on the battery or battery contact with your hands.

Power Management

Power management originated with portable computers because of their heavy dependence upon battery power. Power management for notebook computers is usually simpler to configure than for desktop computers. There are two major hardware standards for power management: Windows 95 supports only **Advanced Power Management (APM)**, and Windows 98/Me/2000/XP also support **Advanced Configuration and Power Interface (ACPI)**.

Advanced Power Management (APM)

APM uses a combination of BIOS configuration options and matching configuration settings in Windows to control power usage by devices such as the display, the CPU, and disk drives. Frequently, Windows-based portable computers come with a special program that enables you to select timing options for power management, different power-management settings for battery and AC power, and options that enable the suspend and resume modes featured in many portable computers.

Systems that use APM power management normally control the power usage of the following parts of a portable system:

■ *Screen brightness*—The brighter the screen, the faster the battery runs down.

■ *Hard disk spin down*—Next to the screen, the biggest user of power in the notebook computer is the hard disk. Allowing the hard disk to spin down during a period of inactivity saves a lot of power.

■ *Adjustable CPU speed*—Reducing the CPU speed, even by a modest amount in MHz, greatly improves battery life in two ways: Slower CPUs use less power, and slower CPUs run cooler, enabling the built-in fans on many portables to run slower or less often. Mobile versions of the Pentium III, Pentium 4, AMD Athlon XP, and the mobile-only Pentium-M processor are designed to support adjustable CPU speeds. Many recent systems vary the CPU speed automatically according to the task the user is performing or whether the portable is running on AC or battery power.

■ *Suspend and resume*—For busy users, suspend and resume can be very useful. The suspend feature enables the user to shut down the computer without closing all the programs; the matching resume feature enables the computer to restart in a few seconds where the user stopped, without having to restart all the programs. Suspend and resume functions depend on

■ Correct BIOS power-management settings

■ Correct settings in Windows-based power management

■ A working RAM or bridge battery and charged main battery

The best power-management settings won't interfere with normal work but will put the computer into power-saving modes during periods of inactivity. A good starting place is to reduce screen brightness and CPU speed immediately and to set the hard disk spin down to take place after about 10 minutes of inactivity. Adjust as needed.

Advanced Configuration and Power Interface (ACPI)

ACPI power management goes far beyond APM to provide power management for all plug-and-play devices installed in a system, and it permits Windows to perform all power-management configurations rather than force the user to modify the BIOS setup to make some of the needed changes. ACPI requires the following:

■ Windows 98/Me/2000/XP

■ An ACPI-compliant BIOS with ACPI features enabled

Because ACPI puts Windows in charge of power management, it's essential that an ACPI-compliant BIOS be installed in a system before a system is upgraded from Windows NT 4.0 or Windows 95 to Windows 98/Me/2000/XP. Contact the portable system vendor for information on which systems can be upgraded to ACPI compliance and what the method is for performing the BIOS upgrade.

After an ACPI-compliant BIOS has been installed, the upgrade should then be performed. Performing the upgrade on a system without ACPI BIOS support will cause the Windows setup program to install only APM power management features.

To determine which power management mode the computer is using, open the Windows Device Manager and view the properties for Computer. If the computer is listed as a Standard PC, it uses APM power management. If the computer is listed as an ACPI PC (see Figure 12.4), ACPI power management is installed.

FIGURE 12.4

A computer with ACPI power management support installed.

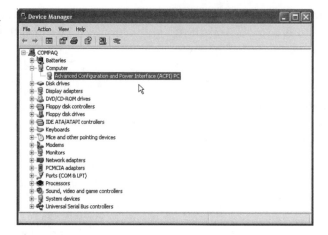

Memory Size and Its Impact on Battery Life

Increasing the amount of RAM in the portable computer also can improve battery life on systems running any version of Microsoft Windows. Microsoft Windows makes heavy use of the hard disk as *virtual memory* when actual RAM is too small for all the programs and data that are in use. The hard disk, because it uses a motor, is a very power-hungry component. Increasing the amount of RAM has these benefits: It delays the need to use the hard disk as virtual memory and increases the amount of memory available as a disk cache (memory used to hold a copy of data read from the disk drives).

PC Cards and Power Usage Issues

As you'll see later in this chapter, PC Cards provide many options for notebook computers. However, PC Cards can decrease your battery's running time per charge. To avoid unnecessary loss of power

- Remove PC Cards from the computer when not needed.
- Use PC Cards that support power management. Use the cards' power management tab on their properties sheets to select whether to shut off the card and whether the device can bring the computer out of standby.

> **caution**
>
> You don't need to buy memory from your computer vendor, but make sure you install memory modules made to work in your computer. The interactive buying guide available at www.crucial.com helps you find good deals on reliable memory for your portable computer.

PC Card (PCMCIA Card) Types and Usage

PC Cards (originally referred to as **PCMCIA** cards) provide a wide range of options for portable computers with PC Card slots.

Most portable computers have at least one Type II PC Card slot, as seen in Figure 12.5. Many have two.

Eject button   Type II PC Card partly inserted

FIGURE 12.5

A typical notebook with a Type II PC Card partly installed (top) and completely installed (bottom). Note the positions of the ejection button.

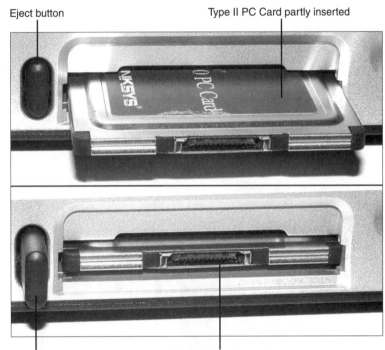

Eject button ready to eject card   PC Card fully inserted

When used with MS-DOS or Windows NT 4.0, PC Cards require special software known as **CSS**, or **Card and Socket Services** (the MS-DOS and Windows NT 4.0 versions are not interchangeable). Windows 95 and newer versions have built-in support for PC Cards.

Most CSS software and the built-in support in Windows 95 and later enable PC Cards to be hot-swapped; the card can be shut down, removed, and replaced with another without shutting down the system. Cards must be "stopped" before being removed or the system can become unstable and the cards or system can be damaged.

PC Card Types I, II, and III and Uses

The Personal Computer Memory Card International Association gave PC Cards their original name of PCMCIA cards and is responsible for developing standards for these cards. There are three types of PC Card slots, each designed for particular types of devices:

- **Type I**—The original version of the PC Card standard. These cards are just 3.3mm thick. Type I cards are typically used for memory.

- **Type II**—The most common PC Card type is 5.5mm. Type II cards are typically used for I/O devices such as Ethernet or wireless networking; modems; USB 2.0, IEEE-1394, or SCSI ports; and proprietary interfaces for external drives. Some hard drives also are available in the Type II form factor.

- **Type III**—Used primarily for PC Card–based hard drives as well as some combo I/O cards, this type is 10.5mm thick. Systems that have two stacked Type II PC Card slots also can use a single Type III card.

All three types of cards have a two-row connector with 68 pins total.

Most systems with PC Card slots feature two stacked Type II slots that can handle all types of cards: a single Type III card, two Type II cards, or two Type I cards at a time. Figure 12.6 compares the thicknesses of these cards.

FIGURE 12.6
Typical Type I, Type II, and Type III PC cards and cross-sections.

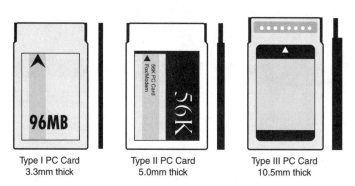

Type I PC Card
3.3mm thick

Type II PC Card
5.0mm thick

Type III PC Card
10.5mm thick

PCMCIA Hardware Resource Requirements

The CSS software used for PC Card support reserves a large area of upper memory (empty space between 640KB and 1MB) for use by PCMCIA cards. I/O port address space and IRQ usage depends on the specific card(s) used. Windows 95 and later versions configure PC Card resources automatically.

CardBus and Zoomed Video (ZV)

Most recent portable systems use a special high-speed type of PC Card slot known as **CardBus**. CardBus slots are compatible with both ordinary (16-bit) PC Cards and 32-bit CardBus cards, but CardBus cards *can't* be used in ordinary PC Card slots.

To verify if a portable system has CardBus support, open the Windows Device Manager and the category marked PCMCIA Adapters. If a CardBus controller is listed, the portable supports CardBus. If not, you can use only 16-bit PC Cards in that system.

Another variation on standard PC Card slots is **Zoomed Video (ZV)** support. Portable systems that support ZV can use PCMCIA cards with a high-speed video connector for processes such as teleconferencing or dual-display support. As with CardBus, use ZV-compatible cards only in compatible systems. However, ZV is not supported by all CardBus slots; to determine if a system with CardBus slots also supports ZV, check with the vendor.

Combo PC Cards

Combo PC Cards contain multiple functions and connections on a single card. The most common combination includes a modem plus Ethernet network interfacing or USB 2.0 plus IEEE-1394a interfacing.

PC Card Dongles

Type I and Type II PC Card cards aren't thick enough to use standard RJ-11 telephone (for modem), SCSI, or RJ-45 UTP network cables. Some Type II PC Cards use a pop-out connector for telephone or network cables; others require the use of a device called a **dongle**—a proprietary extension to the PCMCIA card that enables standard cables to be connected to the card. Figure 12.7 shows a typical 56Kbps PC Card network card with its dongle.

If you lose or damage the dongle, your PC Card is useless until you replace it. For this reason, many vendors are now building Type II PC Cards with a thick outer edge to support integrated 10/100 Ethernet RJ-45 or RJ-11 modem cables. Type III PC Cards are thick enough to provide standard connections, but don't fit into some systems.

Dongle connects to rear of card

FIGURE 12.7

A typical Type II PC Card 10/100 Ethernet card with the dongle used to attach the card to standard Category 5 UTP cable. Photo courtesy Linksys.

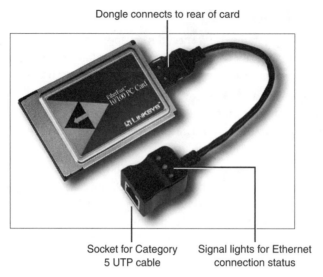

Socket for Category 5 UTP cable

Signal lights for Ethernet connection status

Inserting and Removing PC Cards

Inserting PC Cards into a system is a simple process (refer to Figure 12.5).

1. Hold the PC Card between your forefinger and thumb.

2. Turn the card so that the end with the pin connectors is facing toward the PC Card slot in the computer.

3. Make sure the top side of the PC Card is facing up; the front side normally has a decorative label listing the card model and manufacturer, as in Figure 12.6.

4. Slide the card straight into the PC Card slot in the portable computer until it interfaces with the connectors inside the slot.

5. The Windows taskbar will display a PC Card icon when the card is detected.

6. If this is the first time the PC Card has been installed, insert the driver disk or CD-ROM as directed to complete the installation.

7. Attach any cables or dongles required to make the PC Card ready for use.

To remove the PC Card

1. Look for an ejector button next to the PC Card slot; on some systems, the button is folded into the unit for storage. Unfold the button to prepare it for use.

2. Disconnect any cables or dongles from the card.

3. Right-click the Windows taskbar PC Card icon and select the card you want to remove from the list of cards.

4. Click Stop and wait for the system to acknowledge the card can be removed.

5. Click OK to close the message.

6. Push in the ejector button to eject the PC Card. Pull the PC Card the rest of the way out of the slot and store it in its original case or another antistatic bag.

Mini-PCI Card Types and Usage

Many recent notebook computers with built-in modem and network ports use a reduced-size version of the PCI add-on card standard known as **mini-PCI** to support these ports.

There are three major types of mini-PCI cards:

- Type I
- Type II
- Type III

Type I and Type II cards use a 100-pin stacking connector that plugs directly into the system board. Type II cards, unlike Type I cards, have network or modem connectors built into the card. Type III, which uses an edge connector, has become the most popular of the three formats. Like Type I, **Type III mini-PCI** cards do not incorporate RJ-11 (modem) or RJ-45 (Ethernet network) connectors; Type I and Type III mini-PCI cards use modem and network connectors built into the system.

Although mini-PCI cards can be replaced, they are not available at retail stores; they must be purchased from the portable computer supplier because they are customized to the characteristics of a particular product family. Mini-PCI cards are used to configure different models of a particular portable computer with different features. Because mini-PCI cards can be replaced, this enables you to replace a failed or outdated network/modem component without replacing the entire motherboard.

Figure 12.8 shows a typical Type III mini-PCI modem card and connector compared to a typical Type II PC Card.

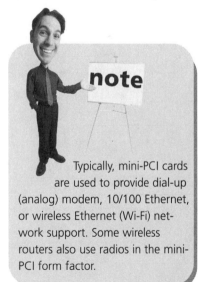

note

Typically, mini-PCI cards are used to provide dial-up (analog) modem, 10/100 Ethernet, or wireless Ethernet (Wi-Fi) network support. Some wireless routers also use radios in the mini-PCI form factor.

Protective plastic covering over components

FIGURE 12.8

A typical mini-PCI Type III modem (left) compared to a typical PC Card Type II network adapter (right).

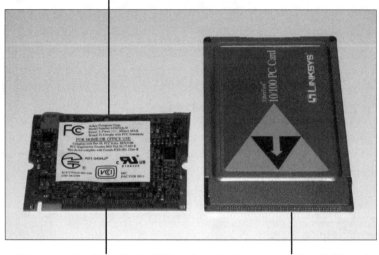

Edge connector (Type III mini-PCI card)   68-pin connector (Type II PC card)

Installing and Removing Mini-PCI Cards

To remove a Type III mini-PCI card, follow this procedure:

1. Turn off the computer.

2. Unplug the computer and remove the battery pack.

3. Locate the mini-PCI card in the unit. It might be accessible from the bottom of the system (see Figure 12.9 for an example), or you might need to remove the keyboard or other components.

4. Remove the cover or other components over the card.

5. Release the spring latches that hold the card in place.

6. Lift the top of the card up until the card is released from the socket.

To install a mini-PCI card

1. Push the mini-PCI card edge connector into place.

2. Push the top of the card down into the socket until the spring clips lock into place.

3. Replace the cover or other components you removed to gain access to the card socket.

4. Reinstall the battery.

5. Plug the computer in.

6. Start the computer. Install any additional drivers required.

Releasing the latches

FIGURE 12.9
Removing a mini-PCI card from a typical notebook computer.

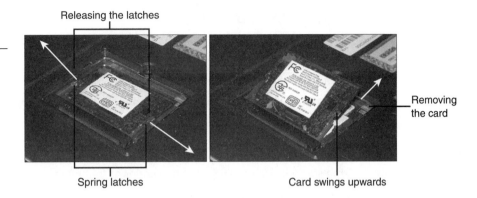

Removing the card

Spring latches

Card swings upwards

Using the Proprietary Expansion Bus

To save weight and space, portable computers do not use standard expansion bus designs, such as the ISA, PCI, or AGP expansion slots used on desktop computers. Instead, many (but not all) portable computers have proprietary connectors (see Figure 12.10) on the rear or bottom of the system case that will connect with either a docking station or a port replicator.

Infrared serial port

FIGURE 12.10
A typical notebook computer with Infrared serial port, SVGA video port, parallel port, and expansion bus for use with a docking station or port replicator (not shown). Dual folding doors, retracted here, protect the expansion bus from damage.

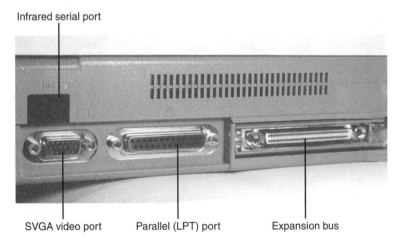

SVGA video port   Parallel (LPT) port   Expansion bus

Docking Stations and Media Slices

A **docking station** expands the capability of a portable computer by adding features such as

- One or more ISA or PCI expansion slots
- Additional I/O ports, such as serial, parallel, PC Card, VGA, or USB
- Additional drive bays
- Connectors for a standard keyboard and mouse

Most docking stations are produced by the vendor of the notebook computer.

Docking stations are also used by PDAs, such as the Palm series and Pocket PC models. These computers use their docking stations primarily for data transfer or battery recharging.

Some thin and light portable computers are designed to use a modular *media slice* for optical and removable-media drives. This unit connects to the bottom of the computer and can be left in place at all times, or can be removed when not needed.

Configuring Docking Stations and Devices

A docking station doesn't require any special hardware configuration, but the devices attached to it often do.

Windows 9x/Me/2000/XP use Plug and Play to support devices available to a portable computer when it is docked; the PnP devices are automatically detected and used.

Port Replicator

A **port replicator** usually connects to the same proprietary expansion bus that can be used by a docking station; many portable computers that do not have docking stations have optional port replicators.

Port replicators don't have expansion slots or drive bays but feature standard I/O ports (serial, parallel, VGA, and USB), keyboard, and mouse connectors. They enable a portable computer user fast, easy connection to a full-sized keyboard, regular mouse or pointing device, desktop VGA monitor,

tip

If in some devices the computer or the operating system doesn't support PnP (Windows NT 4.0 is not a PnP operating system), you can create an alternative hardware profile from the System properties sheet, Hardware Profiles screen. Using this feature requires you to manually enable and disable hardware features in the Docked profile you will create by copying the original configuration.

modem, and printer without needing to attach or remove multiple cables. Because portable cable connectors can wear out, using a port replicator extends the life of the system and makes desktop use faster and easier.

Some company systems use devices similar to conventional port replicators to provide access to the system's I/O ports; these systems provide just the expansion bus, without any normal ports, to save space and weight. This is true of very small portable systems such as the Toshiba Libretto series and others. In these cases, the port replicator is normally supplied with the system instead of being an optional extra.

Port replicators normally are built by the same company that makes the portable computer, but some third-party vendors produce both *dedicated* models (designed to attach to the proprietary expansion bus of a given model) and *universal* versions, which attach through the PC Card slot or USB port and can be freely moved among different brands and models of portable computers.

Software drivers are required for universal port replicators but not for standard port replicators.

Portable Storage

Portable storage devices use the same major internal technologies as desktop storage devices, but differ in matters such as bus connections, cost per MB, and form factor. Systems that have no internal provision for the type of drive desired can attach an external drive to any of the following:

- PC Card slot interface
- Parallel port interface
- USB interface or IEEE-1394a interface (if present)
- SCSI interface (if present)

Drives that support USB 2.0 (Hi-Speed USB), IEEE-1394a, or SCSI interfaces usually require the portable user to install the correct port by means of a CardBus PC Card to use devices of these types. SCSI devices also can be connected by means of a parallel-to-SCSI adapter, although performance is slower than with a normal SCSI device. USB-to-SCSI adapters also are available, and provide good performance when connected to USB 2.0 ports. Some recent portables also include IEEE-1394a or USB 2.0 ports.

Hard Drives

Although notebook computers have hard drives that are comparable in size to recent desktop computers, both form factors and connectors are different on drives made for portable computers and on desktop computers. To save space and weight, portable computers use a 2.5-inch–wide hard drive with a single 44-pin connector for both power and data. Although the technology is based on ATA/IDE, this is a different interface than the 40-pin data and 4-pin power connectors used by 3.5-inch standard desktop ATA/IDE hard drives. Because of the smaller form factor and different connector style, portable hard drives are more expensive per gigabyte than desktop hard drives. Figure 12.11 shows a typical notebook ATA/IDE hard drive and interface.

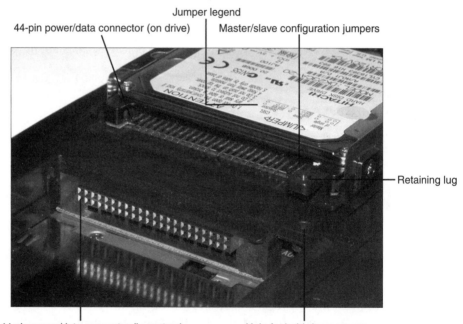

Jumper legend

44-pin power/data connector (on drive)   Master/slave configuration jumpers

FIGURE 12.11

A typical
2.5-inch
ATA/IDE hard
drive for note-
book computers
and its 44-pin
interface.

Retaining lug

44-pin power/data connector (in system)   Hole for hold-down screw

You can purchase bare 2.5-inch notebook ATA/IDE drives to use as replacements for failed or outdated drives, but many vendors sell special kits that include data-transfer software and a data-transfer cable to "clone" the old hard drive's contents to the new hard drive.

Some portable computers have interchangeable drives built into a special drive bay. These drive bays are often able to accommodate the user's choice of

- Hard drive
- Standard or high-capacity removable media drive, such as Zip, LS-120, or LS-240
- Optical drives, such as CD-ROM, CD-RW, DVD-ROM, or rewritable DVD
- Extra batteries

Some models with interchangeable drives allow you to **hot-swap**, which enables the user to exchange drives without shutting down the computer, whereas others require the user to shut down the system, change drives, and then restart the computer.

Portable computers with this capability are more expensive but are also more versatile.

Replacing a Portable Hard Drive

Portable hard drives that are not installed in interchangeable drive bays can be replaced by partly disassembling the computer. The details of the process vary from system to system, but follow this basic procedure:

1. Turn off the system.
2. Unplug the AC adapter or power cord from the system.
3. Remove the battery pack.
4. Determine the location of the hard drive.

Follow the correct procedure, depending on the location of the drive:

1. If the hard drive bay is accessible from the outside of the computer, remove the cover or screws that hold the drive in place.
2. Slide the drive out of the system (refer to Figure 12.11).

OR

1. If the hard drive bay requires disassembly of the computer, remove the keyboard and other components to gain access to the drive.
2. Disconnect the drive from the power/data cable (a single assembly on portable computers).
3. Remove any bracket or hold-down device securing the drive in position.
4. Remove the drive from the system.

To install the new drive in place, reverse the sequence as required by the drive type. A similar process is used to replace other built-in drives (optical, floppy, and removable-media).

After the new drive is installed, start the computer's setup program and make sure the drive is properly detected. Then, use either the operating system's partitioning and.formatting utility (Fdisk and Format for Windows 9x/Me or Setup for Windows 2000/XP) or a drive or system manufacturer–provided setup program to prepare the drive for use.

tip

Note that some manufacturers provide a data-transfer cable for use in transferring data between the old and new drives. Use the data-transfer cable before replacing the old drive with the new drive.

Floppy and Removable-Media Drives

The traditional 1.44MB 3.5-inch floppy drive can be found in four forms on portable computers:

- Built in
- Removable bay
- External proprietary bus
- External (USB port)

Some portable computers have replaced the standard floppy disk drive with the LS-120 or LS-240 SuperDisk drives, which use both proprietary 120MB media and standard 1.44MB media.

Optical Drives

Optical drives, such as CD-ROM, CD-RW, and DVD, are found in four locations on portable computers:

- Built in
- Removable bay
- Docking station
- External connection (via PC Card, USB 1.1/2.0, or IEEE-1394a)

Internal optical drives, including those made for removable drive bays, must be built specially for the portable system they're used with. Unlike ATA/IDE hard drives made for portables, optical drives do not use a common interface that enables them to be freely upgraded or replaced.

Flash Memory Storage

Some portable systems, primarily those in the PDA category, use Flash memory instead of magnetic or optical storage for program and data storage. Some PDAs have fixed amounts of Flash memory, whereas others use industry-standard devices, such as Compact Flash, Smart Media, or the Sony Memory Stick, to store information.

Card readers that attach to the serial, parallel, or USB ports can be used to move data between removable Flash memory devices and conventional PC storage devices. Some PDA and other very compact systems use a docking station or special cable instead.

USB-based solid-state drives are being used in place of floppy drives by some users of portable and desktop computers. These devices are about the size of a keychain and plug directly into the USB port. However, USB drives hold much more than the 1.44MB capacity of a standard floppy disk. Typical USB solid-state drives have capacities of 128MB or more.

Infrared Ports

Most portable computers feature an infrared (IR) port. This port usually follows the **IrDA** standard and can be used for the following tasks if the other device also follows the same standard:

- Networking using the Windows Direct Cable Connection (DCC) program to connect to computers with compatible IR ports
- Printing to laser and other printers equipped with a compatible IR port

Installing the Infrared Port

Windows will generally detect a built-in IR port and add it to the Device Manager. You also can install the port manually with the Add/Remove Hardware Wizard, but you will need to know the port brand and model or use the Have Disk option. In either case, have the operating system CD-ROM available to supply necessary hardware and software drivers for the port.

Infrared Port Hardware and Software Configuration

The IR port usually is considered a serial port by the system's setup program, and it will be assigned a serial port number, IRQ, and I/O port address. It may be configured as COM 2, COM 3, or COM 4, depending on the system. However, Windows will assign it a simulated serial (COM) port number and a simulated parallel (LPT) port number to enable the port to be used for networking with DCC and for printing. The value assigned might not match the actual COM port usage in hardware. You also can select your own serial and parallel port numbers.

⇨   **See** "Serial Ports," **p. 254**, for details.

Printing with the Infrared Port

Printers you want to use with the IR port are configured like any other printers through the Windows Printer Wizard. Simply specify the simulated parallel (LPT) port set aside for use by the IR port as the port to use for printing. Follow this procedure to print with the IR port:

1. Place your portable computer so that its IR port is aimed at the IR port on the printer.

2. Make sure the printer is turned on and is ready to receive a print job.

3. Select the printer in the printer properties sheet for your application, and start the print job.

4. The printer will receive data and print the document.

Because of the low transmission speed of IR ports, expect printing to take longer when you use the IR port than when you use parallel or USB connections.

Memory

Portable systems need extra memory as much as desktop systems do, but portable memory is both more expensive and less versatile than memory for desktop systems.

Generally, portable systems have only one connector for additional memory. Older portable systems might use proprietary memory modules, whereas recent systems use **SODIMMs** (a reduced-size version of an SDRAM or DDR DIMM module).

Portable Memory Module Types

The best memory upgrade for a portable system is to add the largest memory module (in MB) that can be installed in the system. Because a future memory upgrade would require the removal of the original memory module on systems with a single memory upgrade socket, it's best to add all the memory a system can take from the beginning. Figure 12.12 shows how a proprietary module and SODIMM compare to a 72-pin SIMM and 168-pin DIMM module.

FIGURE 12.12

Proprietary (top left) and standard SODIMM (bottom left) memory modules compared to 72-pin SIMM (top right) and 168-pin DIMM memory (bottom right).

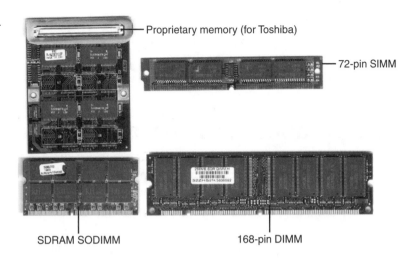

Proprietary memory (for Toshiba)

72-pin SIMM

SDRAM SODIMM

168-pin DIMM

Upgrading Portable Memory

Memory upgrades often can be performed without removing the keyboard, which covers most other internal components. Follow these steps to perform a typical memory upgrade:

1. Remove the cover over the memory upgrade socket on the bottom of the system.

2. Remove any screws or hold-down devices.

3. Remove the old memory upgrade if necessary.

4. Insert the new memory upgrade, making sure the contacts (on the back side or edge of the module) make a firm connection with the connector.

5. If you are installing an SODIMM or small-outline Rambus module, push the top of the module down until the latches lock into place (see Figure 12.13).

Push SODIMM module into slot

Push rear of module until latches lock into place

FIGURE 12.13

Installing an SODIMM module on a typical portable computer.

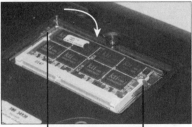

Locking latches

6. If the memory socket uses screws to secure the memory in place, install them.

7. Test the module by starting the system and observing the memory counter; use third-party diagnostics if possible.

8. Close the cover and secure it to complete the upgrade.

Selecting Upgrades for a Portable Computer

With a wide range of standard ports as well as expansion through PC Card and mini-PCI add-on cards, today's portable computers offer a wide variety of expansion possibilities.

When choosing upgrades, consider the following:

- *Can the portable computer attach the upgrade with its existing ports?* If not, the additional cost of the appropriate add-on card should be considered.

- *Does the portable computer have interchangeable drive or device bays?* If so, you can select from vendor-supplied drive and battery upgrades. Although these might be more expensive than external options, they provide better portability.

- *Can you choose a combo PC Card or CardBus card if you need to add ports?* Combo cards enable you to use a single Type II or Type III slot to perform two or more jobs. This saves money and minimizes the need to swap cards.

Study Lab

Don't miss the Study Lab materials found on the CD accompanying this book. Each Study Lab is tailored to the individual chapters in this book, meaning that you'll quickly be able to determine which topics you understand well enough to pass the exam and which topics need more study. The Study Labs are presented in printable PDF format so that you can take them with you to study at work, on the road, or even in your car just before test time!

THE ABSOLUTE MINIMUM

Review the chapter with this listing of major points just before you take your test.

- Portable computers are equipped with onboard components similar to those found in desktop computers, but the components in portable computers are usually built into the systems and replacements often use proprietary interfaces.

- PDAs differ from portable computers by using different operating systems, user interfaces, and processors.

- Active-matrix LCD displays are found on recent portable computers. They offer wider viewing angles, faster response, and better use under a variety of lighting conditions than older dual-scan LCD displays.

- Portables don't have removable graphics/video cards. However, some use graphics integrated into the motherboard chipset, whereas others use a discrete chipset with its own memory. Discrete chipsets have better 3D performance.

- Although damaged LCD display panels can be replaced, you cannot upgrade a system with a dual-scan panel with an active-matrix panel.

- Portable computers use integrated pointing devices such as pointing sticks, touchpads, or trackballs. Replacing failed pointing devices might require replacing the keyboard.

- A mouse or other external pointing device can be attached to most portables, but it might be necessary to disable the integrated pointing device if the integrated device is defective or unwanted.

- Some rechargers can be used anywhere because they automatically adjust to different voltages and AC cycles, whereas others must be replaced before the portable can be used in a location with different power standards than the original location.

- Lithium-Ion (Li-Ion) batteries provide the best combination of light weight and long life of the major rechargeable battery technologies.

- Most portables support either APM or ACPI power management. ACPI power management supports more devices and can be configured in the Windows GUI.

- There are three different types of PC Cards: Type I, Type II, and Type III. Type II cards are the most widely used, but many modem or network cards require a dongle.

- CardBus is a 32-bit version of PC Card, whereas Zoomed Video (ZV) is a version of CardBus used for video capture and display.

- Mini-PCI cards are used by many recent systems with built-in modem or network adapters. Type III is the most common variety.

- A docking station enables a portable computer to use desktop drives and add-on cards, whereas a port replicator enables a portable to connect to a variety of cables with a single connector. A media slice is used by some thin and light portables to provide optional portable optical and removable-media drives. All three rely on a proprietary expansion bus at the rear or the bottom of the system.

- Hard drives use a 44-pin version of the ATA/IDE standard to enable upgrades to larger capacities. Other drives use various proprietary connections.

- Some portables include an infrared port using the IrDA standard. It can be used for printing or data transfer with other devices having IrDA ports.

- Most portables have upgradeable memory. Recent systems usually take SODIMM modules, but older systems use various proprietary modules.

13

SAFETY AND RECYCLING

To clean equipment safely, don't reach under the kitchen sink and grab the first cleaner you see. Instead, use materials designed especially for electronics and computer use, or general-purpose cleaners proven to work well on electronics and computer equipment. Some useful cleaning materials include

- *Antistatic electronic wipes*—Use antistatic electronic wipes for monitor cases and glass surfaces, keyboards, LCD screens, and all types of plastic and metal cases for computers and peripherals. This type of product combines effective cleaning and **antistatic** properties, which protect your computer investment. You can also use these wipes to clean up gunk after it's been loosened up by compressed air.

- *Glass and surface cleaners*—Glass and surface cleaners can be used on monitor glass and LCD screens and on other surfaces. However, they are not the preferred choice because they usually lack any antistatic properties. Endust for Electronics in pump or aerosol sprays is preferred for this use because it cleans and has antistatic properties.

- *Isopropyl alcohol*—Isopropyl alcohol can be used along with foam (not cotton!) cleaning swabs to clean tape drive heads, floppy disk drive heads, and some keyboards. Some cleaning swabs are pre-moistened for convenience.

- *Specialized device cleaning kits for mechanical mice, tape drives, floppy disk drives, and inkjet and laser printers*—Specialized device cleaning kits, as I have recommended in other chapters, are good ways to clean the devices they are built for. These device cleaning kits enabled me to avoid repairing or replacing at least one floppy disk drive and one inkjet printer.

- *Compressed air*—Compressed air is a powerful but "brainless" cleaner. Unlike the cleaners mentioned previously, compressed air cannot trap dirt and dust. Instead, dirt, dust, grit, and assorted fuzz are expelled violently out of their hiding places. If you use compressed air, put plenty of old newspapers under and around the device you are cleaning to catch the gunk compressed air expels from the device being cleaned. Use liquid cleaners or cleaning wipes to pick up residue left behind after using compressed air.

- *Stabilant-22a*—Stabilant-22a (sold by D. W. Electrochemicals) is often recommended for use when assembling or reassembling a system for use in memory module sockets and expansion slots. It cleans the sockets and provides a more effective electrical connection.

Using a Vacuum Cleaner Safely

Vacuum cleaners are great for cleaning homes and offices, but typical models use plastic parts that can build up harmful static electricity. So, instead of

The CD included with this book contains important Study Lab material for this chapter, as well as Chapters 2–22 in this book. The Study Lab for each chapter contains terms to study, exercises, and practice tests—all in printable PDF format (Adobe Acrobat Reader is included on the CD, too). These Study Lab materials will help you gear up for the A+ Exam. Also, the CD includes an industry-leading test engine from PrepLogic, which simulates the actual A+ test so that you can be sure that you're ready when test day arrives. Don't let the A+ test intimidate you. If you've read the chapters, worked through the Study Lab, and passed the practice tests from PrepLogic, you should be well prepared to ace the test!

Also, you'll notice that some words throughout each chapter are in bold format. These are study terms that are defined in the Study Lab. Be sure to consult the Study Lab when you are finished with this chapter to test what you've learned.

using an ordinary office or home vacuum cleaner to clean a computer, purchase a model especially suited for computer use.

Computer-compatible vacuum cleaners have features such as

- Small-sized tips and brushes perfect for cleaning out keyboards and working around motherboards and add-on cards
- Antistatic construction
- Hand-held with an adjustable neck for easy use inside a system

Cleaning Inkjet and Laser Printers

Inkjet cartridges can become clogged with ink, especially if the printer is not shut down properly, and laser printer toner cartridges can leak toner. To learn more about cleaning these types of printers, see Chapter 10, "Printers."

Recycling and Disposal Issues

Nothing lasts forever in the computer business. Whether it is a worn out real-time clock battery, an obsolete monitor, or an empty toner cartridge, there's a right way to get rid of it or to recycle it. Generally, the more "durable" a computer-related item is, the more likely it is that it should be recycled when it reaches the end of its useful life, instead of simply being discarded.

Disposal of Batteries

Batteries no longer contain significant amounts of mercury, a highly toxic chemical responsible for the insanity of many real-life "Mad Hatters" in nineteenth-century England, but today's batteries still contain chemicals that should not go into landfills.

Depending on the type of battery that you have replaced, you might find more than one option for disposal of the old ones:

> **caution**
>
> With any spray cleaner, always spray the product onto the cleaning cloth, and never on the product to be cleaned. Spraying any kind of cleaner directly onto a keyboard or monitor can damage or destroy the product.

> **tip**
>
> Use a vacuum cleaner as an alternative to compressed air whenever possible, especially when working at the client's site because it's neater—there's no flying gunk that can land in awkward places.

- Some stores have drop-off bins for watch and calculator batteries; the popular 3.0V lithium CR-2032 or equivalent battery used on motherboards to maintain the CMOS and RTC settings could be disposed of this way.

- Contact your local EPA for disposal instructions for Li-Ion, Ni-Cad, or Alkaline batteries found in portable computers.

note

To prepare for the A+ Certification Exam, you should know which items are suitable for disposal, which should be recycled, and the proper methods for handling each type of item.

How to Recycle Toner and Printer Cartridges

As you learned in Chapter 10, many manufacturers of laser toner and inkjet printer cartridges want you to recycle the empty cartridges; these companies provide postage-paid envelopes or mailing labels to help you return the empty product.

Otherwise, contact local rebuilders of laser toner or inkjet cartridges. Some of these companies might pay you a small fee per each empty toner cartridge.

How to Dispose of Chemical Solvents and Cans

When you use up the contents of a cleaning product container, check the label for container-disposal instructions. Depending on the product, you might

- Be able to recycle the plastic container in household **recycling**; this is most often true for citrus-based and other mild cleaners

- Be required to follow toxic material disposal procedures; check with your local EPA office for a "Tox-Away Day" and store your empty containers for safe disposal at that time

If you need additional information about disposing of a particular type of container, check the product's **material safety data sheet (MSDS)**.

To learn more about proper disposal of computer materials, see "How to Read an MSDS (Material Safety Data Sheet)," later in this chapter, for details.

Disposing of Obsolete Monitors and Other Computer Equipment

If you send your obsolete PC, printer, or monitor to a landfill, it will have plenty of company. Millions of old units go there every year; it's legal, but it's also a waste of equipment that could teach somebody something or still be useful to someone. Here are some better ways to deal with obsolete computers and peripherals:

- If possible, try to dispose of your working, cast-off computer equipment by giving it to a school or charity. These organizations might be able to wring an additional year or two of useful life out of the equipment, and are usually grateful for the opportunity.

- To dispose of non-working equipment, see if an electronics trade school is willing to take the equipment for classroom use. Some electronic and computer service facilities will allow you to drop off defective monitors with payment of a small disposal fee.

- Use "computer" and "recycling" in a major search engine such as Google.com to find options for constructive disposal of both working and non-working equipment.

How to Read an MSDS (Material Safety Data Sheet)

What happens if a toddler decides to taste the ink in a printer cartridge? The MSDS knows. Many consumable products such as cleaners and printer cartridges have an MSDS, or material safety data sheet. In more and more cases today, this information is available from the manufacturer's Web site on the Internet.

The MSDS can be used to

- Determine safe storage practice

- Determine treatment if the product is accidentally swallowed or contacts the skin

caution

Hard disk drives in castoff machines can be a treasure trove of confidential information for the recipients, even if you format or repartition the drives. Many off-the-shelf data recovery programs such as Norton Unerase, Norton Unformat, Ontrack Easy Data Recovery, and others can pull all kinds of information including credit card, bank, and proprietary company data from an intact hard disk with little difficulty.

Norton WipeInfo and other programs that overwrite data areas of the drive repeatedly are designed to help prevent easy data recovery. However, forensic data-recovery tools intended for use by law-enforcement organizations can be purchased and used by anyone to retrieve data, even if it has been overwritten with Norton or other programs.

For maximum security for your personal or company data, take the hard disks out of any machine you're disposing of and physically destroy them. Open the cover of each hard disk drive and destroy the platters with a hammer.

■ Determine safe disposal methods

■ Determine how to deal with spills, fire, and other hazards

The MSDS is divided into sections 1 through 16. For example, to determine first-aid measures in case of ingestion or inhalation, you would view section 4; to view fire-fighting information, go to section 5 (see Figure 13.1).

For easy reading, many manufacturers use the Adobe Acrobat (.pdf) format; documents in this format can be read by anyone with the free Adobe Acrobat Reader program, obtainable from www.adobe.com.

FIGURE 13.1

A portion of an MSDS for a typical HP laser printer toner cartridge, viewed with Adobe Acrobat.

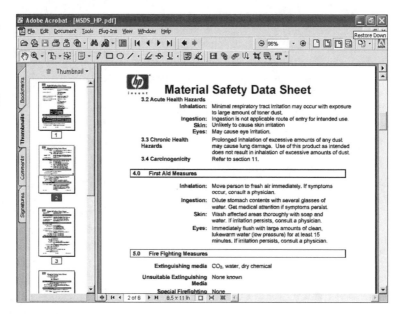

Electro-Static Discharge (ESD)

Anyone who works with electronics, especially disassembled components, needs to be very concerned about ESD. **ESD** is the static-electricity discharge that happens when two differently charged objects (such as your body and a computer component) come in contact with each other. ESD is an invisible killer of memory modules, interface cards, hard disks, and other computer components, because ESD buildup and discharge happens long before you actually notice it.

You might dread shaking hands with a new acquaintance in the winter because you'll get a shock, but ESD discharges far below the 3,000V level that you can actually feel can still destroy chips. As little as 30V of ESD is enough to destroy the current generation of low-powered chips, and you can build up as much as 20,000V of ESD from walking across a carpeted room in the winter if you shuffle along.

ESD damage is "invisible" for another reason: It leaves in its wake equipment that has no visible damage but simply won't work reliably.

ESD damage is a major cause of intermittent failures, which are the bane of computer technicians everywhere. An intermittent failure is the classic "it wasn't working when I called you" kind of problem that "goes away" when you examine the system but recurs from time to time later.

Preventing ESD

You can prevent ESD by taking proper precautions when you do the following:

- Install or remove components
- Store and transport components
- Use computers

One way to prevent ESD is to equalize the electric potential of your body and the components on which you're working.

Unequal electrical potential between you and the device on which you're working is the major cause of ESD. When your body has a higher electric potential than the device or component with which you're working, an ESD from your body to the device or component equalizes the potential—but at the cost of damage or destruction to the component.

note

Although the greatest danger of ESD occurs when you have the system open and are working with components, PC users can also cause ESD problems when working with closed-up systems. I once delivered such a big static shock to a keyboard after a coffee break that I couldn't save my document and had to power down and restart the computer to restore my keyboard to working order.

Protection Devices

You can best equalize the electrical potential of a computer or component that is being serviced by placing the computer or component on an antistatic work mat equipped with a **wrist strap**; attach your wrist strap to the mat. This will help place you and the component at the same level of electrical potential, and thus eliminate the "need" for ESD to occur to equalize the potential.

For additional safety, use the alligator clip on the antistatic mat to attach to the component or computer you are working on. The clip should be attached to unpainted metal on the chassis, such as the frame. This provides superior equalization for the mat, you, and the hardware on the mat.

Table mats connected to a grounded power supply are useful tools for preventing ESD on working computers, especially if users are reminded to touch the mat or grounded keyboard strip first. Antistatic cleaning spray and antistatic carpet spray should be used in any carpeted office to reduce static, especially in the winter when dry heat causes buildup.

Correct Storage for Equipment

Correct equipment storage should have two goals:

- Eliminate the possibility of ESD.
- Protect equipment from impact damage.

To protect equipment from ESD, store equipment in the **Faraday cage** antistatic bags originally supplied with the equipment; retain bags for installed equipment for reuse. Faraday cage antistatic bags feature a thin metallic layer on the outside of the bag, which is conductive and prevents ESD from penetrating to the components inside. Thus, metalized metallic bags should never be used for temporary mats for components; if you lay a component on the outside of the bag, you're laying it onto a conductive surface. Colored antistatic bubble wraps also work well for parts storage, and can also be used as a temporary mat, too. If you use bubble wrap, make sure it is antistatic (see Figure 13.2).

All work mats and wrist straps should have a 1-megohm resistor, as shown in Figure 13.3, to stop high voltage coming through the ground line from injuring the user.

> **caution**
>
> Do *not* leave the computer plugged in while you work. This does *not* minimize the chances of ESD, and you could damage equipment if you attach or remove it. This is because ATX and NLX-based systems still draw power even when they have been shut down.

FIGURE 13.2

A grounded work mat, suitable for use on either a work area or under an office computer in a high-static area, and antistatic Faraday bags.

Faraday cage: metalized plastic

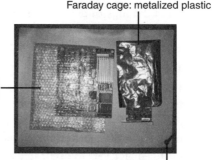

Faraday cage: antistatic bubble plastic with a pocket

1-megohm resistor for protection against high voltage

Store components in appropriate boxes to avoid physical damage. If the original boxes have been discarded, use cardboard boxes that have enough room for the component, the Faraday cage bag around the component, and antistatic padding.

Using a Commercial Wrist Strap

A typical commercial wrist strap and a grounded work mat are shown in Figure 13.3. Both the wrist strap and the work mat include alligator clips that are attached to the system chassis to equalize electrical potential between the wearer and the computer. Wrist straps use hook and loop or other types of adjustable closures; it's important to wear the wrist strap comfortably snug so that the metal plate underneath the resistor touches the skin to provide proper conductivity.

> ### caution
> You should use a commercial wrist strap for most types of computer service, but there is one major exception: *Never* ground yourself when you are working with high-current devices, such as when you discharge a CRT. Grounding yourself to such devices could cause your body to receive a fatal high-current electrical charge.

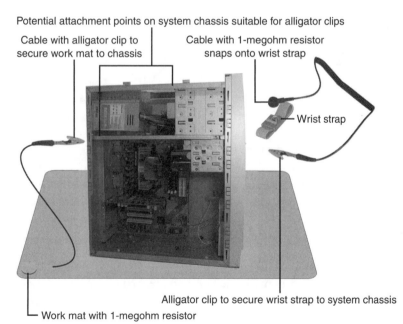

Potential attachment points on system chassis suitable for alligator clips

Cable with alligator clip to secure work mat to chassis

Cable with 1-megohm resistor snaps onto wrist strap

Wrist strap

Alligator clip to secure wrist strap to system chassis

Work mat with 1-megohm resistor

FIGURE 13.3
A typical ESD kit includes a grounded work mat and wrist strap. Both have 1-megohm resistors to protect the user from electric shock and alligator clips to connect the mat and wrist strap to unpainted metal parts on or inside the system.

Additional ESD Precautions

A grounded wrist strap can help prevent ESD, but you should also follow these additional precautions:

- If you must handle expansion cards and other devices with chips without suitable antistatic protection, *never touch the chips*! Most current products use a **CMOS (Complementary Metal-Oxide Semiconductor)** design, which has practically no resistance to ESD; as little as 30V of ESD can damage CMOS-based devices.

- Hold expansion cards by the brackets, never by the motherboard connectors.

- Wear natural fibers, such as cotton and leather-soled shoes, instead of synthetics to avoid ESD buildup.

- Use an antistatic spray (commercial or antistatic fabric softener/water mixture) to treat carpeting to reduce ESD.

- Use antistatic cleaning wipes on keyboards, monitors, and computer cases to reduce static buildup. Turn off the power, and if you use a liquid cleaner, always spray the cloth, never the device!

Hazards

Computer equipment poses several hazards for the technician:

- High-voltage sources, such as computers, and peripherals, such as printers and monitors

- Mechanical devices, such as printer mechanisms

- Laser-light sources, such as laser printers and optical drives

caution

Computers and their peripherals can *kill* or *injure* you if you don't take reasonable precautions. This section discusses typical dangers of computer maintenance and the precautions you can take against these dangers.

High-Voltage Sources

The number-one hazard created by computer equipment is high voltage that can be present while devices are turned on and plugged in and even when some devices are unplugged and turned off. The major sources of potentially dangerous voltage include

- Printers
- Power supplies
- Monitors
- Systems in suspend mode

Printers also pose laser and mechanical hazards to technicians. All these risks are covered in the following section.

Printers

Unlike computers, printers normally do *not* run on safe, low-voltage **DC (direct current)**. Although laser printers typically do use DC current, it is at a high voltage. Most dot-matrix and inkjet printers also use high-voltage **AC (alternating current)**.

Although normal operation is safe, defeating safety features that shut off the laser printer can put you at risk of a shock or a zap in the eyes from a laser beam. In addition to being potential shock sources if opened while running, dot-matrix and inkjet printers also can pinch or crush fingers in their gears and paper feeders if the cover is removed while the printer is in operation.

Any printer should be turned off and unplugged before being serviced. In the event of ink or toner spills, water or other liquids should *not* be used to clean up the mess unless the printer is turned off and disconnected, due to the risk of a potentially fatal electric shock.

The Power Supply

The exterior of practically every power supply is marked something like this:

CAUTION! Hazardous area! Severe shock hazards are present inside this case. Never remove the case under any circumstances. (See Figure 13.4 for a typical example.)

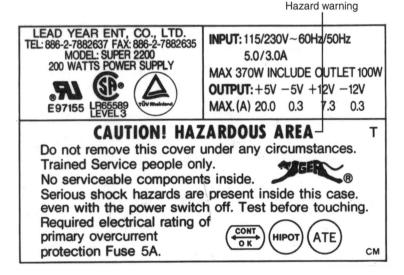

FIGURE 13.4
Hazard warnings on the label for a typical power supply.

Monitors

As with the power supply, the outside of the monitor is safe. However, if you remove the cover of a CRT monitor for servicing or adjustments, you expose the danger. The high-voltage anode (a metal prong covered with a red insulator, found on the wide top of the CRT) holds dangerously high voltage for days after the power is turned off.

Disassembled monitors also pose the following hazards:

- X-rays coming from the unshielded neck of the CRT when the monitor is on
- Dropping the monitor and breaking the CRT

Replace the shielding around the neck of the CRT before using the monitor, and use padding and carefully balance CRTs and monitors during storage and transport to avoid damage. See "Discharging CRTs" later in this chapter for additional information.

Systems in Suspend Mode

Systems based on the ATX or NLX standards typically go into a deep **suspend mode** rather than a true "off" condition when shut down by Microsoft Windows. Some ATX systems have power supplies with a separate on/off switch on the back of the unit, but most do not. For these reasons, you should disconnect the power cord from the system.

I learned about this feature of ATX systems the hard way: I reached down into a system that was supposedly "off" and received a nasty tingle from a modem.

As with other devices, the power can be on unless you disconnect it at the source.

> **caution**
>
> Believe it. You can see the danger if you understand what is in the "cage" at the back of the typical power supply. Past the cooling fan it contains, you'll see coils of heavy wire. These windings retain potentially lethal high-voltage levels for a long time.
>
> Because any power supply you buy as a replacement is likely to have a higher wattage rating and can also have a quieter fan than your current power supply, don't go cheap and wind up dead. Heed the warnings and replace the power supply without opening it to find out why it is broken. Make sure you purchase a UL-rated power supply.

Precautions Against Electric Shock

This section discusses the precautions you should take to avoid the hazards covered in previous sections.

To work with electricity safely, follow these simple precautions:

- Remove jewelry, including rings, bracelets, and necklaces. Metal jewelry provides an excellent path for current.

- Use rubber gloves for extra insulation—rubber gloves prevent your hands from touching metal parts; however, they do not provide sufficient insulation to enable you to work on a live system.

- Work with one hand out of the system if possible, to avoid electricity passing through your chest if your arms complete a circuit.

- Keep your hands and the rest of your body dry; your body's natural shock resistance drops to virtually nil when your skin is damp.

Disconnecting Equipment

Regardless of the level of service you will provide to a component, devices such as printers, computers, monitors, and so on should be disconnected from power as well as turned off before service. This will help prevent shock hazards as well as mechanical hazards.

Do *not* leave the computer plugged in while you work inside it. At one time, an acceptable practice was to leave the computer plugged in but shut down and to keep one hand on the power supply as a ground. This is no longer appropriate because ATX-based units aren't really "off"; they're in a suspend mode and power is still running through memory, expansion cards, and so on.

Discharging CRTs

I don't recommend trying to service CRT-based monitors smaller than 19-inch diagonal measurement; replacement monitors are inexpensive enough to make 17-inch and smaller monitors practically disposable. You should not service any monitor unless you are a certified technician. However, if you must open a CRT-based monitor for service, discharge the high-voltage anode following this procedure:

1. Turn off and unplug the monitor.
2. Remove the housing carefully.
3. Attach a large alligator clip and wire from a long, flat-bladed, *insulated* screwdriver to the metal frame surrounding the monitor.
4. Slide the flat blade of the screwdriver under the insulator until the tip touches the metal anode clip (see Figure 13.5).

FIGURE 13.5

Discharging the high-voltage anode on a typical CRT. Note the ground wire clipped between the metal monitor frame and the screwdriver

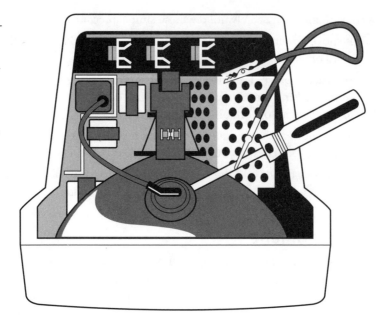

5. Be prepared for noise—anything from crackling to a loud pop—as the anode discharges its stored electricity. Keep the screwdriver in place for several seconds to fully discharge the anode.

6. Slide the screwdriver out without twisting it; you could damage the CRT.

This process must be repeated after each time the monitor is powered up until the housing is replaced.

Study Lab

Don't miss the Study Lab materials found on the CD accompanying this book. Each Study Lab is tailored to the individual chapters in this book, meaning that you'll quickly be able to determine which topics you understand well enough to pass the exam and which topics need more study. The Study Labs are presented in printable PDF format so that you can take them with you to study at work, on the road, or even in your car just before test time!

THE ABSOLUTE MINIMUM

Use this section to review the highlights in this chapter just before you take the exam. You can also use these highlights to determine what parts of the chapter to study in greater detail.

- To clean equipment safely, use materials designed especially for electronics and computer use.

- Avoid ESD buildup by using antistatic cleaners and computer-grade vacuum cleaners.

- Batteries and empty containers used for cleaning products can be environmental hazards; contact the local EPA for help in disposing of them properly.

- You can use local firms or original vendors to recycle inkjet and toner cartridges.

- Alternatives to discarding equipment include donations to schools or charities or paying for recycling at an electronics or computer-servicing facility.

- A product's MSDS (material safety data sheet) provides safe handling and disposal information.

- ESD (electro-static discharge) can damage equipment even if no shock can be felt.

- You can reduce ESD with antistatic parts storage bags, antistatic work mats, wrist straps, and antistatic cleaners.

- CRT monitors, printers, and power supplies are major high-voltage hazards.

- Disconnect high-voltage hazard sources, instead of just turning them off, for maximum safety.

14

STORAGE

Want to keep what you create with your PC? You need storage! Magnetic storage devices such as hard disks, floppy drives, and removable-media drives, and optical storage devices such as CD-ROM, CD-RW, and various types of read-only and rewritable DVD storage are standard with virtually every PC. However, upgrades and additions to storage are frequently made during the life of a computer. Reliable storage of programs and data is a critical factor of customer satisfaction and computer use. In this chapter, you'll learn how to configure and troubleshoot major storage devices.

Common Characteristics of Magnetic Storage Devices

All magnetic storage devices have the following characteristics in common:

- **Read/write heads** use controlled electrical pulses to affect the magnetic structure of the media. Each disk surface has one read/write head, whereas double-sided media use two read/write heads (one per side).

- **Hard drives** use one or more double-sided platters formed from rigid materials such as aluminum or glass that are coated with a durable magnetic surface.

- All disk-based magnetic media is divided up into 512-byte areas called **sectors**.

- Sectors are organized in concentric circles from the edge of the media inward toward the middle of the platter. These concentric circles are called **tracks**.

- All magnetic storage devices require that media be formatted before it can be used. **Formatting** means that a logical magnetic pattern must be placed on the disk to enable data to be organized and located. Most media is preformatted at the factory.

- All disk-based magnetic media store information about where files are located. The method used to organize this information is called the **file system**.

- The file system used by Windows 9x/Me uses a special area near the outer edge of the first side of the media to store a record of where files are located; this is called the **File Allocation Table (FAT)**. Two copies of the FAT are updated whenever a file is created, changed, or deleted.

note

The CD included with this book contains important Study Lab material for this chapter, as well as Chapters 2–22 in this book. The Study Lab for each chapter contains terms to study, exercises, and practice tests—all in printable PDF format (Adobe Acrobat Reader is included on the CD, too). These Study Lab materials will help you gear up for the A+ Exam. Also, the CD includes an industry-leading test engine from PrepLogic, which simulates the actual A+ test so that you can be sure that you're ready when test day arrives. Don't let the A+ test intimidate you. If you've read the chapters, worked through the Study Lab, and passed the practice tests from PrepLogic, you should be well prepared to ace the test!

Also, you'll notice that some words throughout each chapter are in bold format. These are study terms that are defined in the Study Lab. Be sure to consult the Study Lab when you are finished with this chapter to test what you've learned.

■ FAT-based storage is also supported by Windows NT/2000/XP, but these operating systems normally use a more sophisticated and secure file system called **NTFS**. NTFS stores information about each file in the **Master File Table (MFT)**.

■ A storage device that emulates magnetic storage, such as an **optical drive**, requires software drivers that will make it appear as an ordinary drive to the system.

■ Disk-based magnetic media uses **random access** (any sector can be accessed at any time) whereas most tape media uses **sequential access** (the tape must be read from the beginning to locate data). Some advanced tape drives use special techniques to speed access to data, but the data is still read sequentially.

Floppy Disk Drives and Media

Floppy drives are used primarily for backups of small amounts of data and for the creation of bootable emergency disks with some versions of Windows. Systems built from the early 1990s to the present use one of two types of 3.5-inch drives:

■ *1.44MB floppy*—These drives use 3.5-inch double-sided high-density (**DSHD**) media. This type is used by almost all vendors, and supports the 720KB 3.5-inch double-sided double-density (**DSDD**) media used by 3.5-inch drives produced in the 1980s.

■ *2.88MB floppy*—These drives use 3.5-inch double-sided extra-density (**DSED**) media. This type was used primarily by IBM. Very little DSED media is available, but these drives can also be used with 1.44MB and 720KB media.

Figure 14.1 shows the data and power connectors used by 3.5-inch floppy drives.

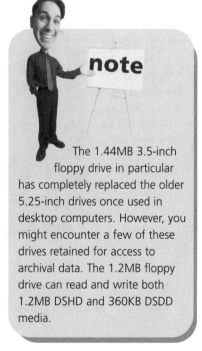

note

The 1.44MB 3.5-inch floppy drive in particular has completely replaced the older 5.25-inch drives once used in desktop computers. However, you might encounter a few of these drives retained for access to archival data. The 1.2MB floppy drive can read and write both 1.2MB DSHD and 360KB DSDD media.

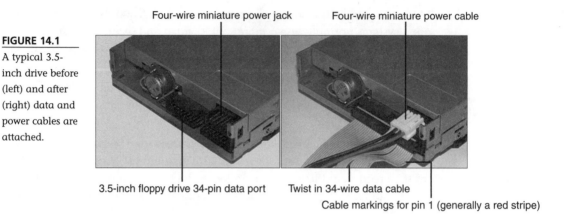

Four-wire miniature power jack   Four-wire miniature power cable

FIGURE 14.1
A typical 3.5-inch drive before (left) and after (right) data and power cables are attached.

3.5-inch floppy drive 34-pin data port   Twist in 34-wire data cable
Cable markings for pin 1 (generally a red stripe)

Distinguishing Marks of Different Disk Types

The reliability of data stored on a floppy disk can be affected by many factors, including the disks themselves. Figure 14.2 compares 1.44MB and 2.88MB floppy disks.

720KB floppy disk (no media-sensing hole)
2.88MB floppy disk (media-sensing hole offset from corner)
1.44MB floppy disk (media-sensing hole near corner)

FIGURE 14.2
A 3.5-inch 720KB floppy disk (left) compared to a 1.44MB floppy disk (right), and a 2.88MB floppy disk (center).

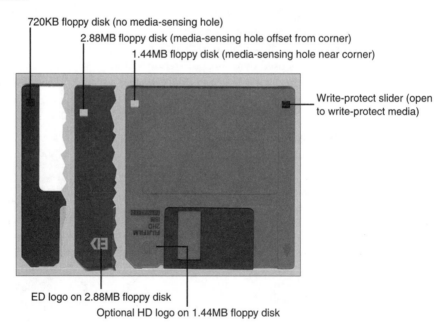

Write-protect slider (open to write-protect media)

ED logo on 2.88MB floppy disk
Optional HD logo on 1.44MB floppy disk

Table 14.1 will help you distinguish between different disk types in use today.

Table 14.1 Physical Characteristics of 3.5-Inch Floppy Media

Disk Type	Capacity	Jacket	Reinforced Hub	Write-Protect	Media Sensor
3.5-inch DSDD	720KB	Rigid with metal shutter	N/A	Open write-protect slider	N/A
3.5-inch DSHD	1.44MB	Rigid with metal shutter	N/A	Open write-protect slider	Opposite write-protect slider
3.5-inch DSED	2.88MB	Rigid with metal shutter	N/A	Open write-protect slider	Offset from write-protect slider

Of the disks pictured in Figure 14.2, only the 3.5-inch DSHD disk is commonly used today. 1.44MB disks are often marked *HD* on their front and always have a media-sensing hole in the opposite corner from the write-enable/protect slider.

BIOS Settings Required for Floppy Disk Drive Support

All 286-based and higher systems built since the late 1980s can support all but 2.88MB floppy drives through ROM BIOS configuration and the use of MS-DOS 3.3 or higher. Systems require specific BIOS support to use 2.88MB drives as well as a high-speed floppy controller on the motherboard or add-on card.

Floppy Disk Drive Hardware Configuration

Floppy disk drive hardware configuration depends on several factors, including

- *Correct CMOS configuration*—The system's BIOS configuration screen must have the correct drive selected for A: and B:.

- *Correct cable positioning and attachment*—The position of the drive(s) on the cable determine which is A: and which is B:. If the cable is not oriented properly, the drive will spin continuously.

note

Some desktop and portable systems might use an LS-120 or LS-240 SuperDisk drive in place of a standard 1.44MB floppy drive. These drives not only can read and write 1.44MB and 720KB 3.5-inch floppy media, but can also use high-capacity 3.5-inch media. The LS-120 SuperDisk uses 120MB media, and the LS-240 SuperDisk can use 120MB or 240MB media. These drives usually plug into the ATA/IDE interface if internal, or the parallel or USB port if external.

The standard floppy disk drive interface uses a single IRQ and single I/O port address range, whether the interface is built in or on an expansion card:

- Floppy Drive IRQ: 6
- Floppy Drive I/O Port Address: 3F0–3F7h

The standard floppy disk drive interface can support two drives: drive A: and drive B:. However, some recent systems support only one floppy drive (A:).

Although the first 5.25-inch floppy drives used jumpers to determine A: and B: assignments, more recent 5.25-inch and all 3.5-inch floppy drives rely on the data cable. The 34-pin floppy disk drive data cable has wires numbered 10 to 16 twisted in reverse between the connectors for drive A: and drive B: (refer to Figure 14.3). The drive beyond the twist is automatically designated as drive A:; the drive connected between the twisted and the untwisted end of the cable (which connects to the floppy controller) is automatically designated as drive B:.

Figure 14.3 compares five-connector universal (3.5-inch/5.25-inch) and three-connector 3.5-inch floppy cables. (The cable connector to the floppy controller is not visible in this photo.)

FIGURE 14.3

Two types of floppy drive cables compared. On the left, a cable designed for 3.5-inch drives only; on the right, a cable designed for 3.5-inch and 5.25-inch drives.

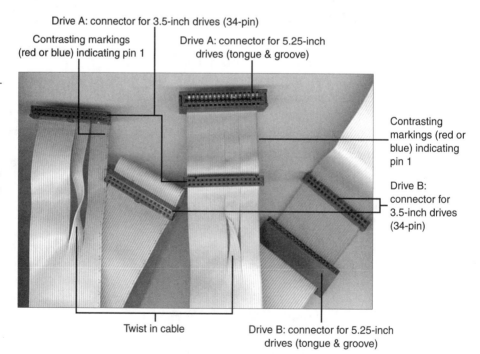

Drive A: connector for 3.5-inch drives (34-pin)

Contrasting markings (red or blue) indicating pin 1

Drive A: connector for 5.25-inch drives (tongue & groove)

Contrasting markings (red or blue) indicating pin 1

Drive B: connector for 3.5-inch drives (34-pin)

Twist in cable

Drive B: connector for 5.25-inch drives (tongue & groove)

Floppy Disk Drive Physical Installation and Removal

To install a 3.5-inch 1.44MB floppy disk drive as drive A:, follow these steps:

1. Select an empty 3.5-inch external drive bay; an external drive bay is a drive bay with a corresponding opening in the case.

2. Remove the dummy face plate from the case front.

3. For a tower system, remove the left side panel (as seen from the front). For a desktop system, remove the top.

4. If the 3.5-inch drive bay is a removable "cage," remove it from the system. This might involve pushing on a spring-loaded tab, as in Figure 14.4 or removing a screw. Some drive bays pull straight out (as here), whereas others swing to one side.

FIGURE 14.4

A typical cage used by many tower cases for 3.5-inch drives.

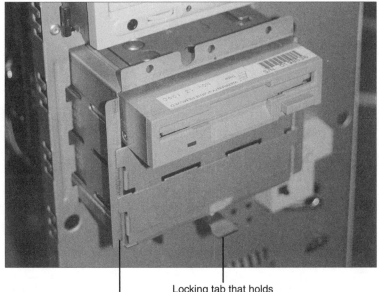

Locking tab that holds removable drive "cage" in place

Removable faceplate on cage

5. Remove the floppy disk drive from its protective packaging. Test the screws you intend to use to secure the drive and ensure they're properly threaded and the correct length.

6. Check the bottom or rear panel of the drive for markings indicating pin 1; if no markings are found, assume pin 1 is the pin closest to the power supply connector.

7. Attach the 34-pin connector at the end of the floppy disk drive data cable with the twist to the data connector on the drive.

8. Run the other end of the floppy disk drive data cable through the drive bay into the interior of the computer. Then, connect it to the floppy disk drive interface on the motherboard or add-on card.

9. Attach the correct type of four-wire power cable to the drive. You might need to slide the drive partway into the drive bay to make the connection.

10. Secure the drive to the drive bay with the screws supplied with the drive or with the computer.

11. Replace the drive bay into the computer if present (see Figure 14.5).

Floppy drive attachment screw

FIGURE 14.5

A removable drive cage with the attachment screws for the floppy disk drive and hard drive. The opposite corner of each drive is also secured with screws (not shown).

Hard drive attachment screw

12. Double check power and data cable keying before starting the computer.

13. Follow these steps in reverse to remove the drive from the system.

BIOS Configuration

Floppy disk drives cannot be detected by the system; you must manually configure the floppy disk drive or floppy disk drives you add to the system.

To configure the floppy disk drive in the ROM BIOS, follow these steps:

1. Verify the correct physical installation as listed previously.

2. Turn on the monitor and the computer.

3. Press the appropriate key(s) to start the BIOS configuration program.

4. Open the standard configuration menu.

5. Select Drive A: or the first floppy disk drive.

6. Use the appropriate keys to scroll through the choices; 3.5-inch 1.44MB is the correct choice for most recent and current systems (see Figure 14.6).

7. No other changes are necessary, so save your changes and exit to reboot the system.

FIGURE 14.6

Viewing floppy drive type options in the BIOS setup program of a typical system.

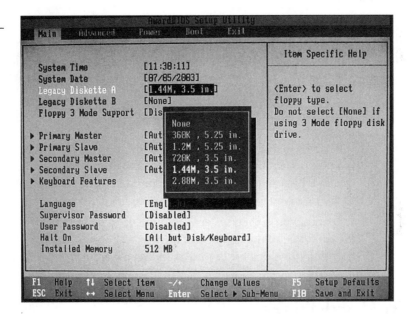

The Care of Floppy Disks, Data, and Drives

You can protect the data on your floppy disks by following these recommendations; most of these suggestions also apply to higher-capacity removable media such as Zip, Jaz, LS-120, and tape backups:

■ Do not open the protective metal shutter on 3.5-inch disks.

■ Store disks away from sources of magnetism (CRT monitors and magnetized tools) or heat.

■ Open the sliding write-protect cover on 3.5-inch disks to prevent the contents of the disk from being changed.

Floppy disk drives are a type of magnetic storage in which the read/write heads make direct contact with the media. This is similar to the way that tape drives work, and just like tape backup, music cassette, or VCR heads, a floppy disk drive's read/write heads can become contaminated by dust, dirt, smoke, or magnetic particles flaking off the disk's media surfaces. For this reason, periodic maintenance of floppy disk drives will help to avoid the need to troubleshoot drives that cannot reliably read or write data.

The following are some guidelines for cleaning a floppy disk drive:

- Approximately every six months, or more often in dirty or smoke-filled conditions, use a wet-type head-cleaning disk on the drive.

  These cleaning kits use a special cleaning floppy disk that contains cleaning media in place of magnetic media, along with an alcohol-based cleaner. Add a few drops to the media inside the cleaning disk, slide it into the drive, and activate the drive with a command such as DIR or by using the Windows Explorer to clean the heads. Allow the heads to dry for about 30 minutes before using the drive.

- Whenever you open a system for any type of maintenance or checkup, review the condition of the floppy disk drive(s). Use compressed air to remove fuzz or hair from the drive heads and check the mechanism for smooth operation.

note

5.25-inch media should be kept in protective paper or cardboard sleeves. To prevent 5.25-inch disks from being erased or altered, cover the write-protect notch on the right side of the disk with opaque tape.

IDE/ATA Hard Disks

Integrated Drive Electronics (IDE) began to replace the older drive interfaces starting in the late 1980s and continues to be, by far, the most popular drive interface used today. IDE drives were originally used in systems designed for ST-412/506 hard drives, and some of their characteristics date back to the need to be compatible with old BIOSs.

IDE was originally designed for hard drives, but several other types of storage devices can also be attached to it:

tip

Some vendors prefer to use the term **AT Attachment (ATA)** instead of IDE for their hard drives. Expect either term to be used on the exam.

- Optical drives (including CD-ROM, CD-R, CD-RW, and all types of DVD drives)
- Removable-media drives, such as Zip, LS-120, LS-240, and others
- Tape backup drives

These types of drives are referred to as **AT Attachment Packet Interface (ATAPI)** drives, and they use the same **master/slave/cable select** jumpers and 40-pin data cable as standard IDE drives do. The system BIOS on recent systems supports minimal functions for these drives, but software drivers are used to provide most functions. These devices should be installed on the secondary IDE channel, and hard drives should be installed on the primary IDE channel.

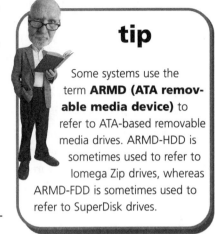

tip

Some systems use the term **ARMD (ATA removable media device)** to refer to ATA-based removable media drives. ARMD-HDD is sometimes used to refer to Iomega Zip drives, whereas ARMD-FDD is sometimes used to refer to SuperDisk drives.

IDE/ATA Hardware Resources

The IDE/ATA hard disk interface, whether found on the motherboard or as an add-on card, uses the following resources. These resources are listed in Table 14.2.

Table 14.2 Standard Hardware Resource Use for IDE/ATA Hard Drive Interfaces

IRQ	I/O Port	Address Range	Notes
Primary Interface	14	1F0–1FFh, 3F6h (newer systems might use additional ranges)	Same as used for ST-506 and ESDI interfaces used in 1980s
Secondary Interface	15	170–177h, 376 (newer systems might use additional ranges)	Not present on older systems

Each IDE hard drive interface, also known as an **IDE channel**, can operate two IDE drives. Therefore, systems with two IDE interfaces can operate up to four IDE drives.

EIDE and ATA Standards

Because the original IDE drives were developed as proprietary drive interfaces for use with brands such as Compaq and Zenith, the first IDE drives had major problems with compatibility and could not be autoconfigured by the BIOS.

Although it can still be difficult to "mix and match" some IDE drives from different vendors, a series of standards for IDE drives are referred to as the *ATA specifications* (AT Attachment). Table 14.3 provides an overview of the differences in the various ATA/IDE specifications.

Table 14.3 ATA/IDE Specifications and Features

ATA Specification	Major Features
ATA-1 (original)	Standardized master/slave jumpers
	IDE Identify command for automatic configuration and detection of parameters
	PIO modes 0–2
	CHS (standard cylinder head sector) and LBA (logical block addressing, sector-translated) parameters
ATA-2	PIO modes 3–4
	Power management
	CHS/LBA translation for drives up to 8.4GB
	Primary and secondary IDE channels
	IDE block mode
ATA-3	S.M.A.R.T. self-diagnostics feature for use with monitoring software
	Password protection
	Improved reliability of PIO mode 4
ATA-4	UDMA-33 (33MBps)
	ATAPI support
	80-wire/40-pin cable
	BIOS support for LBA increased to 136.9GB
ATA-5	UDMA-66 (66MBps)
	Required use of 80-wire/40-pin cable with UDMA-66
ATA-6	UDMA-100 (100MBps)
	Increased capacity of LBA to 144 petabytes (PB; 1PB = 1 quadrillion bytes)

An ATA-7 standard is currently in draft form. It is expected to provide standards for external hard drives and for the Ultra ATA-133 transfer rate (FastDrive; 133MBps) developed by Maxtor and available in current Maxtor drives.

Enhanced IDE is a marketing term used by some vendors to refer to the enhancements listed as ATA-2 in Table 14.3.

Serial ATA

Serial ATA (SATA) is a development of the ATA/IDE standard that provides a pathway to faster drives, greater reliability, and simpler installation than ATA/IDE.

Serial ATA uses a single seven-wire data cable, which uses high-speed serial technology instead of the parallel technology used by ATA/IDE to transmit signals between the drive and host adapter. Unlike ATA/IDE drives, SATA drives use a direct one-to-one connection between the drive and the host adapter. Thus, no jumpers are necessary to configure the drive. Hooray!

Serial ATA uses the same commands as ATA/IDE, so SATA drives and host adapters can be retrofitted to existing systems. SATA drives can be prepared by Windows 98 and more recent versions. Some recent systems include one or more SATA host adapters on the motherboard. On such systems, after the SATA host adapter is enabled in the system BIOS, SATA drives are configured just as ATA/IDE drives are.

note

Some vendors do not support ATA-133 transfer rates (ATA-7) and have added Serial ATA interfaces to their motherboards instead. Although ATA-7 is not yet in its final form, Maxtor drives running at ATA-133 support the ATA-7 transfer rate.

The original version of SATA, SATA-150, has a maximum data transfer rate of 150MBps. Faster versions are expected in the future.

ATA RAID Types

RAID (redundant array of inexpensive drives) is a method for creating a faster or safer single logical hard disk drive from two or more identical physical drives. RAID arrays have been common for years on servers using SCSI-interface drives. However, a number of recent systems feature **ATA RAID** or SATA RAID host adapters on the motherboard. ATA and SATA RAID host adapter cards can also be retrofitted to systems lacking onboard RAID support.

ATA and SATA RAID types include the following:

- *RAID Level 0*—Two drives are treated as a single drive, with both drives used to simultaneously store different portions of the same file. This method of data storage is called striping. Striping boosts performance, but if either drive fails, all data is lost. Don't use striping for data drives.

- *RAID Level 1*—Two drives are treated as mirrors of each other; changes to the contents of one drive are immediately reflected on the other drive. This method of data storage is called mirroring. Mirroring provides a built-in backup method and provides faster read performance than a single drive. Suitable for use with program and data drives.

- *RAID Level 0+1*—Four drives combine striping plus mirroring for extra speed plus better reliability. Suitable for use with program and data drives.

Most motherboards support only RAID 0 and RAID 1. Some host adapters support RAID 0, 1, and 0+1.

ATA or SATA RAID host adapters can sometimes be configured to work as normal ATA or SATA host adapters. Check the system BIOS setup or add-on card host adapter setup for details.

ATA and Serial ATA Cabling

ATA/IDE drives use one of two types of cables, depending upon their speed, whereas Serial ATA drives use one type of cable:

- ATA drives that support PIO modes or Ultra DMA (UDMA) 33 transfer rates can use a 40-wire, 40-pin cable. This is a straight-through cable; master and slave assignments are determined by drive jumpers.

- ATA drives that support UDMA-66 or faster transfer rates must use an 80-wire, 40-pin cable. The connector is the same as the original ATA/IDE cable, but the additional 40 wires are used to provide an electrically cleaner signal. The position of the drives on the cable along with drive jumpers are used to determine master and slave assignments. (See "Drive Jumpers and Cable Select," later in this chapter, for details.) Many of these cables are color coded. In such cases, the blue connector is used for the host adapter, the gray connector is used for the slave drive, and the black connector is used for the master drive.

- SATA drives use a seven-pin cable. No jumpers are used by SATA drives; each drive connects directly to an SATA port on the host adapter or motherboard, so SATA doesn't use master or slave settings.

Figure 14.7 compares these cables to each other. Note the ridged appearance of the 40-wire ATA/IDE cable compared to the smoother 80-wire cable; the 40-wire cable uses thicker wires.

FIGURE 14.7

40-wire and 80-wire ATA/IDE cables compared to an SATA cable.

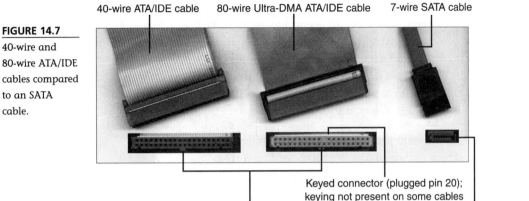

40-wire ATA/IDE cable   80-wire Ultra-DMA ATA/IDE cable   7-wire SATA cable

Keyed connector (plugged pin 20); keying not present on some cables

Keyed connector (raised projection or 'bump'); keying not present on some cables

Keyed connector (L-shaped); used by all SATA cables

➡ For more information on PIO and UDMA transfer rates, **see** "ATA/IDE Performance Optimization," **p. 456**.

IDE Data Cable Keying Standards

Depending upon the design of the ATA/IDE cable and connectors used in a particular system, you might discover difficulties in properly connecting devices:

- Some IDE cables have a raised projection in the middle of the cable connector, which is designed to correspond to a cutout on the IDE drive or host adapter shield around the connector pins. The cables in Figure 14.8 use this keying method.

- Some IDE cable connectors plug the hole for pin 20 and are designed to be used with IDE drives or host adapters that omit pin 20. The cables in Figure 14.8 also support this keying method.

- Some IDE cable connectors don't use either method, making it easy to attach the cable incorrectly. Many vendors continue to use this type of cable because manufacturers can't agree on which of the positive keying methods listed previously should be standard.

Drive Jumpers and Cable Select

With two drives possible per ATA/IDE cable, the ATA/IDE interface uses one of two methods to determine which drive is master and which is slave:

- Drives connected to the 40-pin, 40-wire cable use the master and slave jumper settings shown in Figure 14.9.

■ Drives connected to the 40-pin, 80-wire cable required by UDMA-66 and faster transfer rates use the cable select jumper setting shown in Figure 14.9 along with the position of the drive on the cable: master on black connector, slave on gray connector, and blue connector to host adapter.

Four different jumper positions are available on the bottom or rear of a typical IDE hard drive:

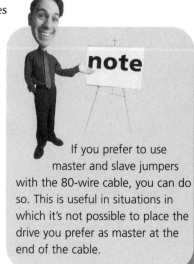

■ One drive installed: Use master jumper or don't jumper any pins (varies by model).

■ Master drive installed with slave; jumper drive as master.

■ Slave drive; jumper drive as slave. Normally, this is used only when two drives are attached to the IDE cable.

note

If you prefer to use master and slave jumpers with the 80-wire cable, you can do so. This is useful in situations in which it's not possible to place the drive you prefer as master at the end of the cable.

■ 80-wire cable in use: Jumper both drives as cable select and connect drives to the appropriate connectors for master and slave.

Figure 14.8 shows two ATA/IDE hard drives configured for cable select.

The Cap Limit jumper shown in Figure 14.8 is used only on systems that cannot use the drive at full capacity.

⇨ To learn more about dealing with hard disk drive size limitations, **see** "Overcoming Hard Disk Capacity Limitations with LBA Mode," **p. 454**.

ATA/IDE Hard Drive Physical Installation

The following steps apply to typical ATA/IDE drive installations. If you are installing an ATAPI drive, you might use a 5.25-inch bay, but the other steps will be the same.

1. Open the system and check for an existing 3.5-inch drive bay; use an internal bay if possible.

2. If a 3.5-inch drive bay is not available but a 5.25-inch drive bay is, attach the appropriate adapter kit and rails as needed, as shown in Figure 14.9.

3. Jumper the drive according to the cable type used: 40-wire cables use master and slave; 80-wire cables use cable select or master and slave.

FIGURE 14.8

Two typical ATA/IDE drives configured for cable select. Some drives, such as the one on the left, require the user to consult a chart on the drive's top plate or in the system documentation for correct settings, whereas others silkscreen the jumper settings on the drive's circuit board.

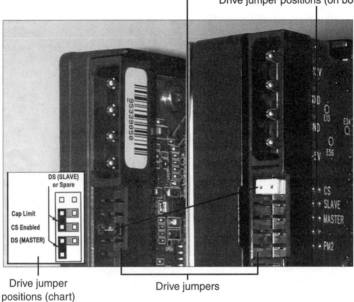

Cable select (CS or CSEL) position

Drive jumper positions (on bottom of drive)

Drive jumper positions (chart)

Drive jumpers

FIGURE 14.9

A typical adapter kit for a 3.5-inch drive. Screw a attaches the frame at hole #1; screw b attaches the frame at hole #2, with corresponding attachments on the opposite side of the drive and frame. Drive rails used by some cases can be attached to the adapter kit.

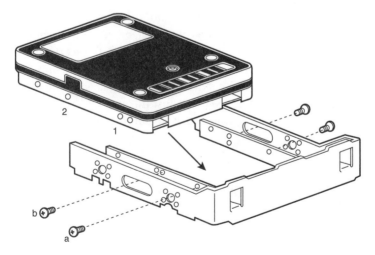

4. Attach the appropriate connector to the drive, making sure to match the colored marking on the edge of the cable to the end of the drive connector with pin 1. Pin 1 might be marked with a square solder hole on the bottom of the drive or silk-screening. If no markings are visible, pin 1 is usually nearest the drive's power connector. Disconnect the cable from the host adapter or other ATA/IDE drive if necessary to create sufficient slack.

5. Slide the drive into the appropriate bay and attach as needed with screws or by snapping the ends of the rails into place.

6. Attach the power connector; most IDE hard drives use the larger four-wire (Molex) power connector originally used on 5.25-inch floppy disk drives. Use a Y-splitter to create two power connectors from one if necessary.

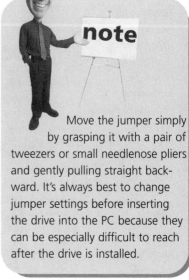

note

Move the jumper simply by grasping it with a pair of tweezers or small needlenose pliers and gently pulling straight backward. It's always best to change jumper settings before inserting the drive into the PC because they can be especially difficult to reach after the drive is installed.

7. Reattach the data cable to the other ATA or ATAPI drive and host adapter if necessary.

8. Change the jumper on the other ATA or ATAPI drive on the same cable if necessary. For example, Western Digital does not use a jumper to indicate a single drive is installed on the cable. Instead, the jumper block is removed, or might be stored across pins that are not used to set the drive's configuration. The Master setting is used only when two drives are on the cable. For example, if you are adding a slave drive to a cable with one drive already attached, you might need to adjust the jumper on the existing drive from single (no jumper) to master. Refer to Figure 14.8.

9. Verify correct data and power connections to IDE drives and host adapters.

10. Turn on the system and start the BIOS configuration program.

Figure 14.10 shows a typical ATA/IDE drive before and after power and data cables are attached.

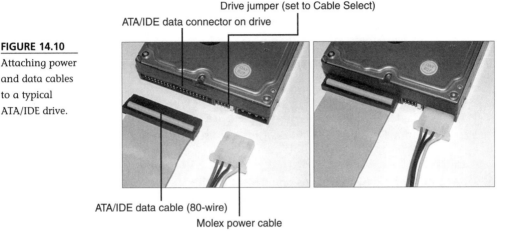

FIGURE 14.10
Attaching power and data cables to a typical ATA/IDE drive.

SATA Hard Drive Physical Installation

The process of installing an SATA drive differs from that used for installing an ATA/IDE drive because there are no master or slave jumpers and the SATA data cable goes directly from host adapter to drive. The following instructions assume the system already has an onboard or add-on card SATA host adapter already installed. If you need to install an SATA host adapter, see the next section for details.

1. Open the system and check for an existing 3.5-inch drive bay; use an internal bay if possible.

2. If a 3.5-inch drive bay is not available but a 5.25-inch drive bay is, attach the appropriate adapter kit and rails as needed, as shown previously in Figure 14.9.

3. Attach the SATA cable to the drive; it is keyed so it can only be connected in one direction.

4. Slide the drive into the appropriate bay and attach as needed with screws or by snapping the ends of the rails into place.

5. Attach the power connector; use the adapter provided with the drive to convert a standard Molex connector to the edge connector type used by SATA. If the drive didn't include a power connector, purchase one.

6. Attach the data cable to the host adapter.

7. Verify correct data and power connections to IDE drives and host adapters.

8. Turn on the system and start the BIOS configuration program if the SATA host adapter is built into the motherboard. Enable the SATA host adapter, save changes, and restart your system.

9. If the SATA drive is connected to an add-on card, watch for messages at startup indicating the host adapter BIOS has located the drive.

10. Install drivers for your operating system to enable the SATA drive and host adapter to function when prompted. See Chapter 15, "Preparing Hard and Floppy Drives with Windows," for details.

Figure 14.11 shows a typical SATA drive. Figure 14.12 shows typical ATA/IDE and SATA host adapter connections on a recent motherboard.

SATA power connector · SATA power cable

FIGURE 14.11

Attaching power and data cables to a typical SATA drive.

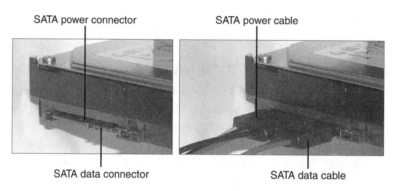

SATA data connector · SATA data cable

ATA/IDE host adapter

FIGURE 14.12

ATA/IDE and SATA host adapters on a recent motherboard.

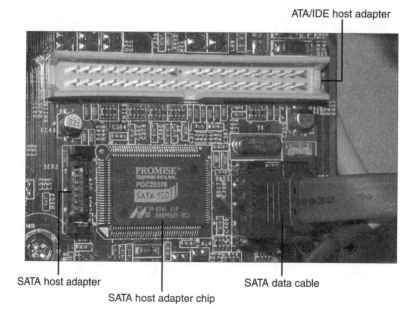

SATA host adapter · SATA data cable

SATA host adapter chip

Installing an SATA Host Adapter

Most systems don't include an SATA host adapter on the motherboard. Thus, to add an SATA drive to many systems, you will also need to install an SATA host adapter card such as the one pictured in Figure 14.13. Follow this procedure:

1. Shut down the system and disconnect the power cable from the outlet to cut all power to the system.

2. Use ESD protection equipment, such as a wrist strap and work mat, if available. (See Chapter 13, "Safety and Recycling," for details.)

3. Open the computer and locate an unused PCI slot.

4. After removing the slot cover, insert the SATA card into the slot. See Chapter 2, "PC Anatomy 101," for basic instructions on adding expansion cards, such as the SATA host adapter described here.

5. Secure the card into place with the screw removed from the slot cover.

6. Connect the card to the SATA drive with an SATA data cable. The cable might be provided with the card or with the drive.

7. Reconnect the power cord and restart the computer.

8. Install drivers when prompted.

9. Restart your computer if prompted.

10. Open the Windows Device Manager to verify that the SATA host adapter is working. It should be listed under the category SCSI Controllers, SCSI Adapters, or SCSI and RAID Controllers (see Figure 14.13).

BIOS Configuration

For ATA/IDE and SATA drives controlled by the motherboard BIOS, the following information must be provided:

- Hard drive geometry
- Data transfer rate
- LBA translation

Hard drive geometry refers to several factors used to calculate the capacity of a hard drive. These factors include the following:

- The number of sectors per track
- The number of read/write heads
- The number of cylinders

FIGURE 14.13

A typical SATA host adapter card that supports two SATA drives. The inset shows how this host adapter appears in the Windows XP Device Manager after installation.

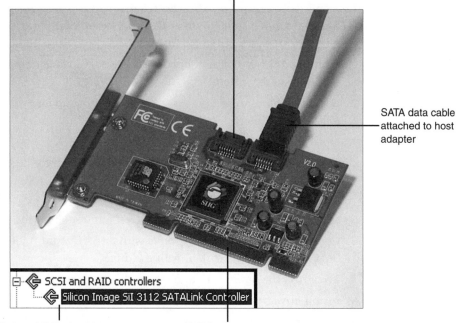

Connector for SATA data cable

SATA data cable attached to host adapter

SCSI and RAID controllers
Silicon Image SiI 3112 SATALink Controller

Windows XP Device Manager entry for host adapter

32-bit PCI slot connector

The surface of any disk-based magnetic media is divided into concentric circles called *tracks*. Each track contains multiple sectors. A sector contains 512 bytes of data, and is the smallest data storage area used by disk drives.

Each side of a hard disk platter used for data storage has a read-write head that moves across the media. There are many tracks on each hard disk platter, and all the tracks on all the platters are added together to obtain the cylinder count.

Figure 14.14 helps you visualize sectors, tracks, and cylinders.

Before the drive can be prepared by the operating system, it must be properly identified by the system BIOS.

note

Although floppy disks also have tracks and sectors, modern operating systems do not require you to specify the track layout of the disk when formatting the media.

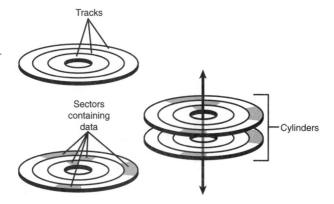

FIGURE 14.14

Tracks, sectors, and cylinders compared.

Depending on the age of the system and the size of the ATA/IDE hard drive, there are two different methods used for configuring an ATA/IDE or SATA drive:

- Manual entry of IDE parameters
- Auto-detection of the IDE hard drive type

Manual Entry of IDE Parameters

This feature started to become common in the BIOS configuration program around 1990, and virtually all systems still allow this today. Systems with this feature have a user-defined drive type that enables you to manually enter the correct cylinders, heads, sectors per track, and special configuration information.

This information is not stored in the BIOS itself, but rather in the CMOS memory, which can be lost due to battery failure or other problems.

Today, this method of defining the hard disk geometry is used primarily when a drive that was prepared using a different disk geometry than that recommended by the manufacturer is being reinstalled in a system or is being moved to another system.

Auto-detection of the IDE Hard Drive Type

Auto-detection is a variation on the user-defined drive type. Auto-detection was developed in the early 1990s, enabling the BIOS to query the drive for the correct configuration information. This information also is placed in the user-defined drive type and stored in the CMOS memory (see Figure 14.15).

note

This information is usually found on a label on most recent hard disks. However, some drives don't provide this information on the disk itself. In such cases, you can check with the hard disk vendor to obtain the correct settings for the drive.

FIGURE 14.15

Configuring an 80GB Western Digital ATA/IDE drive with the auto-detection feature in a typical recent system BIOS.

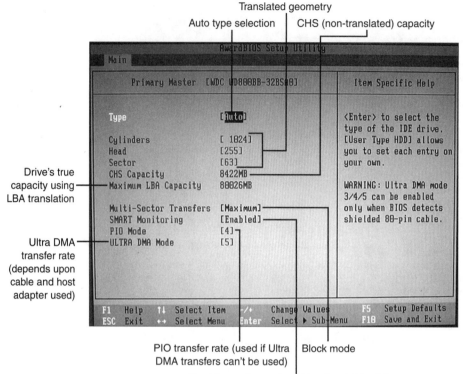

Translated geometry

Auto type selection

CHS (non-translated) capacity

Drive's true capacity using LBA translation

Ultra DMA transfer rate (depends upon cable and host adapter used)

PIO transfer rate (used if Ultra DMA transfers can't be used)

Block mode

Provides early warning of imminent drive failure

Auto-detection is the best way to install a new ATA/IDE or SATA drive because other settings such as LBA translation, block mode (multi-sector transfers), and UDMA transfer rates will also be configured properly.

Some BIOSs perform the automatic detection of the drive type every time you start the system by default. Although this enables you to skip configuring the hard drive setting, it also takes longer to start the system and prevents the use of nonstandard configurations for compatibility reasons.

To save time during the boot process and to allow you to see the actual values used for the drive in the system BIOS, you can use these methods:

- Detect the drive with the BIOS setup program.
- Configure the drive's geometry values manually by entering the manufacturer-supplied values into a user-defined drive type. Then, record the values on a sticker attached to the outside of the drive or the system unit in case the CMOS memory is corrupted and the data must be re-entered.

Depending on the system, removable-media ATAPI (ARMD) drives such as Zip and LS-120 should be configured as Not Present or Auto in the system BIOS setup or as ARMD drives depending upon the BIOS options listed. These drives do not have geometry values to enter in the system. The CD-ROM setting should be used for ATAPI CD-ROM and similar optical drives, such as CD-R, CD-RW, and DVD. Using the correct BIOS configuration for ATAPI drives will enable them to be used to boot the system on drives and systems that support booting from ATAPI devices.

Creating an ATA or SATA RAID Array

An ATA or SATA RAID array generally requires

- *Two or more identical drives*—Some systems enable a single drive to be converted into an array, but this is not recommended. If one drive is larger than the other, the additional capacity will be ignored.

- *A RAID-compatible motherboard or add-on host adapter card*—Both feature a special BIOS, which identifies and configures the drives in the array.

Because RAID arrays use off-the-shelf drives, the only difference in the physical installation of drives in a RAID array is where they are connected. They must be connected to a motherboard or add-on card that has RAID support.

caution

ATA/IDE drives from the earliest days have been designed to work with any valid geometry (combination of sectors per track, heads, and cylinders) that calculates to the maximum size of the drive or less. This sector-translation feature was developed to enable early drives to be installed in systems that lacked a user-definable drive type. (The user was forced to select a drive type with a specified geometry from a list of predefined types.)

If you move a drive from one machine to another *and* the drive type was manually configured, be sure to use the *same* cylinder, head, and sector per track values used to specify the drive when you set it up in another computer or you won't be able to access the drive properly.

After the drive(s) used to create the array are connected to the RAID array's host adapter, restart the computer. Start the system BIOS setup program and enable the RAID host adapter if necessary. Save changes and exit the BIOS setup program.

After enabling the RAID array host adapter, follow the vendor instructions to create the array. Generally, this requires you to activate the RAID array setup program when you start the computer and follow the prompts to select the type of array desired. After the RAID array is configured, the drives are handled as a single physical drive by the system.

Overcoming Hard Disk Capacity Limitations with LBA Mode

When the IDE interface was developed, several limitations on the total capacity of an IDE hard disk existed:

■ MS-DOS limitation of 1,024 cylinders per drive

■ IDE limitation of 63 sectors per track

■ BIOS limitation of 16 heads

These limitations resulted in a total capacity of 504MiB,
or approximately 528 million bytes. By 1994, these limitations were no longer theoretical; users were able to purchase drives that exceeded this size and a BIOS-based way was needed to ensure reliable access to the drives' full capacity.

Previously, systems that were incapable of using the entire capacity of a drive would use a software driver such as OnTrack's Disk Manager, but this approach could be risky to data if the driver or special drive configuration failed.

The most common method for enabling larger IDE hard drives to be used is called **Logical Block Addressing (LBA)**. How does LBA work?

LBA mode alters how the drive is accessed internally. It increases the BIOS limit to 255 heads and works around the MS-DOS limitation of 1,024 cylinders per drive by dividing the cylinders and multiplying the heads by the same factor. Thus, an LBA mode drive has the same capacity as a non-LBA mode drive, but its configuration is different.

For example, assume an ATA/IDE hard drive has a factory-defined configuration of 13,328 cylinders, 15 heads, and 63 sectors per track. To determine the drive capacity, multiply the cylinders by the heads by the sectors per track. Divide the result by 2,048, and the capacity is 6.15GiB

note

Many recent motherboards have four ATA/IDE connectors: Two are used for normal ATA/IDE disk interfacing and the others are intended to be used for an ATA RAID array or as additional standard connectors. Sometimes ATA RAID connectors are made from a contrasting color of plastic than other drive connectors. New systems with two SATA connectors might also support SATA RAID, but the best way to determine if your system or motherboard supports ATA or SATA RAID arrays is to read the manual for the system or motherboard.

caution

If one or more of the drives to be used in the array already contains data, *back up the drives before starting the configuration process!* Most RAID array host adapters delete the data on all drives in the array when creating an array, sometimes with little warning.

(about 6.4GB). However, if you don't enable LBA mode, only the first 1,024 cylinders are recognized by the system, shrinking the drive to 504MiB (528MB).

Which of the three values listed previously is the problem? The cylinder count! When LBA mode is enabled, the following changes take place in the logical geometry of the drive:

- The cylinder count is divided by 15 (13,328/15=888.53—rounded up to 889).
- The head count is multiplied by 15 (15×15=225).

Both of these new logical values fall below the BIOS limits adjusted by LBA. Consequently, the 6.4GB drive is recognized at full capacity. That's a pretty good trick!

Remember, every operating system with a Microsoft logo—from dusty old MS-DOS to the latest Windows version—is incapable of using more than 504MiB of any IDE/ATA or SATA hard drive unless LBA mode is enabled (SCSI has the same limitation, but it's handled a different way).

It's Not Nice to Fool Around with LBA!

If LBA mode is disabled after a drive has been prepared using LBA mode, the drive will not work properly, to put it mildly.

With MS-DOS, the system at some point might try to write to data stored on areas past the barrier of 1,024 cylinders that LBA mode overcomes. Without LBA mode to translate the drive's full capacity, the system will loop back to the beginning of the drive and overwrite the partition table and file allocation table, destroying the drive's contents. Ouch!

If you're running Windows (all 99.9% of you), don't panic. Windows won't boot if you turn off LBA mode, but you won't lose any data.

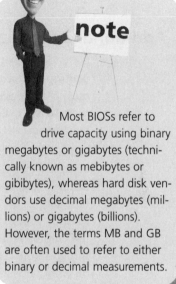

note

Most BIOSs refer to drive capacity using binary megabytes or gigabytes (technically known as mebibytes or gibibytes), whereas hard disk vendors use decimal megabytes (millions) or gigabytes (billions). However, the terms MB and GB are often used to refer to either binary or decimal measurements.

caution

Don't be living "large" with the Award BIOS. Some versions of the Award BIOS (now sold by Phoenix) feature both LBA mode and another translation method called *LARGE*. LARGE and LBA don't work the same way, so you'd have problems moving a drive from a system using LBA to a system using LARGE. Forget LARGE, and stick with LBA: LBA mode is supported by all major BIOS and system makers.

If you're the paranoid type (did I enable LBA mode?), you can use your operating system's disk preparation software to find out if LBA is working. See Chapter 15 for details.

Additional Drive-Size Limitations

Early versions of LBA-mode BIOS could not handle drives of more than 4,095 cylinders (approximately 2.1GB); many more recent systems cannot handle drives with more than 16,384 cylinders (approximately 8.4GB). Support for drives with more than 16,384 cylinders, referred to as **Extended INT13h** or EBIOS support, also requires support in the operating system (Windows 95 or later).

Whenever possible, you should install a system BIOS upgrade to handle limitations of these types. Check out Chapter 6, "BIOS and CMOS Configuration," for the details. If a BIOS upgrade is not available for your system, you can install an ATA host adapter card with an auxiliary BIOS onboard. The BIOS chip on the card can override your existing BIOS to provide the additional support necessary to operate the hard drive at full capacity. An ATA host adapter card is installed using a process similar to that used to install an SATA host adapter card. Like the SATA card, it uses an empty PCI slot.

The upgrade version of Windows 95 and the original OEM version cannot use drives larger than 8.4GB because they use the file system (FAT16) inherited from MS-DOS. The OSR 2.x (Windows 95B/C) versions can use drives up to 32GB in size. Later versions of Windows can use drives over 32GB in size. For more details, see Chapter 15.

ATA/IDE Performance Optimization

If your hard drive is stuck in first gear, so is your system. Fortunately, most systems that support LBA mode also offer several different ways to optimize the performance of IDE drives and devices. These include

- Selecting the correct PIO or DMA transfer mode in the BIOS
- Selecting the correct block mode in the BIOS
- Installing busmastering Windows drivers
- Enabling DMA mode in Windows
- Adjusting disk cache software settings

caution

Even if you love to overclock your processor, video card, or other components, don't mess around with trying hard disk transfer rates faster than your drive is designed to handle! That's a sure way to send your data down the tubes.

PIO and DMA Transfer Modes

IDE hard drives are capable of operating at a wide variety of transfer speeds. Depending on when the drive was built, IDE hard drives are designed to run in one of two modes:

- PIO (Programmed Input/Output) mode
- Ultra DMA (UDMA) mode (also called Ultra ATA mode)

These modes refer to different peak transfer rates the hard drive can achieve. Some systems automatically determine the correct transfer rate, whereas others require you to select the correct speed from a list of options. Selecting transfer rates too fast for the drive can cause data corruption, and selecting rates that are too low can slow down the system.

To achieve a given transfer rate, the hard disk, the host adapter (card or built-in), and the data cable must be capable of that rate. In addition, the host adapter must be configured to run at that rate.

Tables 14.4 and 14.5 list the most common transfer rates. Check the drive documentation or with the drive vendor for the correct rating for a given drive.

Table 14.4   PIO Peak Transfer Rates

Mode	Peak Transfer Rate	Interface Type Required
PIO 0	3.33MBps	16-bit
PIO 1	5.22MBps	16-bit
PIO 2	8.33MBps	16-bit
PIO 3	11.11MBps	32-bit VL-Bus or PCI
PIO 4	16.67MBps	32-bit VL-Bus or PCI

Although PIO modes 3 and 4 require a fast 32-bit IDE interface, not every VL-Bus card is capable of such transfer rates; some require software drivers to achieve mode 3/mode 4 speeds. Check the documentation for the host adapter card or the BIOS configuration screen for systems using a built-in ATA/IDE interface to find out which speeds are supported.

Table 14.5   UDMA (Ultra ATA) Peak Transfer Rates

Mode	Peak Transfer Rate	Interface Type Required
UDMA 2 (UDMA-33)	33.33MBps	32-bit PCI
UDMA 4 (UDMA-66)	66.66MBps	32-bit PCI
UDMA 5 (UDMA-100)	100MBps	32-bit PCI
UDMA 6 (UDMA-133)	133MBps	32-bit PCI

These modes are backward compatible, enabling you to select the fastest available mode if your system lacks the correct mode for your drive. ATA/IDE drives are backward compatible; you can select a slower UDMA mode than the drive supports if your system doesn't support the correct UDMA mode, or you can use PIO modes if your system has no UDMA options in the BIOS. Performance will be slower, but the drive will still work.

Note that UDMA 4 (UDMA-66) and faster modes require the use of a 40-pin, 80-wire cable previously shown in Figure 14.9. If a 40-wire cable is used, UDMA 2 (UDMA-33) is the fastest speed possible.

IDE Block Mode

IDE **block mode** refers to an improved method of data handling. Originally, a hard drive was allowed to read only a single 512-byte sector before the drive sent an IRQ to the CPU. Early in their history, some IDE hard drives began to use a different method called block mode, which enabled the drive to read multiple sectors, or blocks, of data before an IRQ was sent. Virtually all recent drives support block mode. Enable it (also called multisector transfers, as shown in Figure 14.16) in the system BIOS to get the performance expected from the drive.

Most recent systems automatically determine block mode capability when they auto-detect the drive. Others require that you enable or disable block mode manually, and still others enable you to select the number of blocks the drive can read. Some very old ATA/IDE drives do not support block mode and run more slowly when it is enabled. If you must set block mode manually, check with the drive vendor to see whether the drive supports block mode and what options to select if it does.

note

About the only time you might be stuck running at PIO speeds these days is if you're trying to recycle an old hard disk or CD-ROM drive. Just about everything made in the last few years supports the UDMA modes shown in Table 14.5.

tip

Some UDMA drives are shipped with their firmware configuration set to a lower transfer rate than the maximum supported by the drive. This helps avoid data loss that could happen if the drive were connected to a system that doesn't support the drive's maximum transfer rate. Fortunately, these drives usually include a software utility that can ratchet up the speed to the maximum allowed. If you can't find the driver disk or CD, check out the vendor's Web site for the utility and download it.

IDE Busmastering Drivers

A third way to improve IDE hard disk performance is to install busmastering drivers for the IDE host interface. A **busmaster** bypasses the CPU for data transfers between memory and the hard disk interface. This option is both operating system specific and motherboard/host adapter specific.

Only systems running Windows 9x and newer versions—but not MS-DOS, Windows NT 3.51, or Windows NT 4.0 before Service Pack 3—can use busmastering drivers. Most newer systems have motherboards that support busmastering drivers. Check with the motherboard or system vendor for busmastering information.

Busmastering drivers require special support from the motherboard's chipset. The original retail versions of Windows 95 and Windows NT 4.0 don't include busmastering drivers (get them from the motherboard or motherboard chipset vendor), but Windows 95 OSR 2.x (also called Windows 95B), Windows 98, and newer versions include busmastering support for motherboards with the correct Intel chipsets. Motherboards using other chipsets might require that you download the correct driver from the motherboard vendor if you are using Windows 95 OSR 2.x; Windows 98 and newer versions include busmastering drivers for major non-Intel chipsets. In most cases, you must manually install the correct driver. If your motherboard includes a driver CD, it might contain more up-to-date busmastering drivers than those included with Windows.

Because busmastering bypasses the CPU, be sure you are installing the correct drivers. Carefully read the motherboard or system vendor's instructions. You might not be able to use busmastering drivers if you use a CD-R or CD-RW drive connected to the IDE interface. In such cases, use the regular IDE host adapter driver supplied with Windows.

Enabling DMA Transfers for IDE Devices in Windows

All versions of Windows from Windows NT 4.0 (Service Pack 3 and greater) and Windows 95 up through Windows XP enable the user to allow DMA transfers between ATA/IDE devices and the system. DMA transfers bypass the CPU for faster performance and are particularly useful for optimizing the performance of both hard drives and optical drives, such as high-speed CD-ROM drives and DVD drives.

Follow this procedure to enable DMA transfers for a particular IDE device in Windows 9x/Me:

note

The correct busmastering drivers for your system and Windows version must be installed before you can enable DMA transfers.

1. Open the System Properties sheet. Right-click My Computer and select Properties, or open the Control Panel and select System.

2. Click Device Manager.

3. Click the plus sign (+) next to the Disk Drives category (for hard drives) or CDROM (for CD-ROM, CD-R/CD-RW, or DVD drives).

4. Click the drive for which you want to enable DMA transfers, and click Properties. Standard IDE hard drives are listed as Generic; other devices and CD-ROM/optical drives are listed by name.

5. Click Settings.

6. Click the DMA box to put a check mark next to DMA.

7. Click OK.

8. Restart the computer as prompted.

Repeat this procedure for each IDE device.

With Windows 2000/XP, follow this procedure:

1. Open the System Properties sheet. Right-click My Computer and select Properties, or open the Control Panel and select System.

2. Click Hardware, Device Manager.

3. To determine which drives are connected to which host adapter, open the category containing the drives (Disk Drives for hard or removable-media drives or DVD/CD-ROM Drives for optical drives) and double-click the drive to open its Properties sheet. The location value visible on the General tab shows to which host adapter and device number the drive is connected. For example, location 0 (1) indicates the drive is connected to the primary host adapter (0) as the secondary device (1).

4. Click the plus sign next to the IDE ATA/ATAPI Controllers category.

5. Double-click the host adapter for which you want to adjust properties (primary or secondary IDE channel) to open its Properties sheet.

> **caution**
>
> Before enabling DMA or UDMA mode, check the documentation for the drive to see if it supports this mode. Enabling DMA or UDMA on a drive that does not support it can have disastrous effects.
>
> If the drive can't go faster than UDMA 2 although it's rated for higher speeds (see Figure 14.16), you might want to change the cable. You need the 80-wire cable shown earlier in Figure 14.8 to get to UDMA 4 (66MBps) or faster transfer rates. It's also okay to use the 80-wire cable for slower speeds.

6. Click Advanced Settings.

7. To enable DMA for a particular drive, select DMA if available for the Transfer mode. To disable DMA, select PIO only (see Figure 14.16).

FIGURE 14.16

The secondary IDE channel on this system is configured to run one drive in PIO mode and one drive in UDMA mode.

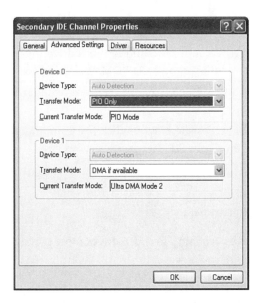

8. Click OK.

9. Restart the computer as prompted.

If DMA is not available, you might need to install the correct busmastering driver for your system.

Adjusting Disk Caching Settings in Windows

Disk caches use a portion of memory to hold information flowing to and from disk drives. The system accesses the cache memory before accessing the main memory. If the information on disk is already in the cache memory, it is accessed far more quickly than if it were read from disk.

Disk cache software is incorporated into Windows 9x and newer Windows versions. (MS-DOS and Windows 9x also include the Smartdrv.exe disk cache program for use at a command prompt.)

The disk cache in Windows 9x and newer versions automatically adjusts to increases in physical RAM—as more RAM is added, the amount of RAM used for disk caching increases. The disk cache also varies in size—the amount of RAM used for disk caching varies with system activity. Windows uses two types of disk caching:

- **Write-behind caching**—This uses the disk cache for both disk reads and disk writes. This frees up an application saving data to disk to proceed to the next task.
- **Read-only caching**—This uses the disk cache for disk reads only. Disk writes go to the drive and cause delays with some applications.

By default, Windows uses write-behind caching for hard drives and read-only caching for floppy, removable-media, and CD-ROM/optical drives.

You can alter Windows 9x and Me's disk-caching settings by following this procedure:

1. Open the System Properties sheet. Right-click My Computer and select Properties, or open the Control Panel and select System.
2. Click Performance.
3. Click File System.
4. Select options as directed next.

To enable Windows to use disk caching for hard drives most effectively, perform the following steps:

1. Select Hard Disk.
2. Select Network Server from the Typical role of this computer menu.
3. Drag the Read-Ahead Optimization selector to Full.

To enable write-behind caching for floppy and other removable disk drives, follow this procedure:

1. Click Removable Disk.
2. Click Enable Write-Behind Caching.

You must make sure all data has been saved to the disk before removing it.

To maximize caching for CD-ROM drives, follow this procedure:

1. Click CD-ROM.
2. Drag the Supplemental Cache Size selector to Large.
3. Select Quad-Speed or Higher from the Optimize Access Pattern menu.

You can disable write-behind disk caching by following this procedure (recommended for troubleshooting only because it slows down the system significantly):

1. Click Troubleshooting.
2. Click Disable Write-Behind Caching.

To complete the changes, click OK and restart the system when prompted.

To adjust disk-cache settings for Windows 2000/XP, follow this procedure:

1. Open the System Properties sheet and click Advanced.

2. Click the Settings button in the Performance section.

3. Click Advanced.

4. Click System Cache to use more memory on a computer that provides server features to other computers or to improve overall disk-caching performance. To avoid reducing system performance, you should enable this feature only on systems with 512MB of RAM or more.

5. Click OK and restart the system as prompted.

SCSI Interface

SCSI (Small Computer System Interface) is a more flexible drive interface than IDE because it can accommodate many devices that are not hard disk drives. The following are common uses for SCSI:

- High-performance and high-capacity hard drives
- Image scanners
- Removable-media drives such as Zip, Jaz, and Castlewood Orb
- High-performance laser printers
- High-performance optical drives, including CD-ROM, CD-R, CD-RW, DVD-ROM, and others

So-called **Narrow SCSI** host adapters (which use an 8-bit data channel) can accommodate up to seven devices of different varieties on a single connector. **Wide SCSI** host adapters use a 16-bit data channel and accommodate up to 15 devices on a single connector.

Multiple Device Support with SCSI Host Adapters

All true SCSI host adapters are designed to support multiple devices, although some low-cost SCSI host adapters made especially for scanners and Zip drives might not support multiple devices (also known as **daisy-chaining**). Several SCSI features permit this:

- External SCSI peripherals have two SCSI ports, enabling daisy-chaining of multiple devices.
- Internal SCSI ribbon cables resemble IDE data cables, only wider.

■ Both internal and external SCSI peripherals enable the user to choose a unique device ID number for each device to distinguish one peripheral from another in the daisy-chain (see Figure 14.17).

FIGURE 14.17

When a SCSI host adapter card with internal and external connectors is used, the SCSI daisy-chain can extend through the card. Note that the devices on each end of the chain are terminated, and each device (including the host adapter) has a unique device ID number.

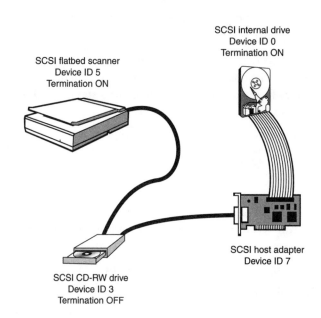

SCSI flatbed scanner
Device ID 5
Termination ON

SCSI internal drive
Device ID 0
Termination ON

SCSI host adapter
Device ID 7

SCSI CD-RW drive
Device ID 3
Termination OFF

Multiple device support enables the different types of devices listed previously to work on a single SCSI host adapter. For example, my office computer features a flatbed scanner, slide scanner, and Zip drive connected to the same card, with room for three additional miscellaneous SCSI devices on that card. To determine which device IDs are in use, you can

■ Physically examine each SCSI device's device ID settings.

■ Scan the SCSI bus with a software program such as Adaptec's SCSI Interrogator or with the BIOS routines built into some SCSI host adapters.

■ View the properties for each SCSI device in the Windows Device Manager.

SCSI Host Adapter Locations and Hardware Resources

Some system boards contain a SCSI host adapter, but most SCSI **host adapters** are add-on cards.

SCSI host adapters do not have standard IRQ or I/O port address settings because they are add-on devices rather than a standard part of the system architecture. Some high-performance ISA SCSI host adapters also use a DMA channel; PCI-based SCSI host adapters do not use a DMA channel. In addition, SCSI host adapters designed to support bootable SCSI hard drives use a memory address for the ROM BIOS chip on the card. Some SCSI host adapters are designed to support only low-speed SCSI peripherals such as scanners and removable-media drives. These host adapters do not use an onboard BIOS. PCI-based SCSI host adapters use Plug and Play (PnP) configuration for all settings.

Note that SCSI cards use the same resources (IRQ, I/O port address, memory address, and DMA), regardless of whether more devices are attached to the card.

SCSI Standards

SCSI actually is the family name for a wide range of standards, which differ from each other in the speed of devices, number of devices, and other technical details. The major SCSI standards are listed in Table 14.6. SCSI host adapters are generally backward compatible, enabling older and newer SCSI standards to be mixed on the same host adapter. However, mixing slower and faster devices can cause the faster devices to slow down unless you use a host adapter with dual buses that can run at different speeds. Table 14.6 lists the speeds and other characteristics of popular SCSI standards.

Table 14.6 Popular SCSI Standards

Popular Name	Speed	Number of Devices	Data Bus	Signal Type
Fast	10MBps	7	8-bit	SE[1]
Fast-Wide	10MBps	15	16-bit	SE
Ultra	20MBps	7	8-bit	SE
Ultra-Wide	20MBps	15	16-bit	SE
Ultra2	40MBps	7	8-bit	LVD[2]
Ultra2Wide	80MBps	15	16-bit	LVD
Ultra 160	160MBps	15	16-bit	LVD
Ultra 320	320MBps	15	16-bit	LVD

[1] *Single-ended*

[2] *Low-voltage differential*

8-bit versions of SCSI use a 50-pin cable or a 25-pin cable; wide (16-bit) versions use a 68-pin cable. 10MBps is the fastest speed supported by ISA cards, which are becoming obsolete. The faster speeds shown in Table 14.6 require a PCI bus card.

SCSI Cables

Just as no single SCSI standard exists, no single SCSI cabling standard exists. In addition to the 50-pin versus 68-pin difference between standard and wide devices, differences also appear in the Narrow SCSI external cables. Figure 14.18 compares internal SCSI cables for wide and narrow applications, and Figure 14.19 compares various types of external SCSI cables and ports.

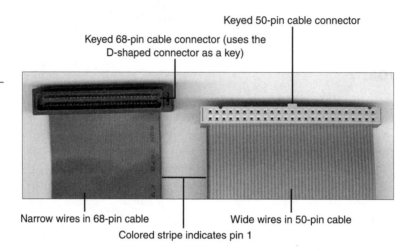

Keyed 50-pin cable connector

Keyed 68-pin cable connector (uses the D-shaped connector as a key)

FIGURE 14.18

A wide (68-pin) SCSI ribbon cable (left) compared to a narrow (50-pin) SCSI ribbon cable (right).

Narrow wires in 68-pin cable

Colored stripe indicates pin 1

Wide wires in 50-pin cable

Compare Figure 14.18 to Figure 14.8 to see the resemblance between SCSI 50-pin ribbon cables and ATA/IDE cables: SCSI 50-pin cables resemble IDE cables but are wider. However, three different types of Narrow SCSI external connectors are available (see Figure 14.19):

- *50-pin Centronics*—Similar to, but wider than, the 36-pin Centronics port used for parallel printers. Also called **LD-50**.

- *50-pin high-density connector* (**HD-50**)—The Wide SCSI 68-pin connector (**HD-68**) uses the same design, but with 34 pins per row instead of 25 pins per row.

- *25-pin DB-25F*—Physically, but not electronically, similar to the DB-25F parallel printer port.

Most recent external 8-bit (narrow) SCSI devices use the HD-50 connector, whereas older models use the LD-50 (Centronics) connector. However, a few low-cost SCSI devices such as the Iomega Zip-100 drive and some SCSI scanners use only the

25-pin connector, which lacks much of the grounding found on the 50-pin cable. Some SCSI devices provide two different types of SCSI connectors. My slide scanner, for example, has a single Centronics 50-pin connector and a single DB-25F connector (refer to Figure 14.21). Consequently, you need to determine what cable connectors are used by any external SCSI devices you wish to connect together.

FIGURE 14.19

Wide (68-pin) and narrow (50-pin, 25-pin) SCSI cable connectors (left) and the corresponding SCSI port connectors (right).

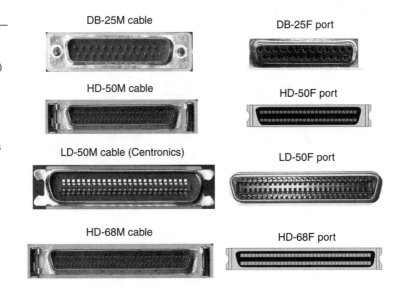

DB-25M cable

DB-25F port

HD-50M cable

HD-50F port

LD-50M cable (Centronics)

LD-50F port

HD-68M cable

HD-68F port

SCSI Signaling Types

In Table 14.6 (previously shown), **SE** stands for **single-ended**, a SCSI signaling type that runs at speeds of up to 20MBps only. SE signaling enables relatively inexpensive SCSI devices and host adapters to be developed, but it reduces the length of cables and the top speed possible.

Ultra2, Ultra2Wide, Ultra 160 and Ultra 320 devices all use a signaling standard called **low-voltage differential (LVD)**, which enables longer cable runs and faster, more reliable operation than the single-ended (SE) standard allows. Some LVD devices can also be used on the same bus with SE devices, but these multimode, or LVD/SE devices, will be forced to slow down to the SE maximum of 20MBps when mixed with SE devices on the same bus. Some advanced SCSI host adapters feature both an SE and an LVD bus to enable the same adapter to control both types of devices at the correct speeds.

Daisy-Chaining SCSI Devices

When you create a SCSI **daisy-chain**, you must keep all these factors in mind:

- Each device must have a unique SCSI **device ID**.

- Each end of the daisy-chain must be terminated. Some devices have an integral switch or jumper block for termination (see Figures 14.20 and 14.21), whereas some external devices require that you attach a terminator (which resembles the end of a SCSI cable) to the unused SCSI connector.

FIGURE 14.20

A SCSI-based internal CD-R drive with (left to right) well-marked jumpers for termination and device ID, power connector, data cable pin 1, and CD-audio cable.

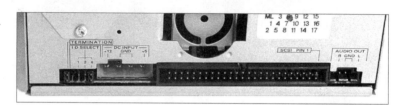

- When daisy-chaining external devices, double check the cable connector type and purchase appropriate cables. You will often need SCSI cables that have different connectors at each end because of the different connector types used (see Figure 14.21).

SCSI Host Adapter Card Installation

For Windows 9x/Me/2000/XP, follow these steps to install a Plug and Play (PnP) SCSI host adapter card:

1. Check the card's documentation and make any required adjustments in the PnP configuration in the BIOS before installing the card. You might need to change the type of IRQ setting used or reserve a particular IRQ for the card.

2. Install the card into the appropriate ISA or PCI expansion slot.

3. Turn on the system.

4. When the card is detected by the system, you'll be prompted for installation software. Insert the appropriate disk or CD-ROM and follow the prompt to complete the installation.

5. Reboot the system and use the Windows Device Manager to view the card's configuration.

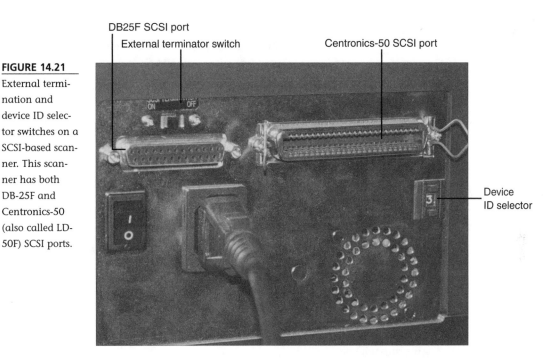

DB25F SCSI port

External terminator switch

Centronics-50 SCSI port

Device ID selector

FIGURE 14.21
External termination and device ID selector switches on a SCSI-based scanner. This scanner has both DB-25F and Centronics-50 (also called LD-50F) SCSI ports.

Choosing an Appropriate SCSI Card for Your Devices

Before you can install a SCSI device, an appropriate SCSI card must be installed in the system. As you have previously seen, SCSI has several standards, and a wide range of cards has been designed for each standard.

Use Table 14.7 to help you choose a SCSI card that is adequate for the devices you want to use with the card. If you plan to buy more advanced devices later, buy a card that exceeds your devices' current requirements, because SCSI is backward compatible. If a customer has an existing SCSI card and wants to add a new SCSI device to it, be sure it meets the minimum requirements for that device.

Table 14.7   SCSI Card Selection Criteria

Devices You Plan to Use	Minimum Features Required
Scanner, Zip drive, CD-ROM	Any SCSI card
CD-R, CD-RW drive	Card with busmastering
Bootable hard drive	Card that matches drive's transfer rate and data bus and has an onboard BIOS

Installing a SCSI Hard Drive

Many SCSI hard drives and some other devices support a feature called **SCAM (SCSI Configuration AutoMagically)**, which automatically assigns SCSI device IDs. Use this option only if all devices on the SCSI host adapter, and the adapter itself, support SCAM.

Most SCSI hard drives will require preparation with a host adapter–specific utility program. If you change host adapters after preparing a SCSI hard drive, its contents might not be readable.

Adjust the system BIOS setting for drive boot order to enable a SCSI drive connected to a bootable host adapter to be bootable. On systems that don't list SCSI as a boot option in the system BIOS, disable the IDE host adapter to enable the SCSI drive to boot.

SCSI hard drives have many additional configuration options not used by other SCSI devices, including

- Negotiation (of speed, bus width, and data transfer type)
- Enable/disable unit attention
- Parity checking for data
- Auto-start delay
- Remote start

Check the drive and host adapter documentation to resolve any conflicts.

CD-ROM, CD-RW, and DVD Drives

Optical drives fall into two major categories:

- Those based on CD technology, including **CD-ROM, CD-R (recordable CD)**, and **CD-RW (rewritable CD)**
- Those based on DVD technology, including **DVD-ROM, DVD-RAM, DVD-R/RW, DVD+R/RW** and **DVD±R/RW**

How CD-ROM and DVD Drives Store Data

The data are stored in a continuous spiral of indentations called **pits** and **lands** on the nonlabel side of the media from the middle of the media outward to the edge. All drives use a laser to read data; DVD stores more data because it uses a laser on a shorter

tip

You should understand both read-only and recordable/rewritable CD and DVD standards to be prepared for the A+ Certification Exam and for your day-to-day work because these drives are found in virtually all recent computers.

wavelength than CD-ROM and CD-RW drives do, allowing for smaller pits and lands and more data in the same space. CD-R and CD-RW drives use special media types and a more powerful laser to write data to the media. CD-R media is a write-once media—the media can be written to during multiple sessions, but older data cannot be deleted. CD-RW media can be rewritten up to 1,000 times.

Similarly, DVD-R and DVD+R media is recordable, but not erasable, whereas DVD-RW and DVD+RW media uses a phase-change medium similar to CD-RW and can be rewritten up to 1,000 times. DVD-RAM can be rewritten up to 100,000 times, but DVD-RAM drives and media are less compatible with other types of DVD drives and media than the other rewritable DVD types, making DVD-RAM the least popular DVD format.

DVD Formats

A number of manufacturers now make various types of writeable DVD drives. There are actually five types of writeable DVD media, and because most drives can use only one or two types, it's essential that you buy the correct type.

- *DVD-RAM*—A rewriteable/erasable media similar to CD-RW but more durable; it can be single or double sided. DVD-RAM is usually kept in a closed disc caddy to protect its surfaces.

- *DVD-R*—A writeable/nonerasable media similar to CD-R; some DVD-RAM and all DVD-RW drives can use DVD-R media.

- *DVD-RW*—A single-sided rewriteable/erasable media similar to CD-RW. DVD-RW drives can also write to DVD-R media.

- *DVD+RW*—A rewriteable/erasable media. Also similar to CD-RW, but not interchangeable with DVD-RW or DVD-RAM.

- *DVD+R*—A writeable/nonerasable media. Also similar to CD-R, but not interchangeable with DVD-R.

DVD-R/RW and DVD+R/RW media is now speed rated because the latest drives can write and rewrite data at faster rates than older drives.

Most DVD+RW and DVD-RW drives, along with some DVD-RAM drives, can also use CD-RW and CD-R media.

All rewritable media (CD-RW, DVD-RAM, DVD-RW, and DVD+RW) must be formatted before it can be used for drag-and-drop file copying. DVD+RW, second-generation and newer DVD-RW, and DVD-RAM drives support quick formatting,

caution

Before using 4x or faster media in older DVD-R/RW drives, make sure you install the firmware update provided by the drive vendor. Otherwise, you will damage your drive if you attempt to use the faster media in the slower drive.

which takes less than a minute. Early DVD-RW and all CD-RW drives require up to an hour to format the media.

Although CD-mastering programs can also use rewriteable media, you should not use such media with these programs, as the media might not be erasable after being mastered. Use CD-R, DVD-R, or DVD+R media for CD- or DVD-mastering tasks.

Multiformat Drives

Many rewritable DVD drives now on the market are referred to as DVD±R/RW, meaning that they can use either DVD-R/RW or DVD+R/RW media. Because DVD-ROM drives and DVD-Video players vary in their compatibility with recordable and rewritable DVD formats, multiformat drives like these ensure compatibility with a wide range of DVD devices.

Some recent DVD-RAM drives have also added write/rewrite compatibility with CD-R/RW and DVD-R/RW media to improve their compatibility with the more popular recordable and rewritable CD and DVD formats.

CD and DVD Capacities

The standard capacity of older CD-ROM drives is 650MB–74 minutes of music. Newer drives and CD-R/CD-RW media support 700MB–80 minutes of music; almost all media on the market today is the 700MB/80 minute media. Standard DVD drives support the DVD-5 standard, which stores 4.7GB on a single-sided, single-layer disk that is the same size as a CD-ROM but holds much more data and must be read by a different type of laser. DVD-RAM media can be single sided (4.7GB) or double sided (9.4GB).

These drives are most commonly connected through the ATA/IDE interface, where they are referred to as *ATAPI devices*, but some older models also connect through SCSI interfaces. Portable drives can use parallel, USB 1.1, USB 2.0 (Hi-Speed USB), IEEE-1394a, or PC Card interfaces—USB 2.0 or IEEE-1394a are the most common interfaces on recent models. Optical drives are installed the same way as other drives using the same interfaces.

CD and DVD Speed Ratings

Drive speeds are measured by an **X-rating**:

- On CD-based drives, 1X equals 150KBps, the data transfer rate used for reading music CDs. Multiply the X-rating by 150 to determine the drive's data rate for reading, writing, or rewriting CD media.

- On DVD-based drives, 1X equals 1.385MBps when working with DVD media; this is the data transfer rate used for playing DVD-Video (DVD movies) content. Multiply the X-rating by 1.385 to determine the drive's data rate for reading, writing, or rewriting DVD media. When DVD drives read, write, or rewrite CD media, they do so at speeds comparable to CD drives.

Most drives run at variable speeds to hold down costs; therefore, a so-called 52X drive produces its maximum 7,500KBps transfer rate only when it is reading the outer edges of the media on a full CD. For drives that work with different types of media, each media type is listed for the drive. For example, a drive that reads CD-ROMs at 50X (maximum), writes CD-R media at 40X, and rewrites CD-RW media at 24X would be said to have a speed rating of 40X/24X/50X; the usual speed order is CD-R/CD-RW/CD-ROM. A DVD drive that can read DVD media at 10X and CD-ROMs at 40X would be referred to as a 10X DVD (40X CD-ROM) drive.

Rewritable DVD drives usually list their speeds in this order:

- DVD write
- DVD rewrite
- DVD read
- CD write
- CD rewrite
- CD read

Installing Optical Drives

The installation of these drives follows the standard procedure used for each interface type. For example, ATAPI/IDE CD-ROM drives are set as master, slave, or cable select (depending upon the cable type); SCSI CD-ROM drives must be set to a unique device ID; and so on. If you want to play music CDs through your sound card's speakers, especially with older versions of Windows, make sure you run the CD audio patch cable supplied with the drive to the CD audio jack on the sound card. Older drives support a four-wire analog cable, whereas newer drives support both the four-wire analog and newer two-wire digital cable. The digital cable provides for faster speed when ripping music CDs (*ripping* is the

note

You might still be able to play CDs on your system provided you don't use an analog or digital patch cable if the installed media player software converts the CD audio into digital audio first. However, this can delay playback and the results might not be as good if you use the analog or digital cable connection to the optical drive.

process of converting music CD tracks into compressed digital music files such as MP3 and WMA). Figure 14.22 shows a typical optical drive before and after connecting power, data, and music cables.

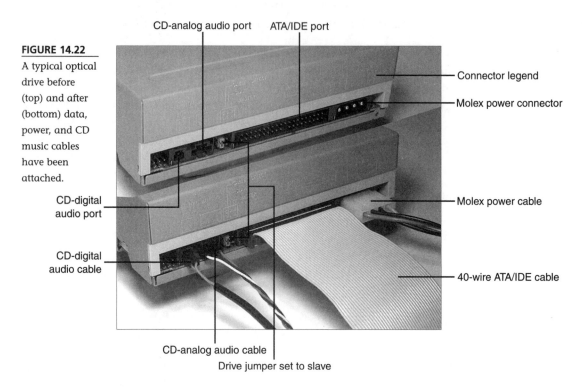

FIGURE 14.22
A typical optical drive before (top) and after (bottom) data, power, and CD music cables have been attached.

CD-analog audio port   ATA/IDE port

Connector legend

Molex power connector

CD-digital audio port

CD-digital audio cable

Molex power cable

40-wire ATA/IDE cable

CD-analog audio cable
Drive jumper set to slave

Enabling CD and DVD Recording Features

All optical drives except for DVD-RAM drives are treated as CD-ROM or DVD-ROM drives by all versions of Windows; DVD-RAM drives are recognized as rewritable drives by all versions of Windows.

Windows XP provides rudimentary CD-R/RW recording capabilities with both CD-R/RW and rewritable DVD drives. However, commercial software such as Nero, Roxio Easy CD and DVD Creator, and others is highly recommended with Windows XP and is required with other versions of Windows in order to use the rewritable/recordable features of CD and DVD drives. Most rewritable drives sold at stores are equipped with some version of one or more of these programs. However, some computer vendors rely on the Windows XP recording feature to support their bundled CD-RW drives.

Windows XP's CD-writing capability is automatically activated for any CD or DVD rewritable drive (although only CD-R/RW media is supported). To write files to the drive, insert a blank disc, drag files to the CD/DVD drive icon using Windows Explorer/My Computer, and click the CD/DVD drive icon. When the drive icon opens, files waiting to be written are listed. Click the task menu option Write These Files to CD. The files are written, albeit much more slowly than if you use a commercial CD-mastering or packet-writing program.

To erase files from a CD-RW disc, place the disc in the drive, open its icon in Windows Explorer/My Computer, select the file(s) to erase, and erase them.

Because Windows XP doesn't format a CD-RW disc the same way a packet-writing program such as DirectCD, InCD, or DLA does, you cannot use a third-party program to erase files from a CD-RW disc written by Windows XP. You must use Windows XP to erase unwanted files. You can then reformat the media as desired with a different program.

IDE/ATAPI Installation Issues

Generally, because data frequently is copied from a CD-ROM drive to the hard drive or from a hard drive to a CD-RW drive, ATAPI CD-ROM drives should be connected to the secondary IDE interface, and hard drives should be connected to the primary IDE interface.

On newer systems with CD-ROM as an available drive type in the system BIOS setup, be sure to set the BIOS drive type as CD-ROM for any optical drive. If you want to use the optical drive as a bootable device for use with Windows 2000/XP or vendor-supplied system recovery CDs, be sure that the optical drive (CD-ROM) is specified as the first device in the boot order.

Removable-Media and Tape Drives

Removable-media drives bridge the capacity gap between floppy disks and hard drives. With capacities ranging from 100MB up to 20GB, they can be used for backup and primary data storage and for data transport between systems. Some types that connect to SCSI or ATA/IDE interfaces can be used as boot drives. Although many types of removable-media drives have been discontinued recently as low-cost rewritable optical storage has become very popular, you need to understand the major types of current and recent removable-media drives to be prepared for the A+ Certification Exam as well as your day-to-day work as a technician.

The major types of removable-media drives you should become familiar with include

- Iomega Zip
- Imation SuperDisk (LS-120, LS-240)
- Iomega Jaz
- Iomega Peerless
- Castlewood Orb

Tape drives are used for backup instead of primary storage. The capacities of current models range from 20GB to as high as 360GB (2:1 data compression assumed). The major types of tape drives in use include

- Travan
- DDS
- VXA
- SLR
- AIT
- DLT
- LTO

Tape drives use various types of magnetic tape. Some tape drive mechanisms can be incorporated into autoloaders or tape libraries for large network backup and data retrieval.

Interface Types

Removable-media and tape drives use the same interface types used by other types of drives:

- Parallel (Zip and SuperDisk LS-120)
- USB (all products listed)
- SCSI (Jaz, Orb, and Zip)
- IEEE-1394a (Jaz, Orb, Zip, and Peerless)
- ATAPI (Zip, SuperDisk, and Orb)

Most current tape drives connect via USB 1.1, 2.0, SCSI, ATAPI, or IEEE-1394a interfaces. Some older models used floppy or parallel-port interfaces.

See the following sections for more details.

Zip

The Iomega **Zip drive** is far and away the most common removable-media drive you are likely to encounter. It is available in three capacities, which among them support all interfaces used by removable-media drives. (Some interfaces have been discontinued.) All Zip drives use only Zip media (see Figure 14.26).

Table 14.8 provides a quick reference to Zip drives produced by Iomega; some third-party vendors also produce Zip drives under license for use in interchangeable drive bays for notebook computers as well as standard internal and external interfaces. All drives listed in Table 14.8 except for the ATAPI version are external drives.

Table 14.8 Iomega Zip Drive Interfaces and Capacities

Drive Capacity	USB 1.1	USB 2.0 (Hi-Speed USB)	Parallel Port	SCSI[1]	ATAPI	IEEE-1394a	Supported Media[2]
100MB	Yes	No	Yes	Yes	Yes	No	100MB R/W
250MB	Yes	No	Yes	Yes	Yes	No	250/100MB R/W[3]
750MB	Yes	Yes	No	No	Yes	Yes	750/250MB R/W[3]
							100MB R/O[4]

[1]Uses DB-25F connectors

[2]R/W—read/write; R/O—read-only

[3]750MB and 250MB versions can read and write the next-lower capacity of media, although performance drops drastically with smaller media

[4]750MB drives can read, but not write, to 100MB media

SuperDisk LS-120, LS-240

The **SuperDisk** drives originally developed by Imation are available in two versions:

- **LS-120**, 120MB SuperDisk media, and also read/write compatible with 1.44MB and 720KB 3.5-inch floppy disks
- **LS-240**, 240MB SuperDisk and 120MB media, and also read/write compatible with 1.44MB and 720KB 3.5-inch floppy disks; can also format 1.44MB floppy disks to hold 32MB of data

Figure 14.23 compares floppy, Zip, and SuperDisk media.

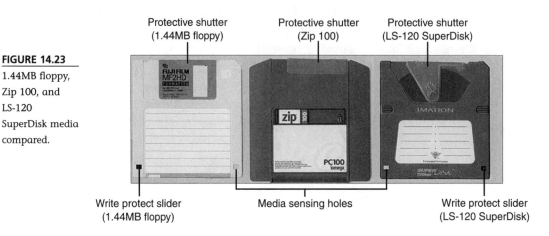

FIGURE 14.23
1.44MB floppy, Zip 100, and LS-120 SuperDisk media compared.

Protective shutter (1.44MB floppy) Protective shutter (Zip 100) Protective shutter (LS-120 SuperDisk)

Write protect slider (1.44MB floppy) Media sensing holes Write protect slider (LS-120 SuperDisk)

SuperDisk drives have been built in various internal and external form factors using parallel, USB, PC Card and ATAPI interfaces, as well as proprietary designs for use in interchangeable drive bays on some notebook computer models.

SuperDisk drives are more versatile than Zip drives because they support standard 3.5-inch media as well as their own SuperDisk media. However, they are not nearly as popular, and most versions have been discontinued.

Orb, Jaz, and Peerless

All three of these removable-media drives have capacities of 1GB or higher, and can be used as primary storage as well as backup storage. These products vary widely in their design and capabilities. Table 14.9 provides an overview.

Table 14.9 High-Capacity Removable-Media Drives

Drive Model and Vendor	Capacities	USB 1.1	USB 2.0	Parallel Port	SCSI	ATAPI	IEEE-1394a
Iomega Jaz	1GB, 2GB	No	No	No	Yes	No	Yes
Iomega Peerless	10GB, 20GB	Yes	No	No	No	No	Yes
Castlewood Orb	2.2GB, 5.7GB	Yes	Yes	No	Yes	Yes	Yes

The Iomega **Jaz drive** (now discontinued) is available in 1GB internal and external and 2GB internal and external versions for SCSI interface only. Both 1GB and 2GB external versions use the HD-50 connector, whereas internal versions use the 50-pin ribbon cable. Jaz drives use only Jaz cartridges; the 2GB version can read and write to both 1GB and 2GB cartridges. Jaz cartridges can be purchased from Iomega and some other vendors.

The Iomega **Peerless drive** (now discontinued) is a unique modular system that uses the following components:

■ 10GB or 20GB Peerless removable hard disk

■ Base

■ Interface module (USB 1.1 or IEEE-1394a)

■ Power cable

The base and interface module are connected to create the base station, which can accept the removable Peerless disk cartridges (see Figure 14.24).

FIGURE 14.24

The major components of the Iomega Peerless drive system.

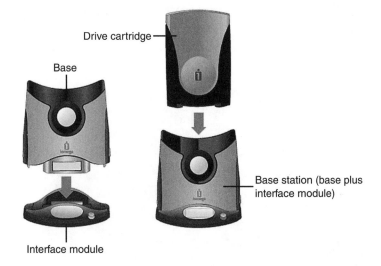

Drive cartridge

Base

Base station (base plus interface module)

Interface module

The Castlewood **Orb drive** is available in two capacities (2.2GB and 5.7GB Castlewood Orb hard disk cartridges). It supports most interface types except for parallel port and USB 2.0. The 5.7GB drive is read-only compatible with 2.2GB media. External Orb drives with SCSI interfaces use the HD-50 connector, whereas internal Orb drives with SCSI interfaces use the HD-68 connector on a ribbon cable.

Tape Drives

Tape drives are available in several types that use various kinds of data cartridges. Tape drives are generally rated in two ways:

■ Native capacity

■ Compressed (2:1) capacity

For example, a VXA-1 tape drive has a native capacity of 33GB, and a compressed capacity of 66GB. Note that the real-world compressed capacity of a tape drive generally falls between the native and 2:1 compressed capacity due to how well different types of data can be compressed. For example, word processing documents and uncompressed bitmap graphics can be compressed by as much as 90% smaller than their original size, but GIF and JPEG graphics and archive files using the ZIP and CAB formats are already compressed and can't be compressed any further during backup.

Tape drives must be used with backup software. Various versions of Windows have limited-capability backup software included, but third-party backup software usually has more capabilities. Some drives are packaged with backup software, but others require the user to purchase tape backup software separately.

Installing and Configuring Removable-Media and Tape Drives

The physical installation of any removable-media or tape drive resembles the process used for installing other drives or devices using the same interface (see Figure 14.25).

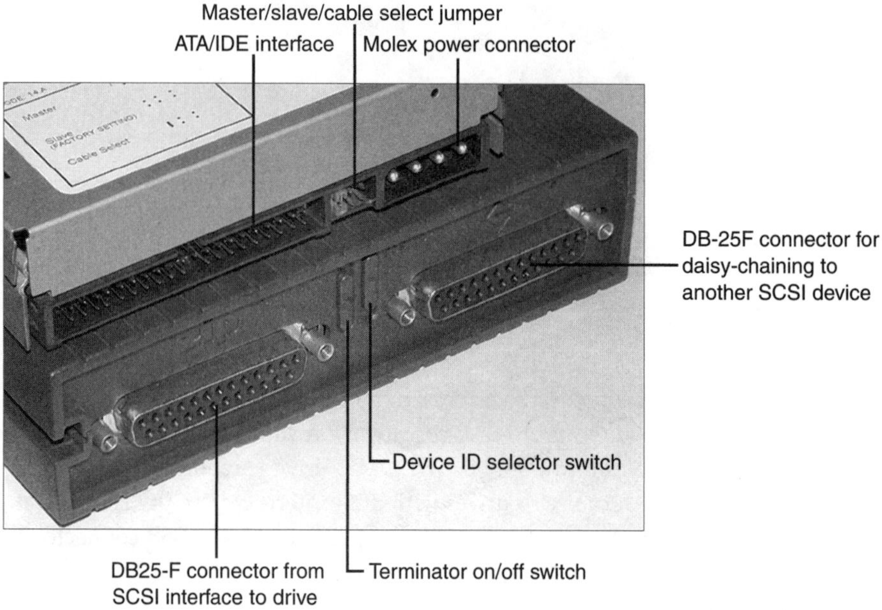

FIGURE 14.25
An internal ATAPI Iomega Zip drive (top) compared to an external SCSI Iomega Zip drive (bottom). Each drive has the same configuration features as other drives in the same category.

Labels: Master/slave/cable select jumper; ATA/IDE interface; Molex power connector; DB-25F connector for daisy-chaining to another SCSI device; Device ID selector switch; DB25-F connector from SCSI interface to drive; Terminator on/off switch

However, there are two significant differences:

- Most removable-media drives depend upon proprietary support software for advanced features; tape drives in particular are useless unless backup software that supports the drive is used. If the drivers are not installed, removable-media drives work, but features such as write protection, disk copying, and others might not be available.

■ You might also need to install the driver and support software for the drive before you install the drive itself. Installing the driver and support software first enables the system to more easily detect the drive. See the documentation for a particular drive for details.

External Hard Drives

An **external hard drive** uses a standard 3.5-inch desktop or 2.5-inch portable drive mechanism to enable large amounts of data to be stored externally.

External drives based on standard desktop 3.5-inch drive mechanisms are larger but less expensive per megabyte and faster than those based on smaller 2.5-inch drive mechanisms originally developed for portable computers.

Interface Types Used by External Hard Drives

External hard drives based on the SCSI interface have been available for many years, but are not widespread in the PC environment. Most recent external hard drives have used the USB 1.1, USB 2.0, or IEEE-1394a interfaces.

Although a USB 2.0 external hard drive can be connected to a USB 1.1 port and function properly, its throughput would be much slower and this is not recommended.

Installing and Configuring External Hard Drives

Typical external drives using USB or IEEE-1394a interfaces are true PnP drives with Windows XP: Plug them in and they are ready for immediate use, because the drives are already formatted with a Windows-compatible file system (usually FAT32). See Chapter 15 for more details about file systems.

Older versions of Windows, particularly Windows 98, might require the user to load drivers from floppy disk or CD before the drive can be recognized.

Study Lab

Don't miss the Study Lab materials found on the CD accompanying this book. Each Study Lab is tailored to the individual chapters in this book, meaning that you'll quickly be able to determine which topics you understand well enough to pass the exam and which topics need more study. The Study Labs are presented in printable PDF format so that you can take them with you to study at work, on the road, or even in your car just before test time!

THE ABSOLUTE MINIMUM

- The most common type of floppy drive is the 1.44MB 3.5-inch drive, which uses DSHD media.

- 3.5-inch floppy drives use a 34-pin cable, which is twisted to enable the system to distinguish drive A: from drive B:.

- Each IDE channel can handle up to two ATA/IDE drives.

- Master and slave jumpers are used with the 40-wire ATA/IDE cable to determine drive priority and can also be used with the 80-wire cable.

- Cable select uses different positions on the 80-wire UDMA-66 cable to determine drive priority. Both drives must be jumpered as cable select to use this feature.

- Serial ATA (SATA) is a high-speed version of ATA that uses a seven-wire cable that runs directly from the host adapter to the drive.

- ATA RAID uses two or more ATA drives to create striped (RAID 0) or mirrored (RAID 1) drive arrays for extra read/write speed or extra reliability.

- LBA (Logical Block Addressing) translation is necessary on all ATA/IDE drives over 528MB (504MiB) to enable Windows to use the entire capacity of the drive.

- Each device in a SCSI daisy-chain must use a unique device ID, and each end of the daisy-chain must be terminated.

- The transfer rates of CD and DVD drives are measured using a X-rating value, but DVD drives use a larger value for X than CD drives do.

- CD/DVD mastering creates a layout from files selected by the user and transferred to a recordable CD or DVD. The process is often called CD or DVD burning.

- Packet writing typically uses rewritable CD or DVD media to store drag-and-drop files, using the drive like a large floppy disk.

- The actual storage capacity of a tape drive varies with whether the data is stored in compressed or noncompressed (native) mode and the amount of compression that can be performed with different types of data.

15

PREPARING HARD AND FLOPPY DRIVES WITH WINDOWS

In the previous chapter, you learned the hardware mechanics behind magnetic and optical storage. In this chapter, you'll learn how data is stored on a disk.

You don't need to do anything to a new floppy disk or Zip disk before you can use it: Just pop it in the drive and copy files to it. Unfortunately, you need to take a few more steps before you can use your new internal hard disk for more than just a paperweight.

Before you can prepare a hard disk for use by an operating system (we'll concentrate on various versions of Windows, because that's what the A+ Certification Exams are concerned with), it must be recognized by the operating system. An ATA/IDE or Serial ATA drive that is plugged into a host adapter on the motherboard must be detected and properly translated by the system BIOS. If you're using an **ATA/IDE**, **Serial ATA**, or **SCSI** hard disk that's plugged into a host adapter card, the BIOS chip on the card detects the drive.

In either case, if the hard drive is not properly recognized by the BIOS, the operating system preparation programs either will not function or will prepare only a portion of the hard disk.

Creating a Boot Disk Suitable for Hard Disk Preparation

You don't need a separate **boot disk** to prepare a hard disk for use if you're adding a hard disk to a computer that's already running Windows; you just use the features built into Windows to prepare the drive for use. However, if you're building a brand-new system or installing a replacement hard disk into a system, you might need to prepare a boot disk you can use in the hard disk preparation process. Here's why: If you can't start the computer with an operating system, you can't prepare the hard disk to use an operating system. No operating system, no useful computer!

The method for preparing a boot disk suitable for hard disk preparation on a new system varies with the operating system. Some operating system versions designed for installation on a new computer include a boot disk already designed to prepare a hard disk, but in many cases you will need to create one yourself on another computer.

The CD included with this book contains important Study Lab material for this chapter, as well as Chapters 2–22 in this book. The Study Lab for each chapter contains terms to study, exercises, and practice tests—all in printable PDF format (Adobe Acrobat Reader is included on the CD, too). These Study Lab materials will help you gear up for the A+ Exam. Also, the CD includes an industry-leading test engine from PrepLogic, which simulates the actual A+ test so that you can be sure that you're ready when test day arrives. Don't let the A+ test intimidate you. If you've read the chapters, worked through the Study Lab, and passed the practice tests from PrepLogic, you should be well prepared to ace the test!

Also, you'll notice that some words throughout each chapter are in bold format. These are study terms that are defined in the Study Lab. Be sure to consult the Study Lab when you are finished with this chapter to test what you've learned.

Windows 9x/Me

With Windows 9x or Windows Me, you can create a suitable hard disk–preparation boot disk by creating an **emergency startup disk (ESD)**—also called the **emergency boot disk (EBD)**—on a computer that already has Windows 95, Windows 98, or Windows Me installed. You will need to have one blank disk available. Windows also refers to this disk as the startup disk.

Follow these steps to create the emergency startup disk:

1. Open the Control Panel and select Add/Remove Programs.

2. Select the Startup Disk tab.

3. Click Create Disk and insert a blank formatted floppy disk into drive A: as prompted.

4. Insert the Windows CD-ROM if prompted; the ESD is created from operating system files that are stored on the CD-ROM (or, on some systems, in the `\Windows\Options\Cabs` folder).

5. Remove the disk when prompted and label it Windows Emergency Startup Disk. Be sure to indicate what release of Windows was used to create the ESD.

If you made the startup disk with Windows 98 or Windows Me, it contains the **Fdisk** and **Format** programs needed to prepare the hard disk, as well as CD-ROM drivers for popular IDE and SCSI hard disk drives. Therefore, when you boot a computer with the Windows 98 or Windows Me ESD, you can Fdisk and Format the hard disk and immediately install Windows from CD.

Ideally, you should use a startup disk that matches your version of Windows. But, if you don't have one, you can use the Windows 98, Windows 98SE, or Windows Me startup disk to

note

If you grabbed a box of Mac-format disks by mistake and can't return them, or dug up an old box of unformatted floppy disks, you will need to format them before you can use them. (Macs use a different disk format than PCs.) Also, you might want to reformat an old floppy disk you've already used if you're planning to store important information on it because the magnetic signals placed on the media by formatting can fade over time.

tip

Notice the word *emergency* in the name of this disk. Even if you don't plan to install a new hard disk anytime soon, take a couple of minutes to make this disk anyway. It can also help you install (or reinstall) Windows if things go bad.

install Windows 95 OSR 2.x (the version shipped in 1996 and later with new hardware), Windows 98/98SE, or Windows Me. The Windows 95 retail upgrade supports hard disks up to 8GB in size, whereas Windows 95 OSR 2.x (95B or 95C) supports hard disks up to 32GB in size, so their boot disks should not be used with later Windows versions.

Adding CD-ROM Drive Support to the Windows 95 Startup Disk

The Windows 95 ESD disk also contains the Fdisk and Format programs. However, because Windows 95 was created at the very end of the "floppy disks are for software distribution" era (you could buy it in a floppy disk or CD-ROM version), its ESD doesn't include CD-ROM support. You must add the following files to the startup disk if you want to use it to start the computer with CD-ROM support:

note

The disk you make with this process is the same ESD that Windows offers to make for you during Windows 9x/Me installation.

- *The MS-DOS CD-ROM device driver for your CD-ROM drive*—This was provided by the drive manufacturer on a disk (if you installed the drive in the field), or it might be on the system's hard disk. The filename will usually contain ATAPI or CD and will end in .sys.

- `Mscdex.exe` *from the* `\Windows\Command` *folder*—This file is used to assign your CD-ROM device a drive letter.

These files must be referred to by the `Config.sys` and `Autoexec.bat` startup files you need to create on the Windows 95 startup disk. After you create the startup disk and copy these files to it, follow this procedure to create the `Config.sys` and `Autoexec.bat` files:

1. Click Start, Programs, Accessories, Notepad.
2. Click New on the Notepad menu.
3. Type the following line into the text-editing window (use the actual name of your CD-ROM device driver in place of *MYCDROM.SYS*):
   DEVICE=*MYCDROM.SYS* /D:CDROM01
4. Click File, Save As.
5. Select A: drive from the Save In pull-down menu.
6. Type **config.sys** in the File Name window.
7. Click Save to save the file.

8. Click New to create a new file.

9. Type the following line into the text-editing window. (Add the /1:x switch and substitute the drive letter you want to specify for the CD-ROM drive for x; otherwise, the next available letter will be used. The /m:10 switch specifies 10 disk buffers to improve data transfer rates from the CD.)
   ```
   mscdex /d:cdrom01 /m:10
   ```

10. Click File, Save As.

11. Select A: drive from the Save In pull-down menu.

12. Type `autoexec.bat` in the File Name window.

13. Click Save to save the file.

14. Click File, Exit to leave Notepad.

Test the disk by leaving it in drive A: and clicking Start, Shut Down, Restart. The system should start from the floppy disk and display the CD-ROM drive letter.

> **tip**
>
> You can create a Windows 98/98SE startup disk from a Windows 98 CD, even if you don't have Windows 98 installed anymore. Open the \Tools\MTSutil\FAT32EBD folder on the Windows 98 or 98SE CD and run the program FAT32EBD.EXE. Insert a blank floppy disk when prompted.
>
> If you're going to use a Windows 98 ESD to prepare a hard disk over 64GB up to 137GB in size, you should go to http://support.microsoft.com/ for the article 263044 "Fdisk Does Not Recognize Full Size of Hard Disks Larger than 64GB" to get a replacement copy of Fdisk.exe to copy to your boot disk. Otherwise, your ESD won't be able to cope properly with a large hard disk.

Windows NT 4.0

The Windows NT 4.0 CD contains the **Winnt.exe** program, which is used to start the Windows NT installation from a DOS prompt. It can also be used to create a set of installation boot floppy disks. To create a set to be used for installing from the Windows NT 4.0 CD

1. Boot a system running a 32-bit version of Windows (NT, 9x, or later).

2. Insert the Windows NT 4.0 CD.

3. Open a DOS prompt session and change to the /I386 folder on the CD.

   or

4. Run this command:

   Winnt.exe/o (on a system running Windows 9x/Me)

   Winnt32.exe/o (on a system running Windows NT/2000/XP)

If you want to create floppy disks that can run an installation from either CD-ROM or floppy disk, use this command instead:

`Winnt.exe/ox` or `Winnt32.exe/ox`

5. Insert blank, formatted floppy disks as prompted until the process is complete.

6. Label the disks.

Use Setup disk 1 to start the system when you want to install Windows NT 4.0. Watch the prompts for when to insert each additional disk and when to insert the Windows NT 4.0 CD.

Windows 2000

The Windows 2000 CD-ROM contains the disk images of four startup disks that might be needed to prepare the hard disk and install Windows 2000. These disks are used only if you cannot boot from the Windows 2000 CD-ROM to start the setup process. Follow these steps to create the setup disks needed to install Windows 2000:

1. Insert the Windows 2000 CD-ROM into the CD-ROM drive on a computer running a 32-bit version of Windows (NT, 9x, 2000, Me, or XP).

2. View the contents of the CD-ROM in the Windows Explorer, or use the Browse option on the Windows 2000 CD-ROM splash screen. Find and open the folder called `Bootdisk`.

3. If you are viewing the CD-ROM from a computer with Windows NT, Windows 2000, or Windows XP, open the program (.exe) file called `Makebt32`; if you are viewing the CD-ROM from a computer using Windows 9x or Me, open the program file called `Makeboot`.

4. A program window opens onscreen, prompting you to insert the first of four blank, formatted floppy disks into drive A:. Follow the prompts to create the floppy disks, labeling them Setup *x* (replace *x* with numbers 1–4) for Windows 2000.

5. Close the window and remove the last floppy disk from drive A: when you are finished.

Use Setup disk 1 to start the system if you cannot boot from the Windows 2000 CD-ROM when you want to install Windows 2000 on a new system. You'll be prompted to insert disks 2–4 and then the Windows 2000 CD-ROM to prepare the hard disk for Windows 2000 and install it.

Windows XP

Like the Windows 2000 CD, the Windows XP CD is also bootable. Generally, any system that is compatible with Windows XP also supports booting from CD. You might need to fiddle around with the boot order in the system BIOS to put the optical (CD-ROM) drive before the hard disk. See Chapter 6, "BIOS and CMOS Configuration," for details.

You can't make the boot disks from the Windows XP CD, but you can download them from Microsoft's Web site. Search `http://support.microsoft.com` for article #310994, "Obtaining Windows XP Setup Boot Disks," for links to the downloadable files for XP Home, XP Professional, and Service Pack 1 versions of both.

note

Although almost any computer capable of handling Windows XP should be able to boot from the Windows XP CD-ROM, it's still a good idea to download the boot disk images from the Microsoft Web site. You never know when you might not be able to boot from the CD!

Understanding File Systems and Partition Types

No matter which version of Windows you use to get a hard disk ready for use, you have two big decisions to make:

- What file system to use
- What partition type to choose

Read on to discover what this means, which versions of Windows support which type, and when to select a particular option.

File Systems Used by Windows

What exactly is a file system, anyway?

A file system describes how data and drives are organized. In Windows, the file system you choose for a hard disk affects the following:

- The rules for how large a logical drive (drive letter) can be, and whether the hard disk can be used as one big drive letter, several smaller drive letters, or must be multiple drive letters
- How efficiently a system stores data; the less wasted space, the better
- How secure a system is against tampering

■ Whether a drive can be accessed by more than one operating system (an important point if you want to install Windows XP and still use the existing Windows 98 operating system in a dual boot configuration, for example)

How quickly do you need to decide this? You must choose a file system during disk preparation, although you can sometimes change to a better one later.

What are your options?

Windows 9x and Windows Me give you these choices:

■ **FAT16**

■ **FAT32**

Windows NT/2000/XP can create the following file systems on a new drive:

■ FAT16

■ FAT32

■ **NTFS**

Allocation Units (Clusters) and File Systems

There are many reasons to choose one file system over another when you prepare a hard disk with Windows, but one of the most important reasons has to do with how Windows creates and keeps track of the files you and Windows make. As you learned in Chapter 14, "Storage," the basic unit of disk management is called the sector. Each and every sector on any hard or floppy disk contains exactly 512 bytes of data if you use standard Windows disk-preparation tools.

Life would be really simple if Windows could use individual sectors when it stores data. Instead, in almost every case, Windows uses various groups of sectors called **clusters** (by old-timers) or **allocation units** (a more recent term that sounds bureaucratic but means exactly the same thing) to

Early versions of Windows 95 only support FAT16. As Mr. T would say, "I pity the fool still using that version of Windows." As you'll learn shortly, FAT16 is a lousy match for large hard disks.

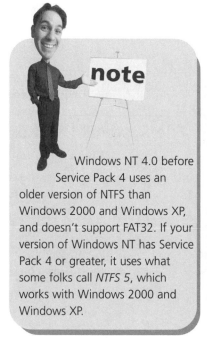

Windows NT 4.0 before Service Pack 4 uses an older version of NTFS than Windows 2000 and Windows XP, and doesn't support FAT32. If your version of Windows NT has Service Pack 4 or greater, it uses what some folks call *NTFS 5*, which works with Windows 2000 and Windows XP.

store data on most types of disk drives. An allocation unit is the smallest amount of disk space an operating system can use to store a file. Even if a file uses less than an allocation unit, the operating system must still allocate the entire allocation unit to that file. Various file systems use varying numbers of allocation units to save a file and, to make matters worse, the allocation unit size varies with the size of the disk.

note

Some magneto-optical drives use a nonstandard sector size.

Why does Windows use allocation units (groups of sectors) instead of individual sectors to store files? Because in most cases the number of sectors is too big for Windows to keep track of on a disk drive.

Here are two examples:

Example #1: A 3.5-inch 1.44MB floppy disk has an allocation unit (cluster) size of 512 bytes. In other words, a sector equals an allocation unit. How many allocation units are there on a floppy disk? Let's do the math:

1. A floppy disk contains 1,457,664 bytes.

2. Divide 1,457,664 by 512 to determine the number of sectors.

3. My calculator says 2,847 sectors (and, in this case, the same number of allocation units).

With floppy disks, Windows uses a file system that can keep track of no more than 4,096 (2^{12}) files on a disk. Because 2,847 (the number of sectors) is less than 4,096, it's no problem to use each sector individually for data storage.

What happens with a hard disk? The 12-bit (2^{12}) file system that Windows uses for floppy disks isn't large enough to handle a hard disk, even a modestly sized one.

Example #2: One of my computers has an old 1.2GB hard disk, which contains 2,503,872 sectors. At 512 bytes per sector, the drive has a capacity of 1,281,982,464 bytes. This hard disk was introduced when Windows 95 was new.

Windows 95 originally used a file system called FAT16, which was designed to handle up to 65,536 (2^{16}) files per drive for hard disks. This number is many times smaller than the number of sectors on the drive. The solution? Divide the sectors into groups called allocation units. The number of allocation units must be at or below the maximum number of files the file system can manage.

How many sectors are needed to make an allocation unit with this drive? Let's try some math, and this time let's use a table (see Table 15.1) to set up the calculations.

Table 15.1 Calculating a Valid Allocation Unit (Cluster) Size

Sector Size (S)	Sectors Per Cluster (C)	Number of Bytes Per Cluster (S×C=B)	Disk Capacity (S×512=D)	Number of Files Per Drive (D/B=N)	Is N <65,536?
512	2	1,024	1,281,982,464	1,251,936	No
512	4	2,048	1,281,982,464	625,968	No
512	8	4,096	1,281,982,464	312,984	No
512	16	8,192	1,281,982,464	156,492	No
512	32	16,384	1,281,982,464	78,246	No
512	64	32,768	1,281,982,464	39,123	Yes

Here's what's going on in Table 15.1. The allocation unit (cluster) size must result in less than 65,536 files per drive so that Windows 95 can manage the hard disk. To calculate this value, we start by taking the sector size (S) and multiplying it by different values of sectors per cluster (C). This calculation (S×C) creates the value in "Number of Bytes Per Cluster" (B). When B is used to divide the disk capacity (D) to determine the number of files per drive (N), N is compared to 65,536 (the maximum number of files that Windows 95 can manage on the drive). A value for N that is equal to or less than 65,536 can be used as the allocation unit (cluster) size for the drive.

As you can see from Table 15.1, this hard disk must use a cluster size of 32,768 (64 sectors) to store a file if the drive is used as a single drive letter. However, smaller hard disk drives using the same FAT16 file system can use smaller cluster sizes. Table 15.2 shows how the cluster sizes vary with hard disk drive sizes. If a large drive is split up into two or more drive letters, the allocation unit size is determined from the size of each drive letter.

Table 15.2 FAT16 Drive and Allocation Unit Sizes

Drive Minimum Size	Drive Maximum Size	Allocation Units		
		Sectors	**Bytes**	**Kilobytes (KB)**
16MB[1]	127MB	4	2,048	2
128MB	255MB	8	4,096	4
256MB	511MB	16	8,192	8

Table 15.2 (continued)

Drive Minimum Size	Drive Maximum Size	Allocation Units		
		Sectors	**Bytes**	**Kilobytes (KB)**
512MB	1,023MB	32	16,384	16
1,024MB (1GB)	2,047MB (2GB)	64	32,768	32[2]

[1]*Drives smaller than 16MB use the FAT12 file system, which uses an 8KB allocation unit size.*

[2]*Windows NT/2000/XP also support a 64KB allocation unit size for drives up to 4,095MB (4GB), but this is not supported by Windows 9x/Me and is not recommended.*

What is the practical impact of larger allocation unit sizes as drive size increases? Because an operating system must use an entire allocation unit to store a file, even if the file is smaller than the allocation unit, larger allocation unit sizes waste disk space.

Let's assume that you want to save a file that requires 5,684 bytes of disk space. How many sectors does this file require? 5684/512=7. However, in the real world, when you save a file on a hard disk, you use allocation units, not individual sectors to save a file. Figure 15.1 shows you how much disk space is wasted when you save this file on drives with varying allocation unit sizes.

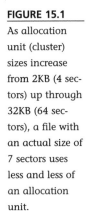

FIGURE 15.1

As allocation unit (cluster) sizes increase from 2KB (4 sectors) up through 32KB (64 sectors), a file with an actual size of 7 sectors uses less and less of an allocation unit.

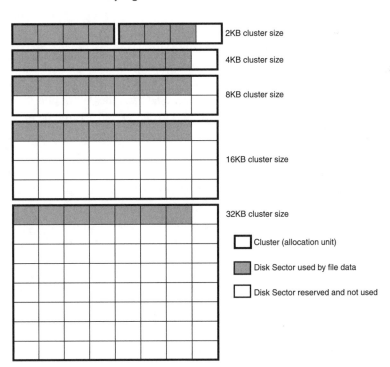

2KB cluster size

4KB cluster size

8KB cluster size

16KB cluster size

32KB cluster size

☐ Cluster (allocation unit)

▨ Disk Sector used by file data

☐ Disk Sector reserved and not used

As you can see from Figure 15.1, the remainder of the allocation unit cannot be used by another file, and is wasted space.

You might be wondering what has happened to enable Windows to use 40GB, 80GB, 120GB, and even larger drives. More efficient file systems that use fewer sectors per cluster is the answer, and in the following sections you'll learn more about these newer file systems.

FAT16

FAT16 (also referred to as FAT) is the oldest and simplest file system used by modern versions of Windows, dating back to MS-DOS versions 3.3 and above. Windows 9x's version of FAT16 is similar to that of MS-DOS, but it permits the use of long filenames and enhanced file attributes, storing the date a file was created, last modified, and last viewed.

FAT16's highlights include

note

Because of the way that computers work, each possible cluster size shown in Table 15.1 and Figure 15.1 is a power of two larger than the previous one. For example, the number 16,384 is also 2^{14}, and cluster size required for the 1.2GB hard disk, 32,768, is also 2^{15}. The number 65,536 (the number of files early versions of Windows 95 can manage) is 2^{16}. This provides the name FAT16 (for the 16-bit file allocation table) used by this version of Windows.

- The 16-bit **file allocation table (FAT)** (which is where the name comes from, by the way), which allows for a maximum of 65,536 allocation units (2^{16}). As you learned in the previous section, an allocation unit (cluster) can be occupied by a file. What about folders (subdirectories)? As far as the FAT is concerned, a folder is a type of file that points to the location of other files, so whenever you create a folder, this counts against the limit as well.

- A limit of 512 entries in the root directory or root folder. Because 32-bit versions of Windows, such as Windows 98, store both the actual long filename and its 8-character plus 3-character short filename (or DOS alias) as separate entries, the actual number of files and folders in the root directory cannot exceed 256 (512÷2) assuming that each file uses only 2 entries. Some long filenames are so long they use up many entries. See Figure 15.2 for an example of a file that uses three entries (one for the DOS alias and two for the long filename, or LFN). So, make sure you store files with long filenames on floppy or hard disks in a folder, not the root directory! If you run out of entries in the root directory, the disk is "full."

FIGURE 15.2

When the file Verisignseal trans.gif is stored, Windows 95 creates a DOS alias from the first six characters of the name and the file extension. The actual long filename (LFN) is also stored, using as many entries as necessary (in this case, two *additional entries*).

A long filename is no big deal today, but when Windows 95 was introduced, it was exciting. Before Windows 95, filenames were limited to eight characters plus a file extension of up to three characters. Because having only eleven characters made naming files difficult, some users created their own file extensions such as .LTR (letter), .MEM (memo), and so forth instead of using the default file extensions. Nonstandard file extensions confuse Windows, which looks at the extension to figure out which program to use to open a file. Fortunately, long filenames give you the freedom to create filenames that make sense without changing the file extension.

- A maximum logical drive size of 2,048MB (2.1GB) because of the limit of 65,536 files/folders per drive; Fdisk must split larger physical drives into multiple logical volumes. So, even a modest 10GB hard disk must be split into at least five drive letters (C, D, E, F, and G)!

- File allocation unit sizes that range from 2,048 bytes (2KB) up to 32KB, depending on the size of the logical drive (refer to Table 15.1).

As you have already learned from Figure 15.1, if you use hard disk drive sizes of 1,024MB or above with the FAT16 file system, the 32KB allocation unit size could cause as much as *30%–40%* of your disk to be wasted!

Now you can create a filename of up to 256 characters, but don't go overboard! The total size of the filename includes the folder names (or path) that lead to the file, such as \My Documents\General\Budget\ 1ˢᵗ Quarter Draft.XLS. You might think the filename is 1ˢᵗ Quarter Draft.XLS, but Windows also counts the characters in the entire path as part of the filename for the purposes of calculating the maximum size of the filename.

note

So, there are lots of reasons *not* to use FAT16 anymore:

- Large allocation unit sizes cause a lot of wasted disk capacity.
- Efficient allocation units (8KB or smaller) require multiple drive letters for drives more than 512MB in size.
- Preparing a hard drive more than 2,047MB in size with FAT16 requires that the drive be divided into multiple drive letters, which can interfere with network drives and CD-ROM drive letter assignments.

To overcome these limitations, FAT32 (large disk support) is the default for preparing drives with the Windows 98 and Windows Me Fdisk program, and it's an option with the Windows 95B and Windows 95C Fdisk program. Note that FAT16 is the only file system supported by the original version of Windows 95 and Windows 95a.

FAT32

FAT32 was introduced with late OEM versions of Windows 95 (Windows 95 OSR 2.0 and above; also referred to as *Windows 95B* or *Windows 95C*). FAT32 is also known as **large disk support**. FAT32 has the following benefits when compared with FAT16:

- The 32-bit file allocation table, which allows for 268,435,456 entries (2^{32}) per drive. Remember, an entry can be a folder or an allocation unit used by a file.
- The root directory can be located anywhere on the drive and can have an *unlimited* number of entries. Hooray!
- The allocation unit (cluster) size is much smaller on similarly sized drives than is possible with FAT16 (see Table 15.3). Smaller allocation unit sizes make FAT32 drives far more efficient, especially for the storage of small files. Note that FAT32 uses an 8KB allocation unit size for drives as large as 16GB; a FAT16 drive using the same 8KB allocation unit size is limited to 511MB as its maximum size.

note

Although long file-names are a terrific convenience, there might be situations in which you access a file created with Windows 95 or later versions of Windows when the long file-name can't be seen, such as if you start the computer with an ESD (boot disk) or use a network connection from a computer running DOS or an older version of Windows. To enable older operating systems to access files created with long filenames, Windows creates a DOS alias name from the first six characters of the filename, adds a number to distinguish it from other files in the same folder that might also have the first six characters in common, and stores it with the file (see Figure 15.2). Systems that can't read long file-names see the DOS alias instead.

■ The maximum logical drive size allowed is 2TB (more than 2 trillion bytes). Large drives no longer must be partitioned into multiple drive letters, although many users still prefer this option for safety.

Table 15.3 FAT16 and FAT32 Disk Usage Compared

Allocation Unit Size	FAT16 Drive Sizes	FAT32 Drive Sizes
4KB	128–255MB	260–8,192MB (8GB)
8KB	256–511MB	8–16GB
16KB	512–1,023MB	16–32GB
32KB	1,024–2,047MB	32GB–2TB

Obviously, FAT32 is a *much* better choice than FAT16 with any hard disk these days. So, what do you need to prepare a hard disk with a bigger, smarter FAT?

You can prepare a drive as a FAT32 drive if the following requirements are met:

■ *Enable FAT-32 support when you start Fdisk*—Fdisk calls this feature "large hard disk support," and when you Fdisk a drive with more than 512MB of capacity, you are offered the opportunity to use this feature.

■ *Have adequate BIOS support*—Fdisk can work with only as much of your drive as it can see. As you learned in Chapter 14, "Storage," **Logical Block Address (LBA)** support is required for any drive more than 504MiB (528MB) used with Windows. To use a drive larger than 8GB, your system must also have an **enhanced BIOS (eBIOS)** that supports extended Int13h functions; these functions are enabled automatically on compatible BIOSs when LBA mode is enabled. Any system built since 1999 should have both LBA and extended Int13h provisions built in.

Virtually all systems shipped with Windows 98 or Windows Me preinstalled will use FAT32 for their hard drives. (Windows 95B– or Windows 95C–based systems often used FAT16.) But, if you're curious, follow this procedure to determine what file system has been used on a hard drive in a system running Windows:

1. Open Windows Explorer.

2. Right-click the drive letter in the Explorer Window and select Properties.

3. The Properties sheet for the drive will list FAT for a drive prepared with FAT16, and FAT32 for a drive prepared with FAT32 (see Figure 15.3).

Unless the system occasionally must be booted with MS-DOS or older versions of Windows, FAT32 is the recommended file system for use with Windows 98 or Me because of its efficient use of disk capacity. If you must boot a Windows 98 or Me system with older versions of Windows, or with MS-DOS, you will need to use the FAT16 file system for any drives you want to access with older versions of Windows or with MS-DOS. However, if a Windows 98 system is accessed over a network, any operating system used on the network can access the files on a FAT32 drive because Windows reads the files before sending them to the other stations on the network.

NTFS

The New Technology File System (NTFS) is the native file system of Windows NT and its descendants (Windows 2000 and Windows XP). NTFS has many differences from FAT16 and FAT32, including

- **Access control**—Different levels of access by group or user can be used with both folders and individual files.
- *Built-in compression for individual files, folders, or an entire drive.*
- *A practical limit for drive sizes of 2TB*—The same as with FAT32, although drives theoretically can reach a maximum size of 2 exabytes (2 billion billion bytes).
- *A recycle bin for each user.*

NTFS 5.0, the version of NTFS used by Windows 2000 and Windows XP (and by Windows NT 4.0 when Service Pack 4 is installed), supports these additional goodies:

- *Support for the* **Encrypted File System (EFS)**—EFS enables data to be stored in an encrypted form. No password, no access to files!
- *Support for mounting a drive*—Drive mounting enables you to address a removable-media drive's contents, for example, as if its contents are stored on your hard disk. The hard disk's drive letter is used to access data on both the hard disk and the removable media drive.
- *Disk quota support*—The administrator of a system can enforce rules about how much disk space each user is allowed to use for storage.
- *Hot-swapping of removable-media drives that have been formatted with NTFS (such as Jaz, Orb and others).*
- *Indexing service support, helping users locate information more quickly when Search is used.*

So, what happens when a system running Windows NT 4.0 gets updated to Windows 2000 or Windows XP? When a Windows NT 4.0 system using NTFS 4.0 is upgraded to Windows 2000 or Windows XP, the NTFS 4.0 file system is upgraded to NTFS 5.0.

If you plan to dual-boot Windows NT 4.0 and Windows 2000, you'd better make sure Windows NT 4.0 has been upgraded to Service Pack 4 or above; older versions of Windows NT 4.0 cannot access an NTFS 5.0 partition. Windows 2000 and Windows XP drives can be prepared with FAT16 or FAT32 partitions, but this is recommended only if the drive will be used in a dual-boot configuration with Windows 98 or Windows Me or a similar operating system that does not support NTFS.

note

Windows 2000 and Windows XP can't create a FAT32 partition larger than 32GB. However, if the partition already exists, they can use it.

Follow these steps to determine what file system was used to prepare a Windows NT, 2000, or XP hard drive:

1. Open Windows Explorer.

2. Right-click the drive letter in the Explorer Window and select Properties.

3. The Properties sheet for the drive will list FAT for a drive prepared with FAT16, FAT32 for a drive prepared with FAT32, and NTFS for a drive prepared with NTFS (see Figure 15.3).

HPFS

The OS/2 **High Performance File System (HPFS)** was supported by Windows NT 4.0 but is not supported by Windows 2000 or Windows XP. HPFS partitions should be converted to NTFS with the Convert.exe program before you upgrade a system running HPFS drives to Windows 2000 or Windows XP.

FIGURE 15.3

A hard disk formatted with FAT16 (top) compared to a hard disk formatted with FAT32 (center) and a hard disk formatted with NTFS version 5 (bottom).

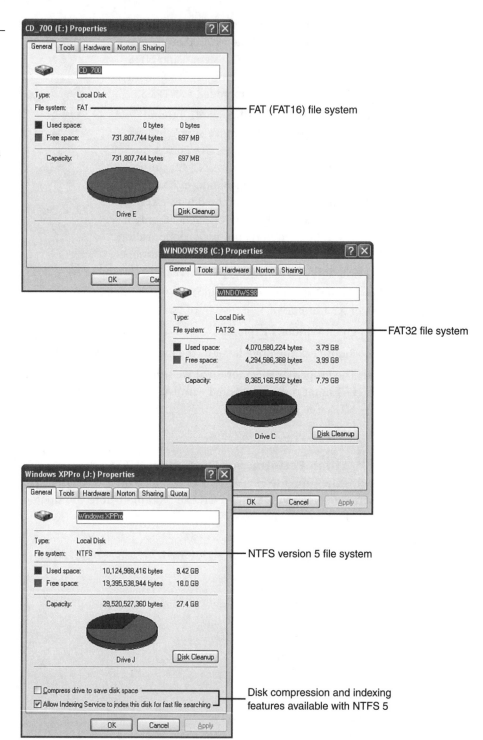

FAT (FAT16) file system

FAT32 file system

NTFS version 5 file system

Disk compression and indexing features available with NTFS 5

Primary and Extended Partitions

There are two steps involved in preparing a hard disk:

- Creating partitions and logical drives
- Formatting partitions and logical drives (which assigns drive letters)

What is a disk partition? A disk partition is a logical structure on a hard disk drive that specifies the following:

- Whether the drive can be bootable
- How many drive letters (one, two, or more) the hard disk will contain
- Whether any of the hard disk's capacity will be reserved for a future operating system or other use

Although the name "disk partition" suggests the drive will be divided into logical sections, every ATA/IDE and SCSI hard disk must go through a partitioning process, even if you want to use the entire hard disk as a single drive letter. All versions of Windows support two major types of disk partitions:

- *Primary*—A **primary partition** can contain only a single drive letter and can be made active (bootable). Although a single physical drive can hold up to four primary partitions, you need only one primary partition on a drive that contains a single operating system. If you install a new operating system in a dual-boot configuration with your current operating system (Windows 98 and Windows XP, for example), a new version of Windows can be installed in a different folder in the same drive, or can be installed in an additional primary partition. If you want to use a non-Windows operating system along with your current operating system, it might require its own primary partition.

- *Extended*—An **extended partition** differs from a primary partition in two important ways:
  - An extended partition doesn't become a drive letter itself but can contain one or more logical drives (sometimes called *logical DOS drives*).
  - Neither an extended partition nor any drive it contains can be bootable.

Only one extended partition can be stored on each physical drive.

If the drive will be used by a single operating system, one of these three ways of partitioning the drive will be used:

- *Primary partition occupies 100% of the physical drive's capacity*—This is typically the way the hard disk on a system sold at retail is used, and is also the default for disk preparation with Windows. This is suitable for the only drive in a system or an additional drive that can be used to boot a system, but should *not* be used for additional drives in a system that will be used for data storage.

- *Primary partition occupies a portion of the physical drive's capacity, and the remainder of the drive is occupied by an extended partition*—This enables the operating system, applications, and data to be stored on separate *logical drives* (drive letters created inside the extended partition), but requires the partitioning process be performed with different settings than the defaults. This configuration is suitable for the only drive or first drive in a multiple-drive system. Systems running early versions of Windows 95 used this method to cope with drives over 2.1GB because of the limitations of the FAT16 file system.

- *Extended partition occupies 100% of the physical drive's capacity*—The drive letters on the extended partition can be used to store applications or data, but not for the operating system. An extended partition cannot be made active (bootable). This configuration is suitable for any drive in a system *except* for the first drive; an extended partition can contain only one logical drive or multiple logical drives.

You can also leave some unpartitioned space on the hard disk for use later, either for another operating system or another drive letter.

Partitioning creates drive letters; formatting creates file systems on the drive letters created during partitioning. Figure 15.4 helps you visualize how these different partitioning schemes can be used on a typical hard disk.

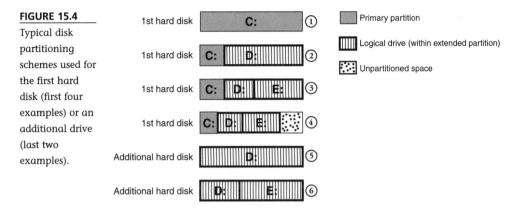

FIGURE 15.4

Typical disk partitioning schemes used for the first hard disk (first four examples) or an additional drive (last two examples).

① All of the hard disk is used as a single bootable drive letter.
② The extended partition contains a non-bootable drive letter.
③ The extended partition contains two non-bootable drive letters.
④ The extended partition contains two non-bootable drive letters and unpartitioned empty space for future use.
⑤ The drive has no primary partition; it cannot be used to boot the system.
⑥ The drive has no primary partition but it has two logical drive letters within the extended partition.

Drive Letters and Partition Types with Windows 9x/Me

If you're adding an *additional* hard disk to a system running Windows 9x/Me, it's critical that you partition it with an extended partition. If you prepare it the same way the original drive is prepared (with a primary partition and possibly logical drives) and if the original system has hard disk drive letters C: and D: or C:, D:, and additional drive letters, the new drive will take over drive letters starting with D:.

Table 15.4 indicates how Fdisk (the disk partitioning program used by Windows 9x/Me) assigns drive letters; study this for a moment and you'll understand why.

Table 15.4 Fdisk Drive Letter Assignments by Priority

Physical Drive	Partition Type	Order
1st	Primary	1st
2nd	Primary	2nd
1st	Extended	3rd
2nd	Extended	4th

What kind of a mess can happen?

Assume that you have a single hard drive divided into C: and D: logical drives. C: is the primary partition; D: is a logical drive inside an extended partition. When you add a second hard drive to expand capacity, you want to use the next available drive letters, starting with E:.

Figure 15.5 compares the results of placing a primary partition and an extended partition (containing one logical drive) on the second hard disk versus preparing the second hard disk as an extended partition with logical drives with Fdisk (the disk partitioning tool used by Windows 9x/Me).

FIGURE 15.5

Comparing an unpartitioned second hard disk (top) with the same drive partitioned with a primary and extended partition (middle) and as an extended partition (bottom). Note how the drive letters are scrambled when the second drive has a primary partition, but the drive letters are in proper sequence when an extended partition is used.

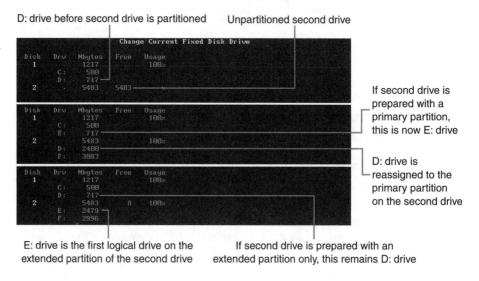

D: drive before second drive is partitioned   Unpartitioned second drive

If second drive is prepared with a primary partition, this is now E: drive

D: drive is reassigned to the primary partition on the second drive

E: drive is the first logical drive on the extended partition of the second drive

If second drive is prepared with an extended partition only, this remains D: drive

Note that setting up a primary partition on the second drive creates an almost unmanageable problem, because you will need to copy all the contents of the "old D:" (now E:) drive to the "new D:" drive, and so on. The chances of data loss are fairly high in such a case. And, the primary partition on the second drive is virtually useless because you would need to use advanced BIOS options or a **boot manager** to use any drive other than C: as a bootable drive.

If you are adding a second (or third or fourth) hard drive to a system running Windows 9x/Me and you want its drive letters to follow the existing drive letters, prepare the new drive with an extended partition occupying 100% of the space on the drive. There's no need to use a primary partition for any drive other than the first hard drive in a system unless you are installing an additional operating system. If an additional drive is added as an extended partition, its logical drives will follow the existing drive letters (refer to Figure 15.5).

> **tip**
>
> If you have an optical or removable-media drive set up as D: and you install a second hard drive, hard disks rule! Your removable-media or optical drive will be kicked up to the next available drive letter. You can use the Device Manager to set these drives to use a different drive letter (all the way to Z:) that isn't likely to be bothered by additional hard disks.
>
> In Windows NT/2000/XP, you can use Disk Management to change the letter of almost any drive, including hard disks, except for the system's default boot drive.

Preparing a Hard Disk for Use with Windows 9x/Me

As you have seen in the previous section, there are several ways to prepare hard disks with Windows 9x/Me:

- As the first hard disk
- As an additional drive
- Entire drive as a bootable (primary) partition
- Part of the drive as a primary partition, the rest as an extended partition with logical drive(s)
- All of the drive as an extended partition with logical drive(s)

No matter which of these methods you use, the same two programs (Fdisk and Format) are used.

Windows 9x/Me use two different programs descended from MS-DOS to prepare a hard disk:

- Fdisk creates or destroys disk partitions and logical drive letters.
- Format prepares drive letters created with Fdisk.

The process that follows is almost identical in any recent DOS or Windows version that uses Fdisk. Fdisk is a command-prompt program, but Format can be performed from a command prompt or from within Windows Explorer.

Partitioning with Fdisk

Depending on whether the drive is being added to your system or is the first drive in an empty system, you can start Fdisk with Start, Run in Windows or by starting your computer with the Windows emergency boot disk. At the command prompt, type **Fdisk** and press Enter.

Press Y to enable Fdisk's Large Disk support so you can create FAT32 partitions. If you answer No, any partitions you create are FAT16 and are limited to a maximum size of 2,047MB (2GB). Use FAT16 *only* if you need to access the drive with an MS-DOS or early-release Windows 95 boot disk.

If you have one physical hard disk installed, the main Fdisk window resembles Figure 15.6.

caution

Think before you start using Fdisk. Fdisk can *destroy* data if you use it on a hard disk containing information instead of on the empty hard disk you just installed in your computer. Sit down and plan out how you will use Fdisk before you start the process, and make sure you won't be interrupted. As you plan out your Fdisk strategy, refer to the examples provided in Figure 15.4 as well as to the discussion that follows.

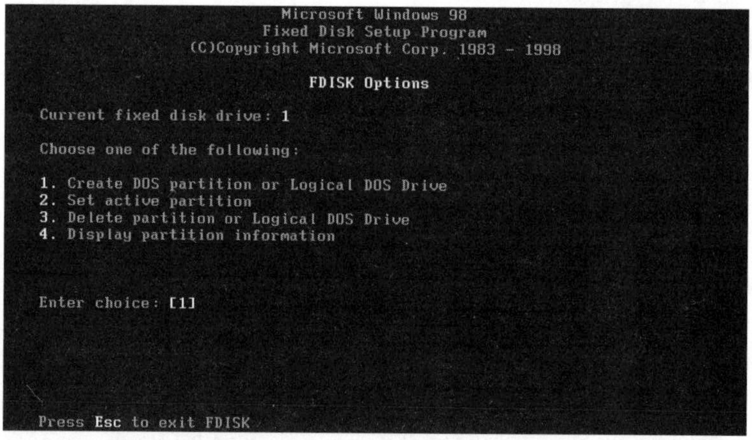

FIGURE 15.6

The Windows 98 Fdisk main menu screen for single-drive systems.

```
                    Microsoft Windows 98
                    Fixed Disk Setup Program
              (C)Copyright Microsoft Corp. 1983 - 1998

                         FDISK Options

Current fixed disk drive: 1

Choose one of the following:

1. Create DOS partition or Logical DOS Drive
2. Set active partition
3. Delete partition or Logical DOS Drive
4. Display partition information


Enter choice: [1]



Press Esc to exit FDISK
```

When two or more physical disks are installed, Fdisk lists a fifth option: Change Current Fixed Disk Drive.

Creating a Primary (Bootable) Partition

If you're installing the first hard drive on an empty system, follow this procedure after booting the system with your startup (emergency) disk and starting Fdisk:

1. Choose Enable Large Disk Support when prompted.

2. From the main menu, select #1, Create **DOS Partition** or **Logical DOS Drive**.

3. From the Create DOS Partition or Logical DOS Drive menu, press Enter to select #1, Create a Primary DOS Partition.

4. Now, it's time to decide which type of partition to make.

   If you want to use the entire drive as C:, press Enter to accept the default (Yes). Follow the prompts to shut down your system and restart it. See "Finishing the Job with the Format Command" later in the chapter for the rest of the process.

   If you want to create at least two drives, type **N** (no) when asked if you want to use the entire capacity of the drive.

5. Enter the amount of space you want to use for the primary partition in either MB or percentages. For example, to use 6GB, enter **6144** (1,024MB=1GB); to use 50% of the drive, enter **50%** and press Enter (see Figure 15.7).

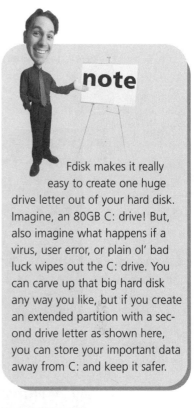

note

Fdisk makes it really easy to create one huge drive letter out of your hard disk. Imagine, an 80GB C: drive! But, also imagine what happens if a virus, user error, or plain ol' bad luck wipes out the C: drive. You can carve up that big hard disk any way you like, but if you create an extended partition with a second drive letter as shown here, you can store your important data away from C: and keep it safer.

FIGURE 15.7

The primary partition on this 1.2GB drive is being set as 800MB by Fdisk.

```
                          Create Primary DOS Partition
Current fixed disk drive: 1




Total disk space is  1223 Mbytes (1 Mbyte = 1048576 bytes)
Maximum space available for partition is  1223 Mbytes (100% )

Enter partition size in Mbytes or percent of disk space (%) to
create a Primary DOS Partition...............................: [ 800]



Press Esc to return to FDISK Options
```

6. Press Esc to return to the main Fdisk menu (refer to Figure 15.6).

7. Because you created a primary partition using only a portion of the disk space, a warning appears to remind you that the primary partition is not yet active; it must be marked active to be bootable.

8. To mark the primary partition as active, type **2** (Set Active Partition) and press Enter to display the Set Active Partition menu.

9. Type the number of the partition you want to make active (normally 1), and press Enter. The status column displays an A for active partition, as in Figure 15.8. Press Esc to return to the main Fdisk menu.

Status set to A (active)

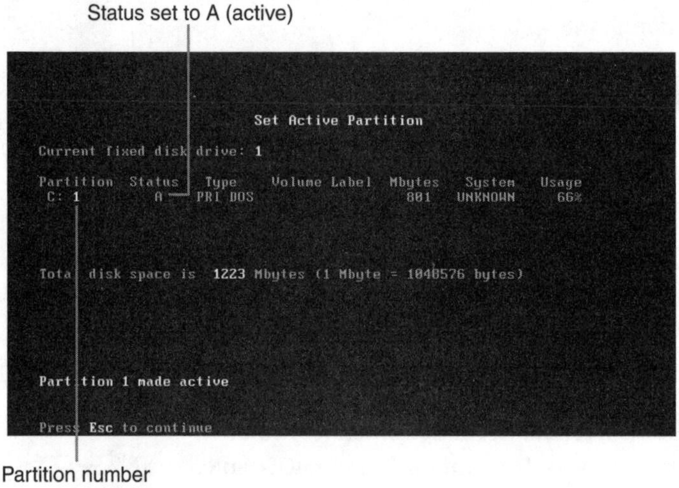

FIGURE 15.8

The 800MB primary partition after Fdisk sets it as Active. To be bootable, this partition must have system files copied to it by the Windows Setup program or by being formatted with the /S (system) option.

Partition number

10. To prepare the rest of the drive for use by Windows, from the Fdisk main menu, select #1, Create DOS Partition or Logical DOS Drive.

11. From the Create DOS Partition menu, select #2, Create an Extended Partition.

12. Press Enter to accept the default (the remaining capacity of the drive); the logical drives are stored in the extended partition.

13. Create one or more logical drives when prompted, specifying the size you want for each letter. The drive letter for each logical drive is listed; note the letters because you need to format each logical drive after you finish using Fdisk and reboot.

14. When the entire capacity of the drive is used, the Fdisk display resembles Figure 15.9. Press the Y key to view the logical drives stored in the extended partition.

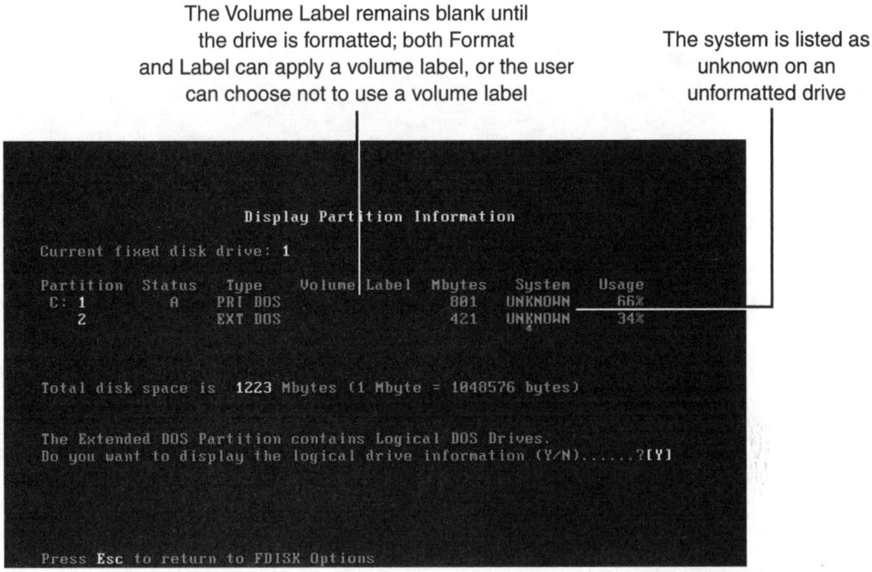

The Volume Label remains blank until
the drive is formatted; both Format
and Label can apply a volume label, or the user
can choose not to use a volume label

The system is listed as
unknown on an
unformatted drive

FIGURE 15.9

This drive contains both a primary and an extended partition; logical drives in the extended partition make this entire drive available to Windows.

```
                    Display Partition Information

Current fixed disk drive: 1

Partition  Status   Type    Volume Label  Mbytes   System    Usage
   C: 1       A     PRI DOS                  801    UNKNOWN    66%
      2             EXT DOS                  421    UNKNOWN    34%


Total disk space is  1223 Mbytes (1 Mbyte = 1048576 bytes)


The Extended DOS Partition contains Logical DOS Drives.
Do you want to display the logical drive information (Y/N)......?[Y]




Press Esc to return to FDISK Options
```

15. After you press Enter again to accept these changes, you're prompted to shut down the system and reboot it. If you ran Fdisk from within Windows, close the Fdisk window, shut down Windows, and reboot. See "Finishing the Job with the Format Command," later in this chapter, to complete the process.

Creating an Extended Partition with Fdisk

Follow these steps to install a fixed disk with an extended partition as an addition to a system with one or more existing drives. (I'm assuming the drive you're installing has no disk partitions, such as a brand-new hard disk.)

1. Select #5 from the main menu after starting Fdisk.

2. Select the drive you want to change from the drives listed. For this example, disk #2 would be selected, as in Figure 15.10.

3. From the main Fdisk menu, select #1, Create DOS Partition or Logical DOS Drive.

caution

Before you continue, I strongly advise you to use the #4 option (Display Partition Information) from the Fdisk main menu to make sure you have selected the new (empty) drive. You should not see any disk partitions on a new hard disk (you might if you are reusing an old hard disk). If you are using a new hard disk and you see disk partitions, you have probably forgotten to select the correct hard disk. Go back to steps 1 and 2 and try it again.

Existing disk partitions on disk #1

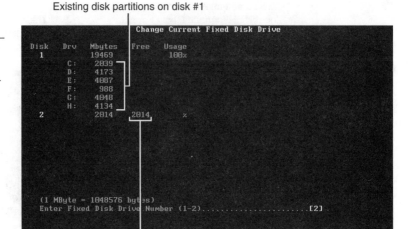

Free space (no disk partitions) on disk #2

4. From the Create DOS Partition menu, select #2, Create an Extended Partition.

5. Press Enter to accept the default (the entire capacity of the drive); the logical drives are stored in the extended partition.

6. Create one or more logical drives when prompted, specifying the size you want for each letter. Note the drive letters that you need to format later are listed.

7. When the entire capacity of the drive is used, you should see a message similar to Figure 15.11.

```
              Create Logical DOS Drive(s) in the Extended DOS Partition
Drv Volume Label   Mbytes  System  Usage
D:                   2014   UNKNOWN  100%
```

```
All available space in the Extended DOS Partition
is assigned to logical drives.
Press Esc to continue
```

8. Exit Fdisk, close Windows if you ran Fdisk from within Windows, and restart the computer.

Finishing the Job with the `Format` Command

The Windows `Format` command finishes the disk preparation process you started with Fdisk. You can use the Windows Explorer to format drives or command-line options.

⇨ For more information about using command-line or Windows Explorer Format options, **see** "Using Format with Floppy and Hard Disks," **p. 517.**

The command-line options listed in Table 15.5 are used with hard disks in Windows. Format offers additional options that work with floppy disks only.

Table 15.5 Common Format Options for Hard Drives

Format Command	Meaning	Used for...	Example	Notes
Format `x:/s`	Formats x: drive with system (boot) files	Any bootable drive (normally C:)	Format `C:/s`	1
Format `x:`	Formats x: drive without system files	Any non bootable drive (D: or higher)	Format `D:`	
Format `x:` `/V:label`	Formats x: drive with specified label	Any drive	Format `D:`	`/V:Mydrive`

[1]*The /s option is not valid with Windows Me. Instead, Windows Me installs the system files to the hard disk during installation.*

Windows NT/2000/XP also support the hard disk Format options shown in Table 15.6. Note that options can be combined.

Table 15.6 Format Options for Hard Drives (NT/2000/XP)

Format Command	Meaning	Example	Notes
Format `x:/FS:` `Filesystem` (FAT, FAT32, NTFS, HPFS)	Formats x: with specified file system	Format `D:/FS:NTFS`	1
Format `x:/C`	Formats x: and compresses all files and folders	Format `D:/C`	2
Format `x:/A:size`	Formats x: with specified allocation unit sizes (KB)	Format `D:/V:Mydrive`	3

Table 15.6 (continued)

Format Command	Meaning	Example	Notes
Format x:/X	Formats x: after dismounting volume	Format x:/X	2, 4

[1]*Windows 2000 and XP don't support HPFS option. Windows NT 4.0 must have Service Pack 4 or greater installed to support FAT32 option.*

[2]*Supported by Windows 2000 and Windows XP only.*

[3]*Not recommended for general use; type* **Format** */?* *to see list of valid values for allocation unit size by file system.*

[4]*Make sure no users or critical processes are trying to use the drive before using this command, or data loss can result.*

To format the hard disk from a command (MS-DOS) prompt, follow these steps:

1. Click Start, Run, Command to open up a command-prompt window.

2. Start the format process with the correct command from Table 15.5 or 15.6. The system displays a warning of possible data loss and enables you to stop if you are about to format the wrong hard disk.

   If you continue, a progress indicator is displayed. If your hard disk has any surface damage, a Trying to recover allocation unit number *xxxxx* message appears as the system marks the damaged area as a "do not use" area. Because modern hard disks have built-in defect management, you should not see any bad allocation units displayed during format. If you do, use the disk manufacturer's own diagnostic utility to replace bad sectors with spare sectors, or to determine if the drive needs to be returned for repair.

3. At the end of the format process, you can add a volume label (up to 11 characters) and see the disk statistics listed, including the drive's total size and the allocation unit size and number available.

Now your drive is ready to use. If it's the first drive in your system, you're ready to install Windows 9x/Me. (See Chapter 16, "Operating System Installation," for details.) If it's an additional drive, you can make folders on it and start storing programs or data there.

Preparing a Hard Disk for Use with Windows NT/2000/XP

Windows NT 4.0, Windows 2000, and Windows XP don't use Fdisk or Format to prepare hard disks for use. Instead, the Windows setup program is used to prepare an empty hard disk on a new system, whereas the **Disk Administrator** (Windows NT) or **Disk Management** portion of the **Microsoft Management Console (MMC)** (Windows 2000/XP) is used to prepare hard disks added to an operational Windows system.

These methods of preparing the hard disk are much different than Fdisk and Format, but help to reduce the always-high risk of user error caused by the command-line operation of Fdisk and Format.

For information about how the Windows NT, Windows 2000, and Windows XP setup programs format empty hard disks on a new system, see Chapter 16.

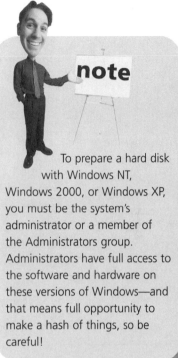

note

To prepare a hard disk with Windows NT, Windows 2000, or Windows XP, you must be the system's administrator or a member of the Administrators group. Administrators have full access to the software and hardware on these versions of Windows—and that means full opportunity to make a hash of things, so be careful!

Using Windows NT Disk Administrator to Prepare a Hard Disk

To use the Disk Administrator to prepare an additional drive as an extended partition

1. Click Start, Programs, Administrative Tools, Disk Administrator.

2. Select Volumes or Disk view from the View menu or with the icons below the top-level menu. Disk view provides a more graphic display.

3. Select the empty hard disk from the listing of disk drives. It will be listed as Disk #1 or above (the Windows boot drive is Disk #0).

4. Click Partition from the top-level menu, and then click Create, Extended.

5. Specify the size of the extended partition with Partition, Create, Create Partition of Specified Size; normally, this is the entire drive. (Leave space only if you want to install another operating system on the drive later.)

6. Click OK.

7. Select the extended partition you just created and click Partition, Create. A Create Logical Drive dialog box appears.

8. To create a single logical drive within the extended partition, enter the full size of the partition in the Create Logical Drive of Size dialog box. To leave room for an additional logical drive, enter a smaller value.

9. Click OK.

10. If you didn't use all the extended partition space in step 8, click the empty space in the extended partition and repeat steps 8 and 9. Repeat until all the space in the extended partition is assigned to logical drives.

11. To create the partition and logical drives specified, click Partition, Commit Changes Now. Look over the settings, and click OK to make the changes. Otherwise, click Cancel or No.

12. Click OK after the partitioning process is complete.

13. To format the logical drive(s), select the first logical drive, and then click Tools, Format. Select the file system (NTFS is recommended unless you plan to boot Windows 9x to access the drive). Enter a volume label to identify the drive (such as Data or NTFS Disk). You can also specify Quick Format to reduce formatting time by skipping checks for bad sectors. Click OK, and then Yes to continue or No to cancel.

14. Read the dialog box showing disk space and any disk errors after the format process is done, and then click OK.

15. Disk Administrator displays the formatted logical drive. Repeat steps 13 and 14 for any additional logical drives.

16. To exit Disk Administrator, click Partition, Exit.

Using Windows 2000 and Windows XP Disk Management to Prepare a Hard Drive

After Windows 2000 or Windows XP is installed on a system, additional hard disks you install are prepared with the Disk Management portion of the Microsoft Management Console. Disk Management is an extension of the Computer Management subset of tools and is a visual, mouse-driven environment.

To prepare a hard disk with Disk Management

1. Right-click My Computer and select Manage to open Computer Management. Disk Management will be expanded under Storage.

2. Click Disk Management. Your current drives appear in the right window, color-coded for easier identification (see Figure 15.12):

   - *Dark blue*—Primary partition
   - *Light blue*—Logical drive
   - *Dark green*—Extended partition
   - *Light green*—Free space
   - *Black*—Unpartitioned space

FIGURE 15.12

This system has one drive prepared as a primary partition and one drive that has no partition.

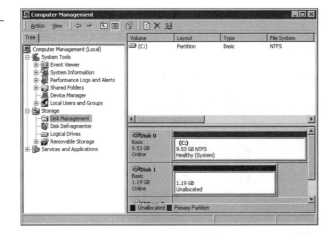

3. Right-click the new drive and select Create Logical Drive to continue.

4. The Create Partition Wizard starts. Click Next to continue.

5. Select Primary Partition if you want to make the partition bootable; select Extended Partition if you are installing the drive for program or data storage (see Figure 15.13). Click Next.

FIGURE 15.13

Logical Drive is not available as a choice until you have created an extended partition.

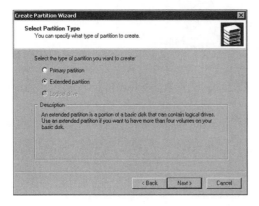

If you select Extended Partition

1. Specify the amount of space. (The default is all available space.) Do *not* select the amount of space for a logical drive because that must be done after the extended partition is created. Click Next.

2. Click Finish to close the wizard; your drive is now marked as Free Space.

To create logical drives

1. Right-click Free Space and select Create Logical Drives to restart the Create Partition Wizard.

2. The logical drive option is already selected. Click Next to continue.

3. Click Next to accept the full capacity of the partition as a logical drive, or enter the size you want the drive to be. Click Next.

4. On the next screen, choose from specifying a drive letter (next available or higher), mounting the drive as a folder on an existing drive, or not assigning the drive a letter or folder. Make your selection (see Figure 15.14) and click Next.

FIGURE 15.14

Unlike Windows 9x/Me, which cannot map hard drive letters around an existing optical or removable-media drive letter, Windows 2000 and Windows XP enable you to leave the optical or removable-media drive at its existing letter (D: on this computer) and choose the next available drive letter (E: or higher) for the new hard disk.

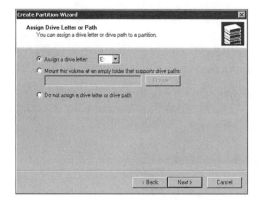

5. Select the Format options desired (see Figure 15.15); the default file system is NTFS (compatible with Windows 2000), but you can also select FAT (compatible with MS-DOS and early Windows 95), FAT32 (compatible with Windows 95B and Windows 98/Me), or skip formatting the drive. You can also enable file and folder compression to save space and provide your own volume

name. Select Quick format (doesn't verify the media) to save formatting time, but if you do, run CHKDSK to test the drive after you format it.

6. On the final screen, scroll through the listed settings and verify they're correct. You can use the Back button to return and make changes, or click Finish to set up and format the drives as listed (see Figure 15.16).

FIGURE 15.15

This drive will be prepared as an NTFS drive.

FIGURE 15.16

Review the complete configuration details for the drive, and use the Back button to make any changes you need.

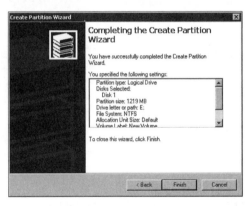

7. The drive will display its name, size, file system, and condition (Healthy) when the format process is complete. You can use the new drive immediately.

8. To close Computer Management, click File, and then click Exit.

Using Format with Floppy and Hard Disks

Format works in very different ways, depending on whether it is used on a hard or floppy disk. When Format is used on a hard drive, it creates a master boot record, two file allocation tables, and a root directory (also referred to as the *root folder*). The rest of the drive is checked for disk surface errors—any defective areas are marked as bad to prevent their use by the operating system. Format appears to "destroy" the previous contents of a hard disk, but if you use Format on a hard disk by mistake, Norton Utilities and some other programs can be used to **unformat** the drive and enable you to recover most, or even all, your information because most of the disk surface is not changed by Format.

If a floppy disk is prepared with Format and the unconditional /U option is used from the command line, or the Windows Explorer Full Format option is used, sector markings (a sector equals 512 bytes) are created across the surface of the floppy disk before other disk structures are created, destroying any previous data on the disk. If the Quick Format or Safe Format option is used, the contents of the disk are marked for deletion but can be retrieved with Norton Utilities or Norton System Works. For more information about using Format with hard drives, see Tables 15.5 and 15.6. For more information about using Format with floppy disks, see Table 15.7.

A floppy disk can be only a single drive letter, but a hard disk can be subdivided into one or more drive letters. Every drive letter created by Fdisk must be formatted.

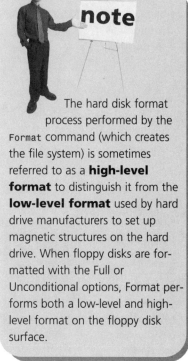

note

The hard disk format process performed by the Format command (which creates the file system) is sometimes referred to as a **high-level format** to distinguish it from the **low-level format** used by hard drive manufacturers to set up magnetic structures on the hard drive. When floppy disks are formatted with the Full or Unconditional options, Format performs both a low-level and high-level format on the floppy disk surface.

Using Format with Floppy Drives

Although most floppy disks today are preformatted at the factory, Format is still useful as a means to

- Erase the contents of a floppy disk quickly, especially if it contains many files or folders.
- Place new sector markings across the disk.
- Create a bootable disk more reliably than by using the Sys command with a preformatted disk (Windows 9x only).

Table 15.7 covers the most important different Format options that apply to floppy disks. For additional Format options available with some versions of Windows, open a command-prompt window, type **Format /?**, and press Enter.

Table 15.7 Major Format Options for Floppy Drives

Command	Meaning	Used for...	Example
Format x:/s	Formats x: drive with system (boot) files (not available with Me/2000/XP)	Makes a bootable floppy disk; assumes floppy disk is same capacity as the drive	Format A:/s
Format x:	Formats x: without system files	Erases the contents of a floppy disk; used for a data floppy disk	Format A:
Format A:/Q	Formats x: without scanning for bad areas; clears FAT and root directory	Erases the contents of a floppy disk; use only if disk is in good condition	Format A:
Format x:/u	Unconditionally formats the floppy disk; wipes out all previous data (not available with 2000/XP)	Rewrites the sector markings on an old floppy disk that might have developed weak areas; /u can be added to any other option	Format A:/s/u
Format x:/v	Allows user to add a volume label to the drive	Label can describe floppy disk's contents or be arbitrary text; can be added to any Format command	Format A:/s/v
Format x: /f:720	Formats a 720KB (DSDD) 3.5-inch disk in a 1.44MB (DSHD) drive[1]	Forces the drive to handle the 720KB floppy disk correctly; some IBM drives without media sensors will format 720KB media as 1.44MB media, but with poor reliability	Format A:/f:720
Format x: /f:360 or Format x:/4	Formats a 360KB (DSDD) 5.25-inch floppy disk in a 1.2MB (DSHD) drive[1]	Allows 1.2MB hard drives to create a floppy disk usable on a 360KB XT-style floppy disk drive; works well for new floppy disks, but might not reliably overwrite tracks made by a 360KB drive	Format B:/f:360 Format B:/4

Format x: and Format x:/s *allow any existing data on the disk to be unerased with a program such as Norton Unformat.*

Format x:/f:360 *and* Format x:/f:720 *are needed only when formatting disks that are not the default size of the drive, which is seldom necessary.*

[1]*Other size options are also available in Windows 2000; the /f:size option is not supported in Windows XP.*

Formatting Floppy and Hard Disks with Windows Explorer

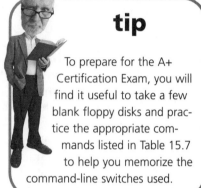

Windows Explorer can be used to format both hard drives and floppy disks. Right-click the drive you want to format, select Format, and the Format options are displayed, as in Figures 15.17 and 15.18.

The Windows Me Explorer Format has some of these same options, but lacks the option to create a bootable floppy. To create a bootable floppy with Windows Me, create an emergency startup disk, or copy the command.com and io.sys files from the \Windows\Command\EBD folder to a blank, formatted floppy disk.

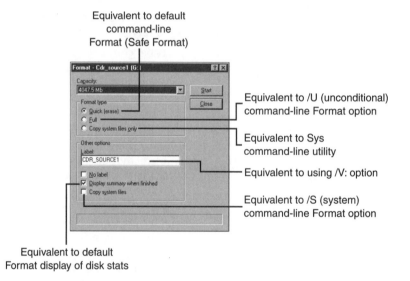

FIGURE 15.17

The Windows 9x Explorer Format menu enables the user to select the same options that can be used with the command-line Format program, and also provides an alternative to the Sys command.

Equivalent to default command-line Format (Safe Format)

Equivalent to /U (unconditional) command-line Format option

Equivalent to Sys command-line utility

Equivalent to using /V: option

Equivalent to /S (system) command-line Format option

Equivalent to default Format display of disk stats

The Windows XP Explorer Format options for floppy disk and hard disk can be seen in Figure 15.18. (Windows 2000's options are almost identical, except for the lack of the MS-DOS startup disk option.)

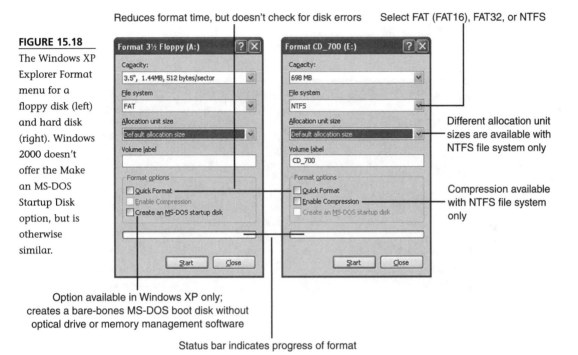

Reduces format time, but doesn't check for disk errors   Select FAT (FAT16), FAT32, or NTFS

FIGURE 15.18
The Windows XP Explorer Format menu for a floppy disk (left) and hard disk (right). Windows 2000 doesn't offer the Make an MS-DOS Startup Disk option, but is otherwise similar.

Different allocation unit sizes are available with NTFS file system only

Compression available with NTFS file system only

Option available in Windows XP only; creates a bare-bones MS-DOS boot disk without optical drive or memory management software

Status bar indicates progress of format

Troubleshooting Drive Preparation Problems

Hard drive preparation is one of the major upgrade tasks of a computer technician. Review this section to prepare yourself for troubleshooting questions on the A+ Certification Exams and to improve your skill in day-to-day troubleshooting.

Troubleshooting Drive Preparation Problems with Fdisk

Fdisk can be used to troubleshoot BIOS configuration and compatibility options with ATA/IDE drives. Some of these options work only on a drive that's already been partitioned with Fdisk. Consequently, if you are concerned about BIOS issues, use the Fdisk defaults to prepare the drive; you can always delete the primary partition and start over again if you have problems.

LBA Mode Troubleshooting

You can use Fdisk to determine problems with either the LBA configuration of the system BIOS or with support for enhanced Int13h functions.

See Figure 15.19: It shows you how to compare the Fdisk values marked A and B with each other and with the rated capacity of a hard drive to find configuration problems with your system.

FIGURE 15.19

If the values listed for A and B don't match each other, as in this example, or don't match the drive capacity, you have a problem with BIOS configuration.

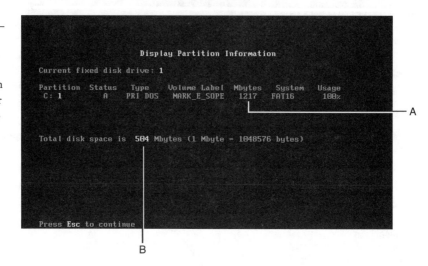

If the value for A on your system lists the full capacity of the drive (greater than 504MB), but the value for B lists the drive capacity as only 504MB, the drive was prepared with LBA mode enabled in the BIOS but LBA has been disabled since the drive was prepared. The drive *cannot* be used at full capacity until LBA mode is enabled, and it will not be bootable if it is the primary or sole drive on the system.

If both A and B indicate the drive is only 504MB, but the actual capacity of the drive is larger, LBA must be enabled in the system BIOS before the drive is prepared.

To restore proper operation in either case, restart the computer, activate the system BIOS setup program, and enable LBA mode. Save the setup changes and restart the computer. Both A and B should display correct values for the drive. For more information about LBA mode, see Chapter 14.

The Disk Management feature in Windows 2000 and Windows XP can recognize a disk at full capacity whether LBA mode is enabled or not. However, LBA mode should be enabled in the system BIOS to maintain compatibility with all Windows versions.

Enhanced Int13h Troubleshooting

If A and B both indicate your hard drive's capacity is 8,064MB (7.88GB) but the drive has a larger rated capacity, this indicates the system BIOS supports LBA mode, but not the Enhanced Int13h functions needed to support drives beyond 7.88GB.

Choose one of the following options for a solution, in order of desirability, best to worst:

■ System BIOS upgrade if the upgrade supports Enhanced Int13h

■ Add-on IDE host adapter card with its own BIOS that supports Enhanced Int13h

■ Hard disk BIOS replacement software that supports Enhanced Int13h (supplied by the drive maker)

Troubleshooting Hard Disks You Can't Partition

If you create partitions but the Format program reports that the drive letter(s) you need to format aren't present, your system might be configured to write-protect the boot sector of the hard disk.

Restart your computer, start the BIOS setup program, and look through the BIOS setup screens for an option called **Write Protect Boot Sector** or **Antivirus Boot Sector**. If this option is enabled, disable it, save the changes in the system BIOS setup, and retry Fdisk.

> **caution**
>
> If your system can't format the hard disk at full capacity, *don't* make any changes to the hard disk until you make one of the changes listed in this section. If you create a partition and then install a BIOS upgrade or other feature to handle the drive's full capacity, you will need to remove the partition you created (and lose any data on that partition) before you can create a partition using the full size of your hard disk.

Note that many recent systems have a type of BIOS-based antivirus protection that can be enabled to stop real viruses but are smart enough to allow boot sector changes by the operating system.

If you partition a hard disk and the system reports that the partition or drive letter is damaged, you might be trying to create a partition larger than the Windows version you're using can handle properly. Reduce the size of the partition and try creating the partition or drive letter again. This can happen both during initial installation of the operating system or with additional drives you install.

Troubleshooting Hard Disks That Can't Boot After Format

If you can't boot from drive C: after formatting it, check the following:

■ Did you use `Format c:/s` with Windows 9x?

The `/s`, as you saw previously, transfers the system files used to boot the system. Use `c:\>DIR /AH` to see whether the system files listed previously are present on the drive. If not, reboot with a floppy disk and run `A:\>SYS` to transfer boot files to the hard disk. Reboot the system without the floppy disk and see whether it starts. With Windows Me, you need to complete the setup program (which installs bootable files to the hard disk as part of the Windows Me installation process).

- Did you make the primary partition (C: drive) **active** with Fdisk?

    If you used Fdisk to create two or more drive letters, you must make the primary partition active. Boot from a floppy disk and rerun Fdisk; select option 2 and make the primary partition active.

- Is the hard disk listed as a bootable drive in boot options in the system BIOS?

    Some BIOSs enable you to skip the hard disk as a bootable drive; make sure the hard disk is listed as a bootable device.

- Is there a floppy disk in drive A:?

    A floppy disk in drive A: prevents booting the system if it is listed before the hard disk in the boot order.

    A floppy disk that is not formatted with the /s option cannot be used to start a system. Remove the floppy disk and restart the computer to allow Windows to start normally with full features.

- Was LBA mode disabled after using it to prepare the hard drive?

    Any drive using Windows 9x/Me can't boot if LBA mode has been disabled after it was originally used to prepare the drive. This is because LBA mode changes the logical layout of the drive, and thus the location of the boot files.

    Using setup defaults or BIOS defaults with some old AMI BIOS versions will disable LBA mode; restart your system and re-enable LBA mode in the BIOS setup program.

- Is there damage to the hard disk's master boot record (see the next section for details)?

Repairing the Master Boot Record

Boot sector viruses and magnetic errors can corrupt the **master boot record (MBR)**, which is used by the BIOS's bootstrap program to locate a bootable drive. A damaged MBR will prevent your system from starting from a bootable hard disk. To repair a damaged or corrupted MBR, you can use one of the following options:

- Windows 9x users can use an undocumented Fdisk switch called `Fdisk/mbr`.

- Windows 2000/XP users can use the Recovery Console command `Fixmbr` on an NTFS-based drive. If the drive is FAT based, `Fixboot` should be used first, followed by `Fixmbr`.

Because damaged MBRs can be caused by a computer virus, systems should be tested with an up-to-date antivirus program before either of these commands is used. If a boot-sector virus is located by an antivirus program, the program's own disk-repair options should be used first.

If this is unsuccessful, you can use the appropriate repair tool to attempt to fix the MBR.

To run Fdisk/MBR, boot from the Windows 9x EBD and type `Fdisk/mbr` at the command prompt; press Enter.

To run Fixmbr, start the Windows 2000 or XP Setup process, select Repair, Recovery Console, and type `Fixmbr` at the Recovery Console prompt. Press Enter. To rewrite the boot sector on a FAT-based drive, type `Fixboot` and press Enter. To repair the master boot record with an NTFS-based drive, type `Fixmbr` and press Enter. (If you boot from a different drive letter than the default Windows drive or a different hard disk than normal, you can specify the hard disk drive letter or drive number with these commands.)

Windows NT 4.0 uses the Diskprobe.EXE program from the Windows NT 4.0 Resource Kit to restore NTFS boot sectors. The **Norton Utilities** Disk Editor can also be used. See Knowledge Base articles 153973 ("Recovering NTFS Boot Sector on NTFS Partitions" provides instructions for using **Diskprobe**) or 121517 ("How to Recover from a Corrupt NTFS Boot Sector" provides DiskEdit instructions) at `http://support.microsoft.com` for details.

note

If you see a message at startup referring to **EZ-BIOS**, **Dynamic Drive Overlay**, or a similar message, that indicates the drive has been prepared using a third-party disk utility, such as DiscWizard, Disk Manager, MaxBlast, Data Lifeguard Tools, or other vendor-supplied hard disk setup programs. If a system has an outdated BIOS that cannot manage the full capacity of the drive, these programs will install a nonstandard MBR and drivers to manage the drive's full capacity. If systems running third-party hard disk management software can't boot, use the repair program provided by the software vendor, not Windows's own MBR repair programs.

Study Lab

Don't miss the Study Lab materials found on the CD accompanying this book. Each Study Lab is tailored to the individual chapters in this book, meaning that you'll quickly be able to determine which topics you understand well enough to pass the exam and which topics need more study. The Study Labs are presented in printable PDF format so that you can take them with you to study at work, on the road, or even in your car just before test time!

THE ABSOLUTE MINIMUM

- An ATA/IDE, SATA, or SCSI hard drive isn't ready for use until its surface has been partitioned and formatted.

- Windows 9x and Me use separate Fdisk and Format programs to perform these tasks.

- Windows NT 4.0, Windows 2000, and Windows XP can partition and format hard disks during installation.

- On installed systems, Windows NT 4.0 uses the Disk Administrator to partition and format hard disks, whereas Windows 2000 and XP use the Disk Management portion of the Microsoft Management Console to partition and format hard disks.

- FAT32 is the recommended file system for use with Windows 9x and Me, unless the drives will be accessed by MS-DOS or early Windows 95 releases, which support only FAT16. NTFS 5 is the recommended file system for use with Windows 2000 and Windows XP.

- Windows NT 4.0 supports NTFS 5 only if Service Pack 4 or later is installed.

- A Windows 9x or Me with Windows 2000 or XP dual-boot system must use FAT32 or FAT16 for any drives to be accessed by both operating systems because Windows 9x/Me can't use any version of NTFS.

- Primary partitions are intended for use in starting a system, and extended partitions contain one or more logical drives that cannot be used to boot the system, although they can hold programs and data.

- A hard disk can hold up to four primary partitions, but only one extended partition.

- The default operation of Fdisk in Windows 9x/Me creates primary partitions only; the Fdisk menu must be used to create extended partitions.

- In Windows 9x/Me, hard disk drive letters follow a fixed sequence based on primary and extended partitions on primary and additional drives.

- If additional hard disks are installed in Windows 9x/Me, they can take over drive letters already in use by removable-media or optical drives if necessary.

- If additional hard disks are installed in Windows 2000/XP, they can use unused drive letters, leaving existing removable-media and optical drive letter assignments intact.

- The Format program uses different command-line options when used with floppy disks and hard drives, but it uses similar menus in the Windows Explorer for both types of drives.

- For maximum utility and data safety, consider creating at least two partitions on your hard drives: one for programs and operating system; one for data.

- Windows contains various tools for repairing damaged boot sectors and master boot records, including `Fdisk/mbr` (Windows 9x/Me), `Fixboot` and `Fixmbr` (Windows 2000/XP), and `Diskprobe` (Windows NT 4.0).

16

OPERATING SYSTEM INSTALLATION

A computer without an operating system is useless. Consequently, it should be no surprise that a big part of the A+ Certification Exam concerns the process of installing operating systems. The process of preparing for an operating system installation includes

- Verifying that your system has sufficient performance and free disk space for the installation
- Verifying that you have drivers for the devices and peripherals you want to use with the operating system
- Preparing the appropriate startup disks (when required) to prepare the hard disk and start the installation
- Determining the location of the operating system if you are installing the new operating system as a dual-boot configuration that will enable you to run either the old or new operating systems

Clean Installation Versus Dual-Boot Installation

There are three ways to install an operating system:

- *On an empty hard disk or a hard disk whose contents you don't want to keep*—This is usually referred to as a **clean install**. The existing operating system (if any) will be replaced by the new operating system. You can also reinstall the same operating system over an existing installation to fix problems with the operating system (this refreshes the system files and settings) without losing user data. However, if you install a different operating system, in most cases your data as well as the old operating system will be wiped out.

- *As a replacement for the existing operating system (retaining existing settings and programs)*—This is usually referred to as an **operating system upgrade**.

- *Into empty space (a partition) on a hard disk with an existing operating system*—This is usually referred to as a **dual-boot installation**, because you can choose the operating system you want to run whenever you start your computer.

Don't let these options confuse you. Whether you're installing a brand-new operating system as the only one on the system, alongside an existing one, or as a replacement, the processes are quite similar.

In all cases, you'd better make sure of the following:

- Does the computer have enough RAM, a fast enough processor, and enough disk space for the operating system?

- Is the hardware inside the PC and connected to it (everything from printers to modems) supported by drivers for the operating system?

note

The CD included with this book contains important Study Lab material for this chapter, as well as Chapters 2–22 in this book. The Study Lab for each chapter contains terms to study, exercises, and practice tests—all in printable PDF format (Adobe Acrobat Reader is included on the CD, too). These Study Lab materials will help you gear up for the A+ Exam. Also, the CD includes an industry-leading test engine from PrepLogic, which simulates the actual A+ test so that you can be sure that you're ready when test day arrives. Don't let the A+ test intimidate you. If you've read the chapters, worked through the Study Lab, and passed the practice tests from PrepLogic, you should be well prepared to ace the test!

Also, you'll notice that some words throughout each chapter are in bold format. These are study terms that are defined in the Study Lab. Be sure to consult the Study Lab when you are finished with this chapter to test what you've learned.

So, what's different about these types of installations?

- New operating system installations are usually performed on empty hard drives. However, you can't take a brand-new drive out of the box and install Windows without preparing the drive. Windows 9x and Me require the user to run Fdisk and Format on a drive before Windows can be installed on a hard drive, whereas Windows NT 4.0/2000/XP incorporate partitioning and formatting into their setup programs.

- New operating system installations are often performed using **original equipment manufacturer (OEM)** versions supplied for a particular type of computer. **OEM versions** often come with a bootable disk used to start the system (or the CD itself is bootable on some recent Windows versions) and require no proof of a previous version. Upgrades require the user to install the operating system to a drive containing the previous version or to provide the previous version during installation to qualify the system for the upgrade installation.

- **Full versions** of Windows 98 Second Edition, Windows Me, Windows 2000, and Windows XP are shipped on **bootable CDs**, but you need to make bootable floppy disks to install Windows 95 and some other versions if you want to use an **upgrade version** to perform a clean install. (Windows 2000 and Windows XP upgrade versions are also bootable.) If your system can't boot from a CD, you can also make (or download) bootable disks for use with later versions of Windows. See Chapter 15, "Preparing Hard and Floppy Drives with Windows," for details.

caution

If you plan to perform a dual-boot installation with Windows, you should install the older version of Windows first, followed by the newer version. Windows 2000 and XP's built-in boot manager works only if Windows 2000 or XP is installed after the older version is installed. If you want to choose from three or more operating systems, or need to install an older version after a newer version is installed, use a third-party boot manager.

note

This chapter covers only basic dual-boot configurations supported by Microsoft. Many other options are available.

■ Dual-boot installations can be started from within the existing Windows installation as are operating system upgrades (this is the method used in this chapter), or you can start them from the bootable CD. In either situation, a dual-boot installation uses unpartitioned free space on the current or on another hard disk as the target. Microsoft Windows NT 4.0/2000/XP all include a simple boot manager to enable the user to determine which operating system to start after a new operating system is installed in a dual-boot configuration.

Making Sure Your System Is Ready for a Particular Windows Version

Got a recent system? Any system built in the last three years can easily achieve (and usually far surpass) the hardware requirements for installing any version of Windows covered on the A+ Certification Operating Systems Exam. However, in the real world, digital dinosaurs that might not be fast enough or have enough free disk space to support some versions of Windows still roam the earth.

Table 16.1 lists the requirements for Windows 95, 98, and Me, and Table 16.2 lists the requirements for Windows NT 4.0 Workstation, Windows 2000 Professional, and Windows XP.

caution

The Windows NT/2000/XP **boot manager** is loaded automatically after you install these versions of Windows in a dual-boot configuration. However, they aren't designed to handle installing another operating system after installing Windows, or to work with Linux or other non-Microsoft operating systems. Use a commercial boot manager if you want to install Windows 9x/Me, Linux, or another operating system after you install Windows NT/2000/XP.

Dual booting, especially if you want to use combinations not supported by Microsoft, is a very complex subject. Don't try it until you read Microsoft's technical notes on the subject and research third-party articles and books, such as *The Multi-Boot Configuration Handbook*, by Roderick Smith (Que Publishing, 2000). Use a search engine such as Google (www.google.com) and use the terms "dual-boot" and the operating system(s) you want to use to find more information.

Table 16.1 Hardware Requirements for Windows 9x/Me by Version

Hardware Component	Windows Version		
	95	**98**	**Me**
Processor	386DX	486-DX2 66MHz	Pentium 150MHz
RAM	4MB	16MB, 24MB[1]	32MB
Free disk space	50MB to 55MB	225MB (typical)[2]	320MB
Floppy drive	1.44MB, 3.5-inch	1.44MB, 3.5-inch	1.44MB, 3.5-inch
CD-ROM drive[3]	Optional	Optional	Required
Display	VGA[5]	VGA[6]	VGA[6]
Microsoft mouse or compatible	Optional	Optional	Required
Multimedia[4]	Optional	Optional	Required

[1]Windows 98 Second Edition requires 24MB of RAM

[2]Can vary between 165MB and 295MB depending upon options and computer configuration

[3]DVD-ROM, CD-RW, and DVD-rewritable can be substituted

[4]Sound card, speakers, or headphones

[5]256-color recommended

[6]16-bit or higher color depth at 800×600 or higher resolutions recommended

Table 16.2 Hardware Requirements for Windows NT 4.0/2000/XP by Version

Hardware Component	Windows Version		
	NT 4.0 Workstation	**2000 Professional**	**XP Home/Pro**
Processor	Pentium[1]	Pentium 133MHz	Pentium 233MHz
RAM	16MB	64MB	64MB
Free disk space	110MB	650MB[2]	1.5GB
Floppy drive	Optional	1.44MB, 3.5-inch	Optional
CD-ROM drive[3]	Required	Optional	Required
Display	VGA	VGA	Super VGA[4]
Microsoft mouse or compatible	Required	Required	Required
Multimedia[5]	Optional	Optional	Required
Keyboard	Required	Required	Required

[1] Intel version; Alpha AXP, MIPS R4x00, and Power PC processors also supported by separate versions

[2]2GB or larger hard disk also required

[3]DVD-ROM, CD-RW, DVD-rewritable can be substituted

[4]800×600 resolution

[5]Sound card, speakers, or headphones

Did you notice how the processor, RAM, and free disk space requirements keep climbing with each new Windows version? All the bells, whistles, and stability of Windows XP have a cost in faster hardware. Thus, before you even consider an upgrade to an older system, you'd better check its stats against what you see in Tables 16.1 and 16.2.

You know what Microsoft is expecting from your hardware. How can you get the gory details about your system? You can use methods discussed in Chapter 2, "PC Anatomy 101," to check your system's hardware against these hardware requirements. For example, Figure 16.1 shows the startup system configuration displayed by a 200MHz Pentium system (top) and a 1.4GHz Athlon system (bottom). Although the Pentium-based system is obsolete by any measure, its clock speed (200MHz), memory size (64MB), and hard disk size (1.6GB) are sufficient to support Windows 9x/Me and Windows NT/2000 (assuming adequate free disk space). However, the 1.4GHz Athlon system comfortably exceeds all requirements for any current version of Windows.

Obtaining Compatible Drivers for Your Version of Windows

Because Windows controls and manages your system's hardware, it is essential that you obtain drivers for your hardware that work with the version of Windows you want to install. If you've already done a Windows install once or twice and found that your modem, your network card, or your printer didn't work unless you supplied the drivers yourself, you already know how essential it is to get drivers in advance.

tip

You might like to recycle old computer parts, but if the processor, hard disk size, and memory size of your PC barely meet the Microsoft requirements, prepare to be annoyed at how slowly your computer runs and how limited its capabilities are. You're much better off if your system greatly exceeds the minimums listed in Tables 16.1 and 16.2.

caution

Note that the installation programs for Windows 2000/Me/XP all test the system for compliance with minimum processor and memory requirements and will not install on systems that don't meet the minimum standards. You can sometimes use optional switches with the setup program to bypass verification, but running these versions of Windows with hardware that doesn't meet the minimum standards is not recommended. In plain English, don't even try it!

FIGURE 16.1

An elderly
Pentium-class
system (top) is
still powerful
enough to run
older versions of
Windows, but a
1.4GHz Athlon
system (bottom)
exceeds the
requirements for
all versions of
Windows includ-
ing XP by a
wide margin.

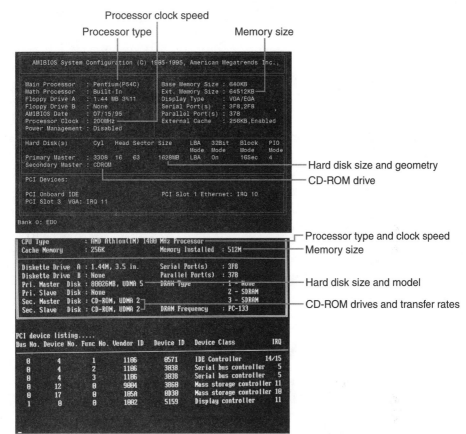

Although newer versions of Windows support broader ranges of hardware than older versions, it would be a big mistake to assume that the version of Windows you want to install can support your motherboard, graphics card, sound card, or other hardware without a bit of help from you. What should you do before you start the installation process?

1. Find out whether your system's hardware is supported by the operating system you want to install.

2. Download the drivers your hardware needs.

3. Install the drivers as prompted during operating system installation or afterward.

There are several ways to determine if you need to download compatible drivers or if you already have them:

■ Check the driver CD or floppy disks provided with existing hardware for compatible drivers.

■ If you are installing Windows 2000 or XP in a dual-boot configuration, start the existing version of Windows, begin the installation process with the Windows 2000 or XP CD, and review the results of the compatibility check performed before continuing. (See Figure 16.2.)

FIGURE 16.2

The Windows XP Upgrade Advisor has determined it supports all the hardware installed on this system (no hardware is listed as having problems), but points out a couple of programs that won't work with XP.

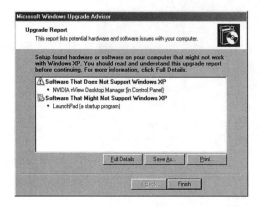

■ If you are thinking about installing Windows XP, you can download the **Upgrade Advisor** and run it from within your existing version of Windows. Get it from `http://www.microsoft.com/windowsxp/pro/howtobuy/upgrading/advisor.asp`.

■ Visit the vendors' Web sites and look for drivers.

■ Use Microsoft's online listing of compatible hardware and software.

Until recently, Microsoft's **Hardware Compatibility List (HCL)** acted as a one-stop-shop for determining which hardware was supported by what version(s) of Windows, and providing drivers as needed. Microsoft is switching away from the HCL database to a catalog listing (lots of pictures, but harder to search) for driver and support information. Consequently, you might need to check out several different Web sites to obtain this information from Microsoft:

■ For Windows NT 4.0 and Windows 98, go to the Windows Logo Program Qualification Service Web site at `https://winqual.microsoft.com/download/default.asp`.

This site also lists text and browsable versions of the HCL for Windows Me/2000/XP Home/XP Pro HCLs. However, there is no listing for Windows 95 hardware. Windows 95 can use some, but not all, Windows 98 drivers.

- For Windows Me/2000/XP, use the product and category search page available at `http://www.microsoft.com/whdc/hcl/search.mspx`.

- For Windows XP only, see the Microsoft Windows Catalog at `http://www.microsoft.com/windows/catalog/`.

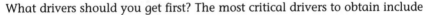

note

This is a secured site (note the https://). You will need to download a security certificate the first time you visit this site.

To obtain drivers for listed products, click the Windows Update link or visit the vendors' Web sites.

What drivers should you get first? The most critical drivers to obtain include

- Modem
- Network card

These are critical to your ability to download updates with Windows Update, and are among the devices that are most frequently not supported by the Windows drivers on the CD. If you don't download these drivers before you install Windows, you might have no way to get them later!

Additional Preparations for Installation

Wanna have a smooooooth operating system installation? Do the following *first*:

- Add enough RAM to the system to meet (good) or surpass (much better) the minimum requirements. More RAM also helps improve the speed of installation, especially after the graphics mode portion of the install starts.

- Disable antivirus settings in the system BIOS; sometimes this is referred to as *write-protect boot sector*. These settings can stop your upgrade in its tracks when it's time to change the boot sector. Re-enable them after installation (see Figure 16.3).

- Change the **boot order** in the BIOS (if necessary) to put the CD-ROM (optical) drive before the hard disk if you can boot from your operating system CD (see Figure 16.3).

FIGURE 16.3

BIOS options that might need to be changed in some systems before installing Windows. This system's options are configured correctly.

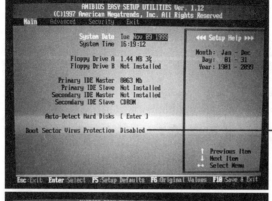

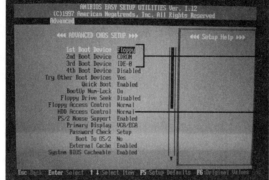

Boot sector virus protection (disable to allow changes by Windows Setup program)

Boot order (move CD-ROM before hard disk to enable booting from Windows CD-ROM)

HDD Access Control (change to normal from write-protected to enable changes by Windows Setup program)

▒ Make sure the Plug and Play (PnP) operating system setting is enabled in the system BIOS for all versions except Windows NT 4.0 (which is the last non-PnP version of Windows). See Chapters 6, "BIOS and CMOS Configuration," and 19, "Installing and Configuring Hardware in Windows," for details.

▒ Scan the Windows CD-ROM and boot floppy media for viruses. Remove any viruses found on magnetic media. Contact Microsoft for a replacement if you find a virus on a Windows CD (hey, it could happen!).

▒ Scan your computer for viruses and remove any viruses found.

▒ Locate your previous version of Windows media if you are installing an upgrade version to an empty drive. The installation program will ask for media to verify you are eligible for the upgrade. Note that compliance checks might not work if you try to use a recovery disk version of Windows (often used by OEMs, such as Compaq and Gateway).

▒ **Back up** the hard disk that will be used for the installation if it contains data you want to retain. Existing data will be lost when the hard disk is

formatted or partitioned. Even if you are going to perform a dual-boot installation (which uses empty space for the new operating system), back up the
drive anyway as a safeguard against user or system error. If a full hard drive
backup isn't possible, back up data files to avoid data loss in case of a problem with the upgrade. For maximum safety, use the byte-by-byte verify
option during backup if available, and test the backup by restoring some files
to an empty hard drive or empty folder.

- Locate or prepare a boot disk suitable for
  preparing the hard disk if your version of
  Windows or computer doesn't support
  booting from the CD, and prepare the
  hard disk as discussed in Chapter 15.
  Make sure the drive is backed up first if it
  contains data you want to keep.

- Make sure you have the product key
  (CD key) for the Windows media you
  want to install.

Backing Up Existing Data and Settings

With hard disk prices so cheap and capacities so
high these days, you might want to go ahead and
get a new one before you install Windows.
However, if you must use a hard disk that contains existing data you want to preserve for a new
OS installation, you should transfer the data you
want to keep from that drive to other media
before you start the installation process. After all,
some of it won't be there later. Files in My
Documents and your Internet Explorer favorites
are wiped out during this type of installation. You can use any of the following
methods:

- Backup programs supplied as part of the operating system
- Third-party backup programs
- Drag-and-drop file transfers to another disk or network location

If you use a backup program, you can save space on the storage media compared to
drag-and-drop file transfers because of data compression, but the data must be

tip

If you don't have the
product key anymore, you
can retrieve the product key
used for an existing installation from the Windows
Registry.

Go to `http://personal-computer-tutor.com/abc2/v15/vic15.htm` for
a roundup of methods for
Windows 9x/Me/2000/XP. Get
downloadable utilities for retriev-
ing the product key from `http://www.angelfire.com/va3/vic3/winkeys.htm`.

Keep in mind that these methods
retrieve the key from an *installed*
copy of Windows—not from the
media!

restored to another drive before it can be used. The backup programs included with various versions of Windows support tape and floppy disk backup, but do not support rewriteable CD or DVD drives. Third-party backup programs support a wider variety of tape drives as well as removable-media, rewriteable CD and DVD drives, and external hard disks.

If you want to back up the settings used by software as well as (or instead of) data, you might prefer to use a system migration tool. If you are installing Windows XP, you can use the Microsoft Windows Files and Settings Transfer Wizard. It can be run from the Windows XP CD-ROM on most other versions of Windows (see Figure 16.4). You can transfer the information to a removable-media drive or other drive letter (this could also include a network drive). After the installation is complete, run the wizard again to bring back your information to your computer.

> **tip**
>
> For versions of Windows other than XP, consider third-party tools such as Aloha Bob's PC Relocator Ultra (www.alohabob.com). This enhanced version of the basic PC Relocator enables you to store digital signatures, desktop and Internet settings, email accounts and data, browser bookmarks and favorites, user profiles, and applications as well as data on removable-media or rewritable/recordable CDs for restoration to another system at a later time.

FIGURE 16.4

The Windows XP Files and Settings Transfer Wizard can transfer files, settings, or files and settings, including the contents of the Fonts, My Documents, and other folders.

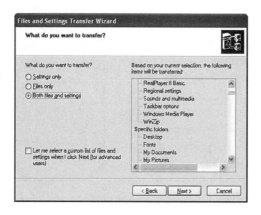

Using an Upgrade Version of Windows for a New Installation

An OEM or full version of the operating system is designed for installation to an empty hard disk (a clean install). You can also use an upgrade version of the operating system for a clean install if you have a qualifying Windows version on CD or floppy disk to provide during the **compliance check** portion of the installation (the compliance check uses the existing Windows installation if you are performing an upgrade or a dual-boot installation). You can use the CD or floppy disks from the previous version (and sometimes two versions back) as qualifying media.

Thus, upgrade versions of Windows Me can use Windows 98 or Windows 95 media to qualify, upgrade versions of Windows 98 can use Windows 95 or Windows/Windows for Workgroups 3.1 media to qualify, and upgrade versions of Windows 95 can use Windows/ Windows for Workgroups 3.1 media to verify eligibility for an installation with an upgrade version.

Windows 2000 can use Windows 9x and Windows NT 4.0/3.51 media to qualify. Windows XP Home can use Windows 98 and Windows Me media, whereas Windows XP Professional can use Windows 98, Windows Me, Windows NT 4.0, Windows 2000, and Windows XP Home Edition media.

Microsoft provides a quick view of eligibility for upgrades to Windows XP Home/Professional at `http://www.microsoft.com/windowsxp/pro/howtobuy/upgrading/matrix.asp`. Although Microsoft refers to the chart on this page as "Eligibility for In-Place Upgrade," media from the eligible versions can also be used to qualify you to use the upgrade for a clean install.

Determining Installation Options

As briefly explained earlier in this chapter, there are three ways you can install an operating system:

- Clean install
- Upgrade
- Dual-boot

caution

Did your version of Windows come on a recovery CD instead of an installable CD? You probably can't use it as a qualifying version.

tip

Always use the CD version of an operating system for the media verification step if possible. The more recent the version of Windows, the more likely it is that it will ask you to insert each and every floppy disk of a Windows floppy disk installation set for verification. This could easily be 10 or more floppy disks with a floppy-based version of Windows 95.

Besides the hassle of swapping floppy disks during verification, a second concern is the possibility of the media going bad. The Windows setup program isn't very forgiving of bad media, and might quit if it cannot read a particular floppy disk during verification.

Even if you no longer use Windows 95, Windows 98, or Windows Me, keep those CDs handy for verification.

This chapter focuses on clean and dual-boot installations. For more information about upgrades, see Chapter 17, "Operating System Upgrades."

Table 16.3 compares these installation methods:

Table 16.3 Install Methods Comparison

Install Option	Start from Windows	Start with Windows CD (Boot)	Retain Existing Programs, Data, and Settings	Avoid Problems with Existing Programs and Settings	Location of Installation
Upgrade	Yes	No	Yes	No	Existing Windows folder
Clean install	No	Yes	No	Yes	Bare drive
Dual-boot	Yes	Yes[1]	[2]	Yes	Unpartitioned free space on hard disk

[1]*Make sure you install Windows to a different folder on the same hard disk or preferably a different disk partition or hard disk if you don't start the installation from within the current version.*

[2]*Does not affect current programs, data, and settings, but software will need to be reinstalled for use with the new operating system.*

Which installation option is best?

- *Upgrade*—If you have a healthy system now and you don't want to keep your old version of Windows, an upgrade will probably go well and will enable you to get back to work within an hour or so.

- *Clean install*—This is the only option available with an empty hard disk. You can also choose this option if your current configuration has problems and you don't mind reinstalling your software and your data (after backing it up, of course). Depending on how much software you need to reinstall, your system could be down for much of the day.

- *Dual-boot*—When you want to use both your existing and new operating systems on the same computer and you have an empty drive or free disk space large enough for the new OS and programs, do a dual-boot installation. Depending on how much software you need to reinstall to the new operating system, your system could be down for much of the day.

Selecting a File System

As you learned in Chapter 15, there are three different **file systems** supported by 32-bit versions of Windows:

- **FAT16** (also known as FAT)
- **FAT32**
- **NTFS**

Which file system should you use for the operating system installation?

- With Windows 9x/Me, you should use FAT32 unless you are installing an early version of Windows 95 that doesn't support FAT32, or if you want to use an MS-DOS boot disk to access the drive. In such cases, use FAT16, but you must create a primary partition less than 2GB in size and install the operating system there. The rest of the hard disk can be used for an extended partition with 2GB or smaller drive letters.

- With Windows 2000/XP, you should use NTFS unless you want to use a Windows 9x/Me boot disk to access the drive. In such cases, use FAT32. With Windows NT 4.0, the choice is between FAT16 and NTFS (FAT32 is not supported). Windows 2000/XP can format a partition up to 32GB as a FAT32 drive; larger drives must be formatted as NTFS.

For more information about these file systems, see Chapter 15.

note

Keep in mind that much of the data security of Windows NT4.0/XP/2000 comes from the use of NTFS. If NTFS is not used to prepare a drive, encryption and compression are not available, nor is user-level or group-level access control.

tip

If you want to use FAT32 with Windows 2000 or XP on a drive greater than 32GB, use the Windows 98 ESD to partition the drive and format it. Windows 2000 and XP can use both formatted and unformatted space for installations.

Installing Windows 9x/Me

So, you've decided to start over again with a clean install of Windows 9x/Me. What's the big picture?

There are three major steps:

1. Partition the hard disk with Fdisk (see Chapter 15).

2. Format the hard disk with Format (see Chapter 15).

3. Run the Windows setup program from floppy disk or CD-ROM.

You want details? Keep reading!

Booting from Emergency Disk or CD-ROM

You can start the Windows 9x/Me installation in one of two ways:

- Boot from the Windows CD (*if* it is bootable and *if* your system is configured to allow it to boot).

- Boot from an **emergency startup disk (ESD).**

Generally, you will need to use an ESD to start the setup process if you are installing an upgrade version of Windows 98 or Me, or almost any version of Windows 95. (There are a few exceptions.) Full versions of Windows 98 and Me enable booting from the Windows CD if your system supports booting from CD and if your CD-ROM or other optical drive is listed before the hard disk in the boot order (refer to Figure 16.3).

If you're wondering whether you can boot from your Windows CD, try it! The worst that can happen is that the system won't boot.

When you boot from the ESD for Windows 98 or Me, the ESD loads CD-ROM drivers that will work with almost any CD-ROM drive. What about Windows 95? Its ESD doesn't include CD-ROM support. Chapter 15 covers the details of how to add CD-ROM support to a Windows 95 boot disk. When you boot with an ESD that has CD-ROM support, you should see a message listing the CD-ROM drive letter at the end of the boot process if you select Boot with CD-ROM Support.

note

Unlike floppy or hard disk booting, CD booting is not mandatory. When you use a bootable CD to start your system, you will see a message prompting you to press a key to boot from the CD. If you don't press a key, the system goes to the next bootable device.

Fdisk

If the hard disk hasn't been partitioned yet, use the Fdisk program on the ESD or the Windows CD to create the partition(s) needed. See Chapter 15 for details.

Format

Each drive letter created with Fdisk must be formatted before it can be used. You do not need to use the /s (system) switch to format the drive before installing Windows, because the Windows setup program copies over the setup files. Note that the /s option is not available with the Windows Me Format program. See Chapter 15 for details.

Running Setup

Whether you're installing Windows 95, Windows 98, or Windows Me, the basic installation process is very similar. The following details are for the Windows 98 installation; I'll mention significant differences with other versions as needed.

Here's the process for installing from a CD-ROM drive:

1. Start SETUP.EXE from the CD-ROM.

2. After Windows 98 and Me check the installed drives for errors, the process continues.

3. If you agree to the **End-User License Agreement (EULA),** click OK, and the installation continues. If you don't, that's the end of the installation!

4. If you are using an upgrade version, provide the CD-ROM or floppy disks for your previous version of Windows when prompted (see Figure 16.5). If you provide floppy disks, Windows will check several before continuing. If you removed your Windows CD to put in the old version for the compliance check, a dialog box pops up to remind you to reinsert it.

FIGURE 16.5

The Upgrade Compliance Check dialog box is displayed if you are installing an upgrade version on a bare drive; use Browse to point to the location of your old Windows CD.

5. Enter the product key; full and upgrade versions put the product key on the back of the CD sleeve or jewel case. OEM versions might have the product key on the packaging around the manual, or sometimes on a sticker on the side or rear of the PC that included this copy of Windows.

6. Select an **installation path**. Use the default (`C:\Windows`) unless you want to set up a dual-boot with a previous version of Windows 9x/3.1 or MS-DOS. In such cases, change the default path from `C:\Windows` to another folder.

7. Select the installation type. Choose from

   - ■ *Typical*—Installs options most useful for desktop users.

   - ■ *Portable*—Installs options most useful for notebook users.

   - ■ *Compact*—Doesn't load options.

   - ■ *Custom*—You can choose the options you prefer.

> **tip**
>
> In a hurry to get your Windows installation done? Choose Compact and you'll save installation time and disk space.
>
> With any installation option, the optional programs and features installed can be changed through the Add/Remove Programs dialog box in Control Panel.

8. Enter your name and company name (you can skip the company name at home).

9. Choose the default options for the selected installation type, or view the list of options and change them as desired.

10. If you have a network card detected by Windows setup, enter your computer name, workgroup name, and a short description—see your network administrator for details (see Figure 16.6).

11. Choose your location (country or region) to set up defaults for currency and date formats. Some Windows versions put the Time Zone selection here, whereas others place this step later in the process.

12. Choose to create a startup disk. Skip this step only if you already have made a Windows ESD from the same Windows release.

▷ For details on creating a startup disk, **see** "Creating a Windows 9x/Me Emergency Startup Disk," **p. 551**.

13. The file-installation process starts. A status bar indicates system progress.

14. The system reboots automatically after completing the file-installation process.

FIGURE 16.6

The computer name must be unique on the network, but the name of the workgroup must be changed to match the name of the work-group you want the computer to join. If you don't see this dialog box, Windows couldn't detect your network card.

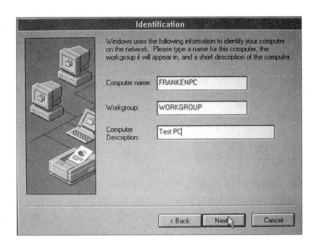

15. The setup program continues after the reboot, detecting hardware and PnP devices.

16. A status bar appears while the system checks for non-PnP hardware in the system.

17. The system restarts after non-PnP hardware is detected and installed.

18. The system loads drivers for hardware after the second reboot.

19. Select the Time Zone when prompted (some versions put this step earlier in the process). The U.S. English version of Windows 98 and Me defaults to the Pacific time zone.

20. Windows sets up the following for you:

    ■ Control Panel

    ■ Programs on Start menu

    ■ Windows Help

    ■ MS-DOS program settings

    ■ Tuning up application startup

    ■ System configuration

21. Windows reboots for a third time.

22. After restarting, Windows prompts you for a username and password (see Figure 16.7). You can leave the password line blank, and Windows 9x/Me

won't care (that's just one of the million or so reasons these versions of Windows are "insecure").

FIGURE 16.7
Entering the
username and
password in
Windows 98.

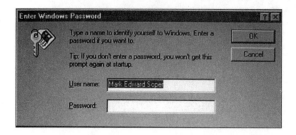

23. If your printer and other external devices are turned on, Windows will usually detect and configure them. You might need to supply drivers for some devices.

24. Windows sets up Internet Explorer and other software.

25. Windows displays the Welcome screen. It's time to install some applications and get to work!

Installing Windows 9x from a Network Drive

Windows 9x and Windows Me can be installed from a network drive. The process can also be automated with scripts with Windows 9x only. Windows 95 and 98 do network and automated installs differently, as you will see.

Installing Windows 95 from a Network Drive

Windows 95 uses the **Netsetup** program found on the Windows 95 full or upgrade CD to copy installation files to a supported network server (running Windows 95, Windows NT, Novell Netware 3.x, 4.x, and others). This program can also create a customized installation script stored as MSbatch.inf, which can be edited with Notepad or other plain-text (ASCII text) editors. The Batch utility can also be used to create setup scripts.

To start the installation from a network drive with an installation script, follow this procedure:

1. Start the computer with a DOS- or Windows-based network client.

2. Connect to the network folder containing the Windows 95 setup files.

3. Start the Windows 95 setup program using this command:
   ```
   Setup MSbatch.inf
   ```

(Change the `.inf` **file** as needed if you use a different name for your organization's installation script file.)

4. The installation proceeds as guided by the specified script file, asking for user input only if the script doesn't specify needed information.

Installing Windows 98 from a Network Drive

Windows 98 can also be installed from a network drive, but it uses different tools than Windows 95 to automate this type of installation.

To start, create the folder you want to use for the installation files and drag and drop the .CAB files into the folder. Use the Batch 98 tool (**Batch.exe**) to create setup scripts (see Figure 16.8). Compared to Windows 95's scripting tools, Batch 98 can customize scripts to practically eliminate user input, supports user profiles, automatically installs network clients and protocols as desired, can enable or disable Windows Update, and can generate scripts for multiple computers, among its major features.

Use the **Dbset.exe** utility to further customize setup scripts; Dbset can add a different user name to each script and customizes other options. It uses a text file for the customization information. The Infinst.exe utility adds device drivers or network drivers to the Windows 98 network folder used for installation so they can be used to support hardware not supported by the Windows 98 CD.

After the Windows 98 network installation folder is customized with installation scripts and additional driver files as needed, log into the folder and start the installation using the same methods as with Windows 95.

tip

Want to make installing Windows 95 even easier? A push installation automates the installation of Windows 95 even further. You can create a login script that starts the Windows 95 setup program automatically, or use other methods.

Windows 95 and Windows NT 4.0 don't include the Windows Script Host, but you can download it and its documentation from `http://msdn.microsoft.com/library/default.asp?url=/downloads/list/webdev.asp`.

To learn more about Windows Script Host, see the following Web sites:

`http://www.iopus.com/guides/wsh.htm`

`http://www.techtutorials.info/winscript.html`

FIGURE 16.8

The Batch 98 main menu (left) and its General Setup Options dialog box (right). Use the Save Settings to INF button to create the script after completing all dialogs and gathering Registry information.

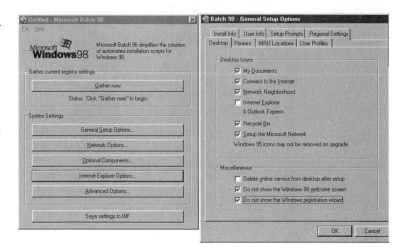

Installing Default Device Drivers

During installation, Windows uses default device drivers located on the Windows installation media for the devices it detects. Does this always work? No way! The Windows CD might not include drivers for all the devices attached to your system, and sometimes Windows selects the wrong drivers for your hardware. Although the Windows setup program prompts you to provide drivers for devices such as monitors and printers, it doesn't prompt you to provide device drivers for other devices. Thus, as soon as you complete a Windows installation or upgrade, open the Device Manager and see which devices need drivers (see Figure 16.9).

Updating Device Drivers

If some of your hardware isn't working correctly after the Windows installation process is over, you can open the Windows Device Manager and update the drivers. See Chapter 19 for details.

caution

As Figure 16.9 makes clear, you can't expect Windows 9x/Me to flawlessly support your hardware without some help. If you have only one computer, make sure you download the drivers you need before you take it out of service for a clean install.

Individual device that needs attention (yellow !)

FIGURE 16.9

The older the version of Windows, the more likely it is that several important devices will not be supported by the drivers on the Windows CD.

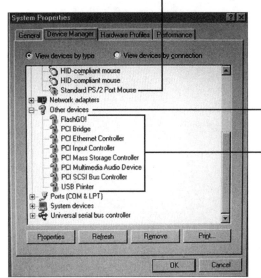

Category used by Windows for devices that need drivers

Devices in Other Devices (need drivers) category

Creating a Windows 9x/Me Emergency Startup Disk

If you used a startup disk from a different version of Windows to start your system, you should create an ESD when prompted by the Windows 9x/Me setup program (see Figure 16.10).

Insert a blank, formatted floppy disk into drive A: when prompted. After the disk is completed, label it and open the write-protect slider to prevent accidental erasure or tampering with the disk's contents. The disk can be used to restore startup files to a damaged Windows installation or to reinstall Windows (which is the only way to restore startup files if you have Windows Me).

⇨ For a step-by-step procedure for adding CD drivers to your Windows 95 startup disk, **see** "Adding CD-ROM Drive Support to the Windows 95 Startup Disk, " **p. 486**.

tip

Although the Windows 98 and Windows Me ESD include CD-ROM device drivers that are designed to operate most typical ATAPI and SCSI CD-ROM and similar optical drives, they might not work in every case. If the default drivers in `Config.sys` don't work for your drive, contact your drive vendor for the correct MS-DOS CD-ROM driver for your drive. Then, manually copy the correct driver file to the ESD and modify the `Config.sys` file to use it. To add CD-ROM support to the Windows 95 ESD, you must create `Autoexec.bat` and `Config.sys` files with the proper program and driver file to enable CD-ROM support.

FIGURE 16.10

Creating a
startup disk.
Even if you have
one from a dif-
ferent version of
Windows, you
should make
one that
matches the ver-
sion of Windows
you install.

Installing Windows NT 4.0

Windows NT 4.0 might be venerable (a polite way of saying "reeeealy old") in computer terms, but it's still around, and understanding how it works is a part of A+ certification. Who knows, you might even need to install it someday!

The process is a little different with Windows NT than with Windows 9x/Me:

1. Boot from the Windows NT 4.0 CD or the bootable setup disks you learned to
   create in Chapter 15.

2. Start the computer with the bootable setup disks.

3. Run the Windows setup program (which prepares the hard disk if necessary).

The following sections cover these steps in detail.

Installing Windows NT 4.0 to a Local Drive

Follow this procedure to perform a clean install of Windows NT 4.0:

1. Insert the Windows NT 4.0 CD into the computer's CD-ROM drive.

2. Turn on the system and allow the computer to boot from the Windows NT
   CD. Adjust the boot order if necessary as discussed in Chapter 6 or as shown
   in Figure 16.3. Use Winnt to start the installation process.

3. If the system won't boot from the Windows NT CD, create boot disks as
   described in Chapter 15 and restart the system with boot disk #1. Insert each
   disk as requested. The setup program starts after the last disk is inserted.

4. After the setup program pokes around your hardware, it prompts you for an
   installation location. Use the default location (c:\Winnt).

5. Create and format disk partition(s) when prompted. Windows NT 4.0 supports FAT16 and NTFS. See Chapter 15 for more information about file systems.

6. Select an installation option: Typical, Portable, Compact, or Custom.

Follow the prompts to complete the remainder of the process, which includes

■ Choose a computer name.

■ Choose **Administrator** account password.

■ Select optional components.

■ Create an Emergency Repair Disk.

■ Select network components (clients, protocols, services).

■ Configure regional settings and date/time.

caution

Windows NT 4.0 must be installed on a primary partition of 7.8GB or less in size. If you install it to a larger hard disk, use the remainder of the disk for an extended partition containing one or more logical drives.

7. If necessary, restart the system in VGA mode to install replacement graphics or other drivers after installation is finished.

Network Drive Installation of Windows NT

Windows NT 4.0 can be installed from a network drive or location. To perform an installation from the network, you need to

1. Create a shared folder on the network.

2. Copy the contents of the \I386 folder and its subfolders to the shared folder with Xcopy or with Windows Explorer.

To perform a clean install of Windows NT from this folder

1. Start the computer with a DOS network client (have fun with Config.sys and Autoexec.bat).

2. Connect to the network folder containing the Windows NT setup files and run WINNT.

When installing upgrades, you can use a Windows network client.

You can automate the network installation with the Setup Manager tool on the Windows NT 4.0 CD. This can be used to create a special text file called Unattend.txt, which contains the responses desired for computer name, time zone, product ID, network settings, file system, and so forth.

Installing Windows NT Default Device Drivers

Windows NT 4.0 automatically installs default device drivers for mass storage, graphics, and other device categories. If additional drivers are needed, in most cases they can be installed after initial configuration is completed.

However, if you need to add replacement **mass storage** (ATA/IDE or SCSI) device drivers, they should be installed during the initial installation process when you're prompted for replacement drivers.

For example, if you need to install Windows NT 4.0 on an ATA/IDE hard disk greater than 8GB, you should download Service Pack 4 or greater and extract the Atapi.sys file or download it directly from the Microsoft FTP site. This file should be copied to a floppy disk. When the system asks if you want it to detect your mass storage devices, press S to skip detection, press S again, and insert the disk. Press Enter twice to add the driver, and use it.

Updating Windows NT Device Drivers

You can update the device drivers used during the installation of Windows NT 4.0 with these methods:

- Specify the driver to use and provide its location instead of letting Windows NT detect your hardware; this is the correct way to handle updated mass storage drivers.

- Create an OEM folder if you use the Setup Manager to automate the installation and create Net or Display folders for network or display drivers.

After the installation, use the Control Panel icons for display, network, and so forth to install the correct drivers.

Creating a Windows NT 4.0 Emergency Repair Disk

During installation, you can (and should!) create a nonbootable emergency repair disk. This is a vital troubleshooting tool in the event your system malfunctions. This disk records the most essential parts of the Windows NT Registry. It can be used by the Windows NT setup program to repair a damaged registry. The disk is unique to each Windows NT installation, so make one for each computer. Even if two or more computers have identical hardware and software, each computer needs its own emergency repair disk.

Installing Windows 2000 Professional or XP

The installation process used by Windows 2000 Professional or Windows XP are similar in many ways to those used by earlier Windows versions. However, there are some differences, as you will see in the following sections.

Although Windows NT 4.0 can be installed as a dual-boot configuration, this is unlikely to be done very often because the operating system is practically obsolete. However, Windows 2000 and Windows XP are excellent candidates for dual-boot installations, so both clean install and dual-boot installations are covered in the following sections.

Local Drive Installation for Windows 2000/XP

Follow this procedure to install Windows 2000/XP on an unpartitioned (empty) drive:

1. If the system can be booted from a CD-ROM drive, insert the Windows CD-ROM into the CD-ROM drive and start the system; press a key as directed by your computer to boot from the CD and the installation program starts automatically. Unlike other Windows installation options, installing Windows this way starts by using a text-mode display. Use the keyboard rather than a mouse to make menu choices.

   If the system does not support booting from a CD-ROM drive, you can create Windows 2000 setup disks. You can download setup disk images for Windows XP, but they are not included on the Windows XP CD. See Chapter 15 for details. Insert the first setup disk and change disks as prompted until the Windows setup program starts.

2. If you are planning to install Windows 2000 or Windows XP on a RAID, Serial ATA, or SCSI drive, press F6 when prompted (look at the status line at the bottom of the screen) and provide the driver disk or CD when prompted (see Figure 16.11).

---

tip

You can also create an emergency repair disk for Windows NT 4.0 after installation with the Rdisk program. Click Start, Run, type

`C:\Winnt\system32\`
`Rdisk.exe /S` (/S backs up

user information) and click OK.

After the information is saved to the `c:\Winnt\repair` folder, insert a floppy disk and click Yes when you're asked if you want to create an emergency repair disk. Store the disk in a safe place, and configure the `c:\Winnt\repair` folder's permissions so that only the Administrators group and System have access.

If Windows NT 4.0 is installed to a different folder, substitute that folder name in these instructions.

As soon as the Windows 2000 or XP setup program starts, you have only a few moments to press F6 if you need to install a third-party SCSI or RAID driver (or Serial ATA driver).

Windows Setup

Press F6 if you need to install a third party SCSI or RAID driver...

Prompt to install mass storage drivers

3. Press Enter when prompted to start the Windows installation process.

4. Press F8 to accept the end-user license agreement.

5. If you are using an upgrade version for the installation, provide the CD from an eligible previous version of Windows as prompted.

6. Select the unpartitioned space on the empty hard drive for the installation; press Enter to install Windows on the unpartitioned space (see Figure 16.12), and skip to step 9.

7. To specify a partition size, press C to continue. Specify the partition size; you can press Enter to accept the default (the entire capacity of the drive) or type a smaller size and press Enter (see Figure 16.13).

8. Select the partition into which to install Windows; specify the partition you created in step 6.

note

If you previously partitioned the hard disk, you can use an existing disk partition. However, it's not mandatory. You can even delete and remake disk partitions with Windows 2000 and Windows XP's setup programs.

Options to install (to a single partition)
or create a smaller partition

FIGURE 16.12

Partitioning
options in the
Windows XP
program.

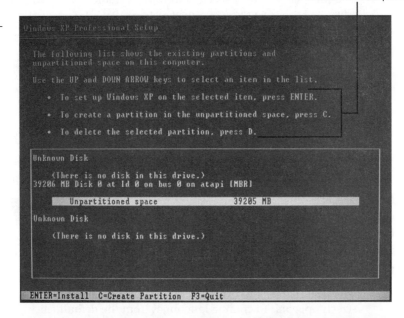

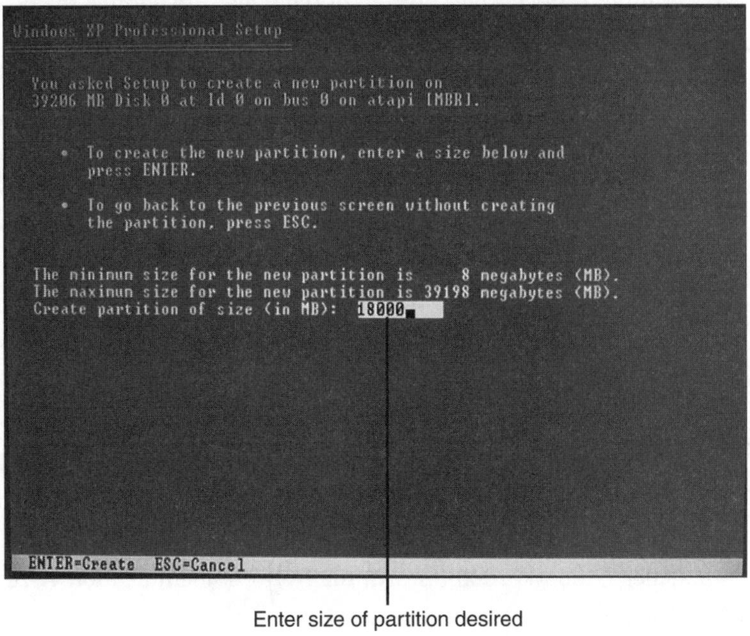

FIGURE 16.13

Creating an
18GB partition
with the
Windows XP
setup program.
You can create
an extended
partition and
logical drives
with the setup
program, or
leave the rest of
the disk empty
until a later
time.

Enter size of partition desired

9. Select NTFS or FAT for the partition (if the partition is under 32GB in size), and press Enter. If you specify FAT, the partition will be FAT16 if it is under 2GB in size and FAT32 if it is 2GB or larger. Windows XP offers the option to perform a quick format (saves time) or a regular format (takes longer but verifies all of the disk surface).

10. Windows formats the partition with the file system you specify and continues the installation process.

11. After copying files, the system reboots.

12. The Windows graphics-mode Setup Wizard starts after the reboot; click Next.

Windows 2000 and Windows XP are practically identical up to this point, but after the graphics mode starts (and your mouse finally works!), their installations are significantly different. See the sections that follow for details.

Completing the Installation of Windows 2000

After the Windows 2000 setup program switches to graphics mode, follow these steps to complete a clean install:

1. After Windows detects your system's hardware, the **Regional Settings** screen appears. To change languages from the default, click the Customize button in the Locales portion of the screen. To change the default keyboard layout, click the Customize button in the Keyboard portion of the screen. The current defaults for both are displayed. Click Next.

2. On the Personalize Your Software screen, enter the user name and company name (if any). Click Next.

3. On the Product Key screen, enter the product key found on the back of the CD-ROM case or sleeve. The installation can't go any further until you enter the product key correctly.

4. Enter the computer name and Administrator password; ask the network administrator for this information. Click Next.

5. On the Date & Time Settings screen, select the date, time, time zone, and whether to use daylight savings time adjustments. Click Next.

6. After components are installed, the Final Tasks screen appears. Click Next.

7. Click Finish on the Completing the Windows 2000 Setup Wizard display, and the system reboots.

8. After Windows 2000 restarts, the Network Identification Wizard starts. Click Next.

9. Complete the Users of This Computer dialog box. Specify either Users Must Enter a User Name and Password to Use This Computer or Windows Always Assumes the Following User Has Logged On to This Computer. Enter the username and password to use for the default user and click Next (see Figure 16.14). If you select Users Must Enter a User Name and Password to Use This Computer, enter the username and password for each user.

FIGURE 16.14

For convenience, select the Windows Always Assumes the Following User Has Logged On to This Computer option. For security, select the User Must Enter a User Name and Password to Use This Computer option.

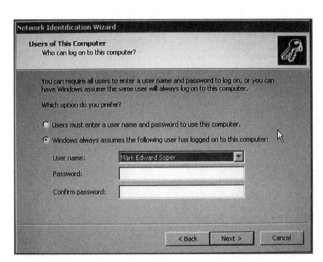

10. Click Finish when done. Windows 2000 logs on the default user (if any) or prompts you for a username and password. This completes the installation of Windows 2000. Now, get to work!

Completing the Installation of Windows XP

After the Windows XP setup program switches to graphics mode, follow these steps to complete a clean install:

1. Click Customize to change regional and language options, Details to adjust text input languages, or Next.

2. Enter your name and organization. Click Next.

3. Windows XP generates a computer name. Change it (if you don't like it) and enter the Administrator Name and password and click Next.

4. If your computer has a modem, provide the correct dialing information when prompted.

5. Verify or change date and time settings. Click Next.

6. If your computer has a network card, you'll see the network settings screen shown in Figure 16.15. When prompted for network settings, select **Typical** if you are networked with other Windows 2000/XP users only and click Next. Then, skip to step 8. Select **Custom** if the network also includes Windows 9x/Me computers or non-Windows computers. Click Next.

FIGURE 16.15

Keep Typical
network settings
(default) if you
don't have an
IEEE-1394 host
adapter and
don't connect to
Windows 9x/Me
computers.
Otherwise, click
Custom to fine-
tune your net-
work
configuration.

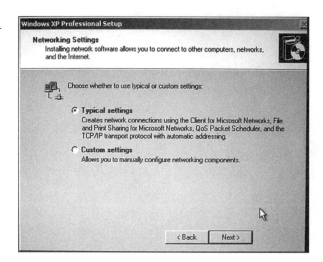

7. If you select Custom and have an IEEE-1394 adapter, it can be used as a net-work adapter. If you don't plan to use it to connect to other computers, clear the check boxes for its network components and click Next.

8. Clear the check box next to QoS Packet Scheduler on the Ethernet adapter configuration screen if you connect to Windows 9x/Me computers; leaving this feature enabled slows down connections with Windows 9x/Me or other non-Windows systems (see Figure 16.16). Click Install to add other network protocols, clients, or services. Click Next when done.

9. Enter the workgroup name or domain name (Windows XP Professional only) the computer will join when prompted. If you select domain, provide the username and password required to join the domain.

10. At the end of the process, the Welcome to Microsoft Windows dialog box is displayed. You can use it to activate your copy of Windows (see Figure 16.17) and set up users.

11. After you complete the steps listed in the Welcome dialog box, the Windows XP desktop is displayed. Restart the computer if prompted to complete instal-lation of some devices.

FIGURE 16.16
Adjusting the
default settings
for this com-
puter's Fast
Ethernet
adapter.

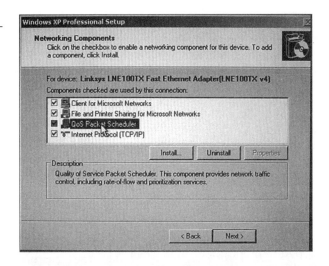

FIGURE 16.17
You have up to
30 days to
activate
Windows XP.

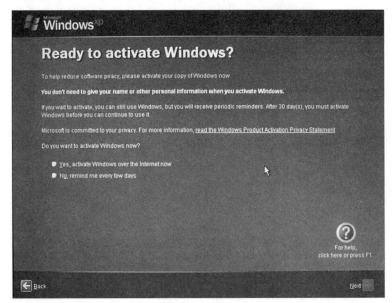

Installing Windows 2000 or XP in a Dual-Boot Configuration

You can select whether to install Windows 2000 or XP as an upgrade to Windows
9x/Me (replacing it) or whether to install Windows 2000 or XP in a separate folder or
separate disk partition, allowing you to dual boot Windows 9x/Me and Windows
2000/XP. If you have hardware or software that can function with Windows 9x/Me
but not Windows 2000/XP, dual booting your old version of Windows with 2000/XP

makes a lot of sense. Just remember that any software or hardware incompatible with Windows XP will need to be run under Windows 9x/Me, which can mean a lot or rebooting if you use that particular piece of software or hardware often.

If possible, install Windows 2000/XP in its own disk partition on the system; installing it on the same disk partition as Windows 9x/Me might prevent these versions of Windows from running correctly.

If you select the dual-boot option, make sure you do not change the file system on the boot drive from the default (FAT16 or FAT32) to NTFS when prompted during installation. Although NTFS has many advantages as described in Chapter 15, NTFS is not compatible with Windows 9x/Me. Thus, you must keep the drive's current file system if you want to use the same disk partition for both Windows 2000/XP and Windows 9x/Me. If you install Windows 2000/XP to its own disk partition (which is what I recommend), you can convert the partition to NTFS during installation.

Installing Windows 2000 to Dual Boot with Windows 9x/Me

To perform a dual-boot installation of Windows 2000 with Windows 9x/Me, follow these instructions:

1. Start Windows 9x/Me.

2. Insert the Windows 2000 CD-ROM.

3. To start the upgrade process, click Yes when the computer asks `Would you like to upgrade to Windows 2000 now?`.

4. On the Welcome to the Windows 2000 Setup Wizard, select Install a New Copy of Windows 2000; click Next.

> **tip**
>
> It's easier to activate Windows over the Internet than to call Microsoft and read the product ID to a bored technician. Just because Windows XP installs network services doesn't mean the network is ready to work at the end of the installation process. My advice? Just say "no" to **product activation** at first startup. Make sure your Internet connection works, and then activate Windows XP on a future restart. You have 30 days to activate it, so take your time and make sure your Internet connection (LAN or dial-up) is working.

> **note**
>
> Although I don't cover the details here, you can also install Windows NT 4.0 as a dual-boot operating system.

5. Agree to the end-user license agreement, and enter the CD-ROM key when prompted.

6. Use the Special Options menu to adjust defaults for location (language), Advanced options (source and destination folders), and Accessibility settings if desired.

7. Use the Advanced button to specify the disk partition to use for Windows 2000 (point to empty space), choose the location of the Windows 2000 files, choose the installation folder name, or copy the setup files to the hard disk for extra speed (see Figure 16.18). Click OK when you're finished.

tip

If you have 20GB or more of unused space on your drive, this is more than enough room for Windows 2000/XP. Use a disk repartitioning program such as PowerQuest's Partition Magic or V Communication's Partition Commander to shrink the size of your existing Windows 9x/Me partitions to make room for a Windows 2000/XP partition. I recommend that you shrink the existing partition enough to leave at least 15GB of space available for the new partition Windows 2000/XP will create during installation.

FIGURE 16.18

The Advanced Options menu enables you to control file and folder names and locations for the Windows 2000 installation.

Advanced Options

You can select advanced options to customize Setup.

Location of Windows 2000 files:
K:\I386   Browse...

Windows installation folder:
\WINNT

☐ Copy all Setup files from the Setup CD to the hard drive
☐ I want to choose the installation partition during Setup

OK   Cancel

8. The file-copying process starts. The computer reboots after setup files are copied.

9. After the system reboots, select Setup from the list of options (which also includes Repair or Exit installation).

10. If the drive has more than one partition, select an empty partition (or unpartitioned space) for installation; you can install into the same partition as Windows 9x or choose a different partition or free space if available (recommended).

note

If **Autorun** has been disabled on your system, you can open the setup program on the Windows 2000 CD-ROM from Windows Explorer to start.

11. When asked to keep the partition as the current file system or to convert the partition to NTFS, keep the current file system unless you have selected a different partition for Windows 2000 than for Windows 9x.

12. Adjust Regional settings if needed; these include location settings (language and country/region), numbers, currency, time, date, and input languages.

13. Adjust the keyboard layout if needed—QWERTY is standard for U.S. locations.

14. Enter your name and organization.

15. If the computer has a network card, you'll be prompted to enter the computer name and administrator password (consult the network manager for this information).

16. Confirm the date and time.

17. Choose the default network components (TCP/IP with Automatic IP Address, Client for Microsoft Networks, and File and Print Sharing) or select options and settings as needed. (Consult the network manager for this information.) See Chapter 21, "Networking and Internet Connectivity," for details about network protocols and configuration.

18. Enter the domain name or workgroup.

19. Click Finish when the configuration tasks are completed. The system reboots.

20. Complete the Network Identification Wizard. Windows 2000 assumes that a single user will log on to the system; change this option to require a name and password if a domain controller (specified in step 14) will be used to verify users.

When you install Windows 2000 with the dual-boot option, a startup menu always appears. The system will start Windows 2000 in 30 seconds unless you select Microsoft Windows, which runs your previous version of Windows (95/98).

Installing Windows XP to Dual Boot

Follow this procedure to install Windows XP as a dual boot with another Windows version. I recommend this for users of Windows 9x/Me, but you can also install Windows XP to dual boot with Windows NT 4.0 or Windows 2000.

1. Start your existing version of Windows.

2. Insert the Windows XP CD-ROM.

3. Unless you've disabled AutoRun, the Windows XP splash screen is displayed. Choose Install Windows XP, Perform Additional Tasks, or Check System Compatibility from the splash screen. Open Setup from Windows Explorer if necessary.

4. Click Check System Compatibility to run the Windows XP Upgrade Advisor. You can run the advisor or go to the compatibility Web site.

5. After completing the Upgrade Advisor check, review any problems it found. Then, click Install Windows XP.

6. Select New Installation (Advanced) and click Next (see Figure 16.19).

FIGURE 16.19

Selecting the New Installation (Advanced) option to install Windows XP as a dual-boot operating system.

tip

Why run the Windows XP Upgrade Advisor if you're performing a dual boot with your old operating system and you need to reinstall your software anyway? There are two good reasons:

- The Upgrade Advisor will tell you if your existing 9x/Me software won't work with XP (so you know it's time for a replacement).

- The Upgrade Advisor will also let you know if some of your hardware might not work with Windows XP (so you can get your own drivers or try Windows 2000 drivers instead).

7. Read the license agreement, click I Accept, and then click Next to continue.

8. Enter the product key from the back of the CD package and click Next to continue.

9. Click the Advanced Options button on the Setup Options screen.

10. Click the I Want to Choose the Install Drive Letter and Partition During Setup box. Click OK and click Next.

11. To update the Windows setup files with new ATA or SCSI drivers, press F6 when prompted and insert the CD or floppy disk containing the driver.

12. After the computer restarts, press Enter when prompted to continue setup.

13. Select unpartitioned space for the installation (see Figure 16.20); Windows XP changes this space to the next available partition number during formatting.

14. Select the file system to use for Windows XP (see Figure 16.21). See Chapter 15 for more details about file systems. If you tested the drive before starting the install procedure, choose the Quick method. Otherwise, choose the regular format (the regular format takes a long time).

Existing operating system partition (Windows 98)

FIGURE 16.20

Preparing to
select empty
space on the
hard disk for the
Windows XP
installation.

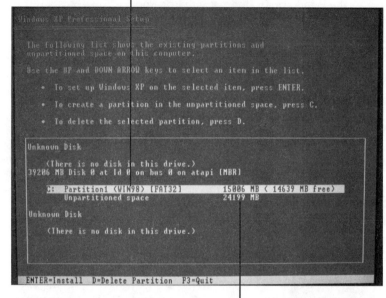

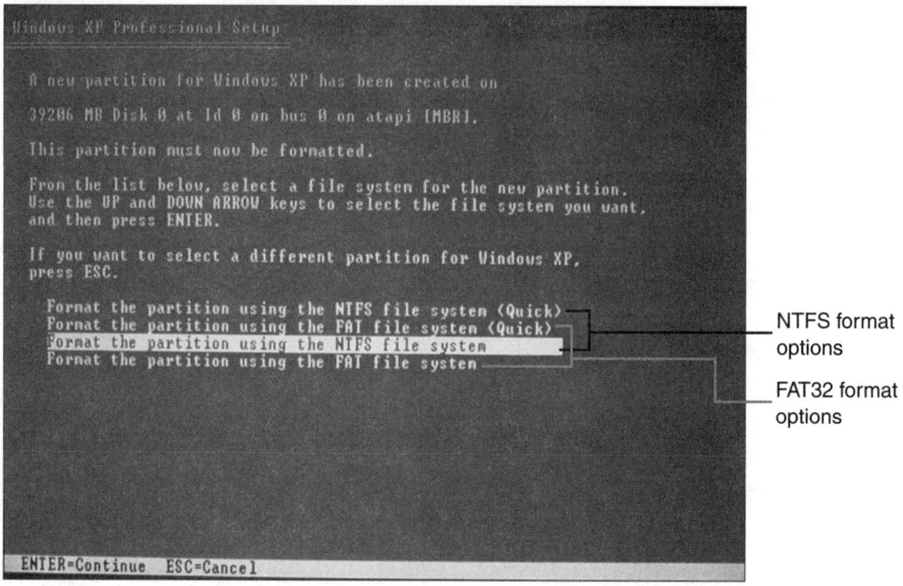

Unpartitioned space (use with Windows XP)

FIGURE 16.21

When a disk
partition is
under 32GB, you
can format it as
a FAT partition
or an NTFS par-
tition with
Windows XP
and 2000.

NTFS format
options

FAT32 format
options

The remainder of the installation is similar to the process used for a clean install.

Installing the Applications You Want to Use

There's one disadvantage to a dual-boot installation: you need to reinstall your favorite software so the new Windows installation can use it. In most cases, applications you use with Windows 9x/Me will also work with Windows XP or 2000, but utility programs such as Norton Utilities/System Works, antivirus programs, and disk-management programs might need to be upgraded to an XP- or 2000-compatible version.

Network Drive Installation with Windows 2000 and XP

You can install Windows 2000 or Windows XP from a network drive using the same basic method as that outlined for Windows NT 4.0. This requires the user to start the computer with a network client and log on to the server to start the process. The Unattend.txt file provides the responses needed to the prompts throughout the installation process. Both Windows 2000 and Windows XP Professional include the Setupmgr.exe program on the distribution CDs to aid in the creation of the Unattend.txt file.

If you want to automate the process, Windows 2000 and Windows XP can both be installed from a network drive automatically using the Remote Installation Services (RIS) program, which can be installed on Windows 2000 Server and Windows Server 2003.

The RIS works along with the Windows Setup Manager Wizard found on the Windows 2000 and Windows XP CD-ROMs. This program is used to create an answer file. As with Windows NT 4.0, the answer file provides the responses needed for the installation.

tip

If you don't have enough empty space on your first hard disk (called disk 0 by Windows XP), you can use empty space on the second hard disk (disk 1) if you have one. The boot manager Windows XP installs will keep everything straight (ditto with Windows 2000). If you want to install Windows XP to the second hard disk, be sure to choose disk 1.

note

Automated deployment is covered in more detail in the book, *Platinum Edition Using Windows XP*, by Robert Cowart and Brian Knittel (Que Publishing, 2003). *Windows XP Under the Hood: Hardcore Windows Scripting and Command-Line Power* by Brian Knittel (Que Publishing, 2002) covers using Windows Script Host and working in the command-line environment. Much of this material also applies to Windows 2000.

Installing Default Device Drivers with Windows 2000/XP

Windows 2000 and Windows XP copy default device drivers to the system during installation. If you need to add new mass storage (ATA or SCSI) drivers, press F6 when prompted and provide the CD or floppy disk containing the drivers.

Updating Device Drivers

You can use the Device Manager to update drivers after installation. Windows XP typically recognizes and installs drivers for more devices than Windows 2000, but you might still need to manually update some drivers or update them with Windows Update. See Chapter 19 for details.

Installing Windows 2000 or XP from a Disk Image and Updating the SID

Like making copies? Sick and tired of installing Windows from scratch on 20 identical PCs? Windows NT/2000/XP can be installed from a disk image of another installation created with a program such as Norton Ghost or PowerQuest Drive Image. This process is called *disk cloning*.

For disk cloning to work, the systems must be identical in every major feature, including

- Same motherboard
- Same ATA/IDE or SCSI host adapter
- Same BIOS configuration

At a Windows software level, the systems must use the same Hardware Abstraction Layer (HAL) and the same Ntoskrnl.exe (NT kernel) file.

The hard disk of the target for a cloned installation must be at least as large as the original system, or larger.

A cloned system is identical in every way to the original, including having the same **Security Identifier Number (SID)**. This can cause conflicts in a network. The SID and other differences in network configuration between the original and a cloned system can be automatically configured with the Sysprep utility from Microsoft. The

caution

Do *not* use disk cloning to make illegal copies of Windows. You can use disk-cloning software legally to make a backup copy of your installation, but if you want to duplicate the installation on another PC, make sure you are cloning a system created with a multiple-computer license for Windows and make sure that you do not exceed the number of systems covered by that license. You can clone standalone computers or those connected to a workgroup (but not a domain).

Sysprep utility is available in separate versions for Windows NT/2000/XP. It is not provided on upgrade versions, but on full and OEM versions of the media.

Sysprep is installed on a system that will be used for cloning before it is cloned. A special mini-Setup Wizard starts on the cloned computer the first time it is run after cloning. Sysprep uses an answer file created with the Setupmgr utility described earlier. When it runs on the cloned system, it creates a unique SID and makes other changes as needed to the network configuration of the system.

The SIDWalker utility can be used to change SIDs manually on Windows NT 4.0/2000.

The Windows XP version of Sysprep has additional features compared to the Windows NT 4.0/2000 versions, including factory (configures computer with customized settings or applications as desired) and auditing (checks system for functionality before delivering it to an end user).

note

The version of Sysprep on the Windows NT 4.0/XP CD-ROM is ready to use. However, although a version of Sysprep is included on the Windows 2000 CD, you should download an improved version from the Microsoft Web site.

Installing Windows from a Recovery CD

Most vendors no longer provide a full installation CD of Windows for computers with preinstalled Windows installations. Instead, a **recovery CD** (or sometimes a hidden hard disk partition) containing a special image of the Windows installation is provided. Systems that store the image on a hidden disk partition might offer the opportunity to create a restore image on a recordable CD (CD-R).

Typically, you have limited choices when you want to restore a damaged installation with a recovery CD or recovery files on a disk partition. Typical options include

- Reformatting your hard disk and restoring it to just-shipped condition (causing the loss of all data and programs installed after the system was first used)

note

A recovery CD is also known as a *system restoration CD*. In any case, these special versions of Windows aren't standalone copies of Windows, meaning you can't use them to install Windows on another PC (unless the PC is identical to the one for which the CD was made).

■ Reinstalling Windows only

■ Reinstalling support files or additional software

Recovery CDs can't be used to perform a clean install of Windows on an empty hard disk. They can fail if third-party hardware has been installed in the computer; it might be necessary to remove third-party hardware before running the recovery CD. Frankly, these limitations make me hate recovery CDs, but sometimes it's all you have.

After you run the recovery CD to restore your system to its original condition, you might need to activate it again if you're running Windows XP.

> **caution**
>
> You might need a CD key or your system's serial number to run the recovery CD program. Keep this information handy.

Restoring User Data Files

After you have installed Windows as a clean installation, you can **restore** the data files you backed up before the installation process.

If you copied them to other media or a network location with drag and drop, you can drag and drop them back to the desired location. However, if you created the backup with a tape drive or other device that uses backup software, you must install the backup software and device to restore the files.

Troubleshooting Your Installation

All versions of Windows covered on the A+ Certification Operating System Exam have troubleshooting tools you can use to determine why an installation isn't working properly. The following sections discuss how to use these tools and methods.

General Installation Troubleshooting

Two of the major problems that can prevent you from completing an installation include

■ *Hardware conflicts*—Change the hardware resource settings on legacy (non-PnP) hardware to values that don't interfere with PnP devices, or remove them for reinstallation later.

■ *Not enough disk space*—To ensure that you can complete the installation, make sure the partition you will use for installing Windows has at least the recommended minimum free disk space.

Troubleshooting the Windows 9x/Me Installation

The four files that provide valuable clues to why a Windows 9x/Me installation or initial startup has failed are

- Detlog.txt
- Netlog.txt
- Setuplog.txt
- Bootlog.txt

All these files are hidden files stored in the root folder of the Windows installation drive (normally C:\). Change the default settings in the Windows Explorer to Show All Files to display these files. You can examine the contents of these files with either Notepad or WordPad.

↪   For more information about displaying all files in the Windows Explorer, **see** "Changing Viewing Options in Windows Explorer," **p. 628**.

If Windows 9x/Me fails to complete its installation, a very long file called Detlog.txt can be used to figure out what happened. Detlog.txt lists the hardware devices that Windows is looking for. If the Windows 9x/Me upgrade process stops, the last entries in Detlog.txt indicate what was being checked at the time of the lockup, enabling you to remove or reconfigure the hardware that caused the installation to fail.

The Netlog.txt file records the network configuration of Windows 9x/Me during initial installation. If network devices do not work, examine this file to see if the end of any lines indicate error messages or error numbers.

Setuplog.txt is a file that records every event of the installation process. If the Windows 9x/Me installation process doesn't finish, check the end of the file to see at what point the installation failed.

An installation might appear to succeed, but it isn't really finished until the system restarts successfully. The Bootlog.txt file records every event during the startup process. Bootlog.txt is generated automatically the first time Windows 9x/Me is started; whenever a new Bootlog.txt is generated, the previous version is renamed Bootlog.prv (replacing any existing Bootlog.prv). As with the other files discussed here, the end of the file is the critical location to look at if Windows can't start. Unlike other files, which are very complex to read, Bootlog.txt is relatively simple: Virtually every START event will have either a matching SUCCESS event, a FAILED event, or no match (if the system locks up after STARTing an event). If Windows 9x/Me locks up, check the end of the file to determine the last driver or process that was STARTed without a matching SUCCESS or FAILED; that is the usual cause of the problem.

Troubleshooting a Windows NT/2000/XP Installation

Windows 2000/XP create various logfiles during installation and startup that can be used to determine if there were any problems encountered. Files marked with an asterisk (*) are also created by Windows NT 4.0 during installation. Most files are found in the root folder of the default Windows system drive.

- `setuperr.log`—Records errors (if any) during installation; check this one first if an installation fails.

- `setuplog.txt`—Records events during the text-mode portion of installation.

- `setupapi.log*`—Records events triggered by an `.inf` file (typically used for hardware installation) from original installation (top of file) to present (bottom of file).

- `setupact.log`—Logs all events created by the GUI-mode setup program (including updates to the system). This file doesn't use internal data/timestamps, so you might want to make a copy of it as soon as you install Windows. It grows with subsequent installations of hotfixes, updates, and so forth.

- `winnt32.log` or `winnt.log`—Created during installation by the corresponding program. By default, lists warnings (level 2), but you can change the level information it stores with the `/debug:level` switch. Windows NT 4.0 creates similar `$winnt.log` files with the `/l` switch.

- `ntbtlog.txt*`—Logs drivers installed during a Safe Mode boot or when bootlog is chosen as a startup option.

These files are all stored in plain-text mode, so they can be viewed with a text editor. Use the methods listed in the previous section for interpreting these files.

If Windows NT/2000/XP is installed on a FAT16 or FAT32 drive, you can start the computer with a Windows 9x/Me boot disk and copy these files to a floppy disk for viewing on another system. If Windows 2000/XP is installed on an NTFS drive, you can use the Windows boot disks or CD to start the system, launch the Recovery Console, and view the files with the `More` command: `More setuplog.txt` displays the contents of the `Setuplog.txt` file.

> **tip**
>
> Start the system in Safe Mode (if possible) and you can use the Windows GUI-based tools such as Notepad to read the files.

Study Lab

Don't miss the Study Lab materials found on the CD accompanying this book. Each Study Lab is tailored to the individual chapters in this book, meaning that you'll quickly be able to determine which topics you understand well enough to pass the exam and which topics need more study. The Study Labs are presented in printable PDF format so that you can take them with you to study at work, on the road, or even in your car just before test time!

THE ABSOLUTE MINIMUM

- ▓ You need to make sure your system meets the performance and free disk space requirements of a particular operating system before you install it.

- ▓ You can install an operating system on an empty disk (clean install), as a replacement (upgrade), or as an additional boot option (dual boot).

- ▓ Upgrades keep existing programs and data, whereas clean installs wipe out existing data and programs. Dual-boot installs don't affect existing programs and data, but can't run programs until they're reinstalled.

- ▓ Windows 9x/Me use `Setup.exe` to start the setup process. Windows 2000 and XP also use `setup.exe`. Windows NT uses `winnt32.exe` or `winnt.exe`.

- ▓ NTFS is the preferred file system for Windows NT/2000/XP installations, whereas FAT32 is the preferred file system for Windows 9x/Me installations except for early Windows 95.

- ▓ Windows 9x/Me installations require the user to run Fdisk and Format first, whereas Windows NT/2000/XP installations can perform partitioning and formatting during installation.

- ▓ Windows NT 4.0 and 2000 can create setup floppy disks if the CD can't be used for booting, but Windows XP requires the user to download bootable floppies if the CD can't be used for booting.

- ▓ After a dual-boot installation, you must install the programs you want to use with the new version of Windows.

- ▓ You can install Windows NT/2000/XP from a disk image onto multiple PCs, but you must change the SID (Security Identifier Number) to avoid duplication.

- ▓ `Detlog`, `netlog`, `setuplog`, and `bootlog` (all .txt files) track activity and changes to a Windows 9x/Me computer during installation and startup. They are useful for troubleshooting.

- ▓ Windows NT uses the `$winnt.log`, `ntbtlog.txt`, and `setupapi.log` files to track installation, setup, and startup activity. Windows 2000/XP use `setuperr.log`, `setuplog.txt`, `setupapi.log`, `setupact.log`, `winnt32.log/winnt.log`, and `ntbtlog.txt` to perform these tasks. They are useful for troubleshooting.

17

OPERATING SYSTEM UPGRADES

No matter how much you like your operating system now, sooner or later you'll probably need to replace it. In this chapter, you'll learn how to upgrade older versions of Windows to Windows 98, Windows 2000 Professional, or Windows XP Professional. If you want to pass the A+ Certification operating systems exam, you need to understand the different parts of the upgrade process. Upgrading makes sense if you want to keep using existing software and settings, but prefer the advantages of a newer version of Windows.

If you prefer to keep your existing Windows 9x/Me or Windows 2000 installation around for awhile and still install Windows 2000 or Windows XP, check back in Chapter 16, "Operating System Installation," for information about dual booting (another important part of the A+ Certification operating systems exam). I cover how to dual boot Windows 98 and MS-DOS in this chapter.

Upgrading to Windows 98

The process of upgrading to **Windows 98** varies, depending upon the version of Windows already installed. The following sections describe typical upgrade processes.

Preparations to Make Before Upgrading to Windows 98

If you are upgrading from **MS-DOS/Windows 3.1** or **Windows 95** to Windows 98, follow these procedures before performing the upgrade:

- Back up hard drives. If a full hard drive **backup** isn't possible, back up data files to avoid data loss in case of a problem with the upgrade. For maximum safety, use the **Byte-by-Byte Verify** option during backup if available, and test the backup by restoring some files to an empty hard drive or empty folder.

- Disable **EMM386.EXE** or other memory managers in Config.sys that provide access to upper memory blocks (UMBs), the memory addresses between 640KB and 1MB that are not occupied by RAM or ROM chips; these can interfere with software installation. Keep Device=Himem.sys and DOS=High options in the Config.sys file.

- Disable Load= and Run= statements in the **Win.ini** file used by Windows 3.1; verify that drivers in the System.ini file used by Windows 3.1 refer to installed hardware only.

- If Windows 98–specific drivers are not available for your video card, set your Windows video type to VGA before the installation because all SVGA cards will also run as VGA.

Microsoft sometimes refers to upgrades as "replace in place" installations.

If you are upgrading from Windows 3.1 to Windows 98, you should also back up the following **.grp files** to a floppy disk:

- Startup.grp
- Oldstart.grp

Then, delete all icons listed in your **Startup folder**; many of these programs will not run properly under Windows 98 and might not be needed.

Upgrading to Windows 98 from MS-DOS

Windows 98 enables you to dual boot with MS-DOS automatically if only MS-DOS is installed on the system before you start the installation process.

.grp files are used by Windows 3.1 to store pointers to programs.

If MS-DOS has CD-ROM support already installed

1. Boot the computer to an MS-DOS prompt.
2. Insert the Windows 98 CD-ROM.
3. Change to the drive letter for the CD-ROM drive.
4. Type **Setup** and press Enter to start the upgrade process. Proceed as described in "Upgrading to Windows 98 from Windows 95" later in this chapter.

To boot back to MS-DOS after installing Windows 98, do one of the following when the system restarts:

- Press the F4 function key.
- Press the Ctrl key and choose Start Previous Version of MS-DOS from the list of options.

Most MS-DOS programs stored in the \DOS folder work as they normally do, but the following disk utilities programs are removed or disabled because they won't work with long filenames:

- Drvspace (MS-DOS 6.22)
- Dblspace (MS-DOS 6.0, 6.2)
- Defrag (MS-DOS 6.x)
- Scandisk (MS-DOS 6.x)

When you try to run any of these programs, a message appears onscreen informing you of the steps you need to follow to run the Windows 98 equivalent.

Upgrading to Windows 98 from Windows 3.1

Installing Windows 98 on a machine that has Windows 3.1 running on it requires that you first decide whether you want to replace Windows 3.1 or create a dual-boot environment that allows you to run your choice of Windows 3.1 or Windows 98.

Using the default installation location for Windows 98 (C:\Windows) replaces your Windows 3.1 installation with Windows 98 and prevents dual booting with your old version of Windows. If you choose a different installation location (for example, C:\Win98), you can dual boot Windows 3.1 as well as MS-DOS as discussed earlier. However, you will need to reinstall any Windows 3.1 applications you still want to use with Windows 98.

The easiest way to start the upgrade to Windows 98 is to follow these steps:

1. Start Windows 3.1.
2. Open the **File Manager**.

tip

The Windows Notepad DOS Edit, Sysedit (Windows 9x/NT 4.0), or MSConfig (Windows Me version) programs can be used to edit plain-text configuration files such as **Config.exe**, **Autoexec.bat**, **Win.ini**, and **System.ini**.

Follow these tips to make needed changes referred to in the previous section:

- To disable a device driver in Config.sys or a command in Autoexec.bat, place the word **REM** at the beginning of the line containing the command or driver. For example,

  device=c:\windows\
  emm386.exe RAM

  can be commented out by editing the line like this:

  REM device=c:\windows\
  emm386.exe RAM

  The system ignores any line preceded by REM in Config.sys or Autoexec.bat.

- To disable a statement in Win.ini or System.ini, use a semicolon instead of the word REM. For example,

  load=printspl.exe

  can be commented out by editing the line like this:

  ; load=printspl.exe

  Be sure to back up any files you edit.

3. Insert the Windows 98 CD-ROM.

4. Open the `Setup.exe` file on the CD-ROM and continue as described in "Upgrading to Windows 98 from Windows 95" later in this chapter.

You can choose to upgrade Windows 3.1 or install Windows 98 in its own folder when you start the Windows 98 upgrade from within Windows 3.1. You can specify any name for Windows 98's own folder, but I recommend using the name `Win98`.

UPGRADING THE WINDOWS 3.1 INSTALLATION TO WINDOWS 98

If you install Windows 98 into the same folder as Windows 3.1, the Windows 3.1 program groups (`.grp` files) and `.ini` files, such as `Win.ini`, `System.ini`, and others, will be used to set up the Windows 98 desktop and Registry. Each `.grp` file becomes a folder of shortcuts visible when you click Start, and then Programs. The `.ini` entries will be transferred to the Windows Registry.

Upgrading to Windows 98 from Windows 95

As with Windows 3.1, the easiest way to start the upgrade process to Windows 98 is to

1. Start Windows 95.

2. Open the **Windows Explorer**.

3. Insert the Windows 98 CD-ROM—this starts the Autorun.exe program in the root folder of the CD-ROM, which displays several options onscreen.

4. To start the upgrade process, answer Yes when the computer asks, `Do you want to upgrade your computer to this new version of Windows 98 now?`.

5. Answering Yes starts the Setup program for you and carries over your existing Windows 95 program groups and preferences to Windows 98. Close the Autorun menu after the Setup program starts so you can make the user entries needed.

According to Microsoft, Windows 95 and 98 cannot be used in a dual-boot configuration, although third-party boot managers, third-party partition managers, and unofficial hacks on the World Wide Web all provide unauthorized methods for bypassing this limitation.

Updating Windows 98

To download the latest security and other updates for Windows 98, click Start, Windows Update to launch the Microsoft Windows Update service. **Windows Update** is customized to the version of Windows on your computer. For details of how it works, see "Installing Windows 2000 Service Packs and Updates," later in this chapter.

Troubleshooting the Windows 98 Upgrade

The four files that provide valuable clues to why a Windows 9x installation or initial startup has failed are

- `Detlog.txt`
- `Netlog.txt`
- `Setuplog.txt`
- `Bootlog.txt`

All these files are hidden files stored in the root folder of the Windows installation drive (normally C:\). Change the default settings in the Windows Explorer to Show All Files to display these files. For more information about displaying all files in the Windows Explorer, see "Changing Viewing Options in Windows Explorer," in Chapter 18, "Using and Optimizing Windows." You can examine the contents of these files with either Notepad or WordPad.

If Windows 9x fails to complete its installation, a very long file called `Detlog.txt` can be used to figure out what happened. `Detlog.txt` lists the hardware devices that Windows 9x is looking for. If the Windows 9x upgrade process stops, the last entries in `Detlog.txt` indicate what was being checked at the time of the lockup, enabling you to remove or reconfigure the hardware that caused the installation to fail.

The `Netlog.txt` file records the network configuration of Windows 9x during initial installation. If network devices do not work, examine this file to see if the ends of any lines indicate error messages or error numbers.

`Setuplog.txt` is a file that records every event of the installation process. If the Windows 9x installation process doesn't finish, check the end of the file to see at what point the installation failed.

An installation might appear to succeed, but it isn't really finished until the system restarts successfully. The `Bootlog.txt` file records every event during the startup process. `Bootlog.txt` is generated automatically the first time Windows 9x is started; whenever a new `Bootlog.txt` is generated, the previous version is renamed `Bootlog.prv` (replacing any existing `Bootlog.prv`). As with the other files discussed here, the end of the file is the critical location to look at if Windows 9x can't start. Unlike other files, which are very complex to read, Bootlog.txt is relatively simple: Virtually every START event will have either a matching SUCCESS event, a FAILED event, or no match (if the system locks up after STARTing an event). If Windows 9x locks up, check the end of the file to determine the last driver or process that was STARTed without a matching SUCCESS or FAILED; that is the usual cause of the problem.

Upgrading to Windows 2000 Professional

You can upgrade to Windows 2000 Professional from any of the following versions of Windows:

- Windows 9x
- Windows NT Workstation 3.51
- Windows NT Workstation 4.0

You cannot upgrade to Windows 2000 Professional from Windows 3.1 or earlier versions, Windows Me, or from any version of MS-DOS.

Preparations to Make Before Upgrading to Windows 2000

It probably won't surprise you to realize that Windows 2000 requires more powerful hardware than its predecessors:

- Pentium 133MHz or compatible processor; dual processors also supported
- 64MB of RAM
- 2GB hard disk with 650MB free space
- CD-ROM or DVD-ROM drive
- VGA or higher-resolution monitor
- Keyboard

Some older systems might require processor, memory, or hard disk upgrades to be qualified to run Windows 2000. You should make sure your computer meets, or exceeds, these standards before you start the upgrade process.

Because upgrading to a new version of Windows retains your existing application software and settings, you should also make sure that both your hardware and software are compatible with Windows 2000. Windows 2000 provides three options you can use to help make sure your system is compatible with Windows 2000. Depending on the installation type, you might not see all these options during the same installation.

■ *Link to the Microsoft Compatibility Web Site*—You can go straight to the Microsoft Compatibility Web site from the Windows 2000 installation if you have a working Internet connection. I recommend performing this task before you start the installation process if possible.

■ *Upgrade Packs for Software*—If your software vendors provide software packs to provide compatibility with Windows 2000, you can install them on the screen after the option to go to the Microsoft Compatibility Web site.

■ *Upgrade (Readiness) Analyzer*—After selecting whether to upgrade to NTFS, the system will run this option to analyze the hardware in your system. You can also download it and run it before you start the installation process.

> **tip**
>
> You can download this tool (also known as the Windows 2000 **Readiness Analyzer**) from `http://www.dewassoc.com/support/win2000/analyzer2.htm` as well as from the Microsoft Download Center at `http://www.microsoft.com/downloads/`. Select Windows 2000 as the Product/Technology and enter **Readiness Analyzer** in the Keywords field.

After you review the results of the Upgrade Analyzer (which can be saved or printed), you can immediately provide a replacement driver for any hardware listed, or provide a replacement driver later. Any hardware listed on the report will not work correctly until a Windows 2000–compatible driver is installed; drivers from earlier versions of Windows will not work.

Before you upgrade to Windows 2000, you should

■ Download any new device drivers you need.

■ Download any new application updates you need.

Create a folder for your updates on your system and uncompress them if needed so they can be used during the upgrade process.

Upgrading to Windows 2000 from Windows NT 4.0

You can upgrade Windows NT 4.0 to Windows 2000 by following these steps:

1. Start Windows NT 4.0.

2. Insert the Windows 2000 CD-ROM.

3. To start the upgrade process, click Yes when the computer asks `Would you like to upgrade to Windows 2000 now?`.

4. On the Welcome to the Windows 2000 Setup Wizard, select Upgrade to Windows 2000 (the default); click Next.

5. Accept the Windows 2000 end user license agreement (**EULA**); click Next to continue.

6. On the Your Product Key screen, enter your 25-character **product key** from the back of the CD case or sleeve that contained your Windows 2000 CD-ROM. Click Next to continue.

7. If the Windows NT 4.0 hard disk is not using NTFS, the Upgrading to the Windows 2000 NTFS File System screen appears. Choose Yes to upgrade your drive to NTFS, or choose No to keep its current file system.

8. Windows 2000 runs the **Upgrade Analyzer** to check hardware and software compatibility, which enables you to display or print a report. If some of your hardware needs new drivers, you can provide updated Plug and Play (PnP) driver files now (recommended) with Have Disk (browse to the folder containing the drivers needed), or click Next if you want to provide file updates later.

9. After you review the Upgrade Analyzer report, you can continue or quit the installation.

10. The system reboots for the first time after copying files.

11. After rebooting, you are prompted to press F6 to load third-party SCSI or RAID drivers; you should also press F6 if you are using a Serial ATA drive. Provide the drivers as needed for your hardware. The Setup program examines your hardware and begins to load driver files, checks your C: drive for errors, and begins to copy files. After your system is configured, Windows 2000 reboots your computer for a second time.

---

tip

If you prefer to find out before starting the installation process if you need updated drivers or applications, visit http://www. microsoft.com/windows2000/ professional/ howtobuy/ upgrading/compat/default.asp and use the Computers, Hardware Devices, and Software buttons to display compatible items and update information when needed. When you search for software, specify the company and application/product fields but use All for the product category to most easily find the information you need. When you search for computers or hardware devices, be sure to specify the full name of the company (Hewlett-Packard, not HP, for example) and the model name/ number. If your search delivers no results, make the search less specific and try again.

12. After the reboot, your drive is converted to NTFS if you selected this option earlier in the setup process. The system is rebooted again.

13. The Setup program detects hardware devices and installs network components.

14. Additional components are installed and configured, including advanced network features, such as COM+.

15. After Final Tasks are performed, the system is rebooted a third time.

16. Log on to the system when prompted to start your upgraded Windows 2000 Professional installation.

If **Autorun** has been disabled on your system, you can open the Setup.exe program on the Windows 2000 CD-ROM from Windows Explorer to start.

Upgrading to Windows 2000 from Windows 9x/Me

You can upgrade Windows 9x to Windows 2000 by following these steps:

1. Start Windows 9x.

2. Insert the Windows 2000 CD-ROM.

3. To start the upgrade process, click Yes when the computer asks, `Would you like to upgrade to Windows 2000 now?`.

4. On the Welcome to the Windows 2000 Setup Wizard, select Upgrade to Windows 2000 (the default). Click Next (see Figure 17.1).

5. Accept the Windows 2000 EULA, and click Next to continue.

6. Enter your 25-character product key from the back of the CD case or sleeve that contained your Windows 2000 CD-ROM. Click Next to continue.

FIGURE 17.1

Select the default Upgrade to Windows 2000 to replace Windows 9x with Windows 2000.

7. Click on the link to visit the Windows Compatibility Web site to check for hardware and software updates if you did not do so before starting the installation process.

8. On the Windows 2000 Setup Web site, click Search for Hardware or BIOS Updates to start the Computer search at the Windows Compatibility Web site. You can also use this tool to search for hardware device or software updates.

9. After downloading and installing any updates you found in the previous step, click the Back button in your browser until you return to the Windows 2000 Setup screen. Click Next to continue.

10. Click the Download the Latest Upgrade Pack for Setup and Compatibility button to check the system against the latest compatibility information; run it from its current location.

11. Accept any security warning that might appear and click Next to continue.

12. Windows returns you to the screen you saw in step 7. Click Next to continue.

13. Select whether to install upgrade packs provided by software vendors to make their software work with Windows 2000, and click Next. If you selected the option to install upgrade packs, specify their location.

14. Select whether to use the NTFS file system on your drive. If you want to dual boot, choose the default of No, but to enjoy the additional benefits of the NTFS file system, choose Yes. If you are unsure, skip this option and convert the drive after installation. Drives other than C: will not be converted during setup.

tip

If you have not accessed the Internet on this computer before, you might be prompted to run the Internet Connection Wizard at this time. See Chapter 21, "Networking and Internet Connectivity," for details.

note

This site lists computer vendors, but not motherboard vendors. If you are looking for updates for a "white-box" generic PC, or if your name-brand PC now uses a third-party motherboard, don't bother to use this search tool. Instead, check the motherboard vendor's site yourself.

Note also that you must manually enter computer, hardware, and software information; Windows doesn't detect the components or software in your system.

15. You can run the Upgrade Analyzer to check hardware and software compatibility and view or print a report; skip this step if you already checked compatibility. If some of your hardware needs new drivers, you can provide updated Plug and Play driver files now (recommended), or click Next if you want to provide file updates later (see Figure 17.2).

FIGURE 17.2

Many hardware devices on this recent motherboard need updated drivers for Windows 2000.

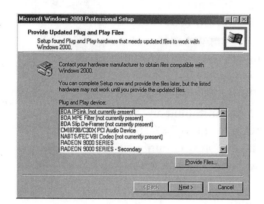

16. The Upgrade Analyzer report lists compatibility concerns for hardware, software designed for MS-DOS, general information, and upgrade pack information. After you review the Upgrade Analyzer report, you can continue or quit the installation.

17. The system reboots for the first time.

18. After rebooting, the Setup program examines your hardware and begins to load driver files, checks your C: drive for errors, and begins to copy files. After your system is configured, Windows 2000 reboots your computer for a second time.

19. After the reboot, a fully graphical desktop appears during the setup process, and your input devices are recognized and set up.

20. Networking components are installed if your system is connected to a local area network (LAN). You might be asked whether the computer is part of a domain or workgroup; specify the domain or workgroup.

caution

If the Upgrade Analyzer indicates it will remove backup files (look under the General Information section), you should press Ctrl-Esc, open Windows Explorer, and make backup copies of any files you want to keep, or cancel the upgrade process until you make the backups you need.

21. Additional components are installed and configured, including advanced network features, such as COM+.

22. After final tasks are performed, the system is rebooted a third time.

23. Press F8 for special startup options, or allow the system to boot normally.

24. After the startup process is completed, you'll be asked to provide a password for the administrator and the last logged-in user. Because the passwords for these two accounts will be identical (a single password is used for both), you'll want to assign a new password to the regular user as soon as possible to maintain security.

25. The Getting Started screen is displayed; you can register your copy of Windows 2000, set up your Internet connection, and tour Windows 2000. Uncheck this option to prevent it from running on each reboot. Do not use the Set Up the Internet option if you already have a working Internet connection.

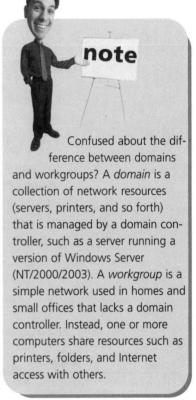

note

Confused about the difference between domains and workgroups? A *domain* is a collection of network resources (servers, printers, and so forth) that is managed by a domain controller, such as a server running a version of Windows Server (NT/2000/2003). A *workgroup* is a simple network used in homes and small offices that lacks a domain controller. Instead, one or more computers share resources such as printers, folders, and Internet access with others.

Installing Windows 2000 Service Packs and Updates

It's a truism that every computer is outdated as soon as you take it out of the store. That's even truer of operating systems. As the recent history of virus and worm attacks has taught us all too well, it's critical to install service packs and updates available for your operating system as soon as you install it (either as a clean installation or as an upgrade). Service packs can add features and driver updates to your Windows installation as well as improve security, whereas updates provide solutions to specific Windows problems.

Windows Update also can provide service packs and updates. So, if you've just installed Windows, the first thing I recommend that you do is download the most recent service pack or order the service pack CD and install it. Then, use Windows Update to download and install additional drivers and fixes.

To see a listing of all service packs for Windows 2000, go to `http://www.microsoft.com/windows2000/downloads/servicepacks/`.

To download and install a service pack for Windows 2000

1. Determine whether the system has any service packs installed. You should perform this check even if you have just installed Windows 2000, because you can install Windows 2000 with service packs included, and some Windows 2000 CDs might contain a service pack. Right-click on the My Computer icon and select Properties. Look at the Windows version section of the General tab for service pack information (see Figure 17.3).

2. Go to the Web site containing the service pack needed.

3. If you have not installed previous service packs, make sure the service pack you want to install also contains the contents of the previous service packs. If not, download and install previous service packs as required.

tip

Microsoft's service packs occasionally cause more significant problems than they solve. Before you select a particular **service pack** to download, you should verify its reliability. Check online technical publications and chat rooms for feedback about the service pack. You might determine that installing an earlier service pack and using Windows Update to install additional patches is better than installing the latest service pack.

FIGURE 17.3

This Windows 2000 system has Service Pack 3 installed.

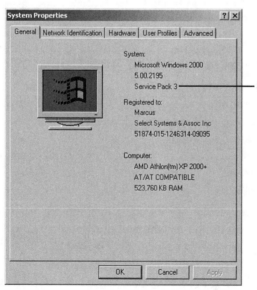

Service pack information

4. Click the link to start the download; you might need to select the correct language for the service pack first.

5. Shut down real-time virus checkers such as Norton Anti-Virus's Auto-Protect.

6. Select **Express Installation** if you want to install the service pack on only one computer (this requires an active Internet connection during the entire process); select **Network Installation** to download the entire service pack for use on multiple computers.

    Follow steps 7 and 8 to perform a Network Installation.

    Follow steps 7a and 8a to perform an Express Installation.

7. Select a location to store the file with Network Installation.

7a. Open the file from its current location to start the installation process with Express Installation.

8. Open the file you downloaded in step 6 to perform a Network Installation of the service pack.

8a. Follow the prompts to complete an Express Installation of the service pack.

9. You should update your system backup disk and back up your files before you install the service pack, and select the option to archive existing Windows 2000 files during the service pack installation.

10. Restart the system when prompted.

To install additional updates for Windows 2000 through Windows Update

1. Click Start, Windows Update.

2. Follow the prompts to install the latest version of the Windows Update software if necessary.

3. Scan for updates. Updates are divided into the following categories:

    ■   *Critical Updates and Service Packs—* These include the latest service pack and other security and stability updates. Some updates must be installed individually; others can be installed as a group.

> **tip**
>
> In some cases, you might need to reinstall third-party applications or utilities after you install a service pack. For example, a service pack might disable a particular third-party program, or a third–party program might stop working until it is upgraded or patched after a service pack is installed. These issues are normally discussed in the technical notes for the service pack or might not be discovered until after the service pack is installed.

■ *Windows Updates*—Recommended updates to fix noncritical problems certain users might encounter; also adds features and updates to features bundled into Windows.

■ *Driver Updates*—Updated device drivers for installed hardware.

4. After you select the updates desired, they are downloaded to your system and installed. You might need to restart your computer to complete the update process.

> **note**
>
> You can perform an Express Installation of the latest service pack only through Windows Update. If you prefer a Network Installation or to install an earlier service pack, you must manually download it as discussed earlier in this section.

Troubleshooting the Windows 2000 Upgrade

Unlike Windows 9x, a Windows 2000 installation doesn't offer an automatic uninstall option. Therefore, it's important to make sure that installation works correctly.

The following problems can prevent you from upgrading a system to Windows 2000:

■ *Hardware conflicts*—Change the hardware resource settings on **legacy hardware** (non-PnP hardware) to values that don't interfere with PnP devices, or remove them for reinstallation later.

■ *Not enough disk space*—To ensure that you can complete the installation, make certain that the partition or drive you will use for the Windows 2000 upgrade or dual-boot installation has at least 1GB of free space (see Figure 17.4). Use the Drive Properties sheet or Fdisk to determine free space.

■ *System configured to dual boot*—Windows 2000 cannot be installed as an upgrade on a computer that is set to dual boot Windows 9x and Windows NT (or Windows 2000). Remove one operating system, or perform a clean install on an empty hard disk after backing up all vital data.

> **tip**
>
> Converting the partition to NTFS during the installation makes more space available for Windows 2000 if the drive was previously formatted as a FAT drive. Do this only if you don't plan to access the drive with Windows 9x/Me.

FIGURE 17.4

This Windows 98 system has just over 1GB of free disk space, barely enough for an upgrade to Windows 2000.

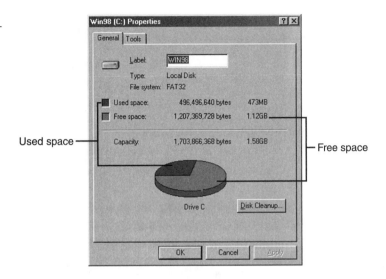

Used space ⎯ Free space

Various problems can take place after you upgrade to Windows 2000 from Windows NT, including

- Printing problems
- Can't connect to network or Internet resources
- Can't select more than 16 colors or higher than base VGA (640×480) resolution

Various problems can take place during or after the upgrade from Windows 9x to Windows 2000, including

- Monitor flickers because a lower refresh rate is in use
- Non-PnP sound card stops working
- Can't select more than 16 colors or higher than base VGA (640×480) resolution or screen is blank
- Can't complete the upgrade installation because the computer can't boot after the initial reboot during the upgrade process

tip

For a more complete list of Windows 9x-to-2000 upgrade problems and solutions (most based on Microsoft Knowledge Base articles), see http://www.labmice.net/Windows2000/install/win9xupgrd.htm.

The preceding examples are just a few of the problems that can happen during and after the upgrade. Because some upgrade problems can prevent you from accessing the Internet for solutions, you should make sure you have performed the following before you start the upgrade process:

- Checked your hardware, applications, and utilities for compatibility using the Upgrade Advisor
- Downloaded updated drivers and application patches
- Removed or disabled applications and utilities that cannot be updated to Windows 2000–compatible versions
- Updated the system BIOS to handle the full capacity of your hard disk and removed nonstandard drivers such as **EZ-BIOS** or **Disk Manager Drive Overlay**

Upgrading to Windows XP Professional

You can upgrade to Windows XP Professional from any of the following versions of Windows:

- Windows 98/98SE
- Windows Me
- Windows NT Workstation 4.0
- Windows 2000 Professional
- Windows XP Home Edition

You cannot upgrade to Windows XP Professional from Windows 95 or earlier operating system versions (including MS-DOS).

> **tip**
>
> EZ-BIOS and Disk Manager Drive Overlay are provided as part of vendor-supplied disk setup programs provided by most major drive vendors (Western Digital, Seagate, Maxtor, and so forth). Contact the maker of your drive for details of how to remove the driver (which is no longer necessary after you update your system BIOS or add an **ATA host adapter card** with an auxiliary BIOS onboard to handle the full capacity of your hard disk; see Chapter 14, "Storage," for details). Keep in mind that you should make a *full* backup of your hard disk in case something goes wrong.
>
> EZ-BIOS is provided by Phoenix Technologies (www.phoenix.com) and Disk Manager Drive Overlay is provided by Kroll Ontrack (www.ontrack.com).

Preparations to Make Before Upgrading to Windows XP

Can you believe it? Windows XP Professional raises the hardware ante compared to previous versions (including Windows 2000) with these requirements:

- Pentium 233MHz or compatible processor or faster; 300MHz or faster recommended
- 64MB of RAM minimum; 128MB or more recommended

- 1.5GB free hard disk space
- CD-ROM or DVD-ROM drive
- Super VGA (800×600) or higher-resolution monitor
- Keyboard and Microsoft mouse or compatible pointing device

As with Windows 2000, some older systems might require processor, memory, or hard disk upgrades to be qualified to run Windows XP. You should make sure your computer meets or exceeds these standards before you start the upgrade process.

Because upgrading to a new version of Windows retains your existing application software and settings, you should also make sure that both your hardware and software are compatible with Windows XP. Windows XP provides three options you can use to help make sure your system is compatible with Windows XP:

- *Downloadable Upgrade Advisor*—You can download the same **Upgrade Advisor** found on the Windows XP CD and run it before you buy Windows XP. I recommend using the Upgrade Advisor before you start the installation process if possible to find and solve any problems with your system early.

- *Upgrade Advisor on Windows XP CD*—If the 30MB download required to get the Upgrade Advisor is too much for your Internet connection, you can run the Upgrade Advisor from the Windows XP CD. Click Check System Compatibility from the Welcome to Windows XP menu; then click Check My System Automatically.

- *Link to the Microsoft Windows Catalog*—You can go straight to the **Microsoft Windows Catalog** (a listing of Windows XP–compatible hardware and software) from the Upgrade Advisor. You can launch it after the downloaded version reports on compatibility issues and from the Windows XP CD after you click Check System Compatibility.

tip

If you've installed Windows XP on a system that is marginal (slow processor, small hard disk, and so forth), you can remove it if you find it's not performing satisfactorily. Try it and see how you like it. If it's not working for you, open the Add/Remove Programs icon in the Control Panel to locate the uninstall program. However, if you want to install Windows XP on another system without hassles, *don't* activate it until you're sure you're happy. Windows XP doesn't need to be activated until 30 days have passed from the install date, so take your time and think it over.

Using the Windows XP Upgrade Advisor

Follow this procedure to run the Windows XP Upgrade Advisor (download version):

1. Connect to the Internet with your existing version of Windows.

2. Use My Computer or Windows Explorer to locate the folder where you downloaded the Upgrade Advisor. Open it to start the process.

3. Follow the prompts to start the advisor and accept the EULA.

   The following steps apply to both the downloaded and Windows XP CD–based versions of the Upgrade Advisor:

4. Download updated files when prompted.

5. After the Upgrade Advisor uses **Dynamic Update** to update itself, it starts to analyze your system.

6. After the analysis is complete, the Upgrade Analyzer displays any incompatible hardware or software it finds (see Figure 17.5).

note

Learn more about the Upgrade Advisor and download it from http://www.microsoft.com/windowsxp/pro/howtobuy/upgrading/advisor.asp. Note that it's a large (over 30MB) download, so use a broadband Internet connection for the download if at all possible.

If you have already installed and registered Windows XP from a CD, you can still use its Upgrade Advisor on another system.

FIGURE 17.5

The Windows XP Upgrade Advisor lists incompatible hardware and software products. Click the Full Details button to learn more.

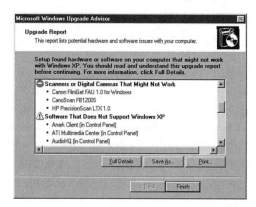

7. When you click Finish, the Upgrade Advisor displays a button you can click to go to the Windows Catalog, which lists compatible products and links to drivers or updates for older products (when available).

Additional Preparations to Make Before the Windows XP Upgrade

Before you upgrade to Windows XP, you should also download any new device drivers or new application updates that you need. Create a folder for your updates on your system and uncompress them if needed so they can be used during the upgrade process.

Upgrading to Windows XP from Older Versions

To start the Window XP upgrade process if you want to replace your old version of Windows, do the following:

1. Insert your Windows XP CD into the CD-ROM drive while your old version is running.

2. Unless you've disabled Autorun, the Windows XP splash screen is displayed. If the splash screen does not appear, use Windows Explorer to open the Setup.exe file on the Windows XP CD. Choose Install Windows XP, Perform Additional Tasks, or Check System Compatibility.

3. If you haven't used the Windows Upgrade Advisor on this system, click Check System Compatibility as discussed earlier in this chapter.

4. After completing the Upgrade Advisor check (if necessary), click Install Windows XP.

5. Select Upgrade (the default setting) to change your installed version of Windows to Windows XP, which enables you to use your existing software and settings without reinstallation.

6. Read the license agreement, click I Accept, and click Next to continue.

7. Enter the product key from the back of the CD package and click Next to continue.

8. The installation process begins; a display on the left side gives an estimate of how long the process will take until completion. The computer restarts several times during the process.

note

During the upgrade process, as with Windows 2000, you can convert the file system to NTFS. Do this to save space on your hard disk (NTFS is more efficient than FAT32) and if you want features such as encryption, file/folder compression, and better security. Remember, though, that if you dual boot with a Windows 9x/Me operating system, they cannot read an NTFS disk.

9. At the end of the process, the Welcome to Microsoft Windows dialog box is displayed. You can use it to activate your copy of Windows and set up users.

10. After you complete the steps listed in the Welcome dialog box, the Windows XP desktop is displayed.

Installing Windows XP Service Packs and Updates

Service Packs for Windows XP? Yes, even Microsoft's latest operating system is a bit out of date now; one service pack is already available, along with a long list of additional updates. Fortunately, just as with Windows 2000, the one-two punch of service pack downloads and Windows Update can bring Windows XP up to date and protect you from the numerous digital bad guys on the Internet.

To download and install a service pack for Windows XP

1. Determine whether the system has any service packs installed. You should perform this check even if you have just installed Windows XP, because you can install Windows XP with service packs included, and newer Windows XP CDs might contain a service pack. Right-click on the My Computer icon and select Properties. Look at the Windows version section of the General tab for service pack information; if a service pack has been installed, it will be listed in the System section of the General tab similar to the way it is listed with Windows 2000 (refer to Figure 17.3).

note

Get the Microsoft Windows XP Professional Service Packs and other updates from `http://www.microsoft.com/` `windowsxp/pro/downloads/` `default.asp`.

The Windows XP Home version of this site is located at `http://www.` `microsoft.com/windowsxp/home/` `downloads/default.asp`.

2. Go to the Web site containing the service pack needed.

3. If you have not installed previous service packs, make sure the service pack you want to install also contains the contents of the previous service packs. If not, download and install previous service packs as required.

4. Read the release notes for the service pack to see if it will cause any problems for your particular configuration, such as problems with networking, winmodems, CD mastering software, and so forth. Take the necessary actions as noted. (Some might require changes before you perform the service pack installation; others might take place afterward.)

5. Click the link to start the download; you might need to select the correct language for the service pack first.

6. Shut down real-time virus checkers such as Norton Anti-Virus's Auto-Protect.

7. Select Express Installation if you want to install the service pack on only one computer (this requires an Internet connection during the entire process); select Network Installation to download the entire service pack for use on multiple computers.

Follow steps 8 and 9 to perform a Network Installation.

Follow steps 8a and 9a to perform an Express Installation.

8. Select a location to store the file with Network Installation.

8a. Open the file from its current location to start the installation process with Express Installation.

9. Open the file you downloaded in step 8 to perform a Network Installation of the service pack.

9a. Follow the prompts to complete an Express Installation of the service pack.

10. You should update your system backup disk and back up your files before you install the service pack, and select the option to archive existing Windows XP files during the service pack installation.

11. Restart the system when prompted.

tip

To save the specific document referenced in the release notes so you can follow up on the problem, use the Save as **Web Archive** option in Internet Explorer. This saves the entire Web page (including graphics) as a single file with an .MHT extension. You can then view the file offline with Internet Explorer if necessary.

tip

In some cases, you might need to reinstall third-party applications or utilities after you install a service pack.

To install additional updates for Windows XP through Windows Update

1. Click Start, All Programs, Windows Update.

2. Follow the prompts to install the latest version of the Windows Update software if necessary.

3. Scan for updates. Updates are divided into the following categories:

■ *Critical Updates and Service Packs*—
These include the latest service pack
and other security and stability
updates. Some updates must be
installed individually; others can be
installed as a group.

■ *Windows Updates*—Recommended
updates to fix noncritical problems
certain users might encounter; also
adds features and updates to features bundled into Windows.

■ *Driver Updates*—Updated device drivers for installed hardware.

4. After you select the updates desired, they
are downloaded to your system and
installed. You might need to restart your
computer to complete the update process.

note

You can perform an
Express Installation of the
latest service pack only through
Windows Update. If you prefer a
Network Installation or need to
install an earlier service pack, you
must manually download it as discussed earlier in this section.

Troubleshooting the Windows XP Upgrade

If a Windows XP upgrade from Windows 9x or Me goes badly, you can uninstall
Windows XP and revert back to your previous Windows version (look for the
Uninstall Windows XP option in the Add or Remove Programs icon in the Control
Panel) *if* you are still using the FAT16 or FAT32
file systems. However, if you need the Windows
XP upgrade, that isn't much of a consolation.
Try the following tips to make the upgrade go
smoothly.

If you are unable to start the upgrade, check the
following:

■ *Free disk space*—You need 1.5GB free at
the minimum; more is better.

■ *Hardware conflicts or problems*—Use
Windows Device Manager to ensure that
all hardware is working correctly before
you start the upgrade or dual-boot
installation.

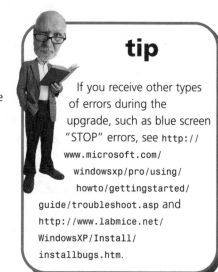

tip

If you receive other types
of errors during the
upgrade, such as blue screen
"STOP" errors, see http://
www.microsoft.com/
windowsxp/pro/using/
howto/gettingstarted/
guide/troubleshoot.asp and
http://www.labmice.net/
WindowsXP/Install/
installbugs.htm.

■ *Processor speed and memory size*—If your system doesn't meet the minimums, upgrade it.

As with upgrades to Windows 2000, various problems can take place after you upgrade to Windows XP from older versions, including

■ Can't connect to network or Internet resources

■ Can't remove programs with Uninstall

■ Certain systems and hardware don't work properly

As with Windows 2000, you should carefully study Microsoft Knowledge Base articles and any tips from your computer vendor to determine if your particular system might have problems with the upgrade to Windows XP.

Because some upgrade problems can prevent you from accessing the Internet for solutions, you should make sure you have performed the following before you start the upgrade process:

■ Checked your hardware, applications, and utilities for compatibility using the Upgrade Advisor

■ Downloaded updated drivers and application patches

■ Removed or disabled applications and utilities that cannot be updated to Windows XP–compatible versions

■ Updated the system BIOS to handle the full capacity of your hard disk and removed nonstandard drivers such as EZ-BIOS or Disk Manager Drive Overlay.

tip

For a more complete list of Windows 9x–to–Windows XP upgrade problems and solutions, see http://www. labmice.net/WindowsXP/ Install/win9xupgrade.htm.

A list of Windows NT/2000 to Windows XP upgrade problems and solutions is available at http://www.labmice.net/ WindowsXP/Install/ win2kupgrade.htm.

tip

EZ-BIOS and Disk Manager Drive Overlay are provided as part of vendor-supplied disk setup programs provided by most major drive vendors (Western Digital, Seagate, Maxtor, and so forth). Contact the maker of your drive for details of how to remove the driver (which is no longer necessary after you update your system BIOS or add a helper card to handle the full capacity of your hard disk). Keep in mind that you should make a *full* backup of your hard disk in case something goes wrong.

Study Lab

Don't miss the Study Lab materials found on the CD accompanying this book. Each Study Lab is tailored to the individual chapters in this book, meaning that you'll quickly be able to determine which topics you understand well enough to pass the exam and which topics need more study. The Study Labs are presented in printable PDF format so that you can take them with you to study at work, on the road, or even in your car just before test time!

THE ABSOLUTE MINIMUM

- The easiest way to upgrade to a newer version of Windows is to start Windows, insert the CD with the newer version, and launch Setup from the older version's file management program (File Manager, My Computer, Windows Explorer).

- All versions of Windows from Windows 98 to Windows XP (including Windows 2000 and Windows Me) support Windows Update, which can be used to install the latest service pack and other security, driver, and feature updates.

- You can upgrade to Windows 2000 from Windows 9x, Windows NT Workstation 3.1, or 4.0. You can upgrade to Windows XP Professional from Windows 9x/Me, Windows NT Workstation 4.0, Windows 2000 Professional, and Windows XP Home Edition.

- Windows 2000 supports several methods for determining if your system is ready for the upgrade, including the Upgrade Analyzer on the Windows 2000 CD and the downloadable Readiness Analyzer. Windows XP has similar features.

- You can search the online compatibility listing for hardware and software to locate driver, BIOS, and software updates you might need for proper Windows 2000 support.

- During the Windows 2000 or Windows XP upgrades, you can convert the drive to the NTFS file system.

- Windows XP must be activated within 30 days of installation, but it can be used without activation during this period.

- Both Windows 2000 and Windows XP support two ways to install service packs: Express Installation (for the current PC only) and Network Installation (downloads the entire service pack for installation on multiple computers).

- Typical reasons for problems with the Windows 2000 or Windows XP upgrades include lack of free disk space, hardware conflicts, and software conflicts.

- You should read the release notes for Windows 2000 or Windows XP (available online) to determine if your system might have problems with the upgrade.

- Many versions of EZ-BIOS and Disk Manager Drive Overlay (programs used to manage hard disks too large for the system's BIOS) are not compatible with Windows 2000 or Windows XP. A BIOS upgrade is preferable.

18

USING AND OPTIMIZING WINDOWS

During the startup process, the following major events take place:

- The system BIOS locates the Io.sys file and starts the **boot sequence**.

- Various **binary** and text-mode configuration and startup files are processed.

- After Windows starts, the **Registry** is processed to complete the configuration of Windows.

The following sections cover these processes in more detail.

Windows 9x/Me Boot Sequence

During the startup process of Windows 9x/Me, the OS accesses several files. These files include

- **Io.sys**—Binary startup file

- **Msdos.sys**—Editable text startup configuration file

- **Config.sys**—Editable text startup device driver and configuration file

- **Autoexec.bat**—Editable text startup configuration file

These files are loaded and processed in the order listed during the initial startup of your system. All these files are located in the root directory of your default startup drive (normally C:). Erasing them is a very bad idea!

Tasks Performed by **Io.sys**

The Io.sys file is loaded into memory by the **bootstrap loader** built into the system BIOS. After it's loaded into memory, Io.sys performs the following tasks:

- Reads the configuration data stored in the Msdos.sys file and starts the computer accordingly. As you'll see later, Msdos.sys can be used to tweak computer operation in many ways.

- Checks for multiple hardware configurations (created by the Hardware Profiles feature in the Windows System properties sheet) and prompts the user to select one. If you don't use mobile system with a docking station or port replicator, don't worry about this one.

- Loads the following files into memory:

    - Logo.sys—Displays the standard or optional Windows splash screen.

note

The CD included with this book contains important Study Lab material for this chapter, as well as Chapters 2–22 in this book. The Study Lab for each chapter contains terms to study, exercises, and practice tests—all in printable PDF format (Adobe Acrobat Reader is included on the CD, too). These Study Lab materials will help you gear up for the A+ Exam. Also, the CD includes an industry-leading test engine from PrepLogic, which simulates the actual A+ test so that you can be sure that you're ready when test day arrives. Don't let the A+ test intimidate you. If you've read the chapters, worked through the Study Lab, and passed the practice tests from PrepLogic, you should be well prepared to ace the test!

Also, you'll notice that some words throughout each chapter are in bold format. These are study terms that are defined in the Study Lab. Be sure to consult the Study Lab when you are finished with this chapter to test what you've learned.

- Drvspace.ini or Dblspace.ini (Microsoft disk compression setup files) if present—These will be present only if the hard drive has been compressed.

- Himem.sys—XMS memory manager.

- Ifshlp.sys—Installable file system driver.

- Setver.exe—Sets up a list of older applications and the DOS versions they expect so they will run properly under Windows.

■ Checks User.dat and System.dat (the Windows Registry) for valid data and opens System.dat. If System.dat is not available, System.da0 (the backup) is opened instead and is renamed System.dat.

Before Io.sys bows out and turns over operation to the next file, it loads the hardware profile you selected and checks the Registry for any drivers located in the following Registry key:

\Hkey_Local_Machine\System\CurrentControlSet

The drivers and parameters referenced there are loaded before the Config.sys file is processed (Windows 9x only) .

tip

Most of these configuration files are hidden by default in the Windows Explorer file management tool, and some are also hidden from the command prompt. To see system and hidden files in the Windows Explorer view, click Tools, Folder Options, View. Select Show Hidden Files and Folders, and clear the check mark next to Hide Protected Operating System Files. (You might want to restore these defaults to protect these files from accidental deletion after you complete your maintenance work on the PC.)

To show hidden files at the command prompt, use the DIR (directory) command with the /AH switch: DIR /AH. The /AH switch displays files that have the hidden file attribute.

Io.sys Default Settings and Values

In Windows 9x, the Io.sys file replaces much of the functionality of Config.sys, so the Config.sys file is sometimes empty or not present.

The following statements, formerly found in Config.sys, are now integrated into Io.sys:

- **Dos=high**—Loads MS-DOS into the High Memory Area (HMA—the first 64KB of extended memory); if Emm386.exe is loaded from Config.sys, DOS=UMB is also used to enable terminate-and-stay-resident (TSR) programs to load into unused upper memory blocks (Windows 9x only).

- Himem.sys—XMS memory manager needed for Windows.

- `Ifshlp.sys`—32-bit file system manager; enables Windows to work with network and real-mode file system APIs.

- `Setver.exe`—Provides MS-DOS version information to programs that need to be told that they are running under a particular version of MS-DOS.

- `files=`—Specifies 60 file handles by default; used only by MS-DOS applications running under Windows 9x.

- `lastdrive=`—Default is Z; used only by MS-DOS applications; value is stored in the Registry.

- `buffers=`—Specifies 30 disk buffers by default; used only by MS-DOS applications that make calls directly to `Io.sys`.

- `stacks=`—Specifies a value of 9,256 (9 stack frames, 256 bytes each); used for compatibility with older programs that need stack frames to properly handle hardware interrupts.

- `shell=command.com`—Indicates command processor to use; `/p` is included by default to make `Command.com` permanent in memory.

- `fcbs=`—Specifies a value of 4; needed only for very old applications running under Windows 9x.

You can edit the `Config.sys` file to override these defaults if necessary.

`Io.sys` Differences in Windows Me

Windows Me is essentially a legacy-free version of Windows 9x. Although it is built on the same basic design, it lacks support for MS-DOS device drivers (loaded from `Config.sys` in Windows 9x) and TSR programs (loaded from `Autoexec.bat` in Windows 9x).

Windows Me uses `Io.sys` for all configuration processes previously performed by `Config.sys`. Windows Me uses `Config.sys` and `Autoexec.bat` only to set up environmental variables that are used to configure the Windows Me Registry such as `PATH=` or `SET=`. Changes you make to `Autoexec.bat` and `Config.sys` in Windows Me are added to the Registry and the changes you made are removed at the next boot.

If you need to load real-mode (MS-DOS) device drivers such as CD-ROM or other drivers for use at a command prompt, you can start the computer with a Windows Me EBD (Emergency Boot Disk) that has a `Config.sys` and `Autoexec.bat` file with the necessary drivers and programs.

Msdos.sys—Configuring Your Boot Options

The first configuration file processed by Io.sys is the Msdos.sys file. In Windows 9x/Me, the Msdos.sys file is not a binary file (as it was with MS-DOS), but is instead a specially formatted text file that controls the boot process.

Like Io.sys, Msdos.sys is a hidden file; to view its contents most easily, open an MS-DOS prompt window and enter the following commands:

C: [changes to C: drive]

CD\ [changes to the root folder of C: drive]

EDIT MSDOS.SYS [opens Msdos.sys with the text editor]

The contents of a typical Msdos.sys file are displayed in Figure 18.1.

FIGURE 18.1

A typical Msdos.sys file; it is located in the root directory of the default Windows 9x/Me boot drive (normally C:).

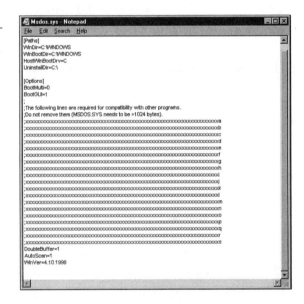

Table 18.1 lists all the possible configuration options for Msdos.sys and their uses. Note that only a few of these options are needed in most cases.

The Msdos.sys file is divided into two sections:

- *Paths*—This section indicates where Windows is installed and what drive is used to start Windows (see Table 18.1).

- *Options*—This section sets the startup options that will be used when booting Windows (see Table 18.2).

When you make changes to add or adjust configuration settings, be sure you do not remove the lines that begin with a semicolon. These lines make the file over 1KB (1,024 bytes), which is required for proper operation of the system.

Table 18.1 Configuration Settings for the [Paths] Section of Msdos.sys

Setting	Typical or Default Value	Use
HostWinBootDrive=	C	Drive letter used to boot Windows
WinBootDir=	C:\Windows	Folder where Windows is installed
WinDir=	C:\Windows	Usually same as WinBootDir
UninstallDir=	C:\	Where uninstall information is stored

Table 18.2 Configuration Settings for the [Options] Section of Msdos.sys

Option	Default Setting	Use
AutoScan=	1	Runs ScanDisk automatically after 1-minute delay if Windows 9x wasn't shut down correctly; set to 0 to disable; set to 2 to run ScanDisk immediately if Windows 9x wasn't shut down correctly.
BootDelay=	2	Delays Windows startup the number of seconds listed; adjust to allow user to press Ctrl or F8 to bring up menu; use 0 to disable.
BootFailSafe=	0	Set to 1 to run Windows in Safe Mode.
BootGUI=	1	Set to 0 to boot Windows to a command prompt.
BootMenu=	0	Set to 1 to display the Windows startup menu.
BootMenuDefault=	1	Selects default boot option if startup menu is displayed.
BootMenuDelay=	30	Selects how long (seconds) to wait after Windows startup menu is displayed to boot.
BootMulti=	0	If set to 1, enables dual-booting with MS-DOS or Windows NT.
BootWarn=	1	If set to 0, disables Safe Mode warning message.
BootWin=	1	Set to 0 to make MS-DOS 5.x or 6.x the default operating system (if installed).
DblSpace=	1	Loads DoubleSpace driver (if installed); set to 0 if DoubleSpace compression hasn't been installed.

Table 18.2   (continued)

Option	Default Setting	Use
DblBuffer=	0	Set to 1 if a SCSI host adapter on the system requires double buffering.
DrvSpace=	1	Loads DriveSpace driver (if installed); set to 0 if DriveSpace compression hasn't been installed.
LoadTop=	1	Loads Command.com and Drvspace.bin at top of conventional memory for compatibility with 16-bit (real mode) network drivers, such as some older NetWare drivers.
Logo=	1	Set to 0 to disable the Windows splash screen; set to 0 also avoids conflicts with some third-party memory managers.
Network=	0	Left over from Windows 95; Windows 98/Me don't support Safe Mode with Networking, so leave this set to 0 or omit option.
WinVer	Varies	Indicates Windows version.

To change the contents of Msdos.sys, which will modify how your system starts, follow this procedure:

1. Using the Windows Find tool (click Start, Find, File or Folders), search your C: drive for Msdos.sys.

2. Msdos.sys should be displayed in the list of files; use the copy on C:\ if more than one is displayed. Right-click the file and select Properties.

3. Uncheck the Read-Only and Hidden attributes and click Apply. Click Close.

4. Double-click Msdos.sys to open it.

5. Because the .sys extension is not associated with a program, the Open With window appears. Scroll down and select Notepad from the programs listed. *Do not* check the Always Use This Program box. Click OK.

6. Add the commands from Tables 18.1 or 18.2 to Msdos.sys with the Notepad text editor, or modify existing commands. Do not remove any of the lines beginning with a semicolon

note

Windows is charmingly inconsistent about the method used to enable (turn on) or disable (turn off) settings. In Msdos.sys, when 1 is used as a value, it enables the option; when 0 is used as a value, it disables the option. However, in the Win.ini and System.ini files also used by Windows, True/False and Yes/No are also used.

that have a long line of x's; these lines are needed to make sure Msdos.sys is large enough (in bytes) to work properly.

7. Save the changes (click File, Save) and close Notepad.

8. Right-click Msdos.sys, recheck Hidden and Read-Only attributes, and click Apply. Click Close; the changes made to Msdos.sys will take effect on the next reboot.

Config.sys in Windows 9x

The Config.sys file—a plain-text file that can be edited with Notepad—in Windows 9x is needed primarily for installing real-mode device drivers for devices that are not supported by Windows 9x's 32-bit device drivers. As you saw earlier, Io.sys contains most of the values formerly found in Config.sys. If you don't like the defaults in Io.sys, you can add the statement you want to change to the Config.sys file with the value you want to change. You also can add a reference to a memory manager to Config.sys.

Follow these steps to open the Config.sys file with the Windows Notepad program:

1. Using the Windows Find tool (click Start, Find, File or Folders), search your C: drive for Config.sys.

2. All copies of Config.sys on C: drive are displayed. The only one that needs to be edited is the one located in the root folder of the C: drive (C:\). Double-click this Config.sys file.

3. Because the file extension .sys is not associated with a program, the Open With window appears. Scroll down and select Notepad from the programs listed. Do *not* check the Always Use This Program box.

4. Click OK to open Config.sys with Notepad.

The Config.sys file on many Windows 9x systems will be empty and waiting for any changes you might need to make. For example, to change the default setting for Files= from the Windows 9x Io.sys default of 60 to a value of 80, follow these steps:

1. Use a text editor such as Notepad to open the Config.sys file.

2. Add the following line:
   Files=80.

3. Save Config.sys and exit Notepad.

4. Restart the computer to put the new value into operation.

To add support for a device that is not supported by Windows 9x's protected-mode device drivers (such as an older CD-ROM drive, for example), add a reference to the device driver to the `Config.sys` file. The following command installs the `Cddriver.sys` file found in the `c:\CDROM` folder into memory and assigns it a device name:

```
Device=C:\CDROM\cddriver.sys /D:MSCD001
```

To enable upper-memory block usage for DOS-based device drivers and TSRs under Windows 9x, add the following to `Config.sys`:

```
Device=C:\Windows\Emm386.exe NOEMS
```

As you learned earlier in this chapter, `Io.sys` adds the `DOS=UMB` reference during its startup process to enable you to use `Devicehigh=` statements in `Config.sys` and `Loadhigh` statements in `Autoexec.bat`.

Autoexec.bat in Windows 9x

The major reasons to add commands to `Autoexec.bat` will be to perform tasks (such as virus scanning or changing the default location of the Windows temporary folder) that should take place before the Windows 9x GUI loads or to change the defaults loaded by `Io.sys`.

For example, to change the default setting for SET TEMP= from the Windows 9x `Io.sys` default of `C:\Windows\Temp` to a different folder such as `D:\Temp`, follow these steps:

1. Use a text editor such as Notepad to open the `Autoexec.bat` file.

2. Add the following lines:

   ```
   SET TEMP=D:\TEMP

   SET TMP=D:\TEMP
   ```

3. Save the changes to `Autoexec.bat` and exit.

4. Use the Windows Explorer to create a folder on D: called `\TEMP`.

5. Restart the computer to put the new settings into operation.

Adjusting Default Memory Configurations (Windows 9x)

Because Windows 9x is built on an MS-DOS foundation, it supports the different types of physical memory specifications that result from the design of the original IBM PC and its many descendants:

- **Conventional memory**—Memory addresses between 0 and 640KB. MS-DOS programs normally run in this area.

- **Upper memory**—Memory addresses between 640KB and 1MB, some of which are already in use for the system BIOS, Plug and Play BIOS, video BIOS, and video RAM. Depending on the system, between 96KB and 160KB of this space is not in use by hardware, but these addresses are not available unless additional memory managers (such as Emm386.exe) are installed during the startup process.

- **Extended memory**—Memory over 1MB. This is the primary memory area used by Windows 9x. Windows 9x/Me loads the XMS (Extended Memory Specification) driver Himem.sys to make this memory available to Windows and compatible MS-DOS programs during Windows startup.

- **High memory**—The first 64KB of extended memory after an XMS driver is loaded. The Io.sys file installs Himem.sys and activates the dos=high option to copy the MS-DOS kernel used by Windows 9x into the High Memory Area (HMA).

- **Expanded memory**—Memory that can be accessed through a 64KB page frame that can be established in unused upper memory blocks. Expanded Memory Specification (EMS) memory originally required special memory boards, but can now be created from XMS memory through the use of Emm386.exe in Config.sys. This type of memory is useful only for older MS-DOS programs.

Memory management takes place during the startup process of Windows 9x. By default, Io.sys converts memory starting at 1MB into XMS using Himem.sys and then uses the dos=high option to move the MS-DOS kernel into the HMA portion of XMS memory.

If you have MS-DOS TSR utilities that you want to install into upper memory blocks (UMBs), you will need to add the following statement to the Config.sys file:

```
Device=C:\Windows\Emm386.exe NOEMS
```

The DOS=UMB statement will be added to the memory configuration by Io.sys to make the UMBs available to MS-DOS TSRs.

If you have MS-DOS applications that need access to EMS memory, you need to add the following statement to the Config.sys file:

```
Device=C:\Windows\Emm386.exe RAM
```

This converts XMS memory into a common pool of XMS/EMS memory that can be used by both Windows and DOS applications. The DOS=UMB statement will be added to the memory configuration by Io.sys to make any UMBs not used by the EMS page frame available to MS-DOS TSRs.

To load any TSRs from Autoexec.bat into UMBs, use the Loadhigh (LH) statement:

```
LH C:\Utilities\MyTools.exe
```

`Win.com` in Windows 9x

The `Win.com` file is responsible for loading the Windows GUI. Normally, `Win.com` is loaded automatically during the Windows 9x startup process. However, if Windows 9x cannot start correctly, `Win.com`'s special startup switches can save the day.

The startup switches discussed in the following section can be used in place of making changes to the `System.ini` file (a specially formatted text file used to adjust how Windows operates). If Windows 9x will start when one or more of these switches is used, add the equivalent statement to the `System.ini` statement until you solve the underlying problem with your Windows installation or your computer.

To use any of the following startup switches with Windows 9x:

1. Start the computer.

2. Press the Ctrl key (Windows 95) or F8 (Windows 98) after the POST (power-on self-test) has been completed to display the Windows 9x Startup menu.

3. Select the Command Prompt Only startup option (not the Safe Mode command prompt). This option processes the Registry, `Config.sys`, and `Autoexec.bat` and boots the system to a command prompt.

4. Enter this command at the prompt and add the desired switches at the end of the command. For example, this command uses four of the possible six switches:
   win/d:fsvx

You can combine the startup switches that can be used with Windows 9x's `Win.com`. They include

- :F—Turns off 32-bit disk access. The equivalent to adding this statement to `System.ini` is 32BitDiskAccess=FALSE.

- :M—Enables Safe Mode. You can also automatically enable this by pressing the F5 key during startup.

- :N—Enables Safe Mode with networking. You can also automatically enable this by pressing the F6 key during startup.

- :S—Specifies that Windows should not use the ROM address space between F000:0000 and 1MB for a break point. The equivalent to adding this statement to `System.ini` is SystemROMBreakPoint=FALSE.

- :V—Specifies that the ROM routine will handle interrupts from the hard disk controller. The equivalent to adding this statement to `System.ini` is VirtualHDIRQ=FALSE.

- :x—Excludes all the adapter area from the range of memory that Windows scans to find unused space. The equivalent to adding this statement to System.ini is EMMExclude=A000-FFFF.

Use the :M (Safe Mode) and :N (Safe Mode with networking) options if you need CD-ROM support while you're in Safe Mode. Safe Mode doesn't process the Config.sys or Autoexec.bat configuration files, so it doesn't provide CD-ROM support. Add the correct CD-ROM device driver to Config.sys and the matching MSCDEX.EXE command to Autoexec.bat, and boot the computer to the command prompt to load the CD-ROM driver into memory. Then, use the :M or :N switches to start Windows 9x with CD-ROM support.

Windows 9x/Me Registry

If you use Windows 9x/Me at the office and at home, you probably notice a lot of differences between the systems, such as screen resolution and color depth settings, installed programs, and so forth.

> **note**
>
> If you need to start Windows Me with special startup switches, use the System Configuration utility. See "Using MSConfig," in Chapter 20, "Troubleshooting Windows and Windows Applications," for details.

The primary files used to keep track of the system configuration are

- System.dat —Stores computer-specific configuration information
- User.dat —Stores user-specific configuration information

Windows Me adds a third configuration file:

- **Classes.dat**—Stores file types and association information (stored in System.dat in Windows 9x)

Collectively, these files form the Windows Registry, the central location where almost everything that's important about how Windows 9x/Me works, as well as the programs and hardware installed for use with Windows, are stored.

These files are found in the default \Windows folder, but because they're system files, they're hidden by default. Unlike Config.sys or Msdos.sys, these files can't be edited or viewed with a simple text editor like Notepad. Instead, Windows uses the Regedit program (see Figure 18.2, later in this section) to view and change the contents of the Registry. To start Regedit, click Start, Run, type **regedit**, and press Enter.

Changes made in **Regedit** are automatically saved when you exit. Under most normal circumstances, the Registry will not need to be edited or viewed. However, Registry editing might be necessary under the following circumstances:

■ To add, modify (by changing values or data), or remove a Registry key that cannot be changed through normal Windows menus or application settings. This might be necessary to remove traces of a program or hardware device that was not uninstalled properly, or to allow a new device or program to be installed.

■ To back up the Registry to a file.

There are five different sections to the Windows Registry, whether it's the Registry used by Windows 9x/Me or the Registry used by Windows NT 4.0/2000/XP:

caution

The Registry should *never* be edited unless a backup copy has been made first, because there is no Undo option for individual edits and no way to discard all changes when exiting Regedit.

■ `HKEY_CLASSES_ROOT`—Linksfile extensions to specific applications installed on the computer (also stored in `HKEY_LOCAL_MACHINE`)

■ `HKEY_CURRENT_USER`—Stores configurations specific to the current user, such as screensaver, desktop theme, and Microsoft Office user information (also stored in `HKEY_USERS`)

■ `HKEY_LOCAL_MACHINE`—Stores hardware and software setup information

■ `HKEY_USERS`—Stores user-specific information for all users of this computer

■ `HKEY_CURRENT_CONFIG`—Stores the settings for the current hardware profile (also stored in `HKEY_LOCAL_MACHINE`)

As you can see from this listing, any setting in Windows is stored in one of two top-level keys (`HKEY_LOCAL_MACHINE` and `HKEY_USERS`). The other three keys provide shortcuts to sections of these two keys.

Microsoft's online Knowledge Base provides numerous examples of using a Registry editor to make manual changes. Figure 18.2 shows a typical Windows 9x Registry, as viewed in Regedit. The left window displays keys, which are displayed as folders. Click a key to open it in the right window. A key can contain multiple values and data, as shown here.

Registry key

FIGURE 18.2

Regedit is being
used to view the
display settings
for the current
configuration.

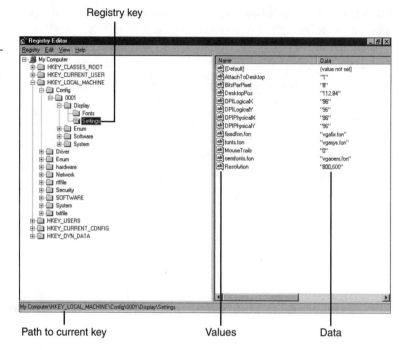

Path to current key   Values   Data

You should edit the Registry *only* with careful instructions from a software or hardware vendor and *only* if other alternatives for solving a problem do not exist.

Follow these steps to back up the Registry to a text file:

1. Start Regedit (click Start, Run, type **Regedit**, click OK).
2. Click Registry.
3. Click Export Registry.
4. Select a folder for the Registry backup.
5. Enter a name for the backup.
6. Select All to back up the entire Registry.
7. Click Save.

As you can see, the Registry is a vital part of Windows: Break the Registry by erasing its files or corrupting its contents, and you've broken Windows. One of the major differences between Windows 95, 98, and Me is how these operating systems help you recover from Registry problems.

Windows 95 makes a backup of the Registry files (System.dat and User.dat) after every start as **System.da0** and **User.da0**. If you can't start Windows, you can recover using the following method:

1. Start your system with the Safe Mode command prompt option.

2. Change to the C:\Windows folder (CD\Windows).

3. Use the Attrib command to remove the read-only, hidden, and system attributes from System.dat and User.dat (Attrib -r -h -s System.dat; Attrib -r -h -s User.dat).

4. Use these commands to replace the damaged Registry files with the backups (Copy System.da0 System.dat; Copy User.da0 User.dat). Answer Y when prompted to overwrite the existing file.

5. Use Attrib to restore the correct file attributes to the new System and User files (Attrib +r +h +s System.dat; Attrib +r +h +s User.dat).

6. Restart the computer.

The Windows 95 method is clumsy, not very intuitive (Attrib's switches always twist my fingers in knots), and prone to error. (Make sure you replace .dat with .da0, not the other way around!) However, it works, assuming you have a good backup.

However, if you start Windows, have a problem with the Registry, restart Windows, and have a problem again, you've just replaced the good Registry you had two startups earlier with a problem Registry!

Windows 98 and Windows Me solve this problem by making multiple backups of the Registry and checking the Registry at startup with **Scanreg**.

Scanreg automatically runs whenever you restart your computer to check your Registry for problems; if any problems are detected, the latest backup copy of your Registry is used instead of the primary copy.

What if the latest backup of the Registry is also corrupted? Don't panic—Windows 98 and Me store five Registry backups by default in the hidden \Windows\Sysbkup folder. The backups are compressed using Windows's own .CAB (cabinet) format, and are numbered rb000 through rb004 (oldest to newest); by default, a backup is made once a day. To restore from an older Registry backup, boot Windows 98 with the Command Prompt Only option or start Windows Me with the Windows Me EBD and change to C: drive, and type **Scanreg/restore** at the command prompt. Select a backup to restore, remove the EBD (if used) and restart the system after completing the restoration process.

note

Scanreg replaces a defective Registry with a backup copy if errors are detected, but it does not remove Registry entries for programs that are no longer on the system.

`Win.ini` and `System.ini` in Windows 9x/Me

Windows 3.x used two specially formatted plain-text configuration files called `Win.ini` (configures the Windows user interface and startup programs) and `System.ini` (configures hardware drivers used with Windows). They're still around in Windows 9x/Me/NT 4.0/2000/XP. Although most 32-bit applications and utilities will change the Registry when installed, some older applications and utilities might need to make changes to the `Win.ini` and `System.ini` files. The `System.ini` file might also need to be changed to allow Windows 9x to run as you learned earlier in this chapter.

If you need to change `Win.ini` and `System.ini`, use a text editor such as Notepad, or run the Sysedit program in Windows 9x (see Figure 18.3), which opens both of the preceding files, plus `Protocol.ini`, `Msmail.ini`, `Config.sys`, and `Autoexec.bat`. To run Sysedit, click Start, Run, type **sysedit**, and click OK.

All four .ini files are stored in the default `\Windows` folder, whereas `Config.sys` and `Autoexec.bat` are stored in the root directory of the boot drive. Sysedit finds them all for you automatically.

FIGURE 18.3
Sysedit (available in Windows 9x only) enables you to edit `Autoexec.bat`, `Config.sys`, and the four major .ini files. These are used by Windows 9x/Me primarily for backward compatibility with older applications.

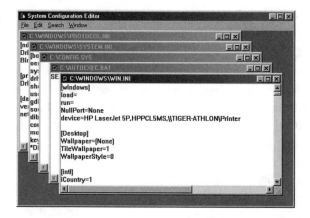

Comparing Windows 9x/Me with Windows NT/2000/XP

Windows NT 4.0, Windows 2000, and Windows XP are three successive versions of what you could call "Windows for business." These versions of Windows, unlike Windows 9x/Me, have no leftover MS-DOS or Windows 3.1 components, and until the development of Windows XP, weren't all that concerned about working with MS-DOS, Windows 3.1, or Windows 9x/Me applications. Instead, these versions of Windows put stability and speed above everything from the moment you push your computer's power switch.

From configuration files to the Windows kernel itself, Windows NT 4.0, Windows 2000, and Windows XP are very different from their predecessors (and sometimes from each other).

Windows NT 4.0/2000/XP Boot Sequence

The following files are required to start these versions of Windows:

- **NTLDR**—The Windows NT 4.0/2000/XP loader program.
- Boot.ini—Options in this file affect how Windows starts up.
- Bootsec.dos—This contains the boot sectors for another operating system if you are multibooting.
- **Ntdetect.com**—This detects the hardware installed on your system.
- Ntbootdd.sys—This device driver is used only if Windows is being started from a SCSI drive whose host adapter does not have an onboard SCSI BIOS enabled.
- **Ntoskrnl.exe**—The Windows kernel, which completes the boot process after being initialized by NTLDR.
- **Hal.dll**—The Hardware Abstraction Layer, a software translator between Windows and system hardware.
- SYSTEM *key in the Registry*—This is read to determine the system configuration.
- *Device drivers*—These are loaded according to the information stored in the Registry.

NTLDR and Starting Windows NT 4.0/2000/XP

After the computer completes the POST and the system BIOS's bootstrap loader locates the NTLDR file, NTLDR

- Enables the user to select an operating system to start (if more than one is installed). NTLDR examines the contents of Boot.ini to find out which operating systems are installed.
- Loads the Windows startup files.
- Uses the Ntdetect.com program to determine what hardware is installed and places a list of the detected hardware into the Windows Registry.

■ Loads Ntoskrnl.exe (the Windows kernel) and the Hardware Abstraction Layer (Hal.dll) into memory and hands over control to Ntoskrnl.exe after loading device drivers appropriate for the system configuration.

The NTLDR and Boot.ini files are located in the root directory (folder) of the default Windows drive if there is only one operating system. If you have a multiboot operating system (another version of Windows and Windows NT 4.0/2000/XP), the NTLDR and Boot.ini files (and Bootsec.dos, if required) are located in the root folder of the original operating system's default drive. For example, if you have Windows 9x installed on the C: drive and Windows XP installed on E:, these files will be in the root folder of the C: drive.

Windows NT/2000/XP Configuration Files

These versions of Windows have two major configuration files:

■ boot.ini

■ The Windows Registry

The following sections discuss these files in more detail.

Windows NT 4.0/2000/XP Boot.ini

The **Boot.ini** file is a specially formatted text file that configures the startup process for Windows NT 4.0/2000/XP. It resides in the default boot drive, even if Windows is installed on another drive.

On a multiboot system, Boot.ini indicates where the different versions of Windows are located. Here's the Boot.ini from my system:

```
[boot loader]
timeout=30
default=multi(0)disk(0)rdisk(0)partition(2)\WINDOWS
[operating systems]
multi(0)disk(0)rdisk(0)partition(2)\WINDOWS="Microsoft Windows XP
Professional" /fastdetect
C:\="Microsoft Windows"
```

The [boot loader] section is configured to start the Windows version (Windows XP) installed on the second partition of the hard disk by default. It also provides a maximum time of 30 seconds to pause the dual-boot menu to enable the user to choose which version of Windows to run.

The [operating systems] section identifies the locations of the Windows versions on the computer. The first line states that Windows XP Professional is located in partition 2 of the first hard disk (disk 0). The second line indicates that the boot files for the previous version of Windows (Windows 98, in this case) are located in the root folder of the C: drive.

Many additional options can be added to `Boot.ini` if necessary for troubleshooting. `Boot.ini` can be viewed with Notepad. However, if you need to configure `Boot.ini` to run your system in a troubleshooting mode, you should use `MSConfig` to view `Boot.ini` and configure it.

Windows NT 4.0/2000/XP Registry

As with Windows 9x/Me, Windows NT 4.0/2000/XP features a Registry, but you shouldn't be surprised to discover that the NT/2000/XP Registry is stored in different files, uses a different Registry editor, and has a different structure than its Windows 9x/Me sibling.

The Windows NT 4.0/2000/XP Registry is stored in different files (known in Windows-speak as **hives**), roughly corresponding to different sections of the Registry. The following files are stored in the SYSTEM32\CONFIG folder beneath the default Windows folder (typically \Windows or \WinNT); the backup file for each is listed in parentheses:

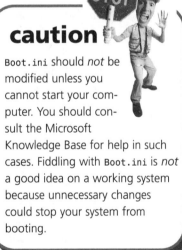

- `default` (`default.LOG`)—Stores `.DEFAULT` settings from the `HKEY_USERS` section of the Registry.

- `SAM` (`SAM.LOG`)—Stores part of the Security Account Manager database from the `HKEY_LOCAL_MACHINE\SAM` section of the Registry.

- `SECURITY` (`SECURITY.LOG`)—Stores part of the Security Account Manager database from the `HKEY_LOCAL_MACHINE\SECURITY` section of the Registry.

- `software` (`SOFTWARE.LOG`)—Stores software settings from the `HKEY_LOCAL_MACHINE\SOFTWARE` section of the Registry.

- `system` (`system.LOG`)—Stores settings from the `HKEY_LOCAL_MACHINE\SYSTEM` section of the Registry.

Windows XP also has two additional Registry hives for each user:

- ntuser.dat (NTUSER.DAT.LOG)—Stores most user-preference settings in the \Documents and Settings\ *username* folder for each user.

- UsrClass.dat (UsrClass.dat.LOG)—Stores user-preference settings for file associations and applications in the \Documents and Settings*username*\Local Settings\ Application Data\Microsoft\Windows folder for each user.

Windows NT 4.0 and Windows 2000 feature two Registry editors: Regedit and **Regedt32**.

> **caution**
>
> SAM and SECURITY sections of the Registry don't contain user-editable keys, so they *appear* to be empty. Don't be fooled—and don't erase the matching Registry files either!

Regedt32 is the primary Registry editor for these versions of Windows; however, Regedt32 does not enable you to search for particular Registry values or data, but only for Registry keys. If you need to search for Registry values or data, use Regedit instead, which has the same look and feel as the Windows 9x/Me version of Regedit.

Windows XP uses Regedit as its sole Registry editor; if you use the Regedt32 command, this command also starts Regedit. Windows XP's Regedit, like the Regedit command in Windows NT 4.0 and Windows 2000, looks like the Windows 9x/Me version.

The Windows NT 4.0 and Windows 2000 Regedt32 Registry editor uses five separate editing windows, which can be resized and repositioned for viewing the Registry, as in Figure 18.4.

Regedt32 also enables you to view the Registry in read-only form, making it the preferred Windows NT 4.0/2000 Registry tool for viewing the Registry's contents.

As with the Windows 9x/Me Registry, the Registry in Windows NT 4.0/2000/XP should *not* be edited by hand unless there is no alternative to solving a particular problem and unless the Registry has been backed up first.

You can use the Export option from the File menu of either Registry editor to make a backup copy with Windows NT 4.0 as well as with newer versions. However, Windows 2000 and Windows XP incorporate special features into their backup programs to make backing up the Registry easier.

To back up the Windows 2000 Registry, use the Windows 2000 backup program. Click Start, Accessories, System Tools, Backup to start it. From the opening menu, select Emergency Repair Disk, and select the option to back up the Registry on the next screen; insert a blank, formatted disk when prompted to complete the process.

Active window   Value and data

Regedt32 menu   Registry key

FIGURE 18.4

FIGURE 18.4

Regedt32
(Windows 2000
version;
Windows NT 4.0
version is simi-
lar). Note the
use of overlap-
ping Windows
for each of the
Registry's major
sections and
additional menu
options com-
pared to Regedit.

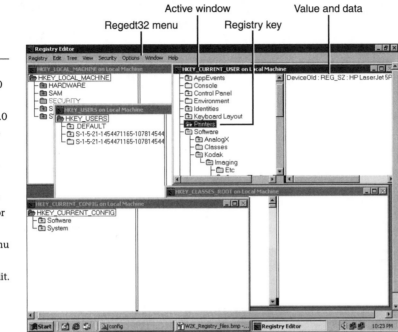

Because the Windows 2000 Registry can occupy as much as 20MB of disk space on some systems, the **Emergency Repair Disk (ERD)** does not contain a copy of the Registry itself but includes other information necessary to help restore the system in case of a crash. The Registry is stored in a folder called RegBack, which is contained in the \WinNT\Repair folder. In the event of a serious system problem, both the Windows 2000 Emergency Repair Disk and the Registry backup in the RegBack folder would be used to restore the system. You should re-create the ERD and Registry backup when-ever you install new hardware or software to keep a record of the latest system configuration.

Windows XP also uses the Windows Backup program to back up the Registry as part of backing up the **System State** (see Figure 18.5). In Windows XP Professional, the System State also includes boot files, COM+ Class Registration database, and files protected by Windows File Protection. This backup is stored on tape or removable media.

FIGURE 18.5

Preparing to
back up the
Windows XP
Registry as part
of the System
State backup
using the
Windows XP
backup
program.

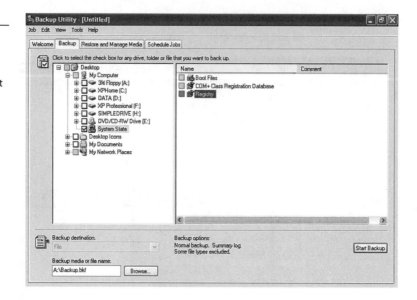

Using the Windows GUI

Although you probably realize by now that you sometimes need to leave the
Windows graphical user interface (GUI) behind to make repairs or perform maintenance, the Windows GUI is where most work gets done. The following sections discuss these elements of the Windows GUI:

- My Computer
- Windows Explorer
- Control Panel
- Taskbar and System Tray (systray)
- Start Menu
- Accessories/System Tools
- Computer Management Console

Network Neighborhood/My Network Places is discussed in Chapter 21, "Networking
and Internet Connectivity," and Chapter 22, "Troubleshooting Principles," and
Device Manager is discussed in Chapter 19, "Installing and Configuring Hardware
in Windows."

My Computer

The **My Computer** icon might be the single most important icon for maintaining and working with Windows. My Computer provides access to the following features and utilities:

- Open My Computer to view the local drives on your system, available network drives, and the Control Panel folder. Additional options are available in various Windows versions.

- Right-click My Computer to choose options such as Properties (which opens the System properties sheet), the Windows Explorer, Search/Find, drive mapping, and creating shortcuts.

My Computer can open a separate window for each object you open, or you can change the contents of the My Computer window to display the contents for each object. You can change this option by clicking View, Folder Options, and selecting Custom from the Folder tab.

In Windows 95, opening My Computer does not start the Windows Explorer unless Internet Explorer 4.0 or above is installed. When Internet 4.0 or above is installed, Windows 95 will work like Windows 98/Me/2000/XP, which open Windows Explorer when My Computer is opened.

The Windows Explorer

The **Windows Explorer** is the file-management utility used by Windows (see Figure 18.6). Windows 98/Me/2000/XP can use Explorer to view both local drive/network and Internet content; Windows 95 and Windows NT 4.0 can view only local or network drives with Explorer unless Internet Explorer (IE) 4.0 or above is installed.

⇨ By default, Windows Explorer doesn't display hidden and system files unless the View options are changed; **see** "Changing Viewing Options in Windows Explorer," **p. 628** for details.

Windows Explorer can be started in any of the following ways:

- From the Start menu, click Start, Programs, Windows Explorer (Windows NT 4.0/9x) or Start, Programs, Accessories, Windows Explorer (Windows Me/2000/XP).

- From the command line, type **Explorer** and press Enter.

- Open My Computer in Windows 98/Me and 2000/XP to start Explorer automatically.

Selected object (C: drive)   Contents of C: drive (default large icons view)

FIGURE 18.6

The Windows
Explorer in
Windows 98
(Classic view);
the selected
object's name
appears in the
Address bar.

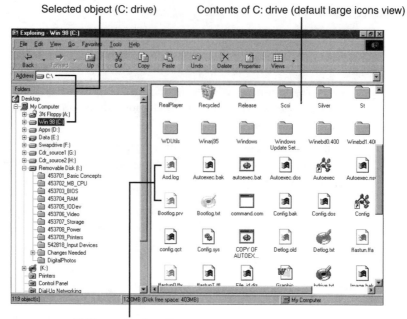

Hidden and system files

To start Windows Explorer from My Computer in Windows NT 4.0/95 if Internet Explorer 4.0 or above is not installed, use either of the following options:

■ *Right-click My Computer and select Explore*—Use this option to display the contents of My Computer in the right Explorer window.

■ *Right-click any object in My Computer and select Explore*—Use this option to display the contents of the object in the right Explorer window.

Classic and Web View

Windows Explorer can be set to display objects in either Classic or Web view. **Classic view** (refer to Figure 18.6) is similar to the original Windows Explorer in Windows 95; **Web view** (see Figure 18.7) requires that Internet Explorer 4.0 or above be installed on Windows 95. It's a standard option with Windows 98/Me and Windows 2000. (Windows Me's Web view adds a zoomable preview window for bitmaps and photos below the file properties display.)

Contents of selected object (Details view)

Selector for large icons (default),
small icons, list, details views

Selected object (C: drive)

FIGURE 18.7

The Web view in
Windows 2000
is being used to
display the con-
tents of the
C: drive. The
properties for
the C: drive (the
selected object in
the left window)
are displayed
in the right
window.

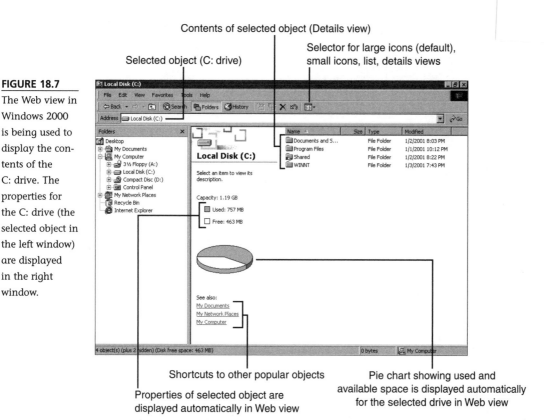

Shortcuts to other popular objects

Properties of selected object are
displayed automatically in Web view

Pie chart showing used and
available space is displayed automatically
for the selected drive in Web view

Common Tasks View (Windows XP)

The Windows XP version of Windows Explorer uses a supercharged version of Web
view known as the **Common Tasks** view as its default (see Figure 18.8). Like Web
view, the Common Tasks view displays the properties of the selected object, but also
displays a preview when available. However, the
most significant new feature is the changeable
task pane in the upper-left side of the display.

The contents and name of the task pane change
according to the characteristics of the selected or
displayed object. For example, display My
Computer, and the task pane is titled System
Tasks, with a choice of options such as View
System Information, Add or Remove Programs,
or Change a Setting. The contents of Other
Places also changes to display related objects.

tip

To switch between
Common Tasks and Classic
view, click the Folders icon
on the toolbar.

FIGURE 18.8

The Common Tasks view of a folder in Windows XP. The Details pane at lower left displays a preview of the selected file as well as its properties. The File and Folder Tasks task pane at upper left changes its name and contents to provide task options suitable for the folder or selected object.

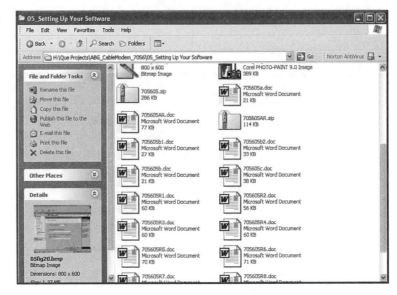

Changing Viewing Options in Windows Explorer

By default, Windows Explorer prevents users from seeing information such as

- File extensions for **registered file types**; for example, a file called LETTER.DOC will be displayed as LETTER because WordPad (or Microsoft Word) is associated with .DOC files.
- The full path to the current folder.
- Files with hidden or system attributes, such as Bootlog.txt and Msdos.sys.
- Folders with hidden or system attributes, such as INF (used for hardware installation).

Concealing this information is intended to make it harder for users to "break" Windows, but it makes management and troubleshooting more difficult.

To change these and other viewing options, follow this procedure:

1. Start Windows Explorer.
2. Click View, Folder Options and select the View tab.
3. Select the options you want (see Figure 18.9). I recommend the following changes for experienced end users:

■ Enable the Display the Full Path in the Title Bar option.

■ Disable the Hide File Extensions for Known File Types option.

If you are maintaining or troubleshooting a system, I also recommend you change the following:

■ Enable the Show All Files setting.

■ Disable the Hide Protected Operating System Files setting.

You should probably change these settings back to their defaults before you return the system to normal use.

4. To apply these settings to all folders, click Like Current Folder.

5. Click OK to apply and close the Folder Options menu.

FIGURE 18.9

The Windows Explorer Folder Options, View menu in Windows 98 (left) and Windows XP (right) after selecting recommended options for use by technicians and experienced end users.

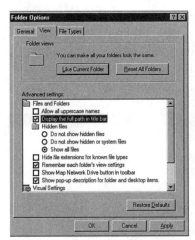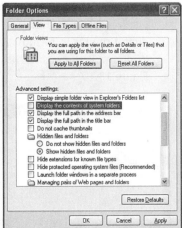

Objects such as files and folders can be displayed in at least four ways within Windows Explorer:

■ *Large icons*—The default (refer to Figure 18.6); Windows XP calls this option Tiles.

■ *Small icons*—Displays more objects onscreen without scrolling vertically; might require the user to scroll horizontally to view multiple columns. Windows XP calls this option Icons.

■ *List*—Displays more objects onscreen than large icons in a single column.

■ *Details*—The same size of icons used by Small or List, plus size and last-modified date details (refer to Figure 18.7).

Windows XP adds two new options:

- *Thumbnails*—Displays a thumbnail (small-sized graphic) sample of previewable files and folders (.BMP, .JPG, and some other graphics file formats and folders containing these files) in the selected folder and uses large tiled icons for non-previewable files. Thumbnail view can be used in any folder.

- *Filmstrip*—Displays a larger preview of the selected graphic file at the top of the right window, and smaller thumbnails below it. Buttons below the large preview can be used to rotate the graphic or to move to another graphic. This view is available in the My Pictures folder or other folders that contain digital photos in formats recognized by Windows Preview, such as .TIF or .JPG (see Figure 18.10).

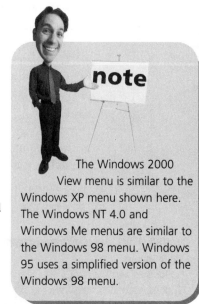

note

The Windows 2000 View menu is similar to the Windows XP menu shown here. The Windows NT 4.0 and Windows Me menus are similar to the Windows 98 menu. Windows 95 uses a simplified version of the Windows 98 menu.

FIGURE 18.10

The new Filmstrip view in Windows XP is used for folders containing digital photos (.TIF or .JPG files). Note that the task pane lists Picture Tasks such as printing photos or copying items to a recordable/rewritable CD.

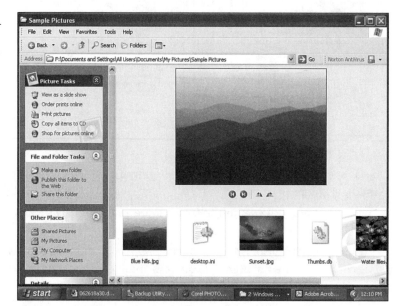

To change the view for the current folder, use the Views button in Figure 18.6 or the View pull-down menu.

Control Panel

The **Control Panel** is the major starting point for adjusting the hardware and user interface settings in Windows. It contains the following hardware-related icons; open the icon to see and adjust the current settings:

- *Add New Hardware (Windows 9x/Me); Add/Remove Hardware (Windows 2000); Add Hardware (Windows XP)*—Installs new PnP and legacy hardware. The Windows 2000 Wizard also troubleshoots and removes hardware.
- *Display*—Adjusts monitor, video adapter, and Windows desktop settings.
- *Game Controllers*—Adjusts settings for joysticks, steering wheels, and other game controllers.
- *Internet Options*—Adjusts Internet settings used by Internet Explorer and other Microsoft products.
- *Keyboard*—Adjusts keyboard repeat rate and language.
- *Modems*—Adjusts, installs, and tests modems and serial ports.
- *Mouse*—Adjusts and installs mouse devices and similar pointing devices.
- *Multimedia*—Adjusts multimedia device settings.
- *Network*—Installs and configures network hardware and software.
- *Power Management*—Enables, disables, and adjusts power management settings.
- *Printers*—Installs and removes printers and adjusts printer settings.
- *Sounds*—Configures sound playback during specified system events.
- *System*—Displays and configures Device Manager and other hardware settings including Performance, and general Windows information, performance, and hardware profiles.
- *Telephony*—Configures telephony device drivers and dialing settings used by modems and similar devices.

Other Control Panel icons such as Add/Remove Programs, Administrative Tools, and Accessibility Options are primarily software related; some user-installed software and devices also add icons to the Control Panel.

note

Windows NT 4.0 doesn't have a unified wizard for adding hardware.

You can open the Control Panel folder from the Start button, My Computer, or the Windows Explorer:

■ *Click Start, Settings, Control Panel*—The Control Panel will open a new window onscreen. (The Control Panel icon is located in the root Start menu in Windows XP.)

■ *Open My Computer and select the Control Panel*—The Control Panel's contents will be displayed in the right window or in a new window, depending on the settings you use for My Computer.

■ *Open the Windows Explorer and select the Control Panel*—The Control Panel's contents will be displayed in the right Explorer window (see Figure 18.11) .

note

Windows Me's default is to display only the most commonly used Control Panel icons. Click View All Control Panel Options to see all the icons.

FIGURE 18.11

The Windows 98 Control Panel as viewed in Windows Explorer.

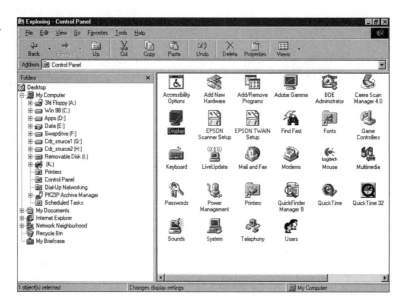

Open any Control Panel icon to see current settings and make adjustments for the devices it controls. If the Classic view is used for the Control Panel folder, double-click an icon to open it. If Web view is used, a single click will open an icon.

Windows XP's Category and Classic Views of the Control Panel

The **Category view** shown in Figure 18.12 is the default in Windows XP. When you click on an icon, it displays various tasks and provides you with a shortcut to classic Control Panel icons (also shown in Figure 18.12). If you're a Windows newcomer, you might prefer the Category view's task-oriented design. However, if you're already familiar with Control Panel, you'll probably prefer to click the Switch to Classic View option in the task pane. The Classic view of the Windows XP Control Panel is very similar to the Windows 98 Control Panel shown in Figure 18.11.

Switches Control Panel to Classic view

FIGURE 18.12

The Windows XP Control Panel in its default Category view, and the sub-menus triggered by each icon. Note that the Add or Remove Programs and User Accounts icons have no submenus.

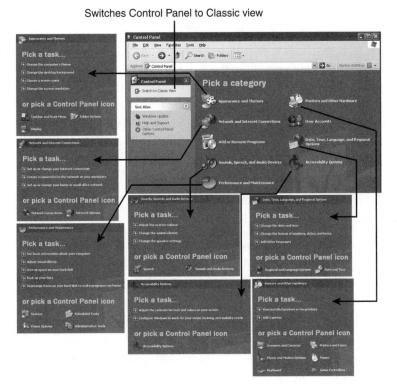

The Switch to Classic View task shown in Figure 18.12 is actually a toggle. No matter which Control Panel view you prefer, the task pane provides the option to switch to the other one.

Shortcuts to Control Panel Icons

Some Control Panel icons can be accessed through properties sheets. If you right-click any of the items in Table 18.3 and select Properties, you will open the Control Panel icon listed.

Table 18.3   Popular Shortcuts to Control Panel Icons

Properties Sheet	Control Panel Icon Opened
My Computer	System
Desktop	Display
Network Neighborhood or My Network Places	Network
Taskbar	Taskbar and Start Menu

Taskbar and System Tray (systray)

Even before you click on the Start menu, most Windows installations already have several programs running in the **System Tray** (also known as the systray or SysTray), which is located in the lower-right corner of the screen, next to the clock. Microsoft also likes to refer to this as the Notification area (refer to Figure 18.14).

Although programs you launch manually can wind up in the System Tray, most programs you find there are started automatically from one of these locations:

- The Startup group in the Start menu
- Load= or Run= statements in Win.ini
- Shell=explorer.exe *filename* in System.ini
- Various Registry keys, such as
  HKEY_LOCAL_MACHINE\Software\Microsoft\Windows\CurrentVersion\Run
  HKEY_LOCAL_MACHINE\Software\Microsoft\Windows\CurrentVersion\RunServices

> **tip**
>
> These and other methods for autolaunching programs, including methods used by spyware, are discussed at http://www.elfqrin.com/docs/autostart-win.html.

Figure 18.13 shows the Run key in the Registry of a Windows XP system with over 20 entries. Running so many programs can slow down the Windows startup process, use up memory and, with Windows 9x/Me, can cause the system to be short of free system resources as soon as the system starts. (See "Using the Windows 9x/Me Resource Meter" in Chapter 20 for details.)

Most systray programs wait for an event (such as a disk insertion or a mouse click) after they are started. To see what each icon in the systray does, right-click the icon.

> **tip**
>
> You can disable startup programs in the systray by using the Microsoft System Configuration utility (Msconfig); see Chapter 20 for details.

The contents of the key

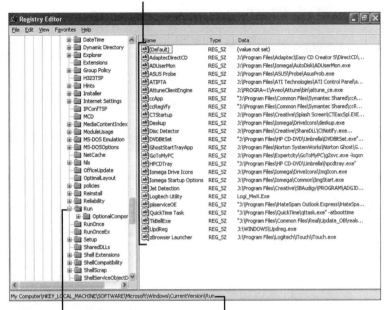

FIGURE 18.13

The contents of
HKEY_LOCAL_
MACHINE\
Software\
Microsoft\
Windows\Current
Version\Run
indicates this
computer starts
over 20
processes at
startup. Other
autostart meth-
ods such as the
Startup group
can start addi-
tional programs
and processes.

The opened key in the Registry   The name of the key

The System Tray is part of the **Taskbar**, which displays running programs that do not insert themselves into the systray. By default, the Taskbar displays one row of program icons, reducing the amount of space given to each program as more and more programs are run. Figure 18.14 shows a typical Windows XP system's System Tray and Taskbar and their properties sheet. To display the Taskbar's properties sheet, right-click on an empty section of the Taskbar and select Properties.

To make the Taskbar more useful if you have many programs running, you can resize it by dragging its top edge: Drag its top edge up to create additional rows or drag the top edge down to the edge of the screen to make it vanish. You can also drag the Taskbar to any side of the screen.

tip

To prevent the Taskbar from being accidentally resized or dragged, enable the Lock the Taskbar option in the Taskbar properties sheet. You can also auto-hide the Taskbar to provide more display area with the Taskbar properties sheet. When the Taskbar is set to autohide, it is displayed only when you move the mouse to the edge of the screen where the Taskbar is hiding or if you press Ctrl-Esc to bring up the Start menu.

Windows XP groups icons from the
same program together to save space in the
Taskbar unless you clear this check mark

FIGURE 18.14

The Taskbar and
System Tray
(Notification
area) on a typi-
cal Windows XP
system and their
properties sheet.
Older versions of
Windows don't
offer the group-
ing and hide
inactive icon
options shown
here.

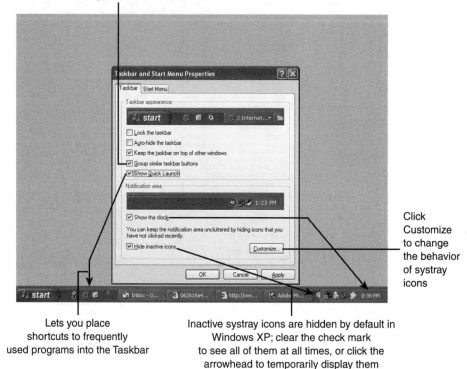

Click
Customize
to change
the behavior
of systray
icons

Lets you place
shortcuts to frequently
used programs into the Taskbar

Inactive systray icons are hidden by default in
Windows XP; clear the check mark
to see all of them at all times, or click the
arrowhead to temporarily display them

Start Menu

With all versions of Windows covered on the A+ Certification Exams, you can add
items to the **Start menu**, remove items from it, create or remove folders, move an
item from one folder to another, and switch between large icons (default) and small
icons.

If Internet Explorer 5.0 or later is installed, you can also right-click on the menu and
select Sort by Name.

Windows XP adds additional customization features, including automatic addition
of the most frequently used programs to a special section of the Start menu.

Adding, Removing, and Sorting Start Menu Items and Folders

The Start menu is comprised of shortcuts to programs and other objects on your system. The method used to add shortcuts to your Start menu varies with the version of
Windows you use.

With Windows 9x and Windows NT 4.0, follow this procedure:

1. Right-click on an empty portion of the Taskbar and select Properties.

2. Click Start Menu Programs.

3. Click Add.

4. You can enter the path to the program (such as `C:\Windows\Pbrush.exe`) or click the Browse button to locate the program for which you are making a shortcut. Click Next.

5. Select the folder to place the shortcut in, or click New Folder to create a new folder for the shortcut. Enter a name for the new folder if desired. Click Next.

6. The shortcut name created by Windows is displayed. To keep the name created by Windows, click Finish. You can also change the name as desired and click Finish.

7. Click OK. The new shortcut (and new folder, if any) appears on your Start button menu.

tip

Along with Add and Remove, most versions of Windows also have an Advanced button (see Figure 18.15), which activates a Windows Explorer view of the Start menu. Use this view if you want to drag shortcuts between folders or nest one folder of shortcuts inside another.

With Windows 2000/Me

1. Right-click on an empty portion of the Taskbar and select Properties.

2. Click Advanced (see Figure 18.15).

3. Follow steps 3–7 for Windows 9x/NT 4.0.

With Windows XP (if the default Windows XP Start menu is used)

1. Right-click on the Start button.

2. To add a shortcut for the current user only, select Explore. To add a shortcut for all users, select Explore All Users.

3. The Start menu folder is opened in the left window (it resembles Figure 18.15); shortcuts on the Start menu are shown in the right window. To see additional Start menu folders, click the plus sign (+) next to Programs in the left window.

4. To create a new folder for the shortcut, click the folder in the left window where you want to create the shortcut to open it in the right window. Right-click an empty area in the right window and select New, Folder. Name the folder as desired.

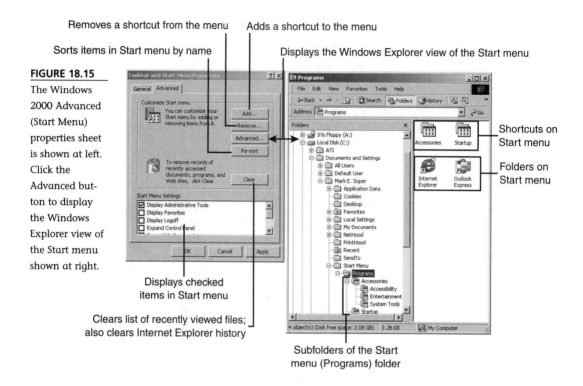

Removes a shortcut from the menu   Adds a shortcut to the menu

Sorts items in Start menu by name   Displays the Windows Explorer view of the Start menu

FIGURE 18.15

The Windows
2000 Advanced
(Start Menu)
properties sheet
is shown at left.
Click the
Advanced but-
ton to display
the Windows
Explorer view of
the Start menu
shown at right.

Shortcuts on
Start menu

Folders on
Start menu

Displays checked
items in Start menu

Clears list of recently viewed files;
also clears Internet Explorer history

Subfolders of the Start
menu (Programs) folder

5. To select a folder for the shortcut, click the folder in the left window. The folder's contents appear in the right window.

6. Click File, New, Shortcut to start the Shortcut Wizard.

7. You can enter the path to the program (such as C:\Windows\Pbrush.exe) or click the Browse button to locate the program for which you are making a short-cut. Click Next.

8. The shortcut name created by Windows is displayed. To keep the name cre-ated by Windows, click Finish. You can also change the name as desired and click Finish.

9. Click OK. The new shortcut (and new folder, if any) appear on your Start but-ton menu.

➪ Windows XP can also be configured to use the **Classic Start** menu (**see** "Adjusting Advanced Start Menu Properties," **p. 639**, for details).

If the Classic Start menu is used

1. Right-click on an empty portion of the Taskbar and select Properties.

2. Select the Start Menu tab and click the Customize button.

3. Follow steps 3–7 for Windows 9x/NT 4.0.

To remove an item from the Start menu, follow the steps to add an item, but instead of adding a new item, click the Remove button and select the shortcut to remove. If you use the Windows Explorer view of the Start menu, press Del to send the shortcut to the Recycle Bin, or Shift-Del to discard the shortcut.

To sort the shortcuts, follow these procedures:

- With Windows 95/NT 4.0, install Internet Explorer 5.0 or greater; then follow the procedure for Windows 98/Me.

- With Windows 98/Me/2000, click Start, Programs, right-click a folder or shortcut, and select Sort by Name.

- With Windows 2000/Me, open the Taskbar and Start Menu properties sheet, click Advanced, and click Re-sort.

- With Windows XP, click Start, All Programs, right-click a folder or shortcut, and select Sort by Name.

> **tip**
>
> It's *much* easier to add shortcuts to the Windows XP Start menu if you switch to the Classic Start menu. Even if you prefer the normal Windows XP menu, I recommend you switch to the Classic Start menu, add the shortcuts you need to make, and switch back to the default menu.

Adjusting Advanced Start Menu Properties

You can adjust the appearance of the Start menu in various ways, depending upon the version of Windows in use. These customizations are available from the Taskbar and Start Menu properties sheets described in the previous section.

Table 18.4 lists the customization options available by Windows version.

Table 18.4   Customizing the Start Menu

Option	95	NT 4.0	98	Me	2000	XP
	\multicolumn{6}{c}{Windows Version}					
Clear shortcuts to recently opened documents	Yes	Yes	Yes	Yes	Yes	Yes
Clear IE browser history	No	No	No	Yes	Yes	Yes[2]
Select objects to appear on Start menu and Taskbar from list	No	No	No	Yes	Yes	Yes
Most frequently used programs are automatically added to Start menu[1]	No	No	No	No	No	Yes
Choice of icon size[3]	Yes	Yes	Yes	Yes	Yes	Yes

[1]*In default Windows XP Start Menu mode only. User can also adjust the number of programs to display.*

[2]*In classic Start Windows XP Start Menu mode only.*

[3]*This option is located on the Taskbar options properties sheet in some versions of Windows.*

Windows XP's Start Menu properties sheet (in default mode) offers more customization options than any previous version. The General tab includes options for

- Icon size
- Whether to place frequently used programs on the Start menu
- Choice of which Web browser and email client to place on the Start menu

Click the Advanced menu to select

- Whether to automatically open submenus
- Whether to highlight newly installed programs
- Which standard items to include on the Start button and whether to list them as links or menus
- Whether to list most recently used documents (see Figure 18.16)

FIGURE 18.16

The Windows XP General (left) and Advanced (right) Start Menu properties sheets.

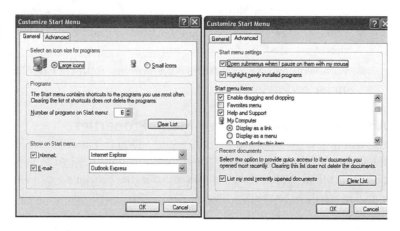

Making Desktop Shortcuts

Some Windows programs add shortcuts to your desktop as well as to the Start menu. However, if you don't have a shortcut on the desktop for a program you frequently use, it's easy to create one.

➪ To add a **desktop shortcut**, right-click the Windows desktop (not on an existing icon); select New, Shortcut, and then follow steps 4–6 for making a Start menu shortcut with Windows 9x as listed in "Adding, Removing, and Sorting Start Menu Items and Folders," **p. 636**.

Accessories/System Tools

The **Accessories folder** in Windows is where to go to find most of the utilities and programs Microsoft supplies with Windows. Of the folders within the Accessories folder, click **System Tools** to find the utilities and programs you need to prevent and solve problems.

The contents of the System Tools folder can vary with the version of Windows installed and the options used during installation. If you install Windows 9x/Me and Windows NT 4.0 with an option other than Typical, some tools might not be installed.

The following sections examine typical selections in the System Tools menu not covered elsewhere in this book:

- Backup
- Character Map
- Disk Cleanup
- Drive Converter (FAT32)
- DriveSpace
- Maintenance Wizard
- Scheduled Tasks
- System Monitor
- Welcome to Windows

To start these tools, click Start, (All) Programs, Accessories, System Tools, and click the tool desired.

Windows Backup

The **Windows Backup** programs supplied with Windows are primarily intended to back up your data. Backup and restore programs differ from conventional file copy routines in these ways:

- Backups are typically compressed; file copies performed with COPY or XCOPY/XCOPY32 generally are not.

- Backups can span a large file onto two or more separate pieces of supported media; COPY and XCOPY/XCOPY32 cannot subdivide a large file.

- Backups must be restored by the same or compatible program; files copied by COPY or XCOPY/XCOPY32 can be retrieved by Windows Explorer and standard Windows programs.

note

Some versions of Windows place these utilities in the Accessories menu rather than the System Tools menu.

If your Windows installation doesn't include a listed utility, open the Control Panel, click Add/Remove Programs, and click the option to install Windows components (sometimes referred to as Windows Setup). Follow the prompts to install the tool needed.

■ Backups can be stored to tape, floppy disk, or other types of removable storage such as Zip drives (but not rewritable CD or DVD); COPY and XCOPY/XCOPY32 can work only with drives that can be accessed through a drive letter or a UNC (Universal Naming Convention) network path. However, COPY and XCOPY/XCOPY32 can be used with CD-RW rewritable DVD, and CD-R media that have been formatted for UDF (drag-and-drop) file copying.

You can also start the Windows Backup program from the Tools menu of the drive properties sheet:

1. Open the Windows Explorer.

2. Right-click a drive.

3. Select Properties.

4. Select Tools.

5. Click Backup Now to start Backup.

> **note**
>
> The Microsoft Backup utility for Windows Me must be installed manually from the add-ons folder of the Windows Me CD. The Microsoft Backup utility for Windows XP Home Edition must also be installed manually from the `\ValueAdd\MSFT\NTBACKUP` folder on the Windows XP Home Edition CD.

The Windows Backup program supports backups to a wide variety of drive types, including tape drives, floppy disk drives, and removable-media drives such as Zip drives, but *not* rewritable CD or DVD drives.

During the backup process, you can specify the following:

■ Which drive(s) to back up

■ Which files to back up, selecting all files or new and changed files only

■ Whether to back up the Windows Registry

■ Where to create the backup—to tape drive, floppy disk, another hard disk, or a removable-media drive

■ How to run the backup—whether to use compression, passwords, and other options

Table 18.5 compares the major features of the Windows Backup programs.

Table 18.5   Windows Backup Versions Compared

	Windows Version					
Feature	95	NT 4.0	98	Me	2000	XP
Manual backup/restore process	Yes	Yes	Yes	Yes	Yes	Yes
Wizard-driven backup/restore process	No	No	Yes	Yes	Yes	Yes
Backs up Windows Registry	Yes	Yes	Yes	Yes	Yes[1]	Yes[1]
Creates Windows Emergency Repair Disk	No	No	No	No	Yes	No
Supports Automated System Recovery (ASR)[2]	No	No	No	No	No	Yes
Supports command-line operation[3]	No	Yes	No	No	Yes	Yes
Features built-in scheduler	No	No	No	No	Yes	Yes

[1]*Backs up Registry as part of backing up System State data.*
[2]*Requires user to perform a special ASR backup, which creates an ASR disk and a special minimal Windows installation that can be used to restore a regular backup. ASR is supported by Windows XP Professional only.*
[3]*Uses the command* NTBACKUP *with various options.*

Windows 95 and NT 4.0's versions of Backup lack wizards, but all other versions feature Backup and Restore Wizards to guide you through the backup and restore processes, or you can cancel the wizard and select the options you want.

Windows Backup will prompt you for additional tape or disk media as needed throughout the backup process. Figure 18.17 illustrates the Windows 98 Backup program; other versions have a similar interface.

FIGURE 18.17

Setting up a backup job with the Windows 98 Backup program.

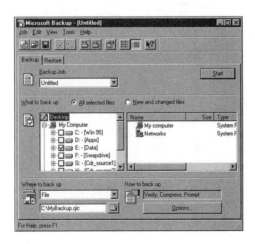

Character Map

Character Map, which is found in all versions of Windows on the A+ Certification Exams, provides an easy way to add an accented, mathematical, scientific, or iconic character to a document. To use Character Map

1. Start your application; then start Character Map.

2. Select the font you want to use from the pull-down menu.

3. Use the preview mode to view the characters in that font (see Figure 18.18).

4. Click Select to choose the character.

5. Repeat steps 2–4 to choose other characters.

6. Click Copy to place the character(s) on the Windows Clipboard.

7. Move the cursor to the desired location in your document.

8. Click Paste to place the character(s).

note

Given the limitations of the Windows Backup programs, many users prefer a third-party solution. If you want to be able to read existing Windows Backup files, but want more features (true disaster recovery, support for CD-R/CD-RW/DVD media, support for more tape drives, and so on), consider backup software made by Veritas (www.veritas.com), such as Backup Exec or BackUpMyPC (made by Veritas for Stomp, Inc.—www.stompinc.com).

FIGURE 18.18

Selecting a character with Character Map. Other characters from other fonts have already been selected for copying.

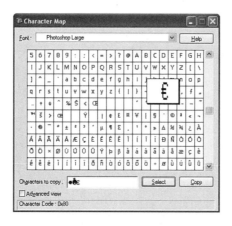

Disk Cleanup

Disk Cleanup was introduced in Windows 98 to provide an easy way to reduce disk clutter. **Disk Cleanup** can be used to

- Compress old (seldom-used) files.

- Remove temporary Internet files and offline Web pages.

- Empty the Recycle Bin.

- Delete other types of temporary files, including those left behind by Microsoft Publisher and the Content Indexer.

Click More Options to remove unused optional Windows components, installed programs, and older System Restore restore points (see Figure 18.19).

FIGURE 18.19

The standard Disk Cleanup (left) and More Options (right) menus. Use the Disk Cleanup menu to remove temporary and other unwanted files, and the More Options menu to remove unneeded programs and restore points.

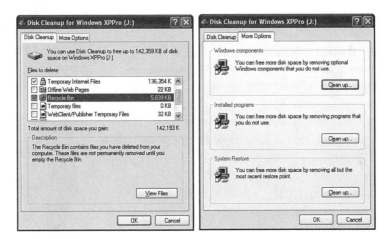

Scheduled Tasks

Starting with Windows 98, you can configure Windows to run a program automatically with the **Scheduled Tasks** Wizard. Start the wizard, select the program you want to run, and specify if you want to run the program daily, weekly, monthly, at startup, when you log on, or one time only. Next, specify what day of the week, what time, and for what period you want to run the task. With Windows 2000 and XP, you can also specify a username and password, which can be used to log onto the system and run the task. At the end of the process, you can display the advanced properties for the task to further customize the process.

Drive Converter

This utility, found only in Windows 98, can convert a drive from the FAT16 file system to the more efficient FAT32 file system.

DriveSpace

Windows 9x features a real-time drive-compression utility called **DriveSpace**. Windows Me can use DriveSpace-compressed drives, but doesn't include the capability to compress a drive with DriveSpace. Windows NT 4.0/2000/XP don't support DriveSpace, but include their own compression features as part of the NTFS file system.

Maintenance Wizard

Windows 98 and Windows Me's **Maintenance Wizard** can be used to schedule and configure the disk defragmentation, ScanDisk error checking, and Disk Cleanup utilities. For more information about these utilities, see the individual entries elsewhere in this chapter.

System Monitor

Windows 9x and Me feature a customizable **System Monitor**, which can be used to monitor the performance of the Dial-Up Adapter, Disk Cache, File System, Kernel, Memory Manager, and Microsoft Network Client. You can select from a variety of measurements in each category, select from line, bar, or numeric charts, adjust the update frequency, and create a logfile. Use System Monitor to help fine-tune the performance of a system or the network (see Figure 18.20).

note

Windows 2000 and XP can convert FAT16 and FAT32 drives to NTFS with the command-line Convert utility. The Windows NT 4.0 version of Convert converts FAT16 drives to NTFS (Windows NT 4.0 doesn't support FAT32).

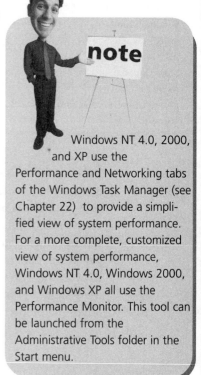

note

Windows NT 4.0, 2000, and XP use the Performance and Networking tabs of the Windows Task Manager (see Chapter 22) to provide a simplified view of system performance. For a more complete, customized view of system performance, Windows NT 4.0, Windows 2000, and Windows XP all use the Performance Monitor. This tool can be launched from the Administrative Tools folder in the Start menu.

FIGURE 18.20

The System
Monitor config-
ured to track
eight different
measurements
of system
performance.

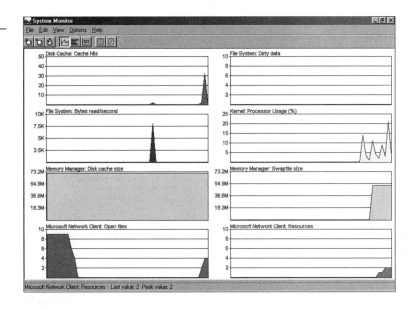

Computer Management Console

Windows 9x/Me have minimal management features
included, because they are designed to be used by
home or small-business users who aren't networked
or have very simple networks. Windows NT 4.0,
2000, and XP, on the other hand, are designed to
work in corporate networks, and have management tools to match.

Windows NT 4.0's management tools are located in
the **Administrative Tools** folder of the Start
menu, whereas Windows 2000 and XP's management tools can be started from the Administrative
Tools folder in Control Panel or from the
Computer Management Console. To open
the Computer Management Console, right-click on
My Computer and select Manage.

The Computer Management Console is a comprehen-
sive management tool that allows the administrator of a Windows 2000 or XP system access to several different administrative tools that can be used to manage your
computer. The major categories in Windows XP (Windows 2000 is similar) include

note

You can also create
your own console with a
customized list of management
tools by running MMC (Microsoft
Management Console) with Start,
Run in Windows 2000/XP.

- *System Tools*—Tools in this category include
  - *Event Viewer*—Tracks system events and problems
  - *Performance*—Displays system performance
  - *Services*—Manages system services
  - *Shared Folders*—Manages network shared folders and users
  - *Local Users and Groups*—Manages groups and users
  - *Performance Logs and Alerts*—Views logs of system performance, events, and problems
  - *Device Manager*—Manages hardware settings

- *Storage*—Tools in this category include
  - *Removable Storage*—Manages flash, disk, and optical removable storage devices
  - *Disk Defragmenter*—Defragments drives
  - *Disk Management*—Prepares hard disks and manages drive letters

- *Services*—Tools in this category include
  - *Services*—Manages services running on the computer
  - *WMI Control*—Manages Windows Management Instrumentation service
  - *Indexing Service*—Manages indexing service

To view details about a managed object, click the object in the left window and the information will appear in the right window. Right-click on an object and select Properties for more detailed information. Figure 18.21 shows the Application event viewer on a Windows XP system being used to view the details of an application error.

Selected management tool

Selected event   Event properties

FIGURE 18.21

Viewing the
details about an
application error
using the
Application
Event Viewer.
The left window
displays other
major compo-
nents of
Windows XP's
Computer
Management
Console.

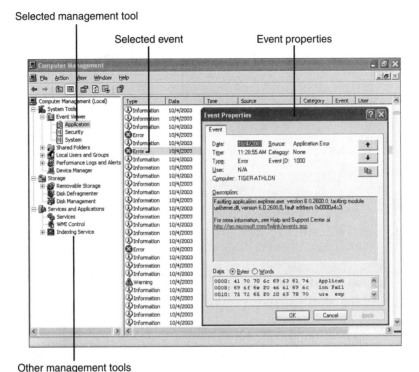

Other management tools

Disk Management

All versions of Windows covered on the A+ Certification Exams feature disk management tools for checking for disk errors, and all but Windows NT 4.0 also include disk
defragmentation tools. These tools are covered in the following sections.

Using ScanDisk and CHKDSK

All versions of Windows covered on the A+ Certification Exams provide integrated
error-checking programs for fixing disk problems. Windows 9x/Me use ScanDisk;
Windows NT 4.0/2000/XP use **CHKDSK**. In Windows Explorer/My Computer, both
are referred to as error checking. To run error checking from the Windows GUI

1. Open the Windows Explorer.

2. Right-click a drive, select Properties, and then click the Tools tab.

3. Click Check Now to start the process (see Figure 18.22).

FIGURE 18.22

The Windows XP
disk Tools menu.
Windows 9x/Me
and Windows
2000 menus are
similar.

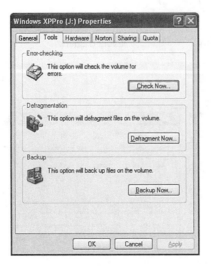

Using ScanDisk

After the ScanDisk process starts, you can select either
Standard or Thorough testing. Thorough testing
takes longer but checks the disk surface for errors as
well as files and folders. Use the Options button to
select whether to check the entire drive, to perform
write testing, or to fix bad sectors in system and
hidden files. Check the Automatically Fix Errors
box to have ScanDisk fix disk and file errors it
detects without user intervention. Click Advanced
to specify how to handle cross-linked files, lost file
fragments, and other problems. Click Start to begin
the test process. A progress bar indicates the
progress of testing.

ScanDisk performs the following tasks:

It's no coincidence that
Error-checking is listed
before Defragmentation and
Backup in the Windows disk Tools
menu. You should check the drive
for errors *first* before you perform
a defrag or backup operation.

- Checks the disk surface of the specified drive
  for read errors

- Repairs problems with the logical disk structure

- Provides disk usage statistics at the end of its operation

If ScanDisk is run from the command prompt while the Windows 9x GUI is active,
the Windows version of ScanDisk will be run. If ScanDisk is run from the command
prompt without the Windows GUI being active, a text-mode version of ScanDisk will

be run. You can also start Windows 9x/Me's ScanDisk by choosing Start, Programs, Accessories, System Tools, ScanDisk.

To see the options available when you run ScanDisk from the EBD or from the command prompt when the Windows GUI is not active, type **Scandisk/?** and press Enter. See the CD Supplement for a detailed list of ScanDisk syntax and command examples.

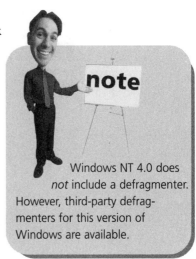

note

You should close active tasks and programs before starting ScanDisk.

Using Windows NT 4.0/2000/XP CHKDSK

With Windows NT 4.0/2000/XP CHKDSK, you can also select whether to automatically fix file system errors and attempt the recovery of bad sectors. If you select the option to automatically fix file system errors, CHKDSK will be scheduled to run at the next restart. This is necessary because CHKDSK requires exclusive access to the drive. CHKDSK performs a three-phase test of the drive.

You can also run CHKDSK from the command prompt. See the CD Supplement for detailed command syntax and usage examples for CHKDSK.

By default, CHKDSK runs automatically at boot time if a drive is dirty (has errors); to adjust this behavior, run CHKNTFS with appropriate options from the command prompt. Use CHKNTFS/? to see the options you can use.

Using Defrag

Over time, the empty space available on a hard disk becomes fragmented as temporary and data files are created and deleted. When a file can no longer be stored in a contiguous group of allocation units, Windows stores the files in as many groups of allocation units as necessary and reassembles the file when it is next accessed. The extra time needed to save and read the file reduces system performance. Starting with Windows 9x, Windows includes a disk defragmentation tool.

In addition to running **Defragment** from the System Tools menu, you can also run it from within Windows Explorer/My Computer:

note

Windows NT 4.0 does *not* include a defragmenter. However, third-party defragmenters for this version of Windows are available.

1. Open Windows Explorer/My Computer.

2. Right-click a drive, select Properties, and then click the Tools tab.

3. Click Defragment Now to start the Defragmentation process. Refer back to Figure 18.22.

There are no configuration options for Windows 9x/Me Defragment. However, you can switch to a full-screen view and display a legend during the operation.

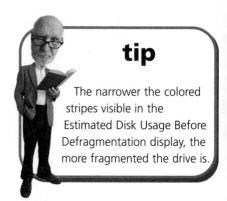

tip

The narrower the colored stripes visible in the Estimated Disk Usage Before Defragmentation display, the more fragmented the drive is.

The Windows 2000/XP defragmenter features an Analyze button that determines whether defragmentation is necessary (see Figure 18.23).

Visual display of drive fragmentation

Indicates whether defragmentation is necessary

FIGURE 18.23

Disk Defragmenter's analysis indicates this drive needs to be defragmented.

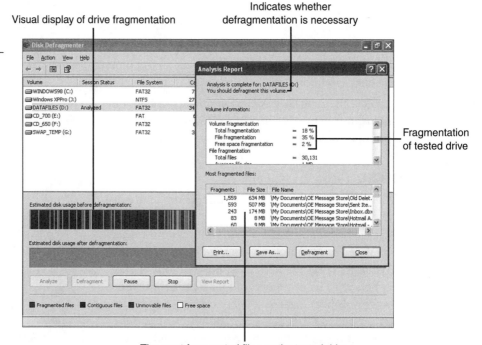

Fragmentation of tested drive

The most fragmented files on the tested drive

File Management

File management skills such as file creation, filenaming, file attributes, compression, encryption, file permissions, and file types are important parts of the A+ Certification Operating System Exam. The following sections discuss these skills.

Creating Files

Data files that can be accessed by registered applications can be created within the Windows Explorer/My Computer interface. To create a new file

1. Open the folder where you want to create the file with My Computer/Windows Explorer.

2. Right-click empty space in the right window and select New to display a list of registered file types (see Figure 18.24).

3. Move the mouse pointer to the file type desired and click it. The new (empty) file is created in the open folder.

4. Enter a new name if desired.

5. To edit the file, double-click it.

Current drive/folder

FIGURE 18.24

Creating a new text document on drive E:.

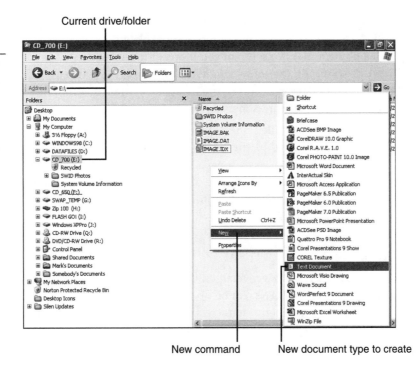

New command   New document type to create

File Types

Broadly speaking, there are two types of files used by Windows and other operating systems:

- Text
- Binary

Text files can be read with an ordinary text editor such as Notepad or Edit. However, most word processing and other types of document files, although they contain text, also contain formatting characters that a text editor cannot properly interpret.

Binary files look like gibberish when viewed in a text editor. Only the operating system (in the case of application binary files) or a compatible application (in the case of binary data files) can interpret their contents.

The following types of files can be started (executed) from a command prompt or from Windows Explorer/My Computer:

- .COM
- .EXE
- .BAT

Both .EXE and .COM files are binary **executable** files, whereas a .BAT file (also called a batch file) is a series of commands that are processed in sequence. Simple batch files contain the same commands that could be entered manually at a command prompt. However, it is also possible to create batch files that have conditional logic and display progress messages.

When an executable filename is entered at a command prompt, the current folder is searched first, followed by the folders in the path. If executable files in the current folder or a folder in the path have .COM, .EXE, and .BAT extensions with the same name preceding the extension, the .COM file is always launched first. For example, assume that the current folder contains DOIT.COM, DOIT.EXE, and DOIT.BAT. DOIT.COM is launched if you enter DOIT.

Naming Files

All versions of Windows covered on the A+ Certification Exams support long file and folder names (**LFN**). LFNs can be up to 255 characters and can contain spaces and most other alphanumeric characters, but cannot contain any of the following characters (which are used by the operating system):

\ / : * ? " < > |

A file can contain more than one period, but only the characters after the last period are considered the extension. In the following example, .doc is the extension: `mydocument.ltr.doc`

By default, the Windows Explorer doesn't show file extensions for registered file types. You can adjust the settings in Windows Explorer to show all file extensions, right-click a file and view properties in Windows Explorer, or use the DIR command from a command prompt to view the extension for a specified file.

Long Filenames and DOS Alias Names

To enable files to be accessed by DOS, older versions of Windows, and operating systems that don't support long filenames, Windows stores a **DOS alias** (also known as the MS-DOS name) as well as the LFN when a file or folder is created.

The DOS alias name is created from the first six letters of the LFN, replacing illegal characters with an underscore, removing spaces, and ignoring additional periods in the LFN. To distinguish between different files with the same DOS alias names, the first DOS alias name in a folder is indicated with a tilde and the number 1 (~1); the second as ~2, and so on. If more than nine files with the same initial letters are saved to a given folder, the first five letters are used for files numbered ~10 and up, and so forth. The three-letter file extension is reused for the DOS alias. Table 18.6 shows the results of creating three files with the same initial files in the same folder. The underlined characters in the original LFN in Table 18.6 are used to create the DOS alias name.

> **note**
>
> If you boot with the Windows 9x/Me EBD or the Windows 2000/XP Recovery Console, LFNs are not visible; only DOS alias names for files and folders are visible.

> **caution**
>
> DOS alias names for existing files can change if the file is renamed or deleted and then re-created.

Table 18.6 Examples of Creating DOS Aliases from LFNs

File Creation Order	Original LFN	DOS Alias
First	Budget Process.xls	BUDGET~1.XLS
Second	Budget Proposal.2003.xls	BUDGET~2.XLS
Third	Budget History+2002.xls	BUDGET~3.XLS

There is a limit of 255 characters for LFNs. However, the path to the file counts against this limit.

Differences in LFN Support by Windows Version

Windows 9x/Me's command-prompt mode uses DOS alias names by default. For example, if you want to change to the My Documents folder from the command prompt, you must use the DOS alias:

`cd\mydocu~1`

Only DOS alias names are shown for files and folders if you use the DIR command when you boot from a Windows EBD. You must use DOS alias names for any disk commands when you boot from a Windows EBD (or a DOS floppy).

However, if you start a command prompt from within the Windows 9x/Me GUI, you can use the LFN *if* you use quote marks around the LFN:

`cd\"My Documents"`

Windows NT 4.0/2000/XP use LFNs by default; DOS alias names are used only for backward compatibility with other operating systems. The command-prompt mode uses LFNs with no special options. example, to change to My Documents, the command would be

`cd\My Documents`

The Recovery Console used by Windows 2000 and XP for troubleshooting and system recovery also supports LFNs.

File Extensions

By default, Windows hides file extensions such as .BAT, .DOC, and .EXE for registered file types. However, you can change this default in Windows Explorer/My Computer.

⇨ **See** "Changing Viewing Options in Windows Explorer," **p. 628**.

note

For a comprehensive list of file extensions and their meanings, I recommend the WhatIs? Web site's "Every File Format in the World" section, which lists more than 3,100 file formats at www.whatis.com.

caution

Don't remove or alter the file extension if you do, Windows won't be able to determine which program it should use to open the file.

Setting and Displaying File and Folder Attributes in Windows Explorer

You've probably heard of **file attributes**, but what are they used for? File and folder attributes are used to indicate which files/folders have been backed up, which files/folders need to be backed up, which files/folders should be hidden from normal display, and which files/folders are used by the system. Windows also supports additional attributes such as when a file/folder was created and last modified. When the NTFS file system is used on a drive, additional advanced attributes (encryption or compression) are also available.

The ATTRIB command can be used to set or display basic attributes for a file/folder from the Windows command line. However, to set or display advanced file attributes, you must use the Windows ExplorerGUI interface.

Basic file attributes include

- *Archive*—Files with the archive attribute have not yet been backed up. When you back up a file with XCOPY/XCOPY32 or any backup program, the archive bit is turned off. Change a file's attribute to archive to force a backup program to back it up if "changed files only" are being backed up.

- *Read-only*—Files with the read-only attribute cannot be deleted or overwritten at an MS-DOS prompt, and cannot be overwritten within a 32-bit Windows application. A read-only file can be deleted within Windows Explorer, but only after the user elects to override the read-only attribute. Change a file's attributes to read-only to provide protection against accidental deletion or changes.

- *System*—Files with the system attribute are used by the operating system, and often have the hidden attribute as well.

- *Hidden*—Files with the hidden attribute cannot be copied with COPY or with XCOPY and cannot be viewed with the normal Windows Explorer settings. Some log files created by Windows (such as Bootlog.txt) are stored with the hidden attribute.

XCOPY32 (which runs only within the Windows GUI) can copy hidden files.

Windows 9x/Me File Attributes

To view the attributes for a file or folder with Windows Explorer

1. Start Windows Explorer.

2. Right-click a file or folder and select Properties.

3. The General tab indicates attributes for the file or folder. In addition to the basic attributes listed previously, Windows 9x/Me can also display the creation date of the file, the date the file was last accessed, and the date the file was last changed (see Figure 18.25).

FIGURE 18.25

This file has the archive attribute set, which can be used by a backup program to detect which files are not yet backed up (archived).

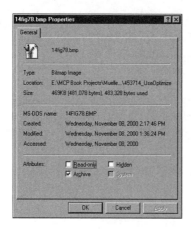

To add an attribute, check the box next to the attribute and click Apply. To remove an attribute, clear the check box next to the attribute and click Apply.

Windows NT 4.0/2000/XP File Attributes

Windows 2000/XP use only three of the basic file attributes used by Windows 9x/Me:

- Read-only
- Hidden
- Archive

Windows NT 4.0 also supports the System attribute.

To view these attributes with the Windows 2000/XP Explorer

1. Start Windows Explorer.

2. Right-click a file or folder and select Properties.

3. The General tab indicates read-only or hidden attributes for the file or folder. In addition to the basic attributes listed previously, Windows 2000/XP can

also display the creation date of the file, the date the file was last accessed, and the date the file was last changed.

To select or deselect the archive attribute, or to set encryption or compression options on a drive using the NTFS file system, click the Advanced button. Figure 18.26 shows the General and Advanced dialogs on a Windows 2000 system (Windows XP is similar).

Encryption and **compression** are available only on Windows 2000 and XP drives formatted with the NTFS file system. (Windows NT 4.0 supports compression, but not encryption.) To set these options for a file or folder in Windows 2000/XP, you can use the Windows Explorer or the command-line programs Compact (to compress a file) or Cipher (to encrypt a file); Windows NT 4.0 also uses Cipher. To encrypt or compress a file with the Windows 2000/XP GUI, follow these steps:

> **note**
>
> Operating system files are stored in the default Windows folder (\Windows or \WINNT). Windows Explorer in Windows 2000/XP is configured *not* to display the contents of these folders by default.

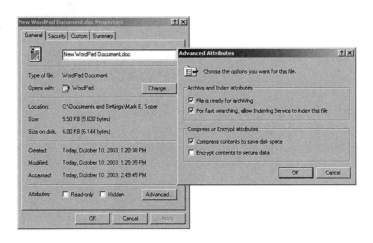

FIGURE 18.26

Compressing a file with Windows 2000. You can select compression or encryption, but not both.

1. Start Windows Explorer/My Computer.

2. Right-click a file or folder and click Properties.

3. Click the Advanced button.

4. Select Compression to reduce the disk space used by the file, or Encryption to restrict access to only the system's administrator or the user who encrypted the file.

5. Click OK to apply either option (refer to Figure 18.26). Files can be compressed or encrypted, but not both.

6. If you are encrypting the file, Windows recommends that you encrypt the folder containing the file (which will also encrypt the file) .

File Permissions

Windows NT 4.0/2000/XP systems that use the NTFS file system feature an additional tab on the file/folder properties sheet called the Security tab. It is used to control **file permissions**.

The Security tab permits you to control access to the selected file or folder by granting or denying permissions shown to selected users or groups:

■ *Full Control*—Enables any and all changes to a file, including deletion.

■ *Modify*—File can be modified.

■ *Read & Execute*—File can be read and executed.

■ *Read*—File can be read.

■ *Write*—File can be overwritten.

The Security tab has two sections. The top section shows the users and groups that have access to the selected file or folder. You can add or remove groups or users. The bottom section lets you specify the permissions available for the selected user or group.

Locating Files and Folders

Windows NT 4.0/9x/Me use the **Find** command to locate files and folders, computers on a network, Internet content and other options, whereas Windows 2000/XP calls this option **Search**. To start the process of locating a file or folder, open the Windows Start menu and click Find (Windows NT 4.0/9x/Me) or Search (Windows 2000/XP).

caution

Only the user who originally encrypted the file (or the system's Administrator) can open an encrypted file and view its contents. Only the Administrator can apply compression to a file or folder.

note

File folders' properties sheets have additional tabs:

• The Sharing tab configures how a folder is shared (if file/print sharing is installed).

• The Customize tab (Windows XP) configures how a folder is displayed in My Computer/Windows Explorer.

Windows NT 4.0/9x/Me use a small, multitabbed window for their Find command; Windows 2000 and Windows XP use the Windows Explorer for their Search command. Each is discussed separately.

Using Windows Find

To find a file or folder with Windows Find

1. Click Start, Find, Files or Folders.

2. Enter the file or folder name (or a portion of the name) in the Named field on the Name & Location tab; you can use **wildcards** such as the following:

   ■ note*—Finds all files or folders starting with note

   ■ *note—Finds all files or folders ending with note

   ■ *note*—Finds all files or folders containing note anywhere in the name

   You also can click the down arrow to reuse a previous search.

3. Select the drives or other locations to search with the Look In menu.

4. Click Find Now to begin the search (see Figure 18.27).

You can also customize the search by specifying text contained in the file, the range of dates to search, the size range of the files to search, the type(s) of files to search, and whether to search only the specified location or the specified location and its subfolders.

If Windows XP is configured to use simple file sharing, the Security tab will not be visible. Simple file sharing is recommended for home and small-business networks, but reduces system security. Simple file sharing is enabled by default if the system is not connected to a domain, but is disabled automatically when the system is connected to a domain (the domain controller is used to control network security).

To disable simple file sharing on a system not connected to a domain, click Start, Control Panel, Folder options; click View and clear the check mark next to Use Simple File Sharing (Recommended) .

Using Windows 2000 Search

The Windows 2000 Search tool offers similar options to the Windows Find tool, although it uses the Windows 2000 Explorer. The following are some differences:

■ Search options are not displayed unless you click the Search Options box.

■ To specify values for each search option, click the check mark box next to the search option.

■ Advanced options also include

■ *Case Sensitive*—This option enables you to specify capital or small letters in your search.

■ *Search Slow Files*—This option will temporarily copy files on removable media to your system's hard disk to speed up searches.

Search term   Search location

FIGURE 18.27

All files containing note in the filename on local or mapped drives are located by a search specifying *note* and My Computer.

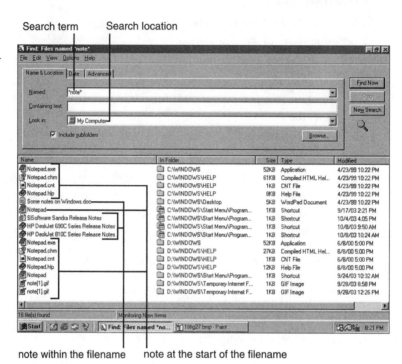

note within the filename   note at the start of the filename

Using Windows XP Search

The Windows XP Search interface is completely different than previous versions of Windows (see Figure 18.28). The task pane on the left side of the screen contains options to search by specific file types (pictures/photos, music, videos, documents) and search-supported tape backups. As with other versions of Windows, you can also specify partial or exact filenames and file text.

Search location

Search term   Files matching search criteria

FIGURE 18.28

The results of
searching the
Windows XP sys-
tem drive (J:) for
files containing
note in the file-
name (right)
and the search
options used
(left).

Advanced search options

Using Command-Prompt Functions and Utilities

Although most computer users seldom use the **command prompt** available in all
versions of Windows covered on the A+ Certification Exams, it's very important for
technicians to know how to use the major command-prompt functions and programs. Command-prompt functions and programs can be used to

- Recover data from systems that can't boot normally.
- Reinstall lost or corrupted system files.
- Print file listings (believe it or not, you can't do this in Windows Explorer or
  My Computer!).
- Copy, move, or delete data.
- Display or configure certain operating system settings.

The following sections discuss the major command-prompt functions and utilities in
more detail.

Starting a Command-Prompt Session

You can start a command-prompt session in Windows by clicking on the Command prompt or MS-DOS prompt option in the Start menu; it's usually located in the Accessories menu on most versions of Windows. However, it's faster to use the Run command:

1. Click Start, Run.
2. *With Windows 9x/Me*

   Type **command** and click OK.

   With Windows NT 4.0/2000/XP

   Type **cmd** and click OK.

Internal Commands Overview

Command.com (Windows 9x/Me) and Cmd (Windows NT 4.0/2000/XP) contain the internal commands listed in Table 18.7. Commands marked (RC) can also be used by the Windows 2000/XP Recovery Console.

> **caution**
>
> Before Windows XP, Search & Find searched all types of files for specified text. However, as initially shipped, Windows XP's Search tool excludes many types of files. Service Pack 1 partially fixes this behavior, as does the Windows XP Application Compatibility Update, October 25, 2001. (Both are available from Windows Update.) To search all file types, you also need to use the Indexing Service and enable the option to index files with unknown extensions. For more information about this problem and its solutions, see Microsoft Knowledge Base article 309173.

Table 18.7 Major Internal Commands

Internal Command	Category	Use	Example
DATE	System management	Views system current date and allows it to be changed	DATE
TIME	System management	Views system current time and allows it to be changed	TIME
COPY[1] (RC)	Disk management	Copies one or more files to another folder or drive	COPY *.* A:\
DEL[1] (RC)	Disk management	Deletes one or more files on current or specified folder or drive	DEL *.TMP
ERASE[1] (RC)	Disk management	Same as DEL	ERASE *.TMP
DIR[1] (RC)	Disk management	Lists files on current or specified folder or drive	DIR *.EXE

Table 18.7 (continued)

Internal Command	Category	Use	Example
MD[1] (MKDIR) (RC)	Disk management	Makes a new folder (subdirectory)	MD TEMP
CD[1] (CHDIR) (RC)	Disk management	Changes your current location to the specified folder (subdirectory)	CD TEMP
RD[1] (RMDIR) (RC)	Disk management	Removes an *empty* folder	RD TEMP
RENAME (REN)[1]	Disk management	Renames a file	REN joe.txt jerry.txt
VER[1]	System management	Lists the version of operating system in use	VER
VOL	Disk management	Lists the current volume label and serial number for the default drive	VOL
SET[1]	System management	Used to set options for a device or program; SET without options displays all current SET variables	SET TEMP=C:\TEMP
PROMPT	System management	Sets display options for the command prompt	PROMPT=$P $G (displays drive letter followed by greater-than sign)
PATH	System management	Sets folders or drives that can be searched for programs to be run	PATH=C:\DOS;C:\WINDOWS
ECHO[1]	Batch files	Turns on or off the echo (display) of commands to the screen	ECHO OFF
CLS (RC)	Batch files, system management	Clears the screen of old commands and program output	CLS
LH (LOADHIGH)	Memory management (Windows 98)	Loads TSR programs above 640K (see preceding memory-management discussion)	LH C:\MOUSE\MOUSE.COM
TYPE[1] (RC)	System management	Views text files onscreen	TYPE AUTOEXEC.BAT

[1]*See the Windows Command Reference on the CD for details and syntax.*

Because these commands are built into the command interpreter, they can also be used from the command prompt if you boot the computer with the Windows 9x/Me Emergency Boot Disk. All but LH (Loadhigh) can also be run from the Windows 2000/XP command prompt.

Using Wildcards to Specify a Range of Files

Command-prompt functions and utilities can be used to operate on a group of files with similar names by using one of the following wildcard symbols:

- ? replaces a single character.
- * replaces a group of characters.

For example, DIR *.EXE displays files with the .EXE extension in the current folder (directory). DEL MYNOVEL??.BAK removes the following files: MYNOVEL00.BAK, MYNOVEL01.BAK, but not MYNOVEL.BAK.

Windows Command-Prompt Utilities

Command-prompt utility programs are found in these locations in Windows 9x/Me:

- C:\Windows\Command
- The Windows 9x/Me Emergency Startup Disk (also called the Emergency Boot Disk [EBD] or Startup disk)

 For more information about the Windows 9x Emergency Startup Disk, **see** "Creating a Boot Disk Suitable for Hard Disk Preparation," **p. 484**.

Most of these commands can also be run from the Windows NT/2000/XP command prompt or from the Windows 2000/XP Recovery Console, which can be started from the Windows CD-ROM or can be installed to the hard disk for troubleshooting startup problems.

note

You can also use command to create a command prompt in Windows NT 4.0/2000/XP. This mode is sometimes referred to as Windows DOS; it is used automatically if you run a DOS program within these versions of Windows. However, creating a command prompt with command is not recommended for most situations because you cannot use the enhancements to internal or external commands available with cmd.

tip

To get help for any internal or external command-prompt function or program, type the program name followed by /?. For example, DIR/? displays help for the DIR command.

These utilities are also referred to as external commands because, unlike the built-in commands stored in Command.com or Cmd, each of these are separate programs.

Table 18.8 lists the major command-prompt utilities supplied with Windows, how each is used, and whether it is part of the Windows 98 Emergency Boot Disk, Windows 95 Startup disk, or the Windows 2000/XP Recovery Console.

Windows NT/2000/XP's command-prompt utilities are typically found in the System32 folder beneath the default Windows folder.

Table 18.8   Major Windows Command-Prompt Utilities

Utility	How Used	Supported at Command Prompt by Windows Versions	Windows 98 EBD	Windows 2000/ XP Recovery Console
ATTRIB.EXE[2]	Changes file attributes	All	Yes[1]	Yes
CHKDSK.EXE	Simple disk repair and statistics reporting tool (replaced by ScanDisk in Windows 98)	All	Yes[1]	Yes
CVT.EXE	Converts FAT16 drive to FAT32 file system	98, Me		N/A
DEBUG.EXE	Debugging utility	All	Yes[1]	No
DELTREE.EXE[2]	Deletes folders and files contained in folders	98, Me		N/A
EXTRACT.EXE	Used to manually uncompress files from Windows .CAB compressed archives	All	Yes	N/A

Table 18.8 (continued)

Utility	How Used	Supported at Command Prompt by Windows Versions	Windows 98 EBD	Windows 2000/ XP Recovery Console
EXPAND.EXE	Used to manually extract files from Windows .CAB archive files	NT, 2000, XP	N/A	Yes
FDISK.EXE	Partitions hard disks	9x, Me	Yes	N/A
MEM.EXE[2]	Displays overall memory usage and programs in conventional memory	All	No	No
MOVE.EXE	Moves files from one location to another	All	No	No
MSCDEX.EXE[2]	Provides access to CD-ROM drives after CD-ROM device drive is loaded in Config.sys	9x, Me (EBD)	Yes[1]	N/A
SCANDISK.EXE	Disk repair and disk statistics tool (replaces CHKDSK)	9x, Me	Yes[1]	N/A
SCANREG.EXE	Registry repair tool	98, Me	No	N/A
UNINSTAL.EXE	Uninstalls Windows 98	98	Yes[1]	N/A
xcopy.exe[2]	Faster version of COPY that can create folders and copy files based on many different criteria	All	No	No

Table 18.8   (continued)

Utility	How Used	Supported at Command Prompt by Windows Versions	Windows 98 EBD	Windows 2000/ XP Recovery Console
xcopy32.exe[2]	Used in place of standard xcopy when run from a DOS Window while the Windows 9x/Me GUI is active; supports long filenames and additional options	9x, Me	No	N/A
DISKCOPY.COM	Makes a bit-by-bit exact copy of a diskette	All	No	No
DOSKEY.COM	Enables user to cycle through previous command-prompt commands for reuse	All	No	Not necessary
EDIT.COM[2]	DOS-based text editor	All	Yes[1]	No
FORMAT.EXE	High-level formatter for hard and floppy drives	All	Yes[1]	Yes
SYS.COM	Transfers system files to formatted hard or floppy drives	9x, Me	Yes[1]	N/A
SETVER.EXE[2]	Enables older software to run without triggering an "incorrect MS-DOS version" error	9x, NT, 2000, XP	No	N/A

[1]*Extracted to RAMDISK created when EBD is used to start computer*

[2]*For more details and command syntax, see the Windows Command Reference on the CD packaged with this book*

Windows 95's Startup disk contains all the Windows 98 EBD files listed in the table except for Debug and Mscdex. You can copy these files manually from the \Windows\System folder to the Startup disk if needed.

For more information about the Windows 2000/XP Recovery Console, see "Windows Recovery Console," in Chapter 20.

The command-prompt utilities listed in Table 18.9 are part of Windows NT 4.0/2000/XP only. For a more complete list, type **HELP** from the Windows NT/2000/XP command prompt. To see command options, type **/?** after each command.

Table 18.9   Windows NT/2000/XP-Only Command-Prompt Utilities

Utility	How Used
Assoc	Displays or changes file extension associations
At	Schedules the running of commands or programs
Cacls	Displays or changes access control lists (ACLs) of files
Chkntfs	Displays or changes the operation of Chkdsk at startup time
Compact	Displays or changes the current compression status of files on NTFS partitions only
Convert	Converts FAT partitions other than the current drive to NTFS
Ftype	Displays or changes file types used in file extension associations
Title	Sets window title for a command-prompt (CMD.EXE) session

Getting Help with a Particular Command

Most command-line functions and utilities provide you with concise help for options; type the command name followed by **/?** to see options for that command.

Optimizing Windows

You can improve the performance of Windows in several ways, including optimizing virtual memory size and location, adjusting the location of temporary files, and defragmenting the hard disk. With Windows NT/2000/XP only, you can also optimize performance by adjusting the priority of applications versus background tasks.

> **tip**
>
> Most Windows 9x command-prompt commands and utilities have similar options to those used by MS-DOS 6.x. The MS-DOS 6.x Help file (which contains more detailed help and examples than those provided by /? help) is stored on the Windows 9x CD-ROM in the OldMSDOS folder. To view the help file, switch to that folder and open Help.com.

With Windows 9x/Me only, you can also optimize performance by adjusting the performance of the Windows disk cache, adjusting file and buffer size settings, and adjusting default memory configurations.

Most of these topics are covered in the following sections.

Adjusting Virtual Memory

If you run short of money, you can borrow some from the bank. However, there's a penalty: interest. Similarly, if your system runs short of memory, it can borrow hard disk space and use it as **virtual memory**. The penalty for this type of borrowing is performance: Virtual memory is much slower than real RAM memory. However, you can adjust how your system uses virtual memory to achieve better performance.

Swapfile Setting in Windows 9x/Me

Windows 9x/Me configures virtual memory through the System properties sheet of the Control Panel. You can access the System properties sheet in one of the following ways:

- Right-click My Computer and select Properties from the right-click menu.
- Click Start, Settings, Control Panel, and open the System icon.

Follow this procedure to view or set virtual memory options in Windows 9x/Me:

1. Open the System properties sheet.
2. Click the Performance tab.
3. Click Virtual Memory (see Figure 18.29).

By default, Windows uses a variable-sized **swapfile** that can grow to the available disk space on the C: drive for virtual memory. You can make the following adjustments:

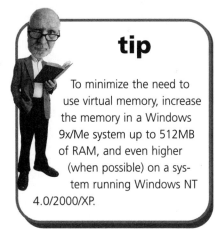

note

Defragmenting the hard disk, adjusting file and buffer size settings, and adjusting default memory configurations are covered earlier in this chapter.

See "Adjusting Disk Caching Settings in Windows" in Chapter 14, "Storage," to adjust disk cache settings in Windows 9x/Me.

tip

To minimize the need to use virtual memory, increase the memory in a Windows 9x/Me system up to 512MB of RAM, and even higher (when possible) on a system running Windows NT 4.0/2000/XP.

■ Set the minimum and maximum sizes of the swapfile (including making the swapfile a fixed size).

■ Set the swapfile to another drive.

■ Disable the swapfile (not recommended).

If you have two or more logical hard drive letters or two physical drives, you might want to set the swapfile to a drive letter other than the default. This can improve performance (especially if you have two physical drives or if the second drive is faster than the original drive) and will prevent the C: drive from running out of space needed for additional program installations or temporary Internet files.

FIGURE 18.29

The Virtual Memory dialog box in Windows 9x shows that this system has been set to use a fixed-size swapfile on the F: drive. (The default is an adjustable-size swapfile on C: drive.)

To avoid disk thrashing (which slows down the system) caused by resizing the swapfile, you can set the swapfile to a fixed size. The swapfile should be set to about three times your system's available RAM; if your system has 64MB of RAM, set your swapfile to 192MB. Use a larger swapfile size if you routinely edit large database or graphics files.

If you make any changes to the swapfile, you need to restart your computer for the changes to take effect.

tip

How large does *your* swapfile get? Before you change your swapfile size, run the Windows System Monitor, open the Memory Manager category, select Swapfile in Use and Swapfile Size and perform typical operations. Make sure you use a custom swapfile size that's larger than the swapfile you actually use during typical operations.

Swapfile (Paging File) Setting in Windows NT/2000/XP

When additional RAM is added to a computer running Windows NT/2000/XP, it is automatically used in place of the **paging file**.

The Windows NT/2000/XP System Monitor can be used to determine whether more RAM should be added to a computer. Follow these steps to monitor performance with the System Monitor:

1. Click the Start button.
2. Click Run.
3. Type **perfmon** and press Enter.

Many different types of performance factors can be measured with the Windows NT/2000/XP Performance Monitor. To see if additional RAM is needed in a system, set up the Paging File % Usage and Pages/Sec counters:

1. Right-click in the blank area beneath the graph and select Add Counters.
2. Choose Paging File as the Performance Object, and then choose Paging File % Usage.
3. Choose Memory as the Performance Object, and then choose Pages/Sec.
4. Click Add.
5. Click Close, and then open the normal program load for this computer.

If the System Monitor indicates that the Paging File % Usage is consistently near 100% or the Memory Pages/Sec counter is consistently above 5, add RAM to improve performance (see Figure 18.30).

Paging file % usage   Memory page/second

FIGURE 18.30

This system has adequate memory at this time, as indicated by the low levels of usage of the Paging File % Usage and Memory Pages/ Sec counters.

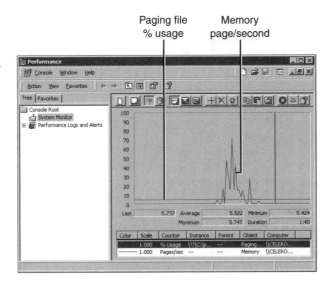

The performance of the paging file can be improved by

- Setting its minimum and maximum sizes to the same amount.
- Moving the paging file to a physical disk (or disk partition) that is not used as much as others.
- Using a striped volume for the paging file. A striped volume is identical areas of disk space stored on two or more dynamic disks that are referred to as a single drive letter. Create a striped volume with the Windows 2000/XP Disk Management tool or Windows NT 4.0 Disk Administrator tool.
- Creating multiple paging files on multiple physical disks in the system.
- Moving the paging file away from the boot drive.

To adjust the location and size of the paging file with Windows NT/2000/XP:

1. Right-click My Computer on the Windows desktop and select Properties or open the Control Panel and open the System icon.
2. Click the Advanced tab.
3. Click the Performance Options button.
4. Click the Change button.
5. Choose the minimum and maximum sizes you want to use for the paging file and its location (see Figure 18.31). Click Set, and then click OK to finish.
6. If you make any changes to size or location, you must restart the computer for the changes to take effect.

FIGURE 18.31

The Virtual Memory dialog box of Windows 2000 enables you to set the size and location of virtual memory.

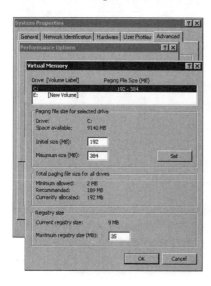

Adjusting the Location for Temporary Files

The default location for temporary files in Windows is the TEMP folder beneath the default Windows folder (\Windows or \WinNT). The location can be adjusted with a pair of SET statements. However, the method used to adjust the default setting varies with the version of Windows in use.

tip

Some applications use SET TEMP=*location*; others use SET TMP=*location* (replace *location* with the actual drive and folder path). Be sure to change both variables if you need to change the setting for temporary files.

Temporary File Settings in Windows 9x/Me

To change the location of **temporary files** to a drive other than the system drive, follow this procedure:

1. Create a folder called TEMP in the root folder of the drive you want to use for your temporary files. You can use Windows Explorer/My Computer or the MKDIR command. For example, if the D: drive will be used for temporary files, you could use this command: MKDIR D:\TEMP.

2. Change to the root folder of the system drive (usually C:) and open the Autoexec.bat file with Notepad or the command-prompt Edit program.

3. If the SET TEMP= and SET TMP= statements are already present, edit them to refer to the drive and folder you want to use for temporary files. For example:
   SET TEMP=*D:\TEMP*
   SET TMP=*D:\TEMP*

   If there are no SET TEMP/SET TMP statements, add them using the drive and folder in place of D:\TEMP.

4. Save the changes to Autoexec.bat.

5. Restart the system to activate the changes.

Temporary File Settings in Windows NT/2000/XP

These versions of Windows don't have Autoexec.bat. Instead, they use the Advanced tab on the System properties sheet to set environmental variables such as SET TEMP and many others. Here's how to make the change (you must be logged on as Administrator):

1. Create a folder called TEMP in the root folder of the drive you want to use for your temporary files. You can use Windows Explorer/My Computer or the MKDIR command. For example, if the D: drive will be used for temporary files, you could use this command: MKDIR D:\TEMP.

2. Open the System properties sheet. You can right-click on My Computer and select Properties or open the System icon in Control Panel.

3. Click the Advanced tab.

4. Click Environmental variables. A new window opens.

5. Click TEMP in the System variables window and click Edit.

6. The Edit System Variable window opens (see Figure 18.32). Clear the variable value (%SystemRoot%\TEMP) and enter the drive and folder you used in step 1 (for example, D:\TEMP). Click OK.

7. Repeat steps 5–6, selecting TMP instead of TEMP.

8. Click OK in the Environment Variables window.

9. Click OK on the System properties sheet.

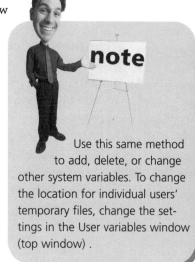

note

Use this same method to add, delete, or change other system variables. To change the location for individual users' temporary files, change the settings in the User variables window (top window) .

FIGURE 18.32

Adjusting the location used for temporary files in Windows 2000.

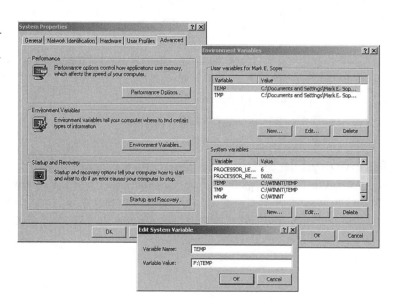

Application Response Settings NT/2000/XP

Windows 2000/XP can be configured to use more memory for **background services** (non-active windows, printing, and so on) instead of the default (**application response**—improves performance for the foreground application). To make this change

1. Open the System properties sheet and click Advanced.

2. Click Performance options.

3. Select Optimize Performance Options for Applications (default) or Background Services.

Windows NT 4.0 uses a slider to adjust the Application Performance from None (balances background and foreground) to Maximum (much more performance for foreground than background) with a middle setting that provides slightly more performance for the foreground application than for background applications.

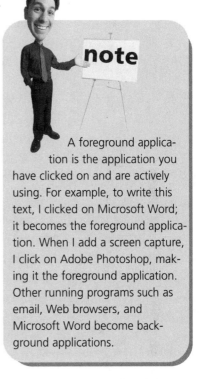

note

A foreground application is the application you have clicked on and are actively using. For example, to write this text, I clicked on Microsoft Word; it becomes the foreground application. When I add a screen capture, I click on Adobe Photoshop, making it the foreground application. Other running programs such as email, Web browsers, and Microsoft Word become background applications.

Study Lab

Don't miss the Study Lab materials found on the CD accompanying this book. Each Study Lab is tailored to the individual chapters in this book, meaning that you'll quickly be able to determine which topics you understand well enough to pass the exam and which topics need more study time. The Study Labs are presented in printable PDF format so that you can take them with you to study at work, on the road, or even in your car just before test time!

THE ABSOLUTE MINIMUM

- The Io.sys, MSdos.sys, Config.sys, Autoexec.bat, and Win.com files are processed in order to start Windows 9x/Me.

- Windows NT 4.0/2000/XP processes NTLDR, Boot.ini, NTdetect.com, Ntoskrnl.exe, and Hal.dll during the startup process.

- The Windows Registry is also read as part of the startup process for all versions of Windows on the A+ Certification Exam.

- Windows uses Regedit as the Registry editor. Windows 2000 and NT 4.0 can also use Regedt32 for some Registry-editing tasks.

- The My Computer icon in the Windows GUI provides access to drives, the Control Panel, and other important Windows components.

- The Control Panel controls major hardware components in Windows.

- The System Tray and Taskbar provide one-click access to currently running programs and utilities.

- The Start menu provides shortcuts to most Windows programs and utilities.

- The Accessories folder provides access to Windows accessories; most system tools are found in the System Tools folder inside the Accessories folder.

- ScanDisk, CHKDSK, Defragment (not in Windows NT 4.0), and Disk Cleanup are Windows's major disk management tools.

- Windows provides both GUI-based and command-line file management tools for displaying files and attributes, copying files, locating files, renaming files, and removing files.

- Major command-line functions and programs include DIR, COPY, XCOPY, XCOPY32, ATTRIB, DEL/ERASE, RENAME, VER, and DELTREE.

- Windows's performance can be improved through adjustments of the default locations for temporary files, swapfile/paging file, and, in Windows 9x/Me, the settings for the disk cache.

19

INSTALLING AND CONFIGURING HARDWARE IN WINDOWS

Whether you're more excited about diving "under the hood" of your PC to upgrade it or you'd prefer digging deeper into the friendly graphical wrappings around the Windows operating system, you can't deny that hardware and Windows go together. Without Windows-specific drivers for your favorite hardware, Windows won't recognize it. And, without Windows, your favorite hardware won't get much done. This chapter shows you how Windows configures and controls printers and other types of hardware.

Printing and Printer Configuration

Before the age of Windows, printer support was all over the map. Some DOS programs such as WordPerfect became legendary for their support of printers hardly anyone had ever seen as well as any printer you could drag home or sign for at the office. Other programs could barely print text with a few of the most popular printers.

Windows changed all that. Windows applications let Windows handle the nitty-gritty details of controlling printer features, and fortunately, Windows is up to the task. Although printers vary widely in resolutions, print technologies, and features, most printers use the standard Windows **Add Printer Wizard** and Printer Properties sheets you'll see later in this chapter for installation and setup.

Installing the Printer

Until you introduce Windows and your printer to each other, about the only document you'll be printing is the self-test sheet.

To install a parallel printer in Windows

1. Open the Printers or Printer and Faxes folder. You can use the Control Panel or a shortcut located on the Start button such as Settings, Printer, or Printer and Faxes.

2. Open the Add Printer Wizard.

3. Specify whether the new printer is connected through a local port or through a network—Windows 2000/XP will automatically detect a Plug and Play (PnP) printer by default.

4. Choose the port (for local printers) or network share (for network printers). If the printer is a network printer, specify whether you want to send MS-DOS print jobs to the printer.

note

The CD included with this book contains important Study Lab material for this chapter, as well as Chapters 2–22 in this book. The Study Lab for each chapter contains terms to study, exercises, and practice tests—all in printable PDF format (Adobe Acrobat Reader is included on the CD, too). These Study Lab materials will help you gear up for the A+ Exam. Also, the CD includes an industry-leading test engine from PrepLogic, which simulates the actual A+ test so that you can be sure that you're ready when test day arrives. Don't let the A+ test intimidate you. If you've read the chapters, worked through the Study Lab, and passed the practice tests from PrepLogic, you should be well prepared to ace the test!

Also, you'll notice that some words throughout each chapter are in bold format. These are study terms that are defined in the Study Lab. Be sure to consult the Study Lab when you are finished with this chapter to test what you've learned.

5. For Windows NT/2000/XP, select the port, and then the brand and model of your printer; for Windows 9x/Me, select the brand and model followed by the port.

   If you have an installation disk or CD-ROM provided by the vendor, click Have Disk and browse to the installation disk or CD-ROM for the printer (see Figure 19.1).

6. Specify whether the printer will be the default printer (if you are installing an additional printer).

7. Specify whether you want to share the printer if prompted.

FIGURE 19.1

Selecting a printer by brand and model (left); if the printer isn't listed, or if you have a driver disk, click Have Disk (right).

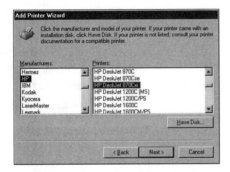

8. Specify whether you want to print a test page. You should do this to make sure your new printer is working properly. This is the default, so Microsoft agrees this is an important step.

9. Windows 2000/XP displays the printer selections. Click Finish if you are done or click the Back button to make changes.

   After you click Finish, the printer will be installed into the Printers folder, and it will be available to all Windows applications.

If you need to install a USB printer, follow the instructions provided with the printer. You typically need to install the driver software provided with a USB printer before you can attach the printer. After the driver software is installed, Windows can detect the printer and complete installation of the driver.

After a printer is installed, it is listed with one of three icons:

- ■ **Local printers** (those connected directly to a port on the PC) are displayed with a plain printer icon. The same icon is also used for so-called "virtual printers," which use special printer drivers to create faxes, Adobe Acrobat .PDF files, or other special types of files.

■ **Remote printers** (those accessed over a network) are displayed with a network cable as part of the icon.

■ **Shared printers** (local printers also accessible over the network by other users) are displayed with an open hand as part of the icon.

See examples of each of these icons in Figure 19.2. A washed-out version of the icon indicates the printer is offline.

tip

Don't panic if you find some unfamiliar icons in your Printers or Printers and Faxes folder. Software such as Adobe Acrobat Distiller and various other print and fax services install printer drivers into this folder. These **virtual printers** enable you to use the File, Print dialog to create Acrobat .PDF files or fax documents.

Remote (network) printer
on server //JULIE   Default printer (local)

FIGURE 19.2
Local, shared, remote (network) and virtual printers in Windows XP.

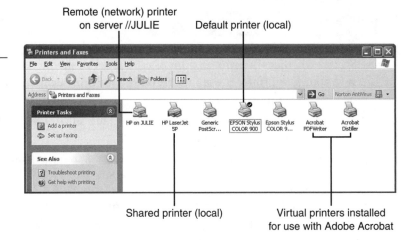

Shared printer (local)   Virtual printers installed
for use with Adobe Acrobat

Setting the Default Printer

If you're lucky enough to have more than one printer installed, you can choose your **default printer** at any time. Which one is your default? Look for the printer with a checkmark next to it in your Printers or Printers and Faxes folder (refer to Figure 19.2). To change to a different default printer

1. Right-click the printer you want to set as the default printer.

2. Select Set As Default from the menu.

To keep your existing printer as the default when you install another printer, make sure you don't select the option to make the new printer the default.

Using the Print Spooler

Your printer can print only one document at a time. So, why doesn't Windows stop you when you send **print job** after print job? Windows automatically uses the default TEMP folder for print jobs, saving them to disk for printing on the printer selected by the user. This process is called print spooling.

Most printers use Windows's own built-in **print spooler**, although some inkjet printers use their own spooler software instead. Normally, the print spooler is transparent to the user, sending print jobs to the printer as they are received and as the printer is available. However, special circumstances, such as a network printer going offline or the need to discard a print job, might require the user to open the print spooler.

To view the print spooler, you can

- Double-click the Printer icon shown in the Windows toolbar; this icon appears whenever one or more print jobs are waiting to print.

- Double-click the icon for your printer in the Printers or Printers and Faxes folder.

The spooler (see Figure 19.3) displays the following information:

- The name of the printer
- The print jobs waiting to print in order (newest at the top), with the following information:
  - Document name
  - Status
  - Owner (user who sent the job)
  - Progress (number of pages or size of document)
  - Time and date the job began printing
  - The number of print jobs waiting to print

To release print jobs stored in the spooler in **offline mode** after the network printer is available, use one of these methods:

1. Open the print spooler.
2. Click Printer.
3. Uncheck Use Printer Offline and the print jobs will go to the printer.

Alternatively

1. Right-click the printer icon in the Printers (Printers and Faxes) folder.

2. Click Use Printer Online.

To discard a print job in the spooler

1. Open the print spooler.

2. Right-click the print job you want to discard.

3. Select Cancel Print and the print job will be discarded.

To discard all print jobs in the spooler

1. Open the print spooler.

2. Click Printer.

3. Click Purge Print Documents or Cancel All Documents (varies by Windows version) to discard all print jobs.

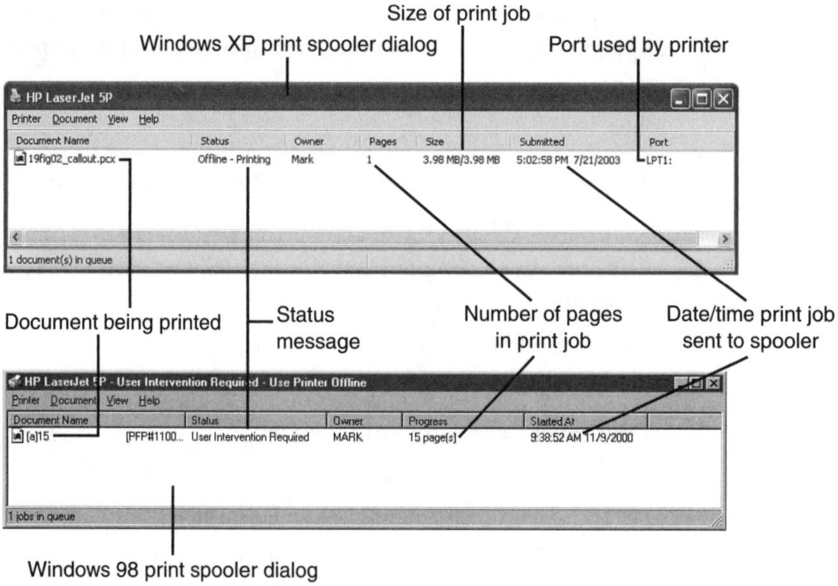

FIGURE 19.3

Windows XP (top) and Windows 98 (bottom) print spoolers in offline mode.

Windows 98 print spooler dialog

Printing to a Network Printer

After you have a network printer configured in Windows, using it is as easy as using a printer plugged into a parallel or USB port. However, getting access to the printer differs according to the version of Windows your computer uses and the version of Windows in use on the printer hosting the computer.

Before you can share a printer connected to a Windows computer with the rest of the network, you need to

1. Open the Network sheet or Local Area Connection Properties sheet and install Windows File and Printer Sharing if it is not already installed (see Figure 19.4).

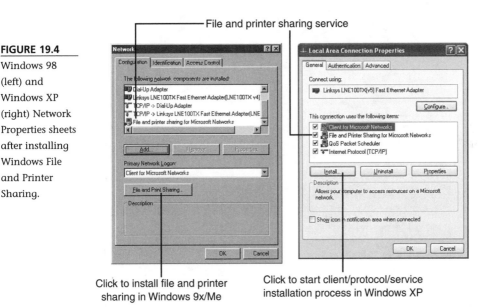

File and printer sharing service

FIGURE 19.4

Windows 98 (left) and Windows XP (right) Network Properties sheets after installing Windows File and Printer Sharing.

Click to install file and printer sharing in Windows 9x/Me

Click to start client/protocol/service installation process in Windows XP

2. Right-click the printer in Windows Explorer and select Sharing (see Figure 19.5). Specify a share name for the printer. Windows 9x/Me also let you specify whether users need a password to use the printer.

3. If the printer is connected to a Windows 2000/XP/NT 4.0 computer, you can enable Windows to provide drivers for users of other versions of Windows. To install additional drivers, right-click the printer and select Properties. Click the Sharing tab, and then the Additional Drivers button after you set the printer as a shared device. Select the driver versions you want to make available (see Figure 19.6). When the remote user selects the printer, Windows will download the correct drivers to the remote user's computer if they are available. If not, the remote user needs to install the correct drivers manually.

FIGURE 19.5

Sharing a printer with Windows 9x/Me; the Sharing tab is used to specify the name and description that the shared printer will display over the network, and the password is used to restrict access to the printer.

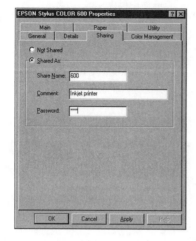

FIGURE 19.6

Selecting Windows 9x/Me and Windows NT 4.0 printer drivers with the Additional Drivers feature in Windows XP.

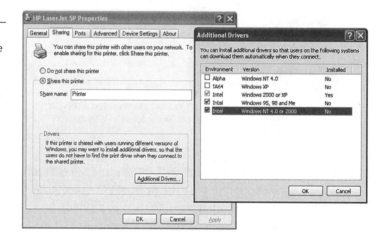

If the computer hosting a shared printer is connected to a computer running Windows NT/2000/2003 Server or Novell NetWare, the server's list of users and groups can be used to restrict access; anyone who wants to use the printer must be on the list of users or groups that have been granted access. The password or server containing the user list is specified in the properties for the shared printer. Computers that use user-level security use the Security tab on the printer's Properties sheet for enabling or disabling access to the printer.

Printer Troubleshooting

Whether you click Print and nothing happens, get streaky output, or have garbage coming out of the printer, Windows provides a variety of tools for dealing with common printing problems:

- Printer Properties sheet
- Printer test
- Spooler options
- Troubleshooters in the Help system

To view the Printer Properties sheet, right-click the Printer icon in the Printers folder and select Properties.

The Printer Properties sheets vary greatly according to which version of Windows you're supporting. Table 19.1 lists the Properties sheets and the versions of Windows that use these sheets. The Properties sheets are explained in the sections following Table 19.1.

note

You can also create a list of users and groups on a Windows 2000 Professional or Windows XP Professional system and use it to restrict printer access. In Windows XP Professional, disable Simple File Sharing in the View section of the Folder Options menu to enable user and group security.

Table 19.1   Standard Printer Properties Sheets

Properties Sheet	Windows Version					
	95	**98**	**Me**	**NT 4.0**	**2000**	**XP**
General	Y	Y	Y	Y	Y	Y
Details	Y	Y	Y	N	N	N
Ports	N	N	N	Y	Y	Y
Sharing	Y	Y	Y	Y	Y	Y
Advanced	N	N	N	N	Y	Y
Security	N	N	N	Y	Y	Y
Scheduling	N	N	N	Y	N	N

- *General*—Features the Print Test Page button, which prints a test page of graphics and text, listing the driver files. Some versions of Windows also provide a shortcut to printer preferences on this tab.
- *Details*—Lists and configures the printer port or network print queue, driver, and print-capture settings. Windows 9x/Me also list the printer driver on this tab.

- *Ports*—Lists and configures local printer ports.

- *Sharing*—This lets the user enable or disable printing. Windows 9x/Me users can also specify a password. Available only if File and Print Sharing is enabled on the system.

- *Advanced*—Schedules availability of printer, selects spooling methods, printer priority, print defaults (quality, paper type, orientation and so forth), printer driver, print processor, and separator page. Windows 2000/XP list the printer driver on this tab.

- *Security*—Enables you to select which users can print and manage print jobs and documents; available only if user-level sharing is enabled, such as if the printer is connected to a computer that is part of a network being managed by a Windows or NetWare server or if Windows XP's Simple File Sharing feature is disabled (see Chapter 21, "Networking and Internet Connectivity," for details).

- *Scheduling*—Schedules availability of printer; selects spooling methods and printer priority.

Other tabs vary by printer brand, model, and type. Some typical optional tabs include

- *Graphics*—Printer's graphics resolution and mode settings. This tab is called Main on some printers.

- *Utility*—Alignment and cleaning options for inkjet printers.

- *Fonts*—Laser printer font cartridges and TrueType font–handling settings.

- *Device Settings*—Varies by printer and Windows version; check here for options not found on other tabs such as memory sizing and options, paper type, fonts, print quality, and other options. Sometimes referred to as Device Options.

- *Paper*—Paper size and orientation settings.

- *Color Management*—Adjusts color output on color printers.

Many print problems can be solved using the Printer Properties sheets.

See Figures 19.7 and 19.8 for examples of these Properties sheets in Windows XP.

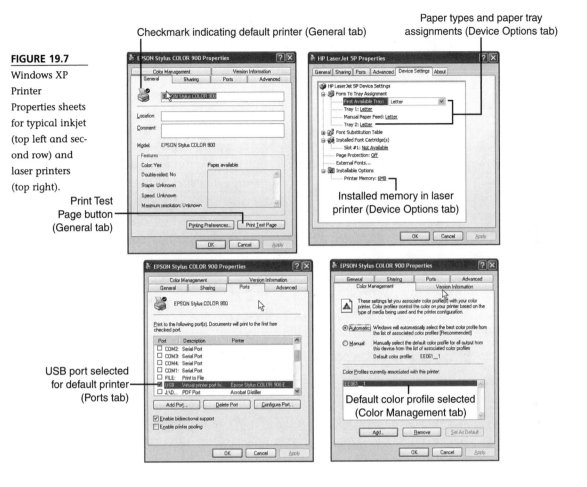

FIGURE 19.7

Windows XP Printer Properties sheets for typical inkjet (top left and second row) and laser printers (top right).

Checkmark indicating default printer (General tab)

Paper types and paper tray assignments (Device Options tab)

Print Test Page button (General tab)

Installed memory in laser printer (Device Options tab)

USB port selected for default printer (Ports tab)

Default color profile selected (Color Management tab)

Can't Print

If you can't print to a local printer, follow this procedure:

1. Check cables to make sure they are tight and in good working order.

2. Check the printer port in the Windows Device Manager and make sure the port is working properly.

⇨ **See** "Using the Windows Device Manager," **p. 703**, for details.

3. Try a test print with the Printer Properties sheet's General tab (refer to Figure 19.7).

4. If you can't get the printer to print a test page, check the appropriate Properties sheets to verify that the correct port and printer driver have been selected; change settings as necessary, and retry the test print.

FIGURE 19.8

The Advanced tab and sub-menus for a typical inkjet printer in Windows XP.

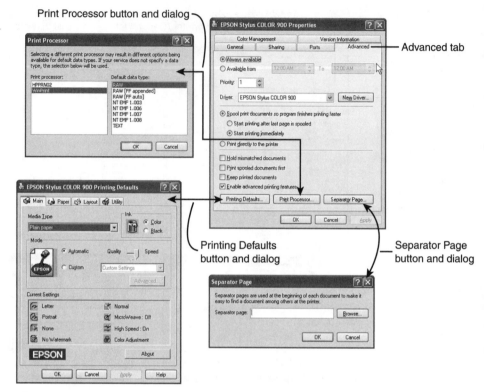

5. Check the print spooler; if the printer was unavailable the last time you tried to print to it, it might be set to offline mode. Make sure the printer is on and clear the offline mode setting.

6. If the paper goes through the inkjet printer and the printhead is moving, but there is no ink on the paper, the printheads might be clogged. Check the Utility tab on the printer driver to locate the head-cleaning utility. Retry printing after cleaning the printhead. If cleaning the printhead doesn't work, replace the inkjet cartridge(s).

7. If you still can't print, use the Windows Print Troubleshooters.

With most versions of Windows, the print troubleshooting process (see Figure 19.9) can be started after you try a test print from the Printer Properties sheet's General tab. Answer No when the dialog asks if the test page printed successfully, and the troubleshooter starts. The troubleshooter can also be started if a regular print job fails or you can just cancel the print job.

➪ You can also start the print or other troubleshooters directly. **See** "Troubleshooting Hardware," **p. 702**, for details.

FIGURE 19.9

Select the best response to each question and the Print Troubleshooter will try to find the solution to your printing problem.

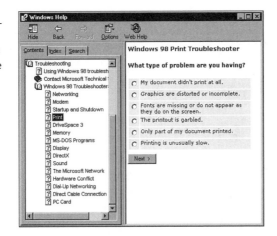

To troubleshoot problems printing to a network printer

1. Try printing from the host computer to the printer. If the computer hosting the printer can't print, use the previous checklist to solve the problem.

2. Make sure you are logged in to the network; no network resources will work if you are not logged in. To log in again, click Start, Shutdown, Logout; then re-enter (or reselect) your username and password at the login screen.

3. If the printer uses share-level security, try to log in to the printer; make sure you provide the correct password.

4. If the printer uses user-level security, make sure you are on the list of authorized users; check with the administrator of the computer or network.

5. Verify that the share name is correct on the Details tab of the printer (see Figure 19.10).

6. Make sure that your print spooler isn't set to offline mode; if the network printer isn't available, offline mode is set by default. A red icon over the Printer icon in the system tray indicates the print spooler is in offline mode.

Poor Print Quality

If you get poor-quality prints from an inkjet printer, use the Printer Properties sheets to perform the following adjustments and tests:

- Ink levels

- Head cleaning

- Paper/media type settings (these should be matched to the print resolution and quality settings for best results)

FIGURE 19.10

Check the server name (\\server) and print queue name (\printer) with the network administrator if you are unable to print; you also might need to obtain a password or make sure you are on the list of approved users for the printer.

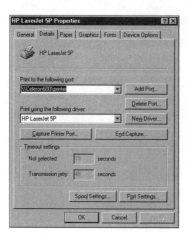

If you get poor-quality prints from a laser printer, use the Printer Properties sheets to perform the following adjustments and tests:

- Check graphics resolution
- Adjust dithering settings for graphics
- Verify proper settings for printer features such as font substitution and graphics output type

Garbage Output and Its Causes

Garbage output from the printer is frequently caused by using the wrong printer driver to communicate with the printer; if the printer is sent commands it cannot understand, it tries to print them anyway.

Some common causes for this problem include

- Failing to select a new printer, connected to the same port as the previous printer, as the default printer
- Forgetting to move the lever on a two-printer to one-computer switchbox

Other causes for garbage output might include

- Selecting a printer driver that would work if the printer were set to the correct emulation mode. For example, if a printer is both LaserJet and Postscript compatible, you might need to manually select which mode to use for printing.

- Turning on the printer after the start of the print job. If the first portion of the print job isn't received, the printer will produce garbage because the printer setup data wasn't received.

- A loose or damaged printer cable. If the printer is connected to the parallel port, make sure the cable is firmly fastened in place to the printer and the computer.

Installing and Configuring Hardware

Virtually all hardware made for use by a Windows computer is now Plug and Play (PnP) compatible. PnP installation means that Windows detects the device during startup, installs the correct software drivers (which might need to be installed prior to connecting or installing the device), and configures the device for correct operation. PnP installations can be performed by all versions of Windows covered on the A+ Certification Operating Systems Exam except Windows NT 4.0. Windows NT 4.0 hardware installations vary with the device, but typically use one of the following methods:

- A setup program included on the driver disk or CD can be used to install the driver.

- The System Control dialog box can also be used to add a new driver for specified device categories. For example, to add a sound card, the user opens the Multimedia category, clicks Devices, Add, and then browses the CD for the required driver.

- Control Panel icons can also be used to add a new driver. For example, to install a new UltraATA or SCSI host adapter, the user selects the SCSI Adapters icon, clicks Drivers, Add, and then browses the CD for the required driver.

To install devices after the system has started with versions of Windows other than Windows NT 4.0, use one of the following options:

- Windows 9x/Me use the Add New Hardware Wizard in the Control Panel.

- Windows 2000 uses the Add/Remove Hardware Wizard in the Control Panel.

- Windows XP uses the Add Hardware Wizard in the Control Panel.

For more information about Control Panel, see Chapter 18, "Using and Optimizing Windows."

Plug and Play Requirements

Windows 9x/Me/2000/XP all support Plug and Play (PnP) installation, but how PnP actually works depends upon the version of Windows in use.

For PnP to function correctly, the following must be true:

■ The device must support **Plug and Play**. Some legacy devices can be switched into Plug and Play mode.

■ The operating system must support PnP.

■ The system BIOS must support PnP. Most BIOSs can be configured to indicate that a PnP-compatible operating system is in use. This setting should be enabled for Windows 9x/Me/2000/XP, but disabled for Windows NT 4.0.

Legacy devices such as serial and parallel ports and PS/2 mouse ports use fixed hardware resources such as Interrupt Request (IRQ), I/O port address, and others. That's not the case with PnP. Whenever a new PnP device is installed, existing device settings can change to enable the new device to be properly installed.

Any PCI or AGP card is designed strictly as a PnP device. Some late-model ISA cards can be configured as either legacy or PnP devices by moving a jumper block, flipping a DIP switch, or running a configuration program.

Installing a PnP Device

The following is the basic procedure for installing a PnP device:

1. Read the documentation for the device to determine if the drivers should be installed before the device is connected or installed. If the drivers should be installed first, install them before proceeding.

2. Install or connect the device to the system.

3. Turn on the system. As soon as the Windows desktop begins to appear, Windows detects the device. If Windows already has a suitable driver, the device will be installed and configured.

If a suitable driver is not already installed, the remainder of the steps vary, depending on the version of Windows you use.

Follow these steps for Windows 95/95a:

1. After the system detects the new hardware, Windows starts the Add New Hardware Wizard.

2. Select Driver from Disk Provided by Hardware Manufacturer, insert the driver disk or CD, and click OK. Change the location where Windows looks for the setup file if necessary.

Follow these steps for Windows 95B/C:

1. After the system detects the new hardware, Windows starts the Update Device Driver Wizard.

2. Insert the driver disk or CD and click OK. Change the location where Windows looks for the setup file if necessary. Click OK to copy the files, and then OK again.

   Remove the setup disk.

Follow these steps for Windows 98/Me:

1. If a suitable driver is not available, Windows starts the Add New Hardware Wizard.

2. Choose from Search for the Best Driver (default) or Display a List of All the Drivers. Then click Next.

3. You can edit the default search options (see Figure 19.11) or specify a location for the driver if you downloaded it. After you have selected the best places to search, click Next to continue.

4. If Search is unable to locate a driver, click Back and select Specify a Location. Click Browse to search the CD-ROM or floppy disk for the correct files.

note

Windows 95a refers to the original retail/update/ OEM release of Windows after installation of Service Pack 1. Installing Service Pack 1 changes the listed version of Windows 95 on the General tab of the System Properties sheet to Windows 95a. Windows 95B and Windows 95C on the General tab of the System Properties sheet indicate that the system has OEM Service Release 2.0 or later installed.

FIGURE 19.11

By default, the Windows 98/Me Add New Hardware Wizard searches the floppy disk drives and CD-ROM drive for hardware drivers (.INF files); select different locations as needed to find the drivers for your device. Select Microsoft Windows Update if an Internet connection is available.

5. Confirm the device name and the driver file location, and click Next to continue. You might need to exchange the driver CD for the Windows CD during installation.

6. Click Finish when prompted. After the device is installed, you might be prompted to reboot the system.

Follow these steps for Windows 2000/XP:

1. If a suitable driver is not available, Windows starts the Add/Remove Hardware Wizard (2000) or Add Hardware Wizard (XP).

2. Choose either Search for a Suitable Driver (default) or Display a List of the Known Drivers.

3. You can edit the default search options or specify a location for the driver if you downloaded it. After you have selected the best places to search, click Next to continue.

4. If Search is unable to locate a driver, click Back and select Specify a Location. Click Browse to search the CD-ROM or floppy disk for the correct files. Windows allows you to disable the device if no suitable driver can be located.

5. You might be able to choose either the recommended driver or an alternative driver from the list of drivers found by Search. Select Install One of the Other Drivers to see alternatives. Select the driver you prefer from the list to continue.

6. The driver will be checked for a **digital signature**, which indicates the driver has been tested by Microsoft for proper operation. If no digital signature is found on the driver, a warning message will be displayed (see Figure 19.15), and you can choose a different driver if you prefer. Click Yes to continue or No to return and choose another driver.

7. Click Finish after installing the device. You will not need to reboot the system.

Installing a Non-PnP Card

Frankly, there aren't a lot of **legacy cards** around anymore. With the end of ISA slots on desktop systems, non-PnP installations with Windows 9x/Me/2000/XP don't happen much anymore. Nevertheless, you should understand how they work in case you're asked about them on the A+ Certification Exam or you encounter an older system in the field.

You need to use the Add New Hardware or Add/Remove Hardware Wizard to install a legacy card, but the default settings the wizard assumes might need to be altered to match the actual settings used by the device.

Follow this procedure to install a non-PnP card under Windows:

1. Use the Windows Device Manager to view the current hardware resource usage (IRQ, DMA, I/O port address, or memory address) for the system. If necessary, select View Resources by Type (refer to Figure 19.18).

2. Compare available resources to those that can be used by the card, and record the available settings. Note that Device Manager shows resources in use. Resources that are not listed are available.

3. Shut down the system.

4. If the card uses jumper blocks or DIP switches to select IRQ, DMA, I/O port, or memory addresses, set the resources to match available resources in the system before you install it.

5. If the card uses a software configuration program, you will need to set the card with its own software before you install it (see step 8).

6. Restart the system, and access the BIOS setup program by pressing the correct key(s).

7. Go to the PnP configuration screen and see if you can set the IRQ and other hardware resources you will use for the card to ISA instead of PnP/PCI. This will prevent Windows from trying to use the resource for existing cards. Save any changes and exit (see Figure 19.12).

Change to Yes to reserve IRQ 3 for a non-PnP device.

FIGURE 19.12

Select the IRQ of the non-PnP card you want to install in the BIOS's PCI/PnP IRQ Resource Exclusion dialog.

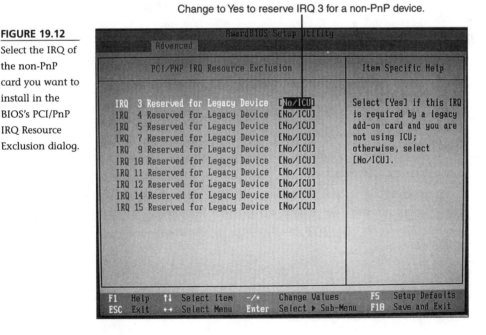

8. If the card uses software configuration, boot the computer to a command prompt. Use the emergency startup disk with Windows 9x/Me. You can also use an MS-DOS or Windows 9x/Me boot disk with Windows 2000/XP. Run the card's setup program and set the card to the available hardware resource settings you noted earlier.

9. Restart the computer normally.

10. After the computer has completed the boot process, open the Control Panel and start the Add New Hardware Wizard (Windows 9x/Me) or Add/Remove Hardware Wizard (Windows 2000) or Add Hardware Wizard (Windows XP). Click Next to continue.

11. For Windows 2000, select Add/Troubleshoot a Device and click Next to continue.

    In Windows 98/Me, the Add New Hardware Wizard searches for PnP devices first and lists any new ones it finds. Select Yes to install newly found devices, or No to install a legacy device. Click Next to continue.

    In Windows 2000, the Add/Remove New Hardware Wizard searches for PnP devices and lists all existing devices. (This enables the wizard to be used to troubleshoot existing devices.) Click Add a New Device and Next to continue.

    In Windows XP, Windows asks if the hardware is already installed. Select Yes if it is installed (Windows XP lists the installed devices), or No if it is not installed yet. Then, click Add a New Device and Next to continue if the device is not listed.

12. If the device is already installed, Windows can search for it. If you know the brand name and model of the device or if you have a driver disk, skip the search process and choose the device type (see Figure 19.13). Click Next to continue.

13. On the next screen, you can select the brand and model, or choose Have Disk and supply the driver disk or CD-ROM.

14. If you chose to search for the device, verify that the correct device has been located, and click Next.

15. In Windows 9x/Me, the system will select default values for the device (which might not work), as shown in Figure 19.14. You can either adjust the device to use those settings or use the Device Manager to choose other settings for the device.

FIGURE 19.13

If your hardware isn't already installed, or if you prefer to specify it yourself, start by selecting the hardware type (Windows 98 shown here).

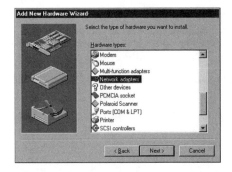

FIGURE 19.14

The default values listed for the device won't work unless the device is already set to use these values. Either change the device or change the settings in Device Manager—your choice!

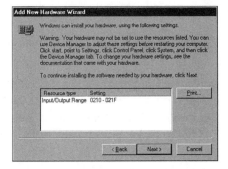

Windows 2000/XP can normally detect the device's actual settings; if the device isn't installed yet, click the Change Setting button and select the correct IRQ and other hardware resources when prompted.

16. In Windows 9x/Me, if the device is set to different values, open the Device Manager tab of the System Properties sheet and change any hardware resource settings that are incorrect to match the actual settings you used.

17. After the software for the device is installed, you might be prompted to shut down and restart the system.

18. After you restart the system, the device will be ready to work.

Aren't you glad PnP was invented?

Signed and Unsigned Device Drivers

Starting with Windows Me, and continuing with Windows 2000 and Windows XP, Microsoft has recommended the use of digitally signed device drivers for hardware.

So, what exactly is a **digitally signed device driver**? It's a device driver that has been tested and approved by the Microsoft **Windows Hardware Quality Lab (WHQL)** for the device and for the version of Windows you're running. The idea behind digitally signed device drivers is to keep you from nuking your Windows installation by installing outdated or buggy drivers for your hardware.

How can you tell if the drivers already installed are digitally signed? Open the Properties sheet for a device in the Windows Device Manager and click the Driver tab. With Windows XP, a device using a digital signature lists Microsoft Windows XP Publisher. However, a device that doesn't use a WHQL-signed driver for that version of Windows lists Not Digitally Signed instead. If you have problems with a device, you should replace **unsigned drivers** with digitally signed drivers.

By default, Windows versions that support driver signing are configured to warn you when you try to install hardware with an unsigned device driver. You can continue the installation or quit. The other options include Ignore, which uses the unsigned drivers without any advisory, and Block, which prevents the installation and displays a message. Figure 19.15 compares these three options and typical dialogs under Windows XP. Windows Me and 2000 are similar.

In a perfect world, using Windows Update or visiting the hardware vendors' Web sites would assure you of a constant stream of these WHQL-approved, good-as-gold device drivers for every device you install. However, the world isn't perfect. With Windows XP, for example, many vendors use Windows 2000 drivers that haven't been tested by WHQL for compatibility with Windows XP. Some vendors use non-signed Windows 98 drivers with Windows Me. These drivers might work perfectly, but they lack the WHQL seal of approval. You also might need to use unsigned drivers downloaded straight from the hardware vendor's Web site for urgent fixes, especially involving brand-new hardware. In such cases, try to avoid beta (prerelease) or test versions of driver software. In general, the latest released versions of a driver are the best to use, but with some older motherboard or video card chipsets, an older driver might work better.

To avoid problems when you install updated drivers, follow these guidelines:

- Download the driver and uncompress it to a known folder location so you can look for Readme files or other information before you install it.

- Uninstall the old driver and use the browse feature of the Detect/Add Hardware Wizard to locate the new driver files when the hardware is redetected. This is often more reliable than installing new drivers over old drivers, particularly with Windows XP, if your old drivers were not digitally signed or were made for Windows 2000.

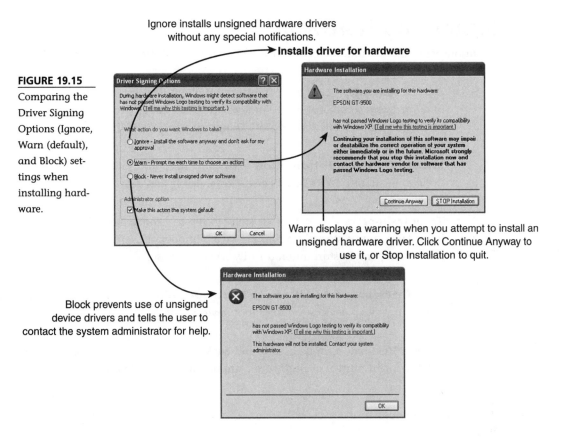

FIGURE 19.15

Comparing the Driver Signing Options (Ignore, Warn (default), and Block) settings when installing hardware.

Ignore installs unsigned hardware drivers without any special notifications.

Installs driver for hardware

Warn displays a warning when you attempt to install an unsigned hardware driver. Click Continue Anyway to use it, or Stop Installation to quit.

Block prevents use of unsigned device drivers and tells the user to contact the system administrator for help.

■ If you install a new driver over an old driver in Windows XP and the hardware has problems, use the Rollback feature on the device's Properties sheet to revert to the old driver.

Installing and Configuring Modems

Use the Modems or Phone and Modem Options icon in Control Panel to detect and install the drivers for a new modem if the modem isn't detected and installed automatically by Windows. (See Chapter 8, "Input/Output Devices and Cables," for details.) Generally, you would use this installation method for legacy devices such as external modems connected to the serial port or internal modems that use an ISA or 8-bit expansion slot.

Click the Modem tab (if required); then click the Add button to detect your modem and install the appropriate drivers. You can also choose your modem from a list.

After the modem has been installed, you can configure its settings through its Properties sheet.

Troubleshooting Hardware

Various versions of Windows include a wide variety of tools for troubleshooting hardware, including

- **Device Manager**—Lists basic information about devices, including driver and hardware configurations. Windows NT 4.0 doesn't have the Device Manager, but uses the Windows NT Diagnostics tool to list hardware information.

- **Microsoft System Information**—Lists advanced information about devices, including **.INF files**, Registry keys, driver files, hardware configurations, and problems.

- **Troubleshooters**—These provide step-by-step assistance in solving problems. They can be started from the Device Manager or the Windows Help system, or they might start automatically when processes such as printing don't work.

- **Add Hardware or Add/Remove Hardware Wizard**—Can be used to unplug hot-swap devices, troubleshoot devices, and install and remove devices.

- **System Restore**—Can be used to roll back the system Registry to a specified point before a particular hardware component or software program was installed.

Table 19.2 provides an overview of the major tools and the versions of Windows that use them.

Table 19.2   Windows Hardware Troubleshooting Tools

Tool	95	98	Me	NT 4.0	2000	XP
Device Manager	Y	Y	Y	N	Y	Y
NT Diagnostics (Winmsd.exe)	N	N	N	Y	N	N
System Information (MSInfo32.exe)	N[1]	Y	Y	N	Y	Y
Troubleshooters	Y	Y	Y	Y	Y	Y
Add or Add/Remove Hardware Wizard	Y	Y	Y	N	Y	Y
System Restore	N	N	Y	N	N	Y
DirectX Diagnostics (DXDIAG.exe)[2]	Y	Y	Y	N	Y	Y
File Signature Verification (Sigverif.exe)	N	N	Y	N	Y	Y
System File Checker (SFC.exe)	N	Y	Y	N	Y	Y

[1]*OSR 2.x CD version uses Hwdiag.exe instead of MSInfo32.exe; older Windows 95 versions lack this feature.*

[2]*Included as part of recent DirectX versions.*

Some of the typical hardware problems that can be isolated with these tools include

- Incorrect parameters for hardware
- Bad or missing drivers
- Conflicts between devices
- Hardware options that don't work

Using the Windows Device Manager

To use the Device Manager

1. Open the System Properties sheet in the Control Panel, or right-click My Computer and select Properties.

2. To continue with *Windows 9x/Me*, click the Device Manager tab; it displays the device categories found in your computer (computer, disk drives, display, keyboards, and so on). Any devices with problems are displayed immediately. Devices with driver problems or conflicts are marked with an exclamation mark in a yellow circle. Disabled devices are shown with a red X.

   To continue with *Windows 2000/XP*, click the Hardware tab and select from the following:

   - *Hardware Wizard*—Runs the Add or Add/Remove Hardware Wizard.

   - *Driver Signing*—Enables you to permit, block, or ignore digital signatures for driver files; helps you determine whether legitimate driver files for Windows 2000 and XP are being used.

   - *Device Manager*—Enables you to view and change hardware properties.

3. Click Device Manager to continue. Any devices with problems are highlighted immediately as described with Windows 9x/Me (see Figure 19.16).

If your computer has devices that are malfunctioning in a way that Device Manager can detect, or has devices that are disabled, they will be displayed as soon as you open the Device Manager. For example, in Figure 19.16, the Ports (COM and LPT) category displays a malfunctioning port, COM 2, indicated by an exclamation mark (!) in a yellow circle. The parallel printer port, LPT1, has been disabled, as indicated by a red X. If the malfunctioning or disabled device is an I/O port, such as a serial, parallel, or USB port, any device attached to that port cannot work until the device is working properly.

Not every problem with a device shows up in Device Manager, but most problems with resource conflicts or drivers will be displayed here.

Malfunctioning Windows device

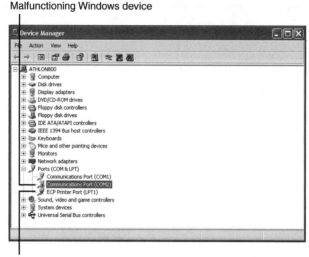

Disabled Windows device

To troubleshoot problems with a device in Device Manager, open its Properties sheet
by double-clicking on the device. Each device has at least three tabs, including
General (displays device status and allows you to enable or disable the device as in
Figure 19.17), Driver (displays device driver files and versions and enables you to
update the driver), and Resources (displays the device's current and alternative settings for IRQ, DMA, I/O port, and memory addresses). Some devices also have an
additional tab to enable adjustment of device-specific settings.

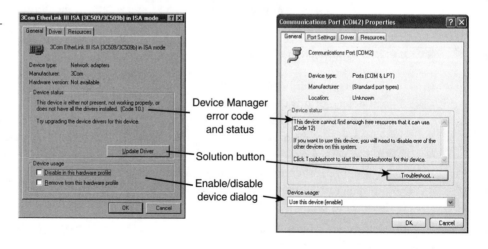

Device Manager
error code
and status

Solution button

Enable/disable
device dialog

When you have a malfunctioning device such as the one in Figure 19.17, you have several options for resolving the problem:

- Look up the Device Manager code to determine the problem and its solution (see Table 19.3).

- Click the solution button (if any) shown on the device's General Properties tab; the button's name and usage depends upon the problem. Table 19.3 lists the codes, their meanings, and the solution button (if any).

- Manually change resources. If the nature of the problem is a resource conflict, you can click the Resources tab and change the settings and eliminate the conflict if possible (see Figure 19.18). Some recent systems that use ACPI power management don't permit manual resource changes in Device Manager and also override any changes you might make in the system BIOS setup program. On these systems, if resource conflicts take place, you might need to disable ACPI power management before you can solve resource conflicts.

- Manually update drivers. If the problem is a driver issue but an Update Driver button isn't available, open the Driver tab and install a new driver for the device.

Table 19.3 Windows Device Manager Codes and Solutions

Device Manager Code Number	Problem	Solution Button[1]	Other Steps to the Solution
1	Incorrect device configuration	Update Driver	If Update Driver fails, delete device listing and run Add New Hardware Wizard.
2	Can't determine correct device bus type or can't install driver	Update Driver	If Update Driver fails, delete device listing and run Add New Hardware Wizard.
3	Bad device driver or system resources low	Update Driver	Press Ctrl+Alt+Del (Task Manager) to check system resources with Windows 2000/XP; run Resource Meter in Windows 9x/Me; if Update Driver fails, delete device listing and run Add New Hardware Wizard.

Table 19.3 (continued)

Device Manager Code Number	Problem	Solution Button[1]	Other Steps to the Solution
4	Bad driver or Registry problem	Update Driver	If Update Driver fails, delete device listing and run Add New Hardware Wizard. Run Scanregw in Windows 98/Me to check Registry.
5	Bad driver	Update Driver	If Update Driver fails, delete device listing and run Add New Hardware Wizard.
6	Resource conflict with another device	Troubleshoot	If the Troubleshooter cannot resolve the conflict, shut down the computer, change the resources used by the device, and restart.
7	Can't configure device	Reinstall Driver	If Reinstall Driver fails, delete device listing and run Add New Hardware Wizard; obtain an updated driver.
8	Various DevLoader (device loader) problems	(none)	Reinstall Windows to re-create a working VMM32.VXD system file.
		Reinstall Driver	If Reinstall Driver fails, delete device listing and run Add New Hardware Wizard; obtain an updated driver.
		Update Driver	If Update Driver fails, delete device listing and run Add New Hardware Wizard; obtain an updated driver.
9	BIOS enumeration problem	(none)	Delete device listing and run Add New Hardware Wizard; contact vendor for correct Registry keys or an updated driver if the problem continues.

Table 19.3 (continued)

Device Manager Code Number	Problem	Solution Button[1]	Other Steps to the Solution
10	Device not present, working properly, or other specified problem	Update Driver	Check physical connection to system (slot connector, cabling, and power); restart system. Run Update Driver if Code 10 reappears. If Update Driver fails, delete device listing and run Add New Hardware Wizard.
11	Windows stopped responding while attempting to start the device	Update Driver	Run ASD (Automatic Skip Driver) for Windows 98/Me only and re-enable the device; if the error shows up again, install new drivers for device and then rerun ASD.
12	No free hardware resources	Troubleshoot or Hardware Troubleshooter	Follow instructions in hardware troubleshooter; might require removal or reconfiguration of other devices to resolve lack of resources.
13	Device not detected by system	Detect Hardware	If Detect Hardware fails, delete device listing and run Add New Hardware Wizard.
14	Must restart computer before device will work	Restart Computer	Shut down computer and restart to activate device.
15	Resource conflict with another device	Troubleshoot or Hardware Troubleshooter	Follow instructions in Troubleshooter to find nonconflicting resources.
16	Some device resources aren't known	(none)	Click Resources tab and manually enter resources required or delete device listing and run Add New Hardware Wizard.
17	Incorrect assignment of resources to multifunctional device	Update Driver	Delete device listing and run Add New Hardware Wizard. Get new driver (.inf) file from vendor if problems persist.

Table 19.3 (continued)

Device Manager Code Number	Problem	Solution Button[1]	Other Steps to the Solution
18	Drivers need to be reinstalled	Reinstall Driver	If Reinstall Driver fails, delete device listing and run Add New Hardware Wizard.
19	Possible bad Registry	Check Registry	Windows 98/Me:
			Run Scanreg; if problem persists, run Scanreg/restore. If problem still persists, remove device and redetect with Add New Hardware Wizard.
			Windows 2000:
			Restart system, press the F8 key, and select Use Last Known Good Configuration from the startup menu.
			Windows XP:
			Windows will restart and use a previous copy of the Registry; if this fails, start Windows in Safe Mode and use System Restore to return to a working condition.
20	Can't load drivers for device	Update Driver	If Update Driver fails, delete device listing and run Add New Hardware Wizard.
21	Windows is removing specified device	Restart Computer	Shut down Windows and computer; wait a few moments and then restart the computer.
22	Device is disabled in Device Manager	Enable Device	Click solution button.
	Device not started	Start Device	Click solution button.
	Device is disabled by driver or program	(none)	Remove device listing and run Add New Hardware Wizard. If the problem persists, use MSCONFIG to disable startup programs (clean boot) and retry; contact the hardware manufacturer for help if problem continues.

Table 19.3 (continued)

Device Manager Code Number	Problem	Solution Button[1]	Other Steps to the Solution
23	Secondary display adapter problems	Properties	Verify primary display adapter works okay.
	Problem with primary display adapter	(none)	Correct problems with primary display adapter and retry.
	Other devices	Update Driver	Click Solution button.
24	Legacy (non-PnP) device was not detected	Detect Hardware	If device still can't be detected, make sure it is properly connected to the system.
	PnP device was not detected	Update Drivers	If device still can't be detected, make sure it is properly connected to the system.
25	Device not completely set up by Windows	Restart Computer	Normally displayed only during first reboots of Windows; if problem persists after Windows is completely installed, you might need to reinstall Windows or remove the device listing and use Add New Hardware.
26	Device not completely set up by Windows	Restart Computer	If problem persists, remove the device listing and use Add New Hardware.
27	Resources can't be specified	(none)	Remove the device listing and use Add New Hardware; obtain updated drivers or help from hardware vendor if problem persists.
28	Drivers not installed	Reinstall Driver	If Reinstall Driver fails, delete device listing and run Add New Hardware Wizard. Obtain updated drivers if necessary.
29	No resources provided by BIOS or device disabled in BIOS	(none)	Restart computer, start BIOS setup program, and configure device in BIOS. Save changes and restart the computer.

Table 19.3 (continued)

Device Manager Code Number	Problem	Solution Button[1]	Other Steps to the Solution
30	IRQ conflict	(none)	Reconfigure device or conflicting device to use a different IRQ. For a legacy device, restart the system and use the PnP menu in the system BIOS to reserve the device's IRQ.
31	A specified device is preventing the current device from working	Properties	Reconfigure other device's properties (displayed when you click solution button) to fix problem; if problem persists, delete device listings and run Add New Hardware Wizard. Obtain updated drivers if necessary.
32	Drivers not available	Restart Computer	Provide installation CD-ROM or log on to network after restarting; if CD-ROM or network doesn't work, resolve its problem so drivers can be accessed.
33	Various hardware errors	(none)	Hardware has failed; replace specified hardware.

[1]*Not available in all versions of Windows*

To see the overall hardware resources in use with Windows 9x/Me

1. Double-click the Computer icon at the top of the list of devices.
2. By default, IRQ usage is displayed; click the DMA, I/O port, and memory buttons to see usage for each of these resources.

To see the overall hardware resources in use with Windows 2000/XP (see Figure 19.18)

1. Click View and select Resources by type.
2. Click the plus sign next to each resource type listed to see its usage.

In Figure 19.18, IRQ and DMA resource usage are displayed in detail. The user can view I/O resource usage by clicking the plus sign, and view memory resource usage by scrolling down to Memory and clicking its plus sign.

FIGURE 19.18

IRQ and DMA usage on a typical Windows 2000 system. Because this computer uses PCI slots and an advanced chipset with ACPI power management that supports IRQ steering, multiple devices share IRQ9 without any problems.

To see the resource and driver information for a particular device

1. Click the plus (+) sign next to the device category containing the device.

2. Click the device.

3. Click Properties.

4. Click the General tab to see if the device is working properly; a device with a problem will display an error message on this tab (refer to Figure 19.17).

5. Click the Driver tab for driver file details; use Update Driver to install new drivers.

6. Click the Resources tab to see which hardware resources the device is using and to see whether there are any conflicts.

If the device has a conflict with another device, you might be able to change the settings in the Control Panel (see Figure 19.19). If the device is a legacy (non-PnP) device, you might need to shut down the system and reconfigure the card manually before you can use the Device Manager to reset its configuration in Windows.

You can also use the Device Manager to disable a device that is conflicting with another device. To disable a device

1. Click the plus (+) sign next to the device category containing the device.

2. Click the device.

3. Click Properties.

4. Click the General tab.

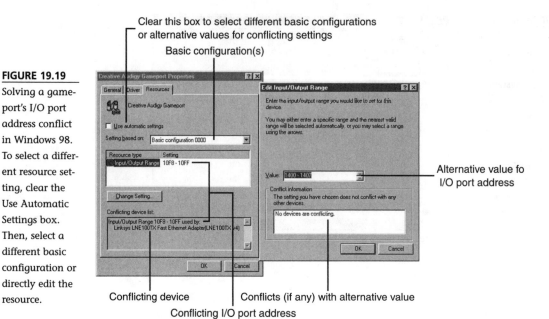

Clear this box to select different basic configurations or alternative values for conflicting settings

Basic configuration(s)

FIGURE 19.19

Solving a game-port's I/O port address conflict in Windows 98. To select a different resource setting, clear the Use Automatic Settings box. Then, select a different basic configuration or directly edit the resource.

Alternative value fo I/O port address

Conflicting device

Conflicting I/O port address

Conflicts (if any) with alternative value

5. Look for the Device Usage display at the bottom of the window. With Windows 9x/Me, click the box next to Disable in This Hardware Profile. You might need to restart the computer. With Windows 2000/XP, click the menu and select Do Not Use This Device (disable). Refer back to Figure 19.17 for details of these dialogs. If you prefer to solve the problem with the device, click the Troubleshooter button to launch the appropriate Windows 2000 or XP troubleshooter.

Depending on the device, you might need to physically remove it from the system to resolve a conflict. To use the Device Manager to remove a device

1. Click the plus (+) sign next to the device category containing the device.

2. Click the device.

3. Click Remove.

4. Confirm that you want to remove the device—the Registry entries for the device are removed, but the drivers remain on the system.

5. Shut down the system when prompted and remove the device. Windows 2000 or XP might not prompt you to shut down the system, but you will need to do so to remove an internal device.

Using Microsoft System Information

The System Information utility in Windows provides you with a powerful way to view your system's

- Basic hardware configuration
- Installed hardware
- Installed software
- Current software environment, including startup programs and running services
- Internet settings
- System problems

Compared to the Device Manager, Microsoft System Information provides more information about your hardware. And, unlike Device Manager, System Information is strictly a reporting tool, so users cannot accidentally change their system configuration by using it.

To use Microsoft System Information for more information about your system's devices, select Start, Programs, Accessories, System Tools, and then click System Information to start the program. If this shortcut isn't available, click Start, Run, type **MSInfo32**, and click OK to start the program.

Need a fast way to find out what's under the hood of your PC? Start System Information and the System Summary screen appears after a few seconds. It displays your operating system version, computer name, motherboard brand and model, processor type and speed, Windows folder, boot drive, username physical and virtual memory, and the location of the pagefile.

note

Windows NT 4.0 doesn't include MSInfo32; however, some versions of Microsoft Office install MSInfo32, and Windows NT 4.0 includes a report tool called WinMSD. WinMSD has fewer features than MSInfo32, but can still be useful in determining information about your system.

Click the plus (+) sign next to Hardware Resources to select from the following options:

- *Conflicts/Sharing*—Lists IRQs or other resources that are shared among devices.
- *DMA*—Lists DMA channels in use by device.
- **Forced hardware**—Lists PnP hardware that has been set manually (see Figure 19.20).

■ *I/O*—Lists I/O port addresses in use by device.

■ *Memory*—Lists memory addresses in use by device.

FIGURE 19.20

Microsoft System Information displays devices with forced hardware settings (PnP devices that are set manually by the user); the Windows 98 version is shown here.

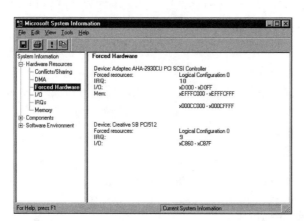

For information about components (video, audio, ports, and so on), click the plus (+) sign next to Components, and click a component category for more information.

In addition to current hardware resource information, Components also lists drivers, Registry keys, and alternative hardware configurations. Devices with problems are flagged. With the Windows 98/Me version, you can toggle between Basic Information and Advanced Information at the top of the screen as needed. The Windows 2000 and XP versions show detailed information at all times (see Figure 19.21).

To learn more about the devices installed on your computer, click Components to open the category, and then navigate through the subcategories and device types to see the name of the device, its driver, its features, and the hardware resources it uses. The exact information provided will vary with the device type. For example, network adapters display IP address and MAC address information, whereas modems display the AT commands they use to activate major features.

tip

Forced Hardware is the Windows term for devices that have been manually configured to use particular hardware resources instead of using the device's normal Windows PnP settings. Forced Hardware settings are not recommended because they can cause conflicts with other devices.

If you see a device listed in the Forced Hardware category, open Device Manager to confirm that it works correctly. If Device Manager reports problems, open the device's Properties sheet, click Resources, and click Use Automatic Settings to enable Windows to configure the device. Restart the computer if necessary.

INF file used to install hardware
Video memory size

FIGURE 19.21

The Windows XP version of the Microsoft System Information utility provides detailed information about installed hardware. Note the details about video memory size, screen resolution, and refresh rates listed for the graphics card.

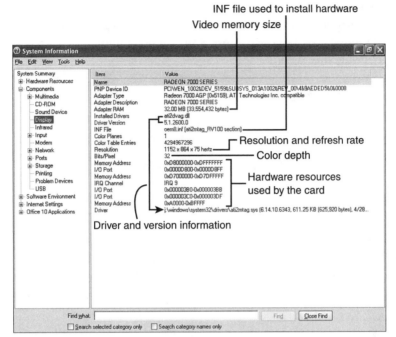

Resolution and refresh rate
Color depth
Hardware resources used by the card
Driver and version information

You can find problems in two ways:

- Click the Problem Devices category.
- Search for the information you know (IP address, IRQ, and so on) with the search tool available in some versions. The Windows XP version calls it Find What.

In many cases, you might find that running System Information is faster than navigating through Computer Management, Internet Explorer or Internet properties settings, Device Manager, and other programs to learn about your system.

Using System Information Tools

System Information isn't just about reporting problems with your system. Click the Tools menu to choose from the utilities listed in Table 19.4 to help fix your system.

caution

Any hardware resources used by forced hardware cannot be reassigned by the PnP features of Windows; try to avoid setting PnP hardware manually unless compatibility issues with specific programs (such as older programs that expect a sound card to use certain resources) or hardware conflicts force you to do so.

If you prefer, or if your version of Windows doesn't include the tool in its System Information menu, use the command in parentheses to run the program from a command prompt or with Start, Run. These commands are explained in more detail following this table.

Table 19.4 System Information Tools

Tool	98	Me	2000	XP
Windows Report Tool	Y	N	Y	N
Update Wizard Uninstall	Y	Y	Y	N
Registry Checker	Y	Y	N	N
System Restore	N	Y	N	Y
DirectX Diagnostics (DXDIAG.EXE)	N	Y	Y	Y
File Signature Verification (SIGVERIF.EXE)	Y	Y	Y	Y
System File Checker (SFC.EXE)	Y	N	N[1]	N[1]
Automatic Skip Driver (ASD.EXE)	Y	Y	N	N
Dr. Watson	Y	Y	Y	Y
(DRWATSON.EXE—98/Me)				
(DRWTSN32.EXE—2000/XP)				
System Configuration Utility (MSConfig)	Y	Y	N	N[2]
Version Conflict Manager	Y	N	N	N
Internet Explorer Repair Tool	Y	N	N	N
Hardware Wizard	N	N	Y	N
Network Connections	N	N	Y	N
Backup	N	N	Y	N
Net Diagnostics	N	N	N	Y
Disk Cleanup	N	N	Y	N

[1]*Can also be run with this command from the command prompt in Windows 2000/XP*

[2]*Can also be run with this command from Start, Run in Windows XP*

Here's more information about the tools listed in Table 19.4:

- *Windows Report Tool*—Complete this when requested by Microsoft support engineers.
- *Update Wizard Uninstall*—Uninstalls updates to Windows performed by the online Update Wizard.

- *System File Checker*—Verifies system files and replaces corrupt or damaged files from the originals stored in CAB files.

- *Signature Verification Tool (File Signature Verification Utility)*—Checks driver and other files for digital signatures (used to verify their authenticity).

- *Registry Checker*—Replaces a corrupt Registry with a backup copy.

- *Automatic Skip Driver (ASD) Agent*—Lists devices that are not working and are skipped by Windows at startup, and allows user to re-enable the device.

- *Dr. Watson*—When loaded into memory, captures details about the system's configuration when a system fault occurs. It can also be loaded from the Startup group.

- *System Configuration Utility (MSConfig)* —Can be used to troubleshoot startup problems by selectively disabling startup programs and services.

- *Version Conflict Manager*—Lists system files that have been replaced with newer versions, and enables backups of those files to be restored.

- *Disk Cleanup*—Can remove temporary files, index files, and (optionally) Windows components and applications to free up disk space. Can also compress older files.

- *DirectX Diagnostic Tool*—Verifies, tests, and reports on the system's DirectX configuration.

- *Hardware Wizard*—Runs the Add/Remove Hardware Wizard.

- *Network Connections*—Opens the Network Properties sheet.

- *Backup*—Runs the Windows 2000 backup program.

- *Net Diagnostics*—Launches verification and testing programs for all types of network connections, including dialup and LAN.

- **System Restore**—Can reset system Registry to its configuration before a particular hardware or software component was installed.

To access these tools, click Tools and select from the tools listed. Some of these tools are discussed elsewhere in this chapter, whereas others are discussed in Chapters 20, "Troubleshooting Windows and Windows Applications," and 21, "Networking and Internet Connectivity."

Using Windows Hardware Troubleshooters

Got a problem? Call a troubleshooter!

The Windows Hardware Troubleshooters can be started in various ways, depending upon the hardware and the version of Windows in use. Troubleshooters can be started from the print dialog if a print job or test print fails, and some can be started with the solution button in the Windows Device Manager. To start others, open the Windows Help or Help and Support System. Look for Troubleshooting or Troubleshooter in the Contents or with Search to find a list of troubleshooters you can use. The Print Troubleshooter shown earlier in this chapter in Figure 19.9 is typical of the Windows troubleshooters. Each troubleshooter is designed to ask you a series of questions. Depending upon your answer to each question, different procedures will be suggested.

If you need to open the Device Manager or a device's Properties sheet to solve a problem, the troubleshooter will provide a shortcut and detailed instructions.

Using System Restore

Ever wish you had a "time machine" so you could go back before you installed a bad driver or troublesome piece of software? Windows Me and XP have one called System Restore. System Restore enables you to fix problems caused by a defective hardware or software installation by resetting your computer's configuration to the way it was at a specified earlier time. The driver or software files installed stay on the system, and so does the data you created, but Registry changes made by the hardware or software are reversed so your system works the way it did before the installation. Restore points can be created by the user with System Restore, and are also created automatically by the system before new hardware or software is installed.

To create a restore point

1. Start System Restore from the System Information Tools menu (see Figure 19.22).

2. Click Create a Restore Point and click Next.

3. Enter a descriptive name for the restore point, such as `Before I installed DuzItAll Version 1.0` and click Create.

4. The computer's current hardware and software configuration is stored as a new restore point.

To restore your system to an earlier condition

1. Start System Restore. If you cannot start the system normally, start it in Safe Mode and select the System Restore link.

2. Click Restore My Computer to an Earlier Time and click Next.

3. Select a date from the calendar (dates that have restore points are in bold text).

Restores computer to a specified restore point

FIGURE 19.22

The main menu
of the System
Restore program
in Windows XP.

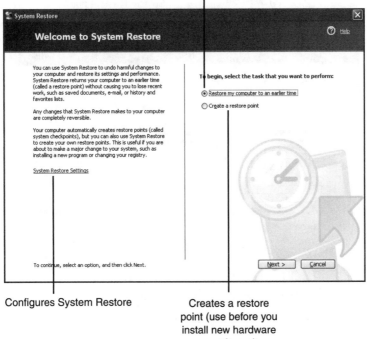

Configures System Restore

Creates a restore
point (use before you
install new hardware
or software)

4. Select a restore point and click Next (see Figure 19.23).

5. Close any open programs and save your work before you click Next to start the process; Windows will shut down and restart.

6. Click OK to close the System Restore program after the computer restarts.

If System Restore is not available, it might be turned off. You can enable or disable System Restore or change the amount of disk space it uses with the System Restore tab on the System Properties sheet; click System Restore Settings from the main menu of System Restore to adjust these settings.

caution

Be wary of using System Restore if you're fighting a computer virus infection. If you (or the system) create a restore point while the system is infected, you could reinfect the system if you revert the system to that restore point. To prevent reinfection, most antivirus vendors recommend that you disable System Restore (which eliminates stored restore points) before removing computer viruses.

Date with restore
point(s) available

Selected restore point

FIGURE 19.23

Choosing a
restore point
with Windows
XP's System
Restore.

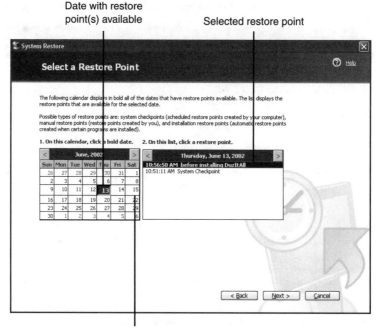

Date with no restore points available

Using File Signature Verification

Behind the scenes in Windows are literally hundreds of system files all designed to work together. Every system file in recent versions of Windows (Me, 2000, XP) are digitally signed by Microsoft. As you learned earlier in this chapter, Microsoft would prefer you kept it that way by using only digitally signed driver files whenever possible. Use the **File Signature Verification** program to keep an eye on your files.

The default setting for File Signature Verification checks for system files that lack digital signatures. Use this feature to determine whether your Windows installation might be corrupted by the use of out-of-date system files that some older programs might have installed. To determine if you are using unsigned driver files, click the Advanced button and select Look for Other Files That Are Not Digitally Signed.

After you configure Advanced options, click OK, and then Start. A status bar informs you of the progress of the scan. Click OK to accept the results of the scan. Click Advanced, Logging, View Log to see detailed results.

To fix problems caused by unsigned files, you can

- Use the Update Driver feature in a device's Properties sheet (Device Manager) after you download a digitally signed file.

- Run System File Checker (SFC) to replace an unsigned system file with the correct version.

Study Lab

Don't miss the Study Lab materials found on the CD accompanying this book. Each Study Lab is tailored to the individual chapters in this book, meaning that you'll quickly be able to determine which topics you understand well enough to pass the exam and which topics need more study. The Study Labs are presented in printable PDF format so that you can take them with you to study at work, on the road, or even in your car just before test time!

THE ABSOLUTE MINIMUM

- Windows, rather than individual applications, is responsible for installing, configuring, and controlling printers.

- If Windows cannot detect your printer during installation, you can choose it from a list or supply the driver disk or CD.

- You should print a test page when you install a new printer to verify proper operation.

- USB printers often require you to install the driver software before installing the printer.

- A local printer is connected directly to your computer.

- A remote printer is a printer you can use via the network.

- A shared printer is connected to your computer and is also available to others on the network.

- The Windows print spooler holds print jobs before they are transferred to the printer, so you can hold or discard them as needed.

- To print to a network printer, you need the appropriate driver files as well as the path to the printer and permission to use the printer.

- Use the printer Properties sheet tabs to test the printer, adjust print quality, select a port, control the printer, and maintain print quality.

- Using an incorrect printer driver produces garbage output.

- Windows NT 4.0 doesn't have a Device Manager or PnP support, whereas Windows 9x/Me/2000/XP have these features to make hardware installation and support easier.

- PnP installations require PnP support in the device, the system BIOS, and the operating system.

- Digital signatures for drivers are usually not required but are recommended for reliable operation.

- A non-PnP installation might require the user to manually configure the hardware resources in the Device Manager after the card is installed.

- By default, the user is warned about unsigned device drivers, but these drivers can also be blocked or can be used without notice by adjusting the Driver Signing Options dialog.

- The Windows Device Manager indicates malfunctioning devices with a yellow exclamation point (!) and disabled devices with a red X.

- The General Properties tab for a device indicates whether it is working.

- Malfunctioning devices have a Device Manager code that can be used for troubleshooting.

- The Driver tab can be used to solve driver problems, and the Resources tab can sometimes be used to solve resource conflicts.

- System Information provides hardware and software information about a system without risk to the system's configuration.

- System Information can also be used to launch various tools such as DirectX Diagnostics and others.

- The System Restore feature lets Windows Me and XP users revert the system Registry to a previous state.

- File Signature Verification determines if unsigned system or device driver files are on the system.

- System File Checker replaces unsigned system files with signed versions.

20

Troubleshootİng Wİndows and Wİndows Applİcatİons

From Windows NT 4.0 to Windows XP, the A+ Certification Operating Systems Exam expects you to understand how to fix problems with a sick operating system. After all, without an operating system, a computer is just a collection of useless circuit boards, plastic, and metal parts.

Problems with Windows can show up at startup or during operation: This chapter covers both types of errors. As you're probably aware by now, Windows 9x/Me are part of the same Windows "family," and you might be more familiar with the errors these versions can produce than with the errors produced by the more business-oriented Windows family of Windows NT 4.0/2000/XP. Whichever version of Windows you use on a day-to-day basis, don't worry. This chapter will help you prepare for the exam and for the real-world challenges beyond the exam.

Startup Errors for Windows 9x/Me

Startup errors can come from a variety of causes:

- Problems with Windows configuration, including boot files, Registry, Win.Ini, System.Ini, Config.sys, and Autoexec.bat files

- Failure to load vital device drivers, such as Himem.sys

- Problems with drives, including virtual memory (swapfile), ATA/IDE, and SCSI configuration

The following sections are designed to help you understand the causes of the most common problems with Windows 9x/Me startup that you might encounter on the A+ Certification Exam and learn the solutions.

error in Config.sys line xx (Windows 9x Only)

Config.sys is used to load **real-mode drivers** in Windows 9x. If you see an error in Config.sys line xx error message, check for one of the following causes:

- A reference to a driver file or folder that isn't present or might be misspelled

- A misspelling of the command in the Config.sys file; for example, Device=C:\Windows\Emm386.exe RAM is correct, whereas Devise=C:\Windows\Emm386.exe RAM is not a recognized command because Devise is not a recognized word

You can use the step-by-step startup from the Windows 9x boot menu referred to earlier to bypass all or selective lines in Config.sys to see if your system performs normally.

note

The CD included with this book contains important Study Lab material for this chapter, as well as Chapters 2–22 in this book. The Study Lab for each chapter contains terms to study, exercises, and practice tests—all in printable PDF format (Adobe Acrobat Reader is included on the CD, too). These Study Lab materials will help you gear up for the A+ Exam. Also, the CD includes an industry-leading test engine from PrepLogic, which simulates the actual A+ test so that you can be sure that you're ready when test day arrives. Don't let the A+ test intimidate you. If you've read the chapters, worked through the Study Lab, and passed the practice tests from PrepLogic, you should be well prepared to ace the test!

Also, you'll notice that some words throughout each chapter are in bold format. These are study terms that are defined in the Study Lab. Be sure to consult the Study Lab when you are finished with this chapter to test what you've learned.

> ⇨ With Windows 98 but not Windows 95, you can also use the MSConfig utility (**see** "Using MSConfig," **p. 747**, to disable the loading of Config.sys or edit its contents).

Bad/Missing Command Interpreter

If you see this error message, check the following possibilities:

- *The **Command.com** file has been deleted from the root folder of the Windows drive (normally C:\)*—Restart the system with the Windows Emergency Boot Disk (EBD) and run Sys C: to restore Command.com and other boot files.

> ⇨ The process of making the EBD for Windows is discussed in Chapter 15, "Preparing Hard and Floppy Drives with Windows," in the section "Creating a Boot Disk Suitable for Hard Disk Preparation," **p. 484**.

- *The Command.com file has been replaced with a Command.com file from a different version of Windows or MS-DOS*—Restart the system with the Windows EBD and run Sys C: to restore Command.com and other boot files.

- *The wrong Command.com file was reloaded into memory after a command-prompt program such as Xcopy (which overwrites Command.com in memory) was run*—If you are not using a multiboot feature to enable you to run MS-DOS on the same system, delete all MS-DOS versions of Command.com on your system (such as in the \DOS folder).

- *A computer virus is present on the system*—Boot with the Windows EBD and run an antivirus program to repair the problem.

note

To help determine the cause of these problems, you might find it helpful to use the System Configuration utility (MSConfig.exe) with Windows 98/Me or the **step-by-step startup** option with Windows 95. These options can help you isolate the particular program or operation that triggers the error.

Himem.sys Not Loaded

If you start Windows 9x with the Safe Mode Command Prompt option, neither the Windows Registry nor the Config.sys files (either of which can run Himem.sys) is processed, so Himem.sys will not be loaded. Restart the computer normally and Himem.sys will be loaded into memory.

> ⇨ **See** "Windows Safe Mode," **p. 728**, for more information about using Safe Mode Command Prompt to start your computer.

Missing or Corrupt `Himem.sys`

If you are starting Windows 9x/Me normally and see a message indicating that `Himem.sys` is missing or corrupt, the file might be damaged or deleted. On Windows 9x/Me, `Himem.sys` is normally found in the `\Windows` folder. To fix a missing or corrupted `Himem.sys` in Windows 98, you can restore `Himem.sys` from the Windows 98 EDB. With Windows 95, you must copy `Himem.sys` from the Windows 95 installation CD-ROM or disks.

Device Referred to in `System.ini/` `Win.ini/`Registry Not Found

The Windows Registry, `System.ini`, and `Win.ini` files are used for hardware and software configuration information for Windows. These configuration files refer to programs and **protected-mode drivers** that must be accessed during the boot process. If you see an error message such as `Device xxx referred to in System.ini/Win.ini/Registry not found`, the most likely cause is that the file being referred to has been removed from the system incorrectly. To avoid this problem, use the appropriate option:

> **note**
>
> It's rare to see a corrupt or missing `Himem.sys` with Windows Me because Windows Me features Windows File Protection, which automatically restores missing or corrupted system files. If the backup copy of `Himem.sys` isn't available, you're prompted to provide the Windows CD to reload the file from CD.

- For hardware, use the Remove button in the Device Manager before you physically remove the hardware from the system. Using Remove removes Registry and .ini file entries for the device so it will not be referred to when the system is restarted.

- Open the Add/Remove Programs icon in the Windows Control Panel, select the program you want to remove, and select Add/Remove (Windows 9x) or Change/Remove (Windows 2000). This starts the uninstall program for applications and utilities listed on the menu.

- Use the program's own **uninstall** option or a third-party uninstall program.

Any of these options should remove both the program and references to it in the Registry and other locations, such as `System.ini` or `Win.ini`.

If the program is removed by deleting its folder, leaving references in the Registry, `System.ini`, or `Win.ini`, use the error message to determine which file contains the reference.

➪ For Windows 98/Me/XP, the easiest way to remove a reference in System.ini, Win.ini, or any startup routine (including the Registry) is to use the **MSConfig** program (**see** "Using MSConfig," **p. 747**, for more information).

Alternatively, you can use a text editor such as Notepad or Edit to remove references to a missing program or device in Windows 9x's System.ini or Win.ini. You can also manually edit the Windows Registry to remove references to a missing device. See Chapter 18, "Using and Optimizing Windows," for information on Registry editors.

Windows Protection Error

A **Windows Protection Error** takes place during the startup process or during the shutdown process when a VxD (32-bit virtual device driver) or .386 driver file is loaded or unloaded. Protection errors also can occur *if* there are driver conflicts, virus infections of Win.com or Command.com, hardware conflicts, bad memory, or a bad motherboard.

To determine if a hardware conflict or driver file is to blame, start the system with the Bootlog (**Logged**) option. If the error recurs, restart the system in Safe Mode. Use EDIT or Notepad to examine the Bootlog, and look at the end of the Bootlog for the last driver file initialized. Search for the driver and examine its properties in My Computer/Windows Explorer to determine what hardware or software it works with. Uninstall the program.

> **caution**
>
> I can't harp on this enough. If you are not fully versed in working with the Windows Registry, you are better off not tinkering with it! Although making changes to the Registry can dramatically enhance system performance, it can also result in dire consequences if you make but a single error while working with a Registry entry. Always, always, always be sure to make a backup of the Registry before you make any changes. More experienced Windows users than you have rendered their PCs inoperable after fiddling with the Registry. You have been warned.

If this doesn't solve the problem, check the system hardware for errors and try reinstalling Windows.

Alternative Startup Methods for Windows 9x/Me

If Windows won't start normally, what next? Try one of the alternative startup methods we cover in the following sections to see if you can get to the Windows Desktop to make changes in your system configuration and get back to work.

To display alternative startup options for Windows, press the Ctrl key with Windows 98/Me; press the F8 key with Windows 95.

Windows Safe Mode

Windows uses Safe Mode to recover from startup problems. There are three different Safe Mode startup options:

- **Safe Mode**—In Safe Mode, the system uses a standard VGA display driver, doesn't process the Config.sys or Autoexec.bat files present on a Windows 9x system, and doesn't load most 32-bit device drivers, including those used for hard disk and CD-ROM access and for networking. This mode loads the Windows GUI and enables the user to access the Windows Explorer and Windows Device Manager, although Windows 9x cannot display hardware resources used when the system is in Safe Mode.

- **Safe Mode with Network Support**—You also can select Safe Mode with Network Support (Windows 9x) or Safe Mode with Networking (Windows 2000/XP) to add bare-bones network support to Safe Mode. This mode also uses the Windows GUI and enables network connections so you can access drivers or needed support items through the network or the Internet.

- **Safe Mode Command Prompt**—When this mode is selected, the computer does not boot to the Windows GUI, but boots to a command prompt without loading the Windows Registry, Config.sys, or Autoexec.bat. If you need to start Windows with special command-line options, choose Command Prompt Only mode instead.

Starting Windows 9x/Me in Safe Mode

Windows 9x/Me automatically starts in Safe Mode if the system didn't start successfully on the previous startup. To run Safe Mode or other startup options, you can display the Windows 9x/Me startup menu by pressing the F8 or Ctrl key on a Windows 9x/Me system as soon as the system's power-on self-test (POST) is complete. Select the Safe Mode option you want to use from the options listed.

note

Remember, if you are running only one operating system, you will have to be quick to boot into Safe Mode. After you have powered the system on, keep your finger over the F8 button and press it immediately after the BIOS hardware startup message moves off the screen. You'll only have a couple of seconds to do this, so be ready. After pressing F8, a menu showing various boot options available to you will appear. Choose Safe Mode from the list of options. If you are dual booting your PC, you will be presented with a boot options menu each time you boot the system.

Using Safe Mode

Safe Mode can be used to start the system if normal startups fail, because Safe Mode uses a minimal set of drivers (for example, VGA instead of chipset-specific SuperVGA drivers) and services. By using only the minimum drivers and services to start the system, potential conflicts that can prevent the system from starting are bypassed.

You can use the Windows Device Manager to remove devices in Safe Mode, but Safe Mode in Windows 9x cannot show you configuration details such as the hardware resources used by each device.

You can access troubleshooters in either version of Windows, and if you start Windows in Safe Mode with Network Support, you might still have access to the Internet for additional help.

Other Startup Options for Windows 9x/Me

Windows 9x/Me offer additional startup options, which include the following:

- *Step-by-Step Confirmation* —Select this option to selectively run or skip commands in `Config.sys`, `Autoexec.bat`, and the Windows Registry.

- *Logged*—Select this option to create a hidden text file called `Bootlog.txt`, which is stored in the root folder of the default Windows drive. `Bootlog.txt` records startup events and is useful for finding problems that prevent Windows from starting.

Windows 9x also offers these additional startup options:

- *Command Prompt Only*—Select this option to start the system at a command prompt after processing `Config.sys`, `Autoexec.bat`, and the Windows Registry. This provides a DOS-like environment suitable for running legacy programs that cannot run with Windows in memory. You can also use it to start Windows 9x with special startup switches (see Chapter 18).

- *Previous Version of MS-DOS*—Loads the previous version of MS-DOS (if still present on the system).

- *Safe Mode Command Prompt*—Starts the system without loading `Config.sys`, `Autoexec.bat` or the Windows Registry to produce a clean-boot environment.

note

With Windows 98/Me (as well as Windows XP), you can use `MSConfig`'s Advanced dialog to start Windows with special startup switches without the need to boot into command-prompt mode first. See "Using `MSConfig`" later in this chapter for details.

Press the function keys listed in Table 20.1 to start Windows 9x/Me with the option listed.

Table 20.1 Windows 9x/Me Startup Option Function Keys

Startup Key	Startup Option Selected	Windows Version	Equivalent to Windows Startup Command
F4	Previous Version of MS-DOS	95, 98	n/a
F5	Safe Mode	95, 98, Me	Win/d:m
Shift-F5	Safe Mode Command Prompt	95, 98	n/a
F6*	Safe Mode with Network Support	95, 98	Win/d:n
Shift-F8	Step-by-Step Confirmation	95, 98, Me	n/a

*Not listed onscreen, but a valid option

Table 20.2 lists some typical uses for the Windows 9x/Me startup menu options.

Table 20.2 Using the Windows 9x/Me Startup Menus for Troubleshooting

Problem	Windows Version	Startup Option to Select	Notes
Windows won't start after you install new hardware or software.	Me	Safe Mode	Boots computer with minimal devices installed; use System Restore (if available) to reset the computer to a previous working condition.
Windows won't start after you install new hardware or software.	9x	Safe Mode	Boots computer with minimal devices installed. Use Device Manager to remove or reconfigure last-installed hardware, or Add/Remove Programs to remove last-installed software. Then, restart the computer. **See** "Using the Windows Device Manager," **p. 703** for details.
Windows won't start after you install a different video card or monitor.	Me, 9x	Safe Mode	Select PCI VGA adapter for the video driver in the Display Properties sheet, and restart the computer. Reinstall the drivers needed for the video card as prompted.

Table 20.2 (continued)

Problem	Windows Version	Startup Option to Select	Notes
Windows can't start normally, but you need access to the Internet to research the problem or download updates.	Me, 9x	Safe Mode with Networking	You can use Windows Update and the Internet, but some devices won't work in this mode. This mode also uses 640×480 and 16-color display mode.
Windows doesn't finish starting normally, and you want to know what device driver or process is preventing it from working.	9x, Me	Enable Boot Logging	This option creates a file called `bootlog.txt` in the root directory of the boot drive (C:\). Restart the computer in Safe Mode and open this file with Notepad or Wordpad to determine the last driver file that loaded. You can update the driver or remove the hardware device using that driver to restore your system to working condition.
Windows is loading programs you don't need during its startup process.	Me, 98	Boot computer in Safe or Normal Mode; click Start, Run, and then type `MSConfig`	Use `MSConfig` to disable one or more startup programs. You can also use `MSConfig` to restore damaged files or to start System Restore to reset your computer to an earlier condition. (`MSConfig` is not included with Windows 95.)

Startup Errors for Windows NT 4.0/2000/XP

Startup errors can come from a variety of causes:

- Corrupt or missing startup/system files
- Problems with Windows configuration, including Registry
- Problems with drives, including virtual memory (swapfile), ATA/IDE, and SCSI configuration

The following sections are designed to help you understand the causes of the most common problems with Windows NT/2000/XP startup that you might encounter on the A+ Certification Exam and learn the solutions.

As you learned in Chapter 18, these versions of Windows use the NTLDR, Boot.ini, NTDETECT.COM, and Ntoskrnl.exe files during the startup process. If these files are corrupted or missing, you will see corresponding error messages:

■ NTDETECT failed—This message is displayed if the NTDETECT.COM file is missing or corrupted.

■ NTLDR is missing—This message is displayed if the NTLDR file is missing or corrupted.

■ Invalid boot.ini—This message is displayed if the boot.ini file is missing or corrupted. The system might boot anyway, particularly if there is only disk partition on the first hard disk. However, if the system is configured as a dual boot or if Windows is not installed on the first disk partition, you need to re-create or recopy the file to enable your system to boot.

■ Windows NT could not start because the following file is missing or corrupt: C:\WinNT\ntoskrnl.exe.—This message is typically displayed in Windows NT 4.0 only; Windows 2000 and XP's system file protection features automatically restore deleted system files such as this one.

To fix these problems, you can

■ Reboot with the Windows CD, select Repair, and run the Emergency Repair option (Windows NT/2000).

■ Reboot with the Windows CD, select Repair, and run the Recovery Console (2000/XP only) and recopy the file from the CD or a backup.

■ Perform a Repair installation of Windows.

> **caution**
>
> What about Windows XP's Automated System Recovery (ASR) feature? This feature reformats your hard disk and reinstalls Windows and your data from a special ASR backup you create with the Windows XP Backup program. You should use ASR *only* if you are unable to get Windows XP running any other way and *only* if you have up-to-date backups of your data.

Using the Emergency Repair Feature with Windows NT 4.0/2000

To run the Emergency Repair feature with these versions of Windows

1. Start the system with the Windows CD; if the system can't boot from the CD, use the Windows setup floppy disks to start the system, and insert the CD when prompted.

2. Select Repair when prompted, and then Emergency Repair.

3. Choose Fast Repair when prompted. Fast repair performs all three options provided with Manual repair: Inspect Startup Environment; Verify System Files; and Inspect Boot Sector. Manual repair lets you select which of these to run.

4. With Windows 2000 and Windows NT 4.0, insert the Emergency Repair Disk (ERD) (if available) when prompted. This disk contains a log file of the location and installed options for this copy of Windows. The Windows 2000 ERD is created with the Windows 2000 Backup program. Windows NT 4.0 uses the RDISK program.

5. After the process replaces damaged or missing files, follow the prompts to remove the ERD and restart the system.

caution

The ERD is *not* interchangeable between systems. If the ERD is missing, use the L (Locate) option instead to find the Windows installation.

Error Messages for Windows NT/2000/XP

Error messages at startup or after the system starts indicate problems with the system configuration. Some of the most common messages are discussed in the following sections.

Missing or Corrupt `Himem.sys`

Windows NT/2000/XP store `Himem.sys` in the `\Windows\System32` or `\WinNT\System32` folder. If `Himem.sys` is accidentally deleted from a system running Windows 2000 or XP, Windows can normally restore it automatically with its built-in System File Protection feature. If this doesn't work, however, you can restore it yourself. With Windows NT 4.0 or XP, boot the system with the Windows CD-ROM and run the Repair option.

System/Application/Security/Directory/DNS Log Is Full Error

When the user logs into a computer running Windows NT 4.0/2000/XP, the `...log is full` error might be displayed if any of the logs listed in the heading for this section are full. The logging feature in these versions of Windows records both routine events and problems involving these services, so the log files should be emptied periodically.

To save and clear the logs

1. Open the Administrative Tools icon in Control Panel.

2. Open Event Viewer (see Figure 20.1).

3. Click the log file reported in the error message.

4. Click Action and select Save File As (if you want to save its current contents); provide a filename.

5. Click Action and select Clear All Events.

You must be the administrator of the system or have been granted permission to use this tool.

FIGURE 20.1

Because Windows 2000 logs all types of events, it won't take long for log files such as the System Log shown here to fill up.

Alternative Startup Methods for Windows NT 4.0/2000/XP

If you are unable to start Windows NT 4.0/2000/XP but don't see an error message, the problem could be caused by a driver or startup program, video driver problems, or problems with the system kernel. Windows NT 4.0/2000/XP offer various optional startup options to help you correct startup problems.

Windows NT 4.0 offers the following startup options:

■ *Normal startup.*

■ **VGA Mode**—Uses a VGA driver in place of a normal display driver to help you diagnose problems caused by the display driver.

■ **Last Known Good Configuration**—Press spacebar when prompted.

Windows 2000/XP offers additional startup options, which include the following:

■ *Enable Boot Logging*—Creates a `bootlog.txt` file.

■ *Enable VGA Mode*—Uses a VGA driver in place of a normal display driver, but uses all other drivers as normal.

■ *Last Known Good Configuration*—Starts the system with the last configuration known to work; useful for solving problems caused by newly installed hardware or software.

■ *Debugging Mode*—Enables the use of a debug program to examine the system kernel for troubleshooting.

■ *Safe Mode*—Starts the system with minimal drives. In Windows XP, Safe Mode can be used to access a previous restore point created with System Restore.

Press the F8 key when you see the prompt at the bottom of the screen during startup to display the startup menu listing these options.

Table 20.3 lists typical problems and helps you select the correct startup option to use to solve the problem.

Table 20.3   Using the Windows 2000/XP Advanced Options Menu

Problem	Windows Version	XP Startup Option to Select	Notes
Windows won't start after you install new hardware or software.	2000, XP	Last Known Good Configuration	Resets Windows to its last-known working configuration; you will need to reinstall hardware or software installed after that time.
Windows won't start after you upgrade a device driver.	2000, XP	Safe Mode	After starting the computer in Safe Mode, open the Device Manager, select the device, and use the Rollback feature to re-store the previously used device driver. Restart your system.
			See "Using the Windows Device Manager," **p. 703**. Uses 640×480 resolution but retains the color settings normally used.
Windows won't start after you install a different video card or monitor.	2000, XP	Enable VGA Mode	Most video cards should be installed when your system is running in VGA Mode (256 colors, 640×480 resolution in 2000; 800×600 resolution in XP). Use Display Properties to select a working video mode before you restart.

Table 20.3 (continued)

Problem	Windows Version	XP Startup Option to Select	Notes
Windows can't start normally, but you need access to the Internet to research the problem or download updates.	2000, XP	Safe Mode with Networking	You can use Windows Update and the Internet, but some devices won't work in this mode. This mode also uses 640×480 resolution, but retains the color settings normally used.
Windows doesn't finish starting normally, and you want to know what device driver or process is preventing it from working.	2000, XP	Enable Boot Logging	This option starts the computer with all its normal drivers and settings and also creates a file called `ntbtlog.txt` in the default Windows folder (usually `C:\Windows` or `C:\WINNT`). Restart the computer in Safe Mode and open this file with Notepad or Wordpad to determine the last driver file that loaded. You can update the driver or remove the hardware device using that driver to restore your system to working condition.
Windows is loading programs you don't need during its startup process.	XP	Boot computer in Normal Mode (or Safe Mode if the computer won't start in Normal Mode); click Start, Run; then type `MSConfig`.	Use `MSConfig` to disable one or more startup programs, and then restart your computer. You can also use `MSConfig` to restore damaged files, or to start System Restore to reset your computer to an earlier condition.

Operating System Error Messages and Solutions

After Windows starts, problems with drivers, software, and resources (Windows 9x/Me) can trigger various types of error messages. The following sections discuss these error messages in greater detail.

General Protection Fault and Illegal Operation Errors

An **illegal operation** can be defined as any software problem that requires Windows 9x/Me to shut down the program to recover from it, including **general protection faults (GPFs)**, page faults, and other problems. An illegal operation is hardly ever caused by the user of the program (you). Instead, illegal operations are caused by the interaction of programs with each other or with Windows itself. One of the most common types of illegal operation errors is the GPF.

GPF errors are caused by two Windows programs attempting to use the same area of memory at the same time; they are more likely to occur with Windows 9x/Me than with Windows NT 4.0/2000/XP because Windows 9x/Me don't protect the memory space used by each program.

To determine the cause of a GPF

- Note which programs were in memory when the GPF happened; generally, an interaction between the last program loaded into memory and programs already in memory is the cause. Take a quick look at the Taskbar and System Tray.
- Consider getting updates to older programs on your system; mismatches between **.dll files** used by new and older programs is a frequent cause of GPFs and other software problems.

Paging Dr. Watson! Capturing System Information

Use the **Dr. Watson** utility supplied with Windows 98/Me to capture information about your system when a GPF or other illegal operations error takes place; you can also use it to generate a snapshot of your system whenever you want.

The Drwatson.exe program is found in the Windows folder in both Windows 98 and Windows Me. You can also click Start, Run, type **Drwatson**, and click OK. Dr. Watson automatically places itself in the system tray when you run it.

To see complete information about the system, as in Figure 20.2, double-click the Dr. Watson icon in the system tray and select the Advanced View. To run it automatically, add a shortcut to it to the Startup group (see Chapter 18 for details). Use the information captured to search the Microsoft Knowledge Base online.

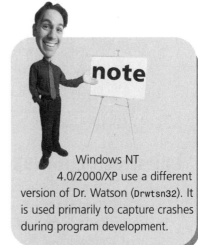

Windows NT 4.0/2000/XP use a different version of Dr. Watson (Drwtsn32). It is used primarily to capture crashes during program development.

FIGURE 20.2

Dr. Watson (left) traps system information when an illegal operation takes place or whenever you ask for a system snapshot. Resource Meter (right) warns you when free system resources (FSR) drops to critical levels.

Using the Windows 9x/Me Resource Meter

A major weakness in Windows 9x/Me is the issue of **free system resources (FSR)**. FSR measures the remaining space in a 64KB segment of memory that is used by the Windows GDI.EXE and USER.EXE programs, which manage the display and objects drawn onscreen. FSR is reduced with every program, window, and object onscreen, and is *not* affected by the amount of RAM installed in your system. Over time, especially with many programs and windows opened, FSR can decline to a level of 15% or less. At 15% or less FSR, the computer can slow down, not permit you to open additional programs or windows, and you might see an illegal operations error.

Use the Windows 9x/Me **Resource Meter** (refer to Figure 20.2) to determine if your computer has enough FSRs to run reliably or allow you to load another program into memory. Click Start, Programs, Accessories, System Tools, Resource Meter to load the Resource Meter. If it is not already installed on your system, install it with the Add/Remove Programs icon in Control Panel.

To run Resource Meter automatically when you start your system with Windows 9x/Me, you can add a shortcut for Resource Meter to the Startup folder as discussed in Chapter 18.

Bluescreen Error (BSOD)

Systems that cannot start the Windows NT 4.0/2000/XP GUI will normally display a **Stop error** when the user attempts to start the system. This is also referred to as the **Blue Screen of Death (BSOD)** because the background is normally blue (or sometimes black) with the error message in white text.

BSOD errors can be caused by any of the following:

- *Incompatible or defective hardware or software*—Start the system in Safe Mode and uninstall the last hardware or software installed. Acquire updates before you reinstall the hardware or software. Exchange or test memory.

- *Registry problems*—Select Last Known Good Configuration as described earlier in this chapter and see if the system will start.

- *Viruses*—Scan for viruses and remove any discovered.

- *Miscellaneous causes*—Check the Windows Event Viewer and check the System log. Research the BSOD with the Microsoft Knowledge Base.

Swapfile (Paging File) and Hard Disk Access Problems

The swapfile (Windows 9x/Me) or paging file (Windows NT 4.0/2000/XP) is a file on a local hard disk that is used as a supplement to memory. A swapfile or paging file must be stored on a local hard disk.

Problems with the swapfile can result from

- *Disk surface problems with the partition used for the swapfile*—These problems can cause the system to halt with various types of errors including page faults, GPFs, and others. Use ScanDisk in Windows 9x/Me or Chkdsk (error-checking) in Windows NT 4.0/2000/XP to check the drive for errors and repair them, and then retry the operation. Check for program-specific causes if the errors occur again.

tip

If you discover that your FSR at startup is under 70%, you might be loading programs you don't need. Use MSConfig to disable startup programs to increase FSR. From the Start menu, select Run, type MSConfig, and press Enter or click OK. Click the Startup tab to see a list of programs currently running on your computer. You might be surprised to find how many unnecessary programs your computer is running. You'll also be hard pressed to separate the necessary applications running on your PC from the unnecessary, resource hogs (spyware, adware, viruses, Trojans, you name it) unless you have a list of those application file names. Fortunately, just such a list exists at http://www.pacs-portal.co.uk/ startup_pages/startup_full.php. Download the full zipped document, open it with an unzipping utility, and look up each of the applications running on your PC. Unless you keep a daily vigil on the applications running at startup, you're almost certain to find anywhere from a handful to more than a dozen nonessential— and possibly dangerous— programs running right under your nose. This Web page also has links to spyware eliminators and to an excellent discussion of startup programs in general.

■ *Lack of space for the swapfile*—By default, Windows uses remaining space on the current Windows drive (normally C:) for the swapfile (paging file). If the remaining space on the C: drive drops below 100MB, some disk operations will become very slow or might cause page faults or GPFs. It's a good idea to keep at least 15% of your hard disk space free if possible. Free up space on the default swapfile drive, change to a different drive for the swapfile, or set the paging file to use multiple drives in Windows NT 4.0/2000/XP. For information on customizing the swapfile (paging file), see Chapter 18.

■ *Serious hardware problems with the hard disk subsystem*—If the wrong 32-bit busmastering drivers are installed for the ATA/IDE hard disk interface in Windows, data loss could result from disk accesses to save data or to swap data in and out of the swapfile.

To disable some or all Windows 9x/Me advanced disk-access features for troubleshooting

1. Open the Windows 9x/Me System Properties sheet.
2. Click the Performance tab.
3. Click File System.
4. Click the Troubleshooting tab.
5. Click the check box for one or more of the entries shown in Figure 20.3 and restart the system.

Disabling the options shown in Figure 20.3 might enable you to run the system until correct drivers can be obtained or hardware conflicts are resolved. Disable options based on the specific problems you are having with Windows 9x/Me. If data is not being written properly to the drives, you could try one of the following options:

note

BSOD errors can also take place after the system starts. In either case, your system is halted. To restart the computer, you must turn off the system and turn it back on. But, before you do that, record the error message text and other information so you can research the problem if it recurs.

tip

Unfortunately, you can't screen-capture a BSOD for printing because a BSOD completely shuts down Windows. However, if you have a digital camera handy, it makes a great tool for recording the exact error message. Just be sure to use the correct range setting to get the sharpest picture possible (normal or closeup, not distant). Don't use flash! If necessary, borrow a friend's PC to view the digital photos and research the error at Microsoft's Knowledge Base (http://search.microsoft.com) if the BSOD keeps happening.

FIGURE 20.3

The File System Properties Troubleshooting menu in Windows 9x/Me enables you to disable disk-access features that might be malfunctioning.

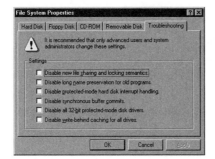

- ■ Disable Write-Behind Caching will send data directly to the drives instead of storing it temporarily in RAM before saving it to disk.
- ■ Disable Synchronous Buffer Commits will force Windows to verify that data written to the drive was written properly.

If disk input/output errors are happening, you could try one of the following options:

- ■ Disable 32-Bit Protected Mode Drivers will return control of the drives to BIOS routines or to 16-bit legacy drivers in Config.sys. Drives that depend solely upon 32-bit drivers will not work, but hard and floppy drives will continue to work. This is equivalent to the Win.com startup switch :F. See Chapter 18 for details.
- ■ Disable Protected-Mode Interrupt Handling will return interrupt handling to the system ROM BIOS. This is equivalent to the Win.com startup switch :V. See Chapter 18 for details.

If you have compatibility problems with 16-bit applications that don't support long filenames, use Disable Long Name Preservation. If you have problems with file locking on a network, use Disable New File Sharing and Locking Semantics. These options will slow down your system and should be used only as workarounds until updated device drivers and applications can be installed.

Drive Configuration Errors

Improperly configured hardware can cause your computer to fail to boot at all. This section discusses typical causes and solutions for hardware configuration problems, including problems caused by incorrect drive configurations, damage to disk data structures, boot sector viruses, and SCSI configuration problems.

Missing Operating System Error

A missing operating system or similar error is generated by the system BIOS's boot loader if it is unable to locate the operating system. Table 20.4 lists typical problems and solutions.

Table 20.4 Missing Operating System Error Causes and Solutions

Problem	Notes	Solution
Incorrect BIOS configuration of the hard disk's geometry (cylinder, head, sectors per track) or LBA mode	If the BIOS values for these settings are altered after the drive is installed, the operating system files can't be located.	See "Auto-detection of the IDE Hard Drive Type" in Chapter 14, "Storage."
Damage to the drive's master boot record	This section of the drive points to the location of boot files if present.	See "Repairing the Master Boot Record" in Chapter 15.
No active partition set for the drive	When Fdisk is used to create multiple partitions (primary plus extended), the primary partition must be set as active by the user.	See "Troubleshooting Hard Disks That Can't Boot After Format" in Chapter 15.

SCSI Error Messages

If Windows is started from a SCSI hard disk instead of from an IDE hard disk, the configuration of the drive is set by the SCSI host adapter, which must support bootable drives. SCSI error messages can be caused by a variety of problems with how devices (including hard disks and other types of devices) are configured on the SCSI bus. SCSI errors are covered in detail because they differ widely from standard drive configuration errors.

Table 20.5 lists typical SCSI error messages and their causes.

caution

Don't play "mix-and-match" with SCSI host adapters and hard disks. To avoid the potential loss of data, use the same brand (and model if possible) of host adapter if a host adapter must be replaced on a system whose SCSI drive already contains data.

Table 20.5   SCSI Error Messages and Solutions

Problem	Solution
Device connected but not ready—No answer was received from a connected SCSI device.	Make sure the device is turned on before the system boots.
	Set the SCSI host adapter to Send Start Unit Command to the device.
	Make sure that there are no duplicate SCSI ID numbers.
Start unit request failed—Device didn't respond to Start Unit Request command.	Disable Send Start Unit command option for that device.
Time-out failure during...—A device attached to the SCSI host adapter caused a time-out.	Check termination on the SCSI bus. Both ends of the SCSI daisy-chain of devices must be terminated.
	Check cables. Loose or damaged cables can cause this problem; retighten cables and restart devices, and then restart the system.
	Disconnect all SCSI devices and restart the system; if the SCSI card without devices runs okay, one or more of the devices is defective.
Driver software error messages—Old DLL or ASPI not loaded.	Download and install new software for the host adapter and ASPI (Adaptec SCSI Programming Interface) or equivalent services for your host adapter.
Can't access data on a SCSI hard disk after attaching it to a new SCSI host adapter— Each brand of host adapter uses its own translation schemes to communicate with a drive.	Reattach the drive to the original SCSI host adapter (if possible) and back up data.
	Attach the drive to the new host adapter and perform a low-level format with the new SCSI host adapter's utility program. This deletes all data on the drive but will allow the drive to communicate with the new host adapter.
A disk read error occurred after creating a boot partition more than 7.8GB in size.	Enable INT13h extensions in the SCSI BIOS or install a SCSI host adapter that supports INT13 extensions.

Post-Startup Errors

Just because Windows starts correctly doesn't mean you're home free. The following sections discuss the causes and solutions for typical errors you might see after the system starts.

Invalid working directory Error

If a Windows or MS-DOS program is set to use a folder that isn't available, the Invalid working directory error might be displayed.

The following are solutions to this error:

- Adjust the program's operation to use a folder that is available using the program's properties sheet.

- If the working folder is on a network drive, make sure the user is logged on the network.

- If the working folder is a removable-media drive, the user must insert the correct disk or CD-ROM before starting the program.

System Lockups

System lockups can result from any of the following causes:

- Programs that stop responding

- Hardware that stops responding or has conflicts

- Exhaustion of Windows's user heap or GDI resources (9x/Me)

Press Ctrl+Alt+Del to display the Close Program dialog box (Windows 9x/Me) or the Windows **Task Manager** application tab (Windows NT 4.0/2000/XP) as shown in Figure 20.4) to determine if a program has stopped working.

FIGURE 20.4

The Windows XP Task Manager (left) and Windows 98 Close Program dialog (right) enable you to shut down a program that has stopped responding.

A program that has stopped responding to the system is labeled as Not Responding

Programs and background tasks in memory are displayed. Programs or tasks with [not responding] at the end of the listing have stopped working; select each one and click Close Program to shut them down. You will need to close each unresponsive program separately.

Can't Log On to Network

A user must be on the list of authorized users to log on to a network managed by a Windows NT/2000/2003 server or Novell NetWare server. To access shared resources on a peer-to-peer Windows 9x/Me network, the user must log on to the network and provide passwords for password-protected resources.

If the user has not logged on to the network, the user should click Start, Shutdown, and Logoff the System. All open programs will be closed, and a new logon screen will be displayed. The user should make sure to enter the correct username and password. Pressing the Escape key or clicking Cancel does not log the user onto the network, although the logon screen is removed from the desktop.

After the correct username and password are entered, the user will have access to any Windows NT/2000/2003/NetWare–managed resources that the user is authorized to use. However, the user will need to provide a password the first time a peer-shared resource on a Windows 9x/Me network is used; if the password is stored in the user's password cache, it will not need to be entered again unless the password for the resource is changed.

TSR Program Error

Terminate-and-Stay-Resident (TSR) programs, such as mouse drivers, CD-ROM drivers, and others, were common when MS-DOS was the predominant operating system. However, all versions of Windows covered by the A+ Certification Exams typically use 32-bit drivers. Only Windows 9x still supports 16-bit drivers through its use of Config.sys and Autoexec.bat and MS-DOS mode.

You can set a particular MS-DOS application that must run from the MS-DOS mode to use TSRs or device drivers by editing the Advanced features of its Program properties sheet (see Figure 20.5). Add or remove drivers, TSRs, or other commands from the default settings listed for Config.sys or Autoexec.bat. The options set here will be run when the program is started and are removed from memory when the user returns to the Windows GUI.

FIGURE 20.5

If you are running an MS-DOS program that needs particular device drivers or TSRs to work in MS-DOS mode (Windows 9x), specify the MS-DOS configuration you need.

Can't Install Applications

If you can't install an application, here are some reasons why—and some solutions!

■ *Not enough disk space on C: drive*—Use the Custom Installation option, if available, to choose another drive, delete old files in the default Temp folder, or delete .chk files created by ScanDisk or Chkdsk in the root folder to free up space.

■ *Computer doesn't meet minimum requirements for RAM or CPU speed*—Check for installation program switches to turn off speed and RAM checks, or, better still, upgrade system to meet or exceed minimums.

■ *No more space available in root folder*—A FAT16 drive with 256 folders and files in the root folder cannot create any more folders or files in the root. Install to another folder, or convert the drive to FAT32 or NTFS to eliminate this limitation.

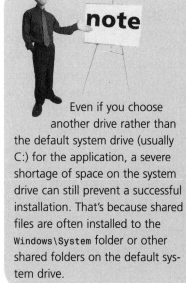

note

Even if you choose another drive rather than the default system drive (usually C:) for the application, a severe shortage of space on the system drive can still prevent a successful installation. That's because shared files are often installed to the Windows\System folder or other shared folders on the default system drive.

Print Spooler Stalled

Windows NT 4.0/2000/XP run the **print spooler** as a **service**. To restart it from the list of local services, with Windows 2000/XP, use this procedure:

1. Open Control Panel and select Administrative Tools.

2. Open the Services shortcut.

3. Scroll to the Print Spooler entry.

4. Right-click and select Restart from the right-click menu.

In Windows NT 4.0, open the Services icon in Control Panel to locate the print spooler. Select Stop, Start.

To fix stalled print spooler problems in Windows 9x/Me

1. Open the C:\Windows\Spool\Printers folder.

2. Delete the files in the folder.

3. Resend any print jobs not completed.

tip

The Spool folder is hidden by default. To display it, change default View settings in Windows Explorer as described in Chapter 18 to show all files and show protected operating system files.

Using Windows Utilities for Troubleshooting

Windows provides many built-in tools for troubleshooting. The following sections describe some of the major utilities.

Using MSConfig

The Microsoft System Configuration Utility, MSConfig (available in Windows 98/Me/XP), enables you to selectively disable programs and services that run at startup. If your computer is unstable, runs out of FSR very quickly with Windows 98/Me, or has problems starting up or shutting down, using MSConfig can help you determine if a program or service run when the system starts is at fault. To start MSConfig

1. Click Start, Run.

2. Type **MSConfig** and click OK.

All versions of MSConfig have a multitabbed interface used to control startup options (see Figure 20.6). The General tab lets you select from Normal, Diagnostic (clean boot), or Selective Startup (you choose which items and services to load). You can also expand or extract files from the Windows XP/Me CD or launch System Restore from the

note

The ScanDisk and CHKDSK disk-testing utilities are discussed in Chapter 18. The Device Manager is discussed in Chapter 19, "Installing and Configuring Hardware in Windows." The Computer Management Console is discussed in Chapter 18.

Windows XP/Me versions of MSConfig. The Advanced option in Windows 98/Me's version displays a dialog box with advanced startup options for Windows.

Other tabs control settings in MSConfig, System.ini (legacy hardware), Win.ini (legacy software and configuration), Boot.ini and services (Windows XP), startup programs, and other version-specific startup options.

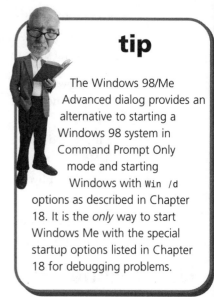

tip

The Windows 98/Me Advanced dialog provides an alternative to starting a Windows 98 system in Command Prompt Only mode and starting Windows with Win /d options as described in Chapter 18. It is the *only* way to start Windows Me with the special startup options listed in Chapter 18 for debugging problems.

FIGURE 20.6

MSConfig's General tab (Windows XP).

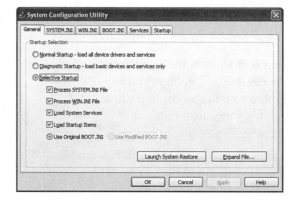

Using System File Checker

System File Checker (SFC) is a Windows 98/2000/XP utility that checks protected system files (files such as .DLL, .SYS, .OCX, and .EXE, as well as some font files used by the Windows desktop) and replaces incorrect versions or missing files with the correct files. Use SFC to fix problems with Internet Explorer or other built-in Windows programs caused by the installation of

tip

You can also run SFC in Windows 98 from the Tools menu in System Information.

obsolete Windows system files, user error, deliberate erasure, virus or Trojan horse infections, and similar problems.

You can run SFC manually, at the next startup, or every time the computer is started.

Using DirectX Diagnostics

Use **DirectX Diagnostics** to determine if DirectX (the software component Windows uses for 3D graphics and sound, game controllers, and multimedia) is working correctly. DirectX Diagnostics has a multiple-tab dialog providing information about the system hardware, DirectX files, display hardware, sound hardware, music hardware, input devices, network settings, and troubleshooters. To run DirectX Diagnostics, click Start, Run, type **Dxdiag**, and click OK.

Command-Prompt Troubleshooting Utilities

The following command-line utilities can be used for troubleshooting various versions of Windows. Table 20.6 lists these tools, the tasks they perform, and the versions of Windows that contain these tools. For more information about starting a command-prompt session, see Chapter 18.

tip

Replace unsigned or defective drivers if you are having problems in DirectX-compatible software (game and multimedia titles). If your computer fails one or more DirectX tests, download and install the latest version of DirectX from Microsoft.

note

Download the latest version of DirectX, get technical help, and learn more about DirectX at the Microsoft DirectX Web site (http://www.microsoft.com/windows/directx/default.asp).

Table 20.6   Windows Command-Prompt Troubleshooting Utilities

Utility	Uses	Windows Versions
Attrib	Changes and displays file attributes	All
Chkdsk	Checks drives for errors	NT 4.0/2000/XP
Chkntfs	Configures automatic disk checking at startup	NT 4.0*/2000/XP
DiskPart	Manages hard disk partitions	XP
Driverquery	Displays driver information	XP
Expand	Expands files from Windows CDs or .CAB files	NT 4.0/2000/XP

Table 20.6 (continued)

Utility	Uses	Windows Versions
Extract	Extracts files from Windows CDs or .CAB files	9x, Me
Ftype	Lists and modifies file associations	NT 4.0/2000/XP
Fdisk	Manages disk partitions	9x, Me
Ipconfig	Displays TCP/IP network settings	NT 4.0/2000/XP
Move	Moves files from one folder to another	All
Ntbackup	Starts backup or restore process	NT 4.0/2000/XP
Print	Sends text files to the printer	All
Recover	Recovers readable data from a bad file	All
Regsvr32	Registers specified .DLL files into the Registry	All
ScanDisk	Checks drive for errors	9x/Me
Shutdown	Shuts down specified local or remote computer	XP
Systeminfo	Displays detailed information about a local or remote computer's installed hardware and software	XP
Sfc (System File Checker)	Checks and verifies system files	98/2000/XP
Tasklist	Displays running tasks by Process ID (PID)	XP
Taskkill	Shuts down task specified by PID	XP
Tree	Displays folder structure of a specified drive or folder	All
Type	Displays contents of a text file	All
Ver	Displays Windows version number	All

Available in Windows NT 4.0 Service Pack 2 or above

Many of these commands are covered in greater detail in Chapter 18 and the Windows Command Reference on the CD packaged with this book.

Windows Recovery Console

The Windows **Recovery Console** is a special command-line interface that is designed for copying files and performing disk repairs. In Windows 2000, you can use the Recovery Console as an alternative to the Emergency Repair process, such as if you need to restore only

> **tip**
>
> You can create a text file with the information displayed from many command-line programs by using the redirect (>) command. For example, to create a file called Mysystem.txt that contains the information reported by Systeminfo, enter this command from the command line:
>
> **Systeminfo>Mysystem.txt**

one system file. Windows XP lacks the Emergency Repair provision, so understanding how to use the Recovery Console is even more important.

The Recovery Console contains some of the same commands that are available in the normal command-line interface, along with additional commands that are necessary only for repairing the installation.

Table 20.7 lists Recovery Console commands and uses.

note

Command.com is the **command interpreter** used by Windows 9x/Me; cmd is the command interpreter used by Windows NT 4.0/2000/XP.

Table 20.7 Recovery Console Commands

Command	Uses
Attrib	Changes file/folder attributes.
Batch	Executes the commands specified in the text file.
Bootcfg	Boot file (boot.ini) configuration and recovery. Can also rebuild a lost boot.ini.
ChDir (Cd)	Displays the name of the current folder or changes the current folder. Requires quotes around folder names with spaces.
Chkdsk	Checks a disk and displays a status report. Use the /r option to repair bad sectors.
Cls	Clears the screen.
Copy	Copies a single file to another drive or folder. Automatically uncompresses files from the Windows CD during the copy process. Can't copy to removable media.
Delete (Del)	Deletes a single file.
Dir	Displays a list of files and subfolders in a folder. Lists file/folder attributes for each item listed.
Disable	Disables a system service or a device driver. Helpful if Ntbtlog.txt (the bootlog) indicates a service or device driver is preventing the system from starting.
Diskpart	Manages partitions on your hard drives. Can be used in interactive mode or with optional switches to add or remove partitions.
Enable	Starts or enables a system service or a device driver.
Exit	Exits the Recovery Console and restarts your computer.
Expand	Extracts a file from a compressed (.cab) file to the hard disk.

Table 20.7 (continued)

Command	Uses
Fixboot	Writes a new partition boot sector onto the specified partition. Often used with `Fixmbr`.
Fixmbr	Repairs the master boot record of the specified disk. Often used with `Fixboot`.
Format	Formats a disk with options for file system and quick format.
Help	Displays a list of the commands you can use in the Recovery Console.
Listsvc	Lists the services and drivers available on the computer.
Logon	Logs on to a Windows installation.
Map	Displays the drive letter mappings. Useful if run before using `Fixboot` or `Fixmbr` to make sure you work with the correct disk or drive letter.
Mkdir (Md)	Creates a directory.
More	Displays a text file.
Net Use	Connects a network share to a drive letter.
Rename (Ren)	Renames a single file.
Rmdir (Rd)	Deletes a directory.
Set	Displays and sets environment variables. Can be used to enable copying files to removable media, use of wildcards, and other options within the Recovery Console if the system security settings are adjusted.
Systemroot	Sets the current directory to the systemroot directory of the system you are currently logged on to.
Type	Displays a text file.

Computer Viruses

A computer virus is a program that attaches itself without the user's knowledge to another program, a part of the computer's storage system, the email system, or another part of the computer's operating system or applications. A computer virus also carries a *payload*, the term for the action the virus takes when it is activated. Viruses can erase files, format the hard disk, install remote control programs that allow an undisclosed user to take over the computer, transmit data to another computer, and other harmful activities.

The essential difference between a **Trojan horse** and a **computer virus** program is that the computer virus program is also able to spread itself from one computer to another; after a single computer in an office has acquired a computer virus, it can easily spread to other computers via floppy disks, network connections, email attachments, and by other means. Both can be detected by up-to-date antivirus software and both pose significant threats to data and systems. For the rest of this section, "virus" will be used to describe both actual computer viruses and Trojan horse programs.

Clues Pointing to Computer Virus Infections

Several clues point to the likelihood that one or more computers and offices are infected with the computer virus:

- The same or similar problems spread from one computer to another and the computers are connected to each other or share data or media.
- Unexpected system slowdown.
- Onscreen messages indicating an infection.
- Loss of system configuration in the CMOS.
- Outbound network traffic coming from unknown programs.

> **caution**
>
> Use Help and the command-specific help (/?) to determine what options you can use in the Recovery Console, even if you're familiar with how the command works from a command prompt. Commands in the Recovery Console often have different options and more limitations than the same commands used at a normal command prompt.

Types of Computer Viruses

Computer viruses come in different types, each with its preferred method of transmission and infection:

- *Executable file virus*—Attaches itself to program files, such as .com,.exe, or .dll.
- *Boot-sector virus*—Attaches itself to the boot sector of media, such as hard drives and floppy disk drives.
- *Macro virus*—Adds unauthorized commands to the macros stored as part of data files created with programs such as Microsoft Word and Microsoft Excel.
- *VB script virus*—Responsible for the ILOVEYOU outbreak and many other recent virus attacks. This type of virus is

> **caution**
>
> Computer technicians who use floppy disk drives for diagnostic software can unwittingly spread boot sector viruses from one computer to another!

spread through corporate and personal email systems and is carried by a Visual Basic script attached to an email message or included in a VB script automatically loaded by a Web page.

- *Blended threat*—Virus or Trojan horse that attacks files, network/Internet connections, servers, and causes multiple types of damage on infected files.

- *Adware/spyware*—Programs that monitor and transmit data without the user's knowledge to a remote computer. Often a concealed part of "free" utility downloads.

Detecting Viruses on Client Computers

In an ideal world, every computer in use would have up-to-date antivirus software that was used on a regular and frequent basis. In the real world, you can't expect clients to achieve this level of protection. Windows does not include any type of antivirus protection.

Because computer viruses target antivirus software on PCs, the best way to check a computer that might contain a computer virus is to start the system with a known "clean" bootable floppy disk or bootable CD-ROM. Then, a known "clean" antivirus program with the latest updates available should be run on the system.

You can create a clean virus detection system for traditional viruses by following as many of these steps as possible:

- Test all new antivirus programs and virus signatures before installation on a computer.

- Keep the computer used for scanning media for viruses behind a secure network firewall.

- Use recordable CDs (CD-R or CD-RW) to store antivirus programs and signature files.

It is good practice to maintain more than one antivirus program, because antivirus programs differ in their capability to detect, eliminate, and protect against different types of viruses. The leaders in the field include Trend Micro (www.trendmicro.com), Symantec (www.symantec.com), and McAfee (www.mcafee.com).

> **tip**
>
> If you are working at the client location and no up-to-date antivirus software is available but the system has an Internet connection, Trend Micro offers free online virus scanning at http://housecall.trendmicro.com.

What to Do When a Virus Is Located on a Client Computer

To prevent reinfection of the computer, take the following steps:

- Disinfect the infected computer by using an up-to-date antivirus program. If the virus can't be removed from the infected file, try a different antivirus program. Delete the infected file only as a last resort.

- Check all other computers that are connected to the infected computer through networks or have shared information through media exchange or email with the infected computer.

- Check all media, including floppy disks, removable media, tape, and CD-R/CD-RW that have been used on the infected computer. Frequently, you'll find more copies of the virus on this media as well. If the virus is not removed from the media, it will reinfect the same computer or infect other computers.

- If the infected computer shares files with a computer at home, encourage the client to check the home computer for viruses. Home computers will frequently reinfect office computers if not checked for viruses.

> **tip**
>
> If a computer running Windows Me or Windows XP has a virus, running System Restore to revert the system to an earlier time could reinfect the computer because the virus could be stored inside the restore point files created by System Restore. Vendors often recommend disabling System Restore before removing a virus, but if you don't want to lose the restore point data, you should at least plan to rescan the computer for viruses if you revert the system to an earlier condition.

Study Lab

Don't miss the Study Lab materials found on the CD accompanying this book. Each Study Lab is tailored to the individual chapters in this book, meaning that you'll quickly be able to determine which topics you understand well enough to pass the exam and which topics need more study. The Study Labs are presented in printable PDF format so that you can take them with you to study at work, on the road, or even in your car just before test time!

THE ABSOLUTE MINIMUM

- Startup errors for all versions of Windows on the A+ Certification Exams can be caused by problems with Windows configuration, missing device drivers, or drive problems.

- You can start Windows with various special startup options such as Safe Mode, Logged, Last Known Good Configuration, and VGA Mode to bypass startup problems and help troubleshoot the system.

- Windows NT 4.0 and 2000 offer the Emergency System Repair option to fix problems with boot files.

- Windows 2000 and XP feature the Recovery Console, a special command-prompt mode for fixing system problems.

- Windows 9x/Me display illegal operation errors as a result of conflicts, low free system resources (FSRs), or other problems.

- The Dr. Watson and Resource Meter utilities can be useful in troubleshooting general protection faults (GPFs) and other illegal operation errors.

- Windows NT 4.0/2000/XP display STOP (Blue Screen of Death, or BSOD) errors when the system has incompatible or defective hardware or software installed, Registry problems, viruses, or other problems.

- Problems with the Windows swapfile (9x/Me) or paging file (Windows NT 4.0/2000/XP) can cause various system problems because the paging file is used as a RAM substitute.

- You can move the paging file or swapfile to another drive or, in Windows NT 4.0/2000/XP, spread the paging file across multiple drives if the default system drive is short of space.

- Windows 9x/Me let you disable advanced disk-access options if necessary to troubleshoot hard disk problems.

- Problems with ATA/IDE and SCSI hard disks can prevent Windows from starting. They can be solved by adjusting system or SCSI BIOS options or adjusting other settings.

- A lack of disk space can cause problems with program installation or system lockups.

- The MSConfig program in Windows 98/Me/XP enables the user to customize the boot process.

- System File Checker in Windows 98/2000/XP checks system files for corruption or unauthorized replacement.

- Command-prompt and Recovery Console utilities can be used to troubleshoot various types of system problems.

- Computer viruses can be spread between systems through media, network connections, and email.

- Antivirus software must be kept up to date and used at all times to prevent infection.

21

NETWORKING AND INTERNET CONNECTIVITY

A network is a group of computers, peripherals, and software that are connected to each other and can be used together. Special software and hardware are required to make networks work.

Two or more computers connected together in the same office are considered a **LAN** (local area network). LANs in different cities can be connected to each other by a **WAN** (wide area network). The **Internet** represents the world's largest network, connecting both standalone computers and computers on LAN and WAN networks all over the world.

This chapter is a little different than other chapters in this book in that it covers topics found on both the A+ Core Hardware and A+ Operating Systems Exams. Because both exams deal with networking topics, covering all the networking topics in a single chapter makes more sense than creating two chapters with overlapping subjects.

Network Operating Systems

As you learned in previous chapters, an operating system is the software that enables you to work with hardware and application programs. A **network operating system (NOS)** is a special type of operating system that enables your computer to communicate with other computers over a LAN, over a WAN, or through the Internet. Novell NetWare and Windows NT/2000/Server 2003 are examples of NOSs.

Although Windows NT 4.0/9x/Me/2000/XP are designed primarily as desktop operating systems, they also include NOS features, such as network client options; support for multiple network protocols, such as TCP/IP and others; and file and print sharing for simple networking. They also can be used with networking hardware to build networks without purchasing additional network software.

Built-In Networking Features in Windows

The Windows versions covered on the A+ Certification Exams include the following NOS features, enabling these operating systems to be used either as network clients or as peer network servers:

- *Client software*—Enables systems to connect with Windows and Novell NetWare networks, among others.

- *Network protocols*—IPX/SPX, NetBEUI, and TCP/IP are all included.

- *File and print sharing*—Enables Windows systems to act as peer servers for Windows and Novell NetWare networks.

note

The CD included with this book contains important Study Lab material for this chapter, as well as Chapters 2–22 in this book. The Study Lab for each chapter contains terms to study, exercises, and practice tests—all in printable PDF format (Adobe Acrobat Reader is included on the CD, too). These Study Lab materials will help you gear up for the A+ Exam. Also, the CD includes an industry-leading test engine from PrepLogic, which simulates the actual A+ test so that you can be sure that you're ready when test day arrives. Don't let the A+ test intimidate you. If you've read the chapters, worked through the Study Lab, and passed the practice tests from PrepLogic, you should be well prepared to ace the test!

Also, you'll notice that some words throughout each chapter are in bold format. These are study terms that are defined in the Study Lab. Be sure to consult the Study Lab when you are finished with this chapter to test what you've learned.

■ *Services*—Enables specialized network services, such as shared printers, network backup, and more.

Network Models

As the network features found in Windows suggest, there are two major network models:

■ Client/server

■ Peer-to-peer

It's important to understand the differences between them as you prepare for the exams and as you work with networks.

> **note**
>
> If you want to create a network with user-based or group-based security, you must set up one or more dedicated servers (computers used only to share resources with other computers) that run full-featured NOSs.

Client/Server

Most departmental and larger networks are **client/server** networks, such as the one illustrated in Figure 21.1. Novell NetWare and Windows NT/2000/2003 Server are examples of client/server networks.

FIGURE 21.1

A server with three workstations, each of which is using a different shared resource: One is using the server's CD-ROM drive, one is printing to the server's printer, and one is copying a file to the server's hard disk.

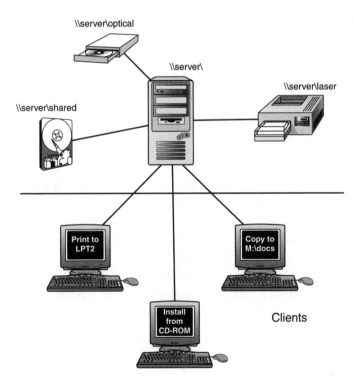

The roles of each computer in a client/server network are distinctive, affecting both the hardware used in each computer and the software installed in each computer.

Servers

A **server** is a computer on the network that provides other computers (called clients or workstations) with access to resources, such as disk drives, folders, printers, modems, scanners, and Internet access.

Because these resources can be used by different computers over the network, they are called shared resources.

Servers can also be used for different types of software and tasks. For example, application servers run tasks for clients, file servers store data and program files for clients, and mail servers store and distribute email to clients.

Servers typically have more powerful hardware features than typical PCs, such as SCSI RAID arrays for hard disk storage, larger amounts of RAM, hot-swap power supplies, and server-optimized network adapters. However, because servers are not operated by an individual user, they often use low-performance integrated or PCI video and might be managed remotely rather than with a keyboard or monitor connected directly to the server.

note

There are two ways to refer to a network resource on a server, as shown in Figure 21.1: the *Universal Naming Convention (UNC)*, in which the servername and the name of the resource are used, such as \\server\shared for the server's hard disk, or a *mapped resource*, in which the server's resource is referred to as if it's built into the client, such as "LPT2" for the network printer (second parallel port) or "drive M:" for the network drive.

Clients

A **client** is a computer that uses the resources on a server. Depending on the network operating system in use, clients and servers can be separate machines or a client can act as a server and a server can act as a client. Clients can refer to servers either by assigning drive letters to shared folders (see "Mapped Drives" later in this chapter) or by using a Universal Naming Convention (UNC) path name to refer to the server. Both of these are illustrated in Figure 21.1.

➯ **See** "The Universal Naming Convention (UNC)," **p. 805**.

Peer-to-Peer

The network features built into Windows allow for peer servers: Computers can share resources with each other, and machines that share resources can also be used as client workstations.

As Figure 21.2 shows, if mapped drive letters and printer ports are used in a peer-to-peer network, the same resource will have a different name, depending on whether it's being accessed from the peer server (acting as a workstation) itself or over the network. In Figure 21.2, the system on the left shares its CD-ROM drive with the system on the right, which refers to the shared CD-ROM drive as F:\. The system on the right shares its printer with the system on the left, which has mapped the shared printer to LPT2.

FIGURE 21.2

A simple two-station peer-to-peer network, in which each computer acts as a peer server to the other.

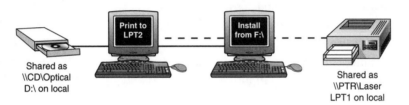

Shared as
\\CD\Optical
D:\ on local

Shared as
\\PTR\Laser
LPT1 on local

The peer server loads file and printer-sharing software to make printers and drives or folders available to others. Because a peer server is also used as a workstation, it is equipped in the same way as a typical workstation or standalone PC.

Internet Connectivity Technologies

One of the best reasons to create a network of any size is to provide access to the Internet. The many types of connectivity technologies that can be used for Internet access are discussed in the following sections.

Dial-Up Internet Connectivity

For home and small-business users, **dial-up networking** is still the most common way of accessing the Internet. Dial-up connections are often referred to as analog connections because the device used to make the connection is an

tip

As you review the following sections, try to determine which type of Internet connections you use at home and at your workplace.

analog modem, which connects to the Internet through an ordinary telephone line. Every time you connect to the Internet with a dial-up modem, you are making a network connection.

Dial-Up Internet Hardware

There have been various standards for analog modems used to make dial-up connections. Before the advent of so-called "56K" standards, the fastest dial-up connection possible was 33.6Kbps. Early proprietary standards for support of connections up to 56Kbps, x2, and K56flex, have been replaced by the ITU v.90 and v.92 (supports call waiting) standards. Virtually all modems in recent systems or available for purchase support either the v.90 or v.92 standards.

For more information about analog modem hardware, see Chapter 8, "Input/Output Devices and Cables."

Although x2, K56flex, v.90, and v.92 modems are all designed to perform downloading at up to 56Kbps, FCC (Federal Communications Commission) regulations limit actual download speed to 53Kbps.

Dial-Up Internet Service Providers

An **Internet service provider (ISP)** provides a connection between the user with an analog (dial-up) modem and the Internet. ISPs that provide dial-up access have several modems and dial-up numbers that their customers can access. The ISP's modems are connected to the Internet via high-speed, high-capacity connections.

An ISP can be selected from many different sources:

- National companies, such as EarthLink or AOL
- Local or regional providers
- Specialized providers such as those that provide filtered, family-friendly access

Choose an ISP based on its rates, its reliability, or special services (such as content filtration or proprietary content) that are appropriate to your needs.

Creating a Dial-Up Connection

With Windows 9x/Me and NT 4.0, a dial-up connection is created and configured through the Dial-Up Networking (DUN) folder. This folder can be accessed by clicking Start, Programs, Accessories, Communications. The folder contains a wizard that can be run to configure the connection and icons for each existing connection.

If dial-up networking is not available in Windows 9x/Me, open the Control Panel, click Add/Remove Programs, click the Windows Setup tab, click Components, click Communications, and select Dial-Up Networking. Follow the prompts and insert your Windows CD if needed to complete installation.

Windows NT 4.0 has a dial-up networking icon listed in My Computer, but if DUN has not been installed, you will be prompted to provide your Windows NT CD to complete DUN installation when you open the DUN icon.

Windows 2000 and Windows XP create DUN connections within the same network folder used for other types of network connections:

- Windows 2000 stores all types of network connections in the Network and Dial-Up Connections folder.

- Windows XP stores all types of network connections in the My Network Places folder.

Requirements for a Dial-Up Internet Connection

All ISPs must provide the following information to enable you to connect to the Internet:

- Client software, including the preferred Web browser, dial-up information, and TCP/IP configuration information

- Dial-up access telephone numbers

- Modem types supported (33.6Kbps, 56Kbps, x2, K56flex, v.90, v.92)

- The username and initial password (which should be changed immediately after first login)

note

If an ISP provides customized setup software, the software will usually create an icon for you in the folder used for DUN connections. This icon contains the settings needed to make your connection.

Even if the client software provided by the ISP configures the connection for you, you should record the following information in case it is needed to manually configure or reconfigure the connection:

- *The dial-up access telephone number*—This might be different for different modem speeds. Users with a 56Kbps modem should know both the standard (33.6Kbps) and high-speed access numbers if different numbers are used.

- *The username and password*—Windows will often save this during the setup of a DUN connection, but it should be recorded in case the system must be reconfigured or replaced.

■ *The TCP/IP configuration*—This is set individually for each dial-up connection through its properties sheet.

To determine this information, right-click the icon for the connection and select Properties.

⇨ For more information, **see** "TCP/IP Configuration," **p. 792**.

ISDN Internet Connectivity

ISDN (Integrated Services Digital Network) was originally developed to provide an all-digital method for connecting multiple telephone and telephony-type devices such as fax machines to a single telephone line and to provide a faster connection for teleconferencing for remote computer users. It can also provide an all-digital Internet connection at speeds up to 128Kbps.

Line quality is a critical factor in determining whether any particular location can use ISDN service. If an all-digital connection cannot be established between the customer's location and the telephone company's central switch, ISDN service is not available or a new telephone line must be run (at extra cost to you!).

The telephone network was originally designed to support analog signaling only, which is why an analog (dial-up) modem that sends data to other computers converts digital signals to analog for transmission through the telephone network. The receiving analog modem converts analog data back to digital data.

ISDN Hardware

In order to make an ISDN connection, your PC (and any other devices that share the ISDN connection) needs a device called an ISDN **terminal adapter** (TA). A TA resembles a conventional analog modem. Internal models plug into the same PCI, ISA, and PC Card slots used by analog modems, and external models use USB or serial ports. External TAs often have two or more RJ-11 ports for telephony devices, an RJ-45 port for the connection to the ISDN line, and a serial or USB port for connection to the computer. For more information about these ports, see Chapter 8.

Setting Up an ISDN Connection

ISDN connections (where available) are provided through the local telephone company. There are two types of ISDN connections:

■ **Primary Rate Interface** (PRI)

■ **Basic Rate Interface** (BRI)

A PRI connection provides 1.536Mbps of bandwidth, whereas a BRI interface provides 64Kbps (single-channel) or 128Kbps (dual- channel) of bandwidth. BRI is sold to small businesses and home offices; PRI is sold to large organizations. Both types of connections enable you to use the Internet and talk or fax data through the phone line at the same time.

An ISDN connection is configured through DUN with Windows NT 4.0/9x/Me or through the network features of Windows 2000 and XP with the same types of settings used for an analog modem connection.

⇨   For more information, **see** "TCP/IP Configuration," **p. 792**.

tip

Many telephone companies have largely phased out ISDN in favor of DSL, which is much faster and less expensive!

note

Downstream refers to download speed; upstream refers to upload speed. SDSL gets its name (Synchronous DSL) from providing the same speed in both directions; ADSL is always faster downstream than upstream.

DSL

DSL (Digital Subscriber Line), like ISDN, piggybacks on the same telephone line used by your telephone and fax machine, but it differs from ISDN in many ways. Like ISDN, DSL requires a high-quality telephone line that can carry a digital signal, but unlike ISDN, DSL is designed strictly for Internet access.

When it comes to connection speed, DSL leaves BRI ISDN in the dust. There are two major types of DSL: ADSL (Asynchronous DSL) and SDSL (Synchronous DSL). Their features are compared in Table 21.1.

Table 21.1 Common DSL Services Compared

Service Type	Supports Existing Telephone Line	User Installation Option?	Typical Downstream Speeds	Typical Upstream Speeds	Typically Marketed To
ADSL	Yes	Yes	384Kbps to 1.5Gbps	128Kbps to 384Kbps	Home, small-business
SDSL	No	No	192Kbps to 1.5Gbps	Same as downstream speed	Larger business and corporate

DSL Hardware

A device known as a DSL modem is used to connect your computer to DSL service. DSL modems connect to your PC through the RJ-45 (Ethernet) port or the USB port. The rear of a typical DSL modem that uses an Ethernet (RJ-45) connection is shown in Figure 21.3.

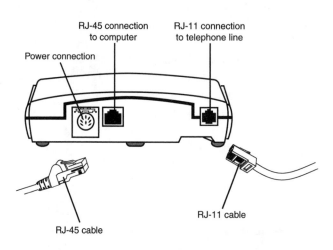

FIGURE 21.3

The rear of a typical DSL modem with a power port (top left), RJ-45 data port to the PC (top center), and an RJ-11 telephone line port (top right). The RJ-45 cable is shown at bottom left, and the RJ-11 cable is shown at bottom right.

Setting Up a DSL Connection

As Figure 21.3 indicates, DSL uses the same telephone lines as ordinary telephone equipment. However, your telephone can interfere with the DSL connection. To prevent this, in some cases a separate DSL line is run from the outside service box to the computer with the DSL modem. However, if your DSL provider supports the self-installation option, small devices called **microfilters** are installed between telephones, answering machines, fax machines, and other devices on the same circuit with the DSL modem. Microfilters can be built into special wall plates, but are more often external devices that plug into existing phone jacks as shown in Figure 21.4.

Some DSL connections are configured as an always-on connection similar to a network connection to the Internet. However, many vendors now configure the DSL connection as a **PPPoE** (point-to-point protocol over Ethernet) connection instead. A PPPoE connection requires the user to make a connection with a username and password.

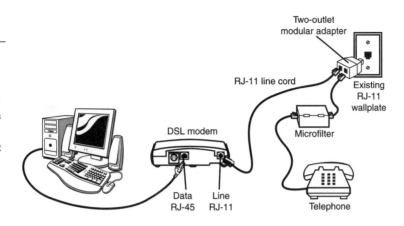

FIGURE 21.4

A typical self-installed DSL setup. The DSL vendor supplies the DSL modem (center) and microfilters that attach between telephones and other devices and the wall outlet (right).

Cable Internet

Cable Internet service piggybacks on the same coaxial cable that brings cable TV into a home or business. A few early cable ISPs used internal cable modems, which supported one-way traffic. (The cable was used for downloads and a conventional telephone line was used for uploads and page requests.) However, one-way **cable modem** service is obsolete and is seldom encountered anymore. Almost all cable Internet service today is two-way and is built upon the fiber-optic network used for digital cable and music services provided by most cable TV vendors.

Cable Internet can reach download speeds anywhere from 500Kbps up to 1.5Mbps. Upload speeds are typically capped at 128Kbps, but some vendors now offer faster upload speeds in some plans.

Windows XP has native support for PPPoE through its Network Connection Wizard. With other versions of Windows, the vendor must provide setup software.

On typical installations that also have cable TV, cable Internet service connects to a cable TV line with a splitter. The splitter prevents cable TV and cable Internet signals from interfering with each other. One coaxial cable from the splitter goes into the set-top cable TV box as usual; the other one goes into a device known as a cable modem. Almost all cable modems are external devices that plug into a computer's 10/100 Ethernet (RJ-45) or USB port. Figure 21.5 shows a typical cable Internet connection.

FIGURE 21.5

A typical cable modem and cable TV installation. The cable modem can be connected to the computer through an RJ-45 cable or a USB cable.

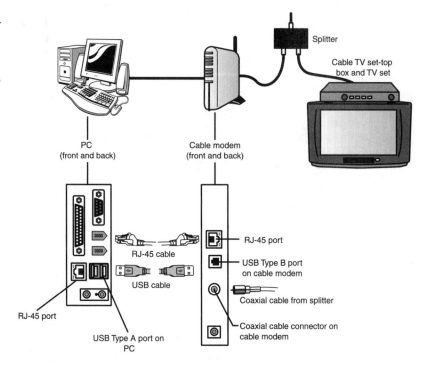

A cable Internet connection can be configured through the standard Network properties sheet in Windows or with customized setup software, depending upon the ISP.

⇨ **See** "TCP/IP Configuration," **p. 792**, for more information.

Satellite

There are two major satellite-based Internet vendors: **DirecWAY** (originally DirecPC) and **Starband**. Both use dish antennas similar to satellite TV antennas to receive and transmit signals between geosynchronous satellites and computers.

> **note**
>
> You can have cable Internet service without having cable TV.

Both services are available in package deals with dual-purpose satellite dishes, which can be used for both Internet and TV reception.

Both DirecWAY and Starband use external devices known as satellite modems to connect the computer to the satellite dish. They connect to the USB or Ethernet (RJ-45) port in a fashion similar to that used by DSL or cable modems.

The FCC requires professional installation for **satellite Internet** service because an incorrectly aligned satellite dish with uplink capabilities could cause a service outage on the satellite at which it's aimed. Setup software supplied by the satellite vendor is used to complete the process.

Wireless

Traditional **fixed wireless** networking uses point-to-point microwave signaling in one of various frequencies from a fixed base to a small external antenna at distances as great as 35 miles from the transmitter. (Distances vary with terrain and height of transmission tower.) Fixed wireless is popular in rural areas and small towns for both Internet and cable TV uses.

If a clear line of sight can be established between the fixed wireless transmitter and the antenna, **two-way service** is available using the antenna to send and receive data. However, if the signal must be bounced off reflectors to be received by the antenna, the service must use a telephone line for page requests and uploads.

After the antenna receives the signal, it transmits the signal through standard RG-6 or RG-59 coaxial cable (the same types of cable used by cable TV) to a wireless broadband router (WBR), a device resembling an external cable modem. A **WBR**, unlike most cable modems, often has an RJ-11 connection for a built-in analog modem or a 9-pin serial port to connect to an external analog modem. These features enable the same WBR to be used with both two-way and **one-way service**.

The WBR connects to the computer through an Ethernet (RJ-45) or USB cable. A fixed wireless network is typically configured through the Standard Network properties sheet in Windows.

➪ For more information, **see** "Wireless Ethernet," **p. 780**.

note

Geosynchronous satellites orbit the Earth's equator at a distance of over 22,000 miles; because of their orbit and altitude, they remain in the same location in the sky at all times. In the Northern hemisphere, you need an unobstructed view of the southern sky to make a connection. In the Southern hemisphere, you need an unobstructed view of the northern sky to make a connection.

note

As an alternative to fixed wireless networks in cities, where buildings cause major problems with line of sight, a growing number of cities and businesses have developed Wireless Ethernet–based wireless networks.

LANs and Internet Connectivity

A LAN is an ideal way to provide Internet access to two or more users. However, a LAN by itself cannot connect to the Internet. Two additional components must also be used with a LAN to enable it to connect to the Internet:

- *An **Internet access device**—*This could be a dial-up modem, but more often a broadband connection such as DSL, cable, ISDN, or wireless is used today. Some satellite modems support networking, but others don't. Check with the vendor for details.

- *A **router**—*This device connects client PCs on the network to the Internet through the Internet access device. To the Internet, only one client is making a connection, but the router internally tracks which PC has made the request and transmits the data for that PC back to that PC, enabling multiple PCs to access the Internet through the network.

Network Protocols

The A+ Certification Exams expect you to understand the major features of the four leading network protocols:

- TCP/IP
- NetBEUI/NetBIOS
- IPX/SPX
- AppleTalk

Although most current networks are based on TCP/IP, you might encounter the others in some older networks. The following sections cover the major features of these networks.

⇨ For information about configuring these protocols, **see** "Networking Configuration," **p. 791**.

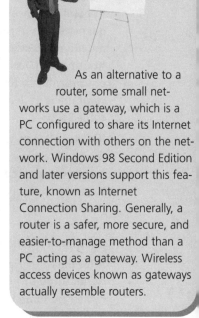

note

As an alternative to a router, some small networks use a gateway, which is a PC configured to share its Internet connection with others on the network. Windows 98 Second Edition and later versions support this feature, known as Internet Connection Sharing. Generally, a router is a safer, more secure, and easier-to-manage method than a PC acting as a gateway. Wireless access devices known as gateways actually resemble routers.

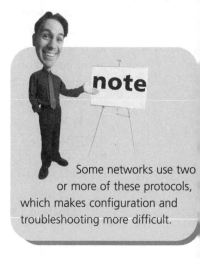

note

Some networks use two or more of these protocols, which makes configuration and troubleshooting more difficult.

TCP/IP

TCP/IP is short for Transport Control Protocol/Internet Protocol. It is a multiplatform protocol used for both Internet access and for local area networks. TCP/IP is used by Novell NetWare 5.x and above and Windows 2000/XP as the standard protocol for LAN use, replacing NetBEUI (used on older Microsoft networks) and IPX/SPX (used on older versions of Novell NetWare). Using TCP/IP as a network's only protocol makes network configuration easier because users need to configure only one protocol to communicate with other network clients, servers, or with the Internet.

tip

Most networking you'll perform in the real world uses TCP/IP. TCP/IP is also the most complex network to configure, especially if you need to use a static IP address. Make sure you understand how it works before you take your exams!

NetBEUI/NetBIOS

NetBEUI (NetBIOS Extended User Interface), the simplest major protocol in use today, is an enhanced version of an early network protocol called **NetBIOS** (NetBIOS itself is no longer used for this purpose). NetBEUI is used primarily on peer networks using Windows, with direct cable connection between two computers, and by some small networks that use Windows NT Servers. NetBEUI lacks features that enable it to be used on larger networks: It cannot be routed or used to access the Internet.

IPX/SPX

IPX/SPX (Internetwork Packet Exchange/Sequenced Packet Exchange) is a suite of protocols created by Novell for use on older versions of Novell NetWare. Unlike NetBEUI and NetBIOS, IPX/SPX is designed for large corporate networks; it can be routed but cannot be used to

note

NetBEUI is not officially supported in Windows XP, although Microsoft provides the NetBEUI protocol on the distribution CD in the `Valueadd\MSFT\Net\ NetBEUI` folder for use with older networks or for troubleshooting. For details on how to install NetBEUI in Windows XP, see the Microsoft Knowledge Base article 301401 available at `http:// support.microsoft.com`.

access the Internet. IPX/SPX is the standard protocol suite used by NetWare 4.x and earlier versions, but NetWare 5.x use this protocol for specialized operations or compatibility with older versions of NetWare only. NetWare 6.0 and later versions don't use IPX/SPX at all.

AppleTalk

Apple developed **AppleTalk** as a low-cost network for use with Apple computers and peripherals such as the Apple LaserWriter laser printer. AppleTalk supports up to 32 nodes per network. AppleTalk connection boxes attach to the serial (printer) port on Macintosh computers and peripherals. Gateway devices that contain both AppleTalk and Ethernet ports enable AppleTalk networks to connect to Ethernet networks.

TCP/IP Applications and Technologies

TCP/IP actually is a suite of protocols used on the Internet for routing and transporting information. The following sections discuss the major application protocols that rely on TCP/IP.

ISP

An ISP (Internet service provider) provides the connection between an individual PC or network and the Internet. ISPs use routers connected to high-speed, high-bandwidth connections to route Internet traffic from their clients to their destinations.

HTTP/HTTPS

Hypertext Transfer Protocol (**HTTP**) is the protocol used by Web browsers, such as Internet Explorer and Netscape Navigator, to access Web sites and content. Normal (unsecured sites) use the prefix http:// when accessed in a Web browser. Sites that are secured with various encryption schemes are identified with the prefix **https://**.

note

Most browsers connecting with a secured site will also display a closed padlock symbol onscreen.

SSL

Secure Socket Layers (SSL) is the encryption technology used by secured (https://) Web sites. To access a secured Web site, the Web browser must support the same encryption level used by the secured Web site (normally 128-bit encryption) and the same version(s) of SSL used by the Web site (normally SSL version 2.0 or 3.0).

HTML

Hypertext Markup Language (HTML) is the language used by Web pages. An HTML page is a specially formatted text page that uses tags (commands contained in angle brackets) to change text appearance, insert links to other pages, display pictures, incorporate scripting languages, and provide other features. Web browsers, such as Microsoft Internet Explorer and Netscape Navigator, are used to view and interpret the contents of Web pages, which have typical file extensions such as .HTM, .HTML, .ASP (Active Server pages generated by a database), and others.

You can see the HTML code used to create the Web page in a browser by using the View Source or View Page Source menu option provided by your browser. Figure 21.6 compares what you see in a typical Web page (top window) with the HTML tags used to set text features and the underlined hyperlink (bottom window). The figure uses different text size and shading to distinguish tags from text, and so do most commercial Web-editing programs used to make Web pages.

Tags such as <P> are used by themselves, and other tags are used in pairs. For example, <A HREF...> is used to indicate the start of a hyperlink (which will display another page or site in your browser window), and </A> indicates the end of a hyperlink.

The World Wide Web Consortium (http://www.w3c.org) sets the official standards for HTML tags and syntax, but major browser vendors, such as Microsoft and Netscape, often modify or extend official HTML standards with their own tags and syntax.

FIGURE 21.6

A section of an HTML document as seen by a typical browser (top window) uses the HTML tags shown in the bottom window for paragraph breaks (<P> tags), font settings (<FONT> tags), and hyperlinks (<A HREF> tags).

FTP

File Transfer Protocol (FTP) is a protocol used by both Web browsers and specialized FTP programs to access dedicated file transfer servers for file downloads and uploads. When you access an FTP site, the site uses the prefix ftp://.

Windows contains ftp.exe, a command-line FTP program; type **FTP**, press Enter, and then type **?** at the FTP prompt to see the commands you can use.

FTP sites with downloads available to any user support anonymous FTP; if any credentials are required, it's typically the user's email address as a password (the username is preset to anonymous). Some FTP sites require the user to log in with a specified username and password.

tip

Although you can use Windows's built-in FTP client for file uploads and downloads with both secured and unsecured FTP sites, you should consider using third-party FTP products such as CuteFTP or WS_FTP Pro. These programs enable you to create a customized setup for each FTP site you visit, and will store passwords, server types, and other necessary information. They also enable faster downloads than typical Web browsers running in ftp:// mode.

Telnet

Telnet enables a user to log in to a particular computer on the Internet and use it as if he were a regular user sitting in front of it, rather than simply downloading pages and files as he would with an http:// or ftp:// connection.

Windows contains a command-line Telnet program. To open a connection to a remote computer, enter a command such as

`telnet a.computer.com`

To use other commands, open a command prompt, type **telnet**, and press the Enter key. To see other commands, type **?/help**.

note

The remote computer must be configured to accept a Telnet login. Typically, TCP port 23 on the remote computer must be open before a login can take place.

DNS

The **domain name system (DNS)** is the name for the network of servers on the Internet that translate domain names such as www.selectsystems.com into the matching IP addresses. If you manually configure an IP address, you typically provide the IP addresses of one or more DNS servers as part of the configuration process.

If you want a unique domain name for either a Web site or email, the ISP that you will use to provide your email or Web hosting service often provides a registration wizard you can use to access the domain name registration services provided by various companies such as VeriSign.

A **domain name** has three major sections, from the end of the name to the start:

- The top-level domain (.com, .org, .net, and so on)
- The name of the site
- The server type; www indicates a Web server, ftp indicates an FTP server, mail indicates a mail server, and search indicates a search server

For example, Microsoft.com is located in the .com domain, typically used for commercial companies. Microsoft is the domain name. The Microsoft.com domain has the following servers:

- `www.microsoft.com` hosts Web content, such as product information.
- `search.microsoft.com` hosts the Microsoft.com search features, enabling users to search all or selected parts of the Microsoft.com domain.
- `ftp.microsoft.com` hosts the File Transfer Protocol server of Microsoft.com; this portion of the Microsoft.com domain can be accessed by either a Web browser or an FTP client.

Many companies have only WWW servers, or only WWW and FTP servers.

Email

All **email** systems provide transfer of text messages, and most have provisions for file attachments, enabling you to send documents, graphics, video clips, and other types of computer data files to receivers for work or play. Email clients are

caution

Can't access the site you're looking for? Got the wrong site? You might have made one of these common mistakes:

- *Don't assume that all domain names end in .com*—Other popular domain name extensions include .net, .org, .gov, .us, .cc, and various national domains such as .uk (United Kingdom), .ca (Canada), and many others.

- *Don't forget to use the entire domain name in the browser*—Some browsers will add the www. prefix used on most domain names, but others will not. For best results, spell out the complete domain name.

note

Some small Web sites use a folder under a domain hosted by an ISP:

`www.anisp.com/~asmallsite`

included as part of Web browsers, and are also available as limited-feature, freely downloadable, or more-powerful commercially purchased standalone email clients. Some email clients, such as Microsoft Outlook, are part of application suites (like Microsoft Office) and also feature productivity and time-management features.

To configure any email client, you need

- The name of the email server for incoming mail
- The name of the email server for outgoing mail
- The username and password for the email user
- The type of email server (POP, IMAP, or HTTP)

To access Web-based email, you need

- The Web site for the email service
- The username and password

Network Topologies

The arrangement of cabling and access devices is referred to as a **network topology**. There are four different types of network topologies (see Figure 21.7):

- **Bus**—All computers share a common cable. This topology is used by 10Base2 and 10Base5 Ethernet.
- **Star**—All computers connect to a central hub or switch (wired) or access point (wireless). This topology is used by 10BaseT, 100BaseT, and 1000BaseT Ethernet and by Wireless Ethernet when configured for the default infrastructure mode.
- **Ring**—All computers connect in a ring. This topology is used by token ring.
- **Peer-to-peer**—All computers on the network can connect directly to each other. This topology is used by Wireless Ethernet when configured for peer-to-peer mode and Bluetooth.

The network goes down if a single computer on a bus-topology network fails, but the other network types stay up if one or more computers fail.

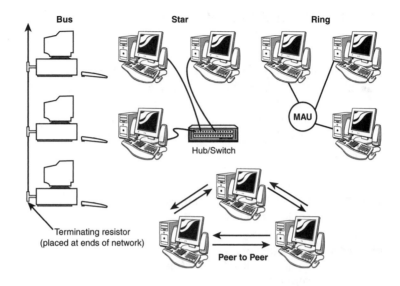

FIGURE 21.7
Bus, star, ring,
and peer-to-peer
topologies
compared.

Network Types

The A+ Certification Exam expects you to be familiar with the key features of major network types such as Ethernet and others. See the following sections for details.

Wired Ethernet Types

The oldest network (30 years old in 2003!) in common use today is **Ethernet**, also known as IEEE-802.3. Most recent wired Ethernet networks use unshielded twisted pair (UTP) cable, but older versions of Ethernet use various types of coaxial cable.

Table 21.2 lists the different types of Ethernet networks and their major features.

➪ For more information about cables and connectors, **see** "Cable and Connector Types," **p. 782**. For more information about network topologies, **see** "Network Topologies," **p. 778**.

note

Ethernet uses theCarrier Sense Multiple Access/ Collision Detect (CSMA/CD) method of transmission access. Here's how it works: A station on an Ethernet network can transmit data at any time; if two stations try to transmit at the same time, a collision takes place. Each station waits a random amount of time and then retries the transmission.

Table 21.2   Wired Ethernet Networks

Network Type	Cable and Connector Type	Also Known As	Maximum Speed	Network Topology Supported	Maximum Distance Per Segment
10Base2	RG-58 coaxial with BNC connector	**Thinnet**	10Mbps	Bus	185 meters
10Base5	Thick coaxial cable with external transceiver	**Thicknet**	10Mbps	Bus	500 meters
10BaseT	UTP Category 3 cable with RJ-45 connector	Ethernet	10Mbps	Star	100 meters
100BaseTX	UTP Category 5 cable with RJ-45 connector	**Fast Ethernet**	100Mbps	Star	100 meters
1000BaseTX	UTP Category 5 cable with RJ-45 connector	**Gigabit Ethernet**	1000Mbps	Star	100 meters

Wireless Ethernet

Wireless Ethernet, also known as IEEE-802.11, is the collective name for a group of wireless technologies that are compatible with wired Ethernet. Wireless Ethernet is also known as **Wi-Fi**, after the Wireless Fidelity (Wi-Fi) Alliance (www.wi-fi.org), a trade group that promotes interoperability between different brands of Wireless Ethernet hardware.

Table 21.3 compares different types of Wireless Ethernet to each other.

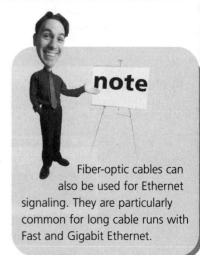

note

Fiber-optic cables can also be used for Ethernet signaling. They are particularly common for long cable runs with Fast and Gigabit Ethernet.

Table 21.3   Wireless Ethernet Standards

Wireless Ethernet Type	Frequency	Speed	Interoperable With
802.11a	5GHz	54Mbps	Requires dual-mode (802.11a/b or 802.11a/g) hardware
802.11b	2.4GHz	11Mbps	802.11g
802.11g	2.4GHz	54Mbps	802.11b

Wireless Ethernet hardware supports both star (infra-structure) network topologies, which uses a wireless access point to transfer data between nodes (required for Internet sharing), and peer-to-peer topologies, in which each node can communicate directly with another node.

Token Ring

A **token-ring** network (also known as IEEE-802.5) includes two or more computers with token-ring adapters, a device known as a **MAU (media access unit)** and an RJ-45 UTP Category 3 or Category 5 or 9-pin STP Type 1 cable between each computer's token-ring adapter and a port on the MAU.

> **note**
>
> Wi-Fi certified hardware is 802.11-family Wireless Ethernet hardware that has passed tests established by the Wi-Fi Alliance. Most, but not all, 802.11-family Wireless Ethernet hardware is Wi-Fi certified.

Externally, the combination of computers, cables, and MAU resemble a star topology. However, inside the MAU, the actual network topology is a ring topology: When a workstation needs to send information, it inserts the information and destination address along with a signal known as a token into the empty frames of information passed continuously within the MAU. The workstation receiving the message changes the token to indicate the message has been received and reinserts the token back into the flow of frames being passed from port to port. This method of information transfer is designed to avoid the collisions inherent in Ethernet.

Token-ring networks originally ran at 4Mbps, but most recent token-ring network hardware runs at both 4 and 16Mbps. Token-ring networks have become far less common in recent years with the rise of high-speed, low-cost Ethernet variants.

Bluetooth

Bluetooth is a short-range, low-speed, wireless network designed to operate in a peer-to-peer mode between PCs and other devices such as printers, projectors, smart phones, and others. Bluetooth runs in the same 2.4GHz frequency used by IEEE-802.11b and g, but uses a spread-spectrum frequency-hopping signaling method to help minimize interference. Bluetooth devices use the peer-to-peer network topology.

Cable and Connector Types

There are four major types of network cables:

- Unshielded twisted pair (UTP)
- Shielded twisted pair (STP)
- Fiber-optic
- Coaxial

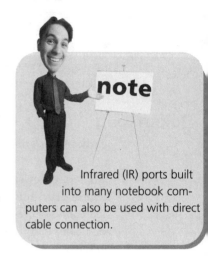

Network cards are designed to interface with one or more types of network cables.

Serial (RS-232) null modem and parallel (LPT) crossover cables can be used with direct cable connection, which is a special type of two-station network included in Windows that uses standard network protocols but does not use network cards.

note

Infrared (IR) ports built into many notebook computers can also be used with direct cable connection.

UTP and STP Cabling

Unshielded twisted pair (UTP) cabling is the most common of the major cabling types. The name refers to its physical construction:four twisted pairs of wire surrounded by a flexible jacket.

UTP cable comes in various grades, of which **Category 5** is the most common of the standard cabling grades. Category 5 cabling is suitable for use with both standard 10BaseT and Fast Ethernet networking, and can also be used for Gigabit Ethernet networks if tested for compliance.

Shielded twisted pair (**STP**) cabling (Category 4) is designed for use on IBM Token-Ring Networks. STP uses the same RJ-45 connector as UTP, but includes wire mesh for electrical insulation between the wire pairs and the outer jacket. It's stiffer and more durable, but also more expensive and harder to loop through tight spaces than UTP. Type 1 STP cable used by older token-ring adapters has a 9-pin connector.

Table 21.4 lists the various types of UTP and STP cabling in use and what they're best suited for.

Table 21.4 Categories and Uses for UTP and STP Cabling

Category	Network Type(s) Supported	Supported Speeds	Notes
1	Telephone, DSL, Home PNA	Up to 100Mbps (HomePNA)	
2	LocalTalk	Up to 4Mbps	Obsolete

Table 21.4 (continued)

Category	Network Type(s) Supported	Supported Speeds	Notes
3	10BaseT Ethernet	Up to 10Mbps	Replace with Category 5 or greater
4	Token ring	Up to 16Mbps	Shielded twisted pair (STP)
5	10BaseT, 100BaseT, 1000BaseT	Up to 1,000Mbps	
5e	10BaseT, 100BaseT, 1000BaseT	Up to 1,000Mbps	Enhanced version of Category 5
6	10BaseT, 100BaseT, 1000BaseT	Up to 1,000Mbps	Handles higher frequencies than Category 5
7	10BaseT, 100BaseT, 1000BaseT	Up to 1,000Mbps	Uses 12-connector GG45 connector (backward compatible with RJ-45)

Figure 21.8 compares Ethernet cards using UTP, thin coaxial, and thick coaxial cables and connectors to each other.

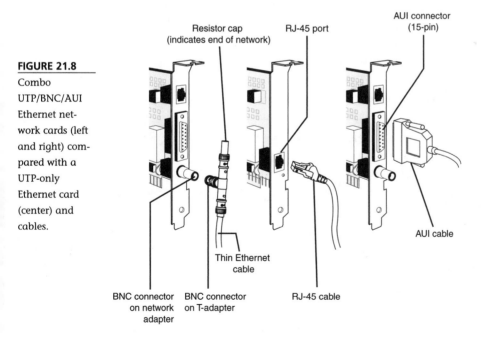

FIGURE 21.8

Combo UTP/BNC/AUI Ethernet network cards (left and right) compared with a UTP-only Ethernet card (center) and cables.

The connector used by Ethernet cards that use UTP is called an RJ-45 connector, and it resembles a larger version of the RJ-11 connector used for telephone cabling. UTP cabling runs between a computer on the network and the hub, which routes signals to other computers (servers or workstations) on the network. It can be purchased in prebuilt form or as bulk cable with connectors, so you can build the cable to the length you need.

⇨ Hubs connect different computers with each other on the network. **See** "Switches and Hubs," **p. 789**, for more information.

To attach UTP cable to a network card or other device, plug it into the connector so that the plastic locking clip snaps into place; the cable and connector will fit together only one way. Squeeze the locking clip toward the RJ45 connector and pull the connector out of the RJ45 jack if you need to remove the cable. Some cables use a snagless connector; squeeze the guard over the locking clip to open the clip to remove the cable.

UTP cable can be purchased in prebuilt assemblies or can be built from bulk cable and connectors.

Fiber Optic

Fiber-optic cabling transmits signals with light rather than with electrical signals, which makes it immune to electrical interference. It is used primarily as a backbone between networks. Fiber-optic cable comes in two major types:

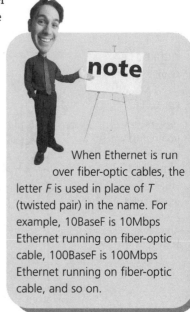

note

- **Single-mode**—Has a thin core designed to carry a single light ray long distances.

- **Multi-mode**—Has a thicker core than single-mode; carries multiple light rays for short distances.

Fiber-optic cabling can be purchased prebuilt, but if you need a custom length, it should be built and installed by experienced cable installers because of the expense and risk of damage. Some network adapters built for servers are designed to use fiber-optic cable. Otherwise, media converters are used to interconnect fiber optic to conventional cables on networks.

When Ethernet is run over fiber-optic cables, the letter *F* is used in place of *T* (twisted pair) in the name. For example, 10BaseF is 10Mbps Ethernet running on fiber-optic cable, 100BaseF is 100Mbps Ethernet running on fiber-optic cable, and so on.

Coaxial

Coaxial cabling is the oldest type of network cabling; its data wires are surrounded by a wire mesh for insulation. Coaxial cables, which resemble cable TV connections, are not popular for network use today because they must be run from one station directly to another rather than to or from a hub/switch.

Coaxial cabling creates a bus topology; each end of the bus must be terminated, and if any part of the bus fails, the entire network fails.

The oldest Ethernet standard, 10Base5, uses a very thick coaxial cable (RG-8) that is attached to a NIC through a transceiver that uses a so-called "vampire tap" to connect the transceiver to the cable. This type of coaxial cable is also referred to as Thick Ethernet or Thicknet.

Thin Ethernet, also referred to as Thinnet, Cheapernet, or 10Base2 Ethernet was used for low-cost Ethernet networks before the advent of UTP cable. The coaxial cable used with 10Base2 is referred to as RG-58. This type of coaxial cable connects to network cards through a T-connector that bayonet-mounts to the rear of the network card using a BNC connector. The arms of the T are used to connect two cables, each running to another computer in the network.

If the workstation is at the end of a network, a terminating resistor is connected to one arm of the T to indicate the end of the network (refer to Figure 21.8). If a resistor is removed, the network fails; if a station on the network fails, the network fails.

Two other types of coaxial cable are common in cable Internet, satellite Internet, and fixed wireless Internet installations:

- *RG-59*—Used in older cable TV or satellite TV installations; 75-ohm resistance. Also used by the long-obsolete Arcnet LAN standard.
- *RG-6*—Uses same connectors as RG-59, but has a larger diameter with superior shielding; used in cable TV/Internet, satellite TV/Internet, and fixed wireless Internet/TV service; 75-ohm resistance.

Plenum and PVC

The outer jacket of UTP, STP, and coaxial cable is usually made of PVC (polyvinyl chloride), a low-cost durable vinyl compound. Unfortunately, PVC creates dense poisonous smoke when burned. If you need to run network cable through suspended ceiling or air vents, you should use more-expensive **plenum** cable, which produces less smoke and a lower level of toxic chemicals when burned.

Connector Types

Most coaxial cables, including RG-58, RG-59, and RG-6 use a **BNC** (Bayonet Neill-Concelman) connector. RG-58 uses a T-adapter to connect to a 10Base2 Ethernet adapter. RG-11 (Thicknet) cable is connected to an Ethernet card by means of an external transceiver, which attaches to the AUI port on the rear of older Ethernet network cards. The transceiver attaches to the cable with a so-called "vampire tap."

10BaseT, 100BaseT, and 1000BaseT Ethernet cards using copper wire all use the **RJ-45** connector shown in Figure 21.8, as do newer token-ring and all ISDN and cable Internet devices.

DSL devices often use the **RJ-11** connector shown in Figure 21.3, as do dial-up modems.

Older token-ring cards use the 9-pin DB-9 Type 1 STP cable; the cable has a male connector and the card has a female connector.

Installing Network Interface Cards

Although many recent computers include a 10/100 Ethernet port or a Wireless Ethernet adapter, you often need to install a network interface card (NIC) into a computer you want to add to a network.

ISA/PCI

To install a Plug and Play (PnP) network card (all PCI cards support PnP, and some ISA cards do as well), follow this procedure:

1. Turn off the computer and remove the case cover.
2. Locate an available PCI expansion slot.
3. Remove the slot cover and insert the card into the slot. Secure the card in the slot.
4. Restart the system and provide the driver disk or CD-ROM when requested by the system.
5. Insert the operating system CD-ROM when requested to install network drivers and clients; you might need to swap the network card driver CD-ROM back into the drive to finish the installation.
6. The IRQ, I/O port address, and memory address required by the card will be assigned automatically.

If you need to install a non-PnP (legacy) network card, see Chapter 18, "Using and Optimizing Windows," for the general process.

USB

Although USB network adapters are also PnP devices, you normally need to install the drivers provided with the USB network adapter before you attach the adapter to your computer. After the driver software is installed, the device will be recognized as soon as you plug it into a working USB port.

Most USB network adapters are bus powered. For best results, they should be attached to a USB port built into your computer or to a self-powered hub. Some adapters support USB 2.0, which provides full-speed support for 100BaseT (Fast Ethernet) signal speeds.

> **note**
>
> You will need to use the operating system CD-ROM to install network drivers and clients when you install any type of network card.

PC Card/CardBus

PC Card network adapters work with both the original 16-bit PC Card slot and the newer 32-bit CardBus slot. However, CardBus cards work only in CardBus slots.

Both PC Card and CardBus cards are detected and installed by built-in support for these adapters in Windows 95 and newer versions. However, Windows NT 4.0 requires that Card and Socket Services compatible with Windows NT 4.0 and with the card(s) you want to install be present if you want to hot-swap the network adapter with another card. If you don't, you can use the enabler software provided by the card vendor.

> **note**
>
> If you are using a wireless USB adapter, you can improve signal strength by using an extension cable between the adapter and the USB port on the computer.

Some PC Card and CardBus network adapters often require that a dongle be attached to the card to enable the card to plug into a network port. See Chapter 12, "Portables," for details.

Configuring Network Interface Cards

Although PCI, USB, PC Card, and CardBus network adapters as well as integrated adapters support PnP configuration for hardware resources, non-PnP ISA adapters require manual resource configuration. You might also need to configure the network adapter for the type of media it uses, for the speed of the connection and, with Wireless Ethernet adapters, the security settings that might be needed to connect with the access point.

Hardware Resources

Typical network interface card hardware resource settings include

- IRQ
- I/O port address range

If the workstation is a diskless workstation, a free upper memory address must also be supplied for the boot ROM on the card. A few older network cards also use upper memory blocks for RAM buffers; check the card's documentation.

Media Type

Most recent Ethernet cards are designed to use only UTP Category 3 or greater network cabling. However, some older cards were also designed to use 10Base5 (Thicknet) or 10Base2 (Thinnet) cabling. Cards that are designed to use two or more different types of cabling are known as combo cards, and during card configuration, you need to select the type of media that will be used with the card. This option is also known as the **Transceiver Type** option. Depending upon the card's drivers, you might need to make this setting through the card's command-line configuration program or the card's properties sheet in the Windows Device Manager.

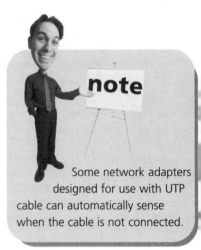

Some network adapters designed for use with UTP cable can automatically sense when the cable is not connected.

Full/Half-Duplex

If the hardware in use on an Ethernet, Fast Ethernet , or Gigabit Ethernet network permits, you can configure the network to run in full-duplex mode. **Full-duplex** mode enables the adapter to send and receive data at the same time, which doubles network speed over the default **half-duplex** mode (where the card sends and receives in separate operations). Thus, a 10BaseT-based network runs at 20Mbps in full-duplex mode; a 100BaseT-based network runs at 200Mbps in full-duplex mode; and a 1000BaseT-based network runs at 2,000Mbps in full-duplex mode.

To achieve full-duplex performance on a UTP-based Ethernet network, the network adapters on a network must all support full-duplex mode, be configured to use full-duplex mode with the device's setup program or properties sheet, *and* a switch must be used in place of a hub.

Wireless Ethernet Configuration

Wireless Ethernet requires additional configuration compared to wired Ethernet, as shown in Table 21.5.

Table 21.5   Wireless Ethernet Configuration Settings

Setting	What the Setting Does
Service Set Identifier (**SSID**)	Names the network. Windows XP can detect SSIDs from unsecured networks.
Channel	Specifies a channel for all stations to use.
Wireless Equivalent Privacy (**WEP**)	Enable to prevent access by unauthorized users. If WEP is disabled (the default with most hardware), anybody can get on the network if they know the SSID.
WEP Encryption Strength	Use the highest setting supported by both WEP and adapters for best security. Small-office home-office hardware might use 64-bit; business-market hardware often uses 128-bit encryption.
WEP Key	Use 10 alphanumeric characters for 64-bit encryption; use 26 characters for 128-bit encryption.
Wi-Fi Protected Access (**WPA**)	An improved security option that replaces WEP in newer hardware. It should be enabled only if all equipment on the network supports WPA. A firmware upgrade might be necessary.

Switches and Hubs

Hubs connect different computers with each other on an Ethernet network based on UTP cabling. A hub has several connectors for RJ-45 cabling, a power source, and signal lights to indicate network activity. Most hubs are stackable, meaning that if you need more ports than the hub contains, you can connect it to another hub to expand its capabilities.

A **hub** is the slowest connection device on a network because it splits the bandwidth of the connection among all the computers connected to it. For example, a five-port 10/100 Ethernet hub divides the 100Mbps speed of Fast Ethernet among the five ports, providing only 20Mbps of bandwidth to each port for Fast Ethernet and 10/100 adapters, and only 2Mbps per port for 10BaseT adapters. A hub also broadcasts data to all computers connected to it.

A **switch** resembles a hub but creates a dedicated full-speed connection between the two computers that are communicating with each other. A five-port 10/100 switch, for example, provides the full 10Mbps bandwidth to each port connected to a 10BaseT card and a full 100Mbps bandwidth to each port connected to a Fast Ethernet or 10/100 card. If the network adapters are configured to run in full-duplex mode, the Fast Ethernet bandwidth on the network is doubled to 200Mbps, and the 10BaseT bandwidth is doubled to 20Mbps. Switches can be daisy-chained in a manner similar to stackable hubs, and there is no limit to the number of switches possible in a network.

> **caution**
>
> If you buy Wi-Fi/ Wireless Ethernet adapters and access points from the same vendor, it might work straight out of the box without adjusting these settings. However, the network will be unsecure, enabling anyone with a compatible Wireless Ethernet card to access the network and compromise its contents. For security, enable security settings and upgrade the hardware to support WPA if possible.

Beyond LANs—Repeaters, Bridges, and Routers

Hubs and switches are the only connectivity equipment needed for a workgroup LAN. However, if the network needs to span longer distances than those supported by the network cabling in use or needs to connect to another network, additional connectivity equipment is needed.

- **Repeater**—A repeater boosts signal strength to enable longer cable runs than those permitted by the "official" cabling limits of Ethernet. Hubs and switches can be used as repeaters.

- **Bridge**—A bridge connects two networks that use the same protocol to each other. For example, a Wireless Ethernet network can be connected to a wired Ethernet network with a bridge.

> **note**
>
> Windows XP features built-in bridging capabilities.

- **Router**—A router is used to interconnect a LAN to other networks; the name suggests the device's similarity to an efficient travel agent, who helps a group reach its destination as quickly as possible. Routers can connect different types of networks and protocols to each other (Ethernet, token ring, TCP/IP, and so on) and are a vital part of the Internet. Router features and prices vary according to the network types and protocols supported.

Networking Configuration

Before a network connection can function, it must be properly configured. The following sections discuss the configurations required for the network protocols covered on the A+ Certification Exams: TCP/IP, IPX/SPX, AppleTalk, and NetBEUI.

Installing Network Protocols in Windows

Depending upon the network protocol you want to install and the version of Windows in use on a particular computer, you can install any of several different protocols through the normal Windows network dialogs, as shown in Table 21.6.

Table 21.6 Windows Support for Network Protocols

	Windows Version				
Network Protocol	NT 4.0	9x	Me	2000	XP
IPX/SPX	Yes	Yes	Yes	Yes	Yes
TCP/IP	Yes	Yes	Yes	Yes	Yes
NetBEUI	Yes	Yes	Yes	Yes	1
AppleTalk	Yes	2	2	Yes	No

[1]Not officially supported in Windows XP, but can be installed manually from the Windows XP CD-ROM's Valueadd\MSFT\Net\NetBEUI folder. See Microsoft Knowledge Base article 301041 for details.

[2]Requires third-party software such as PC MACLAN from Miramar Systems (www.miramar.com).

To install a network protocol in Windows NT 4.0, follow this procedure:

1. Open the Network icon in Control Panel or right-click on Network Neighborhood and select Properties.

2. Click the Protocols tab.

3. Click the Add button.

4. Select the **protocol** you want to add.

5. Click OK.

To install a network protocol in Windows 9x/Me, follow this procedure:

1. Open the Network icon in Control Panel or right-click on Network Neighborhood (My Network Places-Me) and select Properties.
2. Click the Add button.
3. Select Protocol and click Add.
4. Select the protocol you want to add.
5. Click OK.

To install a network protocol in Windows 2000/XP, follow this procedure:

1. Open the Network (Network Connections-XP) icon in Control Panel or right-click on My Network Places and select Properties.
2. Right-click the connection you want to modify and select Properties.
3. Click the Install button.
4. Click Protocol.
5. Select the protocol you want to add.
6. Click OK.

After the protocol is installed, select the protocol and click Properties to adjust its properties setting.

TCP/IP Configuration

The TCP/IP protocol, although it was originally used for Internet connectivity, is now the most important network protocol for LAN as well as larger networks. To connect with the rest of a TCP/IP-based network, each computer or other device must have a unique IP address. If the network connects with the Internet, additional settings are required.

There are two ways to configure a computer's TCP/IP settings:

- **Server-assigned IP address**
- **Static IP address**

Table 21.7 compares the differences in these configurations.

note

Routers, wireless gateways, and computers that host an Internet connection shared with Windows's Internet Connection Sharing or a third-party sharing program all provide DHCP services to other computers on the network.

Table 21.7   Static Versus Server-Assigned IP Addressing

Setting	What It Does	Static IP Address	Server-Assigned IP
IP address	Identifies computer on the network	Unique value for each computer	Automatically assigned by DHCP server
DNS configuration	Identifies domain name system servers	IP addresses of one or more DNS servers, host name, and domain name must be entered	Automatically assigned by server
Gateway	Identifies IP address of device that connects computer to Internet	IP address for gateway must be entered; same value for all computers on network	Automatically assigned by server
WINS configuration	Maps IP addresses to NetBIOS computer names; used with Windows NT 4.0 and earlier versions	IP addresses for one or more WINS servers must be entered if enabled	Can use DHCP to resolve WINS if necessary

All versions of Windows default to using a server-assigned IP address. As Table 21.7 makes clear, this is the preferable method for configuring a TCP/IP network. Use a manually assigned IP address only if a Dynamic Host Configuration Protocol (**DHCP**) server (which provides IP addresses automatically) is not available on the network.

Figure 21.9 shows the tabs used to configure TCP/IP settings in Windows 9x/Me.

Windows NT 4.0's TCP/IP interface is similar to Windows 9x/Me's, but puts the IP address and gateway setting on the IP Address tab and uses an Advanced button from that tab to add gateways.

Windows 2000 and XP's TCP/IP configuration features a General tab used for IP addressing and DNS servers. An Advanced button displays a multi-tabbed dialog for adding gateways, DNS server addresses, adjusting WINS resolution, and adjusting TCP/IP port filtering.

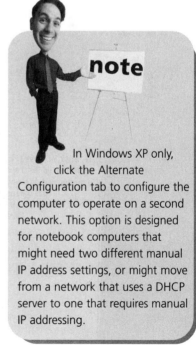

note

In Windows XP only, click the Alternate Configuration tab to configure the computer to operate on a second network. This option is designed for notebook computers that might need two different manual IP address settings, or might move from a network that uses a DHCP server to one that requires manual IP addressing.

FIGURE 21.9

Typical TCP/IP configuration screens for systems when static (user-assigned) IP addresses are in use.

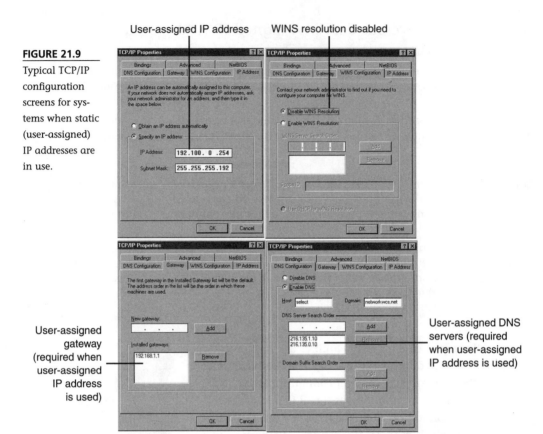

User-assigned IP address

WINS resolution disabled

User-assigned gateway (required when user-assigned IP address is used)

User-assigned DNS servers (required when user-assigned IP address is used)

IP Address

Where you set the IP address varies with the connection type. If you are using a modem with dial-up networking with versions of Windows prior to Windows 2000 and XP, you adjust the IP address on the properties sheet for the connection (see Figure 21.10). For a connection made on a LAN, you change the IP address and other settings with the Networks icon in the Windows Control Panel using the properties sheet for the network adapter (see Figure 21.11).

note

Windows XP uses a unified Network Connections folder and Windows 2000 uses a Network and Dial-Up Connections folder for all types of Internet connections.

FIGURE 21.10

Click the Server Types tab, and select TCP/IP Configuration in the properties sheet for your Dial-Up Networking connection (left) to view or change the IP address (right) with Windows 9x/Me.

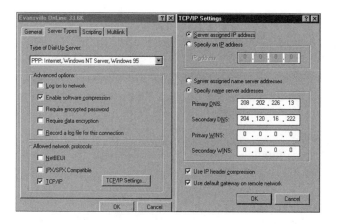

FIGURE 21.11

Select the TCP/IP -> (network card) icon in the Windows Network components list to view or change TCP/IP settings used for your LAN-based Internet connection with Windows 9x/Me.

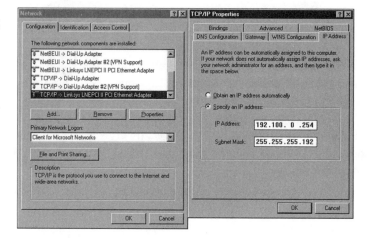

IP addresses use four groups of numbers that range from 0 to 255. The subnet mask is used along with the IP address for routing. Both computers and other networked devices, such as routers and network printers, can have IP addresses, and some devices can have more than one IP address. For example, a router has two IP addresses—one to connect the router to a LAN, and the other that connects it to the Internet, enabling it to route traffic from the LAN to the Internet and back.

WINS Configuration

Windows Internet Naming Service (**WINS**) matches the NetBIOS name of a particular computer to an IP address on the network; this process is also called *resolving* or *translating* the NetBIOS name to an IP address. WINS requires the use of a Window

Server that has been set up to provide the resolving service. If WINS is enabled, the IP addresses of the WINS servers must be entered.

If the IP address is provided by a DHCP server, or if a WINS server is used, you will need to enter the correct WINS settings (refer to Figure 21.9).

The network administrator will inform you of the correct settings to use on this tab.

Gateway

A **gateway** is a computer or device (such as a router) that provides a connection between a LAN and a wide area network (WAN) or the Internet. Computers that use a LAN connection to connect to the Internet need to enter the IP address or addresses of the gateways on this tab (refer to Figure 21.9) if the computer doesn't use DHCP to obtain an IP address.

DNS Configuration

The Internet uses the domain name system (DNS) to map domain names, such as www.microsoft.com, to their corresponding IP address or addresses. A computer using the Internet must use at least one DNS server to provide this translation service. Use the DNS Configuration tab to set up the computer's host name, domain name, and DNS servers (refer to Figure 21.9) if the computer doesn't use DHCP to obtain an IP address.

After you have configured these settings, click OK and reboot the computer if directed to do so.

note

Most ISPs and networks have at least two DNS name servers to provide backup in case one fails. Be sure to enter the IP addresses of all DNS servers available to your network.

IPX/SPX Configuration

Although recent versions of Novell NetWare support TCP/IP as the native network protocol, older versions of Novell NetWare used IPX/SPX, also known as NWLink, as the native network protocol.

You can generally leave this protocol at its default settings. However, if you need to adjust options, you can change the network address (also known as the internal network number; must be unique to each computer) and select the frame type.

AppleTalk Configuration

Windows NT 4.0 and Windows 2000 support printing to AppleTalk printers when the AppleTalk protocol is installed. Select the printer through the Printers dialog as a

local printer. Select AppleTalk Printing Devices as the
port type and select the printer from the list of printers displayed.

NetBEUI Configuration

The only configuration required for a NetBEUI network is that each computer has a unique name
and that all computers in a particular workgroup
use the same workgroup name. To set or change
the computer and workgroup names, use the
Identification tab on the Network properties sheet
in Windows NT 4.0/9x/Me, the Network
Identification tab on the System properties sheet in
Windows 2000, or the Computer Name tab on the
System properties sheet in Windows XP.

note

Windows NT Server and
Windows 2000 Server can
be configured to provide network
services to an AppleTalk network
by installing Services for Macintosh
(SFM). Windows Server 2003 does
not support AppleTalk.

Setting Up Shared Resources

Sharing resources with other network users
requires the following steps:

1. Installing File and Printer sharing
2. Selecting which drives, folders, or printers
   to share
3. Setting permissions on Windows NT
   4.0/2000/XP

The following sections cover performing these
processes manually. With Windows Me and
Windows XP, the Network Setup Wizard can also
perform these steps for you.

caution

Windows Me and
Windows XP have
Network Setup
Wizards, which are
designed to automate
various parts of the network setup
process. Do *not* use these wizards
if you have already configured network settings because the wizards
might undo your changes.

Installing File and Printer Sharing

All versions of Windows covered on the A+
Certification Operating Systems Exam support **file and printer sharing**. File and
printer sharing is installed through the network properties sheet. For Windows 2000
and XP, follow this procedure:

1. Open the properties sheet as described in "Installing Network Protocols in
   Windows," **p. 791**.

2. Click the Install button.

3. Click the Service icon.

4. Click the Add button.

5. Select File and Printer Sharing for Microsoft Networks and click OK.

6. Restart the computer.

For Windows 9x/Me, follow this procedure:

1. Open the properties sheet as described earlier in "Installing Network Protocols in Windows."

2. Click File and Printer Sharing.

3. To share files, click the box next to I Want to Be Able to Give Others Access to My Files. To share printers, click the box next to I Want to Be Able to Allow Others to Print to My Printer(s).

4. Click OK on all open dialogs and restart the computer when prompted.

note

Windows XP uses permissions only on NTFS-formatted drives and only if simple file sharing is disabled.

Shared Folders and Drives

A **shared folder** or drive can be accessed by other computers on the network. On a peer network, each shared folder or drive can be password protected with a different password for each share. Separate passwords can be used to provide full access or read-only access for each resource—to control access levels, you would give some users the read-only password, other users the full-access password, and some users might not receive either password. To use a shared resource, users must log on to the network, and then provide the appropriate password for each shared resource they want to use.

note

Windows NT 4.0 automatically provides file and printer sharing through its Server option on the Bindings tab of the network properties sheet.

On a server-based network, shares are protected by lists of users or groups. Only members who belong to a specific group or are listed separately on the access list for a particular share can access that share. After users log on to the network, they have access to all shares they've been authorized to use without the need to provide additional passwords. Access levels include full and read-only and, on NTFS drives, other access levels, such as write, create, and delete. Windows NT 4.0/2000/XP (when not using **simple file sharing**) also support user and group access control.

To share a folder or drive in Windows XP with simple file sharing enabled

1. Right-click the folder or drive and select Sharing and Security.

2. If you right-click a drive, Windows XP displays a warning. Click the link to continue.

3. Click the box Share This Folder on the Network to share the folder in read-only mode. To share the folder in read/write mode, click the box Allow Network Users to Change My Files. Click OK.

To share a folder or drive in Windows 2000/XP (with simple file sharing disabled)

1. Right-click the folder or drive and select Sharing.

2. Click Share This Folder and specify a sharename. (The default sharename is the name of the drive or folder.) Add a comment if desired.

3. Specify the number of users or use the default (10).

4. Click Permissions to set folder permissions by user or group. See Chapter 18 for details.

5. Click Caching to specify whether files will be cached on other computers' drives and how they will be cached.

6. Click OK.

To share a folder or drive in Windows 9x/Me

1. Right-click the drive or folder you want to share and select Sharing.

2. Click Shared As and specify a sharename. (The default sharename is the name of the drive or folder.) Add a comment if desired.

3. Select the access type. (Read-Only is the default.) You can also select Full (allows changes) or Depends on Password.

4. Supply Read-Only and Full Access passwords. Click OK.

Figure 21.12 compares the Windows 2000 and Windows XP (simple file sharing) and Windows 9x/Me share dialogs. Windows NT 4.0 doesn't support caching, but uses an interface similar to Windows 2000.

Controls access type

Enables sharing

Enables sharing

Share name

Share name

Enables sharing

FIGURE 21.12

The Windows 2000 (left), Windows XP simple file sharing (center), and Windows 9x/Me's Sharing dialogs.

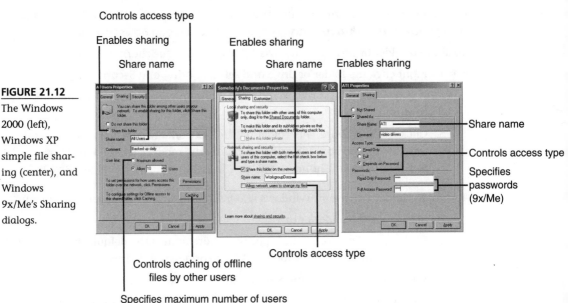

Share name

Controls access type

Specifies passwords (9x/Me)

Controls access type

Controls caching of offline files by other users

Specifies maximum number of users

Shared Printers

Access control for shared printers on both peer- and server-based networks is similar to access control for drives and folders. The following are the differences:

- Only a single level of access (and a single password) are supported on peer networks (Windows 9x/Me).
- Windows NT 4.0/2000/XP can distribute printer drivers for other versions of Windows when clients log on to the server and want to use its shared printers.

To set up a printer as a shared printer

1. Open the Printers or Printers and Faxes folder.
2. Right-click a printer and select Sharing.
3. Select Shared As (9x/Me) or Share This Printer (NT 4.0/2000/XP) and specify a sharename. With Windows 9x/Me only, you can also specify a comment.
4. Specify a password if desired (9x/Me only). Click OK.

With Windows NT 4.0/2000/XP, click Additional Drivers to select additional drivers to install for other operating systems that will use the printer on the network.

Setting Permissions

You can specify file and folder permissions with Windows NT 4.0 and 2000 (and with Windows XP if simple file sharing has been disabled).

➔ **See** "File Permissions," **p. 660**, for details.

Setting Up the Network Client

The client in both peer-to-peer networks and dedicated server networks is a computer that uses shared resources. To access shared resources, a client computer needs

- Network client software
- The name of the network and server(s) with shared resources
- The correct password(s) to access shared resources that use passwords
- The printer drivers for the network printers

With Windows, the Network or Network Connections icon in the Control Panel is used to install network client software and to indicate the name of the network.

Network Neighborhood (Windows NT 4.0/9x/Me) or My Network Places (Windows XP/2000) is used to locate shared resources and to provide passwords. The Printers icon is used to set up access to a network printer.

Installing Network Client Software

Windows NT 4.0/2000/XP incorporate **network client** software for Microsoft Networks.

If you need to install additional network clients, such as for NetWare, in Windows 2000/XP, follow this procedure:

1. Open the Network (Network Connections-XP) icon in Control Panel or right-click on My Network Places and select Properties.
2. Right-click the connection you want to modify and select Properties.
3. Click the Install button.
4. Click the Client icon.
5. Select the client you want to add.
6. Click OK.

To install a network client in Windows 9x/Me, follow this procedure:

1. Open the Network icon in Control Panel or right-click on Network Neighborhood (My Network Places-Me) and select Properties.

2. Click the Add button.

3. Select the Client icon and click the Add button.

4. Select the client you want to add.

5. Click OK.

Installing a Network Printer

Follow this procedure to install a network printer:

note

With Windows NT 4.0, follow the vendor's instructions for installing third-party clients.

1. Open the Printers or Printers and Faxes folder.

2. Click Add Printer or Add a Printer.

3. Click Next (Windows 2000/XP); then select Network Printer.

4. You can browse for the printer on a workgroup network, use Active Directory to search for a printer on a domain-based network, or enter its name (*server**printername*). With Windows XP and 2000, you can also specify the printer's URL. With Windows 9x/Me, specify if the printer will be used with MS-DOS programs. Click Next.

5. After the printer is selected, specify whether you want the new printer as the default printer. Click Next.

6. Specify if you want to print a test page.

7. Click Finish to complete the setup process. Provide the Windows CD or printer setup disk if required to complete the process.

Using Shared Resources

With any type of network, the user must log on with a correct username and password to use any network resources. With a dedicated server, such as Novell or Windows NT/2000/Server 2003, a single username and password is needed for any network resource the user has permission to use.

On a peer-to-peer network, such as a Windows 9x/Me network, additional passwords might be required for each of your resources. On a dedicated server network, such as Novell NetWare or Windows NT/2000/Server 2003, a single password provides a specified user with access to all the shared resources that a particular user is permitted to use. This is called user-level security. A Windows 9x/Me peer server connected to a dedicated server can also use the dedicated server's list of users to control access.

User-level security controls a wider range of activities on a system than does share-level security.

A peer server used on Windows 9x/Me uses a username and password for initial access, and can also use a separate password for each shared resource. This is called share-level security and is harder to maintain. A peer server has three security levels:

- No access (if incorrect password is provided)
- **Read-only access** (can be password protected or left open to all)
- **Full access** (can be password protected or left open to all)

Information can be copied from a shared drive or folder if the user has read-only access; to add, change, or delete information on the shared drive or folder, the user needs full access.

Network printing is performed the same way as local printing after the network printer driver software has been set up on the workstation.

You can identify shared resources with Windows by using Explorer or My Computer. On a system that is sharing resources with other users, a shared drive, folder, or printer will use a modified icon with a hand, indicating that it is being shared (see Figure 21.13).

FIGURE 21.13

The Windows 9x Explorer (left) and Printers folder (right) display shared and nonshared resources. The hand icon indicates which drives and printers are shared with other computers.

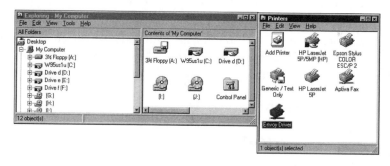

To use a shared resource on a peer server that uses share-level security, the user must provide the correct password for any password-protected share. To use a shared resource on a network that uses dedicated servers with user-level security, the user must log on to the network. The administrator of the server or network has already assigned access levels and permissions to each user or group, so the user can immediately begin using shared resources as permitted.

Shared drives and folders can be referred to by a mapped drive letter, a Universal Naming Convention (UNC) name, or a fully qualified domain name (FQDN). Each of these is explained in the following sections.

Mapped Drives

Windows enables shared folders and shared drives to be mapped to drive letters on clients. In the Windows Explorer/My Computer, these mapped drive letters will show up in the list along with the local drive letters. A shared resource can be accessed either through Network Neighborhood (using the sharename) or through a **mapped drive** letter.

Drive mapping has the following benefits:

- A shared folder mapped as a drive can be referred to by the drive name instead of a long Universal Naming Convention path (see "The Universal Naming Convention [UNC]" later in this chapter for details).

- Shared folders can be accessed by MS-DOS programs only if drive mappings are used.

To map a shared folder to a drive with Windows Explorer, follow this procedure:

1. Right-click the shared folder in the Windows Explorer and select Map Network Drive.

2. Select a drive letter from the list of available drive letters; only drive letters not used by local drives are listed. Drive letters already in use for other shared folders display the UNC name of the shared folder (see Figure 21.14).

FIGURE 21.14

The Map Network Drive menu lists already-mapped folders and drive letters that are still available.

3. Click the Reconnect at Login box (not shown) if you want to use the mapped drive every time you connect to the network. This option should be used only if the server will be available at all times; otherwise, the client will receive error messages when it tries to access the shared resource.

Shared folders can be accessed by either their mapped drive letters or by their folder names in Windows Explorer.

The Universal Naming Convention (UNC)

The Universal Naming Convention (**UNC**) is designed to enable users to access network resources without mapping drive letters to network drives or specifying the type of device that stores the file or hosts the printer. A UNC name has the following structure in Windows:

`\\servername\sharename\path\filename`

A typical UNC path to a document would resemble

`\\Aopen\0\NetDocuments\this_doc.doc`

What does this mean in plain English?

- `\\Aopen` is the server.
- `\0` is the sharename.
- `\NetDocuments` is the path.
- `\this_doc.doc` is the document.

UNC enables files and printers to be accessed by the user with Windows applications. Windows 3.x and MS-DOS users must map drive letters to shared folders to access files and must map printer ports to shared printers to print. Because only 23 drive letters (maximum) can be mapped, UNC enables network resources beyond the D–Z limits to still be accessed.

Some Windows applications will display the UNC path to a file even if the file was accessed through a mapped drive letter, and other Windows applications will refer to the UNC path or mapped drive letter path to the file, depending on how the file was retrieved.

Fully Qualified Domain Names (FQDNs)

TCP/IP networks that contain DNS servers often use FQDNs to refer to servers along with, or in place of, UNC names. The structure of an **FQDN** is

`Name-of-server.name-of-domain.root-domain`

For example, a server called "charley" in the selectsystems.com domain would have an FQDN of

`charley.selectsystems.com`

If you want to access the shared `Docs` folder on `charley.selectsystems.com`, you would refer to it as

`\\charley.selectsystems.com\Docs`

You can also use the IP address of the server in place of the servername. If 192.10.8.22 is the IP address of charley.selectsystems.com, you can access the `Docs` folder with the following statement:

`\\192.10.8.22\Docs`

You can use either UNCs or FQDN along with the Net command-line utility to view or map drive letters to shared folders.

Browser Installation and Configuration

A **Web browser**, such as Microsoft Internet Explorer and Netscape Navigator, is the main interface through which you navigate the Internet. Internet Explorer is a standard component of all versions of Windows covered by the A+ Certification Operating Systems Exam. Updates and newer versions can be downloaded manually from the Microsoft Web site with Windows NT 4.095; with Windows 98/2000/Me/XP, you can also get updates and upgrades through Windows Update. Other browsers can be downloaded in compressed form and installed manually.

Depending on how you connect with the Internet, you might need to adjust the browser configuration.

Typical options you might need to change include

- *Proxies for use with LAN-based or filtered access*—Users who access the Internet through a local area network might be doing so through a proxy server. A **proxy server** receives a copy of the Web site or content the user wants to look at and checks it for viruses or unapproved content before passing it on. The proxy server information is set through the browser's configuration menu.

- *Automatic dial up for convenience*—Internet Explorer and most other browsers can also be set to dial up the Internet automatically whenever you start the browser to make Internet access easier. This option is very useful for dial-up connections but should not be used for connections made through a LAN.

- *Email configuration*—Most browsers include an email client; the settings for the email server and other options must be made to allow email to be seen and replied to within the browser.

- *Disable graphics*—Users with extremely slow connections who view primarily text-based pages can disable graphics for extra speed.

■ *Security settings for Java*—Advanced features, such as Java and ActiveX, make sites more interactive, but might also pose a security risk; these features can be limited or disabled through the Security menu.

You can also adjust default colors and fonts and the default start page.

Generally, you should use all the features possible of the browser unless you have speed or security concerns that lead you to disable some features.

Setting Up Your Browser to Use Your Internet Connection

In most cases, users will want the Internet to be available as soon as they open their Web browser. Because some users have dial-up connections and some networks use proxy servers to provide firewall protection or content filtering, you might need to adjust the browser configuration to permit Internet access.

To view or adjust the browser configuration for Internet Explorer, follow this procedure:

1. Open Internet Explorer.
2. Click Tools, Internet Options.
3. Click the Connections tab.
4. If the Internet connection uses a dial-up modem, select the correct dial-up connection from those listed and choose Always Dial (to start the connection when the browser is opened) or Dial Whenever a Network Connection Is Not Present. Click Set Default to make the selected connection the default.
5. If the Internet connection uses a network, click Never Dial a Connection, and click LAN Settings to check network configuration.
6. Ask the network administrator if you should use Automatically Detect Settings or whether you should specify a particular automatic configuration script.
7. If a proxy server is used for Internet access, it must be specified by server-name and port number. If different servers and port numbers are used for different TCP/IP protocols, such as HTTP, FTP, and others, click Advanced and specify the correct server and port number to use (see Figure 21.15).
8. Click OK to save changes at each menu level until you return to the browser display.

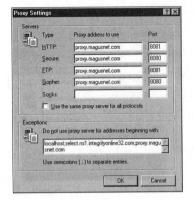

FIGURE 21.15

You can specify different proxy servers, ports, and which servers can be accessed directly by using the Advanced option for proxy server settings.

Enabling/Disabling Script Settings

Some networks use a separate configuration or logon script for Internet access. To specify a script with Internet Explorer, click Tools, Internet Options, Connections, LAN Settings, and Use Automatic Configuration Script. Enter the URL or filename of the script and click OK.

Configuring Browser Security Settings

You can configure Internet Explorer's default security settings for **Java**, **ActiveX**, and other potentially harmful content through the Internet Options' Security tab. Open the **Internet Options** tab with Control Panel, or click Tools, Settings, Internet Options within Internet Explorer.

> **tip**
>
> You can also configure Internet Explorer to automatically detect the settings if your network is configured to provide them. However, if you enable this option and the network is not configured to provide them, Internet Explorer will not be able to connect to the Internet.

There are four default security settings: High, Medium, Medium-Low, and Low. High blocks almost all active content and prevents Web sites from setting cookies (small text files that can track Web site usage). Medium (the default) enables some active content but blocks unsigned ActiveX controls. Medium-low blocks unsafe content but downloads other content without prompts, and low has no safeguards.

Each setting is matched to a **Web content zone**. By default, all sites not in other zones are placed in the Internet zone, which uses Medium security. The local Intranet zone also uses Medium security. Trusted sites use Low security by default; restricted sites use High security by default.

To add or remove sites on the local Intranet, Trusted, or Restricted site list, select the zone and click Sites.

By default, local Intranet sites include all local sites, all sites that don't use a proxy server, and all UNC network paths. Remove check marks to restrict these options. Click Advanced to add or remove a specific site or to require a secured server. Trusted or Restricted sites display the Add/Remove dialog box immediately.

Enabling/Disabling Windows XP Firewall

Windows XP contains a built-in **firewall** designed to prevent unauthorized inbound access to a computer. To enable the firewall for a particular connection, right-click the connection in the Network Connections display, select Properties, and click Advanced. Click the box next to Protect My Computer...to enable the firewall. Click OK to finish.

note

Click Custom from the main Security tab to adjust the default settings for any security level.

Using Network Command-Line Tools

Windows contains several command-line tools for troubleshooting and configuring the network. These include

- Net—Displays and uses network resources.
- Ping—Tests TCP/IP and Internet connections.
- Tracert—Traces the route between a specified Web site or IP address and your PC.
- NSLookup—Displays detailed information about DNS.
- IPConfig—Displays detailed TCP/IP configuration about your Windows NT/2000/XP system.

caution

You should enable the firewall on all computers that use the Internet *except* those that provide shared resources to other computers. Enabling the firewall on these systems blocks access to shared resources.

WinIPCfg is used by Windows 9x/Me to perform tasks similar to IPConfig. Start WinIPCfg from Start, Run. See the "Windows Command Reference" on the CD for more information about these commands.

Study Lab

Don't miss the Study Lab materials found on the CD accompanying this book. Each Study Lab is tailored to the individual chapters in this book, meaning that you'll quickly be able to determine which topics you understand well enough to pass the exam and which topics need more study time. The Study Labs are presented in printable PDF format so that you can take them with you to study at work, on the road, or even in your car just before test time!

THE ABSOLUTE MINIMUM

- A network is a group of computers, peripherals, and software that are connected to each other and can be used together.

- Windows NT 4.0/2000/XP and Windows 9x/Me all contain client software, network protocols, file and print sharing, and services that can be used to create network clients or share resources with other computers.

- Dial-up, ISDN, and DSL all use telephone lines, but ISDN and DSL provide two-way, all-digital Internet connections.

- Cable Internet typically uses high-performance digital cable TV networks, although older, all-coaxial networks support one-way service.

- DirecWAY and Starband provide two-way satellite Internet service.

- Fixed wireless is used in areas beyond the reach of DSL or cable TV, and is often provided by vendors of wireless cable TV.

- TCP/IP is a suite of network protocols used for both Internet access and LAN connections.

- Domain names typically divide into three parts, including the top-level domain (.com, .org), the site name (Microsoft), and the server type (www, ftp, or others).

- The most common network topology is the star topology, used by 10BaseT and faster, UTP-based Ethernet and Wireless Ethernet in infrastructure mode.

- Wireless Ethernet networks that use 802.11a-, 802.11b-, or 802.11g-compatible hardware are often referred to as Wi-Fi networks.

- UTP cables in Category 5 and higher are required for Fast Ethernet (100BaseT) and faster networks.

- Network cards typically require an IRQ and an I/O port address range, and some also need media type and full-duplex settings to complete the configuration process.

- TCP/IP configuration is easiest when a server-assigned IP address is used.

- You can share printers, folders, and other types of resources.

- Shared resources can be referred to with mapped drive letters, UNC names, or FQDN names.

- You can improve system security by enabling the Windows XP Firewall and by using the Security settings in the Internet Explorer browser.

In This Appendix

- Using PrepLogic Practice Exams, Preview Edition Software
- Software Requirements
- Installing PrepLogic Practice Exams, Preview Edition
- Using PrepLogic Practice Exams, Preview Edition
- Using Chapters 22 and 23
- Using the CD Supplement
- Using the Study Guide
- Using the Hands-On Labs
- Using the Beep Codes

A

CD-ROM Instructions

The CD packaged with this book is just as important to your studies as the book's text itself. The CD has the following features:

- The top-rated PrepLogic self-test engine, which is also used by other Que certification books
- Chapters 22 and 23
- CD supplement with additional hardware coverage
- Study Guide for Chapters 2–22
- Hands-On Labs for Chapters 2–22
- Beep codes

The following sections describe these CD features in more detail.

Using PrepLogic Practice Exams, Preview Edition Software

This book includes a special version of PrepLogic Practice Exams—a revolutionary test engine designed to give you the best in certification exam preparation. PrepLogic offers sample and practice exams for many of today's most in-demand and challenging technical certifications. This special Preview Edition is included with this book as a tool to use in assessing your knowledge of the Training Guide material while also providing you with the experience of taking an electronic exam.

This appendix describes in detail what PrepLogic Practice Exams, Preview Edition is, how it works, and what it can do to help you prepare for the exam.

note

Note that although the Preview Edition includes all the test simulation functions of the complete, retail version, it contains only a single practice test. The Premium Edition, available at PrepLogic.com, contains the complete set of challenging practice exams designed to optimize your learning experience.

Exam Simulation

One of the main functions of PrepLogic Practice Exams, Preview Edition, is exam simulation. To prepare you to take the actual vendor certification exam, PrepLogic is designed to offer the most effective exam simulation available.

Question Quality

The questions provided in the PrepLogic Practice Exams, Preview Edition are written to the highest standards of technical accuracy. The questions tap the content of the Training Guide chapters and help you review and assess your knowledge before you take the actual exam.

Interface Design

The PrepLogic Practice Exams, Preview Edition exam simulation interface provides you with the experience of taking an electronic exam. This enables you to effectively prepare for taking the actual exam by making the test experience a familiar one. Using this test simulation can help eliminate the sense of surprise or anxiety you might experience in the testing center because you will already be acquainted with computerized testing.

Effective Learning Environment

The PrepLogic Practice Exams, Preview Edition interface provides a learning environment that not only tests you through the computer, but also teaches the material you need to know to pass the certification exam. Each question comes with a detailed explanation of the correct answer and often provides reasons the other options are incorrect. This information helps to reinforce the knowledge you already have and also provides practical information you can use on the job.

Software Requirements

PrepLogic Practice Exams, Preview Edition requires a computer with the following:

- Microsoft Windows 98, Windows Me, Windows NT 4.0, Windows 2000, or Windows XP
- A 166MHz or faster processor is recommended
- A minimum of 32MB of RAM
- As with any Windows application, the more memory, the better your performance
- 10MB of hard drive space

Installing PrepLogic Practice Exams, Preview Edition

Install PrepLogic Practice Exams, Preview Edition by running the setup program on the PrepLogic Practice Exams, Preview Edition CD. Follow these instructions to install the software on your computer:

1. Insert the CD into your CD-ROM drive. The Autorun feature of Windows should launch the software. If you have Autorun disabled, click Start and select Run. Go to the root directory of the CD and select setup.exe. Click Open, and then click OK.

2. The Installation Wizardcopies the PrepLogic Practice Exams, Preview Edition files to your hard drive; adds PrepLogic Practice Exams, Preview Edition to your Desktop and Program menu; and installs test engine components to the appropriate system folders.

Removing PrepLogic Practice Exams, Preview Edition from Your Computer

If you elect to remove the PrepLogic Practice Exams, Preview Edition product from your computer, an uninstall process has been included to ensure that it is removed from your system safely and completely. Follow these instructions to remove PrepLogic Practice Exams, Preview Edition from your computer:

1. Select Start, Settings, Control Panel.

2. Double-click the Add/Remove Programs icon.

3. You are presented with a list of software installed on your computer. Select the appropriate PrepLogic Practice Exams, Preview Edition title you want to remove. Click the Add/Remove button. The software is then removed from your computer.

Using PrepLogic Practice Exams, Preview Edition

PrepLogic is designed to be user friendly and intuitive. Because the software has a smooth learning curve, your time is maximized because you start practicing almost immediately. PrepLogic Practice Exams, Preview Edition has two major modes of study: Practice Test and Flash Review.

Using Practice Test mode, you can develop your test-taking abilities as well as your knowledge through the use of the Show Answer option. While you are taking the test, you can expose the answers along with a detailed explanation of why the given answers are right or wrong. This gives you the ability to better understand the material presented.

Flash Review is designed to reinforce exam topics rather than quiz you. In this mode, you will be shown a series of questions but no answer choices. Instead, you will be given a button that reveals the correct answer to the question and a full explanation for that answer.

Starting a Practice Test Mode Session

Practice Test mode enables you to control the exam experience in ways that actual certification exams do not allow:

- *Enable Show Answer Button*—Activates the Show Answer button, enabling you to view the correct answer(s) and full explanation(s) for each question during the exam. When not enabled, you must wait until after your exam has been graded to view the correct answer(s) and explanation.

> ▪ *Enable Item Review Button*—Activates the Item Review button, enabling you to view your answer choices, marked questions, and to facilitate navigation between questions.

> ▪ *Randomize Choices*—Randomize answer choices from one exam session to the next. Makes memorizing question choices more difficult, therefore keeping questions fresh and challenging longer.

To begin studying in Practice Test mode, click the Practice Test radio button from the main exam customization screen. This enables the options detailed in the preceding list.

To your left, you are presented with the option of selecting the preconfigured Practice Test or creating your own Custom Test. The preconfigured test has a fixed time limit and number of questions. Custom Tests enable you to configure the time limit and the number of questions in your exam.

The Preview Edition included with this book includes a single, preconfigured Practice Test. Get the complete set of challenging PrepLogic Practice Tests at PrepLogic.com and make certain you're ready for the big exam.

Click the Begin Exam button to begin your exam.

Starting a Flash Review Mode Session

Flash Review mode provides you with an easy way to reinforce topics covered in the practice questions. To begin studying in Flash Review mode, click the Flash Review radio button from the main exam customization screen. Select either the preconfigured Practice Test or create your own Custom Test.

Click the Best Exam button to begin your Flash Review of the exam questions.

Standard PrepLogic Practice Exams, Preview Edition Options

The following list describes the function of each of the buttons you see. Depending on the options, some of the buttons will be grayed out and inaccessible or missing completely. Buttons that are appropriate are active. The buttons are as follows:

> ▪ *Exhibit*—This button is visible if an exhibit is provided to support the question. An exhibit is an image that provides supplemental information necessary to answer the question.

> ▪ *Item Review*—This button leaves the question window and opens the Item Review screen. From this screen you will see all questions, your answers, and your marked items. You will also see correct answers listed here when appropriate.

■ *Show Answer*—This option displays the correct answer with an explanation of why it is correct. If you select this option, the current question is not scored.

■ *Mark Item*—Check this box to tag a question you need to review further. You can view and navigate your Marked Items by clicking the Item Review button (if enabled). When grading your exam, you will be notified if you have marked items remaining.

■ *Previous Item*—View the previous question.

■ *Next Item*—View the next question.

■ *Grade Exam*—When you have completed your exam, click to end your exam and view your detailed score report. If you have unanswered or marked items remaining, you will be asked if you would like to continue taking your exam or view your exam report.

Time Remaining

If the test is timed, the time remaining is displayed on the upper-right corner of the application screen. It counts down minutes and seconds remaining to complete the test. If you run out of time, you will be asked if you want to continue taking the test or if you want to end your exam.

Your Examination Score Report

The Examination Score Report screen appears when the Practice Test mode ends—as the result of time expiration, completion of all questions, or your decision to terminate early.

This screen provides you with a graphical display of your test score with a breakdown of scores by topic domain. The graphical display at the top of the screen compares your overall score with the PrepLogic Exam Competency Score.

The PrepLogic Exam Competency Score reflects the level of subject competency required to pass this vendor's exam. Although this score does not directly translate to a passing score, consistently matching or exceeding this score does suggest you possess the knowledge to pass the actual vendor exam.

Reviewing Your Exam

From Your Score Report screen, you can review the exam that you just completed by clicking on the View Items button. Navigate through the items, viewing the questions, your answers, the correct answers, and the explanations for those questions. You can return to Your Score Report by clicking the View Items button.

Getting More Exams

Each PrepLogic Practice Exams, Preview Edition that accompanies your training guide contains a single PrepLogic Practice Test. Certification students worldwide trust PrepLogic Practice Tests to help them pass their IT certification exams the first time. Purchase the Premium Edition of PrepLogic Practice Exams and get the entire set of all new challenging Practice Tests for this exam. PrepLogic Practice Tests—Because You Want to Pass the First Time.

Contacting PrepLogic

If you would like to contact PrepLogic for any reason including information about our extensive line of certification practice tests, we invite you to do so. Please contact us online at www.preplogic.com.

Customer Service

If you have a damaged product and need a replacement or refund, please call the following phone number:

800-858-7674

Product Suggestions and Comments

We value your input! Please email your suggestions and comments to the following address:

feedback@preplogic.com

License Agreement

YOU MUST AGREE TO THE TERMS AND CONDITIONS OUTLINED IN THE END USER LICENSE AGREEMENT ("EULA") PRESENTED TO YOU DURING THE INSTALLATION PROCESS. IF YOU DO NOT AGREE TO THESE TERMS, DO NOT INSTALL THE SOFTWARE.

Using Chapters 22 and 23

Chapters 22 and 23 are included on the CD in printable Adobe Acrobat (.PDF) format.

Using the CD Supplement

The CD supplement provides coverage of a few test objectives that were not covered in the main text of the book. The list of objectives in Chapter 1, "A+ Objectives for the 2003 Exam Revisions," identifies which topics are covered in the CD supplement. Like Chapters 22 and 23, the CD supplement is also a printable Adobe Acrobat (.PDF) file.

Windows Command Reference

The Windows Command Reference contains detailed usage and syntax guides for major command-prompt commands and utilities for copying, deleting, and viewing files, managing and maintaining disk drives, and others. The list of objectives in Chapter 1, "A+ Objectives for the 2003 Exam Revisions," identifies which topics are covered in the Windows Command Reference. The Windows Command Reference is also a printable Adobe Acrobat (.PDF) file.

Using the Study Guide

The CD contains a printable Study Guide in Adobe Acrobat (.PDF) format for Chapters 2–22. Each chapter's Study Guide contains the following sections:

- *Key Terms and Definitions*—The key terms used in each chapter are defined for you.

- *Practice Test*—In addition to the self-test engine, each chapter's Study Guide also contains a list of multiple-choice questions. Most of these questions are scenario based, requiring you to apply the material you've learned in the chapter to solve real-world problems just as you will on the actual exams.

- *Hands-On Labs*—Each chapter has two or more experiments you can perform to reinforce the major concepts in the chapter. See the next section for details.

- *Answers to Practice Test*—See how you did on the Practice Test.

tip

The CD contains Adobe's free Acrobat Reader for 32-bit Windows PCs.

If you have a PDA such as a PalmOS or Pocket PC, a Nokia Communicator 92xx series (Symbian OS), or have a PC running another operating system such as MacOS, Linux, or others, visit Adobe's Web site (`http://www.adobe.com`) for a free download of the Acrobat Reader version right for your system.

tip

You can print the Study Guide's contents or transfer the PDF files to another computer, making it easy to study anywhere you like.

Using the Hands-On Labs

The Hands-On Labs are an essential part of your preparation for the A+ Certification Exams. They are based, in part, upon the years of hands-on demonstrations and troubleshooting scenarios I developed for Advanced PC Troubleshooting classes I taught around the country.

Each chapter has a series of exercises that are based on the contents of that chapter. Each exercise has a list of required equipment, an objective, and questions for you to answer based on what you learn in each lab.

tip

As you perform the lab experiments for each chapter, turn to that chapter for more information.

The labs are designed to simulate real-world tasks you might perform as an IT or network technician. The labs are open ended, so don't hesitate to use them as a starting point for further explorations of the topics they cover.

Using the Beep Codes

The CD includes actual recordings of sample beep codes from computers using the AMI, Award, Phoenix, and Microid Research (MR) BIOSs saved in .WAV (uncompressed audio) format. .WAV files can be played back by the Windows Media Player and by most other audio playback programs.

The Award, AMI, and MR BIOS beep codes are those played when no video card (or a bad video card) is installed; this is one of the most common problems that will trigger beep codes, and it shows how different BIOS vendors use different types of beep codes to indicate the same problem.

The AMI BIOS uses different numbers of short beeps to indicate 11 different problems, and Award (now known as Phoenix FirstBIOS) uses beep codes sparingly; the video beep code heard here is the only beep code used by the Award BIOS. The MR BIOS beep code is an example of this BIOS's use of high- and low-pitched beep codes to report more than 30 different problems.

The Phoenix BIOS (now known as Phoenix FirstBIOS Pro) doesn't use a beep code to indicate video problems, so I chose the beep code that plays when the RTC (real-time clock) on the motherboard is defective. The Phoenix BIOS uses short and long beeps to report dozens of different system problems.

Index

How can we make this index more useful? Email us at indexes@quepublishing.com

How can we make this index more useful? Email us at indexes@quepublishing.com

N

nanoseconds (ns), memory speeds, 228

narrow SCSI devices, PDF:1002-1003

Narrow SCSI host adapters, 463

native capacity, tape drives, 479

Near Letter Quality (NLQ) mode, 333

Net command-line tool, 809

Net Diagnostics, 717

Net Use command (Windows Recovery Console), 752

NetBEUI (NetBIOS Extended User Interface), 773, 797

NetBIOS, resolving/ translating, 795

NetBIOS Extended User Interface (NetBEUI), 773, 797

Netlog.txt hidden file, 580

network adapters (NICs), printers, PDF:1007

network devices, connecting
broadband Internet access devices, 370-371
infrared adapters, 372-374
WAPs (wireless access points), 369-370

network drives
Windows 9x installations, 548-549
Windows 2000/XP installations, 567
Windows NT 4.0 installation, 553

Network Identification Wizard, 558, 564

Network Installations, service packs, 590

Network Neighborhood, troubleshooting with, PDF:918-920

network operating system (NOS), 760-761

network printers
configuring/installing, 684-687
installing, 802
troubleshooting, 691, PDF:917

network resources, displaying, PDF:1029

network topologies, 778-779

networks
Bluetooth, 781
cables, 782-785
client/server model, 761-762
clients, 801-802
configuring, command-line tools, 809
connectors, 782-786
defined, 759
DNS (domain name system), 776-777
email, 777-778
FTP (File Transfer Protocol), 776
HTML (Hypertext Markup Language), 775
hubs, 789
Internet, 759
cable connections, 769
dial-up connections, 763-765
DSL (Digital Subscriber Line) connections, 767-769
ISDN (Integrated Services Digital Network) connections, 766-767
LAN (local area network) connections, 772
satellite connections, 770-771
wireless connections, 771
LAN (local area network), 759, 790
logons, troubleshooting, 745
peer-to-peer model, 745, 763
protocols, 772
AppleTalk, 774, 796
installing, 791-792

IPX/SPX (Internetwork Packet Exchange/Sequenced Packet Exchange), configuring, 796
NetBEUI (NetBIOS Extended User Interface), 773, 797
TCP/IP (Transport Control Protocol/Internet Protocol), 773-774
shared resources, 802
File and Printer Sharing, 797-798
FQDNs (fully qualified domain names), 805-806
identifying, 803
mapped drives, 804-805
passwords, 798, 803
permissions, 801
setting up, 797
shared drives, 798-799
shared folders, 798-800
UNC (Universal Naming Convention), 805
SSL (Secure Socket Layer), 774
switches, 790
Telnet, 774-776, 793-796
token-ring (IEEE-802.5), 781
troubleshooting, command-line tools, 809
WAN (wide area network), 759
wired Ethernet, 779-780
wireless Ethernet, 780-781

New menu commands
Folder, 637
Shortcut, 640

New, Shortcut command (File menu), 638

NICs (network adapters), printers, PDF:1007

NLQ (Near Letter Quality) mode, 333

NLX motherboards, 112, 114
installing, 121
removing, 119

How can we make this index more useful? Email us at indexes@quepublishing.com

How can we make this index more useful? Email us at indexes@quepublishing.com

How can we make this index more useful? Email us at indexes@quepublishing.com

Windows 95
installing, network drives, 548-549
PnP (Plug and Play) devices, installing, 694
Windows 98 upgrades, 579

Windows 9x
connections, adjusting, PDF:854-855
disk-access features, disabling, 740
drive letters, 503-505
dual-boot configurations, Windows 2000, 562-564
File and Printer Sharing, installing, 798
file attributes, 658
folders, removing, 521, PDF:1020-1021
hard drive preparations, Fdisk program, 505
hardware requirements, OS (operating system) installations, 533
installing, 543
  CD-ROM, 544-548
  device drivers, 550
  ESD (emergency startup disk), 544, 551
  Fdisk, 544-545
  network drives, 548-549
  troubleshooting, 571
launching, 603
  boot sequence, 604-611
  default memory configurations, 611-612
  Win.com file, 613-614
network client software, installing, 801-802
network protocols, installing, 792
partitions, shrinking, 563
peer-to-peer networks, shared resource access, 745
print spoolers, trouble-shooting, 747
shared folders/drives, 799
Start menu, managing items, 637

startup, 727
  Command Prompt Only, 729
  Logged, 729
  Previous Version of MS-DOS, 729-730
  Safe Mode, 728-730
  Step-by-Step Confirmation, 729-730
  troubleshooting, 730-731
startup switches, 613-614
swapfiles, 671-672, 739-741
temporary files, settings, 675
Windows 2000 Professional upgrades, 584-587

Windows 9x/Me Resource Meter, 738-739

Windows 98
installing, network drives, 549
MSConfig troubleshooting utility, 747-748
PnP (Plug and Play) devices, installing, 695-696
SFC (System File Checker), 748
updating, 580
upgrading
  MS-DOS, 577-578
  preparations, 576-578
  troubleshooting, 580-581
  Windows 3.1, 578-579
  Windows 95, 579

Windows 2000, 618
boot sequence, 619
compatibility, 581-582
configuration files, 620-623
connections, adjusting, PDF:855
File and Printer Sharing, installing, 797-798
file attributes, 658-660
hard drives
  Format program, 511-512
  preparations, 512-517
hardware requirements, OS (operating system) installations, 533-534

installing
  device drivers, 568
  disk images, 568-569
  dual-boot configuration, 561-564, 567
  local drives, 555-559
  network drives, 567
  SID (Security Identification Number), 568-569
  troubleshooting, 572
launching, 619-620
logfiles, 572
network client software, installing, 801
network protocols, installing, 792
NTLDR program, 619-620
paging files, 673-374, 739-741
PnP (Plug and Play) devices, installing, 696
print spoolers, trouble-shooting, 746
SFC (System File Checker), 748
shared folders/drives, 799
software upgrade packs, 582
Start menu, managing items, 637
startup, 734-736
temporary files, settings, 675-676
Upgrade (Readiness) Analyzer, 582

Windows 2000 Professional
service packs, installing, 587-590
updating, 587-590
upgrading
  preparations, 581-583
  troubleshooting, 590-592
  Windows 9x, 584-587
  Windows Me, 584-587
  Windows NT 4.0, 582-584

Windows 2000 Search feature, 661-662
Windows Backup, 641-644
Windows Device Manager. See Device Manager

How can we make this index more useful? Email us at indexes@quepublishing.com

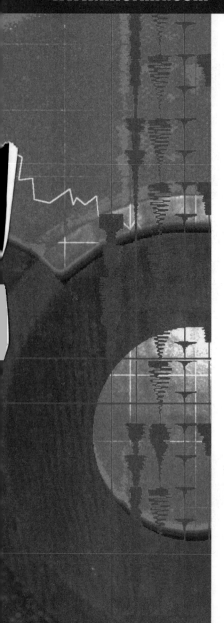

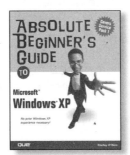

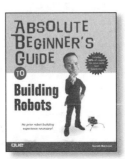